T0211116

Lecture Notes in Computer Science 14261

Founding Editors

Gerhard Goos
Juris Hartmanis

Editorial Board Members

The series Lecture Notes in Computer Science (LNCS), including its subseries Lecture Notes in Artificial Intelligence (LNAI) and Lecture Notes in Bioinformatics (LNBI), has established itself as a medium for the publication of new developments in computer science and information technology research, teaching, and education.

LNCS enjoys close cooperation with the computer science R & D community, the series counts many renowned academics among its volume editors and paper authors, and collaborates with prestigious societies. Its mission is to serve this international community by providing an invaluable service, mainly focused on the publication of conference and workshop proceedings and postproceedings. LNCS commenced publication in 1973.

Lazaros Iliadis · Antonios Papaleonidas ·
Plamen Angelov · Chrisina Jayne
Editors

Artificial Neural Networks and Machine Learning – ICANN 2023

32nd International Conference on Artificial Neural Networks
Heraklion, Crete, Greece, September 26–29, 2023
Proceedings, Part VIII

 Springer

Editors
Lazaros Iliadis ⓘ
Democritus University of Thrace
Xanthi, Greece

Plamen Angelov ⓘ
Lancaster University
Lancaster, UK

Antonios Papaleonidas ⓘ
Democritus University of Thrace
Xanthi, Greece

Chrisina Jayne ⓘ
Teesside University
Middlesbrough, UK

ISSN 0302-9743   ISSN 1611-3349 (electronic)
Lecture Notes in Computer Science
ISBN 978-3-031-44197-4   ISBN 978-3-031-44198-1 (eBook)
https://doi.org/10.1007/978-3-031-44198-1

This Springer imprint is published by the registered company Springer Nature Switzerland AG
The registered company address is: Gewerbestrasse 11, 6330 Cham, Switzerland

Paper in this product is recyclable.

Preface

The European Neural Network Society (ENNS) is an association of scientists, engineers and students, conducting research on the modelling of behavioral and brain processes, and on the development of neural algorithms. The core of these efforts is the application of neural modelling to several diverse domains. According to its mission statement ENNS is the European non-profit federation of professionals that aims at achieving a worldwide professional and socially responsible development and application of artificial neural technologies.

The flagship event of ENNS is ICANN (the International Conference on Artificial Neural Networks) at which contributed research papers are presented after passing through a rigorous review process. ICANN is a dual-track conference, featuring tracks in brain-inspired computing on the one hand, and machine learning on the other, with strong crossdisciplinary interactions and applications.

The response of the international scientific community to the ICANN 2023 call for papers was more than satisfactory. In total, 947 research papers on the aforementioned research areas were submitted and 426 (45%) of them were finally accepted as full papers after a peer review process. Additionally, 19 extended abstracts were submitted and 9 of them were selected to be included in the front matter of ICANN 2023 proceedings. Due to their high academic and scientific importance, 22 short papers were also accepted.

All papers were peer reviewed by at least two independent academic referees. Where needed, a third or a fourth referee was consulted to resolve any potential conflicts. Three workshops focusing on specific research areas, namely Advances in Spiking Neural Networks (ASNN), Neurorobotics (NRR), and the challenge of Errors, Stability, Robustness, and Accuracy in Deep Neural Networks (ESRA in DNN), were organized.

The 10-volume set of LNCS 14254, 14255, 14256, 14257, 14258, 14259, 14260, 14261, 14262 and 14263 constitutes the proceedings of the 32nd International Conference on Artificial Neural Networks, ICANN 2023, held in Heraklion city, Crete, Greece, on September 26–29, 2023.

The accepted papers are related to the following topics:

Machine Learning: Deep Learning; Neural Network Theory; Neural Network Models; Graphical Models; Bayesian Networks; Kernel Methods; Generative Models; Information Theoretic Learning; Reinforcement Learning; Relational Learning; Dynamical Models; Recurrent Networks; and Ethics of AI.

Brain-Inspired Computing: Cognitive Models; Computational Neuroscience; Self-Organization; Neural Control and Planning; Hybrid Neural-Symbolic Architectures; Neural Dynamics; Cognitive Neuroscience; Brain Informatics; Perception and Action; and Spiking Neural Networks.

Neural applications in Bioinformatics; Biomedicine; Intelligent Robotics; Neuro-robotics; Language Processing; Speech Processing; Image Processing; Sensor Fusion; Pattern Recognition; Data Mining; Neural Agents; Brain-Computer Interaction; Neuro-morphic Computing and Edge AI; and Evolutionary Neural Networks.

September 2023

Lazaros Iliadis
Antonios Papaleonidas
Plamen Angelov
Chrisina Jayne

Organization

General Chairs

Iliadis Lazaros — Democritus University of Thrace, Greece
Plamen Angelov — Lancaster University, UK

Program Chairs

Antonios Papaleonidas — Democritus University of Thrace, Greece
Elias Pimenidis — UWE Bristol, UK
Chrisina Jayne — Teesside University, UK

Honorary Chairs

Stefan Wermter — University of Hamburg, Germany
Vera Kurkova — Czech Academy of Sciences, Czech Republic
Nikola Kasabov — Auckland University of Technology, New Zealand

Organizing Chairs

Antonios Papaleonidas — Democritus University of Thrace, Greece
Anastasios Panagiotis Psathas — Democritus University of Thrace, Greece
George Magoulas — University of London, Birkbeck College, UK
Haralambos Mouratidis — University of Essex, UK

Award Chairs

Stefan Wermter — University of Hamburg, Germany
Chukiong Loo — University of Malaysia, Malaysia

Communication Chairs

Sebastian Otte	University of Tübingen, Germany
Anastasios Panagiotis Psathas	Democritus University of Thrace, Greece

Steering Committee

Stefan Wermter	University of Hamburg, Germany
Angelo Cangelosi	University of Manchester, UK
Igor Farkaš	Comenius University in Bratislava, Slovakia
Chrisina Jayne	Teesside University, UK
Matthias Kerzel	University of Hamburg, Germany
Alessandra Lintas	University of Lausanne, Switzerland
Kristína Malinovská (Rebrová)	Comenius University in Bratislava, Slovakia
Alessio Micheli	University of Pisa, Italy
Jaakko Peltonen	Tampere University, Finland
Brigitte Quenet	ESPCI Paris, France
Ausra Saudargiene	Lithuanian University of Health Sciences, Lithuania
Roseli Wedemann	Rio de Janeiro State University, Brazil

Local Organizing/Hybrid Facilitation Committee

Aggeliki Tsouka	Democritus University of Thrace, Greece
Anastasios Panagiotis Psathas	Democritus University of Thrace, Greece
Anna Karagianni	Democritus University of Thrace, Greece
Christina Gkizioti	Democritus University of Thrace, Greece
Ioanna-Maria Erentzi	Democritus University of Thrace, Greece
Ioannis Skopelitis	Democritus University of Thrace, Greece
Lambros Kazelis	Democritus University of Thrace, Greece
Leandros Tsatsaronis	Democritus University of Thrace, Greece
Nikiforos Mpotzoris	Democritus University of Thrace, Greece
Nikos Zervis	Democritus University of Thrace, Greece
Panagiotis Restos	Democritus University of Thrace, Greece
Tassos Giannakopoulos	Democritus University of Thrace, Greece

Program Committee

Abraham Yosipof	CLB, Israel
Adane Tarekegn	NTNU, Norway
Aditya Gilra	Centrum Wiskunde & Informatica, Netherlands
Adrien Durand-Petiteville	Federal University of Pernambuco, Brazil
Adrien Fois	LORIA, France
Alaa Marouf	Hosei University, Japan
Alessandra Sciutti	Istituto Italiano di Tecnologia, Italy
Alessandro Sperduti	University of Padua, Italy
Alessio Micheli	University of Pisa, Italy
Alex Shenfield	Sheffield Hallam University, UK
Alexander Kovalenko	Czech Technical University in Prague, Czech Republic
Alexander Krawczyk	Fulda University of Applied Sciences, Germany
Ali Minai	University of Cincinnati, USA
Aluizio Araujo	Universidade Federal de Pernambuco, Brazil
Amarda Shehu	George Mason University, USA
Amit Kumar Kundu	University of Maryland, USA
Anand Rangarajan	University of Florida, USA
Anastasios Panagiotis Psathas	Democritus University of Thrace, Greece
Andre de Carvalho	Universidade de São Paulo, Brazil
Andrej Lucny	Comenius University, Slovakia
Angel Villar-Corrales	University of Bonn, Germany
Angelo Cangelosi	University of Manchester, UK
Anna Jenul	Norwegian University of Life Sciences, Norway
Antonios Papaleonidas	Democritus University of Thrace, Greece
Arnaud Lewandowski	LISIC, ULCO, France
Arul Selvam Periyasamy	Universität Bonn, Germany
Asma Mekki	University of Sfax, Tunisia
Banafsheh Rekabdar	Portland State University, USA
Barbara Hammer	Universität Bielefeld, Germany
Baris Serhan	University of Manchester, UK
Benedikt Bagus	University of Applied Sciences Fulda, Germany
Benjamin Paaßen	Bielefeld University, Germany
Bernhard Pfahringer	University of Waikato, New Zealand
Bharath Sudharsan	NUI Galway, Ireland
Binyi Wu	Dresden University of Technology, Germany
Binyu Zhao	Harbin Institute of Technology, China
Björn Plüster	University of Hamburg, Germany
Bo Mei	Texas Christian University, USA

DongNyeong Heo	Handong Global University, South Korea
Dongyang Zhang	University of Electronic Science and Technology of China, China
Doreen Jirak	Istituto Italiano di Tecnologia, Italy
Douglas McLelland	BrainChip, France
Douglas Nyabuga	Mount Kenya University, Rwanda
Dulani Meedeniya	University of Moratuwa, Sri Lanka
Dumitru-Clementin Cercel	University Politehnica of Bucharest, Romania
Dylan Muir	SynSense, Switzerland
Efe Bozkir	Uni Tübingen, Germany
Eleftherios Kouloumpris	Aristotle University of Thessaloniki, Greece
Elias Pimenidis	University of the West of England, UK
Eliska Kloberdanz	Iowa State University, USA
Emre Neftci	Foschungszentrum Juelich, Germany
Enzo Tartaglione	Telecom Paris, France
Erwin Lopez	University of Manchester, UK
Evgeny Mirkes	University of Leicester, UK
F. Boray Tek	Istanbul Technical University, Turkey
Federico Corradi	Eindhoven University of Technology, Netherlands
Federico Errica	NEC Labs Europe, Germany
Federico Manzi	Università Cattolica del Sacro Cuore, Italy
Federico Vozzi	CNR, Italy
Fedor Scholz	University of Tuebingen, Germany
Feifei Dai	Chinese Academy of Sciences, China
Feifei Xu	Shanghai University of Electric Power, China
Feixiang Zhou	University of Leicester, UK
Felipe Moreno	FGV, Peru
Feng Wei	York University, Canada
Fengying Li	Guilin University of Electronic Technology, China
Flora Ferreira	University of Minho, Portugal
Florian Mirus	Intel Labs, Germany
Francesco Semeraro	University of Manchester, UK
Franco Scarselli	University of Siena, Italy
François Blayo	IPSEITE, Switzerland
Frank Röder	Hamburg University of Technology, Germany
Frederic Alexandre	Inria, France
Fuchang Han	Central South University, China
Fuli Wang	University of Essex, UK
Gabriela Sejnova	Czech Technical University in Prague, Czech Republic
Gaetano Di Caterina	University of Strathclyde, UK
George Bebis	University of Nevada, USA

Gerrit Ecke	Mercedes-Benz, Germany
Giannis Nikolentzos	Ecole Polytechnique, France
Gilles Marcou	University of Strasbourg, France
Giorgio Gnecco	IMT School for Advanced Studies, Italy
Glauco Amigo	Baylor University, USA
Greg Lee	Acadia University, Canada
Grégory Bourguin	LISIC/ULCO, France
Guillermo Martín-Sánchez	Champalimaud Foundation, Portugal
Gulustan Dogan	UNCW, USA
Habib Khan	Islamia College University Peshawar, Pakistan
Haizhou Du	Shanghai University of Electric Power, China
Hanli Wang	Tongji University, China
Hanno Gottschalk	TU Berlin, Germany
Hao Tong	University of Birmingham, UK
Haobo Jiang	NJUST, China
Haopeng Chen	Shanghai Jiao Tong University, China
Hazrat Ali	Hamad Bin Khalifa University, Qatar
Hina Afridi	NTNU, Gjøvik, Norway
Hiroaki Aizawa	Hiroshima University, Japan
Hiromichi Suetani	Oita University, Japan
Hiroshi Kawaguchi	Kobe University, Japan
Hiroyasu Ando	Tohoku University, Japan
Hiroyoshi Ito	University of Tsukuba, Japan
Honggang Zhang	University of Massachusetts, Boston, USA
Hongqing Yu	Open University, UK
Hongye Cao	Northwestern Polytechnical University, China
Hugo Carneiro	University of Hamburg, Germany
Hugo Eduardo Camacho Cruz	Universidad Autónoma de Tamaulipas, Mexico
Huifang Ma	Northwest Normal University, China
Hyeyoung Park	Kyungpook National University, South Korea
Ian Nabney	University of Bristol, UK
Igor Farkas	Comenius University Bratislava, Slovakia
Ikuko Nishikawa	Ritsumeikan University, Japan
Ioannis Pierros	Aristotle University of Thessaloniki, Greece
Iraklis Varlamis	Harokopio University of Athens, Greece
Ivan Tyukin	King's College London, UK
Iveta Bečková	Comenius University in Bratislava, Slovakia
Jae Hee Lee	University of Hamburg, Germany
James Yu	Southern University of Science and Technology, China
Jan Faigl	Czech Technical University in Prague, Czech Republic

Jan Feber	Czech Technical University in Prague, Czech Republic
Jan-Gerrit Habekost	University of Hamburg, Germany
Jannik Thuemmel	University of Tübingen, Germany
Jeremie Cabessa	University Paris 2, France
Jérémie Sublime	ISEP, France
Jia Cai	Guangdong University of Finance & Economics, China
Jiaan Wang	Soochow University, China
Jialiang Tang	Nanjing University of Science and Technology, China
Jian Hu	YiduCloud, Cyprus
Jianhua Xu	Nanjing Normal University, China
Jianyong Chen	Shenzhen University, China
Jichao Bi	Zhejiang Institute of Industry and Information Technology, China
Jie Shao	University of Electronic Science and Technology of China, China
Jim Smith	University of the West of England, UK
Jing Yang	Hefei University of Technology, China
Jingyi Yuan	Arizona State University, USA
Jingyun Jia	Baidu, USA
Jinling Wang	Ulster University, UK
Jiri Sima	Czech Academy of Sciences, Czech Republic
Jitesh Dundas	Independent Researcher, USA
Joost Vennekens	KU Leuven, Belgium
Jordi Cosp	Universitat Politècnica de Catalunya, Spain
Josua Spisak	University of Hamburg, Germany
Jozef Kubík	Comenius University, Slovakia
Junpei Zhong	Hong Kong Polytechnic University, China
Jurgita Kapočiūtė-Dzikienė	Vytautas Magnus University, Lithuania
K. L. Eddie Law	Macao Polytechnic University, China
Kai Tang	Independent Researcher, China
Kamil Dedecius	Czech Academy of Sciences, Czech Republic
Kang Zhang	Kyushu University, Japan
Kantaro Fujiwara	University of Tokyo, Japan
Karlis Freivalds	Institute of Electronics and Computer Science, Latvia
Khoa Phung	University of the West of England, UK
Kiran Lekkala	University of Southern California, USA
Kleanthis Malialis	University of Cyprus, Cyprus
Kohulan Rajan	Friedrich Schiller University, Germany

Koichiro Yamauchi	Chubu University, Japan
Koloud Alkhamaiseh	Western Michigan University, USA
Konstantinos Demertzis	Democritus University of Thrace, Greece
Kostadin Cvejoski	Fraunhofer IAIS, Germany
Kristína Malinovská	Comenius University in Bratislava, Slovakia
Kun Zhang	Inria and École Polytechnique, France
Laurent Mertens	KU Leuven, Belgium
Laurent Perrinet	AMU CNRS, France
Lazaros Iliadis	Democritus University of Thrace, Greece
Leandro dos Santos Coelho	Pontifical Catholic University of Parana, Brazil
Leiping Jie	Hong Kong Baptist University, China
Lenka Tětková	Technical University of Denmark, Denmark
Lia Morra	Politecnico di Torino, Italy
Liang Ge	Chongqing University, China
Liang Zhao	Dalian University of Technology, China
Limengzi Yuan	Shihezi University, China
Ling Guo	Northwest University, China
Linlin Shen	Shenzhen University, China
Lixin Zou	Wuhan University, China
Lorenzo Vorabbi	University of Bologna, Italy
Lu Wang	Macao Polytechnic University, China
Luca Pasa	University of Padova, Italy
Ľudovít Malinovský	Independent Researcher, Slovakia
Luis Alexandre	Universidade da Beira Interior, Portugal
Luis Lago	Universidad Autonoma de Madrid, Spain
Lukáš Gajdošech Gajdošech	Comenius University Bratislava, Slovakia
Lyra Puspa	Vanaya NeuroLab, Indonesia
Madalina Erascu	West University of Timisoara, Romania
Magda Friedjungová	Czech Technical University in Prague, Czech Republic
Manuel Traub	University of Tübingen, Germany
Marcello Trovati	Edge Hill University, UK
Marcin Pietron	AGH-UST, Poland
Marco Bertolini	Pfizer, Germany
Marco Podda	University of Pisa, Italy
Markus Bayer	Technical University of Darmstadt, Germany
Markus Eisenbach	Ilmenau University of Technology, Germany
Martin Ferianc	University College London, Slovakia
Martin Holena	Czech Technical University, Czech Republic
Masanari Kimura	ZOZO Research, Japan
Masato Uchida	Waseda University, Japan
Masoud Daneshtalab	Mälardalen University, Sweden

Mats Leon Richter	University of Montreal, Germany
Matthew Evanusa	University of Maryland, USA
Matthias Karlbauer	University of Tübingen, Germany
Matthias Kerzel	University of Hamburg, Germany
Matthias Möller	Örebro University, Sweden
Matthias Müller-Brockhausen	Leiden University, Netherlands
Matus Tomko	Comenius University in Bratislava, Slovakia
Mayukh Maitra	Walmart, India
Md. Delwar Hossain	Nara Institute of Science and Technology, Japan
Mehmet Aydin	University of the West of England, UK
Michail Chatzianastasis	École Polytechnique, Greece
Michail-Antisthenis Tsompanas	University of the West of England, UK
Michel Salomon	Université de Franche-Comté, France
Miguel Matey-Sanz	Universitat Jaume I, Spain
Mikołaj Morzy	Poznan University of Technology, Poland
Minal Suresh Patil	Umea universitet, Sweden
Minh Tri Lê	Inria, France
Mircea Nicolescu	University of Nevada, Reno, USA
Mohamed Elleuch	ENSI, Tunisia
Mohammed Elmahdi Khennour	Kasdi Merbah University Ouargla, Algeria
Mohib Ullah	NTNU, Norway
Monika Schak	Fulda University of Applied Sciences, Germany
Moritz Wolter	University of Bonn, Germany
Mostafa Kotb	Hamburg University, Germany
Muhammad Burhan Hafez	University of Hamburg, Germany
Nabeel Khalid	German Research Centre for Artificial Intelligence, Germany
Nabil El Malki	IRIT, France
Narendhar Gugulothu	TCS Research, India
Naresh Balaji Ravichandran	KTH Stockholm, Sweden
Natalie Kiesler	DIPF Leibniz Institute for Research and Information in Education, Germany
Nathan Duran	UWE, UK
Nermeen Abou Baker	Ruhr West University of Applied Sciences, Germany
Nick Jhones	Dundee University, UK
Nicolangelo Iannella	University of Oslo, Norway
Nicolas Couellan	ENAC, France
Nicolas Rougier	University of Bordeaux, France
Nikolaos Ioannis Bountos	National Observatory of Athens, Greece
Nikolaos Polatidis	University of Brighton, UK
Norimichi Ukita	TTI-J, Japan

Oleg Bakhteev	EPFL, Switzerland
Olga Grebenkova	Moscow Institute of Physics and Technology, Russia
Oliver Sutton	King's College London, UK
Olivier Teste	Université de Toulouse, France
Or Elroy	CLB, Israel
Oscar Fontenla-Romero	University of A Coruña, Spain
Ozan Özdenizci	Graz University of Technology, Austria
Pablo Lanillos	Spanish National Research Council, Spain
Pascal Rost	Universität Hamburg, Germany
Paul Kainen	Georgetown, USA
Paulo Cortez	University of Minho, Portugal
Pavel Petrovic	Comenius University, Slovakia
Peipei Liu	School of Cyber Security, University of Chinese Academy of Sciences, China
Peng Qiao	NUDT, China
Peter Andras	Edinburgh Napier University, UK
Peter Steiner	Technische Universität Dresden, Germany
Peter Sutor	University of Maryland, USA
Petia Georgieva	University of Aveiro/IEETA, Portugal
Petia Koprinkova-Hristova	Bulgarian Academy of Sciences, Bulgaria
Petra Vidnerová	Czech Academy of Sciences, Czech Republic
Philipp Allgeuer	University of Hamburg, Germany
Pragathi Priyadharsini Balasubramani	Indian Institute of Technology Kanpur, India
Qian Wang	Durham University, UK
Qinghua Zhou	King's College London, UK
Qingquan Zhang	Southern University of Science and Technology, China
Quentin Jodelet	Tokyo Institute of Technology, Japan
Radoslav Škoviera	Czech Technical University in Prague, Czech Republic
Raoul Heese	Fraunhofer ITWM, Germany
Ricardo Marcacini	University of São Paulo, Brazil
Riccardo Renzulli	University of Turin, Italy
Richard Duro	Universidade da Coruña, Spain
Robert Legenstein	Graz University of Technology, Austria
Rodrigo Clemente Thom de Souza	Federal University of Parana, Brazil
Rohit Dwivedula	Independent Researcher, India
Romain Ferrand	IGI TU Graz, Austria
Roman Mouček	University of West Bohemia, Czech Republic
Roseli Wedemann	Universidade do Estado do Rio de Janeiro, Brazil

Rufin VanRullen	CNRS, France
Ruijun Feng	China Telecom Beijing Research Institute, China
Ruxandra Stoean	University of Craiova, Romania
Sanchit Hira	JHU, USA
Sander Bohte	CWI, Netherlands
Sandrine Mouysset	University of Toulouse/IRIT, France
Sanka Rasnayaka	National University of Singapore, Singapore
Sašo Karakatič	University of Maribor, Slovenia
Sebastian Nowak	University Bonn, Germany
Seiya Satoh	Tokyo Denki University, Japan
Senwei Liang	LBNL, USA
Shaolin Zhu	Tianjin University, China
Shayan Gharib	University of Helsinki, Finland
Sherif Eissa	Eindhoven University of Technology, Afghanistan
Shiyong Lan	Independent Researcher, China
Shoumeng Qiu	Fudan, China
Shu Eguchi	Aomori University, Japan
Shubai Chen	Southwest University, China
Shweta Singh	International Institute of Information Technology, Hyderabad, India
Simon Hakenes	Ruhr University Bochum, Germany
Simona Doboli	Hofstra University, USA
Song Guo	Xi'an University of Architecture and Technology, China
Stanislav Frolov	Deutsches Forschungszentrum für künstliche Intelligenz (DFKI), Germany
Štefan Pócoš	Comenius University in Bratislava, Slovakia
Steven (Zvi) Lapp	Bar Ilan University, Israel
Sujala Shetty	BITS Pilani Dubai Campus, United Arab Emirates
Sumio Watanabe	Tokyo Institute of Technology, Japan
Surabhi Sinha	Adobe, USA
Takafumi Amaba	Fukuoka University, Japan
Takaharu Yaguchi	Kobe University, Japan
Takeshi Abe	Yamaguchi University, Japan
Takuya Kitamura	National Institute of Technology, Toyama College, Japan
Tatiana Tyukina	University of Leicester, UK
Teng-Sheng Moh	San Jose State University, USA
Tetsuya Hoya	Independent Researcher, Japan
Thierry Viéville	Domicile, France
Thomas Nowotny	University of Sussex, UK
Tianlin Zhang	University of Manchester, UK

Tianyi Wang	University of Hong Kong, China
Tieke He	Nanjing University, China
Tiyu Fang	Shandong University, China
Tobias Uelwer	Technical University Dortmund, Germany
Tomasz Kapuscinski	Rzeszow University of Technology, Poland
Tomasz Szandala	Wroclaw University of Technology, Poland
Toshiharu Sugawara	Waseda University, Japan
Trond Arild Tjostheim	Lund University, Sweden
Umer Mushtaq	Université Paris-Panthéon-Assas, France
Uwe Handmann	Ruhr West University, Germany
V. Ramasubramanian	International Institute of Information Technology, Bangalore, India
Valeri Mladenov	Technical University of Sofia, Bulgaria
Valerie Vaquet	Bielefeld University, Germany
Vandana Ladwani	International Institute of Information Technology, Bangalore, India
Vangelis Metsis	Texas State University, USA
Vera Kurkova	Czech Academy of Sciences, Czech Republic
Verner Ferreira	Universidade do Estado da Bahia, Brazil
Viktor Kocur	Comenius University, Slovakia
Ville Tanskanen	University of Helsinki, Finland
Viviana Cocco Mariani	PUCPR, Brazil
Vladimír Boža	Comenius University, Slovakia
Vojtech Mrazek	Brno University of Technology, Czech Republic
Weifeng Liu	China University of Petroleum (East China), China
Wenxin Yu	Southwest University of Science and Technology, China
Wenxuan Liu	Wuhan University of Technology, China
Wu Ancheng	Pingan, China
Wuliang Huang	ICT, China
Xi Cheng	NUPT, Hong Kong, China
Xia Feng	Civil Aviation University of China, China
Xian Zhong	Wuhan University of Technology, China
Xiang Zhang	National University of Defense Technology, China
Xiaochen Yuan	Macao Polytechnic University, China
Xiaodong Gu	Fudan University, China
Xiaoqing Liu	Kyushu University, Japan
Xiaowei Zhou	Macquarie University, Australia
Xiaozhuang Song	Chinese University of Hong Kong, Shenzhen, China

Xingpeng Zhang	Southwest Petroleum University, China
Xuemei Jia	Wuhan University, China
Xuewen Wang	China University of Geosciences, China
Yahong Lian	Nankai University, China
Yan Zheng	China University of Political Science and Law, China
Yang Liu	Fudan University, China
Yang Shao	Hitachi, Japan
Yangguang Cui	East China Normal University, China
Yansong Chua	China Nanhu Academy of Electronics and Information Technology, Singapore
Yapeng Gao	Taiyuan University of Technology, China
Yasufumi Sakai	Fujitsu, Japan
Ye Wang	National University of Defense Technology, China
Yeh-Ching Chung	Chinese University of Hong Kong, Shenzhen, China
Yihao Luo	Yichang Testing Technique R&D Institute, China
Yikemaiti Sataer	Southeast University, China
Yipeng Yu	Tencent, China
Yongchao Ye	Southern University of Science and Technology, China
Yoshihiko Horio	Tohoku University, Japan
Youcef Djenouri	NORCE, Norway
Yuan Li	Military Academy of Sciences, China
Yuan Panli	Shihezi University, China
Yuan Yao	Tsinghua University, China
Yuanlun Xie	University of Electronic Science and Technology of China, China
Yuanshao Zhu	Southern University of Science and Technology, China
Yucan Zhou	Institute of Information Engineering, Chinese Academy of Sciences, China
Yuchen Zheng	Shihezi University, China
Yuchun Fang	Shanghai University, China
Yue Zhao	Minzu University of China, China
Yuesong Nan	National University of Singapore, Singapore
Zaneta Swiderska-Chadaj	Warsaw University of Technology, Poland
Zdenek Straka	Czech Technical University in Prague, Czech Republic
Zhao Yang	Leiden University, Netherlands
Zhaoyun Ding	NUDT, China
Zhengwei Yang	Wuhan University, China

Invited Talks

Developmental Robotics for Language Learning, Trust and Theory of Mind

Angelo Cangelosi

University of Manchester and Alan Turing Institute, UK

Growing theoretical and experimental research on action and language processing and on number learning and gestures clearly demonstrates the role of embodiment in cognition and language processing. In psychology and neuroscience, this evidence constitutes the basis of embodied cognition, also known as grounded cognition (Pezzulo et al. 2012). In robotics and AI, these studies have important implications for the design of linguistic capabilities in cognitive agents and robots for human-robot collaboration, and have led to the new interdisciplinary approach of Developmental Robotics, as part of the wider Cognitive Robotics field (Cangelosi and Schlesinger 2015; Cangelosi and Asada 2022). During the talk we presented examples of developmental robotics models and experimental results from iCub experiments on the embodiment biases in early word acquisition and grammar learning (Morse et al. 2015; Morse and Cangelosi 2017) and experiments on pointing gestures and finger counting for number learning (De La Cruz et al. 2014). We then presented a novel developmental robotics model, and experiments, on Theory of Mind and its use for autonomous trust behavior in robots (Vinanzi et al. 2019, 2021). The implications for the use of such embodied approaches for embodied cognition in AI and cognitive sciences, and for robot companion applications, was also discussed.

Challenges of Incremental Learning

Barbara Hammer

CITEC Centre of Excellence, Bielefeld University, Germany

Smart products and AI components are increasingly available in industrial applications and everyday life. This offers great opportunities for cognitive automation and intelligent human-machine cooperation; yet it also poses significant challenges since a fundamental assumption of classical machine learning, an underlying stationary data distribution, might be easily violated. Unexpected events or outliers, sensor drift, or individual user behavior might cause changes of an underlying data distribution, typically referred to as concept drift or covariate shift. Concept drift requires a continuous adaptation of the underlying model and efficient incremental learning strategies. Within the presentation, I looked at recent developments in the context of incremental learning schemes for streaming data, putting a particular focus on the challenge of learning with drift and detecting and disentangling drift in possibly unsupervised setups and for unknown type and strength of drift. More precisely, I dealt with the following aspects: learning schemes for incremental model adaptation from streaming data in the presence of concept drift; various mathematical formalizations of concept drift and detection/quantification of drift based thereon; and decomposition and explanation of drift. I presented a couple of experimental results using benchmarks from the literature, and I offered a glimpse into mathematical guarantees which can be provided for some of the algorithms.

Reliable AI: From Mathematical Foundations to Quantum Computing

Gitta Kutyniok[1,2]

[1]Bavarian AI Chair for Mathematical Foundations of Artificial Intelligence, LMU Munich, Germany
[2]Adjunct Professor for Machine Learning, University of Tromsø, Norway

Artificial intelligence is currently leading to one breakthrough after the other, both in public life with, for instance, autonomous driving and speech recognition, and in the sciences in areas such as medical diagnostics or molecular dynamics. However, one current major drawback is the lack of reliability of such methodologies.

In this lecture we took a mathematical viewpoint towards this problem, showing the power of such approaches to reliability. We first provided an introduction into this vibrant research area, focussing specifically on deep neural networks. We then surveyed recent advances, in particular concerning generalization guarantees and explainability methods. Finally, we discussed fundamental limitations of deep neural networks and related approaches in terms of computability, which seriously affects their reliability, and we revealed a connection with quantum computing.

Intelligent Pervasive Applications for Holistic Health Management

Ilias Maglogiannis

University of Piraeus, Greece

The advancements in telemonitoring platforms, biosensors, and medical devices have paved the way for pervasive health management, allowing patients to be monitored remotely in real-time. The visual domain has become increasingly important for patient monitoring, with activity recognition and fall detection being key components. Computer vision techniques, such as deep learning, have been used to develop robust activity recognition and fall detection algorithms. These algorithms can analyze video streams from cameras, detecting and classifying various activities, and detecting falls in real time. Furthermore, wearable devices, such as smartwatches and fitness trackers, can also monitor a patient's daily activities, providing insights into their overall health and wellness, allowing for a comprehensive analysis of a patient's health. In this talk we discussed the state of the art in pervasive health management and biomedical data analytics and we presented the work done in the Computational Biomedicine Laboratory of the University of Piraeus in this domain. The talk also included Future Trends and Challenges.

Contents – Part VIII

2RDA: Representation and Relation Distillation with Data Augmentation

Xurui Yang[1,2] and Jian Ye[1,2(✉)]

[1] Institute of Computing Technology, Chinese Academy of Sciences, Beijing, China
{yangxurui20g,jye}@ict.ac.cn
[2] University of Chinese Academy of Sciences, Beijing, China

Abstract. Large pre-trained language models have demonstrated superior performance in natural language processing tasks. However, the massive number of parameters and slow inference speed make it challenging to deploy them on resource-constrained devices. Existing knowledge distillation methods use the point-to-point approach to transfer the knowledge, which restrains the ability to learn the higher-level semantic knowledge from the teacher network. In this paper, we propose Representation and Relation Distillation with Data Augmentation(2RDA), a novel knowledge distillation framework. Unlike previous methods, 2RDA introduces an improved contrastive distillation loss function for data augmentation to solve the problem that data augmentation during the fine-tuning of downstream tasks may lead to the misclassification of positive and negative sample pairs for contrastive learning. Additionally, we guide the student model to obtain structural knowledge by distilling the relational knowledge between samples from a mini-batch through distance loss. 2RDA achieves excellent results and surpasses the state-of-the-art model compression methods on the GLUE benchmark, demonstrating the effectiveness of our approach.

Keywords: knowledge distillation · contrastive learning · data augmentation

1 Introduction

In the past few years, pre-trained language models like BERT [3] and RoBERTa [11] have achieved significant progress in natural language processing (NLP) tasks. However, these bloated models restrict their deployment in limited computational resources. Knowledge distillation (KD) [8] is popular research as a method for model compression [7]. KD is a Teacher-Student network training structure, which completes the process of migrating the knowledge from the complex teacher model to the simple student model at the expense of a slight performance loss.

A constant question in KD development is: What knowledge should the student learn? The common approach [8] requires the student model to learn the

L. Iliadis et al. (Eds.): ICANN 2023, LNCS 14261, pp. 1–12, 2023.
https://doi.org/10.1007/978-3-031-44198-1_1

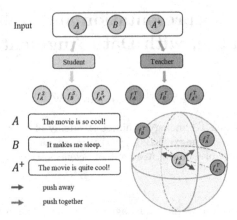

Fig. 1. Schematic of traditional contrastive distillation. In this case, A^+ is a sample after using data augmentation by sample A. The traditional method assumes that f_A^S and f_{A+}^T are not similar representations so that contrastive loss pushes f_{A+}^T away indiscriminately from the other negative samples. This goes against the way in which contrastive learning initially determines positive and negative examples.

probability distribution, but this formal knowledge appears insufficient for building natural language understanding models with such a large number of parameters. Existing research [10,15,17] suggests that a wealth of information can be learned from intermediate representations. However, these distillation strategies only aim to mimic the output values of the teacher layers in the hidden states, ignoring the structural information that is essential to improve the performance of the student model. Recently, some distillation works [5,16] introduced contrastive learning to capture the structural characteristics between the student and teacher. However, when performing contrastive learning with data augmentation, only the same sample is considered to be in the same class, which results in false negatives. For instance, the original data and augmented data should also be close to each other rather than pushed away. False negatives may have a potential inhibition when the student learns semantic representations, as shown in Fig. 1.

Moreover, is there other useful information waiting to be learned by the student? We find that maintaining relations between samples is also the key to preserving deep structure knowledge. Considering only the results of a single sample will neglect structural relations between features, thus affecting the outcome of knowledge distillation.

To bridge the gap, we propose a distillation framework called 2RDA. In KD process, contrastive learning loss for data augmentation is introduced to train the student, considering the impact of augmented data samples for the contrastive learning object. Specifically, We reformulate the rules for determining positive and negative sample pairs, which prevents the sample pairs augmented from the same data from being away from each other. By improved contrastive loss, the student can capture the higher-order output dependence between the intermediate representations of the teacher and student. In addition, we distill the relations from the intermediate representations of the teacher. Student builds structural relations of the output representations and captures the correlations and higher-order output dependencies of each sample through angular loss, rather than only learning the representations themselves. To encourage the student to concentrate on learning a good representation in the early stage without the influence of label signals, we adopt a two-stage training strategy. In the process of transferring knowledge, we distill the transformer layers at the first stage, then the prediction layer at the second stage.

Our contributions are summarized as follows.

- We propose a novel KD framework, 2RDA, which combines distilling the representations through contrastive loss and distilling the relations through angle distance loss.
- We propose a new contrastive loss to distill the intermediate representations. Compared to previous contrastive distillation, the judgment of the positive and negative sample pairs is more fine-grained.
- Our extensive experiments on the GLUE task demonstrate that the 2RDA approach performs better than the state-of-the-art baseline model.

2 Related Work

2.1 Knowledge Distillation

There have been numerous important works throughout the history of KD research. The standard form of knowledge distillation [8] employed the softmax function with a temperature parameter to transfer the probability distribution of categories from the teacher to the student, referred to as soft targets. DistilBERT [14] not only proposed cosine loss to compute the cosine similarity between the hidden state of the teacher and student but also optimized the matrix computation of fully connected layers in the transformer. TinyBERT [10] used a parameter matrix to linearly transform the hidden states of the student layers to extract knowledge from the middle and last layers of the teacher. MiniLM [20] distilled the self-attention module of the final transformer layer of the teacher and introduced teaching assistants to help distill the model. MobileBERT [17] assumed the same number of layers for the teacher-student network and introduced a bottleneck module to keep their hidden layers the same size.

Furthermore, some work is exploring how to introduce contrastive learning into knowledge distillation. The reference [18] first used contrastive learning in compute vision (CV) distillation tasks and demonstrated that contrastive loss maximizes the mutual information of student and teacher output distribution. LRC-BERT [5] introduced contrastive learning at each intermediate layer of the student. It replaced cosine similarity with angular distance to evaluate the similarity of two samples. During the distillation of certain downstream tasks, the training data set was conducted with 20 times data augmentation. However, the existing contrastive distillation constitutes the same sample from the student and the teacher as a positive sample pair, pushing the distance between the data-enhanced samples in the feature space farther away, which may hinder representation learning.

2.2 Contrastive Learning

Contrastive learning [4] uses the data itself as supervised information and manually sets rules to construct positive and negative sample pairs, which is frequently used to learn the high-quality representation of samples. Common contrastive loss functions are NCE loss [6] and infoNCE loss [12].

The core of contrastive learning is how to construct positive and negative example pairs. CLEAR [22] proposed sentence-level feature extraction and tried multiple sentence-level enhancement strategies to pull in the representations in the feature space after data augmentation of the same sentence. In common contrastive knowledge distillation work [5,16,18], the same sample is often used to form positive sample pairs by entering the student model and the teacher model separately. In our approach, we use contrastive learning for distillation in the transformer layer to learn the intermediate representations of the teacher network and address the interference in the judgment of positive and negative sample pairs caused by data augmentation.

3   Method

3.1   Framework Overview

2RDA distillation framework is illustrated in Fig. 2. We use BERT-base [3] as the teacher network, denoted as f^T with 12 transformer blocks. The student network with L transformer blocks is denoted as f^S. In 2RDA, L is set to 4 or 6. Since the teacher has 12 transformer layers and the student has only L transformer layers, we define the mapping function $\phi(l)$, which represents the l-th transformer layer of the student will learn from the $\phi(l)$-th transformer layer of the teacher. Set a mini-batch with n sentences, $\boldsymbol{X} = [x_1, x_2, ..., x_n]$. For sample x_i, we choose the [CLS] token as the hidden representation of the student and teacher, denoted as h_i^S and h_i^T respectively. The hidden representation from the l-th layer of the student is denoted as $\boldsymbol{H}_l^S = [h_{1,l}^S, h_{2,l}^S, ..., h_{n,l}^S]$ $(1 \leq l \leq L)$, and the hidden representation from the l-th layer of the teacher is denoted as $\boldsymbol{H}_l^T = [h_{1,l}^T, h_{2,l}^T, ..., h_{n,l}^T]$ $(1 \leq l \leq 12)$. The output $\boldsymbol{H}_l^S$ of the student is trained to match the output $\boldsymbol{H}_{\phi(l)}^T$ of the teacher.

2RDA transfers the representations and relations in each student transformer layer, which facilitates the formation of structural knowledge. With the help of soft and hard labels in the prediction layer, the student strengthens the ability to predict downstream tasks. The distillation objective of 2RDA consists of three components: (*i*) proposed contrastive distillation loss based on data augmentation $\mathcal{L}_{crda}$; (*ii*) relational distillation loss $\mathcal{L}_{rd}$; (*iii*) standard distillation loss from prediction layer $\mathcal{L}_{pred}$.

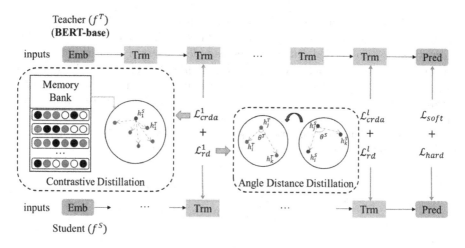

Fig. 2. The main architecture of 2RDA. "Emb", "Trm", and "Pred" represent an embedding layer, a transformer layer, and a prediction layer, respectively. f^T and f^S represent the teacher model and student model, respectively.

3.2   Contrastive Distillation

Memory Bank. Existing works [1,2,6,18] suggested that more negative samples were able to benefit contrastive learning. Thus, for an anchor in contrastive learning, we need a large number of negative samples. In practice, we cannot increase the number of negative samples by merely turning up the batchsize due to the hardware limitations. Thus, we follow the approach of [21] and utilize memory banks $\{M^i\}_{i=1}^L$ to store the intermediate representations from the corresponding layer of the teacher. To reduce the cost of storage space, each memory bank only stores a fixed number of negative samples depending on the capacity. The memory bank employs the queueing mechanism. If the memory bank that stores current layer representations is full, the earliest representations of the current layer will be eliminated, preserving data mobility and training robustness. Since the parameters of the teacher network are fixed during the distillation, the teacher representations of the corresponding sample will not be updated.

Contrastive Loss for Data Augmentation. As a result of introducing the memory bank in contrastive distillation, the number of negative samples is significantly increased. When performing contrastive learning, the current anchor h_i^S is more likely to be compared with the representations after data augmentation by the same sample. Traditional contrastive distillation methods considered these sample pairs as negative pairs, inhibiting the student model from learning better representation information. We propose the improved contrastive loss for data augmentation to address the problem that the previous distillation contrastive method incorrectly the classify categories. For each training sample x, we store the index of its corresponding original data in the training data set. Samples augmented by the same original data have the same index. The index information is also carried out when the samples generate intermediate representations, even in the memory bank. We use $index(h)$ to obtain the index of the representation h. For the anchor h_i^S in a mini-batch during the contrastive learning, it needs to be compared with K samples, where K is the number of representations in the current memory bank M.

For every hidden representation $h_{i,l}^S$ for the sample x_i on the l-th layer , we redefine the contrastive representation loss for data augmentation:

$$\mathcal{L}_{crda}^l = -\sum_{i=1}^{n} \log \frac{\sum_{m=1}^{K} g(h_{i,l}^S, h_{m,\phi(l)}^T) \cdot \exp(f(h_{i,l}^S W, h_{m,\phi(l)}^T)/\tau)}{\sum_{j=1}^{K} \exp(f(h_{i,l}^S W, h_{j,\phi(l)}^T)/\tau)} \tag{1}$$

where

$$g(h_i^S, h_j^T) = \begin{cases} 1, & index(h_i^S) = index(h_j^T) \\ 0, & otherwise \end{cases} \tag{2}$$

where $f(u, v)$ represents the cosine similarity between u and v, and τ is a temperature hyperparameter. The matrix $W \in \mathbb{R}^{d' \times d}$ is a linear transformation, where d and d' represent the hidden size of the teacher network and the student network, respectively. It maps the hidden layer output of the student network to a feature space of the same dimension as the teacher network. The function is adapted from the well-known InfoNCE loss [9]. We add the function g to the numerator, which treats all sample pairs with the same index as positive sample pairs. Our proposed contrastive loss compensates for the gaps caused by the misclassification of sample pairs in conventional contrastive distillation.

3.3   Relational Distillation

Making the individual intermediate representation of the student being close to the teacher in the semantic space is insufficient to capture the complex structural relationships between representations in the high-dimensional space. We also focus on the internal relations between the representations. We follow the work of [13] by introducing angular distillation loss in the intermediate layer in order to transfer the structural relations of the teacher layer. When taking three samples x_i, x_j, x_k from a mini-batch, the cosine angle of these examples in the intermediate representation space is formulated as:

$$\theta(h_i, h_j, h_k) = \frac{h_i - h_j}{||h_i - h_j||_2} \cdot \frac{h_j - h_k}{||h_j - h_k||_2} \tag{3}$$

Since the computational complexity grows cubically with the number of samples, we do not introduce memory bank in relational distillation. We extract the feature relations by minimizing the angular distance of the same three samples of student and teacher in a mini-batch:

$$\mathcal{L}_{rd}^l = \sum_{(x_i, x_j, x_k) \in \mathcal{X}^3} \mathcal{L}_\delta(\theta(h_{i,l}^s, h_{j,l}^s, h_{k,l}^s), \theta(h_{i,\phi(l)}^t, h_{j,\phi(l)}^t, h_{k,\phi(l)}^t)) \tag{4}$$

where $\mathcal{X}^3$ represents the set of all three mutually different samples in a mini-batch, $\mathcal{L}_\delta$ is Huber loss:

$$\mathcal{L}_\delta(s,t) = \begin{cases} \frac{1}{2}(t-s)^2, & |t-s| \leq \delta \\ \delta|t-s| - \frac{1}{2}\delta^2, & otherwise \end{cases} \tag{5}$$

where δ denotes the error threshold hyperparameter, which is set to 1.

3.4   Training Process

Transformer Layer Distillation. Contrastive distillation and angle distance distillation are introduced in every transformer layer of the student. The total loss for all transformer layers is defined as follows:

$$\mathcal{L}_{transformer} = \alpha_1 \sum_{l=1}^{L} \mathcal{L}_{crda}^l + \alpha_2 \sum_{l=1}^{L} \mathcal{L}_{rd}^l \tag{6}$$

where α_1 and α_2 are weight coefficient.

Prediction Layer Distillation. To classify specific downstream tasks, the student learns the soft label of the teacher and their corresponding real label from the data set, which denotes the hard label at the prediction layer. The prediction loss $\mathcal{L}_{pred}$ is defined as:

$$\mathcal{L}_{pred} = \alpha_3 CE(z^S/t, z^T/t) + \alpha_4 CE(z^S, y) \tag{7}$$

where CE represents the soft cross-entropy loss function, z^S and z^T represent the predicted logits of the student and the teacher, respectively. y is the real one-hot label, t means the temperature hyperparametric.

We employ a two-stage training approach. Specifically, in the first stage, we set α_3, α_4 to 0, only to calculate the contrastive loss and relational loss of the transformer layer. In the second stage, we set α_1, α_2 to 0 only to perform prediction layer distillation, empowering the student ability to predict downstream tasks.

4   Experiment

4.1   Datasets

We evaluate 2RDA on the General Language Understanding Evaluation (GLUE) [19] benchmark, which contains 9 sentence-level classification tasks, including Microsoft Research Paraphrase Matching (MRPC), Quora Question Pairs (QQP), Semantic Textual Similarity Benchmark (STS-B), Stanford Sentiment Treebank (SST-2), Question Natural Language Inference (QNLI), Recognizing Textual Entailment (RTE), Corpus of Linguistic Acceptability (CoLA), Multi-Genre Natural Language Inference Matched (MNLI-m) and Multi-Genre Natural Language Inference Mismatched (MNLI-mm). We evaluate 2RDA using the metrics of the GLUE benchmark. Specifically, for QQP and MRPC, the metric is F1-score, the Spearman correlation is adopted for STS-B, the Matthews correlation coefficient is used as the evaluation metric for CoLA, and accuracy is adopted for the rest tasks.

4.2   2RDA Settings

Data Augmentation. We focused our experiments on contrastive knowledge distillation using data augmentation on specific downstream tasks rather than distilling a pre-trained model because distilling a pre-trained model does not lack training corpus. We utilize the training data sets corresponding to specific tasks on GLUE to compress the teacher network. We follow the method and setup for data augmentation proposed by TinyBERT [10] to expand the data by 20 times in each downstream task.

Implementation Details. We use BERT-base [3] as our teacher model. BERT-base contains 12 transformer layers with 768 hidden dimensions, 3072 intermediate dimensions, 12 attention heads per layer, and about 109M parameters. To enable a more comprehensive comparison with previous work, two student model architectures were designed. The first student architecture contains a 4-layer transformer with 312 hidden layer size, 1200 intermediate dimensions, 12 attention heads and about 14.5M parameters, which is denoted as $2RDA_4(L = 4, d' = 312, d_i = 1200, l_{head} = 12)$. The second student architecture($L = 6$, $d' = 768$, $d_i = 3072$, $l_{head} = 12$) with approximately 69M parameters, denoted as $2RDA_6$. We employ the two-stage distillation training for downstream tasks as mentioned in Sect. 3. For the first stage, $2RDA_4$ and $2RDA_6$ initialize the generic distillation weights from $TinyBERT_4$ and $TinyBERT_6$[1], respectively.

Hyperparameters. For each downstream task on GLUE, we fine-tune the BERT-base as the teacher. In the first distillation stage, we distill the transformer layer with the augmented dataset. We set the size of each memory bank to 2048. The training epoch is fixed to 10. For the contrastive learning temperature τ, we set it to 0.05. The parameters α_1 and α_2 in $\mathcal{L}_{transformer}$ are set to 3 and 1, respectively. As for the second distillation stage, we used the student who completed the first distillation stage as input. The epoch is fixed to 5. The temperature t in $\mathcal{L}_{soft}$ is set to 1.2. We set both α_3 and α_4 in $\mathcal{L}_{pred}$ to 1. For the batchsize B and learning rate lr of the two-stage training, we utilize grid search to set the B from {32, 64} and lr from {1e-5, 3e-5, 5e-5}. The mapping function for $2RDA_4$ is $\phi(l) = 3l$ while $\phi(l) = 2l$ for $2RDA_6$. In each task, we select the best model in the dev set to predict the task in the test set. Then we submit the result to the official GLUE to compare with other baseline models.

---

[1] https://github.com/huawei-noah/Pretrained-Language-Model/tree/master/Tiny BERT.

Table 1. Experimental results for the GLUE test set. The subscript indicates the number of transformer layers in each model name. The evaluation findings are obtained from the GLUE benchmark's official website, with the best experimental outcomes highlighted in bold. Results of other baseline models are taken from published papers.

Model	#Params	Speedup	MNLI-(m/mm) (393K)	QQP (368K)	SST-2 (67K)	QNLI (108K)	MRPC (3.7K)	RTE (2.5K)	CoLA (8.5K)	STS-B (5.7K)	Ave.
BERT-base	109M	×1	84.6/83.4	71.2	93.5	90.5	88.9	66.4	52.1	85.8	79.6
DistillBERT$_4$	52.2M	×3.0	78.9/78.0	68.5	91.4	85.2	82.4	54.1	32.8	76.1	71.9
BERT$_4$-PKD	52.2M	×3.0	79.9/79.3	70.2	89.4	85.1	82.6	62.3	24.8	79.8	72.6
TinyBERT$_4$	14.5M	×9.4	82.5/81.8	71.3	92.6	87.7	86.4	66.6	44.1	80.4	77.0
2RDA$_4$(ours)	14.5M	×9.4	**83.5/82.4**	**71.5**	**93.0**	**89.1**	**87.3**	**66.8**	**46.8**	**82.0**	**78.0**
DistillBERT$_6$	67.0M	×2.0	82.6/81.3	70.1	92.5	88.9	86.9	58.4	49.0	81.3	76.8
BERT$_6$-PKD	67.0M	×2.0	81.5/81.0	70.7	92.0	89.0	85.0	65.5	-	-	-
BERT-of-Theseus$_6$	67.0M	×2.0	82.4/82.1	71.6	92.2	89.6	87.6	66.2	47.8	84.1	78.2
TinyBERT$_6$	67.0M	×2.0	84.6/83.2	71.6	93.1	90.4	87.3	70.0	51.1	83.7	79.4
2RDA$_6$(ours)	67.0M	×2.0	**84.7/83.9**	**71.9**	**93.3**	90.5	88.0	70.6	51.4	**84.4**	79.9

4.3 Experimental Results

The experimental results on the GLUE test set are presented in Table 1. We compare the distillation results of 2RDA with popular baseline, such as DistillBERT [14], BERT-PKD [15], TinyBERT [10], BERT-of-Theseus [23]. We do not compare the results with CoDIR [16], which introduced contrastive distillation because CoDIR utilized a more powerful RoBERTa-base [11] as the teacher model, which may lead to unfair comparative results.

By analyzing the experimental results of the 4-layer student model, it can be concluded that 2RDA$_4$ outperforms the other 4 transformer-layer students on all GLUE tasks, retaining 98% of the teacher performance. 2RDA$_4$ exceeds the best competitor, TinyBERT$_4$, by 1% score on Ave. Specifically, 2RDA$_4$ achieves 1.0% higher result for MNLI-m, 0.6% for MNLI-mm, 0.2% for QQP, 0.4% for SST-2, 1.3% for QNLI, 0.9% for MRPC, 0.2% for RTE, 2.7% for CoLA and 1.6% for STS-B. Compared to BERT-PKD$_4$ and DistillBERT$_4$, 2RDA$_4$ outperforms these two student models while only with 30% parameters. Inference time is also an important metric for measuring a model. We can find that our proposed 2RDA$_4$ runs 9.4 times faster than the original teacher model, BERT-base, and has 7.5 times smaller parameters.

We observe similar results when we continue to increase the number of layers to 2RDA$_6$. 2RDA$_6$ still performs the best among the 6-layer student models. 2RDA$_6$ outperforms the experimental results of TinyBERT, rising by 0.5% on Ave. Furthermore, 2RDA$_6$ even outperforms the 12-layer teacher model on certain datasets, which is considered to be an excellent result. The above results demonstrate the effectiveness of the proposed approach for distillation-specific tasks using data augmentation.

4.4 Ablation Studies

Effect of Loss Function. We evaluate different loss function objectives to validate the effectiveness of 2RDA. We use the following settings separately: (1)

Table 2. Ablation study on the different loss functions. The experimental results are based on GLUE dev set. The results are averaged for 3 runs.

Model	MNLI-(m/mm) (393K)	QQP (368K)	SST-2 (67K)	QNLI (108K)	MRPC (3.7K)	RTE (2.5K)	CoLA (8.5K)	STS-B (5.7K)	Ave.
2RDA$_6$	**84.6/84.2**	72.0	92.8	**90.9**	**87.6**	**71.2**	**53.9**	84.4	**80.2**
$\mathcal{L}_1$	81.9/81.4	70.8	90.9	87.6	85.7	68.2	49.6	81.8	77.5
$\mathcal{L}_2$	84.1/83.6	71.8	92.7	90.2	86.4	69.7	52.8	82.5	79.3
$\mathcal{L}_3$	84.6/84.0	**72.4**	**92.9**	90.6	86.8	69.9	52.2	83.7	79.7

2RDA$_6$: This is our proposed distillation technique based on data augmentation. (2)$\mathcal{L}_1$: Remove the contrastive loss function which is used in the first stage. (3)$\mathcal{L}_2$: Remove the angular distance loss function in the first stage. (4)$\mathcal{L}_3$: Use the conventional infoNCE loss instead of $\mathcal{L}_{crda}$ when conducting contrastive learning. The other configurations for settings (2), (3), and (4) are the same as 2RDA$_6$.

The results for the GLUE dev set are shown in Table 2. The results show that 2RDA$_6$ outperforms all other methods in terms of Ave. Specifically, without using contrastive loss, angular distance loss results in 2.7% and 0.9% performance decrease on average. Conventional infoNCE leads to a 0.5% drop on average, indicating that removing or altering any loss targets would decrease the results. The performance loss from setting (4) is relatively minor compared to setting (2) and (3) and still maintains competitive performance on the QQP, MNLI-m/mm, and SST-2 tasks. We speculate it is due to a large amount of training data on the QQP, MNLI-m/mm, and SST-2 tasks, which significantly dilutes the probability of matching augmented samples from the same source data in contrastive learning.

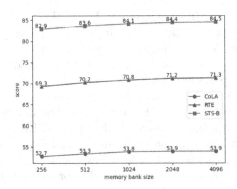

Fig. 3. Analysis of the size of the memory bank on CoLA, RTE, and STS-B dev set. The results are averaged for 3 runs.

Analysis of the Size of Memory Bank. The memory bank size represents the number of negative samples when performing contrastive learning. We explore whether the memory bank size affects the result of contrastive distillation. We set the size of each memory bank to 512, 1024, 2048, and 4096, respectively. Then we analyze the results by comparing them to CoLA, RTE, and STS-B dev set. Other settings are the same as $2RDA_6$.

Figure 3 shows the experimental results. We can observe that using more negative examples for the training set will help to improve the accuracy. Furthermore, it is evident that when the size of the memory bank is increased from 512 to 2048, the accuracy of the model gets improved significantly. However, when the memory bank size exceeds 2048, the improvement is slight. Specifically, when the size is increased from 2048 to 4096, it only contributes 0%, 0.1%, and 0.1% performance improvement on the CoLA, RTE, and STS-B tasks, respectively. However, storing 4096 negative samples for each memory bank will consume a lot of storage space and calculation time. To balance the training time and effectiveness, we set the memory bank size to 2048 in 2RDA.

5 Conclusion

In this paper, we propose a novel knowledge distillation framework, 2RDA, for compressing the BERT into a lightweight student model, which is suitable for data-scarce downstream tasks. 2RDA uses contrastive learning based on data augmentation in the distillation process to better judge the positive and negative sample pairs when transferring representations knowledge from the teacher, which is not considered in existing knowledge distillation methods. In addition, the angular distance penalty is introduced to capture high-level relationships between samples. Our experiments demonstrate that 2RDA can achieve more competitive performance.

Acknowledgement. The research work is supported by National Key R&D Program of China (No. 2022YFB3904700), Industrial Internet Innovation and Development Project in 2021 (TC210A02M, TC210804D), Opening Project of Beijing Key Laboratory of Mobile Computing and Pervasive Device.

References

1. Bachman, P., Hjelm, R.D., Buchwalter, W.: Learning representations by maximizing mutual information across views. In: Advances in Neural Information Processing Systems, NeurIPS, pp. 15509–15519 (2019)
2. Chen, L., Wang, D., Gan, Z., Liu, J., Henao, R., Carin, L.: Wasserstein contrastive representation distillation. In: Proceedings of the IEEE/CVF Conference on Computer Vision and Pattern Recognition, pp. 16296–16305 (2021)
3. Devlin, J., Chang, M.W., Lee, K., Toutanova, K.: BERT: pre-training of deep bidirectional transformers for language understanding. In: Proceedings of NAACL-HLT, pp. 4171–4186 (2019)

4. Fang, H., Wang, S., Zhou, M., Ding, J., Xie, P.: CERT: contrastive self-supervised learning for language understanding. arXiv preprint arXiv:2005.12766 (2020)
5. Fu, H., et al.: LRC-BERT: latent-representation contrastive knowledge distillation for natural language understanding. In: Proceedings of the AAAI Conference on Artificial Intelligence, pp. 12830–12838 (2021)
6. Gutmann, M., Hyvärinen, A.: Noise-contrastive estimation: a new estimation principle for unnormalized statistical models. In: Proceedings of the 13th International Conference on Artificial Intelligence and Statistics, AISTATS, pp. 297–304. JMLR Workshop and Conference Proceedings (2010)
7. Han, S., Mao, H., Dally, W.J.: Deep compression: compressing deep neural networks with pruning, trained quantization and Huffman coding. In: ICLR 2016 - Conference Track Proceedings (2016)
8. Hinton, G., Vinyals, O., Dean, J.: Distilling the knowledge in a neural network. arXiv preprint arXiv:1503.02531 (2015)
9. Hjelm, R.D., et al.: Learning deep representations by mutual information estimation and maximization. In: 7th International Conference on Learning Representations, ICLR (2019)
10. Jiao, X., et al.: TinyBERT: distilling BERT for natural language understanding. In: Proceedings of the Conference on EMNLP, pp. 4163–4174 (2020)
11. Liu, Y., et al.: Roberta: A robustly optimized BERT pretraining approach. arXiv preprint arXiv:1907.11692 (2019)
12. Oord, A.V.D., Li, Y., Vinyals, O.: Representation learning with contrastive predictive coding. arXiv preprint arXiv:1807.03748 (2018)
13. Park, W., Kim, D., Lu, Y., Cho, M.: Relational knowledge distillation. In: Proceedings of the IEEE/CVF Conference on Computer Vision and Pattern Recognition, pp. 3967–3976 (2019)
14. Sanh, V., Debut, L., Chaumond, J., Wolf, T.: Distilbert, a distilled version of BERT: smaller, faster, cheaper and lighter. arXiv preprint arXiv:1910.01108 (2019)
15. Sun, S., Cheng, Y., Gan, Z., Liu, J.: Patient knowledge distillation for BERT model compression. In: Proceedings of the EMNLP-IJCNLP, pp. 4322–4331 (2019)
16. Sun, S., Gan, Z., Cheng, Y., Fang, Y., Wang, S., Liu, J.: Contrastive distillation on intermediate representations for language model compression. In: Proceedings of the Conference on EMNLP, pp. 498–508 (2020)
17. Sun, Z., Yu, H., Song, X., Liu, R., Yang, Y., Zhou, D.: Mobilebert: a compact task-agnostic BERT for resource-limited devices. In: Proceedings of the 58th ACL, pp. 2158–2170 (2020)
18. Tian, Y., Krishnan, D., Isola, P.: Contrastive representation distillation. In: 8th International Conference on Learning Representations, ICLR (2020)
19. Wang, A., Singh, A., Michael, J., Hill, F., Levy, O., Bowman, S.R.: GLUE: a multi-task benchmark and analysis platform for natural language understanding. In: 7th International Conference on ICLR (2019)
20. Wang, W., Wei, F., Dong, L., Bao, H., Yang, N., Zhou, M.: MiniLM: deep self-attention distillation for task-agnostic compression of pre-trained transformers, pp. 5776–5788 (2020)
21. Wu, Z., Xiong, Y., Yu, S.X., Lin, D.: Unsupervised feature learning via non-parametric instance discrimination. In: Proceedings of the IEEE Conference on Computer Vision and Pattern Recognition, pp. 3733–3742 (2018)
22. Wu, Z., Wang, S., Gu, J., Khabsa, M., Sun, F., Ma, H.: CLEAR: contrastive learning for sentence representation. arXiv preprint arXiv:2012.15466 (2020)
23. Xu, C., Zhou, W., Ge, T., Wei, F., Zhou, M.: BERT-of-Theseus: compressing BERT by progressive module replacing. In: Proceedings of the Conference on EMNLP, pp. 7859–7869 (2020)

A Document-Level Relation Extraction Framework with Dynamic Pruning

Hanyue Zhang[1], Li Li[1(✉)], and Jun Shen[2]

[1] School of Computer and Information Science,
Southwest University, Chongqing 400700, China
lily@swu.edu.cn
[2] School of Computer and Information Technology, University of Wollongong,
Wollongong, NSW 2522, Australia

Abstract. Relation extraction (RE) has been a fundamental task in natural language processing (NLP) as it identifies semantic relations among entity pairs in texts. Because sentence-level RE can only capture intra-connections within a sentence rather than inter-connections between or among sentences, researchers shift their attentions to document-level RE to obtain richer and complex relations which may involve logic inference. Prior works on document-level RE suffer from inflexible pruning rules and lack of sentence-level features, which lead to the missing of valuable information. In this paper, we propose a document-level relation extraction framework with both dynamic pruning mechanism and sentence-level attention. Specifically, a weight-based flexible pruning mechanism is applied on the document-level dependency tree to remove non-relational edges dynamically and obtain the weight dependency tree (WDT). Moreover, a graph convolution network (GCN) then is employed to learn syntactic representations of the WDT. Furthermore, the sentence-level attention and gating selection module are applied to capture the intrinsic interactions between sentence-level and document-level features. We evaluate our framework on three benchmark datasets: DocRED, CDR, and GDA. Experiment results demonstrate that our approach outperforms the baselines and achieves the state-of-the-art performance.

Keywords: Document-level Relation Extraction · Dynamic pruning mechanism · sentence-level attention · gating selection

1 Introduction

Relation extraction (RE), which identifies semantic relations among entity-pairs in texts, has been a fundamental task in natural language processing (NLP) [16,20]. Early research [8,24] largely focused on predicting relations between entities within a sentence. In contrast, document-level relation extraction requires integrated information within and across sentences, via capturing complex interactions among mentions of entities. For example, as shown

© The Author(s), under exclusive license to Springer Nature Switzerland AG 2023
L. Iliadis et al. (Eds.): ICANN 2023, LNCS 14261, pp. 13–25, 2023.
https://doi.org/10.1007/978-3-031-44198-1_2

No.1: The Samsung Galaxy S (Super Smar) series is a line of high-end Android-powered mobile devices produced by *Samsung Electronics*, a division of *Samsung* from South Korea.
No.2: ...
No.3: ...
No.4: Since the introduction of the *Samsung Galaxy Note* in 2011, the Galaxy S line has co-existed with Galaxy Note line as being *Samsung Elecreonics*'s flagship smartphones.

Example Relation 1		
Sub: *Samsung*	Rel: *parent organization*	Obj: *Samsung Electronics*
Example Relation 2		
Sub: *Samsung Electronics*	Rel: *manufacturer*	Obj: *Samsung Galaxy Note*
Example Relation 3		
Sub: *Samsung*	Rel: *manufacturer*	Obj: *Samsung Galaxy Note*

Fig. 1. An example adapted from the DocRED dataset. The mentions of a same entity are described with same color.

in Fig. 1, there are two intra-sentence relations (*Samsung, parent organization, Samsung Electronics*), (*Samsung Electronics, manufacturer, Samsung Galaxy Note*) and an inter-sentence relation (*Samsung, manufacturer, Samsung Galaxy Note*). According to an analysis of the Wikipedia corpus, DocRED [18] reveals that at least 40.7% of relations can only be expressed through multiple sentences. Therefore, it is essential to extract relations from the document-level rather than the sentence-level.

To extract document-level relations, most previous research [7,22] mainly constructed a dependency tree module based on heuristic structures. Those methods utilize hand-crafted path-centric pruning rules, which cannot balance the weight of relevant and irrelevant words. This inevitably leads to the missing of valuable information. In addition, many existing methods in literature [9,10] fail to consider the features of both sentence-level and document-level at the same time like human readers. In other words, models usually focus on the features of the words. The lack of sufficient sentence-level and document-level features makes the inferior performance of the extraction result. In summary, there are two research questions in this field: 1) As the method of manually constructing pruning rules is not flexible, the mechanism of dependency tree pruning rules need to be explored. 2) The mechanism of sentence-level attention needs to be explored. For example, the relation3 in Fig. 1 is difficult to be determined by a single sentence, because it requires logical inference with sentences No.1 and No.4. That is to say, the extraction of relations may need to assign critical attention to multiple sentences.

In this paper, we propose a document-level relation extraction framework with a dynamic pruning mechanism and sentence-level attention. Firstly, a weight-based flexible pruning mechanism is applied to the document-level dependency tree to remove non-relational edges dynamically and obtain the weight dependency tree (WDT). Specifically, the irrelevant nodes and edges in the document-level dependency tree are automatically pruned according to the weight of edges, which is achieved through the bi-affine function. Secondly, a graph convolution network (GCN) is applied to the WDT. GCN allows nodes to aggregate features from multi-hop neighbors to enrich syntactic representations. Thirdly, the sentence-level attention and gating selection module are utilized to capture the intrinsic interactions among sentence-level and document-level features. Specifically, sentence-level attention assigns different values to multiple sentences to learn sentence-level attentional features. Meanwhile, the gating selection module balances the sentence-level and document-level features to achieve multiple-grained semantic representations. Finally, Experiments on three benchmark datasets, DocRED [18], CDR [6], and GDA [14], demonstrate that our approach outperforms the baseline methods and achieves state-of-the-art performance. Our contributions can be summarized as follows:

- We propose a dynamic pruning mechanism to automatically remove the irrelevant information from the dependency tree. The dynamic pruning mechanism reduces noise and preserves the topological structural features with an improvement of the model's accuracy.
- To interact with the multiple-grained features, we propose sentence-level attention and gating selection module. The representation of pairwise entities with rich semantics can be obtained according to the balance of sentence-level and document-level features.
- Experiments on three datasets demonstrate that our method achieves state-of-the-art performance. Additionally, we also conduct an ablation study, and the pruning methods analysis of our framework to better understand its working mechanism.

2   Methodology

2.1   Problem Definition

Given an input document $D = \{S_i\}_{i=1}^{N_s}$, it is composed of N_s sentences and a variety of entities $\{e_i\}_{i=1}^{N_e}$. Each entity $e_i = \{m_j\}_{j=1}^{N_m}$ contains N_m mentions, which means entity e_j appears N_m times in the document D. The objective is to predict the relation $r_{ij} \in R$ between pairwise entity (e_i, e_j), where R is a predefined relation typeset. e_i and e_j represent the subject and object, respectively. As illustrated in Fig. 2, the overall architecture consists of four tiers: encoder module (Sect. 2.2), dynamic pruning module (Sect. 2.3), sentence-level attention module (Sect. 2.4), and classification module (Sect. 2.5).

2.2   Encoder Module

Let $D = \{w_i\}_{i=1}^{n}$ be an input document, where w_i is the ith word in it. The encoder layer transforms inputs into fixed-dimensional vectors for the semantic

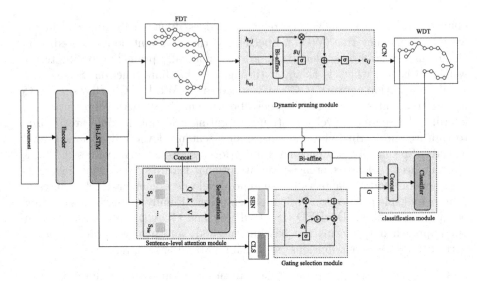

Fig. 2. Architecture of the proposed framework. It consists of four main components: encoder module, dynamic pruning module, sentence-level attention module, and classification module.

features. The special symbol $< S >$ and $< CLS >$ are inserted at the start of each sentence and the entire document, respectively. The contextual representation x_i for each token w_i is obtained from a pre-trained transformer language model:

$$\{x_1, x_2, \ldots, x_n\} = Encoder(\{w_1, w_2, \ldots, w_n\}) \tag{1}$$

Moreover, a two opposite directions LSTM [2] is utilized to uncover the hidden representations:

$$\overleftarrow{h_i} = LSTM(\overleftarrow{h_{i+1}}, x_i) \tag{2}$$

$$\overrightarrow{h_i} = LSTM(\overrightarrow{h_{i-1}}, x_i) \tag{3}$$

where $\overleftarrow{h_i}$ and $\overrightarrow{h_i}$ are the hidden representations of the ith token in two opposite directions. The context-sensitive representations H can be formulated as:

$$H = \{h_1, h_2, \ldots, h_n\} = \{[\overleftarrow{h_1}; \overrightarrow{h_1}], [\overleftarrow{h_2}; \overrightarrow{h_2}], \ldots, [\overleftarrow{h_n}; \overrightarrow{h_n}]\} \tag{4}$$

2.3   Dynamic Pruning Module

Firstly, we propose a structural model that consists of entities and words. Specifically, the sentence-level dependency tree for each sentence is generated via syntactic parsing. Furthermore, the mentions that belong to the same entity in different sentences are combined to generate the document-level dependency tree.

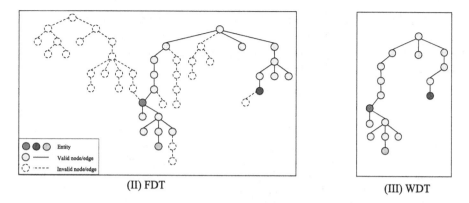

(II) FDT   (III) WDT

No.1: The Samsung Galaxy S (Super Smar) series is a line of high-end Android-powered mobile devices produced by *Samsung Electronics*, a division of *Samsung* from South Korea.
No.4: Since the introduction of the *Samsung Galaxy Note* in 2011, the Galaxy S line has co-existed with Galaxy Note line as being *Samsung Elecreonics*'s flagship smartphones.

(I) DOCUMENT

Fig. 3. An example document with its FDT and WDT.

In this way, the entities are gathered around by context. We treat the document-level dependency tree as non-directional and add self-loop to each node. For an entity e_i with mentions $e_i = \{m_j\}_{j=1}^{N_m}$, LogSumExp pooling [5] is utilized to combine the mentions that belong to the same entity in different sentences and integrate the initial entity embedding $h_{e_i}^0$:

$$h_{e_i}^0 = \frac{1}{N_m} \log \sum_{j=1}^{N_m} exp(h_{m_j}) \tag{5}$$

h_{m_j} denotes the hidden state of mention m_j. The structure model captures the syntactic representations of the dependency tree (document) and its nodes (entities or words). The graph convolution network (GCN) is adopted to encode the structure model. Formally, the layer-wise propagation rule is formulated as:

$$h_{v_i}^{l+1} = \sigma\left(\sum_j \frac{1}{\sqrt{d_i d_j}} \cdot h_{v_j}^l \cdot W^l\right) \tag{6}$$

where $\sqrt{d_i d_j}$ is the degree of node v_i and v_j. σ represents the activation function.

Although the dependency tree provides rich syntactic information, its dependency edges are not all relational relevant. Literature works proposed several hand-crafted rules to remove irrelevant information from the full dependency tree (FDT), such as the shortest dependency path (SDP) [1], or the path-centric pruning dependency tree (PDT) [22]. However, these hand-crafted rules cannot balance the weight of relevant and irrelevant information. Motivated by the situation, a dynamic pruning module is proposed to convert the original FDT into a weight dependency tree (WDT) automatically. Figure 3 demonstrates an example document with its FDT and WDT, the different colors are used to represent different entities. Specifically, a plug-and-play adaptive fusion function is introduced to dynamically adjust the voting weights of edges:

$$g_{ij} = \sigma(h_{v_i} \cdot W_{ij} \cdot h_{v_j}) \tag{7}$$

$$E' = g_{ij} \otimes (h_{v_i} \cdot W_{ij} \cdot h_{v_j}) \tag{8}$$

$$e_{ij} = \sigma(E' + h_{v_i} \cdot W_{ij} \cdot h_{v_j}) \cdot W_e + b_e \tag{9}$$

where σ and $\otimes$ represent sigmoid function and element-wise multiplication. As the sigmoid function is utilized, the range of g_{ij} is [0,1]. The value of g_{ij} measures the confidence level of the edges connecting nodes h_i and h_j. Then, the emphasized feature E' can be calculated through element-wise multiplication. E' represents the representation of reliable edges with relevant information. At the same time, a residual connection is utilized to alleviate the trouble of gradient back-propagation. Then the sigma function is used again to generate the edge weight e_{ij}. Note that $e_{ij} = 0$ when node v_i and v_j are not connected. Edges are softly pruned when their weights are close to 0. To compare with the soft pruning method, we also try the hard value in experiments. Finally, the GCN is employed in the WDT:

$$h_{v_i}^{l+1} = \sigma(\sum_j \frac{1}{\sqrt{d_i d_j}} \cdot e_{ij} \cdot h_{v_j}^l \cdot W^l) \tag{10}$$

Different layers of GCN express features of different abstract levels. In order to cover features of all levels, the hidden states of each layer are concatenated to form the final representation of entity e_i, L represents the number of GCN layers:

$$h_{e_i} = [h_{e_i}^0; h_{e_i}^1; \ldots; h_{e_i}^L] \tag{11}$$

2.4   Sentence-Level Attention Module

Sentence-level attention module is proposed to select the valid sentences in document-level RE. Moreover, a gating selection module is applied to balance the significant sentence features and document features automatically.

The representations of the ith sentence and document are obtained via the special symbols $< S_i >$ and $< CLS >$, respectively. The entities e_i and e_j are concatenated as a query to compute the self-attention of sentences, the formulas are:

$$SEN = Att(q, k, v) = softmax(\frac{qk^T}{\sqrt{d_k}})v \tag{12}$$

$$q = \sigma(W_q \cdot [h_{e_i}; h_{e_j}]) \tag{13}$$

where k and v are the key and value of sentences, respectively. SEN is considered as the entire sentence-level attention feature and is captured from the specific pairwise entities.

Some straightforward relations can be inferred with a single or a few sentences, while *NA* or cross-sentence relations need to be inferred with the entire document. Therefore, there is a need to utilize a gating selection module to automatically adjust and combine *SEN* and *CLS*:

$$G = g_t \otimes SEN + (1 - g_t) \otimes CLS \tag{14}$$

$$g_t = \tanh(W_t \cdot [SEN; CLS] + b_t \tag{15}$$

where G denotes the combined representation with rich semantic information. g_t represents an additional value to balance the features of the document and sentence-level, with a larger g_t indicating that the current relation is intra-sentential and a smaller g_t indicating that the current relation is inter-sentential.

2.5   Classification Module

The pairwise entity with rich structural features is constructed by the bi-affine function and denoted as Z. Finally, G and Z are concatenated and injected into a linear layer:

$$Z = e_i \cdot W_z \cdot e_j + b_z \tag{16}$$

$$p(r|e_i, e_j) = \sigma(W_r \cdot [Z; G] + b_r) \tag{17}$$

the W_r, b_r are learnable parameters. In this paper, we employ dropout to prevent over-fitting. The model parameters are estimated by adaptive-thresholding the loss function proposed by ATLOP [25]. An extra category s_0 is proposed by ATLOP, in which the scores of positive samples is upper than category s_0 and the scores of negative samples is lower than s_0. For simplicity, we set the additional category threshold as zero.

3   Experiments

3.1   Dataset

We conduct experiments on three benchmark datasets, including DocRED [18], CDR [6], and GDA [14]. DocRED is a large-scale human-annotated dataset for document-level RE. It is constructed from Wikipedia and Wikidata while it consists of a train set with 3053 documents, a development set with 998 documents and a test set with 1000 documents. CDR is a widely-used document-level RE dataset that infers the interactions between chemical and disease concepts and it contains 1500 PubMed abstracts with 3116 relational facts. GDA is another biomedical document-level RE dataset that aims to predict the interactions between disease concepts and genes and consists of 30192 biomedical abstracts with 46343 relational facts. The dataset statistics are shown in Table 1.

Table 1. Statistics of the experimental datasets.

Dataset	DocRED	CDR	GDA
# Train	3053	500	23353
# Dev	998	500	5839
# Test	1000	500	1000
# Relations	97	2	2
Avg. # entities per Doc	19.5	7.6	5.4
Avg. # mentions per Ent.	1.4	2.7	3.3

3.2   Experimental Settings

Following previous works [18], F1 and Ign-F1 are adopted as the evaluation metrics, where Ign-F1 calculates F1 excluding the common relations in the training and development/test sets. Our model is implemented on Huggingface's Transformers[1] and DGL [13]. We used cased BERT-base [4] as the pre-trained language model on DocRED, SciBERT on CDR and GDA. AdamW is utilized as optimizer with learning rates $2e-4$. Moreover, we employ mixed-precision training based on the Apex library[2]. The number of GCN layers and dropout rate are set to 3 and 0.5, respectively. We train the model for 30 epochs with a batch size of 8 and evaluate it with a batch size of 32. The hyper-parameters are tuned on the development set.

3.3   Main Results

Table 2 shows the experimental results on the DocRED dataset. In order to compare our model with current state-of-the-art models, the following models are employed as baselines. Some models use different neural architectures to encode the document, such as BERT-RE, BERT-Two-Step [12], CNN, LSTM, BiLSTM, context-aware [18], and ATLOP [25]. Some models construct homogeneous or heterogeneous graphs based on the document, such as DRPRN [7], LSR [9], SSAN [15], HeterGSAN [17], Coref+BERT [19], and GAIN [21]. Our model achieves 62.44% F1 and 60.38% Ign-F1 on the test set. Our model surpasses all baseline models. Specifically, compared with the dependency tree-based model DRPRN, our model surpasses 0.47% and 0.45% in terms of F1 and Ign-F1. Such improvements demonstrate the dynamic pruning mechanism is more suitable for dependent tree than hand-crafted pruning rules. At the same time, compared with the semantic-based model ATLOP, our model outperforms ATLOP by 1.14% and 1.07% in terms of F1 and Ign-F1. The results show the superiority of the proposed model in capturing crucial semantic information.

Table 3 shows the experiment results on two biomedical datasets. We compared with many classical baselines, such as EOG [3], DRPRN [7], LSR [9],

---

[1] https://github.com/huggingface/transformers.
[2] https://github.com/NVIDIA/apex.

Table 2. Main results (%) on the development and test set of DocRED.

Model	PLM	Dev		Test	
		F1	Ign-F1	F1	Ign-F1
CNN	–	43.45	37.99	42.33	36.44
LSTM		50.66	44.41	50.10	43.60
BiLSTM		50.95	45.12	51.06	44.73
context-aware		51.10	44.84	50.64	43.93
BERT-RE	bert-based	54.16	–	53.20	–
BERT-Two-Step		54.42	–	53.93	–
coref+BERT		57.51	55.32	56.96	54.54
SSAN		59.19	57.03	58.16	55.84
LSR		59.00	52.43	59.05	56.97
HeterGSAN		60.18	58.13	59.45	57.12
GAIN		61.22	59.14	61.24	59.00
ATLOP		61.09	59.22	61.30	59.31
DRPRN		61.65	59.82	61.97	59.93
Ours		**61.99**	**60.27**	**62.44**	**60.38**

Table 3. Results (%) on the biomedical datasets CDR and GDA.

Model	CDR	GDA
BRAN	62.1	–
EOG	63.6	81.5
LSR	64.8	82.2
DHG	64.9	83.1
SSAN	68.7	83.7
ATLOP	69.4	83.9
DRPRN	70.8	84.4
Ours	**72.8**	**85.1**

BRAN [11], SSAN [15], DHG [23], and ATLOP [25]. According to Table 3, our model surpasses DRPRN by 2.0% and 0.7% on CDR and GDA, respectively.

4   Analyses

4.1   Ablation Study

In this subsection, an ablation study experiment is conducted to validate the effectiveness of different components of our model. Table 4 shows the results of an ablation study on DocRED. From these ablations, we find that: 1) The

Table 4. Ablation study on DocRED dev dataset. Dyn-Pru: dynamic pruning. Sent-Att: sentence-level attention. Gating: gating selection.

Model	F1	ign-F1
Default	**61.99**	**60.27**
- GCN	60.95	58.60
- Dyn-Pru	58.95	57.44
- Sent-Att	60.34	59.20
- Gating	61.68	59.66
- GCN&Dyn-Pru	58.80	56.65
- Sent-Att&Gating	59.98	58.41
- Dyn-Pru&Sent-Att&Gating	57.50	56.32

Table 5. The performance of different pruning methods on DocRED dev set.

Method	K(Distance)	Parameters	F1	ign-F1
WDT-soft	–	144M	**61.99**	**60.27**
WDT-hard	–	136M	61.12	59.44
PDT	0(SDP)	**120M**	60.01	59.44
	1	150M	61.87	59.95
	2	174M	61.20	58.86
	3	220M	60.38	58.40
	$+\infty$(FDT)	298M	58.95	57.44

decrease in performance caused by the lack of each component clearly indicates that all components are beneficial. The dynamic pruning mechanism, sentence-level attention and gating selection module contribute total 4.49% F1 score. 2) The dynamic pruning mechanism improves the F1 score by 3.04% if compared with FDT structure, and it is the most important component of the proposed model. The results demonstrate that dynamic pruning mechanism is beneficial to remove irrelevant information. 3) The F1 score drops 1.65% and 0.31% when we remove the sentence-level attention and gating selection module, respectively. Thus, automatically balancing the sentence-level and document-level features is essential for document-level RE.

4.2   Pruning Methods Analysis

To show the effect of the dynamic pruning mechanism, we investigated several pruning methods, including shortest dependency path (SDP), path-centric pruning dependency tree (PDT) with different distances ($K = 1, K = 2, K = 3$) and hard pruning method (WDT-hard). Note that $K = 0$ is equivalent to the SDP, $K = +\infty$ is equivalent to the full dependency tree (FDT). The hard pruning method denotes the weight of edges will be assigned with 1 if the probability exceeds a threshold λ. We set λ to 0.5. As shown in Table 5, the decrease in model performance is accompanied by the increase of K. In addition, although the results of $K = 1$ in PDT are similar to the result of WDT, the WDT achieves better performance with fewer parameters. Furthermore, WDT-soft improves the F1 score by 0.87% if compared with WDT-hard. A flexible pruning method is greatly beneficial to improving model performance.

5   Conclusion

We propose a framework for the document-level relation extraction task. The cores of our framework are the dynamic pruning mechanism, sentence-level attention, and gating selection module. In this paper, we generate a document dependency tree and propose a flexible weight-based pruner to remove non-relational edges. Prior work considered pruning methods as hand-crafted rules, while did not consider whether the pruning rules are applicable to the edges outside SDP. Furthermore, we apply sentence-level attention to obtain the attentional features of sentences. The query representation based on entity pairs ensures that all entities keep the closest attention to related sentences. Finally, the gating selection module is utilized to capture the intrinsic interaction between sentence-level and document-level features. Experiments on three public datasets demonstrate that our framework outperforms existing models and achieves state-of-the-art performance. We also conduct further experiments and analyses to discuss the superior performance of our framework components. In future work, we consider extensively exploring applications of our proposed framework, such as the construction of a knowledge graph.

Acknowledgment. This work was supported by NSFC (grant No.61877051).

References

1. Bunescu, R.C., Mooney, R.J.: A shortest path dependency kernel for relation extraction. In: HLT/EMNLP 2005, 6–8 October 2005, Vancouver, British Columbia, Canada, pp. 724–731. The Association for Computational Linguistics (2005)
2. Cai, R., Zhang, X., Wang, H.: Bidirectional recurrent convolutional neural network for relation classification. In: ACL 2016, 7–12 August 2016, Berlin, Germany, Volume 1: Long Papers (2016)
3. Christopoulou, F., Miwa, M., Ananiadou, S.: Connecting the dots: document-level neural relation extraction with edge-oriented graphs. In: EMNLP-IJCNLP 2019, Hong Kong, China, 3–7 November 2019, pp. 4924–4935 (2019)
4. Devlin, J., Chang, M., Lee, K., Toutanova, K.: BERT: pre-training of deep bidirectional transformers for language understanding. In: NAACL-HLT 2019, Minneapolis, MN, USA, 2–7 June 2019, Volume 1 (Long and Short Papers), pp. 4171–4186 (2019)

5. Jia, R., Wong, C., Poon, H.: Document-level N-ary relation extraction with multi-scale representation learning. In: Burstein, J., Doran, C., Solorio, T. (eds.) NAACL-HLT 2019, Minneapolis, MN, USA, 2–7 June 2019, Volume 1 (Long and Short Papers), pp. 3693–3704 (2019)
6. Li, J., et al.: Biocreative V CDR task corpus: a resource for chemical disease relation extraction. Database J. Biol. Databases Curation 2016 (2016)
7. Li, Y., Liu, Y., Gu, X., Yue, Y., Fan, H., Li, B.: Dual reasoning based pairwise representation network for document level relation extraction. In: ICME 2022, Taipei, Taiwan, 18–22 July 2022, pp. 1–6 (2022)
8. Miwa, M., Bansal, M.: End-to-end relation extraction using LSTMs on sequences and tree structures. In: ACL 2016, 7–12 August 2016, Berlin, Germany, Volume 1: Long Papers (2016)
9. Nan, G., Guo, Z., Sekulic, I., Lu, W.: Reasoning with latent structure refinement for document-level relation extraction. In: ACL 2020, 5–10 July 2020, pp. 1546–1557 (2020)
10. Sun, Q., et al.: Dual-channel and hierarchical graph convolutional networks for document-level relation extraction. Expert Syst. Appl. **205**, 117678 (2022)
11. Verga, P., Strubell, E., McCallum, A.: Simultaneously self-attending to all mentions for full-abstract biological relation extraction. In: NAACL-HLT 2018, New Orleans, Louisiana, USA, 1–6 June 2018, Volume 1 (Long Papers), pp. 872–884 (2018)
12. Wang, H., Focke, C., Sylvester, R., Mishra, N., Wang, W.Y.: Fine-tune BERT for docred with two-step process. CoRR abs/1909.11898 (2019)
13. Wang, M., et al.: Deep graph library: towards efficient and scalable deep learning on graphs. CoRR abs/1909.01315 (2019)
14. Wu, Y., Luo, R., Leung, H.C.M., Ting, H., Lam, T.W.: RENET: a deep learning approach for extracting gene-disease associations from literature. In: Proceedings of the RECOMB 2019, Washington, DC, USA, 5–8 May 2019, vol. 11467, pp. 272–284 (2019)
15. Xu, B., Wang, Q., Lyu, Y., Zhu, Y., Mao, Z.: Entity structure within and throughout: modeling mention dependencies for document-level relation extraction. In: AAAI 2021, IAAI 2021, EAAI 2021, Virtual Event, 2–9 February 2021, pp. 14149–14157 (2021)
16. Xu, K., Feng, Y., Huang, S., Zhao, D.: Semantic relation classification via convolutional neural networks with simple negative sampling. In: EMNLP 2015, Lisbon, Portugal, 17–21 September 2015, pp. 536–540 (2015)
17. Xu, W., Chen, K., Zhao, T.: Document-level relation extraction with reconstruction. In: AAAI 2021, IAAI 2021, EAAI 2021, Virtual Event, 2–9 February 2021, pp. 14167–14175 (2021)
18. Yao, Y., et al.: Docred: a large-scale document-level relation extraction dataset. In: ACL 2019, Florence, Italy, 28 July–2 August 2019, Volume 1: Long Papers, pp. 764–777 (2019)
19. Ye, D., et al.: Coreferential reasoning learning for language representation. In: EMNLP 2020, 16–20 November 2020, pp. 7170–7186 (2020)
20. Zeng, D., Liu, K., Lai, S., Zhou, G., Zhao, J.: Relation classification via convolutional deep neural network. In: COLING 2014, 23–29 August 2014, Dublin, Ireland, pp. 2335–2344 (2014)
21. Zeng, S., Xu, R., Chang, B., Li, L.: Double graph based reasoning for document-level relation extraction. In: EMNLP 2020, 16–20 November 2020, pp. 1630–1640 (2020)

22. Zhang, Y., Qi, P., Manning, C.D.: Graph convolution over pruned dependency trees improves relation extraction. In: EMNLP 2018, Brussels, Belgium, 31 October–4 November 2018, pp. 2205–2215 (2018)
23. Zhang, Z., et al.: Document-level relation extraction with dual-tier heterogeneous graph. In: COLING 2020, Barcelona, Spain (Online), 8–13 December 2020, pp. 1630–1641 (2020)
24. Zhong, Z., Chen, D.: A frustratingly easy approach for entity and relation extraction. In: NAACL-HLT 2021, 6–11 June 2021, pp. 50–61 (2021)
25. Zhou, W., Huang, K., Ma, T., Huang, J.: Document-level relation extraction with adaptive thresholding and localized context pooling. In: AAAI 2021, IAAI 2021, EAAI 2021, Virtual Event, 2–9 February 2021, pp. 14612–14620 (2021)

A Global Feature Fusion Network for Lettuce Growth Trait Detection

Zhengxian Wu[1] , Jiaxuan Wu[1], Yiming Xue[1(✉)] , Juan Wen[1] ,
and Ping Zhong[2]

[1] Collage of Information and Electrical Engineering,
China Agricultural University, Beijing 100083, China
{xueym,wenjuan}@cau.edu.cn
[2] Collage of Science, China Agricultural University, Beijing 100083, China

Abstract. Lettuce growth traits are important biological attributes that directly reflect growth conditions. However, most existing approaches simply extract coarse features from RGB images and ignore the significantly varied appearance of different lettuce varieties at diverse growth phases, which brings about the loss of important information. To address these issues, we propose a novel lettuce growth-traits detection model, namely Global Feature Fusion Network (GFFN), based on dense connection and dilated convolution to fully utilize fine-grained and multi-level feature representations from RGB-D images. Firstly, RGB and depth images are combined through channel concatenation to provide rich, learnable information. Next, a dense extractor is proposed to perform progressively refined feature extraction, which gathers fine-grained local context from coarse lettuce representations. Then, a multi-scale receptor aims to merge multi-level feature representations and learn scale and location knowledge. Finally, extensive experiments show that GFFN achieves competitive performance compared to the other mainstream methods in detecting five primary attributes of lettuce growth traits.

Keywords: Growth trait detection · Deep learning · Greenhouse hydroponic lettuce · Computer vision

1 Introduction

Lettuce (Lactuca sativa L.) is a fantastic source of iron, folate, vitamin C, and fiber. It is one of the most widely produced and consumed crops on the planet [1,2]. With the development of intelligent agriculture, the demand for high-yield and high-quality lettuce has increased [3]. In the hydroponic greenhouse, environmental factors have a significant impact on lettuce quality and yield. By detecting several important growth traits, including fresh weight (FW), dry

This work is supported by the National Natural Science Foundation of China (No. 62272463).

L. Iliadis et al. (Eds.): ICANN 2023, LNCS 14261, pp. 26–37, 2023.
https://doi.org/10.1007/978-3-031-44198-1_3

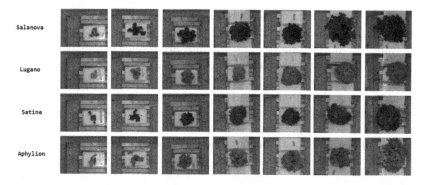

Fig. 1. Four varieties and seven growth cycles of lettuce.

weight (DW), lettuce height (LH), lettuce diameter (LD), and leaf area (LA), experts can evaluate the growing condition of lettuce and control the environmental conditions of a hydroponics greenhouse for a high yield and improved nutritional quality. Hence, a quick and accurate growth trait detection of lettuce is of immense importance for the timely harvest and precise control of growth, yield, and quality.

Conventional methods for identifying lettuce growth traits have invariably relied on destructive sampling [4], which frequently results in large resource-consuming and cannot fulfill the demand for high-yield and high-quality exports on a wide scale. In recent years, the development of a computer vision approach has enabled the automatic detection of lettuce growth traits. Yeh et al. [5] developed an automated vision-based plant growth measurement system to track plant growth and determine the area, height, and volume. Jung et al. [6] analyzed the ability of two different image processing methods, i.e., morphological and pixel-value analysis methods, to measure the fresh weight of lettuce. Mortensen et al. [7] segmented the 3D point cloud image, extracted features, and finally used linear regression and quadratic regression to predict the fresh weight of lettuce. Reyes-Yanes et al. [8] extracted the features from the pre-processed mask image using the torque and constructed a regression model to acquire the correlation between the lettuce size and fresh weight. These methods achieve automatic detection of lettuce growth traits, but they typically rely on hand-crafted features designed by experts with related knowledge. Moreover, hand-crafted features can only reflect the shallow information from the input images and cannot represent the ever-evolving property of lettuce appearance in different growth stages. As shown in Fig. 1, different varieties of lettuce vary significantly in shape and scale in different growth phases. Consequently, using shallow feature representations may lead to a decline in detecting accuracy when changing lettuce varieties or growth phases, which has a negative impact on the model's robustness.

Nowadays, with the improvement in computing power, deep learning provides powerful techniques for modeling complex processes and performing effectively on a large amount of data. Among these techniques, the convolutional neural network (CNN) has emerged as the most outstanding method because of its enormous advantages in image processing [9]. Many areas, such as lane detection [10], face recognition [11], and pest and disease identification [12], have seen extensive usage of CNN. Zhang et al. [13] introduced the convolution neural network (CNN) in studying three growth traits of lettuce (i.e., fresh weight, dry weight, and leaf area). This work indicates that deep learning acquires feature information of specific datasets through the convolution layer, which can effectively extract hidden feature representations of lettuce and overcome the disadvantages of traditional image processing methods in terms of generalization ability and robustness. However, they studied lettuce growth traits by solely using RGB images without considering the depth information. Furthermore, they did not explore leaf color and shape differences in detecting growth traits in different lettuce species. At the same time, due to the limitation of the receptive field of convolutional neural networks, existing CNN-based methods fail to learn from the fast-changing appearances of lettuce at various growth stages.

To address the above-mentioned limitations and further improve the detection performance, in this paper, we propose a new framework, namely Global Feature Fusion Network (GFFN), which learns both fine-grained and multi-level representations for lettuce growth trait detection. To solve the problem of extracting better feature representations from the ever-evolving appearance of lettuce in different growth phases, a dense extractor is proposed to gather fine-grained local context by reusing low-level features. In addition, the multi-scale receptor is designed to learn multi-level features, which provides plenty of knowledge of various scales and shapes. The results show that our proposed method outperforms other mainstream methods in detecting the five primary attributes of lettuce.

The contributions of this work are summarized as follows:

- A lettuce growth trait detection framework, namely Global Feature Fusion Network (GFFN), is proposed, which fully utilizes fine-grained and multi-level representations to improve the detection performance of different lettuce varieties in diverse growth stages.
- A dense extractor (DE) aims to gather fine-grained local context by reusing low-level features. Furthermore, a multi-scale receptor (MSR) is introduced to learn multi-level feature representations to depict information on various scales.
- Experimental results show that the proposed GFFN can effectively extract fine-grained and multi-level feature representations of lettuce, improve the detection performance of lettuce growth traits, and outperform other mainstream methods in detecting five attributes of lettuce growth traits.

2   Proposed Method

In this paper, we propose a Global Feature Fusion Network (GFFN), an end-to-end lettuce growth trait detection method, that fuses fine-grained local features

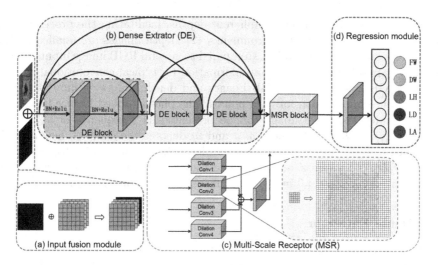

Fig. 2. An overview of our approach. (a) The input fusion module (IFM). (b) The dense extractor (DE). (c) The multi-scale receptor (MSR). (d) The regression module.

Fig. 3. RGB and depth images.

and multi-level features to address the appearance-various issue at different growth stages in the lettuce growth trait detection task. Figure 2 illustrates the overall architecture of our proposed method, which comprises four components: (1) Input Fusion Module (Sect. 2.1) to fuse the input of RGB and depth images into RGB-D. (2) Dense Extractor (Sect. 2.2) to learn fine-grained local features by reusing the coarse-local representations. (3) Multi-Scale Receptor (Sect. 2.3) to extract multi-level feature representations. (4) Regression Module (Sect. 2.4) to learn the relation between lettuce growth traits and the hybrid feature representations. In the rest of the section, we will introduce each component in detail and then present the design of our loss function (Sect. 2.5).

2.1 Input Fusion Module

As shown in Fig. 3, RGB images contain lettuce appearance information, such as color and texture, while depth features can describe 3D geometric information. Depth images offer two significant advantages [14]: (1) It can naturally disambiguate between objects at different depths, facilitating the processing of disturbances in complicated environments. (2) Depth images are unaffected by appearance or changes in lighting. Compared to general RGB image input, which provides learnable two-dimensional information for typical convolutional neural networks, GFFN takes both RGB images and depth images as input to offer extra distance information for each point of the photographed lettuce images.

Specifically, the RGB image can be presented as a sequence of $[r, g, b] = \{(r_{ij}, g_{ij}, b_{ij})\} \in R^{3 \times n \times m}$, where 3, n and m denotes the channel, height, and width of the input RGB image. Besides, depth images are presented in $[d] = \{(d_{ij})\} \in D^{n \times m}$, where n and m denote the image size. For input fusion, we concatenate $[r, g, b]$ and $[d]$ in channel dimensions, as shown in Fig. 2(a).

2.2   Dense Extractor

Existing learnable convolutional neural networks focus on extracting coarse local features, leading to the issue of feature loss. To remedy this, we design a dense extractor (DE) using dense connections, which enhance information exchange between layers and increase low-level feature representation reuse to provide additional information regarding local details. The detailed structure of the dense extractor is shown in Fig. 2(b).

To be specific, the dense extractor consists of three dense extractor blocks that use shortcut connections to transfer the information flow. Each block is constructed with two sets of composite operations: batch normalization (BN), rectified linear unit (ReLU), and convolution (Conv). The input of lth dense extractor block X_l are the fused feature maps, which come from the feature maps of all preceding blocks:

$$X_l = Y_0 + Y_1 + \cdots + Y_{l-1}, \tag{1}$$

where Y_0 and Y_l denote the information of the original RGB-D data and the output of the lth dense extractor block, respectively. The fused feature maps X_l guide the lth dense extractor block to further mine the fine grained representations from the coarse feature presentations. This process can be formulated as:

$$Y_{l1} = Conv_{l1}(RELU_{l1}(BN_{l1}(X_l))), \tag{2}$$
$$Y_l = Conv_{l2}(RELU_{l2}(BN_{l2}(Y_{l1}))), \tag{3}$$

where, $RELU_{li}(\cdot)$, $BN_{li}(\cdot)$, and $Conv_{li}(\cdot)$ presents the ith set of composite operation of RELU, BN, and Conv in l^{th} dense extractor block. In this way, the dense extractor can perform refinement based on the reuse of low-level feature representations to extract fine-grained local features of lettuce.

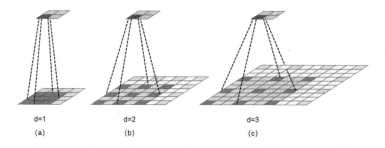

Fig. 4. The receptive fields of convolutional layers with different dilated rate.

2.3 Multi-scale Receptor

Compared to convolutional layers with a fixed kernel size, which learn feature maps, the dilated convolution layer expands the receptive field of the convolution kernel while maintaining the same parameters. Figure 4 illustrates the change in receptive fields with different dilations. By enlarging the dilated rate from 1 to 3 in a 3×3 kernel, the receptive field of convolution is expanded. The receptive fields of convolutions with different dilations can be defined as:

$$\hat{k} = k + (k - 1) \times (d - 1), \tag{4}$$

$$s_i = \prod_{j=1}^{i} stride_j, \tag{5}$$

$$RF_{i+1} = RF_i + (\hat{k} - 1) \times s_i, \tag{6}$$

where k represents the size of the convolution kernel, $\hat{k}$ represents the size of the convolution kernel after dilating, d represents the dilation rate, $stride_j$ represents the step length of the jth layer, and s_i represents the product of the step lengths of all layers from the first layer to the ith layer, and RF_i represents the receptive field of the ith layer.

Motivated by this, the Multi-Scale Receptor (MSR) is proposed to produce multi-level feature representations, and the details of the MSR are shown in Fig. 2(c). Specifically, the MSR consists of four parallel 3×3 convolutions with different dilation factors. The dilations are set up to 1, 6, 12, and 18. Each convolution takes feature maps of the dense extractor as input and produces various scale feature maps as output. The outputs of four convolutional layers with different dilation rates are concatenated together and fed into the final regression module. This process can be formulated as:

$$Y_i = BN(Conv_{d=i}(X_{input})), \tag{7}$$

$$Y_{ouput} = Conv(Y_1 + Y_6 + Y_{12} + Y_{18}), \tag{8}$$

where X_{input} and Y_{ouput} present the output of DE and the output of MSR. $Conv_{d=i}(\cdot)$ denotes the operation of a convolutional layer with a dilation rate i. Y_i denotes the feature maps of the convolutional layer with dilation rate i.

The merging of high-level and low-level feature representations with the same channel numbers can provide plenty of knowledge about various scales, and the location near the lettuce will be perceived.

2.4 Regression Module

At the final stage, the regression module models the relationship between feature maps Y_{output} and lettuce growth traits. To decrease the number of parameters and alleviate over-fitting, we adopt a global average pooling layer to compute the average value of all the elements in the feature map and feed it into the full connection layer, which outputs 5 lettuce growth traits $F = \{f_j\}$, $j \in [1, 5]$.

2.5 Loss Funcation

The loss function calculates the difference between the detection results of each iteration of the model and ground truth, and is described as:

$$loss = \sum_{j=1}^{r}(1 - \frac{\sum_{i=1}^{n}(y_{ij} - f_{ij})^2}{\sum_{i=1}^{n}(y_{ij} - \bar{y}_i)^2}), \tag{9}$$

where r and n are the numbers of growth traits and images, respectively. f_{ij} and y_{ij} represent the ith detection and real growth trait values of the jth image, respectively. $\bar{y}$ represents the mean of the real values of the ith growth trait.

3 Experimental Results

3.1 Dataset

To verify the advance and effectiveness of our proposed GFFN, we perform experiments on a public lettuce dataset [15]. There are 388 images consisting of four varieties: Salanova, Lugano, Satine, and Aphylion. We divide them into 310, 38, and 40 images for training, validation, and evaluation, respectively. The training set is expanded from 310 images to 12,400 images through image rotation, transposition, flipping, and brightness adjustment.

3.2 Implementation Details

In this paper, the proposed method is trained using the adaptive moment estimation (Adam) optimizer [16] in an end-to-end joint manner by backpropagation. In addition, we set the learning rate at 0.001. Due to memory limitations, we uniformly set the batch size as 16, and the input image size as 224×224. In order to effectively converge and avoid wasting memory, we adopt a total epoch number of 50. Moreover, our experiments are implemented using PyTorch with a Python interface. To accelerate the training process, we use the GeForce GTX 1080Ti GPU and CUDA 11.0.

Table 1. The R^2 and $NRMSE$ of ablation experiments The abbreviations IFM, DE, and MSR stand for input fusion module, dense extractor, and multi-scale receptor, respectively.

Metrics	IFM	DE	MSR	Average	FW	DW	LH	LD	LA
R^2 ↑		√	√	89.38	90.04	94.68	87.12	81.59	93.49
	√		√	91.45	94.24	95.31	85.64	87.71	94.35
	√	√		91.50	94.27	95.01	**89.06**	85.67	93.50
	√	√	√	**92.67**	**94.47**	**96.64**	88.16	**88.95**	**95.13**
$NRMSE$ ↓		√	√	20.67	31.13	20.65	15.89	13.59	22.07
	√		√	18.30	23.67	19.40	16.77	11.11	20.56
	√	√		18.46	23.62	20.02	**14.64**	12.00	22.05
	√	√	√	**16.90**	**23.19**	**16.43**	15.23	**10.53**	**19.09**

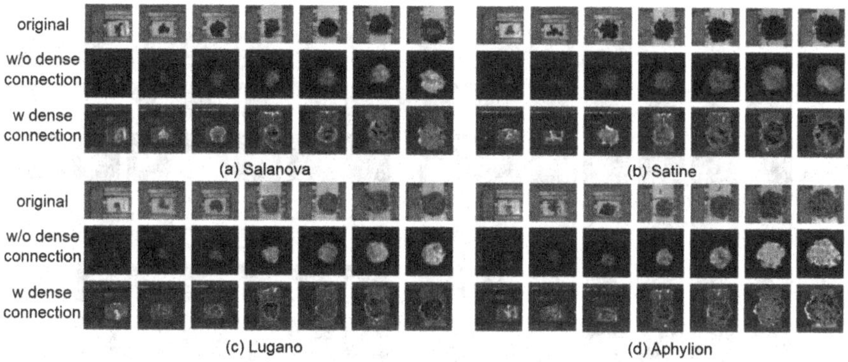

Fig. 5. Illustration of feature maps in dense extractor with and without dense connections. 'w/o' denotes without. 'w' denotes with.

For a fair comparison with other methods, the commonly used coefficient of determination (R^2) and normalized root mean squared error ($NRMSE$) are adopted to evaluate the model's performance. R^2 describes a goodness-of-fit measure for the variances between detected and measured data. $NRMSE$ reflects the relative difference between detected and measured data.

3.3 Ablation Study

To validate the effectiveness of the proposed method, we conducted a series of ablation experiments on a public lettuce dataset. The R^2 and $NRMSE$ comparisons and the feature visualization of DE and MSR are shown in Table 1, Fig. 5 and Fig. 6.

Effectiveness of Input Fusion Module (IFM). From Table 1, the input fusion module improves the average R^2 from 89.38% to 92.67% and the average $NRMSE$ from 20.67% to 16.90%. This result validates that fusing two-dimensional and depth images can provide rich and learnable information.i

Effectiveness of Dense Extractor (DE). The dense extractor makes the performance of the network have an obvious improvement, such as a gain of 1.22% in R^2 and 1.40% in $NRMSE$. Results in FW, DW, LD, and LA are consistently improved, which indicates that the dense extractor can enhance the relationship between different convolutional layers and reuse more coarse information sufficiently to obtain richer details and clearer edges. Furthermore, the effectiveness of the dense extractor can be more thoroughly demonstrated in Fig. 5. For various appearances of lettuce in different growth phases, the feature visualizations of the dense extractor with and without a dense connection illustrate that the dense extractor could focus on more distinguishable regions of lettuce.

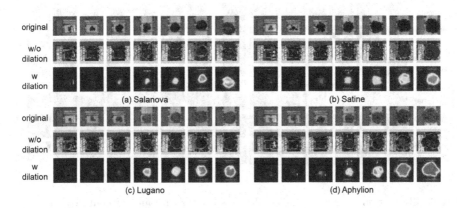

Fig. 6. Illustration of feature maps in multi-scale receptor with and without dilation. 'w/o' denotes without. 'w' denotes with.

Effectiveness of Multi-Scale Receptor (MSR). As shown in Table 1, the multi-scale receptor improves the average R^2 by 1.13% and the average $NRMSE$ by 1.56%, which validates that leveraging multi-level feature representations to detect lettuce growth traits is useful. Figure 6 further illustrated the effectiveness of MSR. Compared with convolutional layers without dilation, the multi-scale receptor eliminates background interference and emphasizes the position and outline of the lettuce.

3.4   Comparison with Mainstream Methods

To demonstrate the validity of our proposed network, we compare the proposed network with other popular detection methods, including Random Forest

Table 2. The R^2 and $NRMSE$ of comparison experiments. The best three results are highlighted in red, **blue**, green.

Metrics	Models	Average	FW	DW	LH	LD	LA
R^2 ↑	SVR	87.62	87.24	88.27	86.83	84.00	91.74
	RF	86.58	88.27	89.01	86.36	81.35	87.90
	VGG16	89.95	92.73	92.35	88.17	81.65	94.83
	Alexnet	89.83	94.50	94.79	86.79	80.99	92.06
	CNN	89.65	90.80	93.88	87.64	**84.22**	91.73
	Resnet18	90.91	93.79	95.07	87.16	83.14	95.36
	Resnet50	90.65	93.32	**96.01**	87.03	82.07	94.81
	Resnet101	**91.28**	93.94	95.68	87.79	83.79	**95.19**
	GFFN	**92.67**	**94.47**	96.64	**88.16**	88.95	95.13
$NRMSE$ ↓	SVR	23.61	35.24	30.68	16.06	12.67	24.86
	RF	24.72	33.78	29.70	16.34	13.68	30.09
	VGG16	19.97	26.59	24.78	15.22	13.57	19.66
	Alexnet	19.57	23.14	20.45	16.09	13.81	24.38
	CNN	21.02	29.93	22.17	15.56	**12.59**	24.87
	Resnet18	18.39	24.58	19.89	15.86	13.01	18.62
	Resnet50	18.49	25.50	**17.88**	15.94	13.42	19.71
	Resnet101	**18.02**	24.28	18.63	15.47	12.76	**18.98**
	GFFN	16.90	**23.19**	16.43	**15.23**	10.53	19.09

(RF) [17], Support Vector Regression (SVR) [18], CNN-based [13], VGG16 [19], AlexNet [20], Resnet-18, Resnet-50, and Resnet-101 [21]. In order to ensure the reliability of the comparative experiments, the convolution neural network-based methods are consistent with the proposed model in the design of hyperparameters. Table 2 shows the comparison of different methods on the R^2 and $NRMSE$.

In Table 2, compared with eight other methods, our method shows impressive performance, and GFFN is much higher than the second-ranked method in DW, LD, and Average. Specifically, compared with RF and SVR, GFFN surpasses them by about 5% and 6% in average R^2 and $NRMSE$, which indicates that our method better extracts hidden feature representations of lettuce images than hand-crafted feature extractors. In comparison with other deep learning-based methods, GFFN further improves the performance of detection, especially in DW and LD. These demonstrate that GFFN can gather fine-grained local and multi-level feature representations and has a strong ability to detect lettuce growth traits. The reason why our method fails to achieve the best score in LA may be that the compact and curved leaves make it easy to hide the lettuce area inside the lettuce, while GFFN prefers to focus on the change of contour. Compared to other popular detection methods, our model is a lot ahead of them on the whole, which further demonstrates the necessity of specially designing the model for appearance-various lettuce at different growth stages.

4   Conclusion

In this paper, we propose a Global Feature Fusion Network (GFFN), which can fully utilize both fine-grained local features and multi-level features from RGB-D images for the automatic detection of lettuce growth traits. To obtain more refined and complete feature representations, we propose a dense extractor to perform refinement from coarse feature representations. To solve the problem of extracting better feature representations from the ever-evolving lettuce appearance, a multi-scale receptor is designed to learn and merge low-level and high-level feature representations, including plenty of scale and location knowledge. Experimental results show that the proposed GFFN outperforms other mainstream methods.

References

1. Kim, M.J., Moon, Y., Tou, J.C., Mou, B., Waterland, N.L.: Nutritional value, bioactive compounds and health benefits of lettuce (Lactuca sativa L.). J. Food Compos. Anal. **49**, 19–34 (2016)
2. Wells, H.F., Bentley, J., et al.: Dietary assessment of us vegetable and dry pulse crops sector-updated1. Electronic Outlook Report from the Economic Research Service (VGS-357-SA1) (2016)
3. Schmilewski, G.: Growing medium constituents used in the EU. In: International Symposium on Growing Media 2007 819, pp. 33–46 (2007). https://doi.org/10.17660/ActaHortic.2009.819.3
4. Ríos, V.M., Gmez Herrera, M.D., Sugita, N.H., Alayn Luaces, P.: Water status response of pineapple using destructive and non-destructive indicators and their relations in two contrasting seasons. J. Saudi Soc. Agric. Sci. **19**(8), 538–547 (2020). https://doi.org/10.1016/j.jssas.2020.10.002
5. Yeh, Y.H.F., Lai, T.C., Liu, T.Y., Liu, C.C., Chung, W.C., Lin, T.T.: An automated growth measurement system for leafy vegetables. Biosyst. Eng. **117**, 43–50 (2014)
6. Jung, D.H., Park, S.H., Han, X.Z., Kim, H.J.: Image processing methods for measurement of lettuce fresh weight. J. Biosyst. Eng. **40**(1), 89–93 (2015). https://doi.org/10.5307/JBE.2015.40.1.089
7. Mortensen, A.K., et al.: Segmentation of lettuce in coloured 3d point clouds for fresh weight estimation. Comput. Electr. Agric. **154**, 373–381 (2018). https://doi.org/10.1016/j.compag.2018.09.010
8. Reyes-Yanes, A., Martinez, P., Ahmad, R.: Real-time growth rate and fresh weight estimation for little gem romaine lettuce in aquaponic grow beds. Comput. Electr. Agric. **179**, 105827 (2020). https://doi.org/10.1016/j.compag.2020.105827
9. Jmour, N., Zayen, S., Abdelkrim, A.: Convolutional neural networks for image classification. In: 2018 International Conference on Advanced Systems and Electric Technologies (IC_ASET), pp. 397–402. IEEE (2018)

10. Qu, Z., Jin, H., Zhou, Y., Yang, Z., Zhang, W.: Focus on local: detecting lane marker from bottom up via key point. In: 2021 IEEE/CVF Conference on Computer Vision and Pattern Recognition, CVPR 2021, pp. 14117–14125 (2021). https://doi.org/10.1109/CVPR46437.2021.01390

11. An, X., et al.: Killing two birds with one stone: efficient and robust training of face recognition CNNs by partial FC. In: 2022 IEEE/CVF Conference on Computer Vision and Pattern Recognition (CVPR 2022), pp. 4032–4041 (2022). https://doi.org/10.1109/CVPR52688.2022.00401

12. Yang, Y.: SDCN: a species-disease hybrid convolutional neural network for plant disease recognition. In: Pimenidis, E., Angelov, P., Jayne, C., Papaleonidas, A., Aydin, M. (eds.) ICANN 2022. LNCS, vol. 13532, pp. 769–780. Springer, Cham (2022). https://doi.org/10.1007/978-3-031-15937-4_64

13. Zhang, L., Xu, Z., Xu, D., Ma, J., Chen, Y., Fu, Z.: Growth monitoring of greenhouse lettuce based on a convolutional neural network. Hortic. Res. $7(1)$, 1–12 (2020). https://doi.org/10.1038/s41438-020-00345-6

14. Fuentes-Jimenez, D., et al.: Towards dense people detection with deep learning and depth images. Eng. Appl. Artif. Intell. 106, 104484 (2021). https://doi.org/10.1016/j.engappai.2021.104484

15. Hemming, S. (creator), de zwart, F. (creator), Elings, A. (creator), Bijlaard, M. (creator), van marrewijk, B. (creator), Petropoulou, A. (creator) (2021). 3rd autonomous greenhouse challenge: Online challenge lettuce images10.4121/15023088

16. Chakrabarty, A., Danielson, C., Bortoff, S.A., Laughman, C.R.: Accelerating self-optimization control of refrigerant cycles with Bayesian optimization and adaptive moment estimation. Appl. Therm. Eng. 197, 117335 (2021). https://doi.org/10.1016/j.applthermaleng.2021.117335

17. Fratello, M., Tagliaferri, R.: Decision trees and random forests. In: Encyclopedia of Bioinformatics and Computational Biology, pp. 374–383. Academic Press, Oxford (2019). https://doi.org/10.1016/B978-0-12-809633-8.20337-3

18. Cho, B.H., Koyama, K., Koseki, S.: Determination of 'Hass' avocado ripeness during storage by a smartphone camera using artificial neural network and support vector regression. J. Food Meas. Charact. $15(2)$, 2021–2030 (2021)

19. Simonyan, K., Zisserman, A.: Very deep convolutional networks for large-scale image recognition. arXiv preprint arXiv:1409.1556 (2014)

20. Krizhevsky, A., Sutskever, I., Hinton, G.E.: Imagenet classification with deep convolutional neural networks. Commun. ACM $60(6)$, 84–90 (2017)

21. He, K., Zhang, X., Ren, S., Sun, J.: Deep residual learning for image recognition. In: Proceedings of the IEEE Conference on Computer Vision and Pattern Recognition, pp. 770–778 (2016)

Adaptive Embedding and Distribution Re-margin for Long-Tail Recognition

Yulin Su[1], Boan Chen[2(✉)], Ziming Feng[3], and Junchi Yan[1]

[1] Shanghai Jiao Tong University, Shanghai, China
{yulinshh,yanjunchi}@sjtu.edu.cn
[2] Fudan University, Shanghai, China
chenboan2022@yeah.net
[3] China Merchants Bank Credit Card Center, Shanghai, China
zimingfzm@cmbchina.com

Abstract. Visual recognition methods assume models will be evaluated on the same class distribution as training data, but real-world data is often heavily class-imbalanced. To address this, the essential idea is to provide discriminative fitting abilities for classes with different sample sizes, i.e., the model achieves better generalization on less frequent classes, while maintaining high classification ability on the recurring classes. In this work, we propose to unify representation learning and classification learning with robust margin adjustment, which enforces a suitable margin in logit space and regularizes the distribution of embeddings. This procedure reduces representation bias in the feature space and reduces classification bias in the logit space at the same time. We further augment the under-represented tail classes on the feature level via re-balanced sampling from the robust prototype, calibrated with the knowledge from well-represented head classes and adaptive embedding uncertainty estimation. We conduct extensive experiments on a common long-tailed benchmark CIFAR100-LT. Experimental results demonstrate the advantage of the proposed AMDRG for the long-tailed recognition problem.

Keywords: Long-Tailed Recognition · Contrastive Learning · Robust Margin Estimation · Data Augmentation

1 Introduction

Deep long-tailed recognition learning unbiased models on imbalanced datasets, has posed great challenges for deep recognition at scale, since they can be easily biased towards dominant classes and perform poorly on tail classes. Early methods for addressing this issue involved resampling [3,18,38], transferring information from head to tail classes [5,26,29], loss reweighing by penalizing errors on rare labels more strongly [32,35,36,39], and enforcing asymmetric logit margins [1,2,8,9,16,25,30]. The main focus of these techniques is on balancing the multi-class classifier. However, these methods do not explicitly control the distribution of the learned embeddings, which can be sub-optimal for tail classes.

L. Iliadis et al. (Eds.): ICANN 2023, LNCS 14261, pp. 38–50, 2023.
https://doi.org/10.1007/978-3-031-44198-1_4

Recently, self-supervised learning has been shown to benefit imbalanced recognition, providing a new direction for long-tailed data classification. To overcome the limitations of existing methods for long-tailed data classification, we propose an AMC-DRG approach that combines logit re-margin and embedding re-margin techniques with a hybrid paradigm for distribution computation and data augmentation. Our approach introduces a combined contrastive loss that efficiently learns representations and extends the prototype supervised contrastive loss with an adaptive margin to address errors due to a small number of samples. We design a hybrid paradigm for distribution computation that includes a linear classifier and a semantic similarity-based classifier. We also directly re-balance the long-tail dataset through data augmentation by generating new features from the distribution of robust prototypes. Empirical results on the CIFAR100-LT dataset demonstrate the effectiveness of our proposed approach in achieving state-of-the-art performance. Our contributions can be summarized as follows:

1. Our combined supervised contrastive loss includes a supervised contrastive loss and a prototype supervised contrastive loss with an adaptive margin, enabling comprehensive and balanced feature learning.
2. Our aligned distribution paradigm, which combines linear and semantic similarity-based classifiers with margin adjustment, expands decision boundaries for tail classes. Additionally, we propose a robust feature generation strategy to re-balance long-tail datasets and alleviate classifier bias.
3. Our approach achieves state-of-the-art performance on the CIFAR100-LT long-tail recognition benchmark.

2   Related Work

The typical methods for solving long-tailed data classification are mainly divided into three classes: data-based, cost-based, and model-based.

2.1   Data-Based Methods

Data-based methods aim to balance the data distribution by augmenting the tail classes. Re-sampling is a common approach, but it can lead to information deficiency or overfitting. Mixup generates additional samples by interpolating input and labels. Knowledge transfer-based methods transfer features learned from head classes to tail classes, but they lack effective controls over the transferring process.

2.2   Cost-Based Methods

The cost-based methods include re-weighting and re-margining, aiming at obtaining balanced gradients during the training. Loss re-weighting upweights the tailed samples and downweights the head samples in the loss function. For example, [13] sets the weights inversely proportional to the number of samples, [7] sets the weights based on the real volumes of different classes, [17] sets the weights on the instance-level, [7] down-weights examples with either very small gradients or large gradients. Loss re-margining handles class imbalance by adjusting the minimal margin between learned features and the model classifier for different classes. [9] uses the mean classification prediction score to guide class-level margin adjustment, [8] adjusts the class-wise margin with the ordinal and variational margins, [30] enforces an additional margin term to enlarge the feature margin for head classes.

2.3 Module-Based Methods

Apart from the aforementioned re-balance strategies, another line of studies proposes to mitigate the negative effects of data imbalance by improving network modules in long-tailed learning. These methods can be divided into three categories: (1) Representation learning [12,19] improves the feature extractor; (2) Decoupled training [2,15,19,23,33] separates the training process into representation learning and classifier learning; (3) Ensemble learning [28,31,34,40] generates a balanced model by assembling and grouping models.

3   Methods

3.1   Problem Setting and Notations

Given an long-tail dataset $\mathcal{X} = \{(x_i, y_i)\}_{i=1}^N$ with N training samples and K classes, x_i is the training image and $y_i \in \{1, 2, \cdots, K\}$ is its label. For different sub-set of X, we denote it as X_k belonging to category k. Defining the number of samples of X_k to $N_k = |X_k|$, we have $N_1 \geq N_2 \cdots \geq N_K$ and $N_1 \gg N_K$ after sorting of N_k. The task of long-tail recognition is to learn a model on the long-tail training dataset $\mathcal{X}_{train}$ that generalizes well on a balanced test split $\mathcal{X}_{test}$. For training, we denote $M(x_i; \theta) = \hat{y}_i$ as the classification model, where x_i is the input, $\hat{y}_i$ is the prediction label and θ is the parameter of the model. The model $M(x_i; \theta) = \hat{y}_i$ contain two components: a feature model $f(x_i) = z_i$ and a classifier $h(z_i) = g_i$, where z_i denotes the feature of input x_i and g_i denotes the logit output of classifier. The prediction label is given as $\hat{y}_i = \arg\max(g_i)$.

3.2   Overview of Our Approach

Figure 1 provides an overview of the AMC-DRG method, which unifies representation learning and label distribution learning within a single training framework with adaptive margin adjustment. Additionally, we propose a robust feature generation scheme to achieve better class balance optimization. In terms of representation learning, our objective is to learn a representation that separates the distributions of samples from different classes effectively. Regarding label distribution learning, we explore two classification methods with logit adjustment: one from a linear-oriented angle and the other from a semantic-oriented angle. For feature augmentation, we optimize the estimated prototype using head-to-tail knowledge transfer and class-wise uncertain estimates, and then generate new

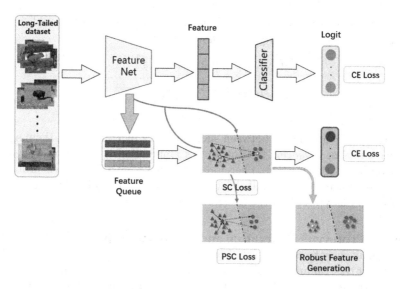

Fig. 1. Overview of AMC-DRG. It consists of three components: a representation learning module, a label distribution learning module, a robust feature generation module.

features from the distribution of the robust prototype. The total objective in our proposed AMC-DRG framework is:

$$
\begin{aligned}
\mathcal{L}_{Total} = \mathbb{E}_{(x,y)\in \mathcal{X}} \left[\mathcal{L}_{SCL} + \mathcal{L}_{PSCL} + \mathcal{L}_{CE}^{cls} + \mathcal{L}_{CE}^{dis} \right] \\
+ \lambda \cdot \mathbb{E}_{(\tilde{z},\tilde{y})\in \tilde{\mathcal{Z}}} \left[\mathcal{L}_{SCL} + \mathcal{L}_{PSCL} + \mathcal{L}_{CE}^{cls} + \mathcal{L}_{CE}^{dis} \right]
\end{aligned}
\tag{1}
$$

where λ is a trade-off between the losses computed from the original data, and losses computed from the generated feature.

3.3 Combined Supervised Contrastive Loss: Representation Learning

In representation learning, we explore two effective contrastive learning strategies and adaptively tailor them with adaptive margin adjustment to learn better image representations from imbalanced data.

Supervised Contrastive Learning. It is an extension to contrastive learning by incorporating the label information to compose positive and negative images. Assuming $\{z_i^+\} = |y_j = y_i, i \neq j\}$ is the number of positive samples of anchor z_i and verse visa, $\tau > 0$ is a scalar temperature parameter, it can be written as:

$$
\mathcal{L}_{SCL} = -\sum_{i=1}^{M} \mathcal{L}_{SCL}(z_i)
\tag{2}
$$

$$
\mathcal{L}_{SCL}(z_i) = \frac{-1}{|\{z_i^+\}|} \sum_{z_j \in \{z_i^+\}} \log \frac{\exp(d(z_i, z_j)/\tau)}{\sum_{z_k, k \neq i} \exp(d(z_i, z_k)/\tau)}
\tag{3}
$$

where $d(\cdot)$ is the distance metrics, calculated by combining the Euclidean similarity d_e and Cosine similarity d_c as shown in Eq. (4):

$$\begin{cases} d_e(z_i, z_j) = \frac{1}{m} \cdot \|z_i - z_j\|_2^2 \\ d_c(z_i, z_j) = \dfrac{z_i \cdot z_j}{\|z_i\| \cdot \|z_j\|} \\ d(z_i, z_j) = d_e(z_i, z_j) - d_c(z_i, z_j) \end{cases} \tag{4}$$

It optimizes the agreements between such positives by contrasting them against negative samples. However, the intra-class embedding is not compact enough merely optimized by Eq. (3). Therefore, we learn a set of balanced prototypes and force each sample to be pulled towards the prototype of its class and pushed away from prototypes of all the other classes.

Balanced Prototype Generation and Prototype Supervised Contrastive Loss. A naive way to create a set of prototypes $\mathcal{P} = \{p_k\}_{k=1}^K$ is to average all the features over the training samples in the same class k. However, exhaustively computing all the features in class k is both (1) computationally inefficient and (2) vulnerable to the bias in the head classes. Hence, we build a dictionary of memory queue $Q = \{Q_k\}_{k=1}^K$ where each key corresponds to the class label and Q_k denotes a queue for class k with the size $|Q_k|$. The centroid of features in Q_k represents the class prototype p_k for class k in the while new labeled features enter Q and some of the old ones are discarded after Q becomes full at every step: $p_k = \frac{1}{Q_k} \sum_{z_i \in Q_k} z_i$. Following [21], we fix the size of Q_k for all classes to the same amount, and adopt momentum encoder $f_{\theta'}$ where θ' is updated by exponential moving average (EMA) of θ. After generating prototypes $\mathcal{P} = \{p_i\}_{i=1}^N$ for class y_i, the prototype supervised contrastive loss function per-class can be designed as Eq. (5), which pulls and pushes between sample and prototype.

$$\mathcal{L}_{PSCL}(z_i) = -\log \frac{\exp(d(z_i, p_i)/\tau)}{\sum\limits_{j=1, j\neq i} \exp(d(z_i, p_j)/\tau)} \tag{5}$$

Embedding Re-margin. Simply optimizing the feature space using Eq. (5) assumes that the test distribution is similar to the empirical train distribution. However, this assumption may not hold true for long-tail recognition due to severe sample imbalance, which can lead to inaccuracies in the distance between the samples and the estimated prototype. To remedy this shortcoming, we set a set of trainable margin parameters $\mathcal{M} = \{m_k\}_{k=1}^K$ for each prototype to adjust distances calculated in Eq. (6), where m_i is a categorical adaptive margin to re-margin the radius of the neighborhood of class i.

$$\mathcal{L}_{PSCL}(z_i) = -\log \frac{\exp((d(z_i, p_i) - m_i)/\tau)}{\sum\limits_{j=1, j\neq i} \exp(d(z_i, p_j)/\tau)} \tag{6}$$

Our adaptive embedding re-margin scheme is designed for learning a representation where its prototype takes into account the estimation error by pushing

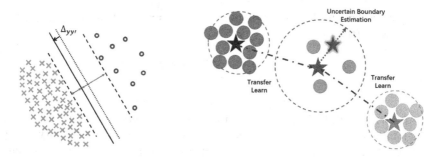

Fig. 2. The scheme of logit adjustment.   **Fig. 3.** Calibration of prototype.

and pulling towards a worst-case possible distribution within an uncertainty area around the estimated prototype. Uncertainty areas are typically larger for tail classes, compared with head classes that have many samples.

$$\mathcal{L}_{PSCL} = -\sum_{i=1}^{N} \omega(c)\mathcal{L}_{PSCL}(z_i) \tag{7}$$

As a whole, we define a prototype supervised contrastive loss in Eq. (7) as a weighted average over per-class losses, where $w(c)$ are class weights. Setting $w(c) = \frac{1}{N_c}$ gives equal weighting to all classes and prevents head classes from dominating the loss.

3.4   Aligned Distribution: Label Distribution Learning

For balanced-dataset learning, we minimize the cross-entropy loss, while in the long-tail setting, the label distribution is highly skewed, a popular strategy involves augmenting the softmax cross-entropy with logit margins. Specifically, these involve an instantiation of the loss:

$$\mathcal{L}_{CE} = -\log \frac{e^{g_y}}{\sum_{y'}^{K} e^{g_{y'}}} = \log[1 + \sum_{y' \neq y}^{K} e^{\Delta_{yy'} + g_{y'} - g_y}] \tag{8}$$

where $\Delta_{yy'}$ is margin between labels y and y', g_y denotes the logit, the prediction label is given as $\hat{y}_i = \arg\max(g_i)$ and the label $y_i \in \{1, 2, \cdots, K\}$. As shown in Fig. 2, such adjustment encourages a large relative margin between logits of rare versus dominant labels.

Linear-Oriented Logit Computation. Computing logit with the linear classifier has been widely adopted by most label distribution training algorithms, we term this type of logit as linear-oriented logit for abbreviation. As mentioned, we define feature model as $f(x_i) = z_i$ and the logit is computed by linear classifier as $g_i^{cls} = h(z_i)$, where z_i denotes feature of input x_i and g_i^{cls} denotes the logit output of classifier. Follow [20, 22], we adopt $\Delta_{yy'} = \log \frac{\mathbf{P}(y')}{\mathbf{P}(y)}$ for logit adjustment, Eq. (8) can be rewritten as:

$$\mathcal{L}_{CE}^{cls} = \log[1 + \sum_{y' \neq y}^{K} e^{\log \frac{\mathbf{P}(y')}{\mathbf{P}(y)} + g_{y'}^{cls} - g_y^{cls}}] \tag{9}$$

Semantic-Oriented Logit Computation. An alternative approach to obtaining logit is to use a similarity-based classifier to measure the similarity of a given representation to a prototype in feature space, which we refer to as semantics-oriented logit. To setup a semantic similarity-based classifier, we utilize the aforementioned class prototypes $\mathcal{P} = \{p_k\}_{k=1}^K$ to serve as the reference for computing logits to the samples in X_{train}. The probability of sample x_i belonging to category k is inversely proportional to the distance between feature z_i and prototype p_k, where a smaller distance between z_i and p_k leads to assign the sample x_i to label k with a larger probability. As a result, we explore semantic-oriented logit as:

$$g_i^{dis} = \frac{\exp(-d(z_i, p_i)/\gamma)}{\sum_{j=1}^K \exp(-d(z_i, p_j)/\gamma)} \tag{10}$$

where γ is a hyperparameter that controls the hardness of the distance-probability conversion. We assign trainable margin parameter $\mathcal{M}$ in Eq. (6) as the margin term $\Delta_{yy'}$. Therefore, for semantic-oriented computation with logit adjustment, Eq. (8) can be rewritten as:

$$\mathcal{L}_{CE}^{dis} = \log[1 + \sum_{y' \neq y}^{K} e^{m_y + g_{y'}^{dis} - g_y^{dis}}] \tag{11}$$

3.5   Robust Feature Generation: Data Augmentation

As described in Fig. 3, to re-balance the training samples, we perform data augmentation by generating new features from the distribution of the robust prototype: we transfer knowledge from the adjacent 2–3 prototypes with more training samples and closer to the given prototype, and further approach the given prototype to the worst-case prototype located at an uncertain boundary.

Head-to-Tail Transfer Learning. We calibrate the distribution for prototypes through head-to-tail transfer learning similar to [37]. The Difference is that we only conduct the calibration in prototypes rather than each sample, which enables more efficient data sampling. For each prototype p_i, we compute the distance between p_i and other classes k which have more training samples as $d_{ik} = \|p_i - p_k\|$. Then, we choose K classes(2 or 3) with smallest distance as a support set $\mathcal{S}$ for prototype p_i. Given the support set $\mathcal{S}$ for each class prototype p_i, we calibrate the distribution of prototype p_i as:

$$\hat{p}_i = (1 - \alpha) \cdot p_i + \alpha \cdot \frac{\sum_{j \in S} \omega_j p_j}{\sum_{j \in S} \omega_j} \tag{12}$$

where α is an optional hyper-parameter to control the calibration, ω_j is a weight term that is inversely proportional to the size of class j. Because we want to learn the distribution knowledge more from the classes with more training samples and closer to the given prototype.

Uncertain Boundary Estimation. To further recover the true distribution of tail classes, we consider the estimation error. The bigger the embedding margin parameter, the larger the uncertainty range of the class embedding. Therefore, the aforementioned trainable margin parameters $\mathcal{M}$ in Eq. (6) can be served as uncertain boundaries. Taking into account the uncertain boundary estimation, we obtain a worst-case possible prototype. In this case, a robust prototype is a compromise between an estimated prototype and a worst-case prototype.

$$\tilde{p}_i = (1 - \beta) \cdot \hat{p}_i + \beta \cdot m_i \tag{13}$$

where β is a trade-off between the estimated prototype and the worst-case prototype, $m_i \in \mathcal{M}$, $\hat{p}_i$ is the calibrated prototype obtained from Eq (12), and $\tilde{p}_i$ is the corresponding robust prototype.

New Feature Generation for Re-balancing Dataset. For each tail class, we obtain the robust prototype with Eq. (13) and generate samples within the robust prototype distribution. The generated dataset is denoted as $\tilde{\mathcal{Z}} = \{(\tilde{z}_i, \tilde{y}_i)\}_{i=1}^N$, where $\tilde{z}_i$ is the sampling feature and $\tilde{y}_i$ is the corresponding label. The sampling number for each class will depend on the inversely class frequency.

4 Experiments

4.1 Experimental Setups

We train our proposed method on CIFAR100-LT [2] with imbalance ratio $\rho = \max_y \mathbf{P}(y) / \min_y \mathbf{P}(y) = 100$, and evaluating the performance on the uniform target label distribution. In our experiments, we use SGD optimizer with momentum 0.9 and weight decay 0.0005 for training. We use ResNet-32 [11] as backbone network to extract image representation. The networks are trained for 600 epochs with the learning rate being decayed by a cosine scheduler from 0.02 to 0. Following MoCo [4,10], we also derive two different augmentation views of an image by using different data augmentations in training phase. The batch size is set to 128, the λ in Eq. (1) is fixed to be 1.0, the τ in Eq. (3) and Eq. (5) is set to 0.07, and the γ in Eq. (10) is 1.0.

4.2 Ablation Studies

Both α (the knowledge transfer ratio) in Eq. (12) and β (the trade-off ratio between the estimated prototype and the worst-case prototype) in Eq. (13) are important parameters. We carry out two ablation studies on the validation set to identify how is the model performance affected when two parameters are changed. According to Table 1 and Table 2, we set $\alpha = 0.2$, $\beta = 0.5$.

Table 1. Different α with $\beta = 0$.

value of α	Top-1
0	51.12
0.1	51.64
0.2	**51.87**
0.4	50.94

Table 2. Different β with $\alpha = 0.2$.

value of β	Top-1
0	51.87
0.1	52.14
0.5	**52.23**
1.0	51.42

4.3   Effectiveness Studies

We conduct experiments to validate the effectiveness of three strategies in our methods, i.e., combined supervised contrastive learning, aligned distribution and robust feature generation.

Effectiveness of Combined Supervised Contrastive Learning. We train our model under four different settings in contrastive learning: (1) supervised contrastive loss(SCL), (2) prototype supervised contrastive loss(PSCL), (3) contrastive Loss and prototype supervised contrastive loss (SCL+PSCL), (4) supervised contrastive loss and prototype supervised contrastive loss with adaptive margin (SCL+PSCL+AM). We report the results in Table 3. It suggests that (SCL+PSCL+AM) learns high-quality features for all classes.

Effectiveness of Aligned Distribution. Table 4 lists results under three variant label distribution learning methods: (1) linear-oriented logit computation (LLC), (2) semantic-oriented logit computation (SLC), (3) linear-oriented and semantic-oriented logit computation (LLC+SLC). The highest accuracy in (LLC+SLC) demonstrates the effectiveness of our aligned distribution strategy.

Effectiveness of Robust Feature Generation. We evaluate the effectiveness of feature generation and two calibration methods for prototype calibration. We test our model under four different settings: (1) no feature generation (No FG), (2) feature generation and prototype calibration of head-to-tail transfer learning (FG+TL), (3) feature generation and prototype calibration of uncertain boundary estimation (FG+UBE), (4) feature generation and both prototype calibration methods (FG+TL+UBE). As shown in Table 5, feature generation strategy further enhances the performance. Moreover, after prototype calibration, the performance gain would be more significant.

Table 3. Top-1 Accuracy with different contrastive losses.

Contr Loss	Top-1
SCL	51.88
PSCL	51.45
SCL+PSCL	52.11
SCL+PSCL+AM	**52.23**

Table 4. Top-1 Accuracy with different logit computations.

Logit Computation	Top-1
LLC	51.97
SLC	50.63
LLC+SLC	**52.23**

Table 5. Top-1 Accuracy w/o feature generation and different prototype calibrations.

Feature Generation	Top-1
No FG	51.74
FG+TL	52.01
FG+UBE	52.03
FG+TL+UBE	**52.23**

4.4 Comparison to State-of-the-Art Methods

For a fair comparison, we re-implement baselines in the same setting for recent state-of-the-arts [6,14,24,27,37]. We report the performance of all baseline methods alxong with AMC-DRG in Table 6. We find that our AMCDRG provides substantial performance gain over all baseline methods.

Table 6. Top-1 classification accuracy over all classes on CIFAR100-LT with ResNet-32. All methods trained in 600 epochs for fair comparison.

Method	Top-1 Accuracy
Hybrid-SPC [27]	44.97
Hybrid-SC [27]	46.72
PaCo [6]	51.66
DRO-LT [24]	46.92
ELM [14]	45.77
GLAG [37]	51.47
AMC-DRG(Ours)	**52.23**

5   Conclusion

In this paper, we propose a novel approach, AMC-DRG, to tackle the long-tail challenge in classification tasks. Our method leverages re-margin schedules that learn representation and distribution jointly within a one-stage training scheme. We incorporate contrastive learning and prototype learning to enhance the embedding training phase, and introduce a hybrid paradigm for distribution computation that includes a linear classifier and a semantic similarity-based classifier. By reducing representation and classification bias towards head classes, our method achieves more balanced performance across all classes. Additionally, we design a robust feature generation module to facilitate data re-balancing. Overall, our approach demonstrates promising results in improving long-tail classification accuracy.

Acknowledgements. This work was partly supported by NSFC (U19B2035) and Shanghai Municipal Science and Technology Major Project (2021SHZDZX0102).

References

1. Cao, D., Zhu, X., Huang, X., Guo, J., Lei, Z.: Domain balancing: face recognition on long-tailed domains. In: Proceedings of the IEEE/CVF Conference on Computer Vision and Pattern Recognition, pp. 5671–5679 (2020)
2. Cao, K., Wei, C., Gaidon, A., Arechiga, N., Ma, T.: Learning imbalanced datasets with label-distribution-aware margin loss. In: Advances in Neural Information Processing Systems, vol. 32 (2019)
3. Chawla, N.V., Bowyer, K.W., Hall, L.O., Kegelmeyer, W.P.: Smote: synthetic minority over-sampling technique. J. Artif. Intell. Res. **16**, 321–357 (2002)
4. Chen, X., Fan, H., Girshick, R., He, K.: Improved baselines with momentum contrastive learning. arXiv preprint arXiv:2003.04297 (2020)
5. Chu, P., Bian, X., Liu, S., Ling, H.: Feature space augmentation for long-tailed data. In: Vedaldi, A., Bischof, H., Brox, T., Frahm, J.-M. (eds.) ECCV 2020. LNCS, vol. 12374, pp. 694–710. Springer, Cham (2020). https://doi.org/10.1007/978-3-030-58526-6_41
6. Cui, J., Zhong, Z., Liu, S., Yu, B., Jia, J.: Parametric contrastive learning. In: Proceedings of the IEEE/CVF International Conference on Computer Vision, pp. 715–724 (2021)
7. Cui, Y., Jia, M., Lin, T.Y., Song, Y., Belongie, S.: Class-balanced loss based on effective number of samples. In: Proceedings of the IEEE/CVF Conference on Computer Vision and Pattern Recognition, pp. 9268–9277 (2019)
8. Deng, Z., Liu, H., Wang, Y., Wang, C., Yu, Z., Sun, X.: PML: progressive margin loss for long-tailed age classification. In: Proceedings of the IEEE/CVF Conference on Computer Vision and Pattern Recognition, pp. 10503–10512 (2021)
9. Feng, C., Zhong, Y., Huang, W.: Exploring classification equilibrium in long-tailed object detection. In: Proceedings of the IEEE/CVF International Conference on Computer Vision, pp. 3417–3426 (2021)
10. He, K., Fan, H., Wu, Y., Xie, S., Girshick, R.: Momentum contrast for unsupervised visual representation learning. In: Proceedings of the IEEE/CVF Conference on Computer Vision and Pattern Recognition, pp. 9729–9738 (2020)
11. He, K., Zhang, X., Ren, S., Sun, J.: Deep residual learning for image recognition. In: Proceedings of the IEEE Conference on Computer Vision and Pattern Recognition, pp. 770–778 (2016)
12. Huang, C., Li, Y., Loy, C.C., Tang, X.: Learning deep representation for imbalanced classification. In: Proceedings of the IEEE Conference on Computer Vision and Pattern Recognition, pp. 5375–5384 (2016)
13. Japkowicz, N., Stephen, S.: The class imbalance problem: a systematic study. Intell. Data Anal. **6**(5), 429–449 (2002)
14. Jitkrittum, W., Menon, A.K., Rawat, A.S., Kumar, S.: ELM: embedding and logit margins for long-tail learning. arXiv preprint arXiv:2204.13208 (2022)
15. Kang, B., et al.: Decoupling representation and classifier for long-tailed recognition. arXiv preprint arXiv:1910.09217 (2019)
16. Khan, S., Hayat, M., Zamir, S.W., Shen, J., Shao, L.: Striking the right balance with uncertainty. In: Proceedings of the IEEE/CVF Conference on Computer Vision and Pattern Recognition, pp. 103–112 (2019)

17. Lin, T.Y., Goyal, P., Girshick, R., He, K., Dollár, P.: Focal loss for dense object detection. In: Proceedings of the IEEE International Conference on Computer Vision, pp. 2980–2988 (2017)
18. Liu, X.Y., Wu, J., Zhou, Z.H.: Exploratory undersampling for class-imbalance learning. IEEE Trans. Syst. Man Cybern. Part B (Cybern.) **39**(2), 539–550 (2008)
19. Liu, Z., Miao, Z., Zhan, X., Wang, J., Gong, B., Yu, S.X.: Large-scale long-tailed recognition in an open world. In: Proceedings of the IEEE/CVF Conference on Computer Vision and Pattern Recognition, pp. 2537–2546 (2019)
20. Menon, A.K., Jayasumana, S., Rawat, A.S., Jain, H., Veit, A., Kumar, S.: Long-tail learning via logit adjustment. arXiv preprint arXiv:2007.07314 (2020)
21. Oh, Y., Kim, D.J., Kweon, I.S.: Distribution-aware semantics-oriented pseudo-label for imbalanced semi-supervised learning. arXiv preprint arXiv:2106.05682 (2021)
22. Ren, J., Yu, C., Ma, X., Zhao, H., Yi, S., et al.: Balanced meta-softmax for long-tailed visual recognition. In: Advances in Neural Information Processing Systems, vol. 33, pp. 4175–4186 (2020)
23. Samuel, D., Atzmon, Y., Chechik, G.: From generalized zero-shot learning to long-tail with class descriptors. In: Proceedings of the IEEE/CVF Winter Conference on Applications of Computer Vision, pp. 286–295 (2021)
24. Samuel, D., Chechik, G.: Distributional robustness loss for long-tail learning. In: Proceedings of the IEEE/CVF International Conference on Computer Vision, pp. 9495–9504 (2021)
25. Wang, F., Cheng, J., Liu, W., Liu, H.: Additive margin softmax for face verification. IEEE Signal Process. Lett. **25**(7), 926–930 (2018)
26. Wang, J., Lukasiewicz, T., Hu, X., Cai, J., Xu, Z.: RSG: a simple but effective module for learning imbalanced datasets. In: Proceedings of the IEEE/CVF Conference on Computer Vision and Pattern Recognition, pp. 3784–3793 (2021)
27. Wang, P., Han, K., Wei, X.S., Zhang, L., Wang, L.: Contrastive learning based hybrid networks for long-tailed image classification. In: Proceedings of the IEEE/CVF Conference on Computer Vision and Pattern Recognition, pp. 943–952 (2021)
28. Wang, X., Lian, L., Miao, Z., Liu, Z., Yu, S.X.: Long-tailed recognition by routing diverse distribution-aware experts. arXiv preprint arXiv:2010.01809 (2020)
29. Wang, Y.X., Ramanan, D., Hebert, M.: Learning to model the tail. In: Advances in Neural Information Processing Systems, vol. 30 (2017)
30. Wu, T., Liu, Z., Huang, Q., Wang, Y., Lin, D.: Adversarial robustness under long-tailed distribution. In: Proceedings of the IEEE/CVF Conference on Computer Vision and Pattern Recognition, pp. 8659–8668 (2021)
31. Xiang, L., Ding, G., Han, J.: Learning from multiple experts: self-paced knowledge distillation for long-tailed classification. In: Vedaldi, A., Bischof, H., Brox, T., Frahm, J.-M. (eds.) ECCV 2020. LNCS, vol. 12350, pp. 247–263. Springer, Cham (2020). https://doi.org/10.1007/978-3-030-58558-7_15
32. Ye, H.J., Chen, H.Y., Zhan, D.C., Chao, W.L.: Identifying and compensating for feature deviation in imbalanced deep learning. arXiv preprint arXiv:2001.01385 (2020)
33. Zhang, S., Li, Z., Yan, S., He, X., Sun, J.: Distribution alignment: a unified framework for long-tail visual recognition. In: Proceedings of the IEEE/CVF Conference on Computer Vision and Pattern Recognition, pp. 2361–2370 (2021)
34. Zhang, Y., Hooi, B., Hong, L., Feng, J.: Test-agnostic long-tailed recognition by test-time aggregating diverse experts with self-supervision. arXiv preprint arXiv:2107.09249 (2021)

35. Zhang, Y., et al.: Online adaptive asymmetric active learning for budgeted imbalanced data. In: Proceedings of the 24th ACM SIGKDD International Conference on Knowledge Discovery & Data Mining, pp. 2768–2777 (2018)

36. Zhang, Y., et al.: Online adaptive asymmetric active learning with limited budgets. IEEE Trans. Knowl. Data Eng. **33**(6), 2680–2692 (2019)

37. Zhang, Z., Xiang, X.: Long-tailed classification with gradual balanced loss and adaptive feature generation. arXiv preprint arXiv:2203.00452 (2022)

38. Zhang, Z., Pfister, T.: Learning fast sample re-weighting without reward data. In: Proceedings of the IEEE/CVF International Conference on Computer Vision, pp. 725–734 (2021)

39. Zhao, P., Zhang, Y., Wu, M., Hoi, S.C., Tan, M., Huang, J.: Adaptive cost-sensitive online classification. IEEE Trans. Knowl. Data Eng. **31**(2), 214–228 (2018)

40. Zhou, B., Cui, Q., Wei, X.S., Chen, Z.M.: BBN: bilateral-branch network with cumulative learning for long-tailed visual recognition. In: Proceedings of the IEEE/CVF Conference on Computer Vision and Pattern Recognition, pp. 9719–9728 (2020)

Adaptive Propagation Network Based on Multi-scale Information Fusion

Qianli Ma[(⊠)], Chenzhi Wang, Zheng Fan, and Yuhua Qian

College of Computer and Information Technology, Shanxi University, Taiyuan, China
mymql@sxu.edu.cn, 202122408075@email.sxu.edu.cn

Abstract. Graph Neural Networks (GNNs) have achieved remarkable success in many aspects, but they still suffer from certain limitations, such as over-smoothing with increasing layer depth, sensitivity to topological perturbations, and inability to be applied to heterophilic graphs. So this paper proposes a **M**ulti-scale Information Fusion **A**daptive **P**ropagation **Net**work (MAPNET) to overcome these limitations. First, a new graph data augmentation method is designed, which deletes unimportant edges and introduces KNN graphs to perturb the graph structure, and adds the graph regularization terms to improve the model's robustness and generalization; second, a multi-scale information fusion adaptive propagation process is designed to enhance the diversity of neighborhoods to alleviate the over-smoothing problem; finally, the edge weights are extended to the negative values to adapt to the heterophilic graphs. Experimental results show that MAPNET partially solves the over-smoothing problem in GNNs. The model outperforms recent models in both semi-supervised and fully supervised node classification tasks on multiple datasets, and has better generalization performance and robustness.

Keywords: Graph neural network · Over-smoothing · Multi-scale information fusion · Adaptive · Node classification · Heterophilic graphs

1 Introduction

Complex networks can describe many real-world systems, such as the social networks, the biological networks, and the internet link networks. In deep learning, the graph neural networks (GNNs) [1] have been widely studied and applied to various tasks, such as the node classification [2], the link prediction [3], and the recommendation [4, 5], due to their excellent ability of graph data processing. Semi-supervised node classification is one of the hottest and most important problems in graph learning. In recent years, many effective node classification methods have been proposed by researchers [6–8]. Despite achieved great success, these algorithms all suffer from the problem of over-smoothing.

APPNP [9], JKNET [10], and GDC [11] are three methods for alleviating the over-smoothing problem in graph neural networks. They respectively use the fusion of PageRank ideas, the utilization of different neighborhood ranges, and a sparse graph diffusion generalized form to aggregate neighborhood information. These methods can alleviate the over-smoothing phenomenon, but they are sensitive to noise attacks and have weak robustness of the models.

L. Iliadis et al. (Eds.): ICANN 2023, LNCS 14261, pp. 51–62, 2023.
https://doi.org/10.1007/978-3-031-44198-1_5

Due to the success of data augmentation in computer vision, more and more scholars have focused the application of data augmentation on graphs. DropEdge [13] increases the diversity of input data by randomly removing a certain percentage of edges. GRAND [14] solves the problems of over-smoothing, non-robustness, and weak generalization through random diffusion and consistency training. NodeAug [15] creates a "parallel universe" for each node to perform data augmentation. These models are effective for homophilic graphs, but their performance on the heterophilic graphs is not good, so using graph neural networks on the heterophilic graphs are increasingly being studied.

In order to address the issues of over-smoothing, weak robustness, and inability to be applied to the heterophilic graphs in GNNs, this paper proposes an Adaptive Propagation Network based on multi-scale information fusion. The novelty of this study lies in several aspects:

- Firstly, new graph data augmentation methods and a new regularization term are designed to enhance the model's robustness and generalization performance.
- Secondly, multiscale neighborhood information fusion is used to alleviate over-smoothing.
- Finally, adaptive propagation weights are used to extend the edge weights to the negative values to adapt to the heterophilic graphs.
- Experimental results show that the proposed model can effectively improve the accuracy of node classification.

2   Related Work

Graph Convolutional Networks (GCN) are the most commonly used type of models in GNNs. The forward propagation of GCN can be defined as:

$$H^{(l+1)} = \sigma\left(\hat{A} H^{(l)} W^{(l+1)}\right) \tag{1}$$

where $H^{(l)} \in \mathbb{R}^{N \times F^{(l)}}$ and $H^{(l+1)} \in \mathbb{R}^{N \times F^{(l+1)}}$ are the input and output node representation matrices of the model. $\hat{A} = \tilde{D}^{-1/2} \tilde{A} \tilde{D}^{-1/2}$ is the symmetric normalized adjacency matrix with self-loops, where $\tilde{A} = A + I$ and $\tilde{D}$ is the diagonal degree matrix. $W^{(l+1)} \in \mathbb{R}^{F^{(l)} \times F^{(l+1)}}$ is the trainable weight matrix, and σ is the activation function, usually ReLU. The above equation can be understood as follows: GCN first propagates the representations of neighbors, and then performs a nonlinear transformation to obtain new node representations.

Due to the differences between the graph data and the Euclidean data, it is not feasible to simply transplant the computer vision methods into the graph neural networks. Therefore, the researchers have begun to explore the methods of data augmentation in graph data, which can be mainly divided into two categories: the manipulating features [23] and the manipulating graph structures [13, 15, 17, 21]. This paper focuses on purposefully deleting and adding edges in graph structures to enhance the data, in order to preserve the correctness of the graph and minimize the impact of noise.

The graph regularization, as an unsupervised term applied to model training, can provide additional supervision information for the model to learn better representations of nodes in the graph. Many methods [13, 14, 21] have already improved the model performance by adding the regularization terms, with the most common one in previous graph representation learning being the graph Laplacian regularization:

$$\mathcal{L}_{\text{lap}} = \sum_{(i,j)\in\mathcal{E}} \left\| h_i^\top - h_j^\top \right\|_2^2 \tag{2}$$

Equation (2) minimizes the difference between the central node and its neighbors, which can provide the structural information for model training. However, the ability of GNN to extract local feature information is similar to that of the graph Laplacian regularization term, so adding the graph Laplacian regularization term to GNN cannot provide additional useful information.

PPNP and its approximation APPNP [9] balance local and global features by overlaying the features from different neighborhoods and using personalized PageRank weights (PPR), and achieve good performance in alleviating over-smoothing. Later, a more generalized information fusion model, graph diffusion convolution (GDC) [11] is proposed: $S = \sum_{k=0}^{\infty} \theta_k T^k$, θ_k and T^k are the weight coefficients and the transition matrices. In this paper, we do not modify the weight coefficients, but replace the transition matrix with an adaptive edge weight matrix.

3 Model Introduction

The model consists of three modules: the graph data augmentation module, the adaptive propagation module, and the regularization module, as shown in Fig. 1 for details. In this section, a data augmentation method is designed to generate S views with different node features but the same topology structure between views during each iteration. Then, the same adaptive propagation network is used to generate S graph embeddings. Finally, the objective function is composed of the cross-entropy and the regularization terms, and the model is trained by minimizing the objective function.

3.1 Importance-Based Data Augmentation

In general, the data augmentation for the topology structure can be broadly divided into the edge deletion and the edge addition. Many previous methods randomly delete edges, such as DropEdge [13] and NASA [21]. However, random edge deletion may remove important edges, so it is generally believed that important edges should have a higher probability of being preserved, while unimportant edges should have a higher probability of being deleted. Then, how to define the importance of edges? In this paper, it is believed that the larger the degree of a node is, the more important the edge connected to it is, because in the propagation process, nodes with a larger degree also propagate more information [15].

Definition 1. *The calculation equation of node importance is $w_{uv}^e = log(d_u)$. The degree of node v_u in edge e_{uv} is used as the measure of importance. The probability of e_{uv} being deleted is inversely proportional to w_{uv}^e. The equation for calculating the probability of an edge being deleted using importance is defined as:*

$$p_{uv}^e = \min\left(\frac{w_{\max}^e - w_{uv}^e}{w_{\max}^e - \mu_s^e} \cdot p_e, p_\tau \right) \tag{3}$$

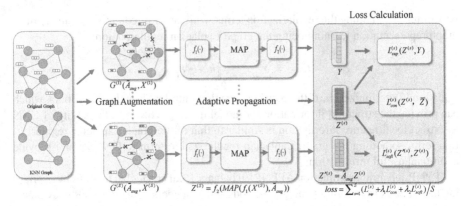

Fig. 1. The structure of MAPNET model

p_{uv}^e is the probability that an edge is deleted, w_{max}^e and μ_s^e are the maximum values and the average values of w_{uv}^e, respectively, and p_e is a hyperparameter that controls the overall probability of deleted edges. p_τ controls the maximum probability of deleted edges. Then, the mask $\varepsilon_{uv} \sim Bernoulli(p_{uv}^e)$ is generated for each edge according to the probability p_{uv}^e, and the edge is determined to be preserved or not based on the mask. According to the above equation, important edges will be more likely to be preserved, while unimportant edges will be more likely to be deleted. Note that p_{uv}^e and p_{vu}^e are not equal, so the undirected graph will become a directed graph after data augmentation, $\tilde{D}_{out}$ is used instead of $\tilde{D}$ in the normalization operation later.

The adding edge process in this paper chooses to add edges to the KNN graph, because in the KNN graph, the features of related points are similar, which is more advantageous than the random adding edge, as shown in Fig. 2(a).

Specifically, in the deleting edge process, if the edges in e_{uv} are deleted, some information will be missing in the node v. In this paper, these missing information is supplemented by using the KNN graph. In the KNN graph, a random node u' adjacent to the node v is selected to connect it and supplement the missing information, that is, deleting e_{uv} and adding $e_{u'v}$.

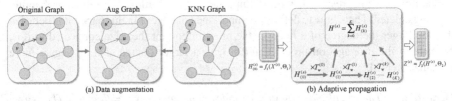

Fig. 2. (a) The data augmentation of graph structure. (b) The Adaptive propagation of multi-scale information fusion.

Definition 2. *Assuming* $\mathcal{N}_v^{\text{remove}} = \{v_u^\varepsilon \in \mathcal{N}_v, \epsilon_u = 1\}$ *is the set of removed points,* $\mathcal{N}_v^{\text{add}} = \{v_{u'} \in \mathcal{N}_v^{KNN}, \epsilon_{u'} = 1\}$ *is the set of added points, The graph augmentation is defined as:*

$$\mathcal{N}_v^{\text{aug}} = (\mathcal{N}_v - \mathcal{N}_v^{\text{remove}}) \cup \mathcal{N}_v^{\text{add}} \tag{4}$$

where v_u^ε represents the source node of the removed edge. $\mathcal{N}_v$ represents the neighborhood of node v_v, and ϵ_u represents the relationship between node v_v and v_u, $\mathcal{N}_v^{KNN}$ represents the neighborhood of node v_v in the KNN graph. After the above operations of removing unimportant nodes and adding similar nodes, the graph structure is perturbed, but it does not significantly affect the correctness of the graph. Moreover, the additional noise can also be used as advantageous information for the node classification in the following process. The KNN graph can be generated outside the training process, so the computational cost can be ignored.

The augmentation of node features uses the most convenient method of dropout, which randomly deletes each component of the node feature. After the above data augmentation method, S views are generated, where the s-th view is denoted as $G^{(s)}(\tilde{A}_{aug}, X^{(s)})$. The topological structure between views is the same, while the node features are different. However, the topological structure is augmented in each epoch, which means that $\tilde{A}_{aug}$ is different in each epoch, named as the dynamic training. The combination of data augmentation and dynamic training makes the model more robust, and reduces its sensitivity to the neighborhood changes.

3.2 Adaptive Propagation of Multi-scale Information Fusion

Here, the specific meaning of multi-scale information is the different orders of neighborhood information. Both APPNP [9] and GPRGNN [16] use multi-order neighborhood information aggregation to alleviate the over-smoothing problem, which can also be regarded as the result of balancing local and global information. The difference is that APPNP uses fixed edge weights in the propagation process, while GPRGNN uses the adaptive weights on the weight coefficients. In this paper, we replaced the traditional fixed edge weights with the adaptive edge weights, and used self-attention mechanism to reduce the number of parameters, The specific process is shown in Fig. 2(b).

The process of dimension transformation on features is only performed at the beginning and end, in order to decouple the feature transformation process from the propagation process. Previous studies have shown that the entanglement between the feature transformation and the feature propagation can exacerbate the over-smoothing phenomenon [12]. After the dimension transformation, the initial embedding $H_{(0)}^{(s)} \in \mathbb{R}^{N \times F'}$ is obtained. It multiplies by the normalized adaptive edge weight matrix $T_w^{(0)} \in \mathbb{R}^{N \times N}$ for the convolution operation to obtain first-order neighborhood information, which is then multiplied by $T_w^{(1)}$ again to obtain second-order neighborhood information. Repeat the above operation to obtain K order neighborhood information $H_{(K)}^{(s)}$, and aggregate and fuse the multi-scale information, then perform the feature transformation to obtain the final embedding $Z^{(s)} \in \mathbb{R}^{N \times C}$. The equation is as follows:

$$H_{(0)}^{(s)} = f_1(X^{(s)}, \Theta_1), \quad H^{(s)} = \sum_{k=0}^{K} \prod_{i=0}^{k} T_w^{(i)} H_{(0)}^{(s)}, \quad Z^{(s)} = f_2(H^{(s)}, \Theta_2) \qquad (5)$$

so the key lies in the computation of the weight matrix $T_w^{(i)}$.

Definition 3. *Let $t_{ij}^{(i)}$ be an element in the matrix $T_w^{(i)}$. If there is no connection between nodes v_i and v_j in $\tilde{A}_{aug}$, set $t_{ij}^{(i)}$ to 0; otherwise, set $t_{ij}^{(i)}$ to the normalized self-attention value of v_i and v_j. The equation for $t_{ij}^{(i)}$ is defined as follows:*

$$t_{ij}^{(i)} = \begin{cases} 0 & a_{ij} = 0 \\ \dfrac{tanh(g^{(i)T}[h_i^{(i)} || h_j^{(i)}])}{\sqrt{d_i d_j}} & a_{ij} = 1 \end{cases} \qquad (6)$$

$g^{(i)} \in \mathbb{R}^{2F'}$ is the self-attention vector and also the parameter to be learned, $||$ denotes the concatenation operation. Here, the *tanh* activation function is used to constrain the value of $t_{ij}^{(i)}$ within $[-1, 1]$. Previous studies have shown that negative values are beneficial for capturing high-frequency signals, which is advantageous for heterophilic graphs [18]. On the other hand, the noise brought by the data augmentation can also be utilized as the information for node classification, which has been verified through experiments that MAPNET achieves good results on the heterophilic graphs. Because the graph structure becomes a directed graph during the data augmentation phase, here we use $\tilde{D}_{out}$ instead of $\tilde{D}$ for normalization. Although each edge has a weight, the number of parameters required for learning is only $\mathcal{O}(KF')$, which is much smaller than $\mathcal{O}(|\mathcal{E}|F')$ without using self-attention mechanism. K is the order of the neighborhood.

3.3 Objective Function

The objective function of MAPNET consists of a supervised loss and two graph regularization terms, one being the consistency regularization and the other being the propagation regularization. In the process, multiple views are generated and multiple embeddings of these views are obtained. And so as to keep the predicted results of multiple embeddings consistent, the consistent regularization training is required. At the same time, in order to make the model comparable to the deep model at a small cost, a propagation regularization term is added.

The supervised loss is commonly known as cross-entropy loss. During the data augmentation phase, the model generates multiple augmented views, so the average cross-entropy loss for each epoch is given by:

$$\mathcal{L}_{\text{sup}} = -\frac{1}{M} \sum_{s=1}^{S} \sum_{i=1}^{M} Y_i^T log P_i^{(s)} \qquad (7)$$

where S is the number of views, M is the number of labeled data, $P_i^{(s)} = softmax(Z_i^{(s)})$ represents the node prediction, and $Z_i^{(s)}$ is the final output embedding representation of the model.

The Consistency regularization forces the model to have similar predictions between the original data and the augmented views, thus making the model robust to the perturbations in node features, while dynamic training techniques make the model robust to the topological structure. The model first calculates the mean prediction of multiple views as the label distribution center: $\overline{P}_i = \frac{1}{S} \sum_{s=1}^{S} P_i^{(s)}$, and then enhances the consistency by reducing the difference between single view predictions and the distribution center. Before calculating the difference, it is necessary to sharpen the label distribution center $\overline{P}_i$, and the purpose of sharpening is to reduce the entropy of $\overline{P}_i$. The sharpening equation is as follows:

$$\overline{P}'_{ij} = \overline{P}_{ij}^{\frac{1}{T}} \Bigg/ \sum_{c=0}^{C-1} \overline{P}_{ic}^{\frac{1}{T}}, (0 \leq j \leq C - 1) \tag{8}$$

where $0 < T \leq 1$ is a parameter controlling the degree of sharpening, with a smaller T resulting in a higher degree of sharpening. When T approaches 0, $\overline{P}'_i$ becomes a one-hot vector.

$$\mathcal{L}_{con} = \frac{1}{N} \sum_{s=1}^{S} \sum_{i=1}^{N} \|P_i^{(s)} - \overline{P}'_i\|_2^2 \tag{9}$$

Minimizing $\mathcal{L}_{con}$ can make the final prediction of each view consistent with the label distribution center, which can reduce the sensitivity of the model to data perturbations and enhance robustness.

Here, we introduce the propagation regularization proposed by Yang [22], which allows the model to achieve deep learning effects at a low cost. First, the final output embedding representation $Z^{(s)}$ is convolved again using $\hat{A}_{aug}$:

$$Z'^{(s)} = \hat{A}_{aug} Z^{(s)} = \tilde{D}_{out}^{-1} \tilde{A}_{aug} Z^{(s)} \tag{10}$$

The final propagation regularization term is expressed as:

$$\mathcal{L}_{soft} = \frac{1}{N} \sum_{s=1}^{S} \sum_{i=1}^{N} \left\|Z_i'^{(s)} - Z_i^{(s)}\right\|_2^2 \tag{11}$$

Minimizing the squared error of $Z'^{(s)}$ and $Z^{(s)}$ and performing the graph convolution with a simple normalization matrix converge to the same point. Therefore, using infinite graph convolution and minimizing propagation regularization are equivalent. The balance between infinite convolution and over-smoothing can be adjusted with the hyperparameters. The final objective function is:

$$\mathcal{L} = \frac{1}{S} \left(\mathcal{L}_{sup} + \lambda_1 \mathcal{L}_{con} + \lambda_2 \mathcal{L}_{soft}\right) \tag{12}$$

λ_1 and λ_2 are the hyperparameters for adjusting the regularization term ratio.

4 Experiment

To evaluate the performance of the proposed MAPNET model, experiments were conducted on eight common benchmark datasets. And then MAPNET is compared with mainstream graph neural network algorithms. Section 4.1 introduced the datasets and mainstream graph neural network algorithms used in the experiments, while Sect. 4.2 performed semi-supervised experiments on each model, Sect. 4.3 performed fully supervised experiments on each model, Sect. 4.4 analyzed the generalization performance of the models, and Sect. 4.5 analyzed experiments regarding over-smoothing and robustness.

4.1 Datasets and Benchmark Algorithms

This section tested the performance of different models in semi-supervised node classification tasks and fully supervised tasks. Specifically, experiments were conducted on six different datasets. Three citation datasets from Kipf [2], namely Cora, Citeseer, and Pubmed, are the homophilic graphs where connected nodes tend to share the same labels. As well as Actor, Texas, and Cornell, these three datasets from WebKB [17] are heterophilic, where connected nodes often have different labels. Following previous studies [16, 18, 20], we selected 9 different neural networks as the baseline algorithm, including MLP, GCN [2], GAT [7], JKNET [10], ChebNet [6], APPNP [9], FAGCN [18], GPRGNN [16], and BrenNet [20].

4.2 Semi-supervised Node Classification

In the semi-supervised experiments, three classic datasets were used. For the semi-supervised node classification, each dataset will be split into standard partitions where each class has 20 labeled nodes, 500 validation nodes, and 1000 testing nodes. Table 1 summarized the prediction accuracy for node classification, it can be observed that the proposed algorithm is generally superior to the compared benchmark algorithms. Specifically, the MAPNET model improved by 3.08%, 3.57%, and 0.39% over GCN, and by 0.88%, 2.35%, and 0.18% over APPNPA on the Cora, Citeseer, and Pubmed datasets, respectively. It can be seen that most models had only a small improvement on the Pubmed dataset, and the performances of BrenNet and GPRGNN were even worse than GCN. A preliminary conjecture is that this is the result of the combination of adaptive mechanisms and multi-scale information fusion. Therefore, FAGCN, which also uses adaptive mechanisms but without multi-scale information fusion, can achieve good results. However due to adding the data augmentation and the regularization terms, MAPNET, which uses both adaptive mechanisms and multi-scale information fusion, has better stability and generalization performance.

Table 1. Semi-supervised classification accuracy (%)

	Cora	CiteSeer	PubMed
BrenNet	83.02 ± 0.53	70.79 ± 1.02	70.60 ± 2.42
GPRGNN	83.50 ± 0.33	71.67 ± 0.36	75.87 ± 1.67
FAGCN	84.10 ± 0.50	72.70 ± 0.80	**79.40 ± 0.30**
APPNP	83.70 ± 0.51	71.52 ± 0.33	79.21 ± 0.50
Chebnet	78.84 ± 0.44	70.99 ± 0.63	76.61 ± 0.61
GAT	83.01 ± 0.69	72.51 ± 0.70	79.02 ± 0.32
GCN	81.5	70.3	79.0
MLP	58.44 ± 0.97	57.25 ± 0.72	70.54 ± 0.57
MAPNET	**84.58 ± 0.51**	**73.87 ± 0.61**	**79.39 ± 0.77**

4.3 Fully-Supervised Node Classification

In the semi-supervised experiments, the entire dataset was used, the ratio of the fully-supervised experimental dataset is 60%/20%/20%. Table 2 summarized the prediction accuracy for node classification. Overall, MAPNET significantly outperforms all other baseline models on the homophilic datasets, with the largest improvement compared to GPRGNN on the Cora and Citeseer datasets, with increases of 1.6% and 1.5%, respectively. On Cora, Citeseer, and PubMed, it achieves improvements of 1.2%, 1.8%, and 0.7%, respectively, compared to BrenNet. It also achieves good results on the heterophilic graphs, with increases of 1.2% and 1.9% compared to GPRGNN on Actor and Cornell, respectively, and increases of 0.9% and 0.2% compared to BrenNet on Actor and Cornell, respectively. The adaptive mechanism performs well on PubMed in dense partitioning, which indicates that it requires a lot of supervision. MAPNET has demonstrated good performance in semi-supervised experiments with few labels and has a higher upper bound than FAGCN.

Table 2. Full-supervised classification accuracy (%)

	Cora	CiteSeer	PubMed	Actor	Texas	Cornell
BrenNet	88.3 ± 1.0	79.1 ± 1.2	88.8 ± 0.7	39.8 ± 1.4	92.3 ± 2.7	92.7 ± 3.0
GPRGNN	87.9 ± 1.1	79.4 ± 1.4	89.4 ± 0.8	39.5 ± 1.2	**93.3 ± 2.6**	91.0 ± 3.8
FAGCN	88.4 ± 1.4	80.8 ± 1.3	84.2 ± 0.7	39.2 ± 1.6	85.7 ± 5.0	81.1 ± 6.4
APPNP	87.1 ± 1.1	79.8 ± 1.2	87.3 ± 0.5	38.9 ± 1.4	91.5 ± 3.7	86.7 ± 4.7

(*continued*)

Table 2. (*continued*)

	Cora	CiteSeer	PubMed	Actor	Texas	Cornell
Chebnet	86.5 ± 1.3	78.2 ± 1.5	88.8 ± 0.5	36.7 ± 1.4	87.6 ± 4.5	85.0 ± 5.8
JKNET	85.7 ± 1.8	77.1 ± 1.9	87.2 ± 0.6	30.3 ± 1.9	77.2 ± 4.3	62.0 ± 6.7
GAT	88.1 ± 1.3	80.6 ± 1.1	87.4 ± 0.6	32.9 ± 3.2	80.5 ± 3.7	78.6 ± 4.7
GCN	87.0 ± 1.3	79.2 ± 1.0	87.0 ± 0.5	32.1 ± 1.4	74.5 ± 5.2	67.5 ± 5.5
MLP	76.4 ± 1.4	75.8 ± 1.1	86.1 ± 0.6	40.2 ± 1.9	91.3 ± 3.2	90.7 ± 3.0
MAPNET	**89.5 ± 1.1**	**80.9 ± 1.2**	**89.5 ± 0.5**	**40.7 ± 1.2**	92.2 ± 3.3	**92.9 ± 2.7**

4.4 Generalization Performance Analysis

This section investigated the impact of data augmentation and regularization on model generalization. The experiments analyzed the cross-entropy loss of the model on the training sets and the validation sets of the Cora dataset. A smaller difference between the losses indicates better generalization performance. Figure 3 shows the generalization performance of the MAPNET model and its two variants: without data augmentation (w/o aug) and without regularization (w/o con and soft). The left compares the loss of (w/o con and soft), which fluctuates significantly and has a large gap. The middle compares the loss of (w/o aug), which fluctuates less but still has a large gap. The right graph shows the complete model, which with both regularization and data augmentation improves the generalization performance. The experimental results demonstrate that the regularization can enhance model stability, while both data augmentation and regularization can help improve the generalization ability.

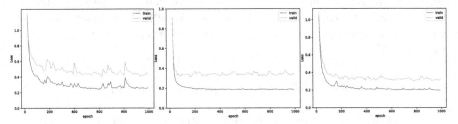

Fig. 3. Generalization performance on Cora, left: (w/o con and soft) and middle: (w/o aug).

4.5 Over-Smoothing and Robustness Study

As the propagation step increases, many GNNs face the problem of over-smoothing. To verify MAPNET's ability of alleviating over-smoothing, experiments with different propagation steps were conducted on the Cora dataset. Figure 4 shows the experimental results on the Cora dataset, indicating that as the propagation step increases, the metrics of GCN and GAT significantly decrease, with GCN's accuracy dropping from 81.5% to

15% and GAT's accuracy dropping from 83% to 20%. MAPNET, APPNP, and GPRGNN can all alleviate the problem of over-smoothing, but MAPNET performs better and has a higher upper limit. For robustness studies, graph structures were perturbed by randomly adding edges, and different methods' classification accuracies on the Cora dataset at different perturbation rates were given in Fig. 4. As shown in the figure, MAPNET is consistently superior to GCN, GAT, and APPNP at all perturbation rates. When 20% new random edges are added to Cora, MAPNET's accuracy only drops by 3.08%, while the classification accuracies of GCN, GAT, and APPNP drop by 6.9%, 13%, and 7.2%, respectively. The study indicates that MAPNET has a robustness advantage over other models.

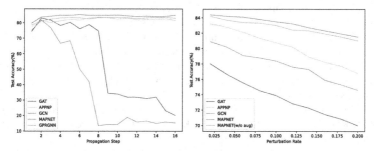

Fig. 4. Analysis of over-smoothing (left) and analysis of robustness (right). Changes in accuracy of each model as the propagation depth and the perturbation rate increase.

5 Summary

This paper proposes a novel graph neural network called MAPNET, aiming to address the issues of over-smoothing, weak robustness, and incapability of handling the heterophilic graphs that exist in traditional GNNs. MAPNET employs importance-based data augmentation to perturb the graph structure, utilizes a multiscale adaptive propagation network to alleviate over-smoothing, and allows negative values to adapt to the heterophilic graphs. Additionally, MAPNET incorporates the regularization terms to enhance robustness and generalization. Experimental results demonstrate that MAPNET outperforms other methods in both semi-supervised and supervised learning tasks, as well as on the heterophilic graphs. In summary, the ideas of MAPNET are feasible and promising for future research.

References

1. Wu, Z., Pan, S., Chen, F., et al.: A comprehensive survey on graph neural networks. IEEE Trans. Neural Netw. Learn. Syst. **32**(1), 4–24 (2021). https://doi.org/10.1109/TNNLS.2020.2978386
2. Kipf, T.N., Welling, M.: Semi-supervised classification with graph convolutional networks. arXiv preprint arXiv:1609.02907 (2016). https://github.com/tkipf/pygcn

3. You, J., Ying, R., Leskovec, J.: Position-aware graph neural networks. In: International Conference on Machine Learning, pp. 7134–7143. PMLR (2019)
4. Fan, W., Ma, Y., Li, Q., et al.: Graph neural networks for social recommendation. In: The World Wide Web Conference, pp. 417–426 (2019). https://doi.org/10.1145/3308558.3313488
5. Berg, R., Kipf, T.N., Welling, M.: Graph convolutional matrix completion. arXiv preprint arXiv:1706.02263 (2017)
6. Defferrard, M., Bresson, X., Vandergheynst, P.: Convolutional neural networks on graphs with fast localized spectral filtering. In: Advances in Neural Information Processing Systems, vol. 29 (2016)
7. Veličković, P., Cucurull, G., Casanova, A., et al.: Graph attention networks. arXiv preprint arXiv:1710.10903 (2017)
8. Hamilton, W., Ying, Z., Leskovec, J.: Inductive representation learning on large graphs. In: Advances in Neural Information Processing Systems, vol. 30 (2017)
9. Klicpera, J., Bojchevski, A., Günnemann, S.: Predict then propagate: graph neural networks meet personalized pagerank. arXiv preprint arXiv:1810.05997 (2018)
10. Xu, K., Li, C., Tian, Y., et al.: Representation learning on graphs with jumping knowledge networks. In: International Conference on Machine Learning, pp. 5453–5462. PMLR (2018)
11. Klicpera, J., Weißenberger, S., Günnemann, S.: Diffusion improves graph learning. arXiv preprint arXiv:1911.05485 (2019)
12. Liu, M., Gao, H., Ji, S.: Towards deeper graph neural networks. In: Proceedings of the 26th ACM SIGKDD International Conference on Knowledge Discovery & Data Mining, pp. 338–348 (2020). https://doi.org/10.1145/3394486.3403076
13. Rong, Y., Huang, W., Xu, T., et al.: DropEdge: towards deep graph convolutional networks on node classification. arXiv preprint arXiv:1907.10903 (2019)
14. Feng, W., Zhang, J., Dong, Y., et al.: Graph random neural networks for semi-supervised learning on graphs. In: Advances in Neural Information Processing Systems, vol. 33 (2020)
15. Wang, Y., Wang, W., Liang, Y., et al.: NodeAug: semi-supervised node classification with data augmentation. In: Proceedings of the 26th ACM SIGKDD International Conference on Knowledge Discovery & Data Mining, pp. 207–217 (2020). https://doi.org/10.1145/3394486.3403063
16. Chien, E., Peng, J., Li, P., et al.: Adaptive universal generalized pagerank graph neural network. arXiv preprint arXiv:2006.07988 (2020)
17. Pei, H., Wei, B., Chang, K.C.C., et al.: Geom-GCN: geometric graph convolutional networks. arXiv preprint arXiv:2002.05287 (2020). https://github.com/graphdml-uiuc-jlu/geom-gcn
18. Bo, D., Wang, X., Shi, C., et al.: Beyond low-frequency information in graph convolutional networks. In: Proceedings of the AAAI Conference on Artificial Intelligence, vol. 35, no. 5, pp. 3950–3957 (2021). https://doi.org/10.1609/aaai.v35i5.16514
19. Yang, L., Li, M., Liu, L., et al.: Diverse message passing for attribute with heterophily. In: Advances in Neural Information Processing Systems, vol. 34, pp. 4751–4763 (2021)
20. He, M., Wei, Z., Xu, H.: BernNet: learning arbitrary graph spectral filters via Bernstein approximation. In: Advances in Neural Information Processing Systems, vol. 34, pp. 14239–14251 (2021)
21. Bo, D., Hu, B.B., Wang, X., et al.: Regularizing graph neural networks via consistency-diversity graph augmentations. In: Proceedings of the AAAI Conference on Artificial Intelligence, vol. 36, no. 4, pp. 3913–3921 (2022). https://doi.org/10.1609/aaai.v36i4.20307
22. Yang, H., Ma, K., Cheng, J.: Rethinking graph regularization for graph neural networks. In: Proceedings of the AAAI Conference on Artificial Intelligence, vol. 35, no. 5, pp. 4573–4581 (2021). https://doi.org/10.1609/aaai.v35i5.16586
23. Ma, Q., Fan, Z., Wang, C., et al.: Graph mixed random network based on PageRank. Symmetry 14(8), 1678 (2022). https://doi.org/10.3390/sym14081678

An Efficient Approach for Improving the Recall of Rough Abstract Retrieval in Scientific Claim Verification

Zhiwei Zhang[1], Jiyi Li[2(✉)] ⓘ, and Fumiyo Fukumoto[2] ⓘ

[1] Binjiang Institute of Zhejiang University, Hangzhou, China
[2] University of Yamanashi, Kofu, Japan
{jyli,fukumoto}@yamanashi.ac.jp

Abstract. Scientific claim verification can help the researchers easily find the target scientific papers with the sentence evidence from a large corpus for the given claim. Because there are a huge amount of papers in the corpus, most of the existing scientific claim verification solutions are always in a two-stage manner that first roughly detects a set of candidate related papers by some naïve but fast methods such as some similarity measures, and then utilizes the large but relatively slow deep neural models for accurate classification. To improve the recall of the overall system by improving the recall of the rough abstract retrieval stage, we propose an approach that also utilizes the neural classification model for the rough retrieval stage. To improve the scalability of the proposal, we propose a distillation-based method to obtain a lightweight model for the rough retrieval stage. The experimental results on the benchmark dataset SCIFACT show that our approach outperforms the existing works.

Keywords: Scientific Claim Verification · Abstract Retrieval · Rationale Selection · Stance Prediction · Distillation

1 Introduction

To investigate a given scientific claim, people want to find the target scientific papers with sentence evidence from a large scholarly document corpus. Scientific claim verification systems can be used for this purpose. To address this research topic, Wadden et al. [18] provided a benchmark dataset named SCI-FACT which consists of *three tasks* (Fig. 1). For a given claim, a scientific claim verification system finds the abstracts which are related to the claim from a corpus (abstract retrieval task); it selects the sentences which are the evidence in the abstract related to the claim (rationale selection task); it also classifies whether the abstract/sentences support or refute the claims (stance prediction task). Scientific claim verification can be an extension of the general claim verification [6,11,12]. There are existing works especially proposed for scientific claim verification with pipeline or joint models [2,9,14,18,19,21,22].

© The Author(s), under exclusive license to Springer Nature Switzerland AG 2023
L. Iliadis et al. (Eds.): ICANN 2023, LNCS 14261, pp. 63–74, 2023.
https://doi.org/10.1007/978-3-031-44198-1_6

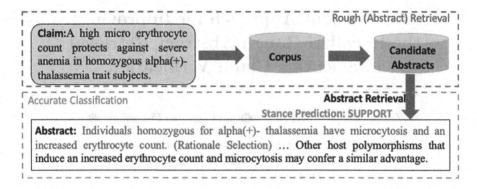

Fig. 1. An example of the general two-stage solution for scientific claim verification.

Because there are a huge amount of papers in the corpus, for the scalability issue, most of these existing works are always in a two-stage manner (Fig. 1), i.e., a *rough retrieval stage* that first roughly detects a very small set of candidate related papers by some naïve but fast methods, e.g., selecting the papers with top-k similarities to the claim by using some similarity measures; and then *an accurate classification stage* utilizes large but relatively slow models based on deep neural networks for accurate classification on the three tasks. For example, for the rough (abstract) retrieval stage, Wadden et al. [18] utilized TF-IDF similarity between a claim or a scientific paper; Pradeep et al. [14] and Wadden et al. [19] utilized BM25 scores or a combination of BM25 and T5 embeddings [15]; Li et al. [9] and Zhang et al. [22] utilized similarities of BioSenVec embeddings [3].

One of the problems of these existing works is that the naïve methods at the rough retrieval stage may be not good enough; if some related papers are not selected as the candidates in this stage, the accurate classification cannot find them even if the deep models are powerful. For the abstract retrieval task of scientific claim verification systems, Recall (**R**) is one of the most important measures because experts can still somewhat check and refine the final results of accurate classification stage, but cannot notice the papers that are not in the candidates obtained by the rough retrieval stage. Therefore, to improve the recall of the overall system by improving the recall of the rough retrieval stage, we propose an approach that also utilizes the deep neural models which can detect the set of related papers with higher classification quality, to the rough retrieval stage. However, the neural based rough retrieval with large model is much slower than the naïve retrieval methods, to improve the speed of rough retrieval so that this proposed solution is practical for a huge amount of papers, we propose a distillation-based method that trains a lightweight student model from the large teacher model which can be a neural model for scientific claim verification from existing works. We utilize the lightweight student model for the rough retrieval stage and the large teacher model for the accurate classification stage. The main contributions of this paper can be summarised as follows.

- We propose a unified approach based on deep neural networks for both rough retrieval and accurate classification stages.
- We proposed a distillation-based method to train a lightweight model for the rough retrieval stage to reach a balance between the recall improvement and speed drop.
- The experimental results on the benchmark dataset SciFact show that our approach outperforms the existing works.

2 Related Work

Automated Fact-verification is now widely studied, while Fact-verification datasets are emerging in various fields. The first Fact-verification dataset was presented by [17]. A later dataset, EMERGENT, a dataset with 300 claims proposed by [4]. Among these claim verification corpora, the manually constructed FEVER dataset [16], which includes 185,000 claims extracted from Wikipedia, is one of the most influential datasets. Recently Wadden et al. [18] proposed a dataset, SCIFACT, which is a Fact-verification dataset containing specialized domain knowledge.

Most existing fact-verification systems are pipeline models that contain three modules: document retrieval, rationale selection and stance prediction. For document retrieval, Hanselowski et al. [5] proposed a heuristic document retrieval module based on TFIDF, Google Search API and named entities, which has been used several times. Rationale selection and stance prediction usually use DNNs, such as kernel graph attention network [11] and neural semantic matching networks [13]. On the other hand, there are Some fact-verification systems use joint optimization strategies. GCAN [12] uses a co-attention mechanism to generate both the verification result and the rationale that made the determination. A model that directly connects two modules through a dynamic attention mechanism was proposed by [9]. In this work, we follow our previous work [22] and combine the three modules for joint training.

For the scalability issue, most of these existing works are always in a two-stage manner, i.e., rough retrieval stage and accurate classification stages. The rough retrieval stage first roughly detects a very small set of candidate related papers by some naïve but fast methods, e.g., selecting the papers with top-k similarities to the claim by using some similarity measures. Wadden et al. [18] utilized TF-IDF similarity between a claim or a scientific paper; Pradeep et al. [14] and Wadden et al. [19] utilized BM25 scores or a combination of BM25 and T5 embeddings [15]; Li et al. [9] and Zhang et al. [22] utilized similarities of BioSenVec embeddings [3]. In this work, we propose an approach that also utilizes the deep neural models for detecting the set of related papers to the rough retrieval stage; we also propose a distillation-based method that trains a lightweight student model from the large teacher model for practical issue.

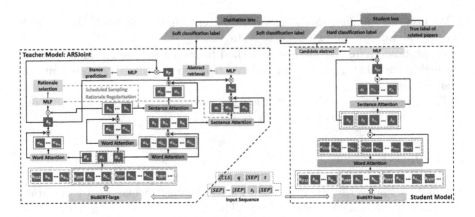

Fig. 2. Framework of the proposed approach.

3 Proposed Approach

3.1 Notation and Definitions

We denote the query claim as q and an abstract of a scientific paper as $a \in \mathcal{A}$. We denote the set of sentences in abstract a as $\mathcal{S} = \{s_i\}_{i=1}^{l}$ and the word sequence of s_i is $[s_{i1}, ..., s_{in_i}]$. The title of the paper $t \in \mathcal{T}$ is used as auxiliary information, the word sequence of t is $[t_1, ..., t_{n_t}]$. Here, $\mathcal{S}$, s_i and t are for a in default and we omit the subscripts 'a' in the notations. The purpose of the *abstract retrieval task* is to detect the set of related abstracts to q; it assigns relevance labels $y^b \in \{0, 1\}$ to a candidate abstract a. The *rationale selection* task is to detect the decisive rationale sentences $S^r \subseteq S$ of a relevant to the claim q; it assigns evidence labels $y_i^r \in \{0, 1\}$ to each sentence $s_i \in \mathcal{S}$. The *stance prediction* task classifies a into stance labels y^e which are in {SUPPORTS=0, REFUTES=1, NOINFO=2}. The sentences in a have the same stance label value.

3.2 Proposed Model

Our method also has rough abstract retrieval and accurate classification stages. The backbone model of our work is ARSJOINT [22] which has good performance in existing works. Our method can also utilize other backbone models (e.g., [9,19]). We utilize ARSJOINT as the teacher model for the rough retrieval stage and in the accurate classification stage. The input sequence of ARSJOINT is defined as $seq = [[\text{CLS}]q[\text{SEP}]t \cdots [\text{SEP}]s_i[\text{SEP}] \cdots]$, obtained by concatenating the claim q, title t and abstract a. The list of word representations $\mathbf{H}_{seq}$ of the input sequence is computed by a pre-trained language model (e.g., BioBERT [8]). The word representations of the claim $\mathbf{H}_q = [\mathbf{h}_{q_1}, \cdots, \mathbf{h}_{q_{n_q}}]$, the title $\mathbf{H}_t = [\mathbf{h}_{t_1}, \cdots, \mathbf{h}_{t_{n_t}}]$, each sentence $\mathbf{H}_{s_i} = [\mathbf{h}_{s_{i1}}, \cdots, \mathbf{h}_{s_{in_i}}]$, and the abstract $\mathbf{H}_S = \mathbf{H}_a = [\cdots, \mathbf{H}_{s_i}, \cdots]$ are extracted from $\mathbf{H}_{seq}$.

The teacher model in Fig. 2 shows its framework. The attention layers on the word (sentence) representations are used to compute sentence (document) representations. Scheduled sampling is used for alleviating the problem of error propagation from the rationale selection module to the stance prediction module. Rationale regularization (RR) is proposed for enhancing the information exchanges and constraints by bridging the sentence attention scores of the abstract retrieval module and the predictions of the rationale selection module. This method jointly trains the model on all three tasks. The joint loss of this model is

$$\mathcal{L} = \lambda_1 \mathcal{L}_{ret} + \lambda_2 \mathcal{L}_{rat} + \lambda_3 \mathcal{L}_{sta} + \gamma \mathcal{L}_{RR}, \tag{1}$$

where $\mathcal{L}_{ret}$, $\mathcal{L}_{rat}$, $\mathcal{L}_{sta}$ and $\mathcal{L}_{RR}$ are the losses of abstract retrieval, rationale selection, stance prediction, and rationale regularization respectively, and λ_1, λ_2, λ_3 and γ are hyperparameters.

In contrast to the existing works that utilize naïve but fast methods (e.g., cosine similarity of document embeddings by BioSenVec) at the rough retrieval stage, we propose a unified approach that also utilizes a deep neural model to select the set of candidate related papers. The problem with this solution is the relatively low classification speed at the rough retrieval stage in the test phase because of the model size. We need a method to make a balance between the classification quality and the speed of the system. The knowledge distillation technique (e.g., [7]) is a proper choice for this purpose. It can migrate the knowledge from a large and complex model (teacher model) to a small and simple model (student model).

Figure 2 shows the framework of our distillation-based model with a teacher model and a student model. We construct an offline distillation method. We first train the teacher ARSJOINT model in the same way with accurate classification; then, we fix its parameters and utilize it to train the student model by using the same training data. Considering that, in the entire teacher model, the module that accounts for the largest percentage of parameters is the language model in the large version (e.g., BioBERT-large) that needs fine-tuning, in the student model, we utilize the base version (e.g., BioBERT-base) that only has one-third of the number of parameters of the large version. Except for the difference in the language model, the student model has a consistent structure with the abstract retrieval module of the teacher model which judges the relevance of an abstract to the claim.

In details of the student model, we build a document $ta = [t, a]$ and concatenate the word representations of t and a into $\mathbf{H}_{ta}^u = [\mathbf{H}_t^u, \mathbf{H}_a^u]$ as the input, here the superscript u denotes the student model. Following ARSJOINT, we also use a hierarchical attention network (HAN) [20] to compute document representations $\mathbf{h}_{ta}^u \in \mathbb{R}^d$, $\mathbf{h}_{ta}^u = \text{HAN}(\mathbf{H}_{ta}^u)$. We also compute the sentence representation of claim $\mathbf{h}_q^u \in \mathbb{R}^d$ with a word-level attention layer (denoted as $g(\cdot)$), $\mathbf{h}_q^u = g(\mathbf{H}_q^u)$. We use a Hadamard product and a Multi-Layer Perception (MLP, denoted as $f(\cdot)$) with Softmax (denoted as $\sigma(\cdot)$) to compute the relevance between $\mathbf{h}_{ta}^u$ and $\mathbf{h}_q^u$. The outputs are the probabilities that whether the abstract is relevant to the claim,

$$[p_0^{bu}, p_1^{bu}] = \sigma(f(\mathbf{h}_q^u \circ \mathbf{h}_a^u)). \tag{2}$$

A cross entropy loss $\mathcal{L}_{ret}^u$ (Student loss in Fig. 2) is used for training.

In addition, in this distillation model, to make the student mimic the teacher model, there is a distillation loss which is the KL-divergence between the soft outputs $\sigma(f(\mathbf{h}_q \circ \mathbf{h}_a))$ of the teacher model and the soft outputs $\sigma(f(\mathbf{h}_q^u \circ \mathbf{h}_a^u))$ of the student model, i.e.,

$$\mathcal{L}_{dist} = \mathrm{KL}(\sigma(f(\mathbf{h}_q \circ \mathbf{h}_a))||\sigma(f(\mathbf{h}_q^u \circ \mathbf{h}_a^u))). \tag{3}$$

The overall loss of our distillation model is

$$\mathcal{L}^u = \lambda_4 \mathcal{L}_{ret}^u + \lambda_5 \mathcal{L}_{dist}. \tag{4}$$

In the test phase, we merge the set $\mathcal{A}^u$ of candidate papers judged by the student model and the set $\mathcal{A}^k$ with the top-k cosine similarity of document BioSenVec embeddings to generate the set $\mathcal{A}^c$ of candidate papers of our rough retrieval method, i.e., $\mathcal{A}^c = \mathcal{A}^u \cup \mathcal{A}^k$. Note that although $|\mathcal{A}^k| = k$ is a fixed pre-defined value, because $|\mathcal{A}^u|$ are diverse for different claims, the number of candidate papers $|\mathcal{A}^c|$ are also diverse.

4 Experiments

4.1 Dataset

We utilize the benchmark dataset SciFact [18][1]. It consists of 5,183 scientific papers with titles and abstracts and 1,109 claims in the training and development sets. Table 1 presents the statistics of the dataset.

4.2 Implementations

We implement our approach in PyTorch. Because the length of the input sequence seq is often greater than the maximum input length of a BERT-based model, we performs a tail-truncation operation on each sentence of seq that exceeds the maximum input length. The MLP in our model has two layers. For the pre-trained language model, we verify our approach by respectively incorporating diverse variants of ARSJOINT which use RoBERTa-large [10] and BioBERT-large [8] trained on a biomedical corpus. It fine-tunes RoBERTa-large and BioBERT-large on the SciFact dataset.

4.3 Baselines

The baselines include VERISCI [18], Paragraph-Joint [9] and ARSJOINT [22]. We use the publicly available code of them. The "Paragraph-Joint Pre-training" model is firstly pre-trained on the FEVER dataset [16] and then fine-tune on the SciFact dataset. The "Paragraph-Joint SciFact-only" is not pre-trained on other datasets.

---

[1] https://github.com/allenai/scifact.

Table 1. Statistics of SCIFACT dataset. The numbers are "number of claims/number of relevant abstracts".

	SUPPORT	NOINFO	REFUTES	ALL
Train	332/370	304/220	173/194	809
Dev	124/138	112/114	64/71	300
ALL	456/508	416/444	237/265	1109

Table 2. Selected Weight hyperparameters Tuned by Optuna.

Model	λ_1	λ_2	λ_3	γ
ARSJOINT w/o RR (RoBERTa)	2.7	11.7	2.2	–
ARSJOINT (RoBERTa)	0.9	11.1	2.6	2.2
ARSJOINT w/o RR (BioBERT)	0.1	10.8	4.7	–
ARSJOINT (BioBERT)	0.2	12.0	1.1	1.9
OUR (For Teacher Model)	9.2	2.3	0.4	10.5

Table 3. Hyperparameter settings following the existing work. k_{tra} and k_{ret} are the number of candidate abstracts for each claim in the training and testing stages. lr_1 and lr_2 are the learning rates of the BERT-based model and other modules of the proposed model.

Name	Value	Name	Value	Name	Value
k_{tra}	12	lr_1	1×10^{-5}	Batch size	1
k_{ret}	30	lr_2	5×10^{-6}	Dropout	0

4.4 Hyperparameter Settings

For our model used in the rough retrieval stage, we use Optuna [1] to tune the weight hyperparameters of the teacher ARSJOINT model, i.e., λ_1, λ_2, λ_3 and γ of the loss $\mathcal{L}$ on 20% of the training set and based on the performance on another 20% training set. We choose the optimal hyperparameters by the recall of the rough retrieval stage. The search ranges of these four hyperparameters are set to [0.1, 12], and the number of search trials is set to 100. The weight hyperparameters tuned by rough retrieval recall of the teacher model for the rough retrieval stage and the weight hyperparameters tuned by classification F1-score for the accurate classification stage are different. Table 2 lists the hyperparameters. In addition, for our method of neural rough retrieval with distillation, we set general values of $\lambda_4 = \lambda_5 = 1$ in $\mathcal{L}^u$. For ARSJOINT model used as the teacher model in our approach, Table 3 lists the hyperparameters. For the hyperparameters of the baselines, we refer to the ones used in [22] to make a fair comparison.

Table 4. Main experimental results, sentence-level evaluation. Our (Neural w/ Dist.) is the abbreviation of Our (Neural Retrieval with Distillation).

(a). Results on development set. The baseline results are from [22].

Rough Retrieval Methods	Accurate Classification Models	Sentence-level					
		Selection-Only			Selection+Label		
		F1	P	**R**	F1	P	**R**
TF-IDF	VERISCI	48.3	54.3	<u>43.4</u>	43.1	48.5	<u>38.8</u>
BioSenVec	Paragraph-Joint SCIFACT-only	58.1	69.3	<u>50.0</u>	50.2	59.8	<u>43.2</u>
BioSenVec	Paragraph-Joint Pre-training	64.7	74.2	<u>57.4</u>	55.2	63.3	<u>48.9</u>
BioSenVec	ARSJOINT w/o RR (RoBERTa)	62.9	70.9	<u>56.6</u>	50.5	56.8	<u>45.4</u>
	ARSJOINT (RoBERTa)	62.0	67.9	<u>57.1</u>	50.7	55.5	<u>46.7</u>
	ARSJOINT w/o RR (BioBERT)	65.3	75.4	<u>57.7</u>	55.1	63.6	<u>48.6</u>
	ARSJOINT (BioBERT)	66.2	76.2	<u>58.5</u>	57.8	66.5	<u>51.1</u>
Our (Neural w/ Dist.)	ARSJOINT w/o RR (RoBERTa)	64.7	72.3	<u>58.5</u>	51.4	57.4	<u>46.4</u>
	ARSJOINT (RoBERTa)	64.4	69.7	<u>59.8</u>	52.1	56.4	<u>48.4</u>
	ARSJOINT w/o RR (BioBERT)	66.9	76.5	<u>59.6</u>	56.8	64.9	<u>50.5</u>
	ARSJOINT (BioBERT)	**68.2**	**77.9**	**<u>60.7</u>**	**58.7**	**67.0**	**<u>52.1</u>**

(b). Results on test set. The results are generated by the leaderboard.

BioSenVec	ARSJOINT (BioBERT)	79.0	82.4	<u>76.0</u>	65.5	68.3	<u>63.0</u>
Our (Neural w/ Dist.)	ARSJOINT (BioBERT)	79.0	81.0	**<u>77.0</u>**	65.4	67.1	**<u>63.8</u>**

4.5 Evaluation Methods

We evaluate the methods by using the abstract-level and sentence-level evaluation criteria given in SCIFACT. *Abstract-level evaluation* evaluates the performance of a model on detecting the abstracts which support or refute the claims. For the "Label-Only" evaluation, given a claim q, the classification result of an abstract a is correct if the estimated relevance label $\hat{y}^b$ is correct and the estimated stance label $\hat{y}^e$ is correct. For the "Label+Rationale" evaluation, the abstract is correctly rationalized, in addition, if the estimated rationale sentences contain a gold rationale. *Sentence-level evaluation* evaluates the performance of a model on detecting rationale sentences. For the "Selection-Only" evaluation, an estimated rationale sentence s_i of an abstract a is correctly selected if the estimated rationale label $\hat{y}^r_i$ is correct and the estimated stance label $\hat{y}^e$ is not "NOINFO". Especially, if consecutive multiple sentences are gold rationales, then all these sentences should be estimated as rationales. For the "Selection+Label", the estimated rationale sentences are correctly labeled, in addition, if the estimated stance label $\hat{y}^e$ of this abstract is correct. We train the model using all training data. In this work, we mainly focus on the Recall (**R**), while we also provide the Precision (P) and F1-score (F1) results as references. On the one

Table 5. Main experimental results, abstract-level evaluation. Our (Neural w/ Dist.) is the abbreviation of Our (Neural Retrieval with Distillation).

(a). Results on development set. The baseline results are from [22].

Rough Retrieval Methods	Accurate Classification Models	Abstract-level					
		Label-Only			Label+Rationale		
		F1	P	**R**	F1	P	**R**
TF-IDF	VERISCI	52.1	56.4	<u>48.3</u>	50.0	54.2	<u>46.4</u>
BioSenVec	Paragraph-Joint SCIFACT-only	59.7	69.9	<u>52.1</u>	55.3	64.7	<u>48.3</u>
BioSenVec	Paragraph-Joint Pre-training	65.1	71.4	<u>59.8</u>	59.9	65.7	<u>55.0</u>
BioSenVec	ARSJOINT w/o RR (RoBERTa)	60.6	66.1	<u>56.0</u>	56.0	61.0	<u>51.7</u>
	ARSJOINT (RoBERTa)	60.8	64.5	<u>57.4</u>	55.7	59.1	<u>52.6</u>
	ARSJOINT w/o RR (BioBERT)	64.2	72.7	<u>57.4</u>	59.9	67.9	<u>53.6</u>
	ARSJOINT (BioBERT)	66.7	75.3	<u>59.8</u>	62.4	70.5	<u>56.0</u>
Our (Neural w/ Dist.)	ARSJOINT w/o RR (RoBERTa)	61.5	66.8	<u>56.9</u>	56.8	61.8	<u>52.6</u>
	ARSJOINT (RoBERTa)	62.3	65.6	<u>59.3</u>	57.3	60.3	<u>54.5</u>
	ARSJOINT w/o RR (BioBERT)	65.9	74.3	<u>59.3</u>	61.7	69.5	<u>55.5</u>
	ARSJOINT (BioBERT)	**67.7**	**75.7**	<u>**61.2**</u>	**63.4**	**71.1**	<u>**57.4**</u>

(b). Results on test set. The results are generated by the leaderboard.

BioSenVec	ARSJOINT (BioBERT)	71.0	73.2	<u>68.9</u>	68.7	70.8	<u>66.7</u>
Our (Neural w/ Dist.)	ARSJOINT (BioBERT)	71.2	72.2	<u>**70.3**</u>	69.0	69.9	<u>**68.0**</u>

hand, we evaluate the approaches on the development set following [9,22]; on the other hand, we also provide some results on the test set through the leaderboard.

4.6 Experimental Results

Table 4(a) and 5(a) show the results on the development set. The proposed method with our neural rough retrieval method has better Recall than the existing works that utilize the naïve rough retrieval methods such as some similarity measures. Especially, in the results using diverse variants of the backbone model ARSJOINT in this work, for accurate classification, comparing the rows with BioSenVec embedding similarities and our neural rough retrieval methods, in the case of the same accurate classification models (ARSJOINT model, w/ or w/o RR, RoBERTa or BioBERT), our method always has better performance. It shows that using better rough retrieval methods can improve the performance of the overall system. Table 4(b) and 5(b) show the results on the test set. Our neural-based method with distillation has better Recall than the baseline with naïve rough retrieval method when using the same accurate classification model.

We then investigate the performance of different methods on selecting the candidate papers at the rough retrieval stage. The most important measure for this stage is the Recall, because if the related papers are not in the set of candi-

Table 6. *Rough retrieval stage*: a trade-off between recall and time cost (seconds) of judging a claim-abstract pair.

Rough Retrieval Method	Recall (**R**)	Time
BioSenVec Embedding Similarity	98.10	$<0.05\,$s
Our w/o Distillation (Neural Retrieval)	99.96	$\approx 0.26\,$s
Our (Neural w/ Dist.)	99.06	$\approx 0.11\,$s

date papers, the model of the accurate classification stage cannot find them and correctly classify them, no matter how powerful the accurate classification model performance is. Table 6 shows that our method has better recall than the typical naïve rough retrieval method of using BioSenVec embedding similarities. It is one of the reason that our approach has better recall of the overall system in Table 4 and 5. We also show the results when directly using the ARSJOINT model to the rough retrieval stage (i.e., Our w/o Distillation). Because our student model is a lightweight version of the ARSJOINT model, our method has somewhat lower recall than it. However, our method only consumes about less than half the time comparing with it. On the other hand, because the document embeddings of the papers can be pre-computed and indexed, the time cost of BioSenVec embedding similarity method is mainly decided by the top-k algorithm, which is expected to be faster than the relevance judgments of neural-based rough retrieval models. Our method has a balance on the classification quality and speed. Note that, we focus on proposing a method that is faster and more efficient than a vanilla neural-based rough retrieval method; it is not necessary to be faster than a naïve (e.g., similarity-based) retrieval methods.

5   Conclusion

In this paper, for improving the recall of two-stage scientific claim verification systems by improving the recall of rough abstract retrieval stage, we propose an approach based on neural networks for both rough retrieval and accurate classification stages. We propose a distillation-based method to train a lightweight model for the rough retrieval stage for a balance on the recall improvement and speed drop.

The limitation of the proposed approach is that it cannot be faster than the existing solutions using naïve rough retrieval methods such as some similarity measures. Note that, we focus on proposing a method that is faster and more efficient than a vanilla neural-based rough abstract retrieval method; it is not necessary to be faster than the naïve (e.g., similarity-based) retrieval methods. The system administrators need to decide whether the classification quality is the preferred factor or the time cost is the preferred factor. On the one hand, the system administrators need to decide whether the classification quality is the preferred factor or the time cost is the preferred factor. On the other hand, in future work, we will investigate smaller student models with satisfied classification quality.

Acknowledgements. This works was partially supported by 23H03402.

References

1. Akiba, T., Sano, S., Yanase, T., Ohta, T., Koyama, M.: Optuna: a next-generation hyperparameter optimization framework. In: Proceedings of the 25th ACM SIGKDD International Conference on Knowledge Discovery & Data Mining, KDD 2019, pp. 2623–2631. Association for Computing Machinery, New York (2019). https://doi.org/10.1145/3292500.3330701
2. Chen, J., Zhang, R., Guo, J., Fan, Y., Cheng, X.: Gere: generative evidence retrieval for fact verification. In: Proceedings of the 45th International ACM SIGIR Conference on Research and Development in Information Retrieval, SIGIR 2022, pp. 2184–2189. Association for Computing Machinery, New York (2022). https://doi.org/10.1145/3477495.3531827
3. Chen, Q., Peng, Y., Lu, Z.: BioSentVec: creating sentence embeddings for biomedical texts. In: 2019 IEEE International Conference on Healthcare Informatics (ICHI), pp. 1–5 (2019). https://doi.org/10.1109/ICHI.2019.8904728
4. Ferreira, W., Vlachos, A.: Emergent: a novel data-set for stance classification. In: Proceedings of the 2016 Conference of the North American Chapter of the Association for Computational Linguistics: Human Language Technologies, pp. 1163–1168 (2016)
5. Hanselowski, A., et al.: UKP-Athene: multi-sentence textual entailment for claim verification. In: Proceedings of the First Workshop on Fact Extraction and VERification (FEVER), pp. 103–108 (2018)
6. Hidey, C., et al.: DeSePtion: dual sequence prediction and adversarial examples for improved fact-checking. In: Proceedings of the 58th Annual Meeting of the Association for Computational Linguistics, pp. 8593–8606. Association for Computational Linguistics, Online (2020). https://doi.org/10.18653/v1/2020.acl-main.761. https://www.aclweb.org/anthology/2020.acl-main.761
7. Hinton, G.E., Vinyals, O., Dean, J.: Distilling the knowledge in a neural network. CoRR abs/1503.02531 (2015). http://arxiv.org/abs/1503.02531
8. Lee, J., et al.: BioBERT: a pre-trained biomedical language representation model for biomedical text mining. Bioinformatics **36**(4), 1234–1240 (2019). https://doi.org/10.1093/bioinformatics/btz682
9. Li, X., Burns, G.A., Peng, N.: A paragraph-level multi-task learning model for scientific fact-verification. In: Veyseh, A.P.B., Dernoncourt, F., Nguyen, T.H., Chang, W., Celi, L.A. (eds.) Proceedings of the Workshop on Scientific Document Understanding co-located with 35th AAAI Conference on Artificial Intelligence, SDU@AAAI 2021, Virtual Event, 9 February 2021. CEUR Workshop Proceedings, vol. 2831. CEUR-WS.org (2021). http://ceur-ws.org/Vol-2831/paper8.pdf
10. Liu, Y., et al.: RoBERTa: a robustly optimized BERT pretraining approach. CoRR abs/1907.11692 (2019). http://arxiv.org/abs/1907.11692
11. Liu, Z., Xiong, C., Sun, M., Liu, Z.: Fine-grained fact verification with kernel graph attention network. In: Proceedings of the 58th Annual Meeting of the Association for Computational Linguistics, pp. 7342–7351. Association for Computational Linguistics, Online (2020). https://doi.org/10.18653/v1/2020.acl-main.655. https://aclanthology.org/2020.acl-main.655

12. Lu, Y.J., Li, C.T.: GCAN: graph-aware co-attention networks for explainable fake news detection on social media. In: Proceedings of the 58th Annual Meeting of the Association for Computational Linguistics, pp. 505–514. Association for Computational Linguistics, Online (2020). https://doi.org/10.18653/v1/2020.acl-main.48. https://www.aclweb.org/anthology/2020.acl-main.48

13. Nie, Y., Chen, H., Bansal, M.: Combining fact extraction and verification with neural semantic matching networks. In: Proceedings of the AAAI Conference on Artificial Intelligence, vol. 33, pp. 6859–6866 (2019)

14. Pradeep, R., Ma, X., Nogueira, R., Lin, J.: Scientific claim verification with VerT5erini. In: Proceedings of the 12th International Workshop on Health Text Mining and Information Analysis, pp. 94–103. Association for Computational Linguistics, Online (2021). https://www.aclweb.org/anthology/2021.louhi-1.11

15. Raffel, C., et al.: Exploring the limits of transfer learning with a unified text-to-text transformer. J. Mach. Learn. Res. **21**(140), 1–67 (2020). http://jmlr.org/papers/v21/20-074.html

16. Thorne, J., Vlachos, A., Christodoulopoulos, C., Mittal, A.: FEVER: a large-scale dataset for fact extraction and VERification. In: Proceedings of the 2018 Conference of the North American Chapter of the Association for Computational Linguistics: Human Language Technologies, New Orleans, Louisiana (Volume 1: Long Papers), pp. 809–819. Association for Computational Linguistics (2018). https://doi.org/10.18653/v1/N18-1074. https://www.aclweb.org/anthology/N18-1074

17. Vlachos, A., Riedel, S.: Fact checking: task definition and dataset construction. In: Proceedings of the ACL 2014 Workshop on Language Technologies and Computational Social Science, pp. 18–22 (2014)

18. Wadden, D., et al.: Fact or fiction: verifying scientific claims. In: Proceedings of the 2020 Conference on Empirical Methods in Natural Language Processing (EMNLP), pp. 7534–7550. Association for Computational Linguistics, Online (2020). https://doi.org/10.18653/v1/2020.emnlp-main.609. https://www.aclweb.org/anthology/2020.emnlp-main.609

19. Wadden, D., Lo, K., Wang, L., Cohan, A., Beltagy, I., Hajishirzi, H.: MultiVerS: improving scientific claim verification with weak supervision and full-document context. In: Findings of the Association for Computational Linguistics: NAACL 2022, Seattle, USA, pp. 61–76. Association for Computational Linguistics (2022). https://doi.org/10.18653/v1/2022.findings-naacl.6. https://aclanthology.org/2022.findings-naacl.6

20. Yang, Z., Yang, D., Dyer, C., He, X., Smola, A., Hovy, E.: Hierarchical attention networks for document classification. In: Proceedings of the 2016 Conference of the North American Chapter of the Association for Computational Linguistics: Human Language Technologies, San Diego, California, pp. 1480–1489. Association for Computational Linguistics (2016). https://doi.org/10.18653/v1/N16-1174. https://aclanthology.org/N16-1174

21. Zeng, X., Zubiaga, A.: QMUL-SDS at SCIVER: step-by-step binary classification for scientific claim verification. In: Proceedings of the Second Workshop on Scholarly Document Processing, pp. 116–123. Association for Computational Linguistics, Online (2021). https://doi.org/10.18653/v1/2021.sdp-1.15. https://aclanthology.org/2021.sdp-1.15

22. Zhang, Z., Li, J., Fukumoto, F., Ye, Y.: Abstract, rationale, stance: a joint model for scientific claim verification. In: Proceedings of the 2021 Conference on Empirical Methods in Natural Language Processing, Punta Cana, Dominican Republic, pp. 3580–3586. Association for Computational Linguistics, Online (2021). https://doi.org/10.18653/v1/2021.emnlp-main.290. https://aclanthology.org/2021.emnlp-main.290

An Explainable Feature Selection Approach for Fair Machine Learning

Zhi Yang[1], Ziming Wang[1], Changwu Huang[1(✉)], and Xin Yao[1,2]

[1] Guangdong Provincial Key Laboratory of Brain-Inspired Intelligent Computation, Department of Computer Science and Engineering, Southern University of Science and Technology, Shenzhen, China
huangcw3@sustech.edu.cn
[2] Research Institute of Trustworthy Autonomous Systems, Southern University of Science and Technology, Shenzhen, China

Abstract. As machine learning (ML) algorithms are extensively adopted in various fields to make decisions of importance to human beings and our society, the fairness issue in algorithm decision-making has been widely studied. To mitigate unfairness in ML, many techniques have been proposed, including pre-processing, in-processing, and post-processing approaches. In this work, we propose an explainable feature selection (ExFS) method to improve the fairness of ML by recursively eliminating features that contribute to unfairness based on the feature attribution explanations of the model's predictions. To validate the effectiveness of our proposed ExFS method, we compare our approach with other fairness-aware feature selection methods on several commonly used datasets. The experimental results show that ExFS can effectively improve fairness by recursively dropping some features that contribute to unfairness. The ExFS method generally outperforms the compared filter-based feature selection methods in terms of fairness and achieves comparable results to the compared wrapper-based feature selection methods. In addition, our method can provide explanations for the rationale underlying this fairness-aware feature selection mechanism.

Keywords: Fairness in machine learning · Group fairness · Feature selection · Feature attribution explanation · Ethics of AI

1 Introduction

Machine learning (ML) algorithms are increasingly adopted in more and more fields and have brought significant impact on our daily lives and society. However, despite the advantages brought by adopting ML models, there is plenty of evidence of discriminatory behavior in algorithmic decision-making. For instance, the software product COMPAS used to predict future criminals was found to be biased against blacks [1]. Many other similar behaviors and findings have also been exposed in other areas and applications [15]. Thus, fairness in ML has received considerable attention and discussions in the last decades [9].

L. Iliadis et al. (Eds.): ICANN 2023, LNCS 14261, pp. 75–86, 2023.
https://doi.org/10.1007/978-3-031-44198-1_7

The widespread concerns about algorithmic fairness have led to growing interest in fairness-aware ML. Hence, many different measurements of fairness have been formalized [5], and different approaches have been proposed to mitigate the unfairness of ML models. According to the model development stage in which the mitigation techniques are adopted, the existing approaches are usually categorized into pre-processing, in-processing, and post-processing methods. Preprocessing approaches try to adjust or transform the training data for removing the underlying bias in the data before feeding it to an ML algorithm [15]. In-processing methods directly account for fairness during the model design stage usually by modifying ML algorithms to address discrimination during the model training phase [22]. Post-processing techniques dedicate to calibrating the predictions of a model after model training to make decisions fairer [17].

Although there are many different fairness-enhancing techniques, each type of method shows its advantages and limitations and there was no conclusively dominating method [17]. The existing pre-processing methods usually either do not consider the fairness measurements explicitly or are limited to the type of bias they can handle. In-processing mechanisms need to modify the downstream ML algorithms, which is nontrivial and requires rich knowledge and experience. Since post-processing approaches are applied to the relatively late stage of the ML process, these methods typically obtain inferior results [23]. Additionally, the existing methods lack explainability for their fairness enhancement mechanisms.

This work focuses on fairness-aware feature selection (FS), which is a type of pre-processing method that aims at mitigating unfairness by selecting a suitable subset of features to train models. We proposed an explainable feature selection (ExFS) approach to mitigate the unfairness by dropping or eliminating the features that contribute most to the unfairness of the model's prediction in an iterative manner, based on an explainable artificial intelligence (XAI) approach. The experiments on several commonly used datasets and ML models show that our proposed method can enhance the fairness of the used model effectively and efficiently. The main contributions of this work are: 1) We implement a method to explain the prediction of the black-box model by constructing an explainable boosting machine (EBM) surrogate model; 2) We propose an approach to explain which features contribute to the unfairness of a model; 3) We design an explainable feature selection (ExFS) method for mitigating unfairness.

The remainder of this paper is organized as follows. Section 2 introduces the commonly used fairness measurements and some related approaches for mitigating unfairness. The proposed explainable feature selection (ExFS) method is described in Sect. 3. Section 4 presents the experimental studies. Finally, the paper is briefly concluded in Sect. 5.

2   Related Work

In this section, we first give the problem setting investigated in this work. Then, some commonly used group fairness measurements and fairness-aware feature selection approaches are introduced under this setting.

2.1 Problem Setting

We consider the most commonly investigated problem in fairness-aware ML literature [11], that is, the binary classification problem that aims to learn a mapping function between user feature vectors $\mathbf{x} \in \mathbb{R}^d$ and class labels $y \in \{0, 1\}$. This task is often achieved by finding a model or classifier $f : \mathbb{R}^d \mapsto \mathbb{R}$ based on the training set $\mathcal{D} = \{(\mathbf{x}^{(i)}, y^{(i)})\}_{i=1}^N$ (where $\mathbf{x}^{(i)} = [x_1^{(i)}, \cdots, x_d^{(i)}] \in \mathbb{R}^d$ are feature vectors and $y^{(i)} \in \{0, 1\}$ are the corresponding labels) such that given a feature vector $\mathbf{x}$ with unknown label y, the classifier can predict its label $\hat{y} = f(\mathbf{x})$. In the context of fairness-aware ML, each $\mathbf{x}$ also has an associated sensitive attribute $s \in \mathcal{S}$ (e.g., sex, race) that indicates the group membership of a user and the model f also needs to be fair with respect to the sensitive attribute. Actually, there can be multiple sensitive attributes. Here we consider a single sensitive attribute case (e.g., the gender of each user $s = \{male, female\}$) and use s_a and s_b to denote two different groups associated with the sensitive attribute. That is, each training data instance $(\mathbf{x}^{(i)}, y^{(i)}) \in \mathcal{D}$ has an associate sensitive feature value $s^{(i)} \in \{s_a, s_b\}$. The goal of fairness-ware ML is to learn a model f that can provide accurate predictions while satisfying fairness requirements.

We introduce some additional notations used in work. The subsets of training dataset $\mathcal{D}$ with values $s = s_a$ and $s = s_b$ are denoted as $\mathcal{D}_a = \{(\mathbf{x}^{(i)}, y^{(i)}) \in \mathcal{D} | s^{(i)} = s_a\}$ and $\mathcal{D}_b = \{(\mathbf{x}^{(i)}, y^{(i)}) \in \mathcal{D} | s^{(i)} = s_b\}$, respectively. Let $X_k = [x_k^{(1)}, \cdots, x_k^{(N)}]^T$ ($k = 1, \cdots, d$) be the k-th feature of the training dataset $\mathcal{D}$, and $S = [s^{(1)}, \cdots, s^{(N)}]^T$ denotes the sensitive attribute associated with $\mathcal{D}$.

2.2 Fairness Measurements

Generally, fairness means the absence of any bias towards individuals or groups based on their inherent or acquired characteristics [15]. Different types of measures for fairness have been proposed, including group and individual fairness [15]. Below, we introduce some widely used group fairness measures.

- Demographic Parity (DP) [4] requires the positive prediction rates across different sensitive groups should be the same, which is evaluated as:

$$m_{DP} = |P(\hat{y} = 1 | s = s_a) - P(\hat{y} = 1 | s = s_b)|. \tag{1}$$

- Equal Opportunity (EOp) [8] requires the true-positive rates across different groups should be the same, which is computed as:

$$m_{EOp} = |P(\hat{y} = 1 | s = s_a, y = 1) - P(\hat{y} = 1 | s = s_b, y = 1)|. \tag{2}$$

- Equalized Odds (EOd) [8] requires both the false-positive and true-positive rates across different groups should be the same, which is assessed as:

$$\begin{aligned} m_{EOd} = &|P(\hat{y} = 1 | s = s_a, y = 0) - P(\hat{y} = 1 | s = s_b, y = 0)| \\ &+ |P(\hat{y} = 1 | s = s_a, y = 1) - P(\hat{y} = 1 | s = s_b, y = 1)|. \end{aligned} \tag{3}$$

2.3 Fairness-Aware Feature Selection (FS)

Feature selection (FS) is an important method to optimize the performance of ML by selecting a suitable feature subset. FS methods are usually categorized into filter, wrapper, and embedded approaches [24]. Recently, there is a growing body of work that uses FS to improve the fairness of ML [6,18], which is referred to as fairness-aware FS [10]. Both filter and wrapper methods have been adopted for mitigating unfairness in ML.

Fairness-Aware Filter FS. It is well known that bias caused by proxy features of the sensitive attribute is one of the main causes of unfairness in ML [17]. Hence, fairness-aware filter approaches intend to identify features that are highly related to the sensitive attribute (i.e., the proxy features) and then drop these features before training a model. Based on this idea, the Pearson correlation coefficient (PCC) and mutual information (MI) [7] can be used to measure the correlation between each feature X_k ($k = 1, \cdots, d$) and the sensitive attribute S.

Fairness-Aware Wrapper FS. This category of methods directly incorporates fairness measures into its objective when evaluating the goodness of the selected subset features. According to the number of objectives, fairness-aware wrapper approaches can be divided into single and multiple objective methods. In single-objective wrapper approaches, the performance (e.g., accuracy, F1-score) and fairness measures (e.g., DP, EOp) of the model are combined to form a single objective that guides the FS process [3], or only the fairness measure is taken as the objective to be optimized [18]. As for multi-objective wrapper methods, both fairness measures and performance metrics are considered as different objectives to be optimized during the FS [18] so as to obtain a set of Pareto optimal solutions. In [18], both single and multi-objective wrapper approaches have been investigated.

However, the above-described fairness-aware filter and wrapper FS approaches both suffer from their drawbacks. On the one hand, a filter method is computationally efficient but its performance may be inferior to a wrapper method due to not considering the adopted model. On the other hand, wrapper methods usually can provide good results but involve high computational costs. Furthermore, neither filter nor wrapper fairness-aware FS approaches can offer the rationale or cause why removing some features can lead to fairness enhancement.

This has motivated us to design the ExFS method which eliminates features based on the feature attribution explanations to the fairness measure. Our proposed method not only utilize the information or knowledge learned by the model but also provides explanations for the underlying reason why dropping the identified features can improve the fairness of the model.

3 Explainable Feature Selection for Mitigating Unfairness

In this section, we propose an explainable feature selection (ExFS) method for mitigating unfairness. Firstly, the used feature attribution explanation method is introduced. Then, we describe the procedure of the ExFS method.

3.1 Feature Attribution Explanation Method

Explainable artificial intelligence (XAI) is an attractive and rapidly developing research area since AI models are increasingly applied in high-stake domains [9]. During the past decades, numerous XAI methods have been proposed to explain the decisions of ML models [2]. With the goal of explaining which feature(s) contribute to the unfairness, we focus on a kind of XAI techniques known as feature attribution explanation (FAE) methods. FAE methods are popular XAI approaches that compute the attribution of input features to the model's output and provide a per-feature attribution score to represent its importance [25].

There are many popular FAE methods, including SHAP [14], LIME [19], EBM [16], etc. SHAP [14] is a post-hoc approach that can provide both global and local explanations. SHAP computes feature importances by removing features in a game-theoretic framework which leads to expensive computational costs. LIME [19] is also a post-hoc approach. It provides local explanations through the perturbation method to identify the importance of each input feature. While EBM [16] is an intrinsic approach that can provide both global and local explanations, it requires a cheap computational cost than others. Thus, we choose EBM as the FAE method used in this work.

EBM belongs to the family of generalized additive models (GAMs) and can be formulated in the following form [16]:

$$g(\mathbf{x}) = \beta_0 + \sum f_k(x_k), \tag{4}$$

where f_k is the shape function of k-th feature that EBM learns through modern ML techniques such as bagging and gradient boosting. EBM is highly intelligible and explainable because the contribution of each feature to a prediction can be revealed by $f_k(x_k)$ and the term contribution of each feature can be sorted and visualized to show which features had the most impact on the prediction [12].

3.2 Explainable Feature Selection (ExFS) Method

Using EBM to Explain Black-Box Model's Predictions: To leverage the explainability of EBM, we use an EBM as a surrogate model to explain the predictions of other black-box models, such as random forest and neural network models. The goal is to use an EBM g to simulate or mimic the input-output mapping of the trained model f. The procedure for constructing an EBM surrogate model is illustrated in Fig. 1. The only difference between building an EBM surrogate and training an EBM directly on the training dataset is that the output (the predicted probability) $\hat{Y}$ of the trained black-box model f are taken as

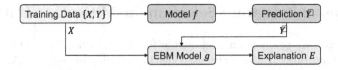

Fig. 1. Illustration of constructing an EBM surrogate model to explain another model.

targets rather than the ground-truth labels Y in the dataset when constructing the EBM surrogate. Then, the EBM surrogate model g can be used to provide explanations for the prediction of model f at any input.

Calculating the Feature Attributions for Fairness Measurement: Let $e(\mathbf{x}) \in \mathbb{R}^d$ denotes the explanation of prediction provided by EBM, which is a vector of contribution score or importance score of each input feature, at input vector $\mathbf{x}$. We use $E_a = \{e(\mathbf{x}^{(i)}) \mid \mathbf{x}^{(i)} \in \mathcal{D}_a\}$, $E_b = \{e(\mathbf{x}^{(j)}) \mid \mathbf{x}^{(j)} \in \mathcal{D}_b\}$ represent the explanation sets for the two subsets (or groups) $\mathcal{D}_a$ and $\mathcal{D}_b$ of dataset $\mathcal{D}$ associated with the sensitive attribute. Based on the individual prediction's explanations, we can attribute DP fairness measurement m_{DP} (in Eq. 1) back to each of the input features [13,21]. We calculate how each feature contribute to the m_{DP} by,

$$FA_{DP} = mean(E_a) - mean(E_b) = \frac{\sum_{\mathbf{x}^{(i)} \in \mathcal{D}_a} e(\mathbf{x}^{(i)})}{|\mathcal{D}_a|} - \frac{\sum_{\mathbf{x}^{(j)} \in \mathcal{D}_b} e(\mathbf{x}^{(j)})}{|\mathcal{D}_b|}. \quad (5)$$

The feature attribution for other group fairness measurements (EOp and EOd) can be derived in a similar way as that for DP described above.

Eliminating Features Based on Explanations: The achieved FA_{DP} is a vector that includes the contributions of each feature to the DP measure, and ΣFA_{DP} indicates the DP value. The larger value of items in FA_{DP} vector indicates the corresponding features contribute more to the fairness measure, i.e., causing unfairness. Hence, we can eliminate features that have large contribution scores to fairness measure for reducing unfairness. In our ExFS method, we recursively eliminate the feature that contributes mostly to the computed fairness measure. The procedure of the ExFS approach is described in Algorithm 1.

4   Experimental Study

In this section, we first present the setup of our experiments and then demonstrate the effectiveness of our method by comparing it with four state-of-the-art methods on three datasets with three different ML models.

4.1   Experimental Setting

Compared Approaches: We compare our approach with four fairness-aware FS methods, as described in Sect. 2.3, namely FS based on Mutual Informa-

---

Algorithm 1. The Procedure of Explainable Feature Selection (ExFS) Method

---

Input: Training dataset $\mathcal{D} = \{(\mathbf{x}^{(i)}, y^{(i)})\}_{i=1}^{N}$, Classification model f, fairness measure
m (e.g., m_{DP}, m_{EOp}, or m_{EOd}), Unfairness tolerance ϵ.
Output: Trained model f that satisfying the fairness requirement.
1: Train the initial model f on dataset $\mathcal{D}$ with the initial set of features.
2: Evaluate the fairness measure m of the trained model f on dataset $\mathcal{D}$.
3: **while** $m > \epsilon$ and $\#Features > 1$ **do**
4:    Construct an EBM surrogate model g for explaining the predictions of model f.
5:    Calculate the feature attributions FA_m for fairness measure m.
6:    Eliminate the feature that has largest contribution to m according to FA_m.
7:    Retrain the model f on the dataset with remaining features.
8:    Evaluate the fairness measure m of the retrained model f.
9: **end while**
10: Return the model f.

---

tion (FS-MI), FS based on Pearson Correlation Coefficient (FS-PCC), FS using
Genetic Algorithm (FS-GA) [18], and FS using NSGA-II (FS-NSGA-II) [18].

Datasets: We validate the proposed method on three commonly used datasets
of binary classification tasks [11]: Adult, Dutch, and Compas, whose sensitive
attributes are sex, sex, and race, respectively.

Models: Experiments were performed on three models: Logistic Regression (LR)
with maximum number of iterations of 1000, Random Forest (RF) with 10 esti-
mators and max-depth of 20 [21], and Multi-layer Perceptron (MLP) with two
hidden layers of size 64 and 32 and maximum number of iterations of 200 [20].

Evaluation Metrics: We used three widely used group fairness metrics as
evaluation criteria, which have been described in Sect. 2.2. We randomly split
each dataset into training and test sets with a ratio of 7:3. All reported results
are the average results on the test set obtained from 15 different random splits.

4.2   Experimental Results

Firstly, we conduct a comparative analysis between our approach and the other
two filter-based methods, as they all gradually drop features until the fairness
measure reaches the threshold. Due to space limitation, we only present the
comparison results of FS process for improving the DP metric in Fig. 2. To stan-
dardize the comparison, all methods drop the sensitive attribute at the beginning
and we set the unfairness tolerance $\epsilon = 0.0$. From Fig. 2, we can see that all methods are effective in reducing the DP value. However, the ExFS method tends to
be the most efficient method for improving the DP metric, especially on the
Adult dataset. In addition, the ExFS method is ultimately capable of achieving
extremely low DP values, which makes it capable of satisfying diverse fairness
requirements, including more stringent ones.

   Then, we provide explanations to demonstrate the operational mechanism of
our method and to explain the reason of fairness measure changes during the

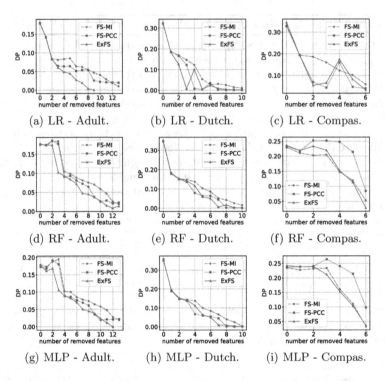

Fig. 2. The comparison results of three filter approaches to enhance DP fairness metric on different datasets using different models.

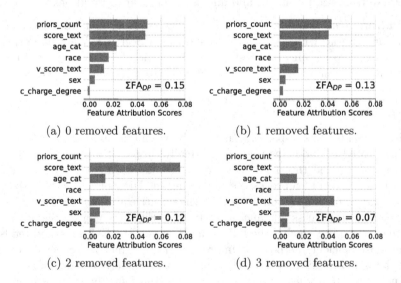

Fig. 3. Feature attribution explanations for DP on Compas dataset using MLP model. (Firstly, the sensitive attribute 'race' is eliminated, then 'priors_count' is removed, and 'score_text' is eliminated subsequently.)

ExFS procedure. The FAE graphs from the ExFS method for each step of the recursive deletion of the first 3 features for the case of Fig. 2(i) are presented in Fig. 3, showcasing part of the attribution process of the ExFS method. As can be seen in Fig. 3(b), when removing the second feature, we selected the 'priors_count' feature that contributed the most to the DP based on the attribution scores provided by FA_{DP}. However, after removing this feature, we can see from Fig. 3(c) that there is no significant change in ΣFA_{DP}. This is due to the sudden increase in the contribution score of the feature 'score_text' (see Fig. 3(c)) following the removal of 'priors_count'. After eliminating the feature 'score_text', the DP value decrease significantly. This demonstrates that FAE of fairness measure can explain why DP value decreases or not during the feature elimination process. Apparently, the ExFS method not only makes the selection process transparent and understandable but also helps us to analyze the reasons for the results generated by this selection. Furthermore, it can be observed from Fig. 3 that the feature ranking based on FAE is not constant. Hence, depending on the ML model used and other hyperparameter settings, the ranking of features that lead to model unfairness may vary. As mentioned in Sect. 2.3, the existing filter-based methods are limited to analyzing the relationship between features in the dataset and are unable to observe or adapt to such changes. Fortunately, the proposed ExFS method can improve the fairness of the model by gaining insight into the features that cause unfairness in the model through FAE and removing the corresponding features purposefully.

Lastly, we conduct a comprehensive comparison between the ExFS method and all the compared methods on DP, EOp, and EOd metrics, respectively, and the results are listed in Table 1. Specifically, for FS-MI and FS-PCC methods, we trained the models and gradually removed the feature with the largest score with sensitive attribute calculated by MI or PCC, and report the corresponding results of the models with the best DP, EOp and EOd metrics obtained in this process, respectively. For FS-GA, FS-NSGA-II, and ExFS methods, we optimize or attribute DP, EOp, and EOd metrics, respectively. Based on the results presented in Table 1, it can be observed that our ExFS approach generally performs better (achieves smaller fairness measurement values) than the two filter-based methods (FS-MI and FS-PCC) on three fairness measurements. At the same time, ExFS achieves comparable results to the two wrapper-based approaches (FS-GA and FS-NSGA-II).

In summary, it can be concluded that our ExFS method generally outperforms the compared filter-based methods in terms of fairness enhancement, and achieves comparable results to the wrapper-based methods. But the wrapper-based methods are somewhat brute-force and black-box approaches. While our ExFs method is transparent and able to provide explanations for the rationale behind removing certain features to achieve fairness enhancement. Furthermore, our method is computationally efficient, which involves a lower computational cost compared to the wrapper-based methods. Since a wrapper-based approach usually requires to evaluate a large number of feature subsets by training a model

Table 1. The comparison results of all investigated fairness-aware feature selection approaches to enhance different fairness measurements. The number in bold face means the corresponding method achieves the best fairness result.

Dataset	Model	Method	Fairness Measurement		
			DP	EOp	EOd
Adult	LR	FS-MI	0.010 ± 0.011	0.012 ± 0.011	0.015 ± 0.008
		FS-PCC	0.020 ± 0.004	0.015 ± 0.013	0.017 ± 0.014
		FS-GA	**0.000 ± 0.000**	**0.000 ± 0.000**	0.021 ± 0.012
		FS-NSGA-II	**0.000 ± 0.000**	**0.000 ± 0.000**	**0.000 ± 0.000**
		ExFS	**0.000 ± 0.000**	**0.000 ± 0.000**	**0.000 ± 0.000**
	RF	FS-MI	0.018 ± 0.007	0.019 ± 0.016	0.024 ± 0.019
		FS-PCC	0.021 ± 0.003	0.014 ± 0.011	0.019 ± 0.008
		FS-GA	**0.000 ± 0.000**	0.054 ± 0.021	0.022 ± 0.016
		FS-NSGA-II	**0.000 ± 0.000**	0.121 ± 0.027	**0.000 ± 0.000**
		ExFS	0.008 ± 0.003	**0.012 ± 0.008**	0.017 ± 0.007
	MLP	FS-MI	0.019 ± 0.008	0.022 ± 0.015	0.021 ± 0.013
		FS-PCC	0.020 ± 0.005	0.016 ± 0.009	0.020 ± 0.010
		FS-GA	**0.000 ± 0.000**	**0.000 ± 0.000**	0.022 ± 0.013
		FS-NSGA-II	**0.000 ± 0.000**	0.111 ± 0.221	0.023 ± 0.011
		ExFS	**0.000 ± 0.000**	**0.000 ± 0.000**	**0.000 ± 0.000**
Dutch	LR	FS-MI	0.011 ± 0.019	0.001 ± 0.002	0.001 ± 0.003
		FS-PCC	0.001 ± 0.001	0.006 ± 0.004	0.009 ± 0.004
		FS-GA	0.003 ± 0.001	**0.000 ± 0.000**	**0.000 ± 0.000**
		FS-NSGA-II	**0.000 ± 0.000**	0.010 ± 0.014	**0.000 ± 0.000**
		ExFS	0.001 ± 0.002	0.002 ± 0.005	0.011 ± 0.005
	RF	FS-MI	0.015 ± 0.015	0.023 ± 0.024	0.043 ± 0.032
		FS-PCC	0.001 ± 0.001	0.008 ± 0.004	0.009 ± 0..004
		FS-GA	**0.000 ± 0.000**	**0.000 ± 0.000**	0.001 ± 0.001
		FS-NSGA-II	**0.000 ± 0.000**	**0.000 ± 0.000**	**0.000 ± 0.000**
		ExFS	0.001 ± 0.001	0.002 ± 0.004	0.010 ± 0.004
	MLP	FS-MI	0.002 ± 0.004	0.018 ± 0.025	0.039 ± 0.028
		FS-PCC	**0.001 ± 0.001**	**0.003 ± 0.003**	**0.004 ± 0.006**
		FS-GA	**0.001 ± 0.002**	0.025 ± 0.034	0.046 ± 0.025
		FS-NSGA-II	**0.001 ± 0.002**	0.045 ± 0.017	0.044 ± 0.026
		ExFS	**0.001 ± 0.001**	**0.003 ± 0.004**	0.005 ± 0.005
Compas	LR	FS-MI	0.058 ± 0.047	0.044 ± 0.051	0.104 ± 0.075
		FS-PCC	0.038 ± 0.049	0.038 ± 0.029	0.063 ± 0.055
		FS-GA	**0.000 ± 0.000**	0.030 ± 0.042	**0.000 ± 0.000**
		FS-NSGA-II	**0.000 ± 0.000**	0.053 ± 0.033	0.070 ± 0.087
		ExFS	0.033 ± 0.047	**0.018 ± 0.037**	0.018 ± 0.045
	RF	FS-MI	0.053 ± 0.043	0.053 ± 0.038	0.082 ± 0.085
		FS-PCC	0.084 ± 0.014	0.102 ± 0.028	0.153 ± 0.030
		FS-GA	**0.005 ± 0.013**	0.077 ± 0.023	**0.023 ± 0.042**
		FS-NSGA-II	0.014 ± 0.029	0.074 ± 0.037	0.055 ± 0.064
		ExFS	0.028 ± 0.036	**0.047 ± 0.046**	0.074 ± 0.066
	MLP	FS-MI	0.032 ± 0.044	0.035 ± 0.039	0.090 ± 0.083
		FS-PCC	0.098 ± 0.022	0.093 ± 0.017	0.159 ± 0.042
		FS-GA	**0.005 ± 0.017**	**0.020 ± 0.035**	0.048 ± 0.061
		FS-NSGA-II	0.029 ± 0.029	0.056 ± 0.035	**0.024 ± 0.040**
		ExFS	0.036 ± 0.041	0.036 ± 0.044	0.062 ± 0.082

on each feature subset, while our ExFS method only needs to retrain the model after each feature elimination.

5 Conclusion

In this paper, we proposed an explainable feature selection (ExFS) approach that is capable of explaining and mitigating unfairness in ML models. The results of our experiments demonstrate the effectiveness of our approach in improving the fairness of ML models. Our proposed ExFS method is transparent and is able to provide explanations for the rationale of why removing some features can lead to fairness enhancement. Furthermore, ExFS is computationally efficient, which requires a lower computational cost compared to wrapper-based methods. The ExFS method fills the gap of the lack of explainability in the investigated fairness-aware feature selection approaches. But, it should be noted that there are still challenges and limitations to the trade-off between fairness and performance of the ML models. In future work, we will focus on how to achieve a trade-off between performance and fairness based on the explanations of the predictions and the fairness measures.

Acknowledgments. This work was supported by the National Natural Science Foundation of China (Grant No. 62250710682), the Guangdong Provincial Key Laboratory (Grant No. 2020B121201001), the Program for Guangdong Introducing Innovative and Entrepreneurial Teams (Grant No.2017ZT07X386), the Shenzhen Science and Technology Program (Grant No. KQTD2016112514355531), and the Research Institute of Trustworthy Autonomous Systems.

References

1. Angwin, J., Larson, J., Mattu, S., Kirchner, L.: Machine bias (2016). https://www.propublica.org/article/machine-bias-risk-assessments-in-criminal-sentencing
2. Arrieta, A.B., et al.: Explainable artificial intelligence (XAI): concepts, taxonomies, opportunities and challenges toward responsible AI. Inf. Fusion **58**, 82–115 (2020)
3. Dorleon, G., Megdiche, I., Bricon-Souf, N., Teste, O.: Feature selection under fairness constraints. In: Proceedings of the 37th ACM/SIGAPP Symposium on Applied Computing, pp. 1125–1127 (2022)
4. Dwork, C., Hardt, M., Pitassi, T., Reingold, O., Zemel, R.: Fairness through awareness. In: Proceedings of the 3rd Innovations in Theoretical Computer Science Conference, pp. 214–226 (2012)
5. Gajane, P., Pechenizkiy, M.: On formalizing fairness in prediction with machine learning. arXiv preprint arXiv:1710.03184 (2017)
6. Grgic-Hlaca, N., Zafar, M.B., Gummadi, K.P., Weller, A.: The case for process fairness in learning: feature selection for fair decision making. In: NIPS Symposium on Machine Learning and the Law, Barcelona, Spain, vol. 1, p. 11 (2016)
7. Guyon, I., Elisseeff, A.: An introduction to variable and feature selection. J. Mach. Learn. Res. **3**, 1157–1182 (2003)
8. Hardt, M., Price, E., Srebro, N.: Equality of opportunity in supervised learning. In: Advances in Neural Information Processing Systems, vol. 29 (2016)

9. Huang, C., Zhang, Z., Mao, B., Yao, X.: An overview of artificial intelligence ethics. IEEE Trans. Artif. Intell. 1–21 (2022). https://doi.org/10.1109/TAI.2022.3194503

10. Khodadadian, S., Nafea, M., Ghassami, A., Kiyavash, N.: Information theoretic measures for fairness-aware feature selection. arXiv preprint arXiv:2106.00772 (2021)

11. Le Quy, T., Roy, A., Iosifidis, V., Zhang, W., Ntoutsi, E.: A survey on datasets for fairness-aware machine learning. Wiley Interdisc. Rev. Data Min. Knowl. Discov. **12**(3), 1–59 (2022)

12. Lou, Y., Caruana, R., Gehrke, J., Hooker, G.: Accurate intelligible models with pairwise interactions. In: Proceedings of the 19th ACM SIGKDD International Conference on Knowledge Discovery and Data Mining, KDD 2013, pp. 623–631. Association for Computing Machinery, New York (2013)

13. Lundberg, S.M.: Explaining quantitative measures of fairness. In: Fair & Responsible AI Workshop@ CHI2020 (2020)

14. Lundberg, S.M., Lee, S.I.: A unified approach to interpreting model predictions. In: Advances in Neural Information Processing Systems, vol. 30 (2017)

15. Mehrabi, N., Morstatter, F., Saxena, N., Lerman, K., Galstyan, A.: A survey on bias and fairness in machine learning. ACM Comput. Surv. (CSUR) **54**(6), 1–35 (2021)

16. Nori, H., Jenkins, S., Koch, P., Caruana, R.: InterpretML: a unified framework for machine learning interpretability. arXiv preprint arXiv:1909.09223 (2019)

17. Pessach, D., Shmueli, E.: A review on fairness in machine learning. ACM Comput. Surv. (CSUR) **55**(3), 1–44 (2022)

18. Rehman, A.U., Nadeem, A., Malik, M.Z.: Fair feature subset selection using multiobjective genetic algorithm. In: Proceedings of the Genetic and Evolutionary Computation Conference Companion, pp. 360–363 (2022)

19. Ribeiro, M.T., Singh, S., Guestrin, C.: "Why should I trust you?": explaining the predictions of any classifier. In: Proceedings of the 22nd ACM SIGKDD International Conference on Knowledge Discovery and Data Mining, pp. 1135–1144. Association for Computing Machinery, New York (2016)

20. Singh, M.: Fair classification under covariate shift and missing protected attribute-an investigation using related features. arXiv preprint arXiv:2204.07987 (2022)

21. Thampi, A.: Interpretable AI: Building Explainable Machine Learning Systems. Manning Publications Co. (2022)

22. Wan, M., Zha, D., Liu, N., Zou, N.: In-processing modeling techniques for machine learning fairness: a survey. ACM Trans. Knowl. Discov. Data **17**(3), 1–27 (2023)

23. Woodworth, B., Gunasekar, S., Ohannessian, M.I., Srebro, N.: Learning non-discriminatory predictors. In: Conference on Learning Theory, pp. 1920–1953. PMLR (2017)

24. Xue, B., Zhang, M., Browne, W.N., Yao, X.: A survey on evolutionary computation approaches to feature selection. IEEE Trans. Evol. Comput. **20**(4), 606–626 (2015)

25. Zhou, Y., Booth, S., Ribeiro, M.T., Shah, J.: Do feature attribution methods correctly attribute features? In: Proceedings of the AAAI Conference on Artificial Intelligence, vol. 36, pp. 9623–9633 (2022)

Anchor Link Prediction Based on Trusted Anchor Re-identification

Dongwei Zhu[1,2], Yongxiu Xu[1,2], Lei Zhang[1,2], Minghao Tang[1,2],
Wenhao Zhu[1,2], and Hongbo Xu[1(✉)]

[1] Institute of Information Engineering, Chinese Academy of Sciences, Beijing, China
{zhudongwei,xuyongxiu,zhanglei,tangminghao,zhuwenhao,hbxu}@iie.ac.cn
[2] School of Cyber Security, University of Chinese Academy of Sciences,
Beijing, China

Abstract. Cross-social network anchor link prediction plays a pivotal role in downstream tasks, such as comprehensively portraying user characteristics, user friend recommendations, and online public opinion analysis, which aims to find accounts that belong to the same natural person on different social networks. It is a common method to use manually marked anchors or anchors inferred through autonomous learning as supervisory information to guide the prediction of subsequent anchor links. However, the credibility of the anchor is not discussed. In this paper, to address this problem, we propose a new framework that can simultaneously complete the identification of trusted anchors and the prediction of anchor links across social networks under a unified framework. The proposed method can effectively identify non-trusted anchor links and improve the accuracy of the anchor link prediction model through the reconstruction of trusted anchors. Extensive experiments have been conducted on two large-scale real-life social networks. The experimental results demonstrate that the proposed method outperforms the state-of-the-art models with a big margin.

Keywords: Social networks · Anchor link prediction · Anchor noise · Network embedding · Feature fusion

1 Introduction

With the development of the online society, people's demand for social network services has gradually increased, and a single social network can no longer meet the needs of users for different network services. In order to enjoy the various forms of services provided by different social networks, people often register accounts on multiple social networks at the same time, such as Facebook, Twitter

Supported by the National Key R&D Plan project of China (2021YFB3100600), the Youth Innovation Promotion Association, Chinese Academy of Sciences (No.2020163) and the Strategic Pilot Science and Technology Project of Chinese Academy of Sciences (XDC02040400).

L. Iliadis et al. (Eds.): ICANN 2023, LNCS 14261, pp. 87–98, 2023.
https://doi.org/10.1007/978-3-031-44198-1_8

and Linkedin. More often than not, users sign up at different social networks for different purposes, and different social network show different views and aspects of people. For example, a user makes connections to their friends on Facebook, but uses Linkedin to connect to his/her colleagues, interested companies and seek job opportunities. These shared users naturally form anchor links bridging different social networks.

Anchor Link Prediction (ALP) aims to recognize the accounts of the same natural person across different networks, and the links between these accounts are anchor links (the accounts are anchor nodes). Users with accounts on multiple social networks allow us to integrate patterns across online social networking sites and solve some problems that cannot be solved with data from only one site, such as the cold start problem and data sparsity in many prediction tasks [1]. Predicting anchor links across different social networks also provides a great opportunity to learn user's migration behavior. In a nutshell, ALP helps us integrate the account information of these natural persons on different social networks (including their friend relationships, behavioral preferences, geographic locations, hobbies, etc.). This allows us to have a more comprehensive understanding of our users and provide them with more attractive services on different social networks.

Early studies address this problem either by leveraging self reported user profiles (e.g., user name, profile, location, gender) and other demographic features [2] or by exploiting user generated contents, such as, tweets, posts, blogs, reviews, and ratings [3]. However, not all networks contain available heterogeneous information. In a homogeneous network, the above approach will not work. User identity data in online social networks has the following unique property: profile structure inconsistency. Different online social networks may employ different structures and schemes to present user profiles. Also, the same attribute can be populated with different information depending on the site and the purpose of the user. Additionally, even on a single social network, user profiles can be deliberately faked, similar to imitating other users [4], which increases the uncertainty and ambiguity of profile characteristics.

In order to solve the above problems, it has been proposed to achieve cross-network anchor link prediction by incorporating social network structural information [5–8]. The complex network structure contains abundant and available information. In addition, with the rise of network embedding, utilizing embedding-based methods for anchor link prediction has become a mainstream trend. Based on the trend, people tend to classify the core methods of anchor link prediction into two parts: embedding and alignment. The embedding part obtains a vectorized representation of network nodes (accounts) according to the network structure. The alignment part obtains latent anchor links by estimating pairwise similarity between the embedding representation vectors of nodes in different networks. According to whether these two parts are processed separately, existing methods can be divided into two categories: unified framework methods [8] and two-stage separate processing methods [9]. Obtaining a better node representation is crucial whether using the unified framework approach or the two-stage approach.

In addition, based on whether to use pre-marked anchor link data, ALP is subdivided into unsupervised, semi-supervised, and supervised methods. Since the desired effect cannot be obtained by using unsupervised methods, semi-supervised and supervised learning methods have become the mainstream methods of anchor link prediction. Whether it is semi-supervised or supervised, manually marked anchor links (or the anchor link inferred by the augmentation algorithm) will be used as a standard to guide the alignment of the two networks. However, due to human factors (mislabeling) or unreasonable design of the augmentation algorithm, these anchor links may contain noise. The use of noisy supervisory data will have a negative impact on subsequent anchor link prediction.

To address the above mentioned challenge, in this paper, we propose a cross-social network anchor link prediction framework based on trusted anchor re-identification technology. The contributions of this paper can be summarized as follows:

- As far as we know, there is no relevant work to study the credibility of anchor links. For the first time, we divided the supervisory data set used to predict anchor links into trusted anchors and non-trusted anchors, and gave a specific definition.
- We propose a trusted anchor re-identification method, which can effectively identify and remove non-trusted anchors from anchor supervision data. This method can effectively reduce the impact of noise in anchor monitoring data.
- We propose a new model that can simultaneously complete the identification of trusted anchors and the prediction of anchor links across social networks under a unified framework.
- We evaluate the proposed framework on two pairs of real-word social networks. The results demonstrate the effectiveness and efficiency of our method compared with several state-of-the-art methods.

2 Problem Statement

In this section, we first introduce the noise problem of anchor data and give the cause of anchor noise. Next, we give a formal definition of trusted anchors and non-trusted anchors. Then the node embedding representation technology and trusted anchor re-identification technology are introduced. Finally, the definition of the cross-social network anchor link prediction problem based on trusted anchor re-identification is given.

2.1 Anchor Noise Problem

In the existing cross-social network anchor link prediction research, the pre-marked anchors are often set to contain no noise by default. In addition, the anchors predicted by the data augmentation algorithm are also directly used in subsequent anchor link prediction. However, whether it is an artificially labeled anchor or an anchor inferred by an augmentation algorithm, it may contain noise, which will have a negative impact on the anchor link prediction model.

2.2 Trusted and Untrusted Anchors

We all know that an anchor is a kind of artificially defined virtual mapping. Both ends of the anchor point to user nodes in two different social networks (indicating that the accounts on these two different social platforms belong to the same person). Therefore, a trusted anchor is defined as a pair of user nodes that play a forward role in the training process of the anchor link prediction model. On the contrary, untrusted anchors are defined as a pair of user nodes that play a negative role.

2.3 Node Embedding Representation and Trusted Anchor Re-identification

Thanks to representation learning technology, people can easily use the characteristics of the node itself and its structural characteristics in the network to obtain high-quality embedded representations of nodes. Similar to most of the existing representation learning methods, we use a d-dimensional embedding representation vector to map each node $v_i \in V$ in the social network via a mapping function $f : V \longrightarrow \mathbb{R}^d$ in the embedding representation space. By calculating the similarity of the two nodes in the embedded representation space, the candidate anchor can be accurately found. Trusted anchor re-identification uses embedded representation technology to re-identify trusted anchors. Through this method, trusted anchors are filtered out and the set of anchor links is reconstructed, and the prediction accuracy of the model is improved by optimizing the quality of the supervision data.

2.4 Anchor Link Prediction Based on Trusted Anchor Re-identification

Given a social network $G = \{V, E\}$, where V is a set of nodes, E is a set of edges. G^S and G^T represent the source network and the target network respectively. Given a user node $a_i \in G^S$ and $a_j \in G^T$ are a pair of anchor nodes. $A=\{(a_i,a_j),...\}$ represents the set of anchors to be verified between the two networks. The task of cross-social network anchor link prediction based on trusted anchor re-identification technology is to use trusted anchor re-identification technology to filter out the trusted anchors in A and accurately predict the potential anchor links between the two networks.

3 Proposed Model

In this paper, we propose a unified framework to predict anchor links across social networks. The representation learning method is used by the framework to integrate the user's attribute characteristics and network structure characteristics at the same time. Then, the representations of the nodes at both ends of the anchor are compared in similarity to determine whether the anchor is

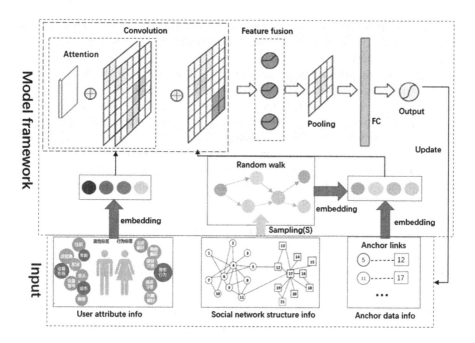

Fig. 1. Overview of model framework.

credible. On this basis, the reconstructed set of trusted anchors will be entered into the model as new supervisory data. The model consists of four parts: feature representation, feature fusion, trusted anchor reconstruction, and anchor link prediction, as shown in Fig. 1. In the first stage, the main related factors are analyzed, feature representations are carried out for different features, and expresses them in a unified form. In the second stage, a CNN-based link prediction model is constructed by combining the feature vectors of user attributes and the feature vectors of user network structure. In the third stage, the trusted anchor data is reconstructed. In the final stage, the trained model is used for anchor link prediction.

3.1 Feature Representation

There are three types of data in social networks: network structure, user text, and photos or videos posted by users. The data of different forms are different in structure and are characterized by high-dimensionality and complexity. Traditional feature representation methods (such as adjacency matrix, one-hot vector, etc.) are difficult to deal with. Therefore, how to extract multiple features and uniformly express them have become a pressing problem to be solved. We select two main features for link prediction: network structure and user attributes.

Feature Representation of Network Structure. Network embedding is used to extract the characteristics of the network structure so that we can reconstruct the network structure. By reconstructing the network, the correlation between users can be captured. Node2vec [10] can learn the homogeneity and structural equivalence of nodes. Therefore, it can capture the potential relationship between users and construct the feature vector of the network structure. In order to obtain a richer and deeper representation of structural features, in node2vec, we adopted a flexible neighborhood sampling strategy [11]. Different sampling strategies will result in different feature representations. Similarly, the goal of node embedding is to maximize the logarithmic probability of sampled node neighbors, that is, to maximize the probability of the nearest neighbor of a given node. The formula is:

$$\max_{f} \sum_{n \in V} \log \Pr(V_s(v)|f(v)) \tag{1}$$

where V is the set of nodes and $f : V \longrightarrow \mathbb{R}^d$ denotes a mapping function. $V_s(v) \in V$ is the neighbor set of node v obtained by sampling strategy S.

Feature Representation of User Attributes. The user attributes and network structure of social networks belong to different characteristic spaces. In order to obtain a unified form of the two features, the user attribute features are extracted through the skip-gram model and converted into low-dimensional vectors. Traditional text embedding methods include VSM and a heat vector. The former is prone to dimensional disasters when expressing a large amount of text, while the latter simply ignores the semantic correlation between words. In contrast, the skip-gram model can map high-dimensional, sparse words to low-dimensional, dense word vectors, and can directly calculate the semantic correlation between words. In this article, the skip-gram model represents user attribute information as a low-dimensional vector, and then mines user attribute characteristics.

3.2 Feature Fusion

After the feature embedding in Sect. 3.1, the network structure space and user attribute space, which are in different forms, have been vectorized. Based on the characteristics of these two aspects, the problem to be solved is how to integrate these two characteristics into a unified form for subsequent modeling and anchor link prediction tasks. Associative with attention mechanism can help the model assign different weights to each attribute, extract more critical information from the attributes, and make more accurate prediction. Moreover, considering that CNN has the ability to capture local features, and can also effectively reduce the computational complexity and the over-fitting problem through the weight sharing and pooling. We have added an attention layer between the input layer and the convolution layer, which selectively considers information about the user's attributes in the input vector. As shown in Fig. 1, the model consists of an input layer, an attention layer, a convolution layer, a feature fusion layer, a pooling layer, a fully connected layer, and an output layer.

3.3   Trusted Anchor Reconstruction

Mislabeling caused by human factors or the irrationality of the design of the augmentation algorithm may introduce noise in the anchor data set. Anchor supervision data containing noise is used to train the model, which will inevitably lead to poor model training effect. Therefore, in this section, we have determined the credibility of all anchors and reconstructed the trusted anchor data set.

Algorithm 1: Anchor link prediction algorithm.

Input: Social networks G^S and G^T ; Anchor links set β; Hyperparameter ξ;
Iteration Γ

Output: Node fusion representation set Ψ_f; Candidate set δ

1 **for** i=1; i $\leq$ β.lenth; i = i+1 **do**
2   Sample a pair of anchor nodes (p, q) from β;
3   Learn the fusion vectors V_p and V_q of p and q ;
4   Calculate the similarity Θ of V_p and V_q by Eq.(2);
5   **if** Θ $<\xi$ **then**
6   update β
7 **end for**
8 Randomly initialize parameter
9 Set epoch, batchsize;
10 Choose kernel size of filter, kernel size of pooling;
11 **for** training data
12 Feed the sample batch of V into CNN for forward propagation;
13 Compute results of Ψ_f from 3.2;
14 Calculate the candidate set $\delta \in G^T$ for each node $\in G^S$;
15 **end for**
16 **repeat**
17   Update parameter by gradient descent algorithm;
18 **until** convergence;
19 **for** test data
20   Get future anchor links from 3.4;
21 **end for**

We use the network structure and user attributes in Sect. 3.1 to obtain the vector of anchor nodes. The similarity between a pair of anchor nodes is converted into a calculation of the similarity between these vectors. Generally speaking, the higher the similarity between the two anchor nodes, the stronger the credibility; on the contrary, low similarity indicates lower credibility. Given any pair of anchor nodes a_i and a_j, whose vectors are $v(a_i)$ and $v(a_j)$, we use the cosine of the angle between the two vectors to measure the similarity between the two nodes.

$$sim(a_i, a_j) = \cos\theta = \frac{\nu(a_i) \times \nu(a_j)}{\nu(a_i) \cdot \nu(a_j)} = \frac{\sum_i^d x_i \cdot y_i}{\sqrt{\sum_i^d x_i} \cdot \sqrt{\sum_i^d y_i}} \qquad (2)$$

where d is the dimension of the vector, x_i and y_i represent the components of $v(a_i)$ and $v(a_j)$, respectively. For each pair of anchor links (a_i, a_j) in A, we first calculate their similarity by the above formula. Then, the untrusted anchors in the anchor data set are eliminated by setting a threshold value and the trusted anchor data set A' is rebuilt for subsequent model training.

3.4 Anchor Link Prediction

For anchor link prediction, we first map the fusion vector of the nodes in the source network and the target network obtained in Sect. 3.2 to a common potential space through the projection function, and then use the trusted anchor link reconstructed in Sect. 3.3 to align the two networks. Finally, the similarity between nodes is calculated by Eq. (2). Obviously, it is more likely that there will be anchor links between more similar nodes in the common potential space. Therefore, for each user in the network G^S, we can find the most relevant user in the network G^T as an anchor candidate. We summarize our algorithm in Algorithm 1.

4 Experiments and Analysis

In this section, detailed experimental settings will be introduced. First of all, we will briefly introduce the data used in the experiment. Next, several baseline methods used for comparison in the experiment are described in detail. Finally, we give several evaluation indicators to evaluate the performance of the model and analyze the experimental results.

4.1 Datasets

For performance evaluation, we employ two real-world social network datasets collected from Foursquare and Twitter [12]. Among them, Twitter contains 5,220 users and 164,916 edges (relationships), Foursquare contains 5,315 users and 76,972 edges (relationships), and there are 1,609 anchor links between the two networks, as shown in Table 1. The ground truth of anchors are provided in Foursquare profiles.

Table 1. Statistics of the datasets used for evaluation.

Network	#Users	#Relations	#Anchor
Twitter	5220	164919	1609
Foursquare	5315	76972	

4.2 Evaluation Metrics

To perform the user identity linkage, we utilize standard metrics [13] $Precision@k(P@k)$ as our evaluation metrics. $Precision@k$ evaluates the linking accuracy, and is defined as:

$$P@k = \sum_i^n 1_i\{success@k\}/n \qquad (3)$$

where $1_i\{success@k\}$ measures whether the positive matching identity exists in $top-k(k <= n)$ list, and n is the number of testing anchor nodes.

4.3 Baselines and Settings

To evaluate the performance of our approach for anchor link prediction, we choose the following baseline models for comparison, including:

- MAG [14]: MAG uses manifold alignment on graph to map users across networks. The dataset Twitter-Foursquare used in MAG is the same as that in our paper. Since the source code of the paper was not published, we tried to reproduce it, so in our paper, there may be some gaps between the reported experimental results and the original results.
- IONE [15]: IONE predicts anchor links by learning the follower-ship embedding and followee-ship embedding of a user simultaneously. However, they did not consider the impact of anchor noise.
- DeepLink [9]: DeepLink is a method used for ALP tasks. The algorithm uses unbiased random walks to generate embedding, and then uses MLP to map users. Similar to MAG, we tried to reproduce its source code, so in our paper, even without considering anchor noise, there may be some gaps between the reported experimental results and the original text.
- HAN [16]: HAN is a GAT-based network embedding model. HAN uses the attention of the vertex level and the attention of the semantic level to learn the importance of the vertex and meta-path respectively, so HAN can capture the complex structural information and rich semantic information of heterogeneous graphs.
- PME [17]: PME constructs the embedding of nodes and relationships in the node space and the relationship space respectively, rather than mapping the embedding of nodes and relationships into the same space. Moreover, it projects various types of links into different subspaces, and finally obtains the overall embedding vector of each node. In this article, we only consider one type of link.

Note that we all use the optimal parameter settings in the original paper for experiments, and we conduct ten experiments on all models separately, and then record their average performance.

To fully demonstrate the effectiveness of our proposed model, we conduct the following experiments: i) Noise anchors with different ratios $N(N = $

Table 2. The P@30 performance of each model under different anchor noise ratios.

Noise(%)	0	10	20	30	40	50	60	70	80	90	100
MAG	32.18	22.62	20.90	19.33	19.89	18.65	16.92	15.05	13.89	12.64	11.56
IONE	60.44	44.12	41.64	38.01	36.48	35.77	33.78	34.03	32.79	31.54	30.88
DeepLink	70.48	53.77	48.63	44.76	43.18	40.48	38.82	36.85	34.52	33.79	31.24
HAN	78.33	62.92	59.91	57.11	56.00	54.91	52.95	51.14	50.09	48.81	48.24
PME	80.95	66.28	64.88	61.61	58.72	54.35	52.51	51.70	49.83	48.79	47.53
ours	**85.17**	**83.90**	**81.24**	**79.28**	**76.57**	**75.06**	**73.73**	**71.94**	**70.42**	**69.75**	**69.03**

$0, 0.1, 0.2, ..., 1)$ are added to the original dataset to compare the changes of P@30 of each model. The specific method of adding anchor noise is as follows: randomly extract one user account from each of the social networks Twitter and Foursquare (these accounts do not belong to the anchor node set) to form a new pair of "anchor" and add them to the anchor data set. As shown in Table 1, there are 5220 users in Twitter and 5315 users in Foursquare. On this basis, the data set is re-divided and the accuracy changes of each model are tested. The results are shown in Table 2.; ii) $P@K(K = 1, 5, 10, 15, 20, 25, 30)$ were studied under the conditions of no noisy anchors, 50% noisy anchors, and 100% noisy anchors, respectively. The results are shown in Fig. 2.

4.4 Analysis of Experimental Results

From the experimental results of the model, it can be seen that with the increase of the proportion of anchor noise, the accuracy of all models is decreasing, and when the anchor noise is first added, the degree of impact on the comparative model is most obvious. This is because anchor noise is directly added to the supervisory data, and the model does not consider the impact of anchor noise, and then all anchor data is used as supervisory data to train the model, resulting in a rapid decline in the predictive power of the model. The reason why the method proposed in this paper is not significantly affected is that before training the model, we first verify the credibility of the input anchor data set, and through the similarity comparison, some of the noise anchors in the data set are removed. In addition, the accuracy of the model we proposed decreases the slowest, which shows that the model has the strongest resistance to anchor noise, that is, the strongest robustness.

Figure 2(a) shows the performance of each model without adding any anchor noise. It can be seen that even without adding any anchor noise, our method still achieves the highest prediction accuracy, which shows that some accurately marked anchors may also have a negative impact on the model. The reason is that the nodes at both ends of these anchors have large differences in attributes and structure in different social platforms, resulting in a low degree of similarity in the representations they learn. Figure 2(b) and Fig. 2(c) show the performance of each model after adding 50% and 100% random noise anchors to the original social network data, respectively. It is not difficult to see that our model performs optimally whether under 50% noisy supervision or 100% noisy supervision.

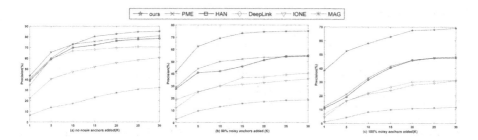

Fig. 2. The performance of each model at $P@K$ with different noise ratios.

We found that with the addition of 100% anchor noise, the P@30 accuracy rate of each model decreased significantly. Among them, the anchor link prediction accuracy of MAG, IONE and DeepLink decreased significantly by 64%, 49% and 56%, respectively, while HAN and PME also decreased by 38% and 41%, respectively, while our method only decreased by 19%. The reason why the accuracy of our model will decrease as the anchor noise is added may be that the node attributes and structure similarity of the introduced random anchor noise are high, which makes our strategy unable to filter it out from the anchor data set. However, even with the addition of 100% random anchor noise, our model can still achieve 69% accuracy, once again proving the effectiveness of our proposed model.

5 Conclusion

In this paper, we propose a new framework that can simultaneously complete the identification of trusted anchors and the prediction of anchor links across social networks under a unified framework. As far as we know from our research, there is no relevant work to conduct in-depth research on the credibility of anchor links. For the first time, we divided the supervised data set used to infer anchor links into trusted anchor links and non-trusted anchor links, and gave specific definitions, hoping to bring some inspiration to relevant researchers. Compared with several state-of-the-art methods, extensive experiments on real social network data sets have proved the effectiveness and efficiency of the proposed method. Future work includes expanding it to multiple networks and exploring its applicability to other types of networks.

Acknowledgment. This work is supported by the National Key R&D Plan project of China (2021YFB3100600), the Youth Innovation Promotion Association, Chinese Academy of Sciences (No.2020163) and the Strategic Pilot Science and Technology Project of Chinese Academy of Sciences (XDC02040400). We thank all authors for their contributions and all anonymous reviewers for their constructive comments.

References

1. Deng, Z., Sang, J., Xu, C.: Personalized video recommendation based on cross-platform user modeling. In: ICME (2013)
2. Iofciu, T., Fankhauser, P., Abel, F., Bischoff, K.: Identifying users across social tagging systems. In: ICWSM 2011 (2011)
3. Novak, J., Raghavan, P., Tomkins, A.: Anti-aliasing on the web. In: WWW 2004 (2004)
4. Narayanan, A., Shmatikov, V.: Myths and fallacies of personally identifiable information. Commun. ACM **53**, 24–26 (2010)
5. Tang, J., Chang, Y., Liu, H.: Mining social media with social theories: a survey. ACM SIGKDD Explor. Newsl. **15**, 20–29 (2014)
6. Goga, O., Loiseau, P., Sommer, R., Teixeira, R., Gummadi, K.P.: On the reliability of profile matching across large online social networks. In: KDD (2015)
7. Shang, Y., et al.: PAAE: a unified framework for predicting anchor links with adversarial embedding. In: The IEEE International Conference on Multimedia and Expo (ICME), pp. 682–687 (2019)
8. Cheng, A., et al.: Deep active learning for anchor user prediction. In: Proceedings of the International Joint Conference on Artificial Intelligence (IJCAI), pp. 2151–2157 (2019)
9. Zhou, F., Liu, L., Zhang, K., Trajcevski, G., Wu, J., Zhong, T.: DeepLink: a deep learning approach for user identity linkage. In: 2018 IEEE Conference on Computer Communications, INFOCOM 2018, Honolulu, HI, USA, 16–19 April 2018 (2018)
10. Grover, A., Leskovec, J.: Node2vec: scalable feature learning for networks. In: Proceedings of the 22nd ACM SIGKDD International Conference on Knowledge Discovery and Data Mining, pp. 855–864. ACM (2016)
11. Xiao, Y., Li, R., Lu, X., et al.: Link prediction based on feature representation and fusion. Inf. Sci. **548**, 1–17 (2021)
12. Zhang, J., Yu, P.S.: Integrated anchor and social link predictions across social networks. In: Proceedings of the Twenty-Fourth International Joint Conference on Artificial Intelligence, Buenos Aires, Argentina (2015)
13. Shu, K., Wang, S., Tang, J., Zafarani, R., Liu, H.: User identity linkage across online social networks: a review. ACM SIGKDD Explor. Newsl. **18**(2), 5–17 (2017)
14. Tan, S., Guan, Z., Cai, D., Qin, X., Bu, J., Chen, C.: Mapping users across networks by manifold alignment on hypergraph. In: Proceedings of the Twenty-Eighth AAAI Conference on Artificial Intelligence, Québec City, Québec, Canada, 27–31 July 2014, pp. 159–165 (2014)
15. Liu, L., Cheung, W.K., Li, X., Liao, L.: Aligning users across social networks using network embedding. In: Proceedings of the Twenty-Fifth International Joint Conference on Artificial Intelligence, IJCAI 2016, New York, NY, USA, 9–15 July 2016, pp. 1774–1780 (2016)
16. Wang, X., et al.: Heterogeneous graph attention network. In: The World Wide Web Conference, WWW 2019, San Francisco, CA, USA, 13–17 May 2019, pp. 2022–2032 (2019)
17. Chen, H., Yin, H., Wang, W., Wang, H., Nguyen, Q.V.H., Li, X.: PME: projected metric embedding on heterogeneous networks for link prediction. In: Proceedings of the 24th ACM SIGKDD International Conference on Knowledge Discovery and Data Mining, KDD 2018, London, UK, 19–23 August 2018, pp. 1177–1186 (2018)

Application of Data Encryption in Chinese Named Entity Recognition

Jikun Dong[1], Kaifang Long[1], Hui Yu[2], and Weizhi Xu[1,3(✉)]

[1] School of Information Science and Engineering,
Shandong Normal University, Jinan, China
2021020969@stu.sdnu.edu.cn, xuweizhi@sdnu.edu.cn
[2] Business School, Shandong Normal University, Jinan, China
[3] Shandong Provincial Key Laboratory for Novel Distributed Computer Software
Technology, Jinan 250358, China

Abstract. Recently, with the continuous development of deep learning, there has been a significant improvement in the performance of named entity recognition tasks. However, privacy and confidentiality concerns in specific fields, such as biomedical and military, limit the availability of data for training deep neural networks. To address the issues of data leakage and the disclosure of sensitive data in these domains, we propose an encryption learning framework. For the first time, we employ multiple encryption algorithms to encrypt the training data in the named entity recognition task, training the deep neural network with the encrypted data. Our experiments, conducted on six Chinese datasets, including three self-constructed datasets, demonstrate that the encryption method achieves satisfactory results. In fact, the performance of some models trained with encrypted data even surpasses that of the unencrypted method, highlighting the effectiveness of the introduced encryption method and partially resolving the problem of data leakage.

Keywords: Chinese named entity recognition · Data encryption · Privacy protection · Natural language processing · Deep neural networks

1 Introduction

Named entity recognition (NER) [1] is an important task in natural language processing (NLP) that identifies useful entities in unstructured text. Deep learning achieves state-of-the-art performance for many NER tasks. However, many datasets used for training the deep learning model contain sensitive information. For example, datasets in the biomedical field usually consist of electronic medical records, which generally include identification information, disease information and treatment plans for patients. Many people or groups worry about the leakage of their private data and are unwilling to disclose it. Therefore, data scarcity is severe in many fields for model training. Most enterprises face problems such as limited data and poor data quality, which hinder the implementation of artificial intelligence (AI) technology. To address the aforementioned problem, federated learning [2] emerged.

However, federated learning has some shortcomings. For example, 1) Data is not centralized. 2) Unstable connections between networks cannot be foreseen or avoided. If a network disconnects, the learning process may time out or exit abnormally. 3) The federated learning system requires multi-party collaboration, leading to issues such as limited model flexibility for users, slow training speed, and high hardware requirements for model training. 4) While federated learning has found application in some practical business scenarios, its large-scale implementation is still distant. To address these challenges, we propose a deep learning framework for the NER task based on multiple data encryptions. Our framework overcomes certain limitations of federated learning and provides improved privacy protection.

Chinese, as an important international language, possesses unique characteristics. The Chinese language, culture, and history are attracting increasing international attention and study. However, there is a scarcity of datasets related to Chinese history in the CNER field. The absence of data and applications presents challenges for scholars who are new to the study of Chinese history and for constructing knowledge graphs in the field. Building upon the aforementioned points, we have developed a new dataset for Chinese history.

Furthermore, we conduct experiments employing various encryption methods on six datasets encompassing biomedicine, news, and history domains. The experiments demonstrate that the performance of the encrypted data is satisfactory. This provides evidence that our approach ensures the accuracy of the deep learning models and mitigates data leakage to a certain extent. Our primary contributions are as follows.

- We introduce hash algorithms and the ciphertext policy attribute-based encryption (CP-ABE) to CNER for the first time. Experiments on six datasets show that our proposed multi-encryption strategy can ensure the performance of the model and protect the data to some degree.
- We have an interesting finding that the performance does not degrade significantly when encrypting the training data for the CNER task.
- We release a new history dataset for CNER. It provides a foundation for recognizing identities from historical documents and building knowledge graphs.

2   Related Work

2.1   Named Entity Recognition

NER aims to rapidly extract entity information of specific types from intricate natural language texts, laying the groundwork for information extraction and structured data generation. The initial approaches to NER encompassed rule-based methods, lexicon-based methods, and statistical machine learning-based methods, including the Support Vector Machine Model (SVM) [3], Hidden

Markov Model (HMM) [4], Conditional Random Field (CRF) [5], among others. Nevertheless, these methods faced challenges related to feature engineering and fell short of attaining the desired NER outcomes.

With the advancement of AI, various neural network approaches have been employed to tackle NER, yielding promising results. During this period, researchers predominantly utilized LSTM-CRF or CNN-CRF models for feature encoding and decoding [6, 7]. However, these methods encountered certain limitations. Firstly, character-based methods neglect the utilization of dictionary information. Secondly, word-based methods can suffer from error propagation resulting from word segmentation errors.

Accordingly, Zhang and Yang [8] introduced a character-word-based hybrid model, which effectively integrates word information into the character-level input sequence. This integration leads to enhanced performance in the NER task. Consequently, many researchers have derived numerous models based on this approach. For instance, Liu et al. [9] proposed the WC-LSTM model, Gui et al. [10] proposed the LR-CNN model, and Ma et al. [11] introduced the Softword method. Ding et al. [12] utilized graph neural networks to improve NER performance. It is widely recognized that NER tasks heavily rely on word embeddings, as the quality of these embeddings significantly impacts the model's performance. The introduction of dynamic word embeddings, such as BERT, has propelled NER performance to new heights. For example, Li et al. [13] developed the FLAT model, while Mengge et al. [14] proposed the Porous Lattice Transformer Encoder based on Lattice LSTM, leveraging the benefits of dynamic word embeddings.

2.2 Data Protection

NER introduces data protection [15] to prevent unauthorized access and disclosure of private information in datasets. This paper addresses data leakage by implementing data desensitization and access control strategies. Data desensitization involves reducing sensitivity and minimizing the risk of leakage through techniques like data replacement, randomization, encryption, and hash transformation. In our study, we utilized hash transformation for data desensitization in the NER dataset. Access control, on the other hand, establishes security rules or policies for users to access and decrypt encrypted data based on permissions or attributes, ensuring authorized access to sensitive information.

3 Method

To prevent unauthorized access and data leakage while enabling users to construct machine learning models according to their specific needs, we propose an NER framework that utilizes multi-encrypted data to address the aforementioned issue. As depicted in Fig. 1, the framework comprises three steps. In the first step, the data provider encrypts the original data using hash algorithms. The second step involves utilizing Ciphertext Policy Attribute-Based Encryption

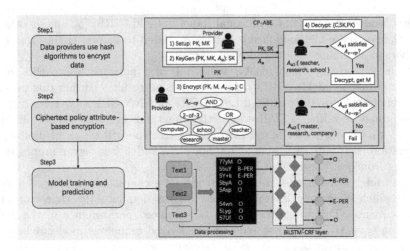

Fig. 1. The overall architecture of the proposed method.

(CP-ABE) based on hash encryption to achieve double-layered data protection, thereby resolving the issue of unauthorized access to the data. In the third step, training and prediction of the model are conducted by legitimate users after obtaining access to the data.

3.1   Data Encryption

Hash functions are utilized to encrypt the data within our model framework, as depicted in Fig. 1. To ensure the authenticity and integrity of the encrypted data during training and to employ multiple encryption methods on the same data, we additionally introduce the Serial Cipher and Base64 methods, in addition to hash functions [16].

Serial Cipher is a symmetric cryptographic algorithm that encrypts plaintext by combining it with a key. Due to its simplicity and fast encryption speed, we view Serial Cipher as an optional data encryption method. Additionally, the coefficients can be adjusted to align Caesar Cipher and Affine Cipher with Serial Cipher, allowing us to categorize these three encryption algorithms together.

Base64 is a widely recognized encoding method for network transmission, specifically designed for 8-bit byte codes. Although it violates encryption key confidentiality, Base64 encoding transforms text data into an unreadable format, providing a way to ensure encryption integrity and enabling multiple encryptions.

The MD5 and SHA-256 algorithms are widely used hash functions in computer security. They convert data of different lengths into fixed values, ensuring dataset security. In our experiment, to demonstrate the feasibility of multiple encryptions on the same data, we use the Base64 algorithm along with the SHA-256 algorithm for encryption.

3.2 CP-ABE

Traditional attribute-based encryption (ABE) [17] systems characterize cipher-texts using attributes and incorporate the access policy within the user's key. Attributes represent characteristics of objects or information files, while the policy is a logical expression composed of attributes and their relationships. CP-ABE [18] employs attributes to depict user eligibility. The data provider formulates the policy for acquiring the ciphertext to determine who can decrypt it. In other words, the attributes are incorporated into the key, while the policy is embedded within the ciphertext.

In Fig. 1, the data provider initializes a public key (PK) and a master key (MK). Using the PK, MK, and user's attribute set (Au), a private key (SK) is generated. An access control policy (Ac-cp) is then constructed based on the user's attributes. Utilizing the PK and the plaintext M (encrypted with the hash algorithm in the figure), a ciphertext (C) is generated according to the access control policy. Finally, the user can decrypt the data using the public and private keys. If the user's attributes are valid, the ciphertext can be successfully deciphered; otherwise, decryption is not possible.

3.3 Model Training and Prediction

As illustrated in the lower right corner of Fig. 1, this section outlines the process by which users train and make predictions using the model on the encrypted dataset. Firstly, the authorized user adheres to the CP-ABE protocol and decrypts the data, utilizing the ciphertext, public key, and private key provided by the data provider, resulting in three data files. Text1 represents the ciphertext encrypted using the hash algorithm, Text2 represents the corresponding label text, and Text3 denotes the length of each sequence in the ciphertext. Based on these three texts, users can obtain the complete training data. If users wish to evaluate the model's performance using their own data, they can encrypt the data using the same hash algorithm mentioned in Text1 prior to making predictions.

Due to the ongoing exploration by researchers, neural networks have experienced rapid development. Li et al. [19] made significant improvements in the performance of biomedical NER through the utilization of recurrent neural networks. Furthermore, the application of deep neural networks, including convolutional neural networks, self-attention mechanisms, and transformers [20,21], has effectively advanced the development of NER. Consequently, users can construct models based on the aforementioned deep neural networks once they acquire encrypted data. In this study, we employ the classical BiLSTM-CRF model as a benchmark. BiLSTM consists of a forget gate, an input gate, and an output gate. These three gate mechanisms interact and update the cell state. The specific formulas are provided below.

$$F^T = \sigma \left(W_\alpha^F X^T + W_\beta^F H^{T-1} + B_F \right) \tag{1}$$

$$I^T = \sigma \left(W_\alpha^I X^T + W_\beta^I H^{T-1} + B_I \right) \tag{2}$$

$$O^T = \sigma \left(W_\alpha^O X^T + W_\beta^O H^{T-1} + B_O \right) \qquad (3)$$

$$\tilde{C}^T = Tanh \left(W_\alpha^C X^T + W_\beta^C H^{T-1} + B_C \right) \qquad (4)$$

$$C^T = F^T \odot C^{T-1} + I^T \odot \tilde{C}^T \qquad (5)$$

$$H^T = O^T \odot Tanh \left(C^T \right) \qquad (6)$$

Here, F^T represents the information that the cell state will forget. I^T and O^T denote the input and output gates, respectively. $\tilde{C}^T$ denotes the current cell state and C^T denotes the final cell state. Where W is the hyperparameter and H denotes the output of the hidden state.

We utilize a CRF [22] to impose constraints on tag transitions following the encoding layer. As depicted in Fig. 2, B-L represents the beginning of a location, I-L represents the middle of a location, and E-L represents the end of a location. S-L indicates a single-entity location, while O denotes a non-entity. Based on the figure, we enforce the following constraints: O cannot transition to I-L and E-L. B-L cannot transition to B-L, S-L, and O. I-L cannot transition to B-L, S-L, and O. E-L cannot transition to E-L and I-L.

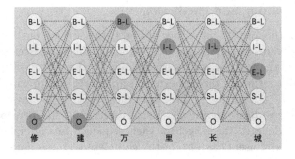

Fig. 2. Label state transitions of conditional random fields in NER.

4   Datasets

This paper aims to compare the model performance before and after data encryption. We utilize six Chinese NER datasets, namely CCKS2017, Resume, MSRA, and History, to validate the authenticity and effectiveness of the experiments. The Table 1 presents the number of sentences and words in each dataset.

CCKS2017 is a clinical medicine NER dataset released by the China Conference on Knowledge Graph and Semantic Computing. Due to the relatively large scale of the CCKS2017 dataset, we partitioned it into a test set, development set, and training set. Resume and MSRA are sourced from social media and news, while the History dataset originates from the field of Chinese history.

Currently, Chinese has emerged as a significant international language. To address the scarcity of historical datasets in the Chinese NER domain, we developed a novel dataset (referred to as History in Table 1). As depicted in Table 2, our dataset encompassed nine label types, which included organization name (ORG), place name (LOC), time (DAT), person name (PER), salutation (POS), official position (APP), book name (EVE), army name (ORGARM), and place of belonging (LOCPER). Additionally, we partitioned the historical dataset into three categories to distinguish specific entities. The first category, named History-9types, comprises nine tag types. The second category, History-3types, includes LOC, APP, and EVE entities. The third category, History-2types, consists solely of PER and POS entities.

Table 1. Statistics of datasets

Datasets	Type	Train	Dev	Test
Resume	Char	124.4K	13.9K	15.1K
	Sent	3.8K	0.46K	0.48K
MSRA	Char	2169.9K	–	172.6K
	Sent	46.4K	–	4.4K
CCKS2017	Char	200.0K	31.8K	33.6K
	Sent	5.9K	0.82K	1.09K
History	Char	289.1K	30.9K	29.9K
	Sent	8.9K	0.97K	0.81K

Table 2. The number of nine entities on the train, dev, and test sets.

	ORGARM	LOC	DAT	ORG	PER
Train	1202	4321	1510	3934	8618
Dev	215	578	179	426	829
Test	212	603	311	396	507
	LOCPER	EVE	POS	APP	–
Train	231	383	3169	834	–
Dev	34	19	441	111	–
Test	32	64	216	118	–

5 Experiments

5.1 Baseline Methods

In this section, we use four models proposed in recent years to verify the effectiveness of encryption algorithms.

BiLSTM-CRF. BiLSTM-CRF [23] was proposed by Lample et al., which is a classical model in NER. Compared with the traditional machine learning models, it shows a dramatic enhancement in performance.

WC-LSTM. WC-LSTM (2019) [9] is a word-character-based model proposed by Liu et al. for addressing the shortcomings of Lattice LSTM.

Multi-digraph Model. Multi-digraph (2019) [12] is a model proposed by modifying the gated graph neural network (GGNN), which can effectively integrate word information into characters.

SoftLexicon. SoftLexicon (2020) [11] is a novel approach to utilizing dictionary information proposed by Ma et al. Its encoding framework is very flexible and can enormously improve the performance of entity recognition.

5.2 Implement Details and Evaluation Metrics

During training, our implement details follow the baseline models. In addition, we use precision (P), recall (R) and F1 score (F1) to evaluate the performance of our model.

Table 3. Performance on three public datasets

Model	CCKS2017			Resume			MSRA		
	P	R	F1	P	R	F1	P	R	F1
LSTM-CRF	88.45	87.35	87.90	**93.73**	93.44	93.58	89.52	**87.41**	88.45
+ Serial Cipher	**89.25**	87.13	**88.18**	93.53	93.13	93.33	89.10	87.25	88.16
+Base64	88.66	87.11	87.88	93.68	93.62	**93.65**	**89.74**	87.34	**88.53**
+MD5	89.21	86.96	88.07	93.46	**93.80**	93.63	89.68	87.18	88.41
+Has256-Base64	87.74	**87.48**	87.61	93.50	93.56	93.53	88.14	86.19	87.15
WC-LSTM	88.96	87.33	88.14	95.14	**94.79**	94.96	**93.67**	**92.20**	**92.93**
+ Serial Cipher	**90.55**	86.14	88.29	**95.36**	94.66	**95.01**	93.66	92.02	92.83
+Base64	89.59	**87.38**	**88.47**	93.64	93.87	93.75	89.33	87.58	88.45
+MD5	89.43	87.33	88.37	93.65	94.05	93.85	88.81	86.92	87.86
+Has256-Base64	88.96	87.21	88.08	93.57	93.74	93.66	90.23	87.34	88.76
Multi-digraph	89.50	88.40	88.94	94.62	94.97	94.79	90.82	**91.20**	91.01
+ Serial Cipher	88.43	86.01	87.20	**95.04**	**95.28**	**95.16**	88.21	85.73	86.95
+Base64	**89.66**	88.86	**89.26**	94.44	94.91	94.68	91.30	90.68	90.99
+MD5	89.22	88.94	89.08	94.37	94.66	94.52	90.54	87.19	88.83
+Has256-Base64	88.73	**89.18**	88.95	94.74	95.03	94.89	**91.38**	90.86	**91.12**
SoftLexicon	89.67	87.23	88.43	95.30	**95.77**	**95.53**	**93.72**	**91.88**	**92.79**
+ Serial Cipher	90.08	**88.34**	**89.20**	95.48	94.66	95.07	88.42	84.32	86.32
+Base64	89.74	86.89	88.29	94.25	93.50	93.87	88.44	84.63	86.49
+MD5	**90.52**	86.98	88.72	**95.50**	94.97	95.23	88.23	84.52	86.33
+Has256-Base64	90.46	86.42	88.39	95.26	94.97	95.12	87.83	84.68	86.23

5.3 Overall Performances

Table 3 presents the results obtained from three public datasets: CCKS2017, Resume, and MSRA. Table 3 displays the results of four distinct models. The initial experiment involves training and prediction using plaintext, while the subsequent four experiments involve training and prediction using ciphertext. The ciphertext is encrypted using the following methods: Serical Cipher, Base64, MD5, and Has256-Base64. For CCKS2017 and Resume, some results obtained from the ciphertext training methods even outperform those obtained from the plaintext training method. For the MSRA dataset, when training on Has256-Base64 encrypted data using Multi-digraph, the P and F1 exhibit improvements of 0.56% and 0.11% respectively, compared to the plaintext training method. The performance degradation is almost negligible when training on LSTM-CRF. However, the experimental performance degradation observed for WC-LSTM and SoftLexicon models may stem from the under-utilization of lexical knowledge by the encryption methods and the lack of development sets.

Table 4 presents the results obtained from the History dataset. The table demonstrates that the performance of the four encryption algorithms, when trained with the LSTM-CRF model, shows minimal degradation compared to the unencrypted data. Furthermore, certain encryption algorithms even outperform the unencrypted data. For instance, the Has256-Base64 encryption algorithm improves the P by 1.19% and 2.60% on the History-9types and History-2types datasets, respectively, compared to the unencrypted data. The serial encryption algorithms result in a 0.79% improvement in P, and the MD5 encryption algorithms yield a 1.78% improvement in R on the History-3types dataset. Training the WC-LSTM model with Serial Cipher encrypted data results in a 0.89% increase in R compared to the unencrypted dataset on the History-3types dataset. Furthermore, P, R, and F1 are 2.28%, 0.55%, and 1.20% higher, respectively, than the unencrypted data on the History-2types dataset. Training the Multi-digraph model with the Base64 algorithm results in a 3.11% increase in P and a 1.27% increase in F1 compared to the unencrypted data on the History-9types dataset. However, when trained with the SoftLexicon model, we observe a significant decrease in the effectiveness of the encryption algorithm. This is due to the SoftLexicon model deviating from the conventional use of vocabulary knowledge, resulting in poor performance.

Table 4. Performance on History datasets

Model	History-9types			History-3types			History-2types		
	P	*R*	*F1*	*P*	*R*	*F1*	*P*	*R*	*F1*
LSTM-CRF	76.01	**60.68**	**67.48**	76.15	50.45	**60.69**	72.40	**60.58**	**65.96**
+ Serial Cipher	76.04	60.27	67.24	**76.94**	49.36	60.09	71.32	52.97	60.79
+Base64	76.06	60.59	67.45	73.60	51.85	60.84	72.14	60.17	65.61
+MD5	76.88	59.90	67.34	72.18	**52.23**	60.61	73.18	58.51	65.03
+Has256-Base64	**77.20**	59.90	67.46	74.25	50.32	59.98	**75.00**	57.68	65.21
WC-LSTM	**82.43**	**68.48**	**74.81**	**83.19**	61.15	70.48	82.45	62.38	71.02
+ Serial Cipher	82.30	68.08	74.52	81.99	**62.04**	**70.63**	**84.73**	**62.93**	**72.22**
+Base64	77.84	61.12	68.47	73.02	51.72	60.55	73.47	61.27	66.82
+MD5	76.27	62.10	68.46	72.99	51.94	60.71	74.15	60.30	66.51
+Has256-Base64	76.67	61.61	68.32	75.57	50.45	60.50	72.50	61.27	66.42
Multi-digraph	75.31	71.70	73.46	**76.14**	59.36	**66.71**	75.31	76.35	**75.82**
+ Serial Cipher	77.24	68.73	72.74	69.54	61.66	65.36	71.54	**77.18**	74.25
+Base64	78.42	71.37	**74.73**	69.06	**62.55**	65.64	74.90	75.52	75.21
+MD5	75.79	**71.82**	73.75	69.79	60.64	64.89	**76.23**	70.54	73.28
+Has256-Base64	**78.66**	63.42	70.22	73.87	60.51	66.53	75.46	74.00	74.72
SoftLexicon	**82.65**	**70.11**	**75.86**	82.47	**67.13**	**74.02**	85.71	**73.03**	**78.86**
+ Serial Cipher	80.31	66.33	72.65	82.23	63.06	71.38	82.30	71.37	76.44
+Base64	73.00	52.99	61.40	73.36	51.85	60.76	71.99	56.15	63.09
+MD5	75.26	58.28	65.69	73.01	54.87	62.59	79.62	63.21	70.47
+Has256-Base64	75.24	57.83	65.39	74.43	53.76	62.43	76.97	64.73	70.32

5.4 Analysis

Performance Analysis. To fully illustrate the effectiveness of our experiments, we analyze the performance on the CCKS2017 dataset and the History-9types dataset.

In Fig. 3, we compare the P, R, and F1 of the LSTM-CRF model with and without encryption. The first value on the abscissa represents the results obtained when training the LSTM-CRF model on unencrypted data, while the last four values represent the results obtained by using four different encryption algorithms on the LSTM-CRF model. From subfigure (a) in Fig. 3, it is evident that using Serial Cipher and MD5 encryption on the LSTM-CRF model yields higher performance compared to no encryption. Additionally, from subfigure (b) in Fig. 3, it can be observed that the encrypted data has no significant impact on the accuracy of the model.

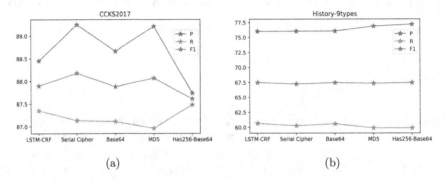

(a)   (b)

Fig. 3. Comparison of P, R and F1 on the LSTM-CRF model with four encryption algorithms and without encryption.

Security Analysis. This paper utilizes hash functions and CP-ABE to ensure data security. The hash functions possess characteristics such as weak collision resistance, strong collision resistance, and resistance to modification. The most significant feature of hash functions is their irreversibility, making it difficult for users to decrypt the plaintext, thereby ensuring data security to a great extent. Furthermore, additional encryption can be applied on top of hash encryption to enhance security, such as using Has256-Base64. Lastly, CP-ABE is employed to ensure the legitimacy of users who obtain the ciphertext generated by other encryption methods. CP-ABE relies on the computational difficulty of discrete logarithms, making it challenging for unauthorized users, proxy servers, and other entities to access the data. Based on the aforementioned analysis, the feasibility and security of our framework can be ensured.

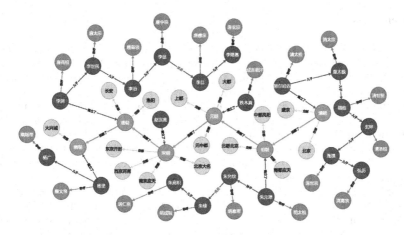

Fig. 4. Diagram of the relationship of partial entities in the History dataset.

5.5   Relations Between Entities

We train a NER model using a dataset of Chinese historical texts to enhance its performance in downstream tasks, specifically accurate identification of entities in unstructured text. Figure 4 illustrates a simplified knowledge graph constructed by extracting partial entity types from the text using the model.

The red nodes represent Chinese dynasties, including the Qing Dynasty, Ming Dynasty, and Tang Dynasty. The red edges denote transitions between dynasties, such as the Qing Dynasty overthrowing the Ming Dynasty and the Tang Dynasty overthrowing the Sui Dynasty. The yellow nodes represent the capital cities of each dynasty. Due to capital city migration, a red node may have connections to multiple yellow nodes. Black nodes describe the leaders of the countries, while black edges indicate father-son or brother relationships. Green nodes represent aliases of emperors.

6   Conclusion

This paper introduces the use of hash algorithms and CP-ABE in the NER task for the first time. This method effectively addresses the issue of data leakage in specific domains. In addition, we introduce a novel dataset to address the scarcity of historical datasets. Our experiments on six datasets validate the effectiveness of our method in achieving satisfactory results. Moreover, future work can focus on enhancing experimental performance by training BERT models using encrypted data.

Acknowledgements. This work was supported in part by Natural Science Foundation of Shandong Province (No. ZR2022MF328 and No. ZR2019LZH014), and in part by National Natural Science Foundation of China (No. 61602284 and No. 61602285).

References

1. Sang, E.F., De Meulder, F.: Introduction to the CoNLL-2003 shared task: language-independent named entity recognition. arXiv preprint cs/0306050 (2003)
2. Liu, Y., Kang, Y., Xing, C., Chen, T., Yang, Q.: A secure federated transfer learning framework. IEEE Intell. Syst. **35**(4), 70–82 (2020)
3. Habib, M.S., Kalita, J.: Language and domain-independent named entity recognition: experiment using SVM and high-dimensional features. In: Proceedings of the 4th Biotechnology and Bioinformatics Symposium, p. 2007 (2007)
4. Zhou, G., Su, J.: Named entity recognition using an HMM-based chunk tagger. In: Proceedings of the 40th Annual Meeting of the Association for Computational Linguistics, pp. 473–480 (2002)
5. Sobhana, N., Mitra, P., Ghosh, S.K.: Conditional random field based named entity recognition in geological text. Int. J. Comput. Appl. **1**(3), 143–147 (2010)
6. Wu, F., Liu, J., Wu, C., Huang, Y., Xie, X.: Neural Chinese named entity recognition via CNN-LSTM-CRF and joint training with word segmentation. In: The World Wide Web Conference, pp. 3342–3348 (2019)
7. Huang, Z., Xu, W., Yu, K.: Bidirectional LSTM-CRF models for sequence tagging. arXiv preprint arXiv:1508.01991 (2015)
8. Zhang, Y., Yang, J.: Chinese NER using lattice LSTM. In: Proceedings of the 56th Annual Meeting of the Association for Computational Linguistics, pp. 1554–1564 (2018)
9. Liu, W., Xu, T., Xu, Q., Song, J., Zu, Y.: An encoding strategy based word-character LSTM for Chinese NER. In: Proceedings of the 2019 Conference of the North American Chapter of the Association for Computational Linguistics: Human Language Technologies, pp. 2379–2389 (2019)
10. Gui, T., Ma, R., Zhang, Q., Zhao, L., Jiang, Y.G., Huang, X.: CNN-based Chinese NER with lexicon rethinking. In: IJCAI, pp. 4982–4988 (2019)
11. Ma, R., Peng, M., Zhang, Q., Huang, X.: Simplify the usage of lexicon in Chinese NER. In: Proceedings of the 58th Annual Meeting of the Association for Computational Linguistics, pp. 5951–5960 (2020)
12. Ding, R., Xie, P., Zhang, X., Lu, W., Li, L., Si, L.: A neural multi-digraph model for Chinese NER with gazetteers. In: Proceedings of the 57th Annual Meeting of the Association for Computational Linguistics, pp. 1462–1467 (2019)
13. Li, X., Yan, H., Qiu, X., Huang, X.J.: FLAT: Chinese NER using flat-lattice transformer. In: Proceedings of the 58th Annual Meeting of the Association for Computational Linguistics, pp. 6836–6842 (2020)
14. Mengge, X., Yu, B., Liu, T., Zhang, Y., Meng, E., Wang, B.: Porous lattice transformer encoder for Chinese NER. In: Proceedings of the 28th International Conference on Computational Linguistics, pp. 3831–3841 (2020)
15. Sivakumar, T.K., Sheela, T., Kumar, R., Ganesan, K.: Enhanced secure data encryption standard (ES-DES) algorithm using extended substitution box (S-Box). Int. J. Appl. Eng. Res. **12**(21), 11365–11373 (2017)
16. Stinson, D.R., Paterson, M.: Cryptography: Theory and Practice. CRC Press (2018)
17. Goyal, V., Pandey, O., Sahai, A., Waters, B.: Attribute-based encryption for fine-grained access control of encrypted data. In: Proceedings of the 13th ACM Conference on Computer and Communications Security, pp. 89–98 (2006)
18. Wan, Z., Deng, R.H.: HASBE: a hierarchical attribute-based solution for flexible and scalable access control in cloud computing. IEEE Trans. Inf. Forensics Secur. **7**(2), 743–754 (2011)

19. Li, L., Xu, W., Yu, H.: Character-level neural network model based on Nadam optimization and its application in clinical concept extraction. Neurocomputing **414**, 182–190 (2020)

20. Vaswani, A., et al.: Attention is all you need. In: Advances in Neural Information Processing Systems, pp. 5998–6008 (2017)

21. Sun, M., Wang, L., Sheng, T., He, Z., Huang, Y.: Chinese named entity recognition using the improved transformer encoder and the lexicon adapter. In: Pimenidis, E., Angelov, P., Jayne, C., Papaleonidas, A., Aydin, M. (eds.) ICANN 2022. LNCS, vol. 13530, pp. 197–208. Springer, Cham (2022). https://doi.org/10.1007/978-3-031-15931-2_17

22. Forney, G.D.: The Viterbi algorithm. Proc. IEEE **61**(3), 268–278 (1973)

23. Lample, G., Ballesteros, M., Subramanian, S., Kawakami, K., Dyer, C.: Neural architectures for named entity recognition. In: Proceedings of NAACL-HLT, pp. 260–270 (2016)

Attractor Dynamics Drive Flexible Timing in Birdsong

Fjola Hyseni[1,2(✉)] ⓘ, Nicolas P. Rougier[1,2,3] ⓘ, and Arthur Leblois[1] ⓘ

[1] CNRS, IMN, UMR 5293, 33000 Bordeaux, France
fjola.hyseni@u-bordeaux.fr
[2] LaBRI, Université de Bordeaux, Talence, France
[3] Inria Bordeaux Sud-Ouest, Talence, France

Abstract. Timing is a critical component of a wide range of sensorimotor tasks that can span from a few milliseconds up to several minutes. While it is assumed that there exist several distributed systems that are dedicated for production and perception [1], the neuronal mechanisms underlying precise timing remain unclear. Here, we are interested in the neural mechanisms of sub-second timing with millisecond precision. To this end, we study the control of song timing in male Zebra Finches whose song production relies on the tight coordination of vocal muscles. There, the premotor nucleus HVC (proper name) is responsible for the precise control of timing. Current models of HVC rely on the synfire chain, a pure feed-forward network. However, synfire chains are fragile regarding noise and are only functional for a narrow range of feed-forward weights, requiring fine tuning during learning. In the present work, we propose that HVC can be modelled using a ring attractor model [2], where recurrent connections allow the formation of an activity bump that remains stable across a wide range of weights and different levels of noise. In the case of asymmetrical connectivity, the bump of activity can "move" across the network, hence providing precise timing. We explore the plasticity of syllable duration in this framework using a reward-driven learning paradigm and a reward-modulated covariance learning rule applied to the network's synaptic weights [3]. We show that the change in duration induced by the learning paradigm is specific to the target syllable, consistent with experimental data.

Keywords: Timing · Songbirds · Attractor

1 Introduction

Timing is crucial for a wide range of sensorimotor tasks. However, there are numerous uncertainties regarding the underlying mechanisms. For instance, sensory and motor timing may or may not rely on the same circuitry, there could be different mechanisms for different scales of timing (subsecond, suprasecond etc.) and it can be considered as a dedicated or intrinsic system [4,5]. In this study, we focus on motor timing at the scale of tens to hundreds of milliseconds.

L. Iliadis et al. (Eds.): ICANN 2023, LNCS 14261, pp. 112–123, 2023.
https://doi.org/10.1007/978-3-031-44198-1_10

Addressing this question has led to the design of several computational models such as ramping models, internal clocks, population clocks, labeled-line models and multiple-oscillator models [6,7]. Ramping model-like patterns of activity during timing tasks [8–10] have been observed in multiple brain areas, but it is unclear whether they are indeed timekeepers or whether they reflect motor preparation instead. On the other hand, internal clocks provide a linear readout of time, assuming the presence of a pacemaker-integrator system, the location of which remains unclear [7]. Lastly, population clock models assume that time is encoded in the dynamically changing population of neurons, but have the limitation of lacking an intrinsic metric of time. They are, however, well suited for pattern timing underlying speech and birdsong.

Birdsong relies on the tight coordination of vocal muscles with a precise timing at the scale of tens to hundreds of milliseconds. In songbirds, a localized timing area has been identified in the premotor nucleus HVC (proper name). HVC projects to a downstream motor nucleus controlling syringeal and respiratory muscles. Neurons in HVC projecting to downstream motor nucleus fire in a time-locked manner during singing, producing a single 10 ms long burst of 3–6 spikes [11]. Manipulating HVC temperature modifies song duration, with a dilation and song stretching when HVC is cooled [12], supporting the hypothesis of HVC as a population clock model.

The dynamics of neuronal activity in the nucleus HVC of songbirds have been previously modelled with networks of excitatory neurons organized in a sequentially connected chain of neuronal populations, referred to as *synfire chain* [13], belonging to the class of population clocks. However, the purely feedforwad connectivity pattern of synfire chains does not appear compatible with the connectivity patterns revealed experimentally in cortical networks. More specifically, unidirectional connectivity between groups of neurons is incompatible with the high level of reciprocal connectivity typically observed in cortex [14]. Additionally, synfire chain networks are sensitive to noise and not very robust to weight variability, requiring very precisely tuned synaptic strengths to avoid runaway excitation or decay.

An alternative hypothesis is that the gradual propagation of an activity bump is driven in HVC by attractor dynamics. In particular, a linear attractor, also referred to as ring attractor, can drive a drifting activity bump with robust and resilient properties thanks to recurrent connections [2]. However, it remains unclear if the ring attractor can account for the properties of HVC neuronal dynamics and the behavioral adaptation of song timing. In previous studies [15,16], timing flexibility in motor timing in adult songbirds has been investigated, through targeting a syllable for modification using a Conditional Auditory Feedback (CAF) protocol (based on reinforcement learning). The results showed that birds can change the targeted element of their stereotyped song with specificity, i.e. with no effect on other syllables. Upon confrontation of these results with three modelling approaches, only synfire chains and not attractors, could account for specificity in adaptive learning. Conversely, we propose and provide evidence that a structured attractor, such as the ring attractor, can simulate adaptive learning and provide results consistent with behavioral data.

2   Methods

2.1   Ring Attractor

We first consider a neural population of 1000 units whose mean firing rate is expressed as $m(x,t)$ with x being the position ($[-\pi/2, \pi/2[$) over a closed one-dimensional manifold (ring, with period π) and t representing time. The evolution of $m(x,t)$ is governed by equation:

$$\tau\frac{d}{dt}m(x,t) = -m(x,t) + G(I_{ext}(x,t) + I_{syn}(x,t) - T + \sqrt{\tau_n}\sigma_n\eta(x,t)), \quad (1)$$

where τ is the neuronal membrane time constant. On the right hand side (rhs) of Eq. (1), I_{ext} is the external constant input, I_{syn} the synaptic input and T represents the threshold. The last rhs term is a zero-mean Gaussian white noise. For the nonlinear gain function $G(I)$, the simple semi-linear form is adopted:

$$G(I) = \begin{cases} 0 & I < 0 \\ I & 0 < I < 1 \\ 1 & I > 1 \end{cases} \quad (2)$$

We use the following expression for the synaptic input:

$$I_{syn}(x,t) = \sum_{x'=1}^{N} \frac{1}{N}W(x-x')m(x',t), \quad (3)$$

where $\sum_{x'=1}^{N}$ denotes a summation over all neuronal indices. The weight matrix W is choosen of the following form:

$$W(x-x') = W_0 + W_2\frac{1}{\sigma\sqrt{2\pi}}e^{-\left(\frac{x-x'+\beta}{2\sigma}\right)^2}, \quad (4)$$

where W is defined based on the neurons' preferred timing (see Fig. 1(A)) and not on the spatial topology, as HVC microcircuitry does not display spatio-temporal organization (see Fig. 1(B)). The parameter W_0 stands for the global inhibition, W_2 the excitation factor, σ the standard deviation and β is the bias term which makes the connectivity pattern asymmetric.

2.2   Implementing a Reward-Covariance Reinforcement Learning Rule

Equations of the learning rule are implemented based on a reward-covariance learning rule [3], to adaptively change W:

$$\Delta W_{ij} = \gamma Re_{ij} \qquad \text{with} \quad e_{ij} = \int_0^t \frac{dt'}{\tau_e}e^{-(t-t')/\tau_e}\eta_i(t')m_j(t'), \quad (5)$$

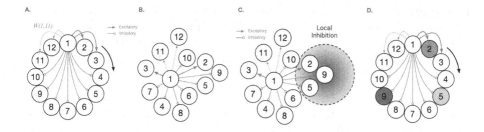

Fig. 1. Simplified illustration of the ring connectivity and consequences of local inhibition. (A) The connectivity is represented using the preferred timing as a neighbourhood proxy for the placement of neurons. (B) The same connectivity is represented using the physical location of neurons. (C) Injection of a local inhibition in nucleus HVC. (D) The same local inhibition shown when neurons are ordered according to their preferred timing. In this spatial representation, the effect is not local, but rather distributed, which makes the network more robust.

j and i represent the pre- and postsynaptic neurons, respectively. The learning rate γ is chosen to match learning rates observed in songbirds experiments, R the reward value and e_{ij} the eligibility trace, τ_e is the eligibility time constant, η_i the noise of the postsynaptic and m_j the rate of the presynaptic neuron. R takes a value of 0 or 1, when the syllable is targeted for modification and 0 when it is not. At the end of each learning trial, a reward of 1 is given if the targeted syllable duration is lower (higher) than the updated target duration. This paradigm is based on the one introduced in [16], where $I^{(tar)}$ denotes the current duration of the syllable, and $\bar{I}^{(tar)}$ represents the running average of the target syllable duration, which is updated after every trial according to the following:

$$\bar{I}^{(tar)} \leftarrow 0.995\bar{I}^{(tar)} + 0.005I^{(tar)}, \tag{6}$$

across the 1000 learning trials. Additionally, prior to learning, we run 50 trials with no reinforcement to determine a baseline distribution of syllables. Following learning, we run 50 more trials without reinforcement and with the updated weight matrix W ($W_{initial} + \Delta W$). Significant change between these two duration distributions is determined by performing independent t-tests.

2.3 Analysis

The quality of the model is evaluated regarding several objectives.

– The speed of the bump, which acts as a proxy for the accuracy of the timing,
– the mean syllable duration when noise is present, and
– the capacity for the model to shorten or lengthen a syllable duration without interferring with others.

Bump Speed. At any time, the position $C(t)$ of the bump of activity can be measured using the center of mass (COM) of the whole population, based on equations for COM in systems with periodic boundary conditions. This center $C(t)$ is further discretized into $\bar{C}(t)$ such as to coincide with the nearest unit position:

$$\bar{C}(t) = argmin_i(C(t) - x_i). \tag{7}$$

The speed of the bump is then computed as the displacement (in the neuronal feature space) of the center of mass over time.

Syllable Definition and Duration. A syllable corresponds to a fixed segment of the ring. Mean syllable length in zebra finches has been reported to be 110 ± 56 ms [17]. We choose a syllable duration close to the mean reported value and for simplification, we chose equal size segments such that for s syllables and n neurons, syllable i is defined by $[\frac{i}{s}n, \frac{i+1}{s}n]$. Syllable duration is then measured from when the center of the activity bump $\hat{C}(t)$ crossed the lower limit of the segment up to when it crossed the upper limit of the segment.

Simulation. All simulations were performed using Euler integration with a timestep (dt) of 0.25 ms. Multiple runs were performed to identify an appropriate (high enough) value for dt that does not alter the outcome. Parameter values for the simulations are detailed in Table 1.

Table 1. Values of the parameters used in Eqs. (1)–(5).

Parameters	Values	Parameters	Values
N (number of neurons)	1000	T (threshold)	0.9
dt (timestep)	0.25 ms	W_0	−5
duration	2 s	W_2	7
τ (membrane time constant)	10 ms	β (bias in the weight matrix)	0.05
I_{ext} (external constant input)	1.1	σ (Eq. (4))	0.067
τ_{noise} (time constant of the noise)	1 ms	σ_{noise}	0.01
γ (learning rate)	0.004	τ_e (eligibility trace time constant)	35 ms

3   Results

In the ring attractor model, recurrent connections allow for the formation of an activity bump that remains stable across a wide range of weights. In the presence of a fully symmetric connectivity and a constant stimulus, the activity bump settles in one of the stationary states and remains there until another input or a high enough perturbation is exerted. However, since the purpose of this model is to generate a sequential activity, we investigate how propagation across these states can be achieved.

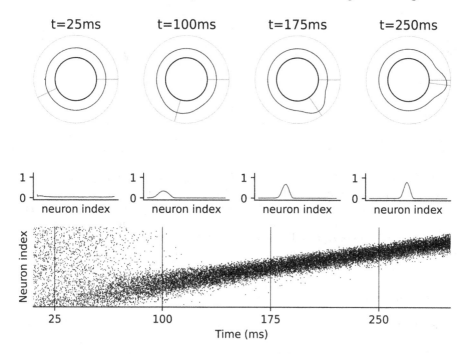

Fig. 2. Activity propagation in the ring. The first two panels show the position of the bump of activity (normalized firing rate) in the network at a particular point in time. The third panel serves to present the possible spiking pattern this rate network would be compatible with. They were generated using a homogenous Poisson process.

3.1 Moving Bump

Three ways to ensure bump propagation have been identified. These include an external drive in the form of a moving stimulus, adaptation and an asymmetric connectivity profile. In the case of a moving stimulus, the velocity/speed of this stimulus has a linear relationship with the speed of the bump.

Intrinsic Drive: Adaptation and Bias. Adaptation [2] can make the bump move by generating a local, strong, delayed negative feedback, and hence suppressing localized activity. This causes higher activity in the nearby unadapted region. Moreover, making the connectivity pattern asymmetric by adding a bias also ensures bump propagation. The activity bump's center of mass encodes time such that at time $t(x)$, neuron x is maximally activated and as it moves across the network different neurons will be more active at different points in time (Fig. 2). The magnitude of the bias also exhibits a quasi-linear relationship with bump speed, such as the higher the bias, which assures the feedforwardness of the network, the higher the speed of movement of the bump (Fig. 3). The rest of the presented results is for the asymmetric connectivity profile.

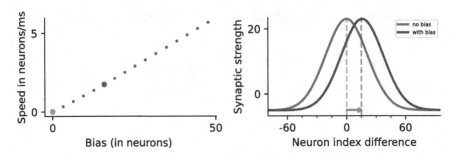

Fig. 3. An asymmetric connectivity pattern makes the bump of activity move across the network. (A) The speed of the bump is driven by the amplitude of the bias. This is a quasi-linear relationship. (B) Connectivity profile for each presynaptic neuron to the postsynaptic neurons with no bias and bias. (Neuron index difference = *presynaptic − postsynaptic*) This bias is the one we use for the rest of the results presented. Self-connections are set to 0 but not illustrated in the figure.

3.2   Robustness

We design a test protocol to evaluate the robustness of the network under possible biological perturbations. We simulate the local injection of a drug inducing the inhibition of neuronal activity (e.g. Muscimol) with an effect that spreads spatially according to a Gaussian spatial distribution into the network, as shown in Fig. 1(C, D). The formula of diffusion of the inhibitory substance is that of a Gaussian distribution and it is added to the main equation as an external inhibitory input:

$$I_i = \alpha \frac{1}{\sigma\sqrt{2\pi}} e^{-\frac{1}{2}\left(\frac{x-\mu}{\sigma}\right)^2}.$$

We test distributions with different spatial widths (σ) or amplitudes (α). We show that the perturbation is diminished across time and, if not too high, there is no disruption in sequence generation and the speed of the bump is conserved. This allows us to make a prediction for the HVC behavior in presence of such inhibition. More precisely, this would mimic inhibition with a GABA-A agonist, Muscimol in HVC and the prediction states that there will only be a delay in the initiation of the sequence (song), but no further disruption as shown in Fig. 4, meaning the timing accuracy would be sustained.

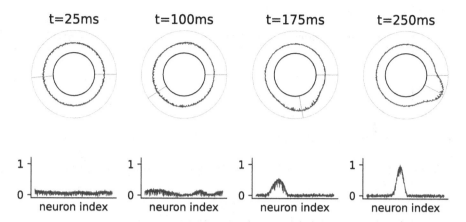

Fig. 4. Influence of a local inhibition. A local inhibition in the model (i.e. an inhibition that only affects a distributed sub-population) induces a delay in the initial formation of the bump even though the model can recover after tens of milliseconds. After this initial delay, the timing is correct.

3.3 Local Plasticity and Comparison with Experimental Data

To validate the model and to address the second question of whether the ring attractor is able to give account for experimental evidence witnessed in the CAF protocol [16], we use a reward covariance rule [3] for the conditioning. Consistent with behavioral data, the duration of a syllable can be modified in response to a perturbed reward profile (Fig. 5) and this change is specific to the target syllable. No interference was present in adjacent or non-adjacent syllables, both in the case of targeting for a duration increase or decrease (Fig. 6).

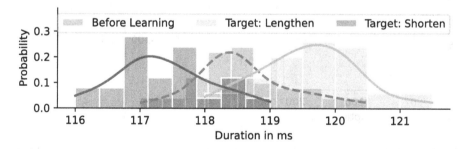

Fig. 5. Syllable duration distribution before and after reinforcement learning (for decrease, increase) of the targeted syllable.

The change in synaptic weights (ΔW), driving the change in syllable duration, is illustrated in Fig. 7. For instance, when the duration is targeted for shortening, connections from the presynaptic neurons to the postsynaptic neurons prior (neuron 450 to 500) are weakened and the ones to the postsynaptic

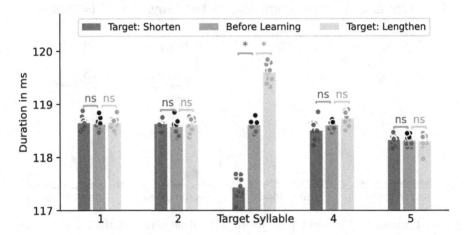

Fig. 6. Adaptive learning is specific to the targeted syllables. 10 runs (of 1000 trials) of learning, aiming to achieve syllable duration reduction (red)/ increase (blue) are run. Baseline mean duration is in gray. For each of the 10 runs in the three conditions, a mean duration is computed from the duration distribution; these are shown as points in the bar plot. Hence, the bars represent the mean duration across the 10 runs. * stands for p < 0.001. Only the target syllable is significantly affected after reinforcement learning. (Color figure online)

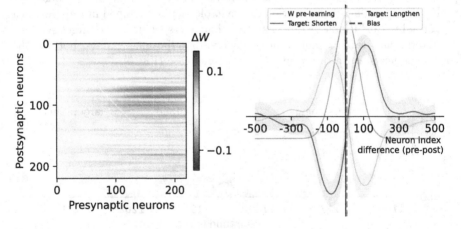

Fig. 7. How do the weights change to achieve specific adaptive learning? On the left: ΔW of a single run (target: decrease syllable duration), zoomed in at the area of pre and post-synaptic neurons encoding the target syllable. On the right: the change in synaptic weights across 10 runs of learning with respect to the presynaptic neurons encoding the target syllable, both when the target is reducing (red) the duration and increasing (blue) it. The thicker line represents the mean across runs and the filled in area the SD extracted from the means across the postsynaptic neurons of the ΔW for each of the 10 runs. (Color figure online)

ahead (neuron 500 to 550) are strengthened, changing slightly the slope of the bump and making it move faster in that area (defined by the presynaptic neurons).

4   Discussion and Conclusion

Attractor dynamics have been used to model a wide range of cognitive processes including memory representation, sequence generation, decision making, integration etc. [18]. A group of criteria have been proposed to claim possible attractor dynamics in different networks in the brain. HVC activity corresponds to the sequence generation category, and abides at least 4 out of 5 of these criteria, namely: i) Possession of a low-dimensional set of states that correspond to attractors in the state space (a one dimensional output in HVC) [11]. ii) Robustness to perturbation and return to the low-dimensional state after it. Electrical stimulation [19] in HVC perturbs song timing, but once removed, it is quickly restored. iii) Invariance and persistence of the states over time, in particular across states. In adult zebra finches, even in the absence of HVC main inputs [20,21], HVC neuronal activity underlying song production persists. Moreover, HVC singing-related activity can be evoked outside singing, e.g. during sleep [21]. iv) Isometry [22]. The fifth condition, pertaining to anatomical and structural correlates, remains to be studied and investigated further. However, there are three reasons that make us speculate it may be true as well. First, based on the resulting HVC dynamics, the underlying pattern could include reciprocal connectivity and relies on stronger connectivity between neurons firing at the same time in song. Secondly, as a local circuit encoding motor timing, HVC is expected to rely on regimes with strong internal connections capable of self-sustained activity [7]. Thirdly, evidence from mammalian visual cortex show that neurons with similar tuning, exhibit stronger connections.

As an attractor, the resulting model is robust to noise and weight variability. Moreover, it is compatible with HVC's sparse coding and exhibits specific learning, consistent with experimental findings. It is also able to derive an experimental prediction regarding possible neural dynamics in the HVC, in the presence of a local GABA-A agonist (Muscimol), which remain to be tested. However, the duration of the burst of activity observed in HVC in zebra finches (approx 10 ms) can only be reproduced with artificially short neuronal time constants (1 ms) in the rate model exposed here. For a more accurate representation of the spiking dynamics in the network and a short-duration burst of activity spreading across the nucleus, it may be necessary to model the network with spiking neurons, e.g. using leaky integrators and relying on adaptation to minimize burst duration [23].

Some observations in the ring attractor lead to important questions in the songbird literature. For instance, activity propagation is possible not only through an asymmetric connectivity, but also adaptation, which is an intrinsic neuronal property. In this setting, we question whether the timing in birdsong is intrinsic (i.e. coming from adaptation) or a combination of intrinsic and experience based factors (bias) [24,25]. Furthermore, the connectivity pattern may be learned through sensory (auditory) stimulation of the nucleus during the sensory period of learning as HVC neurons can respond to auditory stimulation and may display mirror-like activity pattern during singing and auditory stimulation [26]. However, it still remains an open question.

Finally, songbirds are also known for being a good model for the neural mechanisms of vocal production in humans [27]. Therefore, similar neural mechanisms may underlie speech and song timing control. The dynamics of cortical neurons driving speech production may thus also be accurately represented by the present model.

References

1. Hazeltine, E., Helmuth, L.L., Ivry, R.B.: Neural mechanisms of timing. Trends Cogn. Sci. **1**(5), 163–169 (1997). https://doi.org/10.1016/s1364-6613(97)01058-9
2. Hansel, D., Sompolinsky, H.: Modeling feature selectivity in local cortical circuits. Book Chapter (1998)
3. Williams, R.: Simple statistical gradient-following algorithms for connectionist reinforcement learning. Mach. Learn. **8**, 229–256 (1992). https://doi.org/10.1007/BF00992696
4. Robbe, D.: Lost in time: rethinking duration estimation outside the brain. PsyArXiv (2021). https://doi.org/10.31234/osf.io/3bcfy
5. Ivry, R., Schlerf, J.: Dedicated and intrinsic models of time perception. Trends Cogn. Sci. **12**(7), 273–80 (2008). https://doi.org/10.1016/j.tics.2008.04.002
6. Goel, A., Buonomano, D.V.: Timing as an intrinsic property of neural networks: evidence from in vivo and in vitro experiments. Philos. Trans. R. Soc. B: Biol. Sci. **369**(1637), 20120460 (2014). https://doi.org/10.1098/rstb.2012.0460
7. Buonomano, D.V., Laje, R.: Population clocks: motor timing with neural dynamics. Trends Cogn. Sci. **14**(12), 520–527 (2010). https://doi.org/10.1016/j.tics.2010.09.002
8. Durstewitz, D.: Self-organizing neural integrator predicts interval times through climbing activity. J. Neurosci. **23**, 5342–5353 (2003). https://doi.org/10.1523/JNEUROSCI.23-12-05342
9. Simen, P., Balci, F., Souza, L., Cohen, J., Holmes, P.: A model of interval timing by neural integration. J. Neurosci. Official J. Soc. Neurosci. **31**, 9238–9253 (2011). https://doi.org/10.1523/JNEUROSCI.3121-10.2011
10. Balci, F., Simen, P.: A decision model of timing. Curr. Opinion Behav. Sci. **8**, 94–101 (2016). https://doi.org/10.1016/j.cobeha.2016.02.002
11. Hahnloser, R., Kozhevnikov, A., Fee, M.: An ultra-sparse code underlies the generation of neural sequences in a songbird. Nature **419**, 65–70 (2002). https://doi.org/10.1038/nature00974
12. Long, M., Jin, D., Fee, M.: Support for a synaptic chain model of neuronal sequence generation. Nature **468**, 394–399 (2010). https://doi.org/10.1038/nature09514
13. Jin, D., Ramazanoğlu, F., Seung, H.: Intrinsic bursting enhances the robustness of a neural network model of sequence generation by avian brain area HVC. J. Comput. Neurosci. **23**, 283–299 (2007)
14. Perin, R., Berger, T.K., Markram, H.: A synaptic organizing principle for cortical neuronal groups. PNAS **108**, 5419–5424 (2011). https://doi.org/10.1073/pnas.1016051108

15. Ali, F., Otchy, T.M., Pehlevan, C., Fantana, A.L., Burak, Y., Ölveczky, B.P.: The basal ganglia is necessary for learning spectral, but not temporal, features of birdsong. Neuron **80**(2), 494–506 (2013). https://doi.org/10.1016/j.neuron.2013.07.049

16. Pehlevan, C., Ali, F., Ölveczky, B.: Flexibility in motor timing constrains the topology and dynamics of pattern generator circuits. Nat. Commun. **9**, 977 (2018). https://doi.org/10.1038/s41467-018-03261-5

17. Glaze, C.M., Troye, T.W.: Temporal structure in zebra finch song: implications for motor coding. J. Neurosci. **26**, 991–1005 (2006). https://doi.org/10.1523/JNEUROSCI.3387-05.2006

18. Khona, M., Fiete, I.: Attractor and integrator networks in the brain. Nat. Rev. Neurosci. **23**, 744–766 (2022). https://doi.org/10.1038/s41583-022-00642-0

19. Vu, E., Mazurek, M., Kuo, Y.: Identification of a forebrain motor programming network for the learned song of zebra finches. J. Neurosci. **14**, 6924–6934 (1994). https://doi.org/10.1523/JNEUROSCI.14-11-06924.1994

20. Naie, K., Hahnloser, R.: Regulation of learned vocal behavior by an auditory motor cortical nucleus in juvenile zebra finches. J. Neurophysiol. **106**, 291–300 (2011). https://doi.org/10.1152/jn.01035.2010

21. Elmaleh, M., Kranz, D., Asensio, A., Moll, F., Long, M.: Sleep replay reveals premotor circuit structure for a skilled behavior. Neuron **109**, 3851–3861 (2021). https://doi.org/10.1016/j.neuron.2021.09.021

22. Lynch, G., Okubo, T., Hanuschkin, A., Hahnloser, R., Fee, M.: Rhythmic continuous-time coding in the songbird analog of vocal motor cortex. Neuron **90**, 877–892 (2016). https://doi.org/10.1016/j.neuron.2016.04.021

23. Brette, R., Gerstner, W.: Adaptive exponential integrate-and-fire model as an effective description of neuronal activity. J. Neurophysiol. **94**, 3637–3642 (2005)

24. Fehér, O., Wang, H., Saar, S., Mitra, P.P., Tchernichovski, O.: De novo establishment of wild-type song culture in the zebra finch. Nature **459**, 564–568 (2009). https://doi.org/10.1038/nature07994

25. Araki, M., Bandi, M.M., Yazaki-Sugiyama, Y.: Mind the gap: neural coding of species identity in birdsong prosody. Science **354**, 1282–1287 (2016). https://doi.org/10.1126/science.aah6799

26. Prather, J., Peters, S., Nowicki, S., Mooney, R.: Precise auditory-vocal mirroring in neurons for learned vocal communication. Nature **451**, 305–310 (2008). https://doi.org/10.1038/nature06492

27. Prather, J., Okanoya, K., Bolhuis, J.: Brains for birds and babies: neural parallels between birdsong and speech acquisition. Neurosci. Biobehav. Rev. **81**, 225–237 (2017). https://doi.org/10.1016/j.neubiorev.2016.12.035

Boost Predominant Instrument Recognition Performance with MagiaSearch and MagiaClassifier

Hao Zhou[iD], Zhen Li[iD], Shusong Xing[iD], Zujun Gu[iD], and Binhui Wang[(✉)][iD]

College of Software, Nankai University, Tianjin, China
wangbh@mail.nankai.edu.cn

Abstract. The objective of this study is to overcome the performance limitations of existing instrument recognition systems in a cost-effective manner. Identifying predominant instruments accurately is a critical problem in music information retrieval, and it directly affects the performance of various advanced techniques. To address this, we propose a novel instrument recognition system that integrates a fast search technique, named MagiaSearch, to discover reliable SpecAugment parameters applicable to instrument recognition and a deep net classifier, named MagiaClassifier, which uses Swin Transformer V2 as the backbone model. Our experiments demonstrate that MagiaSearch effectively searches for reliable SpecAugment parameters applied to log mel spectrograms of instrument audio, MagiaClassifier enhances the performance of instrument recognition systems, and combining MagiaSearch and MagiaClassifier, we achieve a significant accuracy of 88.76% for major instrument recognition tasks in 11 categories in the IRMAS dataset.

Keywords: Musical Instruments Recognition · Deep Learning · SpecAugment

1 Introduction

Predominant musical instrument recognition aims to develop intelligent and automated classification systems that can accurately identify the primary musical instrument from polyphonic digital audio. This subproblem is critical in music information retrieval since it forms the foundation for several advanced techniques such as music source separation and music auto-tagging. To achieve reliable instrument recognition, it is necessary to develop robust algorithms that can effectively differentiate between different instruments based on their spectral characteristics.

In previous studies, numerous studies have explored instrument recognition from various perspectives. In traditional instrument classification, researchers typically use handcrafted acoustic features to train conventional machine learning models, as demonstrated in previous works such as [13]. In recent years,

L. Iliadis et al. (Eds.): ICANN 2023, LNCS 14261, pp. 124–136, 2023.
https://doi.org/10.1007/978-3-031-44198-1_11

however, the growing popularity of deep learning has led to the use of more complicated audio spectrograms for instrument classification research, as shown in studies such as [4,6,19], among others.

Despite these advancements, previous studies have been constrained by various factors, such as the limited representational capability of the backbone model, suboptimal parameters, and ineffective data augmentation methods. Improving the representational capacity of the backbone model is crucial to enhancing the system's performance. However, finding an optimal parameter search strategy for augmentation methods can be challenging.

In this study, we mainly analyze the selection of the backbone model, data augmentation methods and their parameter search strategies to improve the performance ceiling of the classification system. The Swin Transformer V2, based on a hierarchical self-attention mechanism, has achieved state-of-the-art performance on several image recognition benchmarks, as reported in [12], and is selected as the backbone model in this study to optimize the instrument classification system at the model structure level. We named this new instrument classifier MagiaClassifier.

Furthermore, we utilize SpecAugment, an advanced data augmentation technique in audio signal processing, and demonstrate its applicability in the instrument classification problem. We propose a novel and efficient method to determine the optimal parameters for SpecAugment on musical instrument audio spectrograms. Specifically, we introduced MagiaSearch, a fast search method that efficiently explores the parameter space in an approximate grid search manner using a reliable classifier, MagiaClassifier, and a set of reliable scoring methods. The scoring procedure only requires the forward inference process of deep neural networks and no backpropagation, making it both fast and economical. To evaluate the effectiveness of MagiaSearch, we compare its outcomes with those of other empirical and random parameter settings. Our experimental results demonstrate the effectiveness of MagiaSearch in determining the near-optimal parameters for SpecAugment in instrument recognition tasks.

The instrument recognition system we proposed integrates MagiaSearch and MagiaClassifier, achieving a remarkable classification accuracy of 88.76% on the prestigious IRMAS [1] dataset. We believe that our approach can lay the foundation for future research and contribute to the development of more accurate and efficient systems in the field of instrument recognition.

2   Related Work

In this study, we address the instrument recognition problem from three aspects: feature extraction strategy, classification model, and data augmentation. One of the most critical aspects of instrument classification is the selection of an appropriate feature extraction scheme [2]. Audio spectrograms are widely used for this purpose, including techniques such as MFCCs, log mel spectrograms and others. Early researchers, such as Eronen et al. [3], employed MFCC in music genre and instrument categorization tasks. Later, Deng et al. [2] demonstrated that the MFCCs feature scheme is more effective for classification than the MPEG-7 feature set (including harmonic centroid, harmonic deviation, harmonic spread, harmonic variation, spectral centroid, log-attack-time, and temporal centroid). More recent studies, such as those conducted by Xu et al. [21] and Wang et al. [20], have shown that log mel spectrograms offer superior performance for classification. Consequently, we use log mel spectrograms as the feature extraction method in this study.

In addition, the ability of the backbone model to represent features plays a significant role in the performance of musical instrument recognition systems. In the past, researchers addressed the challenges of instrument classification using machine learning models such as those developed by Martin et al. [14], Eronen et al. [15], and Marques et al. [13]. However, with the advent of deep learning, sequence models were introduced to model audio data by several researchers, such as Fanelli et al. [4]. In recent years, studies by Solanki et al. [19] and Saeed et al. [18] have utilized convolutional neural networks as their core models. Several studies have employed the UNet architecture for instrument recognition, including the work of Hung et al. [9]. Additionally, there are studies that have incorporated uncomplicated attentional mechanisms in instrument recognition, such as Gururani et al. [7]. With the growing popularity of self-attention mechanisms in sequence modeling, researchers have attempted to adopt the Transformer model as the backbone model for instrument classifiers, as demonstrated in the work by Gong et al. [6]. The Swin Transformer V2 is a visual transformer that differs from convolutional neural networks in that its basic building block is a self-attentive layer rather than a convolutional kernel. It has demonstrated exceptional performance on tasks such as image classification, object detection, and semantic segmentation of images. This study explores the potential of employing the Swin Transformer V2 as a backbone model for musical instrument categorization systems and attempts to migrate the Swin Transformer V2 to the field of musical instrument recognition.

Typically, researchers enhance the accuracy of classification results and the generalization ability of models by augmenting input features. SpecAugment [16] is a data augmentation technique specifically designed for spectral graphs. Studies have demonstrated that SpecAugment can mitigate model overfitting issues and significantly improve the performance of audio signal processing systems. Additionally, the computational cost of SpecAugment is relatively low, and this augmentation technique can be used online during model training. In their respective experiments, Zeyer et al. [22], Zhou et al. [23], and Gaido et al. [5] all utilized SpecAugment and achieved positive outcomes.

3   Methodology

Although SpecAugment has demonstrated superior performance in numerous studies, the instrument recognition field lacks well-defined rules and procedures for tuning its parameters. In that case this paper proposes MagiaSearch, a novel and efficient fast search scheme for SpecAugment parameters. Through

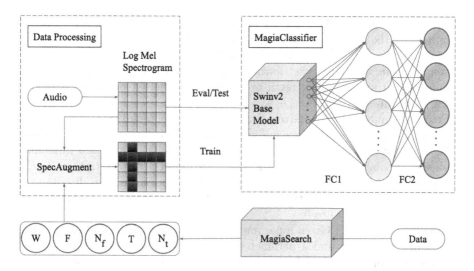

Fig. 1. The architecture of the proposed system, consisting of a Data Processing module, MagiaSearch, and MagiaClassifier.

the search results of MagiaSearch and our model MagiaClassifier, we achieve SOTA accuracy on IRMAS. Our proposed architecture consists of a data processing module, MagiaSearch, and MagiaClassifier, as illustrated in Fig. 1.

3.1 Data Processing

The IRMAS-TrainingData packet sourced from the IRMAS dataset is utilized as the experimental dataset in this paper. The dataset consists of audio recordings of 11 instruments, including vocals, with each sample possessing a duration of three seconds and corresponding to a predominant instrument type.

We use the log mel spectrogram as the input feature for the model. First, the Fourier transform is applied to a 3-second audio sample to determine the frequency distribution of signals inside the sample. The results of the Fourier transform are then concatenated along the time axis to produce a spectrogram. To be compatible with the human ear's perception of sound, we transform the Hz scale of the frequency axis of the spectrogram to the mel scale, and the amplitude indication are converted to decibel scale, resulting in a log mel spectrogram. Next, we normalize the log mel spectrogram to ensure that its values fall within the range of floating-point numbers, with a mean of 0 and a variance of 1.

After calculating log mel spectrograms with consistent parameters, we employed the SpecAugment data augmentation technique to augment the training set. Examples of a log mel spectrogram and the outcomes of its SpecAugment application can be found in [16]. Given a log mel spectrogram with a time step of τ and a number of mel frequency channels of ν, the SpecAugment for it consists of three parts:

- Time warping(TW). Given a parameter W such that $W \in [0, \tau]$, where W represents the upper bound of time warp length, we randomly select a time step w_0 from a uniform distribution on $(W, \tau - W)$, and select another time step w from a uniform distribution on $(-W, W)$, where w represents the number of time steps to stretch or compress to the left or right. Then, we warp the time step w_0 to $w_0 + w$.
- Frequency masking(FM). Given a parameter N_f representing the number of frequency masking operations and a parameter F such that $F \in [0, \nu]$, where F represents the upper bound of frequency masking length, we randomly select a frequency masking length f from a uniform distribution on $[0, F]$, and select a starting mel frequency channel f_0 from a uniform distribution on $[0, \nu - f)$. We then set the values of continuous mel frequency channels in the range $[f_0, f_0 + f)$ to 0.
- Time masking(TM). Given a parameter N_t representing the number of time masking operations and a parameter T such that $T \in [0, \tau]$, where T represents the upper bound of time masking length, we randomly select a time masking length t from a uniform distribution on $[0, T]$, and select a starting time step t_0 from a uniform distribution on $[0, \tau - t)$. We then set the values of continuous time steps in the range $[t_0, t_0 + t)$ to 0.

3.2   MagiaClassifier

In this study, we use the Base version of Swin Transformer V2 as the backbone model for our instrument classification system. To match the input features, the backbone model has a base resolution of 256×256 and is composed of 12 basic blocks, with a patch size of 4×4 and a self-attention window size of 8×8. The model is pre-trained on the ImageNet-1k dataset. To adapt the model for the task of Predominant Musical Instrument Recognition, we introduce a multilayer perceptron (MLP) after the last hidden layer of Swin Transformer V2. It is worth noting that the final linear layer of the MLP, which consists of two linear layers, contains the 11 output nodes that correspond to the 11 distinct instrument categories. The first linear layer of the MLP uses rectified linear unit (ReLU) activation, while the second layer employes softmax activation. This approach enables accurate categorization of instrument classes during model inference process, improving classification performance. Our proposed model architecture effectively integrates the strengths of Swin Transformer V2 with MLPs to achieve state-of-the-art performance in the task of Predominant Musical Instrument Recognition.

3.3   MagiaSearch

In recent years, it has become widely recognized that data augmentation plays a crucial role in enhancing the performance of deep learning models. In the field of instrument recognition, SpecAugment has demonstrated outstanding performance. The parameters of SpecAugment are critical factors that significantly influence its performance, however, a comprehensive evaluation of these parameters is noticeably lacking. To address this research gap, we propose an experimental scheme that systematically searches for the parameters of SpecAugment in the context of instrument recognition.

Although previous studies have not extensively explored the search for optimal SpecAugment parameters suitable for instrument recognition, the study by Hwang et al. [10] provides valuable references for exploring the parameter space for instrument recognition. Hwang et al. conducted a search experiment for the mel spectrogram augmentation parameter in speech recognition, utilizing a metric called the Deformation Per Deteriorating Ratio (DPD). DPD is defined as the ratio of the difference between the spectrogram deformation rate and the Character Error Rate (CER) of speech recognition.

However, our approach differs from Hwang et al. in terms of metrics. Specifically, we define Accuracy Deformation Per Deteriorating Ratio (ADPD) as the ratio of the difference between the spectral deformation rate and the decline in instrument recognition accuracy, along with a small constant to avoid division by zero in the denominator. The definition ADPD is shown in Eq. 1, where c is a small positive constant. We aim to find the SpecAugment parameter that is applicable to instrument identification by using this metric.

$$ADPD_{aug} = \frac{AD_{aug}}{|E_{aug} - E_{none}| + c} \tag{1}$$

In this study, we introduce a notation where the subscript aug represents the category of the augmentation subtechnique, AD_{aug} defines the spectral graphical variation rate for the augmentation subtechnique aug, E_{aug} denotes the expectation of the instrument recognition accuracy after applying the augmentation technique aug, and E_{none} denotes the expected instrument recognition accuracy before applying the augmentation subtechnique.

In sharp contrast to the methodology adopted by Hwang et al. [10], which employed the Google Speech API to evaluate CER, our objective is to investigate the recognition accuracy of musical instrument categories. To quantify the recognition accuracy, we employ Eq. 2, where N denotes the total number of samples, y_i denotes the ground truth label, and $\hat{y}_i$ denotes the predicted label obtained from the classifier. In particular, we utilize the MagiaClassifier to measure the recognition accuracy, without leveraging any data augmentation techniques during the training process.

$$Accuracy = \frac{1}{N} \sum_{i}^{N} 1(y_i = \hat{y}_i) \tag{2}$$

For parameter search, we use the test set to compute $ADPD_{aug}$. We independently research and evaluate the settings of SpecAugment's time warping, frequency masking, and time masking subtechniques, assigning each set of determined parameters for a subtechnique a score. We compare the recognition results to the actual labels and calculate the accuracy, referred to as E_{aug}.

We compute AD_{aug} differently for each augmentation subtechniques, as shown in Table 1. Please note that the definitions of the variables W, F, N_f, ν, T, N_t, and τ can be found in Sect. 3.1. Our definition of AD_{aug} is similar but not identical to D_{aug} of Hwang et al. [10]. To alleviate the impact of errors, we conducted M repetitions of the experiment and obtained the average data. The optimal set of parameters for each sub-technique that yields the superior performance of $ADPD_{aug}$ was selected as the output of the search process.

Table 1. AD_{aug} Formula

	Time Warping	Frequency Masking	Time Masking
Parameter	W	F, N_f	T, N_t
AD_{aug}	$\frac{W}{\tau}$	$\frac{F \times N_f}{\nu}$	$\frac{T \times N_t}{\tau}$

Our proposed parameter search method utilizes a forward propagation approach, which incurs very small computational overhead after fine-tuning the MagiaClassifier. The overall time complexity of our search methodology is represented as $O(f(n) + b(n) + nmf(n))$, where n denotes the sample size used for scoring and m represents the number of parameter values to be retrieved. Here, $O(f(n))$ and $O(b(n))$ correspond to the time complexity of forward and backward propagation, respectively; $O(f(n) + b(n))$ corresponds to the time complexity of fine-tuning; and $O(nmf(n))$ corresponds to the time complexity of searching for augmentation strategy parameters. Backward propagation has a higher time complexity than forward propagation since it involves computing and updating gradients for each parameter in the neural network, while forward propagation processes the input only once. In comparison, the conventional tuning method requires fine-tuning and scoring for each set of predetermined parameters, resulting in a search time complexity of $O(2nmf(n) + nmb(n))$. Evidently, $O(2nmf(n) + nmb(n))$ is significantly larger than $O(f(n) + b(n) + nmf(n))$. Therefore, our proposed strategy is substantially more cost-effective than the conventional tuning scheme.

4 Experiment

The experiments were divided into three parts. In the first part, we utilized MagiaSearch to search for the optimal parameters of each sub-technique of SpecAugment. The second part aimed to find the best combination of SpecAugment sub-techniques. Finally, we compared the results obtained by MagiaSearch with those obtained using empirical and random parameter values in the third part.

4.1 SpecAugment Parameter Search

In this experiment, the MagiaClassifier's backbone model was initially pre-trained on the ImageNet-1k dataset. It was then reassembled as MagiaClassifier and fine-tuned for 100 epochs using the IRMAS dataset. We shuffled the data, resulting in a different ordering compared to Sect. 4.2. The IRMAS dataset was split into training, validation, and test sets in the ratio of 7 : 1 : 2, and solely spectrogram normalization was applied as a pre-processing step. An early stopping mechanism was incorporated to terminate the training if the accuracy on the validation set failed to improve within 5 epochs. In the context of parameter search, we selected the model with the highest score on the validation set, while the score on the test set was denoted as E_{none}.

This study proposes a parametric search strategy to address the challenge of instrument recognition. Specifically, we employ Eq. 1 to compute the $ADPD$ for each parameter set independently and select the optimal value based on the resulting curve. For time warping, we explore the value domain of W in 2-step increments within the range of $[0, \tau/2)$, as illustrated by the search curve in Fig. 2(a).

To obtain the optimal value F_{best} for frequency masking, we traverse the value domain of F in 2-step increments within the range of $[0, \nu]$ with a fixed N_f value of 1. The search curve for F_{best} is depicted in Fig. 2(b). Then score each pair of F_i and N_{fi} values that satisfy the constraint $F_i * N_{fi} = F_{best}$.

Similarly, we scan the value of T in 2-step increments within the range of $[0, \tau]$ with a fixed N_t value of 1. The search curve for T_{best} is shown in Fig. 2(c). Then score each pair of T_i and N_{ti} values that satisfy the constraint $T_i * N_{ti} = T_{best}$.

Given the stochastic nature of SpecAugment, we conducted our score calculations M times, commencing from different starting random states, and the scores were taken as mean values. The optimal parameter values obtained from our search are summarized in Table 2.

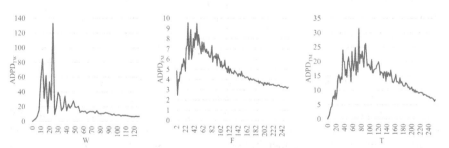

(a) Curve of Time Warp Parameter Search
(b) Curve of Frequency Masking Parameter Search
(c) Curve of Time Masking Parameter Search

Fig. 2. Curve of SpecAugment Parameter Search

Table 2. Results of SpecAugment Parameter Search

Parameters	W	N_f	F	N_t	T
Result	24	1	28	1	74

4.2 SpecAugment Subtechnology Combination Search

In this experiment, we utilize the optimal parameter values from the previous parameter search as augmentation techniques. We aim to explore the combination of the three SpecAugment augmentation techniques to determine the optimal combination for the proposed architecture. The outcomes of this experimentation are showcased in Table 3. In the table, the mode denoted by "None" signifies the absence of any augmentation technique. Moreover, the scores for macro precision, macro recall, macro F1, etc., were unavailable in [17]. Therefore, we denoted them with "Unavailable" in the table.

We fine-tune the MagiaClassifier for each augmentation technique combination using the IRMAS dataset and a $7:1:2$ split between the training, validation, and test sets. Before fine-tuning, we pre-trained MagiaClassifier on the ImageNet-1k dataset, which is consistent with Sect. 4.1. During the training phase, we apply SpecAugment using AdamW as the optimizer with an initial learning rate of $2e-5$ and a weight decay factor of 0.05. We trained MagiaClassifier for 100 epochs and applied early stopping if the validation set accuracy did not improve within 5 epochs. We selected the model with the highest validation set accuracy and evaluated its performance on the test set, ensuring the robustness and efficacy of our approach. It is critical to emphasize that the model solely utilizes the optimized SpecAugment parameters and lacks any prior knowledge of the IRMAS-TrainingData, without sharing weights with Sect. 4.1.

Our results show that time warping provides the greatest performance gain when used alone, followed by time masking. Combining all three augmentation techniques leads to the highest model accuracy of 0.8876, which represents a performance gain of 0.0603 compared to no augmentation technique. Our study includes a comparative analysis of our findings with those of prior research [17] on IRMAS. Our results demonstrate that the proposed MagiaClassifier significantly enhances the instrument recognition accuracy on IRMAS from 0.79 to 0.8248. Moreover, combining the outcomes of MagiaSearch and MagiaClassifier further improves the instrument recognition accuracy on IRMAS from 0.79 to 0.8876, underscoring the significant impact of our proposed methodology in enhancing the performance of instrument recognition systems. We note that prior research only focused on six types of instruments, whereas our study covered all eleven types of instruments in IRMAS, making our work much more challenging and complex.

Table 3. Results of SpecAugment Subtechnology Combination Search

Mode	Accuracy	Macro Precision	Macro Recall	Macro F1
Baseline	0.79	Unavailable	Unavailable	Unavailable
None	0.8273	0.8248	0.8196	0.8192
TW	0.8756	0.8801	0.8700	0.8713
FM	0.8499	0.8451	0.8438	0.8431
TM	0.8567	0.8552	0.8524	0.8509
TW+FM	0.8552	0.8559	0.8523	0.8500
TW+TM	0.8484	0.8488	0.8407	0.8404
FM+TM	0.8560	0.8552	0.8503	0.8503
TW+FM+TM	**0.8876**	**0.8853**	**0.8848**	**0.8831**

4.3 Comparison of SpecAugment Parameters

Our study involved a comparison of the output of MagiaSearch with several empirical and random parameters of SpecAugment, as illustrated in the Sect. 4. The empirical parameters were sourced from Li et al. [11], Hidaka et al. [8], Park et al. [16] and Zhou et al. [23], while Completely Random parameters refer to the random sampling of W, F, N_f, T, N_t parameters of SpecAugment once for each sample on which SpecAugment is applied, so that their values are expressed as the set of sampled values $Z_W \in \{n \in \mathbb{Z} \mid 0 \leq n \leq 127\}$, $Z_F \in \{n \in \mathbb{Z} \mid 0 \leq n \leq 256\}$, $Z_{N_f} \in \{n \in \mathbb{Z} \mid 0 \leq n \leq 10\}$, $Z_T \in \{n \in \mathbb{Z} \mid 0 \leq n \leq 256\}$ and $Z_{N_t} \in \{n \in \mathbb{Z} \mid 0 \leq n \leq 10\}$, where Z represents the set of positive integers. This approach ensured a comprehensive evaluation of MagiaSearch's ability to optimize the parameters of SpecAugment.

In this experiment, the experimental configuration and the datasets remained the same as what we used in Sect. 4.2. In particular, we employed MagiaClassifier as the backbone model for conducting experiments with each parameter set, rather than using the original models described in the source papers for each parameter set. Consequently, we anticipate observing similar results across similar parameter sets. Table 4 demonstrates that MagiaSearch obtained the best score, outperforming the other parameter sets, followed by the parameter set from Park et al. [16], which yielded results very similar to those of MagiaSearch. In sharp contrast, Completely Random yielded the worst score, highlighting that the performance of SpecAugment in instrument recognition is highly dependent on suitable parameter values. Our MagiaSearch algorithm offers a more resource-efficient approach for obtaining optimal SpecAugment parameter values than traditional search methods, as outlined in Sect. 3.3.

Table 4. Comparison of SpecAugment Parameters

Source	W	F	N_f	T	N_t	Accuracy
Li et al. [11]	5	15	1	10	1	0.8491
Hidaka et al. [8]	0	5	2	11	2	0.8658
Park et al. [16]	80	27	2	100	2	0.8816
Zhou et al. [23]	0	18	5	10	3	0.8552
Random	Z_W	Z_F	Z_{N_f}	Z_T	Z_{N_t}	0.7421
MagiaSearch	24	28	1	74	1	**0.8876**

5 Conclusion

This study aims to cost-effectively break the performance ceiling for predominant instrument recognition tasks. A proposed method involves transforming audio data into a log mel spectrogram and using MagiaClassifier and MagiaSearch to improve the instrument recognition system's performance. The Swin Transformer V2 serves as the backbone model for MagiaClassifier, while SpecAugment is used for data augmentation. The experiments demonstrate the effectiveness of MagiaSearch and MagiaClassifier, with the proposed architecture achieving a test set accuracy of 88.76 percent, surpassing the performance ceiling.

Future research opportunities include exploring the parameters of other data augmentation techniques, such as SpecAugment++, developing specialized models to address the spectrogram problem, and replacing ImageNet-1k with spectrogram data during pre-training. Additionally, model and parameter studies can be extended to other music information retrieval areas, such as instrument source separation, to further improve the performance of music information retrieval systems.

References

1. Bosch, J.J., Janer, J., Fuhrmann, F., Herrera, P.: A comparison of sound segregation techniques for predominant instrument recognition in musical audio signals. In: ISMIR, pp. 559–564 (2012)
2. Deng, J.D., Simmermacher, C., Cranefield, S.: A study on feature analysis for musical instrument classification. IEEE Trans. Syst. Man Cybern. Part B (Cybern.) **38**(2), 429–438 (2008)
3. Eronen, A.: Comparison of features for musical instrument recognition. In: Proceedings of the 2001 IEEE Workshop on the Applications of Signal Processing to Audio and Acoustics (Cat. No. 01TH8575), pp. 19–22. IEEE (2001)
4. Fanelli, A.M., Caponetti, L., Castellano, G., Buscicchio, C.A.: Content-based recognition of musical instruments. In: Proceedings of the Fourth IEEE International Symposium on Signal Processing and Information Technology, pp. 361–364. IEEE (2004)

5. Gaido, M., Gangi, M.A.D., Negri, M., Turchi, M.: End-to-end speech-translation with knowledge distillation: Fbk@iwslt2020. In: Proceedings of the 17th International Conference on Spoken Language Translation, IWSLT 2020, Online, 9–10 July 2020, pp. 80–88. Association for Computational Linguistics (2020)
6. Gong, Y., Chung, Y.A., Glass, J.: AST: audio spectrogram transformer. In: Proceedings of the Interspeech 2021, pp. 571–575 (2021)
7. Gururani, S., Sharma, M., Lerch, A.: An attention mechanism for musical instrument recognition. In: Proceedings of the 20th International Society for Music Information Retrieval Conference, ISMIR 2019, Delft, The Netherlands, 4–8 November 2019, pp. 83–90 (2019)
8. Hidaka, S., Wakamiya, K., Kaburagi, T.: An investigation of the effectiveness of phase for audio classification. In: 2022 IEEE International Conference on Acoustics, Speech and Signal Processing (ICASSP), ICASSP 2022, pp. 3708–3712. IEEE (2022)
9. Hung, Y.N., Chen, Y.A., Yang, Y.H.: Multitask learning for frame-level instrument recognition. In: 2019 IEEE International Conference on Acoustics, Speech and Signal Processing (ICASSP), ICASSP 2019, pp. 381–385. IEEE (2019)
10. Hwang, Y., Cho, H., Yang, H., Won, D.O., Oh, I., Lee, S.W.: Mel-spectrogram augmentation for sequence to sequence voice conversion. arXiv preprint arXiv:2001.01401 (2020)
11. Li, X., Zhang, Y., Zhuang, X., Liu, D.: Frame-level SpecAugment for deep convolutional neural networks in hybrid ASR systems. In: 2021 IEEE Spoken Language Technology Workshop (SLT), pp. 209–214. IEEE (2021)
12. Liu, Z., et al.: Swin transformer V2: scaling up capacity and resolution. In: Proceedings of the IEEE/CVF Conference on Computer Vision and Pattern Recognition, pp. 12009–12019 (2022)
13. Marques, J., Moreno, P.J.: A study of musical instrument classification using Gaussian mixture models and support vector machines. Cambridge Research Laboratory Technical Report Series CRL **4**, 143 (1999)
14. Martin, K.D., Kim, Y.E.: Musical instrument identification: a pattern-recognition approach. J. Acoust. Soc. Am. **104**(3), 1768 (1998)
15. Martin, K.D.: Sound-source recognition: a theory and computational model. Ph.D. thesis, Massachusetts Institute of Technology (1999)
16. Park, D.S., et al.: SpecAugment: a simple data augmentation method for automatic speech recognition. In: Proceedings of the Interspeech 2019, pp. 2613–2617 (2019)
17. Racharla, K., Kumar, V., Jayant, C.B., Khairkar, A., Harish, P.: Predominant musical instrument classification based on spectral features. In: 2020 7th International Conference on Signal Processing and Integrated Networks (SPIN), pp. 617–622. IEEE (2020)
18. Saeed, A., Grangier, D., Zeghidour, N.: Contrastive learning of general-purpose audio representations. In: Proceedings of the ICASSP, pp. 3875–3879. IEEE (2021)
19. Solanki, A., Pandey, S.: Music instrument recognition using deep convolutional neural networks. Int. J. Inf. Technol. **14**, 1659–1668 (2019)
20. Wang, H., Zou, Y., Chong, D.: Acoustic scene classification with spectrogram processing strategies. In: Proceedings of 5th the Workshop on Detection and Classification of Acoustic Scenes and Events 2020 (DCASE 2020), Tokyo, Japan (Full Virtual), 2–4 November 2020, pp. 210–214 (2020)
21. Xu, Y., Kong, Q., Wang, W., Plumbley, M.D.: Large-scale weakly supervised audio classification using gated convolutional neural network. In: Proceedings of the ICASSP, pp. 121–125. IEEE (2018)

22. Zeyer, A., Bahar, P., Irie, K., Schlüter, R., Ney, H.: A comparison of transformer and LSTM encoder decoder models for ASR. In: 2019 IEEE Automatic Speech Recognition and Understanding Workshop (ASRU), pp. 8–15. IEEE (2019)
23. Zhou, W., Michel, W., Irie, K., Kitza, M., Schlüter, R., Ney, H.: The RWTH ASR system for TED-LIUM release 2: improving hybrid hmm with SpecAugment. In: Proceedings of the ICASSP, pp. 7839–7843. IEEE (2020)

Can Machine Learning Support Improvement in Effective Nutrition of Patients in Critical Care Units?

Elias Pimenidis[1]([envelope]) [ID], Kamran Soomro[1] [ID], Antonios Papaleonidas[2] [ID], and Anastasios Panagiotis Psathas[2] [ID]

[1] University of the West of England, Bristol BS16 1QY, UK
{Elias.pimenidis,Kamran.Soomro}@uwe.ac.uk
[2] Democritus University of Thrace, Xanthi, Greece
{papaleon,anpsatha}@civil.duth.gr

Abstract. This work presents the roadmap for the development of a research impact case study as it evolves with research carried out at the University of the West of England, in the United Kingdom (UK). The focus of the research is using Machine Learning algorithms in supporting decision making in terms of appropriate nutrition and other key factors in treating patients in Critical Care Units (CCUs) of hospitals in the UK. A first stage of the research has sought to improve the accuracy and timeliness of patient referrals to dietitians, upon arrival at the CCU. The results have shown that among various machine learning classifiers using data from various physio-logical measures of CCU patients a Support Vector Machine (SVC) classifier was the best performing model (AUC: 0.78). An electronic dashboard has been developed to support a decision maker at the CCU to process referrals efficiently and support enhanced patient care. The research has been extended to a different area of interest, this time focusing on paediatric CCU patients. The aim here it to use similar research methodologies to attempt to estimate energy expenditure for very young patients. This bears the challenge of having to use limited sized datasets, which the researchers attempt to address with explainable Artificial Intelligence.

Keywords: Critical Care Units · Machine Learning · Patient nutrition · Energy Expenditure

1 Introduction

Critical care units (CCUs) are specialist hospital wards that treat patients who are seriously ill and need constant monitoring.

Such patients might have problems with one or more vital organs or be unable to breathe without support. Other reasons that patients might need intensive care will be because of a serious accident, a serious short-term condition (heart attack or stroke), a serious infection, or major surgery.

Patients are monitored and treated by specially trained health care professionals. They are connected to various equipment that are combined with smart beds that all

© The Author(s), under exclusive license to Springer Nature Switzerland AG 2023
L. Iliadis et al. (Eds.): ICANN 2023, LNCS 14261, pp. 137–146, 2023.
https://doi.org/10.1007/978-3-031-44198-1_12

together provide measurement of important bodily functions, such as heart rate, blood pressure and the level of oxygen in the blood. Other equipment supports feeding and administration of medication while a patient might not be able to receive these in the usual way [1].

The aim of any health organization is to treat patients appropriately to ensure their speedy and full recovery. Beyond the obvious benefits to the patients a full and speedy recovery offers operational benefits to the hospitals, improves their efficiency, and ensures that they can treat more patients effectively, reduce any backlogs and improve the wellbeing of the communities they serve.

Such an efficiency can be achieved at the point of entry to the hospital where a sound estimate can provide nurses and admin staff the ability for the timely discharge of a patient at the point that they are fit to leave.

The bureaucratic steps of discharging a patient - contacting social services, making sure patients have a bed in place - often only begin when that patient is fit to leave and can take several days. By giving an estimated date for discharge from the moment patients arrive, nurses can look ahead and book social care in advance [2].

Although Artificial Intelligence is being used widely in medicine and in various procedures at hospitals. An area that has not benefited from the use of AI is that of nutrition management in Critical Care Units.

Hospitals are currently running at 95 per cent capacity, but about 15 per cent of beds are taken up by patients who are medically fit to leave. Discharging patients more quickly would allow the NHS to move from disastrously high capacity to normal levels of bed occupancy [2].

1.1 Preparing a Patient to be Discharged from CCU

Estimating whether a patient is fit to leave the hospital will vary on their initial condition at admission. This is more challenging with very sick patients that are admitted at CCU. The estimate / prediction of being able to leave will be much more complex in such situations. What could speed up the recovery and offer consistent and reliable data upon which reasonably accurate estimates can be made, is suitable nutrition. The involvement of dietitians and timely referrals to them are essential in providing CCU patients with suitable nutrition [3, 4] Soomro et al. 2022). Patients admitted in CCUs due to pathological health issues present staff with complex situations due to multiple health conditions that often become conflicting as to the treatments that they are due to receive and nutrition that they need to be provided with. There are various methodologies for patient feeding in CCUs. There are different approaches that primarily focus on adult patients. One of the main challenges is that of offering each patient a dietitian review at admission to the CCU. This is often difficult to achieve due to limited resources. Although hospitals and CCUs use smart beds to capture a plethora of patient data, often this cannot be utilized to allow for more informed decision making as to prioritize patients for referrals to dietitians. In most cases a rule of thumb, based on key physiological data and some critical medical condition data, is used to determine priority to access to dietitians.

With the advent of smart beds, many physiological measurements are automatically collected for all patients under critical care in the CCU. This data is currently available to CCU staff, but due to cognitive overload they often miss patients that require attention and there are no automated mechanisms in place to help them identify such patients.

Many patients are also sedated and need regular monitoring and external feeding. Furthermore, the data collected from patients is stored in many different places in the information system and is often distributed across various information systems within the same hospital. An automated system that can offer automatically monitoring and analysis of patient data and flag patients that need attention to the staff can significantly improve quality of patient care. The aim of the first phase of this project was to explore the feasibility of developing a system that can automatically screen CCU patients that need to be referred to a dietitian.

This will enable staff at the CCU to improve the quality of a patient's healthcare, and at the same time improve the efficiency of utilizing the limited number of beds available more efficiently. Compared to other nations, the UK has a very low total number of hospital beds relative to its population. The average number of beds per 1,000 people in OECD EU nations is 5, but the UK has just 2.4. Germany, by contrast, has 7.8. Combined with staffing shortages, an insufficient core bed stock means that hospitals are less able to cope with large influxes of patients, for example during winter or periods of high demand. This has ultimately impacted hospitals' ability to provide safe and timely care and remains a major factor in growing backlogs for the NHS [5].

2 Related Work

CCUs are specific hospital wards where the sickest patients are admitted and where large amounts of detailed clinical data are collected (usually every hour) for the duration of the patient's stay. Many CCUs have moved from paper to clinical information systems to capture all this data from the patients' monitor, ventilator, and other equipment such as drug infusions into a very extensive database, which we have the potential to utilise much more extensively than the 'expensive recording system' that currently exists. Over the past few years medical professionals are becoming increasingly aware that CCUs are not using these systems and this data to their advantage, with much of the data being captured not being analysed or used for maximal benefit. In an era of limited healthcare systems such as the NHS in the UK, these digital resources have the potential to both optimize patient outcomes and make systems more efficient and effective [6].

Data analysis and machine learning systems have been explored on several research cases and have been utilized widely in health care and CCUs. They are usually used to automate processes where problems are well known and fully defined and there the deliverables to efficiency and accuracy achieved are well within the expected levels [7, 8]. In this project, the potential of utilizing the data that is produced by the information system is not fully known. The opportunity of working with problems that the benefits that might be accrued are not known are frequent in the field of AI; the availability of such rich data to work with as it is the case here is attractive and challenging at the same time.

The goal for CCUs is to optimize the patients' survival, clinical outcomes and to reduce harm caused by our therapies (iatrogenic harm). All CCUs have several recognized targets to improve outcomes such as maintaining an optimal level of sedation (not too high or low), maintain lung volumes delivered by the ventilator within a specific range to minimize lung injury and trying to deliver a minimum amount of nutrition to patients whilst they are critically ill. Yet these seemingly simple targets, are often not achieved. Dietitians translate the science of nutrition into everyday information about food and advise people on their food and nutrition choices. During critical illness, a patient's nutritional needs can change daily, and it is a dietitian's job to ensure they receive the correct amount of nutrition to help their recovery. Most of the time, nutrition for these patients is delivered through a tube into a patient's stomach or blood supply [9].

Data that is produced by clinical information systems is not always fit to be processed by machine learning algorithms. Researchers must determine its quality and suitability for exposure to advanced analysis techniques. Data will normally need to be filtered and cleaned to develop a suitable experimental repository which will be compatible with the problem to be analysed by suitable techniques. Such data will be mined to reveal potential associations that will enhance the detail, quality and significance of the information that could be passed on to the clinicians at CCUs [10].

3   A Digital Dashboard to Support Referrals to Dietitians

A prototype data dashboard was developed to demonstrate how an automated system could assist staff in screening patients, shown in Fig. 1. The dashboard shows the patient ID, and any relevant treatments that they are receiving. Feeding is provided according to guidelines and based on the schedule provided by dietitians. Users can select to view details of patients that are recommended for referral to dietitians upon arrival at the CCU. The dashboard provides a quick overview of all patients in the CCU at any one time, also showing those that require a referral. The background to identifying the need for referral is based on a simple rule of thumb that can be applied mentally by a nurse at the CCU. This considers the patient's Body Mass Index (BMI) and whether the patient is affected by any of a few critical medical conditions. The wealth of data that the hospital will have collected on the patient remains largely unutilised in such a decision-making process and patients are not prioritized in any other way.

3.1   Applying Machine Learning to Our Problem

To overcome the limitation of the simplistic rule of the thump algorithm applied, the researchers shifted their focus on applying Machine Learning algorithms to the rich data that had been supplied by the CCU at the Bristol Royal Infirmary. This involved the adult CCU initially with a view to exploring data from the paediatric CCU at a later stage. The challenge of the data is that it does not originate from one source, but from many databases within the hospital. Some of them will have data drawn from CCU smart beds, while others will have inputs from other sections of the hospital. In addition, data might have free text notes added by medical staff as observations after examinations or procedures that a patient might have undergone. Therefore, the data required a lot of cleaning and filtering.

Fig. 1. A screenshot of the dashboard based on rule of thumb algorithm

Currently, CCUs are not using these systems and data to their advantage, with much of the captured data left unanalysed. In an era of limited NHS resources, these digital resources have the potential to both optimize patient outcomes and make systems more efficient and effective.

Data analysis and machine learning systems have been used widely in hospitals, primarily to automate processes where problems are well known and fully defined, and there the deliverables to efficiency and accuracy achieved are well within the expected levels.

CCUs aim to optimize the patients' survival, clinical outcomes and to reduce harm caused by therapies. All CCUs have recognized targets to improve outcomes, such as maintaining an optimal sedation level, maintaining lung volumes delivered by the ventilator within a specific range and delivering a minimum amount of nutrition to patients whilst they are critically ill. Yet, these targets are often not achieved [2, 3, 5].

The authors have conducted research with machine learning algorithms that establish a better basis for prioritizing referrals to dietitians, when compared with traditional rules of thumb.

The work has led to the development of an interactive dashboard that would support decision making by CCU staff in managing those referrals. Figures 2 and 3 below show screenshots of this more advanced dashboard, whose data analysis and patient referrals are based on the use of machine learning algorithms.

The main challenge to this work is the lack of synchronous access to data as it is collected from the patients. The collection of data used with the machine learning algorithms is made up of different sources and online access to them is limited as the database systems that capture and store them vary in structure and access. Moreover, the data captured from all the different systems in a hospital is not directly usable for machine learning due to its status and consistency of format. This inevitably leads to the use of standalone offline systems that risk the decision-making lagging behind the latest developments (and health measurements collected) for some patients.

3.2 Developing a More Efficient Dashboard

Figures 2 and 3 below show screenshots of an enhanced dashboard that allows a member of staff at a CCU to use machine learning based analysis to identify patients requiring priority to dietitian referral. The output is much more accurate with results on records of more than 5000 patients' data processed, revealing patients that were missed with the previous rule of thumb algorithm. The dashboard itself is much more versatile and allows the user to zoom in and study patient details, project groups requiring priority referrals and search the results that the system has produced for groups of patients diagnosed with specific medical conditions. The dashboard is versatile and allows for easy update on the algorithms used to process the data to facilitate maintainability and ease of further development along with the progress of the research.

Our team had the opportunity to present this part of the work by invitation a specialist interest nutrition group meeting that took place at the 36th annual conference of the Paediatric Critical Care Society in the UK, in September 2022. Although the data used in this work was from adult CCU, the audience at the presentation was receptive, positive, and impressed.

This presentation has inspired the next phase of our research which is now focused on paediatric CCU patients, still focusing on the challenges of nutrition, but this time addressing the more direct problem of estimating energy expenditure for a patient and therefore allowing a dietitian to prescribe appropriate nutrition accurately, based on the medical condition of the patient.

3.3 Machine Learning Behind the New Dashboard

The data in the hospital database is stored in a meta-model that is described else-where [3]. It comprises treatments and interventions by clinical staff at the CCU. The patient's medical history at the point of admission in the CCU is also included and their key serious medical conditions are identified. The first step in the ML process involved extracting features from this meta-model for further processing. To this end the data was first anonymised by removing the unique patient ID and replacing it with a pseudonymous number. The timestamps for the various interventions were also replaced by pseudo-dates to further anonymise the data. Relevant attributes for various interventions were extracted as separate features [4]. The BMI of the patients was calculated from their height and weight and outliers as well as missing values were filtered as part of the cleaning process. Furthermore, if a patient's record contained a note from a dietitian, indicating that the patient had been referred to a dietitian, the corresponding target variable was set to

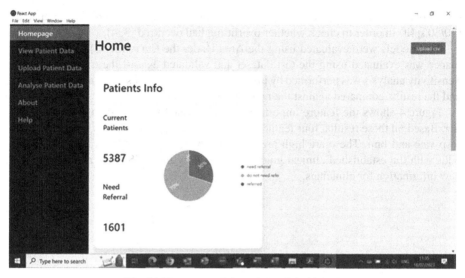

Fig. 2. Homepage of the enhanced dashboard

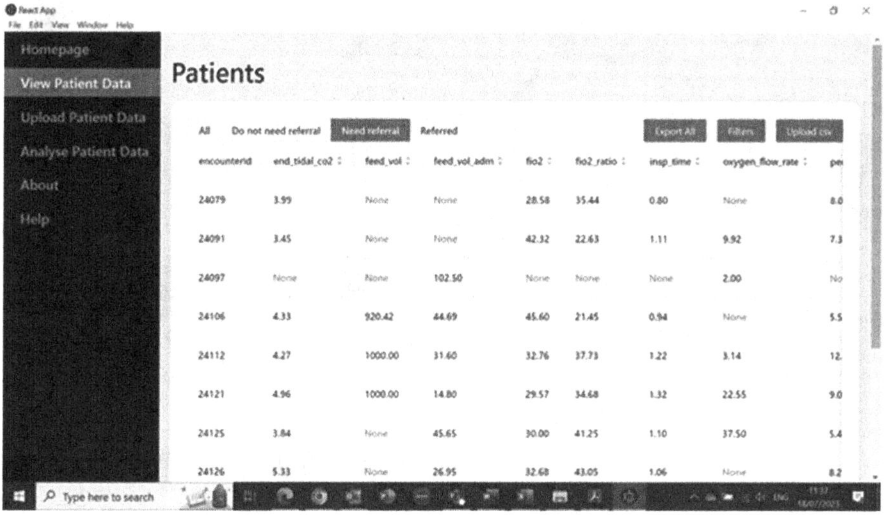

Fig. 3. Patients requiring referrals, with full data available.

1, otherwise it was set to 0. This allowed the problem to be formulated as supervised classification problem. Missing values for included features were replaced with 0.

Various supervised classification models were chosen for this step. Since the target classes were unbalanced in this case (80% non-referrals vs 20% referrals), the AUC rather than the overall accuracy was chosen as the performance metric. Based on hyper-parameter tuning coupled with 10-fold cross validation, the best performing models for each algorithm were compared using the AUC. Training vs test sets were also compared (70/30 split) in order to check whether overfitting had occurred [3, 4].

The models were evaluated using the Area Under the Curve (AUC). Their performance was evaluated using the test dataset and validated against the training dataset. Sensitivity analysis was performed by imputing the missing values using a KNN Imputer and the results compared against the non-imputed datasets.

Figure 4 shows the feature importance as determined by a Random Forest Classifier. Based on these results, four features were shortlisted: feed_vol, oxygen_flow_rate, resp_rate and bmi. These are high predictors of the target variable. This finding is at odds with the established clinical guidelines issued by the NHS Trust and constitutes new information for clinicians.

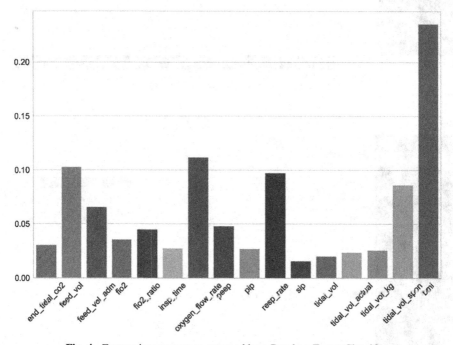

Fig. 4. Feature importance as returned by a Random Forest Classifier.

A sensitivity analysis was also performed by filling in the missing values using a K-Nearest Neighbour algorithm to impute the missing values. Table 1 shows the hyperparameters for the best performing classifiers. The four measurements in particular; feed_vol, oxygen_flow_rate, resp_rate and bmi; are high predictors of the target variable. This finding is at odds with the established clinical guidelines issued by the NHS Trust and constitutes new information for clinicians.

Table 1. Parameters giving the best results for the various models.

Classifier	Best parameters
random forest	max depth: 7
svc	kernel: rbf
linear discriminant	solver: svd

4   The case of Energy Expenditure in a Paediatric CCU

Only 113 children were admitted to a Paediatric Intensive Care Unit (PICU) per 100 000 (0.11% of all children in England). Most of those children (42.5%) being below one year of age [11]. Nutritional management of the critically ill child (CIC) is, therefore, a very specialist and challenging area in paediatric dietetic practice. To be able to feed such children appropriately, to support their recovery, their energy requirements must be predicted as accurately as possible. Many predictive equations have been used and studied in the paediatric critical care setting to calculate energy requirements. Current guidelines in the UK recommend indirect calorimetry to establish energy requirements. There is a considerable cost in doing so and most PICUs do not have a calorific calorimeter. Alternatively, there are other methods whose accuracy is established in adults and older children. These use equipment whose accuracy in small children is questionable.

To address these requirements and challenges we have embarked in collaborating with dietitians from the paediatric CCU of Southampton Hospital in the UK. The aim of this work is to explore whether a machine learning model can accurately estimate energy requirements in critically ill children. We will using pseudo anonymised data sets of quantitative variables of interest from critically ill children. This is a unique project and challenge. One of the main challenges International that of the data provided. The sample size is limited and coming from one hospital it induces further limitations. We have been given data that comprises tens of thousands of observations, but only for a limited number of different patients. To be able to overcome this challenge we will attempt to use explanations, based on the experienced gathered from a resurgence of explainable AI. Explainable AI has been explored in explaining medical decision-making [12], and explaining predictions of classifiers, before.

5   Summary – Conclusions

The work presented here is research applied to the support the requirements of Critical Care Units in improving the accuracy of decision making as to nutrition of very ill patients.

Whether the patients are adults or children, nutrition is crucial in supporting their recovery and allowing them to progress into improving their health. Properly recovered patients will usually leave a CCU earlier and will stand a better opportunity of a full recovery, thus avoiding a return to the hospital for the same ailment. This will in turn have a positive impact on bed utilization and reducing the risk healthcare systems reaching stress levels when seasonal demand is high.

The first of the two cases presented here has demonstrated that accuracy and speed of decision making at the CCU in referring patients to dietitians as a priority, can be improved by using machine learning algorithms to process patient data at arrival to the CCU.

The second research endeavour entails different challenges as to the nature of the data available and the complexity of the case. The research team is cautiously optimistic that using explainable AI the data challenges will be overcome and possibly suitable algorithms can help analyze the data and achieve accurate predictions to the energy expenditure of very young ill children.

Acknowledgement. Elias Pimenidis and Kamran Soomro, would like to acknowledge Dr Luise Marino for introducing them to the case of Energy Expenditure in PICUs.

References

1. Intensive Care conditions. https://www.nhs.uk/conditions/intensive-care/. Accessed 10 July 2023
2. Hayward, E.: AI cure for bed blocking can predict hospital stay. The Times (2022). https://www.thetimes.co.uk/article/ai-cure-for-bed-blocking-can-predict-hospital-stay-fpvjn5ql6. Accessed 17 July 2023
3. Soomro, K., Pimenidis, E.: Automated screening of patients for dietician referral. In: Iliadis, L., Angelov, P.P., Jayne, C., Pimenidis, E. (eds.) EANN 2020. PINNS, vol. 2, pp. 319–325. Springer, Cham (2020). https://doi.org/10.1007/978-3-030-48791-1_24
4. Soomro, K., Pimenidis, E., McWilliams, C.: Supporting patient nutrition in critical care units. In: Iliadis, L., Jayne, C., Tefas, A., Pimenidis, E. (eds.) EANN 2022. CCIS, vol. 1600, pp. 128–136. Springer, Cham (2022). https://doi.org/10.1007/978-3-031-08223-8_11
5. BMA, NHS hospital beds data analysis (2022). https://www.bma.org.uk/advice-and-support/nhs-delivery-and-workforce/pressures/nhs-hospital-beds-data-analysis. Accessed 17 July 2023
6. Gholami, B., Haddad, W.M., Bailey, J.M.: In the Intensive Care Unit Artificial Intelligence Can Keep Watch, North American, October 2018, pp. 31–35 (2018). https://spectrum.ieee.org
7. Saeed, M., et al.: Multiparameter intelligent monitoring in intensive care II: a public-access intensive care unit database. Criti. Care Med. **39**(5), 952–960 (2011)
8. Salman, I., Vomlel, J.: A machine learning method for incomplete and imbalanced medical data. In: 20th Czech-Japan Seminar on Data Analysis and Decision Making Pardubice. University of Ostrava, Czech Republic (2017)
9. NHS, The role of a dietitian. https://www.healthcareers.nhs.uk/explore-roles/allied-health-professionals/roles-allied-health-professions/dietitian. Accessed 10 July 2023
10. Lee, C.H., Yoon, H.-J.: Medical big data: promise and challenges. Kidney Res. Clin. Pract. **36**(1), 3–11 (2017). https://doi.org/10.23876/j.krcp.2017.36.1.3
11. PICANEt Homepage, PICANet State of the Nation Report 2022. https://www.picanet.org.uk/annual-reporting-and-publications/. Accessed 19 July 2023
12. Miller, T.: Explanation in artificial intelligence: insights from the social sciences. Artif. Intell. **267**(2), 1–38 (2019)

Cross-Domain Transformer with Adaptive Thresholding for Domain Adaptive Semantic Segmentation

Quansheng Liu[1], Lei Wang[1], Yu Jun[1(✉)], and Fang Gao[2(✉)]

[1] School of Information Science and Technology, University of Science and Technology of China, Hefei, China
liuqs29@mail.ustc.edu.cn, {wangl,harryjun}@ustc.edu.cn
[2] School of Electrical Engineering, Guangxi University, Nanning, China
fgao@gxu.edu.cn

Abstract. The goal of unsupervised domain adaptive semantic segmentation (UDA-SS) is to learn a model using annotated data from the source domain and generate accurate dense predictions for the unlabeled target domain. UDA methods based on Transformer utilize self-attention mechanism to learn features within source and target domains. However, in the presence of significant distribution shift between the two domains, the noisy pseudo-labels could hinder the model's adaptation to the target domain. In this work, we proposed to incorporate self-attention and cross-domain attention to learn domain-invariant features. Specifically, we design a weight-sharing multi-branch cross-domain Transformer, where the cross-domain branch is used to align domains at the feature level with the aid of cross-domain attention. Moreover, we introduce an adaptive thresholding strategy for pseudo-label selection, which dynamically adjusts the proportion of pseudo-labels that are used in training based on the model's adaptation status. Our approach guarantees the reliability of the pseudo labels while allowing more target domain samples to contribute to model training. Extensive experiments show that our proposed method consistently outperforms the baseline and achieves competitive results on GTA5→Cityscapes, Synthia→Cityscapes, and Cityscapes→ACDC benchmark.

Keywords: Domain Adaptation · Semantic Segmentation · Transformer · Attention mechanism

1 Introduction

Image semantic segmentation is crucial for scene understanding. However, training deep segmentation models requires a large amount of pixel-annotated data, which is expensive to obtain. To alleviate the model's reliance on fully labeled data, using synthetic data to expand the training set is a common solution. However, due to the distribution shift between synthetic and real data (lighting conditions, image styles, etc.), models may struggle to generalize to the real domain.

L. Iliadis et al. (Eds.): ICANN 2023, LNCS 14261, pp. 147–159, 2023.
https://doi.org/10.1007/978-3-031-44198-1_13

Unsupervised domain adaptation (UDA) methods have been proposed to address this issue by transferring the knowledge learned in the annotated source domain to the unlabeled target domain. This allows the model to adapt to the target domain without using target domain labels. Currently, most UDA semantic segmentation methods are based on self-training [4,7,12]. These approaches utilize the model trained on the source domain to generate pseudo-labels for the target domain, which are then used as a form of supervision to optimize the model for target domain adaptation.

Recently, Transformer models have emerged as a preferred choice for various computer vision tasks due to their superior performance compared to convolutional neural network (CNN) models. A series of works [4,5] have showcased significant improvements in UDA segmentation tasks by adopting Transformer.

The self-attention mechanism is the key to the Transformer, allowing the model to expand its receptive field to the entire image and selectively attend to informative regions of the input sequence. However, in UDA settings where there are distribution shifts between the training data, relying solely on self-attention for feature extraction can lead to poor robustness, making the pseudo-labels noisy that hinder the model's generalization on the target domain.

We noted that despite variations in image appearance between the source and target domains, they share similarities in semantic context. Cross-domain attention [21] has shown to be effective in utilizing such contextual information for domain alignment. However, in semantic segmentation tasks, cross-domain attention has yet to be thoroughly explored. Moreover, pixel-level pseudo-labels are more vulnerable to noise than image-level pseudo-labels. Due to the neglect of adaptation difficulty variations among different categories, previous UDA methods that used fixed thresholds [12,23] for pseudo-label filtering could not effectively utilize unlabeled samples in the target domain.

To address these issues, we propose a weight-sharing multi-branch cross-domain Transformer network that integrates self-attention with cross-domain attention. Cross-domain attention promotes feature alignment across domains, while self-attention captures spatial dependencies within the same domain. Additionally, a category-specific adaptive threshold strategy is proposed to balance the quality and quantity of pseudo-labels without manual parameter tuning.

To summarize, our main contributions can be listed as follows:

- We designed a multi-branch domain-adaptive Transformer that combines self-attention and cross-domain attention to facilitate domain alignment at the feature level and promote the learning of domain-invariant knowledge.
- To address the noisy-pseudo labels during self-training, we proposed an adaptive thresholding strategy for adjusting the pseudo-label threshold of each category based on their individual learning status.
- We conducted comprehensive experiments and ablation studies on different UDA benchmarks to validate the effectiveness of our proposed methods.

2   Related Works

2.1   Unsupervised Domain Adaptation Semantic Segmentation

UDA methods for semantic segmentation can be divided into two categories: domain alignment and self-training. Domain alignment methods [3,13,16] aim to align the features from the source and target domains by adversarial training, making them indistinguishable to a domain discriminator. Domain alignment can be performed at the input, output, or feature level. Currently, self-training has become the mainstream method for unsupervised domain adaptation tasks. These methods [4,12,24] use separate teacher segmentation model to generate pseudo-labels for the unlabeled target domain images, which are then used for further training. To denoise pseudo-labels, dynamic thresholding methods [1,6] have been introduced. However, most of these methods require the adjustment of hyperparameters for different tasks. In contrast, the proposed adaptive method does not introduce any additional hyperparameters.

2.2   Vision Transformers

Transformer [15], originally developed for NLP, has been successfully applied to computer vision tasks in the form of Vision Transformers, with representative examples including ViT [2] and Swin [9]. In the field of semantic segmentation, Segformer [20] proposed a hierarchical network design for feature extraction and efficient self-attention. For domain adaptation tasks, CDTrans [21] utilizes cross-attention for domain alignment within the Transformer framework for image classification. However, its input is restricted to predefined positive image pairs, which is not practical for dense prediction tasks like segmentation. In this paper, we propose to use cross-domain attention to calculate segmentation loss in the mixed intermediate domain, which allows the model to simultaneously focus on context dependencies between source and target domains.

3   Method

In this section, we first formalize the UDA setting and then introduce the design of our cross-domain Transformer and the adaptive thresholding strategy. The overall framework of our method is shown in Fig. 1.

3.1   Problem Settings

For the unsupervised domain adaptation (UDA) semantic segmentation task, we have images from labeled source domain $D^S = \{(x^S, y^S)\}$ and unlabeled target domain $D^S = \{(x^T)\}$. Both domains share the same label set. The objective of the task is to learn a student feature extractor f and segmentation head h_{cls} that can achieve decent results on the target domain.

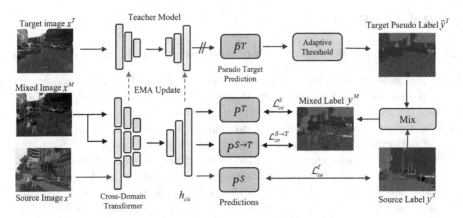

Fig. 1. Overview of our proposed Cross-Domain Transformer and Adaptive Thresholding Strategy in self-training framework.

In self-training UDA pipeline [4], the teacher model $f_{\theta'}$ and the student model f_θ are trained simultaneously. In the source domain, we train the student model in a fully supervised manner with the segmentation loss denoted by:

$$\mathcal{L}_{ce}^S = \mathrm{CE}(h_{cls}(f(x^S), \tilde{y}_i^T) \tag{1}$$

where CE stands for the cross-entropy loss. In the target domain, we generate pseudo-labels based on the prediction result of the teacher model and use it to calculate the pixel-level loss function. Meanwhile, in order to reduce the domain gap, we refer to DACS [12] for mixing the image from the source and target domain to obtain the mixed image x^M and the corresponding labels y^M. Then the loss for the target domain is defined as:

$$\mathcal{L}_{ce}^T = w \cdot \mathrm{CE}(h_{cls}(f(x^M), \tilde{y}_i^M) \tag{2}$$

where w is the loss weight on the target domain.

3.2   Cross-Domain Transformer

The proposed cross-domain Transformer adopts the architecture of Mix Transformer (MiT) network [20], but with the addition of cross-domain attention to address the specific challenges of domain adaptation. Additionally, a multi-branch cross-domain network is designed to enable feature-level integration between samples from the two domains.

Cross-Domain Attention. In the self-training frameworks, the student Transformer network uses the Self-Attention module for feature extraction in both the source and target domains. Self-attention mechanism facilitates the model to capture global semantic relationships within images by expanding the model's

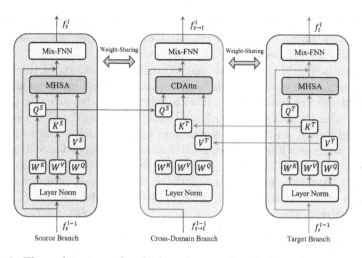

Fig. 2. The architecture of multi-branch cross-domain Transformer network.

receptive field. The self-attention mechanism on the source domain and target domain can be given as:

$$Attn_s(Q_s, K_s, V_s) = \text{Softmax}(\frac{Q_s K_s^T}{\sqrt{d_{head}}})V_s$$
$$Attn_t(Q_t, K_t, V_t) = \text{Softmax}(\frac{Q_t K_t^T}{\sqrt{d_{head}}})V_t \qquad (3)$$

where d_{head} is the dimension of the attention head, Q_s, K_s, V_s are the queries, keys, and values vector from the source domain image x^S, and Q_t, K_t, V_t are from the target domain image x_t.

However, the effectiveness of self-attention relies on the assumption of consistent data distributions. In the presence of domain shift, self-attention may not accurately respond to objects in the target domain. To capture the contextual relationships between different domains and learn domain-invariant features, we introduce the cross-domain attention mechanism (CDAttn). Unlike the traditional self-attention mechanism that only considers the context within the same domain, the cross-domain attention incorporates queries from different domains. Specifically, the query vector Q_s from the source domain image and the key-value pairs K_t and V_t from the target domain are used to generate attention weights within the image pairs. The cross-domain attention is given as:

$$Attn_{s \to t}(Q_t, K_s, V_s) = \text{Softmax}(\frac{Q_s K_t^T}{\sqrt{d_{head}}})V_t \qquad (4)$$

Multi-branch Cross-Domain Transformer. To promote the fusion of cross-domain features during training, we propose a weight-sharing three-branch cross-domain Transformer based on the MiT [20] architecture.

As shown in Fig. 2, the cross-domain Transformer consists of three weight-sharing branches: the source branch f_S, the source-to-target cross-domain branch $f_{s \to t}$, and the target branch f_t, each with independent dataflow. At the initial stage, $f_{s \to t}$ takes the images pair $\{x^S, x^M\}$ as input, while x^S and x^M are respectively passed into f_s and f_t. The source and target branches aim to learn representative patterns within their respective domains using self-attention. Meanwhile, the cross-domain branch $f_{s \to t}$ integrates features from both domains using cross-domain attention, allowing the model to learn domain-invariant features.

Features extracted from those three branches are denoted as F_s, F_t, and $F_{s \to t}$, respectively, where $F_s = f_s(x^S)$, $F_t = f_t(x^M)$ and $F_{s \to t} = f_{s \to t}(x^S, x^M)$. To achieve feature-level domain alignment, we utilize the cross-domain features $F_{s \to t}$ to generate predictions on the mixed domain, which yields the training loss for the cross-domain branch:

$$\mathcal{L}_{ce}^{S \to M} = \frac{1}{H \times W} \sum_{i=1}^{H \times W} \text{CE}(h_{cls}(f_{s \to t}(x_i^S, x_i^T)), \, \tilde{y}_i^M) \tag{5}$$

where CE denotes the cross-entropy loss, h_{cls} represents the classification head, and $\tilde{y}^M$ is the mixed labels. As the multi-branch network does not introduce extra trainable modules compared to the MiT backbone, the entire model can reuse the weights pretrained on ImageNet-1K.

3.3   Hyperparameter-Free Self-adaptive Threshold

In the self-training domain adaptation method, pseudo-labels generated by the teacher model contain varying degrees of noise due to domain shifts. We note that the existing pseudo-label selection strategy [6,12] lacks consideration for inter-class variation and requires manual hyper-parameter tuning. To this end, we propose a self-adaptive thresholding module that dynamically modifies the threshold for pseudo-label selection. Inspired by previous research [18], we divide the pseudo-label confidence threshold into global and local components, both of which are updated based on the model's prediction confidence. Furthermore, the adaptive thresholds are adjusted in a class-specific manner based on their adaptation status, which allows the model to learn from potentially correct pseudo-labels in the early stages and gradually filter out unreliable predictions as the model gains confidence in its predictions. We visualize the evolution of the category threshold during training in Fig. 3.

Global Threshold. The global threshold τ_t is an indicator of the model's overall adaptation status on the target domain. In practice, τ_t is set as the Exponential Moving Average (EMA) of the maximum prediction confidence in the current training batch, which estimates the average prediction confidence for

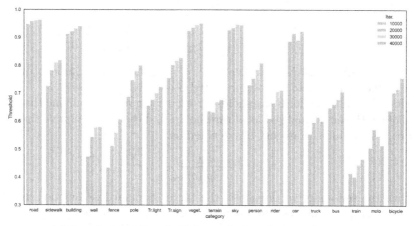

(a) Pseudo-label threshold for each class during adaptation.

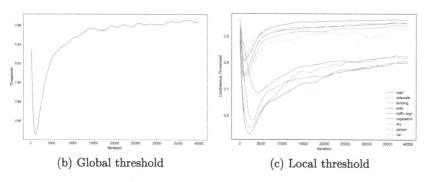

(b) Global threshold   (c) Local threshold

Fig. 3. Overview of the adaptive thresholding strategy.

all target domain pixels. To handle the issue of noisy pseudo-labels generated in the early stages of training, we start with a strict global threshold of $\tau_0 = 1$. As training progresses, τ_t is gradually increased according to the following rules:

$$\tau_t = \begin{cases} 1, & t = 0, \\ \lambda\tau_{t-1} + (1-\lambda)\frac{1}{N_T}\sum_{i=1}^{N_T}\max(q_i), & t \neq 0, \end{cases} \quad (6)$$

where N_T denotes the total number of pixels in the target domain, q_i represents the class-wise confidence score of the corresponding pixel, and λ is the weight for the EMA update.

Local Threshold. It is observed that in the target domain, the extent of distribution shift varies across different categories. Therefore, we introduce a local threshold to further modify the global threshold in a class-specific way. Specifically, we compute the expectation of the maximum prediction confidence for each category in the current training batch and update the local threshold $\tilde{p}_t(c)$ in an EMA manner:

$$\tilde{p}_t(c) = \begin{cases} 1, & t = 0 \\ \lambda \tilde{p}_{t-1}(c) + (1-\lambda)\frac{1}{N_{T,c}}\sum_{i=1}^{N_{T,c}} q_i(c), & t \neq 0, \end{cases} \qquad (7)$$

where $N_{T,c} = |X_c|$, and $X_c = \{x_i | x_i \in X^T, c = \arg\max_{c \in C} q_i(c)\}$ denotes set of pixels in the current batch whose predicted pseudo label is class c.

After obtaining the local thresholds for each category, we combine the global threshold with the normalized local thresholds, and the final adaptive threshold $\tau_t(c)$ corresponding to category c is denoted as:

$$\tau_t(c) = \frac{\tilde{p}_t(c)}{\|\tilde{p}_t(c)\|_\infty} \cdot \tau_t \qquad (8)$$

With the self-adaptive threshold, the target domain loss function and the cross-domain branching loss function could be modified accordingly:

$$\mathcal{L}_{ce}^T = \frac{1}{H \times W} \sum_{i=1}^{H \times W} \mathbb{1}(max(q_i^t) > \tau_t(\arg\max_c(q_{i,c}^t))) \cdot \mathrm{CE}(q_i^t, \tilde{y}_i^T)$$

$$\mathcal{L}_{ce}^{S \to T} = \frac{1}{H \times W} \sum_{i=1}^{H \times W} \mathbb{1}(max(q_i^{s \to t}) > \tau_t(\arg\max_c(q_{i,c}^{s \to t}))) \cdot \mathrm{CE}(q_i^{s \to t}, \tilde{y}_i^T) \qquad (9)$$

where $\tilde{y}^T(i)$ is the corresponding pseudo label, $F_{s \to t}$ and $F_{s \to t}$ are the cross-domain and target domain branches in the student model. $q_i^t = h_{cls}(F_t(x_i^M))$ and $q_i^{s \to t} = h_{cls}(F_{s \to t}(x_i^S, x_i^M))$ are the class predictions of the two branches.

3.4   Overall Training Objective

We integrate the cross-domain Transformer network with the self-training framework and utilize an adaptive confidence threshold for pseudo-label filtering, which leads to the combined objective function $\mathcal{L}_{total}$. It consists of three parts: domain-specific losses $\mathcal{L}_{ce}^S$ and $\mathcal{L}_{ce}^T$, as well as cross-domain prediction loss function $\mathcal{L}_{ce}^{S \to T}$, as given in Eq. (9). The overall training objective can be formulated as:

$$\mathcal{L}_{total} = \mathcal{L}_{ce}^S + \mathcal{L}_{ce}^T + \mathcal{L}_{ce}^{S \to T} \qquad (10)$$

4   Experiment

4.1   Implantation Details

Datasets and Benchmarks. To demonstrate the superiority of our proposed method, we conducted experiments in different benchmarks, including the two sim-to-real benchmark GTA5→ Cityscapes and Synthia→Cityscapes, as well as the normal-to-adverse benchmark Cityscapes → ACDC.

The GTA and Synthia datasets consist of synthetic urban scene images generated by graphics engines, while the Cityscapes dataset contains real street scene images, all annotated with 19 common semantic categories. The ACDC dataset contains images under four adverse conditions: rain, snow, fog, and night. Except for Synthia, all datasets share the same 19 categories for semantic segmentation.

Table 1. Quantitative comparison results on GTA5→Cityscapes.

Method	BB	Road	S.walk	Build.	Wall	Fence	Pole	Tr.Light	Sign	Veget.	Terrain	Sky	Person	Rider	Car	Truck	Bus	Train	M.bike	Bike	mIoU
Source Only	C	75.8	16.8	77.2	12.5	21.0	25.5	30.1	20.1	81.3	24.6	70.3	53.8	26.4	49.9	17.2	25.9	6.5	25.3	36.0	36.6
AdaptSegNet [13]	C	86.5	36	79.9	23.4	23.3	23.9	35.2	14.8	83.4	33.3	75.6	58.5	27.6	73.7	32.5	35.4	3.9	30.1	28.1	42.4
AdvEnt [16]	C	89.4	33.1	81.0	26.6	26.8	27.2	33.5	24.7	83.9	36.7	78.8	58.7	30.5	84.8	38.5	44.5	1.7	31.6	32.4	45.5
CyCADA [3]	C	86.7	35.6	80.1	19.8	17.5	38.0	39.9	41.5	82.7	27.9	73.6	64.9	19.0	65.0	12.0	28.6	4.5	31.1	42.0	42.7
CBST [24]	C	91.8	53.5	80.5	32.7	21.0	34.0	28.9	20.4	83.9	34.2	80.9	53.1	24.0	82.7	30.3	35.9	16.0	25.9	42.8	45.9
PatchAlign [14]	C	92.3	51.9	82.1	29.2	25.1	24.5	33.8	33.0	82.4	32.8	82.2	58.6	27.2	84.3	33.4	46.3	2.2	29.5	32.3	46.5
FDA [22]	C	92.5	53.3	82.4	26.5	27.6	36.4	40.6	38.9	82.3	39.8	78.0	62.6	34.4	84.9	34.1	53.1	16.9	27.7	46.4	50.5
DACS [12]	C	89.9	39.7	87.9	30.7	39.5	38.5	46.4	52.8	88.0	44.0	88.8	67.2	35.8	84.5	45.7	50.2	0.0	27.3	34.0	52.1
CorDA [17]	C	94.7	63.1	87.6	30.7	40.6	40.2	47.8	51.6	87.6	47.0	89.7	66.7	35.9	90.2	48.9	57.5	0.0	39.8	56.0	56.6
ProDA [23]	C	87.8	56.0	79.7	46.3	44.8	45.6	53.5	53.5	88.6	45.2	82.1	70.7	39.2	88.8	45.5	59.4	1.0	48.9	56.4	57.5
Source Only	T	71.5	18.0	84.2	34.4	30.9	33.4	44.3	23.5	87.4	41.3	86.6	64.0	22.5	88.3	44.5	39.1	2.3	35.2	31.6	46.5
DAFormer [4]	T	95.7	70.2	89.4	53.5	48.1	49.6	55.8	59.4	89.9	47.9	92.5	72.2	44.7	92.3	74.5	78.2	65.1	55.9	61.8	68.3
Ours	T	96.2	73.1	89.6	53.0	52.7	52.6	54.5	65.1	89.2	47.4	90.2	73.9	46.9	93.1	81.8	83.7	68.5	55.9	63.4	70.0
Oracle	T	98.0	84.2	92.6	59.4	59.7	61.9	66.7	76.6	92.5	66.4	94.9	79.6	60.7	94.6	84.0	88.6	81.2	63.2	75.0	77.9

Training Details. We used the same experimental settings as DAFormer, with the MiT-B5 [20] backbone used as the encoder and the decoder also derived from DAFormer. During training, both source and target domain images were randomly cropped into patches of 512×512 augmented with techniques including random flipping and color jittering. These images were then grouped into batches of size 2 and passed into a multi-branch cross-domain Transformer. We used the AdamW optimizer with a learning rate of 6×10^{-5}. Additionally, the momentum update parameter for the pseudo-label threshold, λ, is set to 0.999. During the inference phase, the batch size is set to 1, and only the target domain branch is used, while the other branches are dropped to ensure efficiency.

4.2   Comparison with Different UDA Methods

Quantitative Comparison. We evaluated our proposed method against existing UDA methods on various benchmarks including GTA5→Cityscapes, Synthia →Cityscapes, and Cityscapes→ACDC, and compared its performance against existing UDA methods. Results are shown in Tables 1, 2, and 3. Following the common UDA settings [4,19], all the results on Cityscapes were calculated on the validation set, and the performance on ACDC datasets is reported on the test set. C denotes CNN-based model, while T represents Transformers.

The results show that our model surpasses the baseline model DAFormer [4] in all three benchmarks, achieving an improvement of 1.7% for GTA5→Cityscapes, 0.6% for Synthia→Cityscapes, and 4.9% for Cityscapes→ACDC. The introduction of cross-domain attention is found to further improve the model's adaptability to the target domain, facilitating the model to focus on more contextual content during prediction and learn domain-invariant knowledge. The model shows higher segmentation performance for specific categories such as *signal sign*, *bus*, *train*, and *fence* in GTA5→Cityscapes, and significant improvement for categories such as *person*, *truck*, and *bus* in Cityscapes→ACDC.

Qualitative Results. As shown in Fig. 4, we visualize the segmentation results on GTA5→Cityscapes and Cityscapes→ACDC benchmarks. The white boxes

Table 2. Quantitative comparison results on Synthia→Cityscapes.

Method	BB	Road	S.walk	Build.	Wall*	Fence*	Pole*	Tr.Light	Sign	Veget.	Sky	Person	Rider	Car	Bus	M.bike	Bike	mIoU*	mIoU
Source Only	C	64.3	21.3	73.1	2.4	1.1	31.4	7.0	27.7	63.1	67.6	42.2	19.9	73.1	15.3	10.5	38.9	40.3	34.9
PatchAlign [14]	C	82.4	38	78.6	8.7	0.6	26.0	3.9	11.1	75.5	84.6	53.5	21.6	71.4	32.6	19.3	31.7	46.5	–
AdaptSegNet [13]	C	84.3	42.7	77.5	–	–	–	4.7	7.0	77.9	82.5	54.3	21.0	72.3	32.2	18.9	32.3	46.7	–
AdvEnt [16]	C	85.6	42.2	79.7	8.7	0.4	25.9	5.4	8.1	80.4	84.1	57.9	23.8	73.3	36.4	14.2	33.0	48.0	41.2
CBST [24]	C	68.0	29.9	76.3	10.8	1.4	33.9	22.8	29.5	77.6	78.3	60.6	28.3	81.6	23.5	18.8	39.8	48.8	42.6
FDA [22]	C	79.3	35	73.2	–	–	–	19.9	24.0	61.7	82.6	61.4	31.1	83.9	40.8	38.4	51.1	52.5	–
DACS [12]	C	80.6	25.1	81.9	21.5	2.9	37.2	22.7	24.0	83.7	90.8	67.6	38.3	82.9	38.9	28.5	47.6	54.8	48.3
CorDA [17]	C	**93.3**	**61.6**	85.3	19.6	5.1	37.8	36.6	42.8	84.9	90.4	69.7	41.8	85.6	38.4	32.6	53.9	62.8	55.0
ProDA [23]	C	87.8	45.7	84.6	37.1	0.6	44.0	54.6	37.0	**88.1**	84.4	74.2	24.3	**88.2**	51.1	40.5	45.6	62.0	55.5
Source Only	T	51.5	20.3	79.2	19.3	1.8	40.9	29.9	22.7	79.1	82.4	63.0	24.9	75.8	33.7	18.9	24.9	46.6	35.2
DAFormer [4]	T	84.5	40.7	**88.4**	41.5	6.5	**50.0**	55.0	54.6	86.0	**89.8**	73.2	48.2	87.2	53.2	53.9	**61.7**	67.4	60.9
Ours	T	84.7	44.3	88.2	**45.1**	**7.6**	48.7	**56.1**	**54.7**	87.3	87.4	**74.3**	**48.6**	87.6	**53.9**	**56.8**	60.2	**68.0**	**61.6**
Oracle	T	98.0	84.2	92.6	59.4	59.7	61.9	66.7	76.6	92.5	94.9	79.6	60.7	94.6	88.6	63.2	75.0	78.0	82.1

Table 3. Quantitative comparison results on Cityscapes→ACDC.

Method	BB	Road	S.walk	Build.	Wall	Fence	Pole	Tr.Light	Sign	Veget.	Terrain	Sky	Person	Rider	Car	Truck	Bus	Train	M.bike	Bike	mIoU
AdvEnt [16]	C	72.9	14.3	40.5	16.6	21.2	9.3	17.4	21.3	63.8	23.8	18.3	32.6	19.5	69.5	36.2	34.5	46.2	26.9	36.1	32.7
BDL [8]	C	56.0	32.5	68.1	20.1	17.4	15.8	30.2	28.7	59.9	25.3	37.7	28.7	25.5	70.2	39.6	40.5	52.7	29.2	38.4	37.7
CLAN [10]	C	79.1	29.5	45.9	18.1	21.3	22.1	35.3	40.7	67.4	29.4	32.8	42.7	18.5	73.6	42.0	31.6	55.7	25.4	30.7	39.0
FDA [22]	C	74.6	73.2	70.1	63.3	59.0	54.7	52.3	47.0	44.9	44.8	43.3	39.5	34.7	29.5	28.6	28.5	28.3	28.2	24.8	45.7
MGCDA [11]	C	73.4	28.7	69.9	19.3	26.3	36.8	53.0	53.3	75.4	32.0	84.6	51.0	26.1	77.6	43.2	45.9	53.9	32.7	41.5	48.7
DANNet [19]	C	**84.3**	**54.2**	77.6	38.0	30.0	18.9	41.6	35.2	71.3	39.4	86.6	48.7	29.2	76.2	41.6	43.0	58.6	32.6	43.9	50.0
DAFormer [4]	T	58.4	51.3	**84.0**	**42.7**	**35.1**	**50.7**	30.0	**57.0**	74.8	52.8	51.3	58.3	32.6	82.7	58.3	54.9	**82.4**	**44.1**	50.7	55.4
Ours	T	81.7	40.4	78.1	37.7	31.9	43.9	**57.8**	56.0	**82.5**	54.9	**86.6**	**61.6**	**39.1**	**84.2**	**66.6**	**73.3**	76.5	41.0	**52.0**	**60.3**

highlight the areas with significant improvements. It can be observed that our model demonstrates superior performance to the baseline in segmenting classes such as *road* and *traffic light* in the former benchmarks, which further verifies the results in Table 1. These two classes of objects have similar contextual relationships in both source and target domains, and the introduction of cross-domain attention allows the model to focus more on similar contexts, resulting in more accurate pixel-level predictions. The effectiveness of our approach is further demonstrated in the Cityscapes→ACDC task under various adverse conditions, where our method significantly outperforms the baseline in segmenting the *sky* class and exhibits improvements in classifying *sidewalk* and *traffic light* (Table 4).

Table 4. Ablation study of proposed modules.

Baseline	ATS	CDAttn	mIoU	mIoU
✓			68.3	–
✓	✓		68.8	+0.5
✓		✓	69.7	+1.4
✓	✓	✓	70.0	+1.7

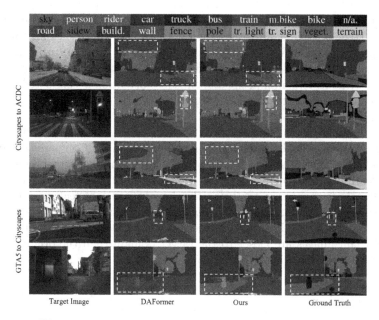

Fig. 4. Qualitative visualization of the experiment results.

4.3   Ablation Study

We showcase the effectiveness of different modules in our model through ablation experiments. As shown in Fig. 4, the Adaptive Thresholding Strategy (ATS) improves the baseline model by 0.6% compared to the original threshold method. The Cross-Domain Attention (CDAttn) network alone achieves a performance boost of 1.2%, indicating that additional attention to cross-domain context can further facilitate the learning of domain-invariant features. The experiments show that the two modules narrow the domain gap from different perspectives, and their combination results in further performance improvement.

To assess the effectiveness of the proposed cross-domain transformer as shown in Fig. 2, we compared it with two different cross-domain transformer

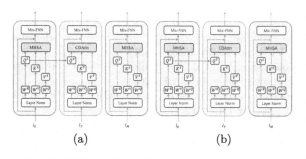

Fig. 5. Different Cross-Domain Attention Design.

Table 5. Comparison of designs.

Design	mIoU
Baseline	68.3
Design-TS	68.6
Design-SMT	68.4
ours	69.5

designs that use different forms of cross-attention between the source and target domains. Design-TS (Fig. 5(a)) uses the target domain's query Q_t instead of Q_s for computing cross-attention, which is opposite to our design. In Design-SMT (Fig. 5(b)), the input of the cross-domain branch is the original target domain image x^T without domain mix-up, and the cross-attention is conducted between the source domain and the original target domain.

Table 5 records the performance of different designs on the GTA→Cityscapes task. Our proposed model outperforms the other designs, highlighting the importance of cross-attention between source and mixed domain. Compared to design-TS, we observed that the direction of attention has an impact on cross-domain feature learning. Specifically, attention directed from the source domain to the target domain is capable of capturing the domain-invariant features effectively, resulting in superior performance in comparison to the design that prioritizes the source domain. Additionally, the results of the Design-SMT indicate that mixed-domain images are closer to the target domain than the original source images, thereby facilitating better domain adaptation.

5   Conclusion

In this paper, we propose a weight-sharing multi-branch cross-domain Transformer to integrate self-attention with cross-domain attention for domain-invariant feature learning. Additionally, we introduce a category-specific adaptive threshold strategy for balancing the quality and quantity of pseudo-labels. Experiments on different benchmark tasks verify the effectiveness of the proposed method.

Acknowledgements. This work was supported by the Natural Science Foundation of China (62276242), National Aviation Science Foundation (2022Z071078001), CAAI-Huawei MindSpore Open Fund (CAAIXSJLJJ-2021-016B, CAAIXSJLJJ-2022-001A), Anhui Province Key Research and Development Program (202104a05-020007), USTC-IAT Application Sci. & Tech. Achievement Cultivation Program (JL06521001Y), Sci. & Tech. Innovation Special Zone (20-103-14-LZ-001 004-01). Fang was supported by the Guangxi Science and Technology Base and Talent Project under Grant (2020AC19253).

References

1. Araslanov, N., Roth, S.: Self-supervised augmentation consistency for adapting semantic segmentation. In: CVPR, pp. 15379–15389 (2021)
2. Dosovitskiy, A., Beyer, L., Kolesnikov, A., et al.: An image is worth 16×16 words: transformers for image recognition at scale. In: ICLR (2021)
3. Hoffman, J., Tzeng, E., Park, T., et al.: CyCADA: cycle-consistent adversarial domain adaptation. In: ICML, pp. 1989–1998 (2018)
4. Hoyer, L., Dai, D., Van Gool, L.: DAFormer: improving network architectures and training strategies for domain-adaptive semantic segmentation. In: CVPR, pp. 9924–9935 (2022)

5. Hoyer, L., Dai, D., Van Gool, L.: HRDA: context-aware high-resolution domain-adaptive semantic segmentation. In: Avidan, S., Brostow, G., Cissé, M., Farinella, G.M., Hassner, T. (eds.) ECCV 2022. LNCS, vol. 13690, pp. 372–391. Springer, Cham (2022). https://doi.org/10.1007/978-3-031-20056-4_22

6. Jiang, Z., et al.: Prototypical contrast adaptation for domain adaptive semantic segmentation. In: Avidan, S., Brostow, G., Cissé, M., Farinella, G.M., Hassner, T. (eds.) ECCV 2022. LNCS, vol. 13694, pp. 36–54. Springer, Cham (2022). https://doi.org/10.1007/978-3-031-19830-4_3

7. Li, J., Zhou, P., Xiong, C., Hoi, S.C.: Prototypical contrastive learning of unsupervised representations. arXiv preprint arXiv:2005.04966 (2020)

8. Li, Y., Yuan, L., Vasconcelos, N.: Bidirectional learning for domain adaptation of semantic segmentation. In: CVPR, pp. 6936–6945 (2019)

9. Liu, Z., et al.: Swin transformer: hierarchical vision transformer using shifted windows. In: ICCV (2021)

10. Luo, Y., Zheng, L., Guan, T., et al.: Taking a closer look at domain shift: category-level adversaries for semantics consistent domain adaptation. In: CVPR, pp. 2507–2516 (2019)

11. Sakaridis, C., Dai, D., Van Gool, L.: Map-guided curriculum domain adaptation and uncertainty-aware evaluation for semantic nighttime image segmentation. PAMI **44**(6), 3139–3153 (2020)

12. Tranheden, W., Olsson, V., Pinto, J., Svensson, L.: DACS: domain adaptation via cross-domain mixed sampling. In: WACV, pp. 1379–1389 (2021)

13. Tsai, Y.H., Hung, W.C., Schulter, S., et al.: Learning to adapt structured output space for semantic segmentation. In: CVPR, pp. 7472–7481 (2018)

14. Tsai, Y.H., Sohn, K., Schulter, S., et al.: Domain adaptation for structured output via discriminative patch representations. In: CVPR, pp. 1456–1465 (2019)

15. Vaswani, A., et al.: Attention is all you need. In: NeurIPS, vol. 30 (2017)

16. Vu, T.H., Jain, H., Bucher, M., et al.: Advent: adversarial entropy minimization for domain adaptation in semantic segmentation. In: CVPR, pp. 2517–2526 (2019)

17. Wang, Q., Dai, D., Hoyer, L., Van Gool, L., et al.: Domain adaptive semantic segmentation with self-supervised depth estimation. In: ICCV, pp. 8515–8525 (2021)

18. Wang, Y., Chen, H., Heng, Q., et al.: FreeMatch: self-adaptive thresholding for semi-supervised learning. arXiv preprint arXiv:2205.07246 (2022)

19. Wu, X., Wu, Z., Guo, H., et al.: DANNet: a one-stage domain adaptation network for unsupervised nighttime semantic segmentation. In: CVPR, pp. 15769–15778 (2021)

20. Xie, E., Wang, W., Yu, Z., et al.: SegFormer: simple and efficient design for semantic segmentation with transformers. In: NeurIPS, vol. 34, pp. 12077–12090 (2021)

21. Xu, T., Chen, W., Wang, P., et al.: CDTrans: cross-domain transformer for unsupervised domain adaptation. arXiv preprint arXiv:2109.06165 (2021)

22. Yang, Y., Soatto, S.: FDA: Fourier domain adaptation for semantic segmentation. In: CVPR, pp. 4085–4095 (2020)

23. Zhang, P., Zhang, B., Zhang, T., et al.: Prototypical pseudo label denoising and target structure learning for domain adaptive semantic segmentation. In: CVPR, pp. 12414–12424 (2021)

24. Zou, Y., Yu, Z., Kumar, B., Wang, J.: Unsupervised domain adaptation for semantic segmentation via class-balanced self-training. In: ECCV, pp. 289–305 (2018)

Delineation of Prostate Boundary from Medical Images via a Mathematical Formula-Based Hybrid Algorithm

Tao Peng[1,2,3]($\boxtimes$), Daqiang Xu[4], Yiyun Wu[5], Jing Zhao[6], Hui Mao[7], Jing Cai[2]($\boxtimes$), and Lei Zhang[8,9]($\boxtimes$)

[1] School of Future Science and Engineering, Soochow University, Suzhou, China
sdpengtao401@gmail.com

[2] Department of Health Technology and Informatics, Hong Kong Polytechnic University, Hong Kong, China
jing.cai@polyu.edu.hk

[3] Department of Radiation Oncology, UT Southwestern Medical Center, Dallas, TX, USA

[4] Department of Radiology, The Affiliated Suzhou Hospital of Nanjing Medical University, Suzhou Municipal Hospital, Suzhou, Jiangsu, China

[5] Department of Ultrasound, Jiangsu Province Hospital of Chinese Medicine, Nanjing, Jiangsu, China

[6] Department of Ultrasound, Beijing Tsinghua Changgung Hospital, Beijing, China

[7] Department of Dermatology, Huangshi Central Hospital, Huangshi, Hubei, China

[8] Graduate Program of Medical Physics and Data Science Research Center, Duke Kunshan University, Kunshan, Jiangsu, China
lei.zhang@dukekunshan.edu.cn

[9] Graduate Program of Medical Physics, Duke University, Durham, NC, USA

Abstract. The precise extraction of the contour of prostate on transrectal ultrasound (TRUS) is crucial for the diagnosis and treatment of prostate tumor. Due to the relatively low signal-to-noise ratio (SNR) of TRUS images and the potential of imaging artifacts, accurate contouring of the prostate from TRUS images has been a challenging task. This paper proposes four strategies to achieve higher precision of segmentation on TRUS images. Firstly, a modified principal curve-based algorithm is used to obtain the data sequence, with a small amount of prior point information adopted for coarse initialization. Secondly, an evolution neural network is devised to find an optimal network. Thirdly, a fractional-order-based network is trained with the data sequence as input, resulting in a decreased model error and increased precision. Finally, the parameters of a fractional-order-based neural network were utilized to construct an interpretable and smooth mathematical equation of the organ border. The Dice similarity coefficient (DSC), Jaccard similarity coefficient (OMG), and accuracy (ACC) of model outputs against ground-truths were $95.9 \pm 2.3\%$, $94.9 \pm 2.4\%$, and $95.3 \pm 2.2\%$, respectively. The results of our method outperform several popular state-of-the-art segmentation methods.

Keywords: Prostate segmentation · transrectal ultrasound image · automatic selection polygon tracking · evolution network · fractional-order-based neural network · explainable mathematical formula

© The Author(s), under exclusive license to Springer Nature Switzerland AG 2023
L. Iliadis et al. (Eds.): ICANN 2023, LNCS 14261, pp. 160–171, 2023.
https://doi.org/10.1007/978-3-031-44198-1_14

1 Introduction

The precise segmentation of organs in ultrasound images is vital for a wide range of modern clinical applications [1]. Numerous ultrasound segmentation techniques have been proposed, but achieving accurate segmentation remains challenging due to factors such as poor image quality and significant variations in prostate shapes and intensity distributions among different patients [2, 3].

Various approaches have been developed to address these challenges. Jaouen et al. [4] introduced an active surface-based method for prostate segmentation in TRUS images, utilizing initial points from base and apex images to accurately model and locate the region of interest (ROI), thus enhancing precision. However, this model necessitated extensive human intervention for parameter initialization. In recent years, deep learning-based segmentation methods have gained prominence. For instance, Lu et al. [5] presented a grading-based approach for segmenting prostate cancer in ultrasound images, employing a region labeling-based ROI detection module and an attention module. Nonetheless, the accuracy of this model could be compromised when detecting lesion regions. Beitone et al. [6] proposed an ensemble learning structure with a fusion network, but this method faced high computational costs and was potentially influenced by the outcomes of the three CNN-based pre-processing architectures. Sloun et al. [7] developed a deep learning structure for prostate segmentation, using MRI images to aid physicians in determining ultrasound image ground truth. However, this model's performance could be affected by indistinct ROI contours.

To tackle these challenges and offer a comprehensive solution, we propose an innovative hybrid approach with several advantages. This paper is organized as follows: Section 2 presents the methodology of our hybrid approach, including (i) the combination of an Automatic Selection Polygon Tracking method (ASPT) with a modified neural network; (ii) the integration of the Principal Curve (PC)-based projection step into the Neutrosophic Adaptive Mean Shift Clustering (NAMSC) method based on bandwidth [8], allowing for the automatic determination of the number of vertices/clusters without human intervention; (iii) the introduction of a Distributed-based Memory Differential Evolution (DMDE) method to aid in identifying the optimal neural network, incorporating multi-mutation operators to enhance population diversity; (iv) the presentation of a Fractional-order Backpropagation Neural Network with L2 regularization (FBNNL), which retains the memory and heredity benefits of the fractional gradient descent algorithm, inspired by Chen et al.'s work [11]; and (v) the development of an explicit mathematical model for a smooth prostate periphery, realized through FBNNL, to achieve a refined segmentation result, addressing the issue of non-smooth contours generated by PC-based variants [12]. Section 3 discusses the experiments and results, demonstrating the effectiveness of our approach, while Section 4 concludes the paper and highlights potential future research directions.

2   Methods

2.1   Background

Existing automatic methods [13] for segmenting ultrasound images face significant difficulty and typically result in a DSC of approximately 0.9. In response to this issue, our proposed technique capitalizes on the prior knowledge of Pn reference points, which guide our model and aid in achieving accurate ROI localization. Traditional PC-based algorithms are subject to the number of preset vertices, whose operators [14] are manually determined, influencing the algorithm's subsequent outcome. Automatic determination of vertices represents a significant challenge, as does the smoothing of the outcome generated by a PC-based algorithm comprised of line segments.

2.2   Contour Extraction Model

Our approach to contour extraction involves a series of four steps. Initially, we leverage several reference points (P_n) and ASPT methodology to generate a data sequence D consisting of P_n and their relevant projection parameter t. Subsequently, we utilize an optimized differential evolution (DE) network to determine the optimal neural network capable of delivering the best results. To minimize model error and enhance the accuracy, we integrated FBNNL training, with D serving as the input. Lastly, we utilize FBNNL's parameters to develop a coherent mathematical formula that accurately represents the prostate boundary, lending to smoothness and explainability to the procedure.

(1) **Obtaining Data Sequence**. Our method combines two renowned techniques (namely, NAMSC and PC-based projection) to facilitate the generation of the input sequence through the ASPT approach. The primary advantage of our ASPT algorithm is that it automatically establishes the amount of vertices of the PC, a feature missing in conventional PC-based methods [9] (as seen in Fig. 1). By contrast, PC-based methods require manual intervention, thereby making them prone to inconsistency and errors. Ultimately, our ASPT algorithm enhances the precision of this process, making it more efficient in generating an accurate output.

Neutrosophic Mean Shift Clustering (NAMSC) Method: The MSC method, developed by Cheng et al. [15], has been successfully employed to cluster datasets. Nevertheless, the precision of the segmentation outcome can be compromised by unforeseen issues like image noise and intensity variations [16]. These indeterminate entities can be better addressed when employing a neutrosophic approach, which is highly effective at processing noise [8]. To optimize the cluster amount, we utilize the NAMSC algorithm, which leverages a neutrosophic filter to enhance the mean shift clustering technique.

Principal Curve (PC)-Based Projection Step: Upon completion of the NAMSC step, the principal curve f is automatically selected, after determining the vertices/clusters. This technique was previously established by Hastie et al. [17] and involves constructing a self-consistent and smooth curve, which passes through the center of a multidimensional data set. To obtain a sequence of points, pi, that correspond to appropriate neighborhood sets, such as the vertex set V or segment set S of f, we employ the projection step. Furthermore, we utilize the projection index t to refer to the sequence of pi projecting to f reliably. Figure 2 illustrates the outcomes of the partition.

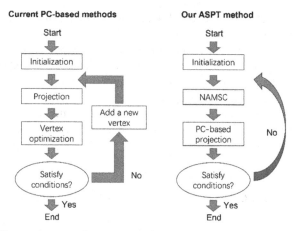

Fig. 1. Difference between the current PC-based methods [9] and our ASPT method.

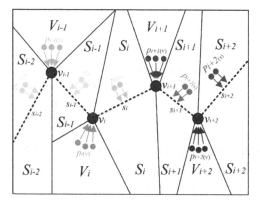

Fig. 2. An example partition output of the principal curve's vertices and segments. Orange and blue arrows illustrate the projection direction from p_i to v_i and s_i.

(2) Optimal Neural Network Selection. Random selection of neural network (NN) parameters often leads to local minima while training [20], undermining the NN's performance. One solution is to utilize the Differential Evolution network (DE) [21], renowned for its exceptional global search abilities. Nonetheless, the DE's performance can be enhanced by means of various methodologies, including the incorporation of an optimal storage mechanism to efficiently store parameters, the use of an appropriate transform scheme, and the population difference strengthen method. To that end, we present a new methodology called distributed-based memory DE (DMDE), which leverages distributed- and memory-based structures and employs multi-mutation operators to improve performance.

Distributed-Based Scheme. This method relies on the principles of the distributed-related structures [10], which we use to shift the best individual from each parallel subpopulation to the later sub-dataset within the ring topology structure. Through this process, we seek to improve the search potential of our technique, and improve the accuracy of the results.

Memory-Based Scheme. In this study, a vital feature of the memory-based DE (MDE) is its capacity to save and utilize best mean crossover rates (uCR) and mean mutation factors (uF) from the previous cycle, thereby increasing the likelihood of finding an optimal individual during the following cycle.

Multi-mutation Operators. To enhance the population difference, multi-mutation operators are introduced to produce mutual vector individual vc_i^{G+1}, shown in Eq. (1).

$$vc_i^{G+1}$$
$$= \begin{cases} x_{i_1}^G + random_1 \times (x_{i_2}^G - x_{i_3}^G), & if \ random[0, 1] < p_G \\ x_{i_1}^G + random_2 \times (x_{i_2}^G - x_{i_3}^G) + random_3 \times (x_{i_4}^G - x_{i_5}^G), \ otherwise \end{cases}$$
(1)

where *random* means a random number between [0, 1]. Integer i_k ($k \in [1, 5]$) is stochastically chosen between $[1, N_p]$ in which N_p means the number of answers. In the mutation phase, condition probability p_G is shown in Eq. (2).

$$p_G = p_{min} + \frac{G \times (p_{max} - p_{min})}{Gmax}$$
(2)

where p_{min} and p_{max} are the minimum- and maximum- conditional probability, respectively.

(3) Training. To lower expected-outcome bias, state-of-the-art backpropagation neural networks (BPNN) rely upon the gradient descent algorithm (GDA) [23]. To remedy GDA's overfitting tendencies and optimize its heredity, our team incorporates the fractional gradient descent algorithm and L2 regularization into BPNN, thereby creating a novel algorithm, FBNNL. In this study, we framed FBNNL with a network structure of three layers, employing Sigmoid [24] and ELU [25] activation functions throughout the forward training process.

(4) Interpretable Mathematical Formula-Based Expression of Contour. Upon obtaining the optimal FBNNL, a mathematical equation that interprets the smooth contour of the prostate is defined as,

$$z(t) = z(A(t)), B(t)) = \left(\frac{2 \times C(A(t)) + 1}{2 \times C(A(t)) + 2}, \frac{2 \times C(B(t)) + 1}{2 \times C(B(t)) + 2} \right)$$
(3)

where t indicates the projection parameter. $B(t)$ and $A(t)$ means y- and x-axis coordinates of vertices of the resulting contour. $C(A(t))$ and $C(B(t))$ are the result in the output layer that are similar to a regression function on t, respectively, expressed by,

$$(C(A(t)), B(y(t)))$$
$$= \left(\frac{1}{2 \times (\sum\limits_{ei=1}^{H} \frac{1}{1+e^{-(tw_{1i}-a_i)}} w_{2i,1} - b_1) - 1)}, \frac{1}{2 \times (\sum\limits_{ei=1}^{H} \frac{1}{1+e^{-(tw_{1i}-a_i)}} w_{2,i,2} - b_2) + 1)} \right)$$
(4)

where Eq. (3) and Eq. (4) are expressed by the parameters of FBNNL. a and w_1 are the threshold and weight in a hidden layer, respectively. Moreover, b and w_2 are the threshold and weight in the output layer, respectively.

2.3 Datasets

Our segmentation plan was evaluated on two separate prostates transrectal ultrasound (TRUS) datasets, which are elaborated as below:

Data A# [26]: a prostate dataset from Jiangsu Province Hospital of Chinese Medicine in Nanjing, China.

Data B# [27]: a dataset including 266 brachytherapy patients from Tsinghua Changgung Hospital, Beijing, China. This dataset was randomly split into training, validation, and testing groups, with a 7:1:2 ratio. The partition of each dataset and the combined set is shown in Table 1.

Data C#, addressing the disequilibrium of training slices in the two datasets, was generated by randomly rotating Data A#'s training data using rotation methods. Every slice is rotated twice between $[-15°, 15°]$.

Manual contours from three physicians were used as ground truth. Three universal metrics [28]: DSC, Accuracy (ACC), and Jaccard similarity coefficient (OMG) were used to evaluate the performance of our proposed method.

Table 1. The partition of each dataset

	Total set	Training set (raw + augmentation)	Validation set	Testing set
Data A#	393	215 (raw) + 430 (aug)	70	108
Data B#	945	675	66	204
Data C# (Combined set)	-	1320	136	312

3 Results

3.1 Model Robustness Evaluation

We first conducted an analysis to determine the effectiveness of noise reduction of our algorithm on audio files recorded in noisy environments. The audio files were deliberately corrupted using various levels of background noise to simulate real-world conditions. The SNR levels ranged from 0.9 to 1.0 [29] to mimic the levels typically found in noisy environments. The algorithm was then applied to each audio file to assess its performance in reducing noise while preserving the integrity of the original sound. The results of the analysis, depicted in graphs, demonstrate that the noise reduction algorithm was highly effective at all SNR levels tested.

In this section, we analyzed the impact of varying degrees of background image noise on the performance of the model. Figure 3 clearly depicts the model's ability to perform well as the signal-to-noise ratio (SNR) decreases. The decline is notable on the Data C# dataset, with the mean values of ACC, DSC, and OMG decreasing by 4.49%, 4.35%, and 4.97%, respectively, as the SNR reduces from 1 to 0.6. At an SNR of 1, our model had a

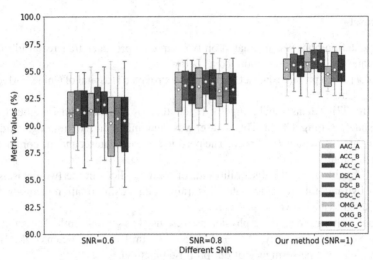

Fig. 3. Metric values of different SNRs. We display the evaluation outcomes for ACC, DSC, and OMG utilizing boxplots with blue, green, and pink hues correspondingly. Within these boxplots, the mean and median values are denoted by white dots and red lines, respectively. Datasets A, B, and C serve as distinct data sources. The detailed outcomes are shown. (When SNR = 0.6, for *Data A#*, ACC = 90.9 ± 3.7%, DSC = 91.3 ± 3.2%, OMG = 90.2 ± 4.4%; When SNR = 0.6, for *Data B#*, ACC = 91.4 ± 3.2%, DSC = 92.4 ± 2.7%, OMG = 90.6 ± 3.7%; When SNR = 0.6, for *Data C#*, ACC = 91.2 ± 3.4%, DSC = 91.9 ± 3%, OMG = 90.4 ± 4%; When SNR = 0.8, for *Data A#*, ACC = 93.3 ± 3%, DSC = 93.6 ± 3%, OMG = 93.1 ± 2.8%; When SNR = 0.8, for *Data B#*, ACC = 93.7 ± 2.9%, DSC = 94 ± 2.5%, OMG = 93.4 ± 2.6%; When SNR = 0.8, for *Data C#*, ACC = 93.5 ± 2.9%, DSC = 93.8 ± 2.8%, OMG = 93.3 ± 2.7%; When SNR = 1(our method), for *Data A#*, ACC = 95.1 ± 2.3%, DSC = 95.6 ± 2.3%, OMG = 94.7 ± 2.7%; When SNR = 1(our method), for *Data B#*, ACC = 95.5 ± 2.2%, DSC = 96.1 ± 2.3%, OMG = 95.1 ± 2.4%; When SNR = 1(our method), for *Data C#*, ACC = 95.3 ± 2.2%, DSC = 95.9 ± 2.3%, OMG = 94.9 ± 2.4%;)

performance of ACC = 95.3 ± 2.2 (%), DSC = 95.9 ± 2.3 (%), and OMG = 94.9 ± 2.4 (%) in Data C#. At an SNR of 0.6, our model attains a performance of ACC = 91.2 ± 3.4 (%), DSC = 91.9 ± 3 (%), and OMG = 90.4 ± 4 (%). Even with noisy data, the mean values of all the metrics on the combined Data C# were above 90.4%, indicating the superior performance of the proposed method under noisy conditions. Figure 4 shows the original ultrasound image and the model-generated prostate contours from a randomly selected example slice.

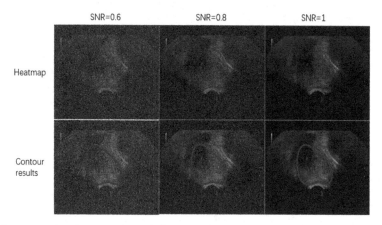

Fig.4. Randomly selected example slice for qualitative visualization under different SNRs.

3.2 Ablation Study (AS)

We utilized the ASPT method to obtain a data sequence that served as the input for the neural network-based FBNNL after determining the optimal FBNNL. The final outcomes were obtained upon the FBNNL's training. To evaluate the influence of FBNNL, an ablation test was performed in this section to assess the contribution of the three key modules (BPNN, FGDC, and L2 regularization), as illustrated in Fig. 5. Table 2 shows the architecture of each method.

Figure 5 shows that choosing BPNN (baseline) resulted in the lowest metric values. Following BPNN, we included other metrics (FGDC or L2 regularization). On the combined testing dataset (Data C#), ACC, DSC, and OMG increased by 2.07%~3.92%, 2.07%~4.8%, and 2.32%~4.97%, respectively. The proposed technique (BPNN+ FGDC +L2 regularization) provides the best performance, with ACC, DSC, and OMG of 95.3 ± 2.2%, 95.9 ± 2.3%, and 94.9 ± 2.4%, respectively.

Table 2. Components of the AS methods

AS	Structures
AS1	BPNN (Baseline)
AS2	BPNN+ FGDC
AS3	BPNN+L_2 regularization
AS4 (our method)	BPNN+ FGDC +L_2 regularization

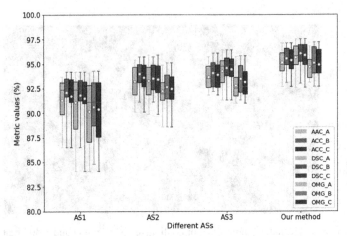

Fig. 5. Metrics values of different ASs. The detailed outcomes are shown. (AS1 for *Data A#*, ACC = 91.3 ± 3.4%, DSC = 91.1 ± 3.9%, OMG = 90.1 ± 4.3%; AS1 for *Data B#*, ACC = 92.1 ± 3.2%, DSC = 91.8 ± 3.2%, OMG = 90.6 ± 4.2%; AS1 for *Data C#*, ACC = 91.7 ± 3.3%, DSC = 91.5 ± 3.6%, OMG = 90.4 ± 4.2%; AS2 for *Data A#*, ACC = 93.2 ± 2.5%, DSC = 93.3 ± 2.6%, OMG = 92.2 ± 2.4%; AS2 for *Data B#*, ACC = 94 ± 2.3%, DSC = 93.5 ± 2.5%, OMG = 92.6 ± 2.6%; AS2 for *Data C#*, ACC = 93.6 ± 2.4%, DSC = 93.4 ± 2.6%, OMG = 92.5 ± 2.5%; AS3 for *Data A#*, ACC = 93.6 ± 2.2%, DSC = 94.2 ± 2.5%, OMG = 92.8 ± 2.4%; AS3 for *Data B#*, ACC = 94 ± 2.3%, DSC = 94.6 ± 2.4%, OMG = 93.5 ± 2.4%; AS3 for *Data C#*, ACC = 94.4 ± 2.4%, DSC = 94.4 ± 2.4%, OMG = 93.1 ± 2.4%; Our method for *Data A#*, ACC = 95.1 ± 2.3%, DSC = 95.6 ± 2.3%, OMG = 94.7 ± 2.7%; Our method for *Data B#*, ACC = 95.3 ± 2.2%, DSC = 96.1 ± 2.3%, OMG = 95.1 ± 2.4%; Our method for *Data C#*, ACC = 95.5 ± 2.2%, DSC = 95.9 ± 2.3%, OMG = 94.9 ± 2.4%;)

3.3 Comparison with SOTA Methods

Figure 6 displays the performance of various cutting-edge methods, such as Transformer [31], A-LugSeg [32], and H-SegMed [33]. Transformer [31] is a globally attentive architecture that excels at segmenting ROIs in medical images. A-LugSeg [32] and H-SegMed [33] are our previous works, where A-LugSeg is based on coarseness-to-refinement structures, while H-SegMed uses prior points to guide ROI localization. As shown in Fig. 6, compared to the Transformer and A-LugSeg methods, both our method and H-Segmed method showed higher mean values of all metrics (ACC, DSC, and OMG) and lower standard deviation of the corresponding metrics. Our approach demonstrates the highest overall performance.

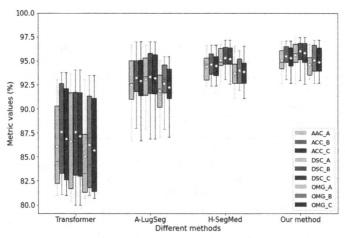

Fig. 6. Boxplots showcase ACC (blue), DSC (green), and OMG (pink) metrics for our method and SOAT methods. The detailed outcomes are shown. (Transformer for *Data A#*, ACC = 86.1 ± 5.5%, DSC = 86.6 ± 5.8%, OMG = 85.1 ± 5.4%; Transformer for *Data B#*, ACC = 87.6 ± 5.7%, DSC = 87.6 ± 5.7%, OMG = 86.3 ± 5.7%; Transformer for *Data C#*, ACC = 86.9 ± 5.6%, DSC = 87.2 ± 5.8%, OMG = 85.7 ± 5.6%; A-LugSeg for *Data A#*, ACC = 92.5 ± 3.8%, DSC = 93.1 ± 3.8%, OMG = 91.9 ± 3.4%; A-LugSeg for *Data B#*, ACC = 93.3 ± 3.3%, DSC = 993.4 ± 3.9%, OMG = 92.6 ± 3.2%; A-LugSeg for *Data C#*, ACC = 92.9 ± 3.6%, DSC = 93.2 ± 3.8%, OMG = 92.3 ± 3.3%; H-SegMed for *Data A#*, ACC = 94.4 ± 2.4%, DSC = 95.1 ± 2.3%, OMG = 93.8 ± 2.4%; H-SegMed for *Data B#*, ACC = 94.7 ± 2.2%, DSC = 95.4 ± 2.1%, OMG = 94 ± 2.4%; H-SegMed for *Data C#*, ACC = 94.4 ± 2.4%, DSC = 94.4 ± 2.4%, OMG = 93.1 ± 2.4%; Our method for *Data A#*, ACC = 95.1 ± 2.3%, DSC = 95.6 ± 2.3%, OMG = 94.7 ± 2.7%; Our method for *Data B#*, ACC = 95.5 ± 2.2%, DSC = 96.1 ± 2.3%, OMG = 95.1 ± 2.4%; Our method for *Data C#*, ACC = 95.3 ± 2.2%, DSC = 95.9 ± 2.3%, OMG = 94.9 ± 2.4%). (Color figure online)

4 Conclusion

In this paper, we have introduced a hybrid approach for prostate segmentation in transrectal ultrasound (TRUS) images, addressing challenges such as poor image quality and variations in prostate shapes and intensity distribution among patients. Our methodology differs from existing techniques in several aspects. The ASPT method incorporates a PC-based projection step into the NAMSC, allowing for the automatic determination of vertices without human intervention. Moreover, we have developed a distributed-based memory differential evolution method to optimize the neural network. We devised a neural network featuring FBNNL, which inherits the memory and heredity advantages of the fractional gradient descent algorithm. Lastly, we have addressed the issue of non-smooth contour by proposing an explainable mathematical model for a smooth prostate periphery. In future research, we plan to explore the generalizability of our model to various imaging modalities, assess the model's robustness and accuracy under diverse conditions, and transition from a semi-automatic algorithm to a fully automatic model for real-time clinical applications.

References

1. Zong, J., Qiu, T., Li, W., Guo, D.: Automatic ultrasound image segmentation based on local entropy and active contour model. Comput. Math. Appl. **78**, 929–943 (2019)
2. Panigrahi, L., Verma, K., Singh, B.K.: Ultrasound image segmentation using a novel multi-scale Gaussian kernel fuzzy clustering and multi-scale vector field convolution. Expert Syst. Appl. **115**, 486–498 (2019)
3. Huang, K., Zhang, Y., Cheng, H.D., Xing, P., Zhang, B.: Semantic segmentation of breast ultrasound image with fuzzy deep learning network and breast anatomy constraints. Neurocomputing. **450**, 319–335 (2021)
4. Jaouen, V., et al.: Prostate volume segmentation in TRUS using hybrid edge-Bhattacharyya active surfaces. IEEE Trans. Biomed. Eng. **66**, 920–933 (2018)
5. Lu, X., et al.: Ultrasonographic pathological grading of prostate cancer using automatic region-based Gleason grading network. Comput. Med. Imaging Graph., 102125 (2022)
6. Beitone, C., Troccaz, J.: Multi-eXpert fusion: an ensemble learning framework to segment 3D TRUS prostate images. Med. Phys. **49**, 5138–5148 (2022)
7. van Sloun, R.J.G., et al.: Deep learning for real-time, automatic, and scanner-adapted prostate (Zone) segmentation of transrectal ultrasound, for example, magnetic resonance imaging–transrectal ultrasound fusion prostate biopsy, European urology. Focus. **7**, 78–85 (2021)
8. Guo, Y., Şengür, A., Akbulut, Y., Shipley, A.: An effective color image segmentation approach using neutrosophic adaptive mean shift clustering. Measurement **119**, 28–40 (2018)
9. Wu, R., Wang, B., Xu, A.: Functional data clustering using principal curve methods. Commun. Stat., 1–20 (2021)
10. Ge, Y., et al.: Distributed differential evolution based on adaptive mergence and split for large-scale optimization. IEEE Trans. Cybern. **48**, 2166–2180 (2018)
11. Chen, M.-R., Chen, B.-P., Zeng, G.-Q., Lu, K.-D., Chu, P.: An adaptive fractional-order BP neural network based on extremal optimization for handwritten digits recognition. Neurocomputing. **391**, 260–272 (2020)
12. Biau, G., Fischer, A.: Parameter selection for principal curves. IEEE Trans. Inf. Theory **58**, 1924–1939 (2012)
13. Wang, Y., et al.: Deep attentive features for prostate segmentation in 3D transrectal ultrasound. IEEE Trans. Med. Imaging **38**, 2768–2778 (2019)
14. Moraes, E.C.C., Ferreira, D.D., Vitor, G.B., Barbosa, B.H.G.: Data clustering based on principal curves. Adv. Data Anal. Classif. **14**, 77–96 (2020)
15. Cheng, Y.: Mean shift, mode seeking, and clustering. IEEE Trans. Pattern Anal. Mach. Intell. **17**, 790–799 (1995)
16. Guo, Y., Şengür, A.: A novel image segmentation algorithm based on neutrosophic similarity clustering. Appl. Soft Comput. **25**, 391–398 (2014)
17. Hastie, T., Stuetzle, W.: Principal curves. J. Am. Stat. Assoc. **84**, 502–516 (1989)
18. Kégl, B., Linder, T., Zeger, K.: Learning and design of principal curves. IEEE Trans. Pattern Anal. Mach. Intell. **22**, 281–297 (2000)
19. Celebi, M.E., Celiker, F., Kingravi, H.A.: On Euclidean norm approximations. Pattern Recogn. **44**, 278–283 (2011)
20. Zeng, Y.-R., Zeng, Y., Choi, B., Wang, L.: Multifactor-influenced energy consumption forecasting using enhanced back-propagation neural network. Energy **127**, 381–396 (2017)
21. Leema, N., Nehemiah, H.K., Kannan, A.: Neural network classifier optimization using differential evolution with global information and back propagation algorithm for clinical datasets. Appl. Soft Comput. **49**, 834–844 (2016)
22. Zhang, J., Sanderson, A.C.: JADE: adaptive differential evolution with optional external archive. IEEE Trans. Evol. Comput. **13**, 945–958 (2009)

23. Xiao, M., Zheng, W.X., Jiang, G., Cao, J.: Undamped oscillations generated by Hopf bifurcations in fractional-order recurrent neural networks with Caputo derivative. IEEE Trans. Neural Netw. Learn. Syst. **26**, 3201–3214 (2015)
24. Han, J., Moraga, C.: The influence of the sigmoid function parameters on the speed of backpropagation learning. In: Mira, J., Sandoval, F. (eds.) From Natural to Artificial Neural Computation, pp. 195–201. Springer, Heidelberg (1995)
25. Hara, K., Saito, D., Shouno, H.: Analysis of function of rectified linear unit used in deep learning. In: 2015 International Joint Conference on Neural Networks (IJCNN), pp. 1–8 (2015)
26. Peng, T., Wu, Y., Qin, J., Wu, Q.J., Cai, J.: H-ProSeg: hybrid ultrasound prostate segmentation based on explainability-guided mathematical model. Comput. Methods Programs Biomed. **219**, 106752 (2022)
27. Peng, T., et al.: H-ProMed: ultrasound image segmentation based on the evolutionary neural network and an improved principal curve. Pattern Recogn. **131**, 108890 (2022)
28. Niu, S., Chen, Q., de Sisternes, L., Ji, Z., Zhou, Z., Rubin, D.L.: Robust noise region-based active contour model via local similarity factor for image segmentation. Pattern Recogn. **61**, 104–119 (2017)
29. Liu, Y., He, C., Gao, P., Wu, Y., Ren, Z.: A binary level set variational model with L1 data term for image segmentation. Sig. Process. **155**, 193–201 (2019)
30. Benaichouche, A.N., Oulhadj, H., Siarry, P.: Improved spatial fuzzy c-means clustering for image segmentation using PSO initialization, Mahalanobis distance and post-segmentation correction. Digit. Sig. Process. **23**, 1390–1400 (2013)
31. Gao, Y., Zhou, M., Metaxas, D.: UTNet: a hybrid transformer architecture for medical image segmentation. In: International Conference on Medical Image Computing and Computer-Assisted Intervention, pp. 61–71 (2021)
32. Peng, T., Gu, Y., Ye, Z., Cheng, X., Wang, J.: A-LugSeg: automatic and explainability-guided multi-site lung detection in chest X-ray images. Expert Syst. Appl. **198**, 116873 (2022)
33. Peng, T., Tang, C., Wu, Y., Cai, J.: H-SegMed: a hybrid method for prostate segmentation in TRUS images via improved closed principal curve and improved enhanced machine learning. Int. J. Comput. Vis. **130**, 1896–1919 (2022)

Diversifying Non-dissipative Reservoir Computing Dynamics

Claudio Gallicchio$^{(\boxtimes)}$ (ID)

Department of Computer Science, University of Pisa,
Largo Bruno Pontecorvo, 3, Pisa, Italy
gallicch@di.unipi.it

Abstract. The Euler State Network (EuSNs) model is a recently proposed Reservoir Computing methodology that provides stable and non-dissipative untrained dynamics by discretizing an appropriately constrained ODE. In this paper, we propose alternative formulations of the reservoirs for EuSNs, aiming at improving the diversity of the resulting dynamics. Our empirical analysis points out the effectiveness of the proposed approaches on a large pool of time-series classification tasks.

Keywords: Euler State Networks · Reservoir Computing · Echo State Networks

1 Introduction

Reservoir Computing (RC) [17,19,22] is a popular technique for efficiently training Recurrent Neural Networks (RNNs) by utilizing the stable neural dynamics of a fixed recurrent reservoir layer and a trainable readout for output computation. This approach has been successful in various applications, in particular for implementing distributed learning functionalities in embedded systems [2,3,6] and as a reference paradigm for neuromorphic hardware implementations of recurrent neural models [20,21].

The effective operation of RC neural networks depends largely on the stability of its dynamics, which can be achieved through a global asymptotic stability property known as the Echo State Property in the widely used Echo State Network (ESN) model [14,15]. This property ensures that the dynamics of the reservoir remain stable, while at the same time it limits its memory and state-space structure, thus preventing the transmission of input information across multiple time steps.

Recently, a new approach to overcome the limitations of fading memory in standard ESNs has been proposed, which involves discretizing an Ordinary Differential Equation (ODE) while ensuring stability and non-dissipative constraints. This approach computes the reservoir dynamics as the forward Euler

This work is partially supported by the EC H2020 programme under project TEACHING (grant n. 871385), and by EMERGE, a project funded by EU Horizon research and innovation programme (grant n. 101070918).

solution of an ODE, hence the resulting model is called the *Euler State Network* (EuSN) [7,9]. As their dynamics are neither unstable nor lossy, EuSNs are capable of preserving input information over time, making them better suited than ESNs for tasks involving long-term memorization. The EuSN approach has already been shown to exceed the accuracy of ESNs and achieve comparable performance levels to fully trainable state-of-the-art RNN models on time-series classification tasks, while still maintaining the efficiency advantage of RC [9]. At the same time, the study of the architectural organization of the EuSN reservoir system is still largely unexplored.

In this paper, we deepen the analysis of EuSN architectures and propose ways to improve the diversification of reservoir dynamics. Our first proposal is to introduce a variability factor by using different integration rates in different reservoir neurons. The second variability factor is to consider different diffusion coefficients, which result in different strengths for the self-feedback connections in the reservoir neurons. We analyze the effects of these factors, individually and in synergy, on the resulting dynamical characterization of the reservoir system and in a wide range of experiments on time-series classification benchmarks.

The rest of this paper is organized as follows. In Sect. 2 we summarize the fundamental aspects of the RC methodology and of the popular ESN model, while in Sect. 3 we introduce the crucial concepts behind non-dissipative RC dynamics and the EuSN model. Then, in Sect. 4, we illustrate the proposed approach to enhance the diversification of reservoir dynamics in EuSNs. Our empirical analysis on several time-series classification benchmarks is given in Sect. 5. Finally, Sect. 6 concludes the paper.

2 Reservoir Computing

Reservoir Computing (RC) [17,22] refers to a category of efficiently trainable recurrent neural models in which the internal connections pointing to the hidden recurrent layer, the *reservoir*, are left untrained after randomization subject to asymptotic stability constraints. The neural architecture is then completed by an output layer, the *readout*, which is the only trained component of the model. Within such a class, we introduce the popular Echo State Network (ESN) [14,15] model, which employs the tanh non-linearity and operates in discrete time-steps.

To set our notation, let us consider a reservoir that comprises N_h neurons, and that is stimulated by a driving (external) N_x-dimensional input signal. Accordingly, we denote the reservoir state and the input at time step t respectively as $\mathbf{h}(t) \in \mathbb{R}^{N_h}$, and $\mathbf{x}(t) \in \mathbb{R}^{N_x}$. We refer to the general case of leaky integrator ESNs [16], and describe the dynamical operation of the reservoir by the following iterated map:

$$\mathbf{h}(t) = (1 - \alpha)\,\mathbf{h}(t-1) + \alpha\,\tanh(\mathbf{W}_h\,\mathbf{h}(t) + \mathbf{W}_x\,\mathbf{x}(t) + \mathbf{b}), \tag{1}$$

where $\mathbf{W}_h \in \mathbb{R}^{N_h \times N_h}$ is the reservoir recurrent weight matrix, $\mathbf{W}_x \in \mathbb{R}^{N_h \times N_x}$ is the input weight matrix, $\mathbf{b} \in \mathbb{R}^{N_h}$ is the bias vector, and $\tanh(\cdot)$ denotes the element-wise applied hyperbolic tangent non-linearity. Moreover, $\alpha \in (0, 1]$

represents the leaking rate hyper-parameter, influencing the relative speed of reservoir dynamics with respect to the dynamics of the input. Before being driven by the external input signal $\mathbf{x}(t)$, the reservoir state is typically initialized in the origin, i.e., $\mathbf{h}(0) = \mathbf{0}$.

After their initialization, the weight values of $\mathbf{W}_h$, $\mathbf{W}_x$, and $\mathbf{b}$ are kept fixed in accordance with the Echo State Property (ESP) [23], which ensures global asymptotic stability of the reservoir dynamical system. In practice, the recurrent weights in $\mathbf{W}_h$ are typically randomly drawn from a uniform distribution over $(-1, 1)$ and then adjusted to limit the resulting spectral radius[1] $\rho(\mathbf{W}_h)$ to values smaller than 1. The value of $\rho(\mathbf{W}_h)$ has a direct influence on the dynamical properties of the resulting reservoir, and in particular on the extent of its fading memory. As such, it is a crucial hyper-parameter of the ESN model. As the spectral radius re-scaling of (a potentially large) matrix $\mathbf{W}_h$ can represent a computational bottleneck, in this paper we resort to an efficient initialization scheme introduced in [10], which leverages results in random matrix theory to provide a fast initialization of the recurrent weights in $\mathbf{W}_h$. The input weight matrix $\mathbf{W}_x$ and bias vector $\mathbf{b}$ are also randomly initialized, and then re-scaled to control their magnitude. A widely used approach consists in drawing their values from uniform distributions over $(-\omega_x, \omega_x)$ and $(-\omega_b, \omega_b)$, respectively, where ω_x and represents the input scaling hyper-parameter, and ω_b is the bias scaling hyper-parameter.

The ESN architecture also includes a trainable dense readout layer which, in the case of time-series classification tasks, is fed by the last reservoir state corresponding to each input time series. As the reservoir parameters are kept fixed, the readout is often trained in closed form [17], e.g., by pseudo-inversion or ridge regression.

Finally, it is worth remarking that the ESN model relies on the ESP stability property to regulate the reservoir dynamics. This property ensures that when the network is fed with a long input time-series, the initial state conditions eventually fade away, and the state encoding produced by the reservoir becomes stable. However, this characterization is linked to the fading memory and suffix-based Markovian organization of the reservoir state space (see, e.g., [8, 11, 13]). These properties make it difficult to transfer information across multiple time-steps, limiting the effectiveness of ESNs for tasks that require long-term memory retention of the input information.

3   Non-dissipative Reservoir Computing

To overcome the limitations of a fading memory reservoir system, an alternative approach based on discretizing ODEs subject to stability and non-dissipativity conditions has recently been proposed [7, 9]. The resulting RC model is derived from the continuous-time dynamics expressed by the following ODE:

$$\mathbf{h}'(t) = \tanh(\mathbf{W}_h \mathbf{h}(t) + \mathbf{W}_x \mathbf{x}(t) + \mathbf{b}), \tag{2}$$

---

[1] The spectral radius of a matrix $\mathbf{A}$ is defined as the maximum length of an eigenvalue of $\mathbf{A}$.

requiring that the corresponding Jacobian has eigenvalues with ≈ 0 real parts. In addition to stability, such a critical condition implies non-dissipative system dynamics, which can be leveraged to effectively propagate the input information over multiple time-steps [5,12]. Crucially, the requested condition on the eigenvalus of the Jacobian of Eq. 2, can be easily met *architecturally* by the use of an antisymmetric recurrent weight matrix, i.e. requiring that $\mathbf{W}_h = -\mathbf{W}_h^T$. In such a case, indeed, the eigenvalues of both $\mathbf{W}_h$ and the Jacobian are on the imaginary axis (see, e.g., [5,9] for further details). Interestingly, this property does not need to be learned from data, rather it can be enforced in the neural processing system by design. In other words, provided that the antisymmetric condition holds, the recurrent weight matrix $\mathbf{W}_h$ can be initialized with random weights and then left untrained, as in standard RC approaches. Finally, the resulting constrained ODE system is discretized by Euler forward method, yielding the following state transition equation ruling the behavior of a discrete-time recurrent neural layer:

$$\mathbf{h}(t) = \mathbf{h}(t-1) + \varepsilon \tanh\Big((\mathbf{W}_h - \gamma\mathbf{I})\mathbf{h}(t-1) + \mathbf{W}_x\mathbf{x}(t) + \mathbf{b}\Big), \qquad (3)$$

where $\mathbf{W}_h = -\mathbf{W}_h^T$ is the antisymmetric recurrent weight matrix, while ε and γ are two (typically small) positive hyper-parameters that represents respectively the *step size* of integration, and the *diffusion* coefficient used to stabilize the discretization [12]. As in standard ESNs, the weight values in $\mathbf{W}_h$, $\mathbf{W}_x$ and $\mathbf{b}$ are left untrained after initialization, and the resulting RC model is named *Euler State Network* (EuSN). In particular, the weight values in $\mathbf{W}_h$ in Eq. 3 can be obtained starting from a random matrix $\mathbf{W}$ whose elements are drawn from a uniform distribution in $(-\omega_r, \omega_r)$, with ω_r representing a recurrent scaling hyper-parameter, and then setting $\mathbf{W}_h = \mathbf{W} - \mathbf{W}^T$, which grants the antisymmetric property. The weight values in $\mathbf{W}_x$ and $\mathbf{b}$ are initialized as described in Sect. 2 for ESNs. Moreover, as in standard ESNs, the state is initialized in the origin, i.e., $\mathbf{h}(0) = \mathbf{0}$, and the neural network architecture is completed by a readout layer that is the only trained component of the model. It has already been shown in the literature that the EuSN model is extremely efficient at propagating input information across many time steps, providing an exceptional trade-off between complexity and accuracy in time-series classification tasks. Overall, EuSNs make it possible to retain the efficiency typical of untrained RC networks while achieving - and even exceeding - the accuracy of fully trained recurrent models (see [7,9] for an extended comparison in this regard). In this paper, starting from the basic EuSN model, we show how its dynamics can be enriched by simple architectural modifications that affect the variety of its dynamic behavior.

4   Diversifying Dynamics in Euler State Networks Reservoirs

We start our analysis by noting that the reservoir system of an EuSN, as described in Eq. 3 has an effective spectral radius intrinsically close to unity.

In fact, using standard arguments in RC area, we can observe how the Jacobian of the system in Eq. 3, analyzed around the origin and for null input, takes the following form:

$$\mathbf{J} = (1 - \varepsilon\gamma)\,\mathbf{I} + \varepsilon\,\mathbf{W}_h, \tag{4}$$

whose eigenvalues have a fixed real part, given by $1 - \varepsilon\gamma$, and imaginary part given by a small perturbation of one of the eigenvalues of $\mathbf{W}_h$. Using $\lambda_k(\cdot)$ to denote the k-th eigenvalue of its matrix argument, we have that:

$$\lambda_k(\mathbf{J}) = 1 - \varepsilon\gamma + i\,\varepsilon\beta_k, \tag{5}$$

where $\beta_k = Im(\lambda_k(\mathbf{W}_h))$. All eigenvalues are thus concentrated (vertically in the Gaussian plane) in a neighborhood of $1 - \varepsilon\gamma$. Given that both ε and γ take small positive values, we can notice that all the eigenvalues in Eq. 5 are close to 1 by design, and the eigenvalues of $\mathbf{W}_h$ have only a minor perturbation impact. This is illustrated in Fig. 1 (top, left). As analyzed in [9], this characterization can be interpreted as an architectural bias of the EuSN model towards critical dynamics. Notice that this bias is fundamentally different from the suffix-based Markovian nature of reservoir dynamics typical of the conventional ESN [8].

Despite the application success of the EuSN model already in its original form (as evidenced by the results in [7,9]), the dynamic characterization of the model seems to be improvable. In particular, while one of the keys to the success of RC is that it can cover a wide range of dynamic behaviour by randomizing the reservoir parameters, in the case of EuSNs randomization does not seem to be fully exploited. This can be seen firstly from the squeezing of the Jacobian eigenvalues on a line, and secondly from the observation that the reservoir state transition function in Eq. 3 contains a self-loop term modulated by the same γ value for all neurons. Accordingly, in the following, we introduce variants of the basic EuSN model in which different neurons can have different values of the step size parameter ε and the diffusion parameter γ.

Step Size Variability. We consider EuSN reservoir neurons with different values of the step size. The resulting state transition function is given by:

$$\mathbf{h}(t) = \mathbf{h}(t-1) + \boldsymbol{\varepsilon} \odot \tanh\Big(\big(\mathbf{W}_h - \gamma\mathbf{I}\big)\mathbf{h}(t-1) + \mathbf{W}_x\mathbf{x}(t) + \mathbf{b}\Big), \tag{6}$$

where $\boldsymbol{\varepsilon} \in \mathbb{R}^{N_h}$ is a vector containing the step size of integration of the different neurons, and $\odot$ denotes component-wise (Hadamard) multiplication. As an effect of this modification, the neurons in the EuSN reservoir exhibit dynamics with variable integration speed, potentially offering greater richness to the encoding produced by the system. Moreover, the resulting Jacobian is given by:

$$\mathbf{J} = diag(\mathbf{1} - \gamma\boldsymbol{\varepsilon}) + diag(\boldsymbol{\varepsilon})\mathbf{W}_h, \tag{7}$$

where $diag(\cdot)$ indicates a diagonal matrix with specified diagonal elements, and $\mathbf{1} \in \mathbb{R}^{N_h}$ is a vector of ones. The resulting eigenvalues are no longer characterized by the same real part, and present a more varied configuration, as illustrated in

Fig. 1 (top, right). In the following, we use EuSN-ε to refer to an EuSN network whose reservoir is ruled by Eq. 6.

Diffusion Variability. We consider EuSN reservoir neurons with different values of the diffusion coefficient. In this case, the state transition function is given by:

$$\mathbf{h}(t) = \mathbf{h}(t-1) \ + \varepsilon \tanh\Big((\mathbf{W}_h - diag(\boldsymbol{\gamma}))\mathbf{h}(t-1) + \mathbf{W}_x\mathbf{x}(t) + \mathbf{b}\Big), \quad (8)$$

where $\boldsymbol{\gamma} \in \mathbb{R}^{N_h}$ is a vector containing the diffusion term of the different neurons. Differently from the previous case of EuSN-ε, all the reservoir neurons operate at the same integration speed, but the reservoir topology is enriched by different strengths of the self-loops. The resulting Jacobian is given by:

$$\mathbf{J} = diag(\mathbf{1} - \varepsilon\boldsymbol{\gamma}) + \varepsilon\,\mathbf{W}_h, \quad (9)$$

whose eigenvalues variability is illustrated in Fig. 1 (bottom, left). In the following, EuSN-γ is used to refer to an EuSN network whose reservoir is described by Eq. 8.

Full Variability. We finally introduce an EuSN in which each reservoir neuron presents its own step size of integration and diffusion coefficient. This configuration includes both variability factors introduced by EuSN-γ and EuSN-γ, and is denoted by EuSN-ε, γ. In this case, the reservoir state transition function reads as follows:

$$\mathbf{h}(t) = \mathbf{h}(t-1) \ + \boldsymbol{\varepsilon} \odot \tanh\Big((\mathbf{W}_h - diag(\boldsymbol{\gamma}))\mathbf{h}(t-1) + \mathbf{W}_x\mathbf{x}(t) + \mathbf{b}\Big), \quad (10)$$

and the resulting Jacobian is given by:

$$\mathbf{J} = diag(\mathbf{1} - \boldsymbol{\varepsilon} \odot \boldsymbol{\gamma}) + diag(\boldsymbol{\varepsilon})\,\mathbf{W}_h, \quad (11)$$

The reservoir exhibits both dynamics with multiple scales of integration speed and diverse self-loops. Moreover, while preserving the architectural bias toward eigenvalues of the Jacobian near 1, these show wider variability, as illustrated in Fig. 1 (bottom, right).

5   Experiments

We have experimentally evaluated the performance of the proposed EuSN variants (introduced in Sect. 4), in comparison to the base EuSN setup (described in Sect. 3) and the conventional ESN model (described in Sect. 2).

Datasets. The performed analysis involved experiments on a large pool of diverse time-series classification benchmarks. The first 20 datasets have been taken from the UEA & UCR time-series classification repository [4], namely:

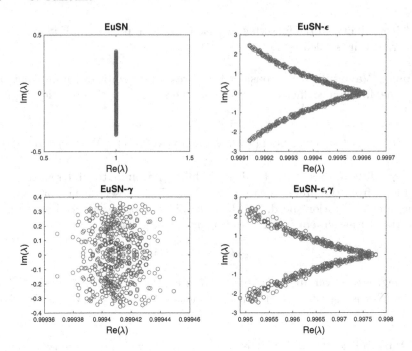

Fig. 1. Eigenvalues of the Jacobian for a 500-dimensional reservoir in EuSN (top left), EuSN-ε (top right), EuSN-γ (bottom left), and EuSN-ε, γ (bottom right). The plots correspond to a system with $\omega_r = 1$, $\varepsilon = 0.01$, $\gamma = 0.01$. Variable values of the step size were randomly sampled from a uniform distribution on $[\varepsilon, \varepsilon + 0.1]$. Variable values of the diffusion were randomly sampled from a uniform distribution on $[\gamma, \gamma + 0.1]$.

Adiac, Blink, CharacterTrajectories, Computers, Cricket, ECG5000, Epilepsy, FordA, FordB, HandOutlines, HandMovementDirection, Handwriting, Heartbeat, KeplerLightCurves, Libras, Lightning2, Mallat, MotionSenseHAR, ShapesAll, Trace, UWaveGestureLibraryAll, Wafer, and Yoga. We have also run experiments on the *IMDB* movie review sentiment classification dataset [18], and on the *Reuters* newswire classification dataset from UCI [1], which were used in the publicly online available forms[2]. For these two tasks, we applied a preprocessing step in order to represent each sentence by a time series of 32-dimensional word embeddings[3]. For all datasets, we used the original splits into training and test,

---

[2] IMDB: https://keras.io/api/datasets/imdb/.
Reuters: https://keras.io/api/datasets/reuters/.

[3] For each dataset individually, every sentence was represented by a sequence of words from the 10k most frequent ones in the corresponding database, with a truncation to a maximum length of 200. To obtain the word embeddings, we trained an MLP network with a preliminary embedding layer of 32 units, followed by a hidden layer of 128 units with ReLU activation, and finally by a dense output layer. The MLP architecture was trained on the training set using the RMSProp optimizer for 100 epochs and early stopping with patience = 10 (on a validation set containing the

Table 1. Information on the time-series classification benchmarks used in our experiments, including the number of sequences in the training set (# Seq Tr) and in the test set (# Seq Ts), the maximum length of a sequence in the dataset (Length), the number of input features (Feat.), and the number of output classes (Classes).

Name	# Seq Tr	# Seq Ts	Length	Feat.	Classes
Adiac	390	391	176	1	37
Blink	500	450	510	4	2
CharacterTrajectories	1422	1436	182	3	20
Computers	250	250	720	1	2
Cricket	108	72	1197	6	12
ECG5000	500	4500	140	1	5
FordA	3601	1320	500	1	2
FordB	3636	810	500	1	2
HandOutlines	1000	370	2709	1	2
HandMovementDirection	160	74	400	10	4
Handwriting	150	850	152	3	26
Heartbeat	204	205	405	61	2
IMDB	25000	25000	200	32	2
KeplerLightCurves	920	399	4767	1	7
Libras	180	180	45	2	15
Lightning2	60	61	637	1	2
Mallat	55	2345	1024	1	8
MotionSenseHAR	966	265	1000	12	6
Reuters	8982	2246	200	32	46
ShapesAll	600	600	512	1	60
Trace	100	100	275	1	4
UWaveGestureLibraryAll	896	3582	945	1	8
Wafer	1000	6164	152	1	2
Yoga	300	3000	426	1	2

applying a further 67% - 33% stratified splitting of the original training data into training and validation sets. Relevant information on the used datasets is reported in Table 1.

Experimental Settings. In our experiments, we considered EuSN with a number of recurrent units N_h ranging between 10 and 500. We explored values of ω_r, ω_x and ω_b in $\{10^{-3}, 10^{-2}, \ldots, 10\}$, ε and γ in $\{10^{-5}, 10^{-4}, \ldots, 1\}$. For EuSN set-

---

33% of the original training data). After this, the output of the embedding layer for each sentence in the dataset was used as input feature in our experiments with the RC models.

Table 2. Results on the time-series classification benchmarks. For every task, it is reported the accuracy on the test set achieved by ESN, EuSN, EuSN with variable step size (EuSN-ε), EuSN with variable diffusion (EuSN-γ), and EuSN with both variable step size and diffusion (EuSN-ε, γ). Results are averaged (and std are given) over 10 random guesses. Best results for each task are highlighted in bold.

Task	ESN	EuSN	EuSN-ε	EuSN-γ	EuSN-ε, γ
Adiac	$0.307_{\pm 0.07}$	$0.690_{\pm 0.01}$	$\mathbf{0.691}_{\pm 0.01}$	$0.634_{\pm 0.01}$	$0.649_{\pm 0.01}$
Blink	$0.620_{\pm 0.02}$	$0.943_{\pm 0.01}$	$0.934_{\pm 0.01}$	$0.946_{\pm 0.01}$	$\mathbf{0.969}_{\pm 0.01}$
CharacterTrajectories	$0.964_{\pm 0.00}$	$\mathbf{0.993}_{\pm 0.00}$	$0.989_{\pm 0.00}$	$0.989_{\pm 0.00}$	$0.985_{\pm 0.00}$
Computers	$0.652_{\pm 0.00}$	$0.638_{\pm 0.02}$	$0.707_{\pm 0.01}$	$\mathbf{0.716}_{\pm 0.01}$	$0.607_{\pm 0.02}$
Cricket	$0.976_{\pm 0.01}$	$0.933_{\pm 0.02}$	$0.993_{\pm 0.01}$	$\mathbf{1.000}_{\pm 0.00}$	$\mathbf{1.000}_{\pm 0.00}$
ECG5000	$0.921_{\pm 0.00}$	$\mathbf{0.938}_{\pm 0.00}$	$0.932_{\pm 0.00}$	$0.937_{\pm 0.00}$	$\mathbf{0.938}_{\pm 0.00}$
FordA	$0.591_{\pm 0.02}$	$0.691_{\pm 0.01}$	$0.656_{\pm 0.01}$	$0.677_{\pm 0.01}$	$\mathbf{0.700}_{\pm 0.02}$
FordB	$0.519_{\pm 0.00}$	$\mathbf{0.652}_{\pm 0.01}$	$0.639_{\pm 0.01}$	$0.555_{\pm 0.02}$	$0.645_{\pm 0.01}$
HandOutlines	$0.690_{\pm 0.02}$	$0.912_{\pm 0.01}$	$0.908_{\pm 0.00}$	$\mathbf{0.919}_{\pm 0.00}$	$0.911_{\pm 0.00}$
HandMovementDirection	$0.551_{\pm 0.03}$	$0.585_{\pm 0.03}$	$\mathbf{0.664}_{\pm 0.01}$	$0.612_{\pm 0.02}$	$0.641_{\pm 0.04}$
Handwriting	$0.297_{\pm 0.01}$	$0.312_{\pm 0.01}$	$\mathbf{0.447}_{\pm 0.01}$	$0.390_{\pm 0.01}$	$0.365_{\pm 0.01}$
Heartbeat	$0.660_{\pm 0.01}$	$0.719_{\pm 0.01}$	$0.738_{\pm 0.01}$	$0.738_{\pm 0.02}$	$\mathbf{0.762}_{\pm 0.01}$
IMDB	$0.874_{\pm 0.00}$	$0.876_{\pm 0.00}$	$\mathbf{0.877}_{\pm 0.00}$	$0.873_{\pm 0.00}$	$0.876_{\pm 0.00}$
KeplerLightCurves	$0.321_{\pm 0.07}$	$0.452_{\pm 0.07}$	$\mathbf{0.489}_{\pm 0.04}$	$0.452_{\pm 0.02}$	$0.459_{\pm 0.05}$
Libras	$0.669_{\pm 0.05}$	$\mathbf{0.845}_{\pm 0.01}$	$0.835_{\pm 0.01}$	$0.765_{\pm 0.01}$	$0.781_{\pm 0.01}$
Lightning2	$0.607_{\pm 0.00}$	$0.623_{\pm 0.00}$	$0.720_{\pm 0.04}$	$0.605_{\pm 0.02}$	$\mathbf{0.772}_{\pm 0.03}$
Mallat	$0.649_{\pm 0.01}$	$0.842_{\pm 0.04}$	$0.883_{\pm 0.01}$	$0.905_{\pm 0.01}$	$\mathbf{0.913}_{\pm 0.01}$
MotionSenseHAR	$0.870_{\pm 0.02}$	$0.864_{\pm 0.01}$	$0.883_{\pm 0.03}$	$0.863_{\pm 0.02}$	$\mathbf{0.956}_{\pm 0.01}$
Reuters	$0.739_{\pm 0.00}$	$0.777_{\pm 0.00}$	$0.779_{\pm 0.00}$	$0.776_{\pm 0.00}$	$\mathbf{0.780}_{\pm 0.00}$
ShapesAll	$0.592_{\pm 0.02}$	$0.806_{\pm 0.01}$	$\mathbf{0.822}_{\pm 0.01}$	$0.804_{\pm 0.01}$	$0.803_{\pm 0.01}$
Trace	$0.648_{\pm 0.07}$	$0.980_{\pm 0.00}$	$0.991_{\pm 0.01}$	$0.986_{\pm 0.01}$	$\mathbf{0.999}_{\pm 0.00}$
UWaveGestureLibraryAll	$0.833_{\pm 0.01}$	$0.952_{\pm 0.00}$	$0.962_{\pm 0.00}$	$\mathbf{0.963}_{\pm 0.00}$	$0.957_{\pm 0.00}$
Wafer	$0.984_{\pm 0.00}$	$0.989_{\pm 0.00}$	$\mathbf{0.994}_{\pm 0.00}$	$0.992_{\pm 0.00}$	$0.988_{\pm 0.00}$
Yoga	$0.702_{\pm 0.03}$	$0.755_{\pm 0.02}$	$0.834_{\pm 0.01}$	$\mathbf{0.846}_{\pm 0.01}$	$0.783_{\pm 0.01}$

tings with step size variability, we explored values of $\Delta\varepsilon$ in $\{10^{-5}, 10^{-4}, \ldots, 1\}$, and generated values of ε from a uniform distribution in $[\varepsilon, \varepsilon + \Delta\varepsilon]$. A similar setting was used for exploring the case with diffusion variability. For comparison, we ran experiments with standard ESNs, exploring values of $\rho(\mathbf{W}_h)$ in $\{0.3, 0.6, 0.9, 1.2\}$, α in $\{10^{-5}, 10^{-4}, \ldots, 1\}$, ω_x and ω_b as for the EuSN models. In all the cases, the readout was trained by ridge regression (with regularization coefficient equal to 1).

For each model individually, the values of the hyper-parameters were fine-tuned by model selection, by means of a random search with 1000 iterations. After the model selection process, for each model the selected configuration was

Table 3. Average ranking across all the time-series classification benchmarks.

Model	Avg Rank
EuSN-ε, γ	2.208
EuSN-ε	2.208
EuSN-γ	2.583
EuSN	2.750
ESN	4.458

instantiated 10 times (generating random reservoir guesses). These 10 instances were trained on the entire training set and then evaluated on the test set. Our code was written in Keras[4], and was run on a system with 2×20 Intel(R) Xeon(R) CPU E5-2698 v4 @ 2.20 GHz.

Results. The achieved results are given in Table 2, which reports the test accuracy of each tested model, averaged over the 10 repetitions. The results in the table show the practical effectiveness of the architectural variants proposed in this paper, which overall achieve the best result in the vast majority of the cases examined. In particular, the variant comprising the maximum variability explored in the paper, i.e., EuSN-ε, γ is the one that is found to be superior in most cases. Taken individually, the variability on the step size (EuSN-ε) is slightly less effective than the full variability, while the variability on the diffusion term (EuSN-γ) is the one that individually results in less effectiveness. It is interesting to note that although in some cases the difference in performance between the best proposed variance and the baseline EuSN model is minimal, in many cases (including Blink, Computers, Cricket, HandMovementDirection, Handwriting, Heartbeat, Lightning2, Mallat, MotionSenseHAR, and Yoga) the improvement achieved is definitely relevant. Furthermore, the results show clear confirmation of the accuracy advantage of the EuSN approach over traditional ESNs. In the few cases where ESNs exceed the accuracy of standard EuSNs (Computers, Cricket, MotionSenseHAR), the proposed EuSN variants achieve even higher accuracy.

Our analysis is further supported by the ranking values given in Table 3, which indicate that on average on the considered datasets, EuSN-ε, γ and EuSN-ε models perform the best, followed by EuSN-γ and standard EuSN, while ESN has the worst performance.

6   Conclusions

In this paper we have empirically explored the effects of (architecturally) introducing dynamical variability in the behavior of Euler State Networks (EuSNs), a recently introduced Reservoir Computing (RC) methodology featured by non-dissipative dynamics. Diversity has been enforced by using reservoir neurons with

---

[4] Source code available at https://github.com/gallicch/VariabilityEuSN.

variable step size of integration (EuSN-ε), and with different diffusion coefficient (EuSN-γ). Both the approaches impact on the organization of the diversification of the dynamical behavior of the model, as pointed out by analyzing the eigenvalues of the resulting Jacobian. Moreover, results on several time-series classification benchmarks showed the efficacy of the proposed variants, and of their synergy, as the EuSN model with both the introduced variability factors (EuSN-ε, γ) resulted in the highest accuracy in a larger number of cases. Notwithstanding the clear advantage of basic EuSNs over conventional Echo State Networks in the explored tasks, from a practical point of view, the results suggest the convenience in exploring EuSNs in conjunction with at least the EuSN-ε, γ variant.

Future work will focus on theoretical analysis of the effects of the dynamic variability factors introduced in this paper, and their application in pervasive artificial intelligence contexts.

References

1. Apté, C., Damerau, F., Weiss, S.M.: Automated learning of decision rules for text categorization. ACM Trans. Inf. Syst. (TOIS) **12**(3), 233–251 (1994)
2. Bacciu, D., et al.: Teaching-trustworthy autonomous cyber-physical applications through human-centred intelligence. In: 2021 IEEE International Conference on Omni-Layer Intelligent Systems (COINS), pp. 1–6. IEEE (2021)
3. Bacciu, D., Barsocchi, P., Chessa, S., Gallicchio, C., Micheli, A.: An experimental characterization of reservoir computing in ambient assisted living applications. Neural Comput. Appl. **24**(6), 1451–1464 (2014)
4. Bagnall, A., Vickers, J.L.W., Keogh, E.: The UEA & UCR time series classification repository. www.timeseriesclassification.com
5. Chang, B., Chen, M., Haber, E., Chi, E.H.: AntisymmetricRNN: a dynamical system view on recurrent neural networks. arXiv preprint arXiv:1902.09689 (2019)
6. Dragone, M., et al.: A cognitive robotic ecology approach to self-configuring and evolving AAL systems. Eng. Appl. Artif. Intell. **45**, 269–280 (2015)
7. Gallicchio, C.: Reservoir computing by discretizing ODEs. In: Proceedings of ESANN (2021)
8. Gallicchio, C., Micheli, A.: Architectural and Markovian factors of echo state networks. Neural Netw. **24**(5), 440–456 (2011)
9. Gallicchio, C.: Euler state networks. arXiv preprint arXiv:2203.09382 (2022)
10. Gallicchio, C., Micheli, A., Pedrelli, L.: Fast spectral radius initialization for recurrent neural networks. In: Oneto, L., Navarin, N., Sperduti, A., Anguita, D. (eds.) INNSBDDL 2019. PINNS, vol. 1, pp. 380–390. Springer, Cham (2020). https://doi.org/10.1007/978-3-030-16841-4_39
11. Grigoryeva, L., Ortega, J.P.: Echo state networks are universal. Neural Netw. **108**, 495–508 (2018)
12. Haber, E., Ruthotto, L.: Stable architectures for deep neural networks. Inverse Prob. **34**(1), 014004 (2017)
13. Hammer, B., Tiňo, P.: Recurrent neural networks with small weights implement definite memory machines. Neural Comput. **15**(8), 1897–1929 (2003)
14. Jaeger, H.: The "echo state" approach to analysing and training recurrent neural networks - with an erratum note. Technical report, GMD - German National Research Institute for Computer Science (2001)

15. Jaeger, H., Haas, H.: Harnessing nonlinearity: predicting chaotic systems and saving energy in wireless communication. Science **304**(5667), 78–80 (2004)
16. Jaeger, H., Lukoševičius, M., Popovici, D., Siewert, U.: Optimization and applications of echo state networks with leaky-integrator neurons. Neural Netw. **20**(3), 335–352 (2007)
17. Lukoševičius, M., Jaeger, H.: Reservoir computing approaches to recurrent neural network training. Comput. Sci. Rev. **3**(3), 127–149 (2009)
18. Maas, A.L., Daly, R.E., Pham, P.T., Huang, D., Ng, A.Y., Potts, C.: Learning word vectors for sentiment analysis. In: Proceedings of the 49th Annual Meeting of the Association for Computational Linguistics: Human Language Technologies, pp. 142–150. Association for Computational Linguistics, Portland, Oregon, USA, June 2011. http://www.aclweb.org/anthology/P11-1015
19. Nakajima, K., Fischer, I. (eds.): Reservoir Computing. NCS, Springer, Singapore (2021). https://doi.org/10.1007/978-981-13-1687-6
20. Van der Sande, G., Brunner, D., Soriano, M.C.: Advances in photonic reservoir computing. Nanophotonics **6**(3), 561–576 (2017)
21. Tanaka, G., et al.: Recent advances in physical reservoir computing: a review. Neural Netw. **115**, 100–123 (2019)
22. Verstraeten, D., Schrauwen, B., d'Haene, M., Stroobandt, D.: An experimental unification of reservoir computing methods. Neural Netw. **20**(3), 391–403 (2007)
23. Yildiz, I., Jaeger, H., Kiebel, S.: Re-visiting the echo state property. Neural Netw. **35**, 1–9 (2012)

Efficient Reinforcement Learning Using State-Action Uncertainty with Multiple Heads

Tomoharu Aizu[✉], Takeru Oba, and Norimichi Ukita

Toyota Technological Institute, Nagoya, Aichi, Japan
{sd23401,sd21502,ukita}@toyota-ti.ac.jp

Abstract. In reinforcement learning, an agent learns optimal actions for achieving a task by maximizing rewards in an environment. During learning, the agent decides its action for *exploration* or *exploitation* at each time. In exploration, the agent searches for a new experience defined by the state, action, reward, and next state. In exploitation, on the other hand, the agent tries to maximize the rewards based on the experiences. Exploration-exploitation trade-off is an important issue in reinforcement learning. In previous work, this trade-off is achieved based on how uncertain what the agent already learns about the environment. While only simple criteria for this uncertainty are explored in the literature, this paper evaluates more uncertainty criteria for efficient reinforcement learning. Our novel uncertainty criteria uses agent's multiple decisions at the same time. In addition, we also propose to employ the advantage of the multiple decisions for bridging the gap between exploration and exploitation by our novel exploitation mode. Extensive experiments verify the effectiveness of our approaches for efficient learning. We also show the learning efficiencies of different learning strategies in order to know which strategy is better for each task.

Keywords: reinforcement learning · exploration-exploitation trade-off · deep learning

1 Introduction

In reinforcement learning, an agent learns optimal actions for achieving a task by maximizing rewards in an environment including the agent itself. The basic cycle of reinforcement learning is as follows. (1) The environment sends the agent a state representing the environmental situation. (2) The agent sends its action to the environment. (3) The environment sends a reward representing the expected appropriateness of the action. The agent memorizes the triplet of the state, action, and reward to choose better actions in future states based on past experiences represented by the triplets.

When the agent chooses an action, it has two modes. These modes are called exploration and exploitation. In exploration, the agent decides its actions to find new experiences. In exploitation, the agent decides the actions based on its experiences to maximize future rewards. In reinforcement learning, the exploration-exploitation trade-off is important for efficient learning.

This exploration-exploitation trade-off is studied in the literature [10,12,14]. For example, the bandit problem is tackled with several approaches such as UCB in [13]. In the bandit problem, it is easy to determine the trade-off because the environment is static. In many other practical tasks, however, the environment is dynamic. Thus, the appropriate trade-off varies from state to state, and the variation of its states is enormous. To cope with this difficulty, an agent decides its action to go to less-experienced states in [12,14]. However, the number of experiences is inappropriate for determining whether or not the experience is enough. For example, we can learn simpler states with fewer experiences.

If we know whether or not enough experience is accumulated in each state, the exploration-exploitation trade-off can be achieved. This sufficiency is judged based on how uncertain the appropriateness of each action is in [10]. With this state-action uncertainty, an agent selects either exploration or exploitation; if the uncertainty is higher, exploration is selected. In [10], the uncertainty becomes higher if the consistency between predicted rewards in continuous times is lower. This is because, since the reward may not change significantly for a short period, the experience is considered insufficient if the predicted rewards are inconsistent between continuous times. At an early learning stage, however, the uncertainty estimated from continuous rewards is not reliable because important differences between similar states are not learned yet.

To avoid the aforementioned unreliability of rewards at different times and explore more uncertainty measures, this paper proposes more uncertainty criteria using rewards estimated at the same time. The multiple rewards at the same time are estimated by differently-trained policies. In our work, the different policies are provided by multiple network heads in Bootstrapped DQN (BDQN) [9] shown in Fig. 1, which is one of the state-of-the-art networks for reinforcement learning. In Q-learning including BDQN, given the state, the expected cumulative reward is estimated as the Q-value with its corresponding action. BDQN estimates multiple Q-values, each of which is estimated by each head, for each action at the same time. While only the highest Q-value is selected for action decision, our method uses multiple Q-values for uncertainty estimation. In addition, our methods also use estimated actions for uncertainty estimation.

As with our method, BDQN is employed for uncertainty estimation in [6,11]. In these methods, however, the exploration-exploitation trade-off is not discussed, while this trade-off is the focus of this paper. Furthermore, we found that a large gap between exploration and exploitation makes it difficult to smoothly transit from one to the other for stable learning, as also mentioned in [13]. Based on this finding, we propose a novel exploitation mode for bridging this gap in order to achieve a better exploration-exploitation trade-off.

Our contributions proposed in this paper are summarized as follows:

1. State-action uncertainty criteria defined with multiple heads in a Q-learning network such as BDQN.

2. Novel learning mode using the advantage of multiple heads for bridging the gap between exploration and exploitation.
3. New measure to evaluate efficiency and robustness in reinforcement learning.

2 Related Work

One of the easiest ways to solve the exploration-exploitation trade-off is ϵ-greedy method [13]. In this method, an agent selects exploration with probability ϵ and exploitation with probability $1 - \epsilon$. ϵ decreases gradually to select exploitation more often as learning progresses. However, it is not easy to manually optimize the hyper-parameter ϵ for arbitrary tasks.

To resolve this problem, the state-action uncertainty [10,11,16] is useful, as mentioned in Sect. 1. In VDBE [16], TD error in Q-learning is used as the uncertainty so that the probability of selecting exploration depends on the state unlike pre-defined scheduling using ϵ. The agent could learn optimal actions without large effects from ϵ. While multiple heads are used in [10] as well as in our method, only a simple uncertainty criterion (i.e., the variance of Q-values given by the multiple heads) is used with a limited number of networks (i.e., two heads). In this paper, on the other hand, more complex decisions given by more heads and uncertainty criteria are explored for efficient learning.

Since our focus in this paper is the trade-off and gap between exploration and exploitation, other components in reinforcement learning (e.g., exploration algorithm) are simply implemented. There are many methods that try to challenge the trade-off [8,15]. For example, several exploration algorithms are proposed to go to less-experienced states [4,5]. While these algorithms can improve exploration efficiency, there is still a gap between exploration and exploitation.

3 Proposed Method

3.1 Exploitation with Multiple Heads

BDQN [9] has one shared network and multiple separated networks called heads, as shown in Fig. 1 in which the number of the heads is H. Each head predicts Q-values, each of which corresponds to each action, at each time. These heads are randomly and independently initialized before learning so that different heads select different actions based on different policies.

For exploitation in [9], the same head is continuously selected through each episode, as shown in Fig. 2 (a). This exploitation guarantees that actions decided by the same head (i.e., the same policy) are temporally consistent (e.g., smoothly transit). In BDQN [9], however, only exploitation is implemented with no exploration. This learning strategy decreases learning efficiency at an early learning stage.

In our method, on the other hand, random action selection is employed as exploration. While exploration enables efficient learning in conjunction with exploitation, there is a huge gap between the action selection criteria of exploration and exploitation. That is, random actions selected in exploration vary significantly, but temporal actions selected by exploitation shown in Fig. 2 (a) are consistent. While such random actions are efficient at an early learning stage, the temporally-consistent actions allow us to deeply search for better actions at a late stage.

For bridging this gap mainly at a middle learning stage, this paper proposes an intermediate mode in which actions are provided by randomly-selected heads instead of the same head used in DBQN. This mode is called *step exploitation*, which is shown in Fig. 2 (b), while we call exploitation in BDQN *episode exploitation*. The different heads select different actions, as mentioned before. This step exploitation allows us to decide the action of an agent based on past experience while avoiding (possibly inefficiently) repeating similar actions selected by the same head.

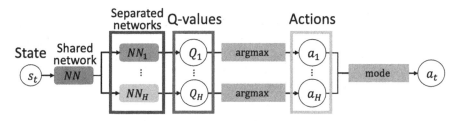

Fig. 1. Structure of BDQN [9], which has multiple heads. Each head predicts the Q values of all actions. In test time, each head outputs an action, and the agent gathers all actions and selects the most frequent action as the output action.

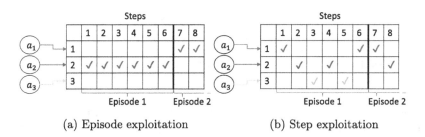

(a) Episode exploitation   (b) Step exploitation

Fig. 2. *Episode exploitation* and *step exploitation*. In step and episode exploitations, one head is selected in each step and episode, respectively.

3.2   Uncertainty Estimation Using Multiple Heads

As proposed in Sect. 3.1, exploration, step exploitation, and episode exploitation are used for different purposes. These three modes should be selected based on learning progress. This learning progress is evaluated with the uncertainty between the decisions of multiple heads in our method. This is because this uncertainty score is expected to converge to smaller values by training the heads with a large amount of experience; since all the heads are trained with the same experience at each time, their policies converge to the same goal. We verify the effectiveness of the following three criteria for uncertainty estimation.

Uncertainty Estimation Using Q-Values. In accordance with [11], the uncertainty is estimated from Q-values provided by the different heads. In our method, the variance of the Q-values of all the heads (enclosed by the red rectangle in Fig. 1) is regarded as the uncertainty. Given the state at the current time t (denoted by s_t), the variance, $\sigma^2(s_t)$, is expressed as follows:

$$\sigma^2(s_t) = \frac{\sum_{a \in A} var(\boldsymbol{Q}(s_t, a))}{|A|}, \tag{1}$$

where A and $|A|$ denote a set of all possible actions and the number of its elements, respectively. $\boldsymbol{Q}(s_t, a)$ is a H-dimensional vector $(Q_1(s_t, a), \cdots, Q_H(s_t, a))$ where $Q_i(s_t, a)$ is the Q-value of the i-th head. With $Q(s_t, a)$, $var(\boldsymbol{Q}(s_t, a)) = \frac{1}{H} \sum_{i=1}^{H} (Q_i(s_t, a) - \overline{Q(s_t, a)})^2$ and $\overline{Q(s_t, a)} = \frac{1}{H} \sum_{i=1}^{H} Q_i(s_t, a)$.

Uncertainty Estimation Using Action Entropy. While uncertainty estimation using Q-values is explored in [11], this paper proposes a novel uncertainty criterion using actions selected by the multiple heads. Unlike Q-values represented by continuous values, the actions are represented as discrete labels. The uncertainty of such discrete action labels (enclosed by the orange rectangle in Fig. 1) is expressed by their entropy as follows:

$$E(s_t) = -\sum_{a \in A} p(s_t, a) \log_2 p(s_t, a), \tag{2}$$

where $p(s_t, a)$ denotes a probability that a-th action is selected by all the heads. In our method, $p(s_t, a) = \frac{H_a}{H}$ where H_a is the number of heads each of whose best action is a.

While Eq. (1) uses raw Q-values, Eq. (2) is computed from the best actions selected by the argmax of the Q-values. Since the selected best actions are simple representations so that the probability values of all actions are omitted, this representation is robust to noise in the probability values. However, the probability values may be advisable for uncertainty estimation. For example, assume that $H = 3$, $A = \{a_1, a_2\}$, $Q(s_t, a_1) = (0.51, 0.49, 0.51)$, and $Q(s_t, a_2) = (0.49, 0.51, 0.49)$. In this toy example, the policies of all three heads seem almost equal. As with this interpretation, the variance in Eq. (1) is small. However, the entropy in Eq. (2) is not small because both a_1 and a_2 are probable (i.e., $p(s_t, a_1) = \frac{2}{3}$ and $p(s_t, a_2) = \frac{1}{3}$). As discussed above, uncertainty criteria in Eq. (1) and Eq. (2) have advantages and disadvantages.

Uncertainty Estimation Using Action Frequencies

Deterministic Model Selection. In addition to the entropy-based action uncertainty described in Sect. 3.2, we also propose uncertainty estimation using the frequencies of actions selected by multiple heads. In the entropy based on Eq. (2), only the best actions selected by the multiple heads are used. In frequency-based uncertainty, on the other hand, the frequencies of other actions are also used.

Remember that H and H_a denote the numbers of all heads and those each of whose best action is a where $a \in A$. m_a denotes the largest H_a. At an early learning stage, m_a is small, and exploration is required. m_a becomes larger as the learning progresses, and then exploitation is beneficial.

In addition to the largest H_a (i.e., m_a), the frequency-based criterion also evaluates the variety of H_a. This variety score denoted by k_a is defined so that the number of different actions is selected by the multiple heads. For example, given $H = 5$, if the actions selected by the heads are $\{a_1, a_1, a_2, a_1, a_5\}$, $k_a = |\{a_1, a_2, a_5\}| = 3$. Contrary to m_a, k_a is smaller and larger when the learning progresses sufficiently and insufficiently, respectively.

With a combination of m_a and k_a, the learning mode is chosen as shown in Table 1. The learning mode is chosen by thresholding the uncertainty criteria, m_a and k_a, as well as $\sigma^2(s_t)$ and $E(s_t)$. How to determine the thresholds is described in Sect. 3.3.

Table 1. Learning strategies.

	m_a is small	m_a is large
k_a is large	exploration	step exploitation
k_a is small	step exploration	episode exploitation

Probabilistic Model Selection. While the learning mode is chosen deterministically with the thresholds in Table 1, we also propose a probabilistic selection method for choosing the learning mode. The "max and min values" of m_a and k_a are "H and 1" and "$|A|$ and 1," respectively. Larger and smaller m_a correspond to lower and higher uncertainties, respectively. Contrary to m_a, larger and smaller k_a correspond to higher and lower uncertainties, respectively.

Based on these properties, our probabilistic method considers m_a to be large with $(\frac{m_a-1}{H-1} \times 100)\%$. With this probabilistic selection, for example, if m_a is just in the middle between the min and max values, m_a is considered small and large with 50% and 50%, respectively. Similarly, k_a is considered to be large with $(\frac{k_a-1}{|A|-1} \times 100)\%$.

3.3   Uncertainty Thresholds for Choosing Learning Modes

For choosing a learning mode (i.e., exploration, step exploitation, or episode exploitation) at each step by using the uncertainty score (i.e., Eq. (1), Eq. (2),

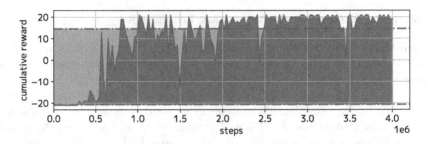

Fig. 3. Learning efficiency. The blue line is the learning curve. The red and brown lines indicate the results of human subjects and a random agent, respectively. The orange area is between the red and brown lines. (Color figure online)

m_a, and k_a), appropriate thresholds of the uncertainty score are required for deterministic mode selection. However, it is not easy to manually determine the thresholds that are appropriate to any task. This difficulty comes from the variable range of the uncertainty scores because the uncertainty scores derive from rewards that are defined depending on the task. The variable range of the task-dependent reward function leads to the variable ranges of Q-values and uncertainty scores based on Eq. (1).

To automatically determine the thresholds independently of the reward function, the uncertainty score computed in the first learning step is regarded as the initial uncertainty score. This initial score is decreased by being multiplied by constant decay rates in order to determine two thresholds dividing the score range into three intervals. In the first, second, and third intervals, exploration, step exploitation, and episode exploitation are used, respectively. In our experiments, the two decay rates are $\frac{1}{2}$ and $\frac{1}{4}$. With these two decay rates, the first, second, and third intervals of $\sigma^2(s_t)$ are $\frac{1}{2}\sigma_i^2 \leq \sigma^2(s_t)$, $\frac{1}{4}\sigma_i^2 \leq \sigma^2(s_t) < \frac{1}{2}\sigma_i^2$, and $\sigma^2(s_t) < \frac{1}{4}\sigma_i^2$, respectively, where σ_i^2 denotes the initial score.

Unlike the uncertainty score in Eq. (1), the range in Eq. (2) is known in accordance with the number of heads so that the uncertainty is maximum when all heads output different actions. This max score is decreased by being multiplied by constant decay rates in order to determine the thresholds. In our experiments, the two decay rates for the entropy are $\frac{2}{3}$ and $\frac{1}{3}$.

As mentioned in Sect. 3.2, the ranges of m_a and k_a are also known: $1 \leq m_a \leq H$ and $1 \leq k_a \leq |A|$. To split these ranges into large and small values in Table 1, half of each max value is regarded as the threshold in our experiments.

3.4 Evaluation Measure of Learning Efficiency

While the learning performance is evaluated only with the reward in the last step in the literature [2,7], this measure cannot evaluate how efficiently/fast learning is done. For evaluating the learning efficiency, we propose to use the learning curve in which the vertical and horizontal axes are the learning steps and cumulative rewards, respectively. The more efficient the learning is, the larger the area under the learning curve indicated by blue. Note that, as with the uncertainty score (1), this area also depends on the range of the reward function. For normalization, $\frac{A_l}{A_n}$ is used as our proposed evaluation score, where A_l and A_n denote the areas of the blue and orange regions in Fig. 3, respectively.

| Breakout | Pong | Ms. Pacman | Boxing | Star Gunner |

Fig. 4. Sample images of Breakout, Pong, Ms. Pacman, Boxing, and Star Gunner.

Table 2. Learning efficiency scores, $\frac{A_l}{A_n}$, defined in Sect. 3.4.

	Breakout	Pong	Ms. Pacman	Boxing	Star Gunner
Step exploitation	**5.312**	0.731	0.167	**5.523**	**0.499**
Episode exploitation	1.275	**0.744**	**0.184**	5.036	0.438

4 Experimental Results

4.1 Tasks

We used Atari 2600 Games Environment [3], which is a common benchmark of reinforcement learning [1,2,7]. This benchmark has a variety of tasks, so it is enough to check the ability to adapt to several kinds of tasks. In our experiments, five tasks, including Breakout, Pong, Ms. Pacman, Boxing, and Star Gunner are used (Fig. 4). All experiments are evaluated with three seeds per task for seed-independent evaluation. In all learning procedures, the number of learning steps was 4e+6. For evaluation purposes, the scores that the agent can get in tasks were computed every 25,000 steps.

4.2 Efficiency of Step Exploitation

The effect of our proposed step exploitation is validated by comparing it with the standard episode exploitation. The results are shown in Table 2. For pure evaluation of the difference between step and episode exploitations, in each experiment, only a single learning mode (i.e., either step exploitation or episode exploitation) is used without exploration.

In Pong and Ms. Pacman, episode exploitation learns more efficiently than step exploitation. On the other hand, in Boxing, Star Gunner, and Breakout, step exploitation can learn more efficiently. In particular, our step exploitation outperforms episode exploitation significantly in those tasks. This difference may depend on the agents' action space except in Breakout. The agent has only six and nine actions in Pong and Star Gunner, respectively, while 18 actions in Boxing and Ms. Pacman. Our interpretation is that, if the number of possible actions is small, even episode exploitation works well because it is not difficult to explore the possible actions without random action selection. That is why episode exploitation is better in Pong and Ms. Pacman.

Table 3. Efficiency of uncertainty scores for reinforcement learning. In Episode [10], the modes are changed in every episode. In ϵ-greedy and time uncertainty [10], exploration and episode exploitation are used. In our methods, exploration, step exploitation, and episode exploitation are used. The best and second-best values are colored by red and **blue**, respectively.

	Breakout	Pong	Ms. Pacman	Boxing	Star Gunner
ϵ-greedy [13]	**6.649**	0.735	**0.184**	4.557	0.487
Episode [10]	2.677	**0.781**	0.161	4.027	**0.488**
Temporal uncertainty [10]	1.117	0.601	0.082	1.489	0.221
Q-values variance (Ours)	2.496	0.830	0.147	**4.823**	0.519
Actions entropy (Ours)	4.118	0.698	0.185	4.665	0.392
Deterministic action (Ours)	4.352	0.739	0.170	5.405	0.433
Probabilistic action (Ours)	6.777	0.615	0.178	4.524	0.445

4.3   Efficiency of Uncertainty

The effects of uncertainty scores for efficient learning are evaluated, as shown in Table 3. In our proposed methods, exploration, step exploitation, and episode exploitation are selected as proposed in Sect. 3.

Our methods are the best in all tasks. Especially, our methods outperform others with a large margin in Pong and Boxing.

For detailed evaluation, the temporal histories of the uncertainty scores during learning are shown in Fig. 5. The variance of Q-values, Eq. (1), decreases in Pong, while it increases in Boxing despite our expectation. This difference leads to a difference in learning efficiency; when the variance of Q-values is used, the best score is obtained in Pong but not in Boxing.

The above difference comes from the difficulty of the task. In Pong, possible actions are only moving upward and moving downward. Furthermore, the variation of scene states is also limited. In Boxing, on the other hand, various actions are possible. In such a difficult task, the best action is not deterministically determined, but there are multiple appropriate actions, each of which is modeled by each head. This varied learning in the multiple heads results in the increases of Q-values in Boxing.

On the other hand, the entropy of action frequencies, Eq. (2), is not decreased both in Pong and Boxing, as shown in Fig. 6. This may be caused due to excessive information reduction by argmax for action selection.

4.4   Learning Strategies

Naturally, as mentioned before, our three learning modes are sorted in order of randomness (i.e., random exploration, step exploitation, and episode exploitation) so that exploration is done at an early learning stage, then step exploitation is selected, and finally episode exploitation optimizes the policy. However, it is also reported that the best order of the learning modes depends on the task in [10]. This report motivates us to verify the learning efficiencies in different orders of the learning modes.

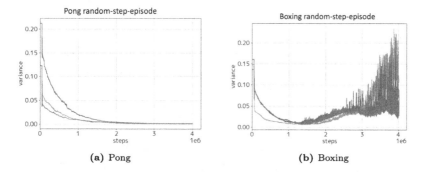

Fig. 5. Variances of Q-values in Pong and Boxing.

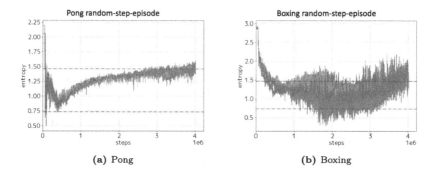

Fig. 6. Entropies of selected actions in Pong and Boxing.

Table 4. Learning efficiencies obtained by different orders of the learning modes selected based on the variance of Q-values.

	Breakout	Pong	Ms. Pacman	Boxing	Star Gunner
random-step-episode	2.496	0.830	0.147	**4.823**	0.519
random-episode-step	6.291	0.683	**0.177**	5.024	0.460
step-random-episode	1.870	**0.722**	0.178	4.526	**0.508**
step-episode-random	0.771	0.395	0.115	1.215	0.146
episode-random-step	**5.480**	0.707	0.141	3.808	0.370
episode-step-random	0.873	0.365	0.135	1.665	0.157

Table 5. Learning efficiencies obtained by different orders of the learning modes selected based on the entropy of action frequencies.

	Breakout	Pong	Ms. Pacman	Boxing	Star Gunner
random-step-episode	4.118	0.757	0.185	5.179	**0.392**
random-episode-step	4.897	0.710	**0.177**	**4.785**	0.358
step-random-episode	**5.027**	**0.738**	0.140	4.114	0.277
step-episode-random	0.682	0.376	0.141	3.269	0.433
episode-random-step	6.888	0.704	0.134	4.071	0.269
episode-step-random	0.827	0.401	0.140	3.499	0.295

Table 6. Learning efficiencies obtained by different orders of the learning modes selected based on the deterministic model selection.

	Breakout	Pong	Ms. Pacman	Boxing	Star Gunner
random-step-episode	4.352	**0.739**	0.170	**5.405**	**0.433**
random-episode-step	**5.504**	0.755	0.191	5.247	0.393
step-random-episode	4.961	0.692	**0.189**	5.318	0.453
step-episode-random	0.792	0.350	0.083	1.093	0.188
episode-random-step	6.238	0.719	0.151	5.068	0.417
episode-step-random	0.821	0.319	0.085	0.830	0.240

Table 7. Learning efficiencies obtained by different orders of the learning modes selected based on the probabilistic model selection.

	Breakout	Pong	Ms. Pacman	Boxing	Star Gunner
random-step-episode	6.777	0.615	0.178	4.524	**0.445**
random-episode-step	6.517	0.709	0.154	4.924	0.475
step-random-episode	6.843	**0.676**	**0.164**	4.599	0.387
step-episode-random	1.047	0.326	0.139	2.615	0.329
episode-random-step	**6.800**	0.632	0.157	4.488	0.381
episode-step-random	0.943	0.477	0.123	2.855	0.296

The results are shown in Tables 4, 5, 6, and 7. The order of the learning modes is shown in the leftmost column of all the Tables. For example, "random-step-episode" denotes that random exploration and episode exploitation are selected with the highest and lowest uncertainties, respectively.

We can see that the learning efficiency is bad if the exploration is selected with lower uncertainty. While the distributions of the learning efficiency scores are complex in these Tables, overall, the best orders are r-s-e, r-e-s, and s-r-e. Among these three orders, the best result depends on the task. Further experiments (e.g., experiments with other tasks) will be important future work.

By using our proposed efficiency measure method, we can compare the agent learning efficiency with other agent learning methods. Since the order of the best learning modes is reasonable, the efficiency measure method is good for measuring efficiency. On the other hand, to use this method, we have to prepare the result that the agent only selects random actions and human manipulation. Other methods will be needed to measure learning efficiency.

5   Conclusion

We proposed a novel exploitation mode, mode selection criteria using uncertainties from Q-values and actions, and a new measure for evaluating learning efficiency. The novel exploitation mode was effective for learning optimal actions in some tasks. The calculating uncertainty methods worked well. For future work, we need to search for more effective methods for learning with other networks.

References

1. Badia, A.P., et al.: Agent57: outperforming the Atari human benchmark. In: ICML, pp. 507–517 (2020)
2. Badia, A.P., et al.: Never give up: learning directed exploration strategies. In: ICLR (2020)
3. Bellemare, M.G., Naddaf, Y., Veness, J., Bowling, M.: The arcade learning environment: an evaluation platform for general agents (extended abstract). In: IJCAI, pp. 4148–4152 (2015)
4. Bellemare, M.G., Srinivasan, S., Ostrovski, G., Schaul, T., Saxton, D., Munos, R.: Unifying count-based exploration and intrinsic motivation. In: NIPS, pp. 1471–1479 (2016)
5. Burda, Y., Edwards, H., Storkey, A.J., Klimov, O.: Exploration by random network distillation. In: ICLR (2019)
6. Chen, R.Y., Sidor, S., Abbeel, P., Schulman, J.: UCB and InfoGain exploration via Q-ensembles. CoRR abs/1706.01502 (2017)
7. Dabney, W., Ostrovski, G., Barreto, A.: Temporally-extended ϵ-greedy exploration. In: ICLR (2021)
8. Gimelfarb, M., Sanner, S., Lee, C.: Epsilon-BMC: a Bayesian ensemble approach to epsilon-greedy exploration in model-free reinforcement learning. In: UAI, pp. 476–485 (2019)
9. Osband, I., Blundell, C., Pritzel, A., Roy, B.V.: Deep exploration via bootstrapped DQN. In: NIPS, pp. 4026–4034 (2016)

10. Pislar, M., Szepesvari, D., Ostrovski, G., Borsa, D.L., Schaul, T.: When should agents explore? In: ICLR (2022)
11. da Silva, F.L., Hernandez-Leal, P., Kartal, B., Taylor, M.E.: Uncertainty-aware action advising for deep reinforcement learning agents. In: EAAI, pp. 5792–5799 (2020)
12. Strehl, A.L., Littman, M.L.: An analysis of model-based interval estimation for Markov decision processes. J. Comput. Syst. Sci. **74**(8), 1309–1331 (2008)
13. Sutton, R.S., Barto, A.G.: Reinforcement Learning: An Introduction, 2nd edn. The MIT Press, London (2018)
14. Tang, H., et al.: #Exploration: a study of count-based exploration for deep reinforcement learning. In: NIPS, pp. 2753–2762 (2017)
15. Tarbouriech, J., Pirotta, M., Valko, M., Lazaric, A.: A provably efficient sample collection strategy for reinforcement learning. In: NeurIPS, pp. 7611–7624 (2021)
16. Tokic, M.: Adaptive ϵ-greedy exploration in reinforcement learning based on value difference. In: KI, vol. 6359, pp. 203–210 (2010)

Exploring the Role of Feedback Inhibition for the Robustness Against Corruptions on Event-Based Data

René Larisch[ID], Lucien Berger, and Fred H. Hamker[(✉)][ID]

Department of Computer Science, Chemnitz University of Technology,
Strasse der Nationen 62, 09111 Chemnitz, Germany
{rene.larisch,lucien.berger,fred.hamker}@informatik.tu-chemnitz.de

Abstract. In event-based vision, visual information is encoded by sequential events in space and time, similar to the human visual system, where the retina emits spikes. Thus, spiking neural networks are to be preferred for processing event-based input streams. As for classical deep learning networks, spiking neural networks must be robust against different corruption or perturbations in the input data. However, corruption in event-based data has received little attention so far. According to previous studies, biologically motivated neural networks, consisting of lateral inhibition to implement a competition mechanism between the neurons, show an increase in the robustness against loss of information of input data. We here analyze the influence of inhibitory feedback on the robustness against four different types of corruption on an event-based data set. We demonstrate how a 1 : 1 ratio between feed-forward excitation and feedback inhibition increases the robustness against the loss of events, as well as against additional noisy events. Interestingly, our results show that strong feedback inhibition is a disadvantage if events in the input stream are shifted in space or in time.

Keywords: STDP · unsupervised learning · event-based data

1 Introduction

How visual information is processed by the biological visual system is a long-standing research area, investigating the functionality in different brain areas along the visual pathway: from the retina via the primary visual cortex (V1), up to higher cortical areas. This research also lead to the development of a new type of camera generating a stream of events in space and time. These so-called event-based cameras are inspired by the functionality of the retina [17] and have become increasingly popular in recent years (see [4], and [17] for a review). Due to the encoding of visual information in single events, spiking neural networks (SNN) are suitable to process the camera output, also visible by the increase of SNNs, trained and evaluated on different event-based datasets [4]. One of the most used event-based datasets is the neuromorphic version of the

L. Iliadis et al. (Eds.): ICANN 2023, LNCS 14261, pp. 197–208, 2023.
https://doi.org/10.1007/978-3-031-44198-1_17

MNIST dataset, the so-called N-MNIST dataset [18]. Therefore, different SNNs were published, which train directly on the N-MNIST data set in a supervised manner via a surrogate learning rule [12,19] or unsupervised with a spike-timing dependent plasticity (STDP) learning rule [7].

As with the biological visual system, SNNs have to be robust against adversarial perturbations [2] or against a certain level of input corruptions [6]. In event-based datasets, the visual information of an object is not only encoded in the spatial dimension but also in time, adding an additional dimension where information can be altered. While adversarial perturbations on neural networks for static images and their defenses are well studied (see [1] for an extensive review), adversarial perturbations for event-based processing have received only a little attention [2]. Moreover, improving the robustness of SNNs against corruptions in event-based datasets has not been sufficiently addressed.

Neural networks, trained with Hebbian-like plasticity, showed, that competition between neurons during training (as implemented by feedback inhibition) lead to a more diverse input representation in the network [11]. Further, feedback inhibition leads to a more robust behavior against corruptions on static images, such as the loss of input information [8,10]. This indicates a possible role for feedback inhibition to improve the robustness against corruptions on an event-based dataset as well.

To evaluate if inhibition is a suitable mechanism to improve the robustness, we use a V1-like SNN, which we published previously [11], trained it on the N-MNIST dataset, and test it on five different types of corruptions on the N-MNIST dataset. To verify if the feature representation of the network is independent of the strength of inhibition, as presented in previous work [11], we trained our SNN with two different excitation-to-inhibition ratios during the training phase. After that, we deactivated (or blocked) the inhibitory feedback synapses for both SNNs. We observe that with active inhibition, the model with stronger inhibition shows higher accuracy than the model with weaker inhibition, whereas blocked inhibition leads to a similar accuracy for both models. We applied the following corruptions: By deleting single events, either randomly out of the input stream or in a specific area, we test the robustness against the loss of information, similar to previous works [8,10]. We expand our analyzes by adding randomly new events to the input event stream, adding noisy information, and shifting single events randomly in space and time to distort the contextual information between the single events, without changing the total number of events.

We observe higher robustness against the loss of information, as well as against additional noisy events if strong inhibitory feedback occurs in the network. In contrast to that, if the input information is distorted by shifting events in space or time, strong inhibitory feedback decreases the robustness. To the best of our knowledge, we present the first study of a biologically grounded spiking neural network to evaluate the role of feedback inhibition for robustness against different types of corruptions on an event-based dataset.

2   Methods

2.1   Spiking Neural Network

The implemented spiking neural network (SNN) follows our previous publication, where we combined two phenomenological spiking learning rules to train a model of simple cells in Layer 4 of the primary visual cortex [11].

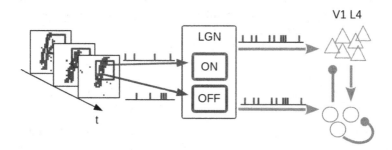

Fig. 1. The architecture of the spiking neural network. The ON-events (indicated green) and OFF-events (indicated red) arrive separately on the LGN ON- and OFF-populations. The excitatory population (orange triangles) and the inhibitory population (blue circles) receive input from both LGN populations. Orange arrows indicate excitatory synapses and blue arrows inhibitory synapses. (Color figure online)

The SNN consists of a population of LGN ON and OFF- neurons, which process separately the ON and OFF events from the input data set and send them to the excitatory and inhibitory populations (see Fig. 1). With an input size of 12×12 pixels, where each pixel corresponds to one LGN neuron in the ON or OFF path, our network consists of 288 LGN cells in total. The excitatory population consists of 144 neurons and the inhibitory population of 36 neurons, to match the 4 : 1 ratio between excitatory and inhibitory neurons as reported for the neocortex [14]. Outgoing synapses from populations transmit excitatory or inhibitory signals, depending on the transmitting neuron type, following Dale's principle.

We use an adaptive integrate and fire (AdEx) neuron model, following the one of Clopath et al. (2010) [3] for the excitatory and inhibitory neurons. The membrane potential (u) follows Eq. 1, with C as the membrane capacity, g_L a leak conductance, E_L as the resting potential, V_T the spiking threshold, Δ_T as a slope factor and I as the input current.

$$C\frac{du}{dt} = -g_L(u - E_L) + g_L\Delta_T e^{\frac{u-V_T}{\Delta_T}} - w_{ad} + z + I \tag{1}$$

Additionally, w_{ad} describes the hyperpolarization adaption current with $\tau_{w_{ad}}$ as a time constant and a as an additional parameter. It changes over time following: $\tau_{w_{ad}}\frac{dw_{ad}}{dt} = a(u - E_L) - w_{ad}$. The after-spike depolarization is modelled by the dynamics of variable z as $\tau_z\frac{dz}{dt} = -z$.

If the membrane potential u exceeds the spiking threshold V_T and the neuron releases a spike, u is reset to the resting potential E_L, w_{ad} is increased by the parameter b and z is set to I_{sp}.

Further, the AdEx model can be parameterized to recreate different spiking patterns [16]. Thus, the AdEx model can be considered a good compromise between computational efficiency and biological plausibility.

The SNN is trained in a fully unsupervised fashion with a voltage-based STDP learning rule [3] and a symmetric inhibitory STDP learning rule [24]. The voltage-based STDP rule is used on all excitatory synapses (LGN to E, LGN to I, E to I) and follows Eq. 2, describing the change of the weight (w_{ij}) from the presynaptic neuron i to the postsynaptic neuron j.

$$\frac{dw_{ij}}{dt} = A_{LTP}\overline{x}_i(u_j - \theta_+)^+(\overline{u}_+ - \theta_-)^+ - A_{LTD}\frac{\overline{\overline{u}}_j}{u_{ref}}X_i(\overline{u}_- - \theta_-)^+ \quad (2)$$

The weight increase and weight decrease depend on the presynaptic spike trace ($\overline{x}_i$), the presynaptic spike event (X_i) as well as on postsynaptic membrane potential (u_j), and two temporal averages of it ($\overline{u}_+$ and $\overline{u}_-$). Additionally, the parameters θ_+ and θ_- are thresholds, that the membrane potential or its temporal averages must exceed to enable a change. Both parameters, A_{LTP} and A_{LTD}, are the learning rates for long-term potentiation and long-term depression, respectively.

The symmetric STDP rule from Vogels et al. (2011) [24] is used for all inhibitory synapses (I to E and I to I). Therefore, the inhibitory weight w_{ij} between a presynaptic neuron i and a postsynaptic neuron j changes as follows

$$\frac{dw_{ij}}{dt} = \begin{cases} \eta(\overline{x}_j - \rho) & \text{, for presynaptic spike} \\ \eta(\overline{x}_i) & \text{, for postsynaptic spike} \end{cases} \quad (3)$$

where $\overline{x}_i$ and $\overline{x}_j$ are spike traces of the presynaptic and postsynaptic neuron, respectively, η the learning rule, and ρ a homeostatic parameter to control the strength of inhibition. For each spike of the corresponding neuron, the spike trace increases by one and decays by $\tau\frac{d\overline{x}}{dt} = -\overline{x}$.

The SNN has been implemented in Python 3.8, using the ANNarchy simulator (v.4.7.2) [23], with a simulation time step of $dt = 1\,\text{ms}$. The implementation of the SNN, the training, and the evaluation of the corruptions are available on GitHub[1]

2.2   Dataset

Our network has been trained on the event-based version of the MNIST dataset, called N-MNIST [18]. To load the dataset we used the Tonic python package [13]. Each sample in the N-MNIST dataset has a spatial resolution of 34×34 pixel but differs in length of time from 300 ms up to 350 ms. Using a neuromorphic vision

---

[1] https://github.com/hamkerlab/Larisch2023_EventBasedSNN.git.

sensor, the MNIST dataset was shown on a monitor, performing three movement saccades to record the movement with the camera. Due to this, an event-based version of each sample in the MNIST training and test set was created. Similar to the original MNIST dataset, the samples of the N-MNIST dataset contain a border with no relevant information, meaning no events during the complete presentation time. Due to this, we removed a border of 5 pixels, leading to a spatial resolution of 24×24 pixels.

2.3   Training

As it has been shown in our previous work, stable receptive fields emerge at around 400.000 [11] stimulus presentations. Thus, we trained the SNN on the same number of randomly chosen samples from the N-MNIST training set. Due to the input size of the network, after selecting a sample, a spatial window of 12×12 pixels were randomly selected. This leads to the emergence of localized receptive fields for each neuron. So a neuron encodes a local feature instead of a complete number. We separated ON and OFF events into separate event streams to determine the spike times of each LGN neuron in the ON-population and OFF-population.

Recording with the neuromorphic sensor leads to a high temporal sampling rate and recording events on a microsecond time scale. Due to a simulation time step of 1 ms in our network, we accumulate all events appearing in one 1 ms in that way, that all events appearing at the same position in a 1 ms window are represented by one event. Due to this 0.35% from the ON events and 0.1% of the OFF events are accumulated. Accumulating was performed separately for ON and OFF events. The resulting event stream in the spatial window and 350 ms presentation time is given to the network.

2.4   Different Strengths of Inhibition

It has been shown in previous work, that the quality of the input representation is independent of the excitatory to inhibitory ratio during the network training [11]. However, the accuracy and robustness against corruption decreases if inhibition is set off, after learning [8,10]. To evaluate if either the inhibitory strength or the resulted encoded features (due to the emerged receptive fields) is important for the robustness, we trained the SNN with two different strengths of feedback inhibition. To do that, we changed the ρ parameter in the inhibitory learning rule for the feedback connections. With a $\rho = 12$, we achieved a nearly $1 : 1$ excitation to inhibition ratio (called $EI1/1$ model), whereas a $\rho = 20$ leads to a three-time stronger excitation than inhibition ratio (called $EI3/1$ model). Each of both model variants is trained and evaluated on the corruptions ten times. Additionally, we deactivated (or blocked) the feedback inhibitory synapses in both model configurations and evaluated them on the corruptions again (called $EI1/1$ *blockInh* and $EI3/1$ *blockInh*, respectively).

2.5   Measuring Accuracy

To measure the quality of the input encoding in our network, we used a linear support vector machine (SVM), fitted on the spike rate (the number of spikes) of the excitatory population on each training sample, and evaluated the SVM on the spike rate on the test set to measure the prediction accuracy. To record the spike rate on the training set, we presented the complete N-MNIST training set again, after the training of the SNN was finished and froze the weights in the SNN. Due to the small input size of the SNN, we split each sample along the spatial dimension of 24 × 24 pixels into four non-overlapping windows. For each window, we record the spike rate for each neuron over the complete presentation time of 350 ms. By concatenating the recorded spike rates of the four windows, we created the sample vector for each sample, which is used to fit the SVM. The same procedure was done on the N-MNIST test set as well to obtain the sample vectors for evaluation. A similar procedure was done in previous works [10,22]. The previous paper has shown, that the input encoding quality of the inhibitory population is lower than that of the excitatory population [22], due to this only used the spike rates of the excitatory neurons. We report here the average over the ten repetitions with the corresponding standard deviation of the mean value. Additionally, we measured the Precision and Recall value for each of the ten classes to investigate, which class is better represented in the SNN. We report here only the mean values.

2.6   Evaluate Robustness Against Corruptions

To evaluate the robustness of our SNNs against corruptions on the event-based dataset, we used the Tonic python package [13], which provides different possibilities to manipulate the event stream. We applied five different corruptions on the event input stream (see Fig. 2), where each of the corruptions was applied on

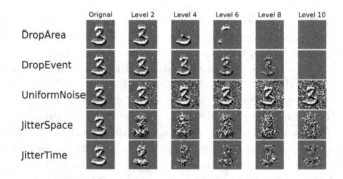

Fig. 2. Samples of the five perturbations used in this study for five different levels of the corresponding perturbation, where level 0 means no perturbation and level 10 maximum perturbation. Each sample shows the accumulated events in the corrupted input stream for a 15 ms time frame. White pixels indicate ON-events and black pixels indicate OFF-events.

ten different levels of corruption strength. The first corruption drops all events in a randomly chosen spatial area of the input stream (called DropArea), whereby the size of the area increases in ten percent steps, in relation to the spatial size of the input. In the second corruption, a randomly chosen number of events of the complete event stream is dropped randomly (called DropEvent). We change the number of events in steps of ten percent from 10% to 100%. The third corruption adds events randomly in the event stream, following a multivariate uniform distribution (called UniformNoise). Due to the fact, that the original Tonic implementation did not check if a new event is created for a position in space and time where an event already exists, we created for this corruption our own implementation to ensure, that only new events will be created, which are not existing already in the event stream. We increased the number of added events from 1.000 to 10.000.

Whereas the other corruptions changed the number of events in the input stream, the last two corruptions shift the position of each event along the two spatial dimensions and the time dimension. The shift of the spatial position follows a multivariate Gaussian distribution, in which the standard deviation determines the shift (called JitterSpace). We increased the standard deviation for both spatial dimensions equally from one up to ten pixels. To shift an event along the time dimension, the shift follows a one-dimensional Gaussian distribution. Therefore, we increased the standard deviation from one to 100 ms. Events that shifted before time point zero or after time point 350 (what is the presentation length of one sample), are no longer part of the event stream.

We recorded the spiking activity of each excitatory neuron for each of the ten levels of corruption strength as described above. To evaluate how strongly the response vector is influenced by each corruption, we first fitted a linear SVM with the sample vectors, recorded on the normal, not corrupted N-MNIST training set. Then, we used the sample vectors recorded on each corruption level as an input to the SVM to predict the sample class. A stronger corruption of the input stream should lead to a stronger corruption in the sample vector and to a wrong classification by the SVM.

3   Results

After training, we visualized the receptive fields of the excitatory and inhibitory populations by rearranging the input weights from the ON and OFF LGN populations (see Fig. 3). Due to the small input size, the receptive fields resemble simpler features instead of complete numbers and partial 2D-Gabor functions, as expected by a simple cell model. Despite that, also curved receptive fields are visible.

On the normal, non-corrupted, N-MNIST dataset, the $EI1/1$ model achieved an accuracy of $95.12\% \pm 0.83$, achieving better accuracy values than the unsupervised STDP network proposed by [7] or the liquid state machine (LSM), whose connection to the readout layer is trained with Spatio-Temporal Backpropagation (STBP), proposed in [20] (see Table 1). In contrast to that, the SNN with

Fig. 3. Left, receptive fields of 18 randomly chosen excitatory cells. Right, receptive fields of 18 randomly chosen inhibitory cells.

Table 1. Accuracy values on the N-MNIST dataset

Model	Learning type	Learning rule	Accuracy in %
LSM [20]	Supervised	STBP	94.43
SNN [7]	Unsupervised	STDP	76.01
$EI1/1$ model	Unsupervised	STDP	95.12 ± 0.83
$EI3/1$ model	Unsupervised	STDP	91.02 ± 2.79

weaker inhibition achieves only an accuracy value of $91.02\% \pm 2.79$. If inhibition is blocked, the accuracy of both network types drops to $91.42\% \pm 2.2$ and $90.65\% \pm 1.66$, respectively. We also measured the Precision and Recall score for each of the ten classes to investigate, how well the single classes are recognized (see Table 2). The $EI1/1$ model and the $EI3/1$ model achieve the highest scores by detecting samples of class 2 and the low scores by detecting class 9. The $EI3/1$ model shows for class 4 and class 6 high differences between the Recall and Precision scores from $9 - 10$, while the scores for Recall and Precision for the $EI1/1$ model show only a difference of ≈ 1. This shows that stronger inhibition improves the discriminability between class representations and improves the accuracy.

By applying the first corruption type, the SNN with strong inhibition shows the highest robustness, whereas both models without inhibition and the model with weak inhibition show similar robustness (see Fig. 4). However, at an area size of 30%, the accuracy of all models drops strongly and is nearly linear with increasing area size.

Table 2. Precision and Recall for the ten different classes. Top row: $EI1/1$ model. Bottom row: $EI3/1$ model.

Model	Metric	1	2	3	4	5	6	7	8	9	10
$EI1/1$ model	Precision	95.87	97.9	96.03	94.26	97.23	94.19	96.19	95.84	92.49	91.57
	Recall	97.98	98.71	92.04	93.14	95.6	94.44	97.08	94.49	91.55	93.73
$EI3/1$ model	Precision	92.23	97.39	90.87	84.57	94.44	91.45	95.97	93.72	86.1	89.68
	Recall	96.63	98.39	87.67	93.38	91.91	79.98	94.13	92.21	83.14	87.97

If events are randomly deleted out of the event stream, again the $EI1/1$ model shows to be most robust, having an accuracy around 90%, if 50% of the events drop. In contrast to the first corruption, the $EI3/1$ model is more robust than both models without inhibition.

Whereas the first two corruptions deleted events, the third corruption adds additional events randomly into the input stream. Similar to the first two corruptions, strong feedback inhibition leads to a more robust encoding, whereas weak inhibition improves the robustness only just a little in comparison to both models without inhibition.

By shifting the events in space, a strong decrease in performance is observable for all models, regardless of the strength of feedback inhibition or the existence of inhibition. Additionally, at higher pixel drifts, stronger inhibition leads to a stronger drop in the accuracy values, whereas weak or no inhibition shows similar robustness.

However, stronger inhibition leads to higher robustness, if the events only shifted by 20 ms in time. This effect reverses for larger shifts around 40 ms or higher. Both models with shutdown inhibition show similar robustness against the shift in time. By shifts around 80 ms, the accuracy for some models increases again. Due to the fact, that events that are shifted before the original starting time point or behind the last time point of 350 ms are deleted, we assume that with larger shifts more and more events are deleted from the event stream rather than distort the stimulus information in time.

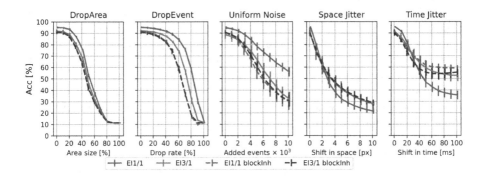

Fig. 4. Accuracy for five different corruptions and levels. $EI1/1$ model indicated by the blue solid line, $EI3/1$ model indicated by the solid red line, $EI1/1$ blockInh model is indicated by the dotted gray line and the $EI3/1$ blockInh model is indicated by the dotted dark red line. (Color figure online)

4 Discussion

We evaluated how inhibition influences the robustness of a spiking neural network against corruptions on an event-based dataset. To do so, we trained a spiking neural network, which was built to resemble layer-4 of the primary visual cortex [11], on the event-based N-MNIST dataset [18].

Our results show that models with shutdown inhibition have similar robustness against all five corruptions. This indicates that the resulting receptive fields in these networks showing a similar quality in terms of input encoding, regardless of the strength of inhibition during the training phase [11]. With a 1 : 1 excitation to inhibition ratio, the robustness against changes in the number of input events, by dropping events or adding new events, improves. Dropping events leads to a loss of information and a reduced amount of input current to the network. Due to this, the network activity should decrease with further dropped events. It has been shown previously, that feedback inhibition is damping the neuronal gain function [11]. Due to this, we assume that dropping events leads only to a weak drift away from the activity occurring upon the original stimuli, resulting in a robust neuronal representation. Adding new events randomly in space and time, occluding the stimuli and increasing the amount of input current shall increase the input current leading to a higher activity of the inhibitory neurons to increase the amount of feedback inhibition, received by the postsynaptic excitatory neuron.

In contrast to those corruptions, shifting events in space and time leads to a distortion of stimulus information, but does not change the total input current (except for long shifts in time). Our results show, that strong inhibition did not provide better robustness against this type of perturbation, on the contrary, it weakens the robustness. We assume that strong inhibition leads to an attractor-like dynamic in our network [15]. The distorted input information, through shifted events, did not match with the connectivity structure of inhibition inside of the network. Due to this, inhibitory interneurons induce another attractor state, forcing the network to another internal representation. It has been shown in previous studies, that lateral excitatory connections as well as top-down feedback signals can increase robustness on distorted stimuli [21], two connectivity structures our network did not include. Lateral excitation between the excitatory cells may stabilize the neural representation and lead to more robust attractor states, while top-down feedback may provide more stabilizing contextual information [5].

Previous studies about robustness improvements, especially against adversarial attacks, propose methods that increase the number of training samples, like adversarial training [2]. Despite their success to increase robustness, adding adversarial samples to the training set increases training time and could lead to a bias toward the used perturbations for adversarial training, making it less robust against new attacks [25]. In contrast to that, feedback inhibition as a network motif can improve the robustness independently of the training data. While we only investigated the robustness against input corruptions, it has been discussed in previous works that inhibitory feedback also can improve the robustness against adversarial attacks [9].

In summary, our work supports the potential of feedback inhibition to increase the robustness against corruptions on an event-based dataset. The presented weakness against shifting events shows, that further research on the effect of more complex network motifs for robustness is warranted.

Acknowledgements. This research has been funded by the Saxony State Ministry of Science and Art (SMWK3-7304/35/3-2021/4819) research initiative "Instant Teaming between Humans and Production Systems"

References

1. Akhtar, N., Mian, A., Kardan, N., Shah, M.: Advances in adversarial attacks and defenses in computer vision: a survey. IEEE Access **9**, 155161–155196 (2021). https://doi.org/10.1109/ACCESS.2021.3127960
2. Büchel, J., Lenz, G., Hu, Y., Sheik, S., Sorbaro, M.: Adversarial attacks on spiking convolutional neural networks for event-based vision. Front. Neurosci. **16** (2022). https://doi.org/10.3389/fnins.2022.1068193
3. Clopath, C., Büsing, L., Vasilaki, E., Gerstner, W.: Connectivity reflects coding: a model of voltage-based STDP with homeostasis. Nat. Neurosci. **13**(3), 344–352 (2010). https://doi.org/10.1038/nn.2479
4. Gallego, G., et al.: Event-based vision: a survey. IEEE Trans. Pattern Anal. Mach. Intell. **44**(01), 154–180 (2022). https://doi.org/10.1109/TPAMI.2020.3008413
5. Gilbert, C.D., Li, W.: Top-down influences on visual processing. Nat. Rev. Neurosci. **14**(5), 350–363 (2013). https://doi.org/10.1038/nrn3476
6. Hendrycks, D., Dietterich, T.: Benchmarking neural network robustness to common corruptions and perturbations. In: Proceedings of the International Conference on Learning Representations (2019)
7. Iyer, L.R., Basu, A.: Unsupervised learning of event-based image recordings using spike-timing-dependent plasticity. In: 2017 International Joint Conference on Neural Networks (IJCNN), pp. 1840–1846 (2017). https://doi.org/10.1109/IJCNN. 2017.7966074
8. Kermani Kolankeh, A., Teichmann, M., Hamker, F.H.: Competition improves robustness against loss of information. Front. Comput. Neurosci. **9** (2015). https:// doi.org/10.3389/fncom.2015.00035
9. Kim, E., Rego, J., Watkins, Y., Kenyon, G.T.: Modeling biological immunity to adversarial examples. In: 2020 IEEE/CVF Conference on Computer Vision and Pattern Recognition (CVPR), pp. 4665–4674 (2020). https://doi.org/10.1109/ CVPR42600.2020.00472
10. Larisch, R., Teichmann, M., Hamker, F.H.: A neural spiking approach compared to deep feedforward networks on stepwise pixel erasement. In: Kůrková, V., Manolopoulos, Y., Hammer, B., Iliadis, L., Maglogiannis, I. (eds.) ICANN 2018. LNCS, vol. 11139, pp. 253–262. Springer, Cham (2018). https://doi.org/10.1007/ 978-3-030-01418-6_25
11. Larisch, R., Gönner, L., Teichmann, M., Hamker, F.H.: Sensory coding and contrast invariance emerge from the control of plastic inhibition over emergent selectivity. PLOS Comput. Biol. **17**(11), 1–37 (2021). https://doi.org/10.1371/journal.pcbi. 1009566
12. Lee, C., Sarwar, S.S., Panda, P., Srinivasan, G., Roy, K.: Enabling spike-based backpropagation for training deep neural network architectures. Front. Neurosci. **14** (2020). https://doi.org/10.3389/fnins.2020.00119
13. Lenz, G., et al.: Tonic: event-based datasets and transformations, July 2021. https://doi.org/10.5281/zenodo.5079802, Documentation available under https:// tonic.readthedocs.io

14. Markram, H., Toledo-Rodriguez, M., Wang, Y., Gupta, A., Silberberg, G., Wu, C.: Interneurons of the neocortical inhibitory system. Nat. Rev. Neurosci. **5**(10), 793–807 (2004). https://doi.org/10.1038/nrn1519

15. Miconi, T., McKinstry, J.L., Edelman, G.M.: Spontaneous emergence of fast attractor dynamics in a model of developing primary visual cortex. Nat. Commun. **7**(1), 13208 (2016). https://doi.org/10.1038/ncomms13208

16. Naud, R., Marcille, N., Clopath, C., Gerstner, W.: Firing patterns in the adaptive exponential integrate-and-fire model. Biol. Cybern. **99**(4), 335–347 (2008). https://doi.org/10.1007/s00422-008-0264-7

17. Nunes, J.D., Carvalho, M., Carneiro, D., Cardoso, J.S.: Spiking neural networks: a survey. IEEE Access **10**, 60738–60764 (2022). https://doi.org/10.1109/ACCESS.2022.3179968

18. Orchard, G., Jayawant, A., Cohen, G.K., Thakor, N.: Converting static image datasets to spiking neuromorphic datasets using saccades. Front. Neurosci. **9**, 437 (2015)

19. Patiño-Saucedo, A., Rostro-González, H., Serrano-Gotarredona, T., Linares-Barranco, B.: Event-driven implementation of deep spiking convolutional neural networks for supervised classification using the spinnaker neuromorphic platform. Neural Netw. **121**, 319–328 (2020). https://doi.org/10.1016/j.neunet.2019.09.008

20. Patiño-Saucedo, A., Rostro-González, H., Serrano-Gotarredona, T., Linares-Barranco, B.: Liquid state machine on spinnaker for spatio-temporal classification tasks. Front. Neurosci. **16** (2022). https://doi.org/10.3389/fnins.2022.819063

21. Spoerer, C.J., McClure, P., Kriegeskorte, N.: Recurrent convolutional neural networks: a better model of biological object recognition. Front. Psychol. **8** (2017). https://doi.org/10.3389/fpsyg.2017.01551

22. Teichmann, M., Larisch, R., Hamker, F.H.: Performance of biologically grounded models of the early visual system on standard object recognition tasks. Neural Netw. **144**, 210–228 (2021). https://doi.org/10.1016/j.neunet.2021.08.009

23. Vitay, J., Dinkelbach, H., Hamker, F.: ANNarchy: a code generation approach to neural simulations on parallel hardware. Front. Neuroinform. **9** (2015). https://doi.org/10.3389/fninf.2015.00019

24. Vogels, T.P., Sprekeler, H., Zenke, F., Clopath, C., Gerstner, W.: Inhibitory plasticity balances excitation and inhibition in sensory pathways and memory networks. Science **334**(6062), 1569–1573 (2011). https://doi.org/10.1126/science.1211095

25. Zhang, H., Chen, H., Song, Z., Boning, D., Dhillon, I., Hsieh, C.J.: The limitations of adversarial training and the blind-spot attack. In: International Conference on Learning Representations (2019). https://openreview.net/forum?id=HylTBhA5tQ

Extracting Feature Space for Synchronizing Behavior in an Interaction Scene Using Unannotated Data

Yuya Okadome[1,2(✉)] and Yutaka Nakamura[2,3]

[1] Faculty of Engineering, Tokyo University of Science, Katsushika, Japan
okadome@rs.tus.ac.jp
[2] Guardian Robot Project, RIKEN Information R&D and Strategy Headquarters, Seika, Japan
[3] Graduate School of Engineering Science, Osaka University, Toyonaka, Japan

Abstract. Human-human interaction includes synchronizing behaviors, such as nodding and turn-taking. Extracting and implementing these synchronization behaviors is crucial for the communication robot which can do "feeling good" conversations. In this research, we propose a framework for extracting the synchronization behavior from a dyadic conversation based on self-supervised learning. "Lag operation" which is the time-shifting operation for the features of a subject is applied to the conversation data, and a neural network model is trained based on the operating data and label of the amount of operation. The representation space is obtained after the training, and the timing-dependent behaviors are expected to isolate in the space. The proposed method is applied to about four hours of conversation data, and the representation of the test data is calculated. Data with social behaviors such as "eye contact", "turn-taking", and "smile" are extracted from the isolated region of the representation. Designing the behavior rules of the communication robot and investigating the proposed framework characteristics are our future projects.

Keywords: Human-human communication · Synchronizing behaviors · Deep learning · Unannotated data

1 Introduction

The development of communication robots that can mutually interact with a human has gained immense attention lately [2,9]. For human-human communication, a bi-directional interaction, i.e., a "full-duplex" interaction is always happening among people. Although this synchronization is fundamental to a social robot, sufficient bi-directional communication is not generally developed for the actual interaction scene. To realize a communication agent with a synchronizing motion, it is necessary to generate a real-time reaction by observing an interaction scene among people.

L. Iliadis et al. (Eds.): ICANN 2023, LNCS 14261, pp. 209–219, 2023.
https://doi.org/10.1007/978-3-031-44198-1_18

The timing of the expression of social behavior must be considered for an adequate real-time reaction. Certain behaviors including nodding [14] and smiling [15] are synchronized at an appropriate timing during human-human communication. Implementing the timing of synchronization behaviors in the agent is necessary for natural interaction. Surveying when the human behaviors are in synchronization is crucial to extract the behavioral rules.

To investigate the behavior synchronization, methods calculating the correlation between the temporal data from a sensor [6], e.g., microphone and video, and evaluation of video clips by subjects [3] are considered. Since a correlation is calculated from two temporal behaviors such as voice and neck angle, it is not easy to extract the relationship between several variables. In addition to many video clips, evaluating "Are they synchronized?" is difficult if subjects annotate videos with some labels. It is crucial to automatically extract synchronized behavior in a database that contains interaction data.

In this research, we propose an data extraction framework of the synchronization behavior of human-human interaction based on self-supervised learning [5,12,13,16]. The aim of the method is to construct the distinctive feature space and to extract data including the synchronization behavior from the specific region in the space. The proposed framework handles dyadic conversation, i.e., involving two subjects in a conversation scene. To generate augmented data for learning a neural network model, features from one subject are combined with the time-shifted features from the other one, and this operation is called a "lag operation". Certain behaviors, such as nodding, can affect the impression [17], and the timing of such synchronizing behavior is mutated due to the lag operation. The amount of time-shift is learned and estimated by using a deep neural network approach, and the representation space is obtained by projecting data with the learned network.

We apply the proposed framework to the gathered dyadic conversation data, and the neural network model is trained on the data. After learning the model, the representation space of input features is obtained. There are separated and un-separated features in the space, i.e., there is the structure. The density ratio (score) on the learned representation space is calculated based on a kernel density estimation [4] and used as the criterion of data extraction. The data is extracted from the separated and un-separated regions. Synchronizing behaviors (e.g., nodding, smiling, etc.) are included in the separated region. Conversely, unsynchronized features (e.g., thinking, out of sight, etc.) are in the un-separated area. Inspired by these, data including synchronization behavior can be extracted by using the proposed framework. For future work, rules of behavior for communication agents are designed from the extracted data.

2   Related Works

Interpersonal synchronization during the conversation is investigated in some research. As for the nodding synchronization during the face-to-face dyadic conversation, the phase of head movement of subjects is analyzed [14]. The analysis method of a facial expression using an EMG signal [18] is also proposed, and the research shows the synchronization of smiles is quite rapid. In many research, the synchronization of two subjects is analyzed using the calculation of correlation and modeling signals as the temporal data [6]. The sequentially occurring events which are related to some variables (e.g., raising the face, nodding, and then smiling at each other) are not considered in these approaches.

The technique of self-supervised learning has been developed to obtain the representation from un-annotated information. Self-supervised learning is mainly used for a small number of labeled data, and the network model weights are obtained by pre-training with un-annotated data and automatically generated labels. For self-supervised learning approaches, a transformation ϕ, e.g., a traditional image process (e.g., rotating and flipping) [5, 8, 13] and by breaking down an image like a puzzle [11, 16], is applied to input image. A neural network is trained on the converted data and the automatically generated label, i.e., which image processes are applied, and where is the correct position of broken image patches.

3   Problem Settings

Thanks to the recent development of devices (e.g., camera and microphone), massive interaction data can be collected. Data is gathered from dyadic conversations, wherein the features of two subjects at time t are $x_L(t), x_R(t)$. Since the interaction data include the social information, past information must be considered for its context. T time-step features of the two are defined as $X_L^T(t) = [x_L(t - i)|i = 0, ..., T], X_R^T(t) = [x_R(t - i)|i = 0, ..., T]$. Figure 1 shows the relationship between $x(t)$ and $X(t)$ at time t. Note that the time indices of the features of subjects $\cdot_L, \cdot_R$ remain consistent. After obtaining data, the annotation labels are added generally, and a function for the task is learned under the label. Since the procedure of annotation is expensive, the number of annotated data is small.

In this research, we aim to develop data processing for the interaction data $\phi(X_R^T(t), X_L^T(t))$ and a framework for extracting the synchronizing behavior. $\phi(X_R^T(t), X_L^T(t))$ is an input feature for self-supervised model, and ϕ is designed for which the characteristics of interaction data must be considered.

4   Methods

In this section, the proposed learning framework trained with the amount of time-shift label is described. A part of the behavior of two subjects is assumed to be synchronized, and the conversion for interaction data ϕ_{TL} is designed as the lag operation. The purpose of self-supervised learning is to extract features from the converted data.

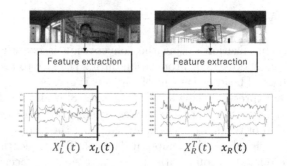

Fig. 1. Relationship between $x(t)$ and $X(t)$.

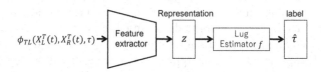

Fig. 2. Input and output variables for self-supervised learning.

4.1 Lag Operation

Corresponding to the time indices of both features $X_L^T(t), X_R^T(t)$, time-shifted feature is defined as $X_L^T(t), X_R^T(t+\tau)$. Thus, the lag operator ϕ_{TL} becomes

$$\phi_{TL}(X_L^T(t), X_R^T(t), \tau) = \{X_L^T(t), X_R^T(t+\tau)\}, \tag{1}$$

where τ is the amount of lag operation, i.e., time-shift. τ is sampled from the set of time-shift $\mathcal{T}$. Without the loss of generality, conversion target X_R is swapped with X_L due to the symmetry of temporal data.

Figure 2 shows the input features, output variables, and estimation model. $\phi_{TL}(X_R^T(t), X_L^T(t), \tau)$ is input to the model, and the model output the representation z. z is input into lag estimator f to estimate the shift $\hat{\tau}$ indicating the amount of time-shift.

4.2 Loss Function

$\tau \in \mathcal{T}$ is used as the label of self-supervised learning. To classify the amount of lag operation, the following loss function,

$$L(z^p, \tau^B, \hat{\tau^B}) = \alpha L_c(\tau^B, \hat{\tau^B}) + \beta L_d(z^p, \tau^B), \tag{2}$$

is calculated. z^p, B, τ^B and $\hat{\tau}^B$ are the representation, batch size, amount of lag operation for each data, and estimated amount of time-shift, respectively. α and β are the constant weights for each term. L_c and L_d are the classification loss to estimate τ and distance-based loss to determine placements of representations, respectively.

L_c is defined as the cross-entropy loss

$$L_c(\tau, \hat{\tau}) = \frac{1}{b} \sum_{b=1}^{B} \sum_{i \in \mathcal{T}} p(\tau = i) \log(p(\hat{\tau} = i)) \tag{3}$$

to estimate the discrete label τ. To learn the distance of each feature, L_d is defined as the soft-nearest neighbor loss [10]

$$L_d(z^p, \tau^B) = -\frac{1}{b} \sum_{b=1}^{B} \log \left(\frac{\sum_{\substack{j \in 1 \cdots B \\ j \neq b \\ \tau_j^B = \tau_b^B}} \exp^{-\frac{d(z_b^P, z_j^P)}{T}}}{\sum_{\substack{k \in 1 \cdots B \\ k \neq b}} \exp^{-\frac{d(z_b^P, z_k^P)}{T}}} \right), \tag{4}$$

where T and $d(\cdot)$ are the temperature variable and distance function, respectively. In this paper, the L2-norm $d(x_b, x_j) = ||x_b - x_j||^2$ is used. Representations with the same τ are placed to close area in representation space by L_d. By employing both L_c and L_d, problems of classification and placement are handled simultaneously. Developing the loss function for self-supervised learning with interaction data is the future work.

4.3 Score of Synchronization Behaviors

Probability density is estimated based on the learned representation space regarding the amount of lag operation in each case, and the density ratio of the representation with $\tau = 0$ is calculated, and the ratio is estimated via the kernel density estimation [4]. The density ratio is used as the score, and the synchronization behavior is expected to be extracted based on the score.

The set of data with τ is defined as $x^\tau = \{\phi_{TL}(X_L^T(t), X_R^T(t), \tau) | \tau \in \mathcal{T}, t = 1, ..., N\}$. The representation z^τ is extracted from x^τ, and the probability density is calculated as $K(z^\tau, h) = \frac{1}{Nh} \sum_{i=1}^{N} k\left(\frac{z^\tau - z_i^\tau}{h}\right)$, where $k(\cdot)$ is the kernel density function. In this research, the Gaussian kernel function is used. h and N are the bandwidths of the kernel function and sample size of the dataset, respectively. The density ratio for z^0, i.e., the representation with $\tau = 0$, is calculated as

$$R(z^0, z^\tau, h) = \frac{K(z^0; z^0, h)}{1/(|\mathcal{T}| - 1) \sum_{i \neq 0} K(z^0; z^i, h)}. \tag{5}$$

This ratio is used as the "score" of representations.

z^0 is isolated in the space if R is large, and z^0 and z^i are closely placed if R is close to 1. When two subjects interact with each other, R is expected to be large.

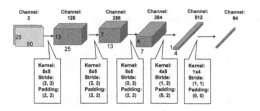

Fig. 3. Network Architecture of self-supervised learning.

5   Experiment of the Synchronizing Behavior Extraction

In this experiment, self-supervised learning is applied to the collected conversation data for learning the representation. Face and voice features are extracted from videos during dyadic conversations. After the learning, isolated data is extracted from the representation space to verify if data with synchronizing behavior such as nodding can be extracted.

5.1   Data Processing

In this experiment, fifteen sessions are collected. The total time length of the sessions is about four hours as one session lasts for about $10 - 20$ minutes. A video with face information is recorded with an omnidirectional camera (Xacti CX-MT100). A dynamic microphone is placed near the mouth to observe the voice of each subject.

Input features for the model are generated from the data obtained. From the video and audio data, three-dimensional face rotation (roll, pitch, and yaw) and the corresponding velocities, two-dimensional gaze rotation (x- and y- axes of an image) and the corresponding velocities, fourteen-dimensional facial action unit (FAU), and voice activity detection (VAD) results are extracted. The video and audio sampling rates are set to 30 fps and 48KHz, respectively.

Face Feature Extraction. By applying OpenFace [1] to the video, face position and features can be estimated. From the results of OpenFace, face and gaze rotation as well as FAU can be obtained.

Voice Activity Detection. Voice activity is detected by distinguishing the voice and noise, including breath and microphone-touching. For detecting the voice activity of each subject, inaSpeechSegmenter [7] is applied to the gathered voice. inaSpeechSegmenter is a detection method based on the deep learning model, and its output is classified into the labels of "noise", "no energy", "music", and "speech". Appropriate sections of "speech" are selected and labeled as a result of VAD, and the power of "speech" is recorded.

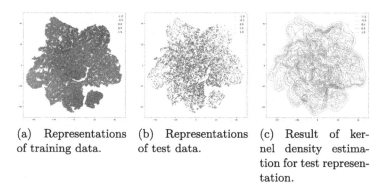

(a) Representations of training data.

(b) Representations of test data.

(c) Result of kernel density estimation for test representation.

Fig. 4. Compressed representation space with t-sne. Blue, orange, green, red, and purple dots represent the amount of lag operation $\tau = -1.0, -0.5, 0, 0.5, 1.0$. (Color figure online)

Combining Features. By combining the face motion, gaze motion, FAU, and VAD, the input feature of the self-supervised learning model is generated. To obtain the face-related features, each feature is down sampled from 30 fps to 10 fps for smoothing signals. The power of voice is down sampled to $10Hz$ to calculate the maximum power for the past $48,000/10 = 4,800$ samples. These features are combined for each subject, and the input features $[x_L(t), x_R(t)]$ for the learning model are generated. As a result, twenty-five-dimensional explanatory variables are obtained for each subject.

5.2 Experimental Settings

Thirteen sessions are used as the training dataset, and the remaining two are the test dataset. Test data is input into the learned model, and representations are output.

The length of past information T is empirically set to $T = 50$, i.e., a five-second context is used. To prevent the duplication of information, features are sampled for every five frames. Therefore, data in training and test dataset is defined as $[X_L^{50}(t), X_R^{50}(t)|t = 50, 55, 60, ...]$. The number of samples for the training and test datasets is $30,176$ and $2,467$, respectively.

Figure 3 shows the network architecture employed in this experiment. The architecture is a five-layer convolutional neural network, and the features of each subject are handled as a two-channel image. The set containing the amount of lag operation for self-supervised learning is $\mathcal{T} = [-1s, -0.5s, 0s, 0.5s, 1s]$ with the maximum time-shift of one second. The constant variables in Eq. 2 is set to $\alpha = 1.0, \beta = 0.2$. Adam optimizer is used to learn the network, and the learning rate is set to 5×10^{-4}.

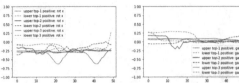
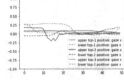
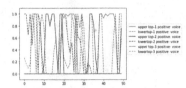
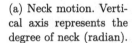

(a) Neck motion. Vertical axis represents the degree of neck (radian).

(b) Gaze motion. Vertical axis represents the degree of gaze (radian).

(c) Voice activity. Vertical axis represents the power of voice.

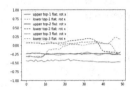
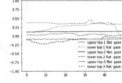
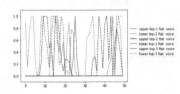

(d) Neck motion. Vertical axis represents the degree of neck (radian).

(e) Gaze motion. Vertical axis represents the degree of gaze (radian).

(f) Voice activity. Vertical axis represents the power of voice.

Fig. 5. Examples of the features of extracted samples. The horizontal axes represent the frames of input data. Red, blue, and green lines are three positives and three flats. Solid and dotted lines reflect features of "upper subject" and "lower subject", respectively. (Color figure online)

5.3   Results of the Behavior Extraction Experiment

The representation space is obtained by learning with the training dataset. Features after conversion $\phi_{TL}(\cdot, \cdot, \tau)$ are expected to have time-dependent characteristics if isolated in the representation space. In contrast, converted features with small behaviors are not separated, i.e., each representation with τ is mixed. Note that, since the tendency of extracted data of two test sessions is similar, the following results are discussed in the one test session.

Representation Space. Fig. 4 shows the representation space compressed by t-SNE [19]. For τ, parts of training and test data are separated. There are many unseparated data in the space, and these representations are placed at "similar" positions even if different τ are applied.

Test data is not "clearly" separated when compared with the training data. Since human behaviors are different for each subject, separating the test data is more difficult the separating the training data. More conversation data is necessary to obtain a generalization ability.

Results of Feature Extraction. Score $R(z_{test}^0, z_{train}^\tau, h)$ in Eq. 5 is calculated based on the representation space. z_{train} and z_{test} are the representations of training and test data.

The representation with highly isolated (positive) data in the space and unseparated mixed (flat) data are extracted. The detailed criteria for feature

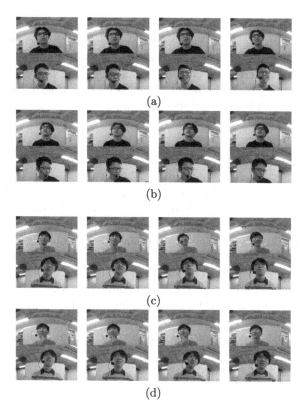

Fig. 6. Example of extracted data. (a) shows the top-1 positive of test session 1, (b) shows the top-1 flat of test session 1, (c) shows the top-1 positive of test session 2, and (d) shows the top-1 flat of test session 2.

extraction in this experiment are described in the next section. Figure 5 shows the neck and gaze motions and VAD of the top three extracted positives and flats, respectively. The motions in the figure are rotation around the x-axis, i.e., pitch motion. As for the neck motion, flats are small change, and angular values are larger than positives. Since subjects do not look ahead of this point, these extracted data do not form the interaction scenes.

Regarding the eye motion, solid and dotted lines of positives demonstrate an intersection for the subjects, i.e., making the eye contact. In the case of flats, an eye contact does not happen since the lines are parallel. Eye contact is a synchronizing behavior since the datapoints are isolated in space.

In VAD, turn-taking happens in positives since solid and dotted lines are activated alternatively. Only one subject continues to talk in flats. The red solid line is activated at around 25 frames in flat, while the dotted line is not activated until 40 frames. In comparison with the results of gaze and neck motions, no synchronizing behaviors are observed in flats.

Figure 6 shows an example of the extracted video clips in the test sessions. As seen in the top-1 positive (Fig. 6(a) and (c)), a subject reacts to speaking of another subject. For Fig. 6(a), the eye contact and smiling happen after the half of the clip duration, and large neck motion and smiling happen after the half of the clip for the Fig. 6(c). Conversely, there is no synchronizing behavior since the movement is small the entire time in top-1 flat (both Fig. 6(b) and (d)) even if the session is different.

6   Conclusions

In this research, we proposed the automatic extraction framework of the synchronizing behavior of human-human interaction based on self-supervised learning. In the framework, the lag operation, wherein the time index of one subject is shifted, is applied to a dyadic conversation data. Synchronizing behavior is separated in the representation space by learning about the label of the amount of time-shift. The score is added to the data based on the kernel density estimation.

The proposed method is applied to the conversation dataset and validated to extract the behaviors from the test data. After learning with the lag-operated data, synchronizing behavior is selected based on the score criterion. Extracted data includes social behaviors, such as "eye contact", "turn-taking", and "smile". Our framework decides whether synchronization occurs or not based on the relationship of certain variables.

Extracting the rules of crucial behaviors for an interaction are important to evaluate the next one. The rules are applied to the behavior of communication robots to develop the robot that can "smoothly" communicate with a human. In addition to rule extraction, the details of the proposed framework must be inspected. It is necessary to investigate whether the tendency of extraction is consistent on increasing the number of conversation sessions or using a certain conversation pair.

Acknowledgment. The authors would like to thank laboratory members at Osaka University for collecting dyadic conversation data. This work was supported by JSPS KAKENHI Grant Numbers 19H05693 and 23K169770.

References

1. Baltrusaitis, T., Zadeh, A., Chong Lim, Y., Morency, L.-P.: OpenFace 2.0: facial behavior analysis toolkit. In: 2018 13th IEEE International Conference on Automatic face & Gesture Recognition (FG 2018), pp. 59–66. IEEE (2018)
2. Bartneck, C., Forlizzi, J.: A design-centred framework for social human-robot interaction. In: 13th IEEE International Workshop on Robot and Human Interactive Communication, pp. 591–594 (2004)
3. Ben-Youssef, A., Clavel, C., Essid, S., Bilac, M., Chamoux, M., Lim, A.: UE-HRI: a new dataset for the study of user engagement in spontaneous human-robot interactions. In: Proceedings of the 19th ACM International Conference on Multimodal Interaction, pp. 464–472 (2017)

4. Bishop, C.M., Nasrabadi, N.M.: Pattern Recognition and Machine Learning, vol. 4. Springer, New York (2006)
5. Chen, T., Kornblith, S., Norouzi, M., Hinton, G.: A simple framework for contrastive learning of visual representations. In: International Conference on Machine Learning, pp. 1597–1607. PMLR (2020)
6. Delaherche, E., Chetouani, M., Mahdhaoui, A., Saint-Georges, C., Viaux, S., Cohen, D.: Interpersonal synchrony: a survey of evaluation methods across disciplines. IEEE Trans. Affect. Comput. 3(3), 349–365 (2012)
7. Doukhan, D., Carrive, J., Vallet, F., Larcher, A., Meignier, S.: An open-source speaker gender detection framework for monitoring gender equality. In: Acoustics Speech and Signal Processing (ICASSP), 2018 IEEE International Conference on. IEEE (2018)
8. Feng, Z., Xu, C., Tao, D.: Self-supervised representation learning by rotation feature decoupling. In: Proceedings of the IEEE/CVF Conference on Computer Vision and Pattern Recognition, pp. 10364–10374 (2019)
9. Forlizzi, J.: How robotic products become social products: an ethnographic study of cleaning in the home. In: Proceedings of the ACM/IEEE International Conference on Human-Robot Interaction, HRI 07, pp. 129–136, New York, NY, USA (2007). Association for Computing Machinery
10. Frosst, N., Papernot, N., Hinton, G.: Analyzing and improving representations with the soft nearest neighbor loss. In: International Conference on Machine Learning, pp. 2012–2020. PMLR (2019)
11. Goyal, P., Mahajan, D., Gupta, A., Misra, I.: Scaling and benchmarking self-supervised visual representation learning. In: Proceedings of the IEEE/CVF International Conference on Computer Vision, pp. 6391–6400 (2019)
12. Grill, J.-B., et al.: Bootstrap your own latent: a new approach to self-supervised learning. arXiv preprint arXiv:2006.07733 (2020)
13. Jaiswal, A., Ramesh Babu, A., Zaki Zadeh, M., Banerjee, D., Makedon, F.: A survey on contrastive self-supervised learning. Technol. 9(1), 2 (2021)
14. Kwon, J., Ogawa, K.-I., Ono, E., Miyake, Y.: Detection of nonverbal synchronization through phase difference in human communication. PLoS ONE 10(7), 1–15 (2015)
15. Li, R., Curhan, J., Hoque, M.E.: Predicting video-conferencing conversation outcomes based on modeling facial expression synchronization. In: 2015 11th IEEE International Conference and Workshops on Automatic Face and Gesture Recognition (FG), vol. 1, pp. 1–6. IEEE (2015)
16. Noroozi, M., Favaro, P.: Unsupervised learning of visual representations by solving jigsaw puzzles. In: Leibe, B., Matas, J., Sebe, N., Welling, M. (eds.) ECCV 2016. LNCS, vol. 9910, pp. 69–84. Springer, Cham (2016). https://doi.org/10.1007/978-3-319-46466-4_5
17. Osugi, T., Kawahara, J.I.: Effects of head nodding and shaking motions on perceptions of likeability and approachability. Perception 47(1), 16–29 (2018). PMID: 28945151
18. Riehle, M., Kempkensteffen, J., Lincoln, T.M.: Quantifying facial expression synchrony in face-to-face dyadic interactions: temporal dynamics of simultaneously recorded facial EMG signals. J. Nonverbal Behav. 41(2), 85–102 (2017)
19. Van der Maaten, L., Hinton, G.: Visualizing data using T-SNE. J. Mach. Learn. res. 9(11) (2008)

F-E Fusion: A Fast Detection Method of Moving UAV Based on Frame and Event Flow

Xun Xiao[1], Zhong Wan[2], Yuan Li[1], Shasha Guo[3], Junbo Tie[1],
and Lei Wang[2(✉)]

[1] College of Computer, National University of Defense Technology,
Changsha 410071, Hunan, China
{xiaoxun520,liyuan22,tiejunbo11}@nudt.edu.cn
[2] Defense Innovation Institute, Academy of Military Sciences, Beijing, China
leiwang@nudt.edu.cn
[3] College of Electronic Engineering, National University of Defense Technology,
Hefei, China
guoshasha13@nudt.edu.cn

Abstract. In recent years, the widespread application of UAVs has caused threats to public security and personal privacy. This paper presents a fast and low-cost method for UAV detection and tracking from fixed-position cameras. In our method, we capture event data and video frames through Dynamic Vision Sensor (DVS) and conventional camera respectively. We use the combination of Dynamic Neural Field (DNF) and clustering algorithm to locate the moving objects in the scene from the event data collected by DVS. Then we obtain high-resolution images from the corresponding regions of the video frame according to the calculated positions for classification. Compared with YOLO or R-CNN, our proposed method reduces the computational overhead by calculating the location of moving objects through event flow. Experimental results show that our method has more than 40 times faster recognition speed on the same platform than YOLO v3. The data and the code of the proposed method will be publicly available at https://github.com/Xiaoxun-NUDT/F-E-fusion.

Keywords: Spiking Neuron Network · Dynamic Vision Sensor · Dynamic Neural Field

1 Introduction

In recent years, with the rapid development of UAV technology, UAVs have become smaller, cheaper, easier to operate and more versatile. Based on these advantages, UAVs have been widely used in many fields, such as transportation, aerial photography, agriculture [2019] and energy [2020]. However, the widespread use of UAVs has also caused a series of problems, the most serious of which is to threaten public security and personal privacy. Although UAV

L. Iliadis et al. (Eds.): ICANN 2023, LNCS 14261, pp. 220–231, 2023.
https://doi.org/10.1007/978-3-031-44198-1_19

manufacturers have set up no-fly zones near airports, commercial centers and other important places. However, some UAVs have bypassed this limitation. [2019] analyzed more than 100 serious UAV incidents in the vicinity of worldwide airports. On the other hand, UAVs with video recording capability also pose a threat to personal privacy. [2020] introduced the privacy issues caused by UAV photography.

How to effectively counter the invading UAV has become an urgent problem. Anti-UAV mainly includes two steps: detection and radio interference. Detecting invading UAVs is the first step. The existing methods based on radar [2021], radio frequency [2020], or sound [2018] have the limitations of high equipment cost, easy to be disturbed and low accuracy.

With the development of deep learning and computer vision, object detection has become an important research direction in computer vision. The rapid development of computer vision makes it possible for UAV detection systems based on vision. Now we can use many mature object detection models, such as YOLO [2016], SSD [2016] and R-CNN [2017].

However, there are some problems in the existing models. They all have large model parameters, which bring high storage and computational overhead. In addition, large model parameters make the calculation time longer, which is easy to cause delays when detecting the position of high-speed flying UAVs. These limits the use scenario and detection accuracy of the model. Therefore, it is very necessary to reduce the computational overhead for edge scenes and high-speed UAV detection.

Inspired by the two-stage object detection algorithm, this paper presents a two-stage UAV detection method for fixed-position cameras. In the first stage, we use the characteristic of the DVS camera that is only sensitive to brightness changes to find all the changed areas in the scene. For a fixed-position DVS camera, The change in brightness is most likely caused by the movement of the object. In the second stage, to distinguish whether the brightness changes in the first stage are caused by UAVs or other objects such as birds. We need to use the classifier to classify the moving objects found in the first stage. Due to the limited resolution and color channel of existing DVS [2017; 2017; 2020], the classification accuracy of small objects cannot satisfy the requirements. So we need to supplement it with high-resolution pictures captured with conventional cameras.

In this way, we only focus on moving objects in the scene, not the whole background area, which reduces the computational redundancy. Experimental results show that our method can effectively detect and track intruding UAVs. The main contributions of this paper can be summarized as:

- We proposed a new two-stage UAV detection method, which combines the advantages of DVS camera and conventional camera. We utilize the feature that the DVS camera is only sensitive to moving objects to locate moving objects in the scene, which reduces the computational overhead of traditional algorithms in the object positioning stage.
- We implemented an SNN-based moving object extractor and noise event filter, which can directly process the event sequence recorded by DVS.

- We propose an event-based multi-object tracking method based on a clustering algorithm, which can realize dynamic continuous tracking of multiple moving objects.

2   Background

2.1   Dynamic Vision Sensor

Dynamic Vision Sensor is a neuromorphic sensor. It uses an event-driven approach to record changing brightness in the scene. When the objects in the scene cause a relative movement to the DVS camera, DVS will generate a series of pixel-level event outputs, with each event in the form of (x, y, t, p). Specifically, the x and y are the coordinate positions of the pixel. The t is the timestamp of the event, which indicates the time when the event is triggered. Moreover, the p is the polarity of the event, which represents the illumination changes of the pixel. Compared with conventional cameras, DVS cameras only record event data generated by moving objects in the scene.

2.2   Dynamic Neuron Field

Dynamic Neuron Field is a mathematical model, which can be used to describe the homogenization behavior among population neurons. In essence, it is a group of spiking neurons with winner-take-all connections. Neurons with similar characteristics have excitatory synaptic connections, while neurons with different characteristics have inhibitory synaptic connections. In this connection mode, due to the existence of activation threshold and global inhibition connection, noise events are difficult to cause neuron activation and be filtered out. But for a specific spike sequence, it will be selectively amplified. In extreme cases, such amplification can even realize the self activation between neurons, that is, neurons still keep activation after stopping input. The population connection mode of this neuron is shown in Fig. 3. Here we use one-dimensional DNF as a demonstration.

3   Related Work

3.1   Vision-Based UAV Detection

For vision-based UAV detection, YOLO is the most widely used deep learning model. [2019] introduced YOLO V3 for UAV detection. Aiming at the problem that UAV is too small in the scene, it advocates the last four scales of feature maps instead of the last three scales of feature maps to predict bounding boxes of objects, which can obtain more texture and information to detect small objects. Benefiting from the improvement of YOLO v4 to YOLO v3, [2020] achieved better results on the YOLO v4 model. In addition, [2021] constructed a multimodal dataset named Anti-UAV using the information in the visible and infrared

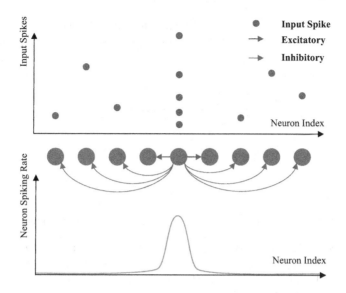

Fig. 1. Schematic representation of a 1-dimensional Dynamic Neural Field. The lateral connections are all-to-all and the synaptic weights are defined by the kernel function that depends on the distance between the pre and post-synaptic neurons.

bands. [2022] propose an anti-UAV dataset called DUT Anti-UAV that contains detection and tracking subsets. They evaluate state-of-the-art methods on their dataset, including 14 detectors and 8 trackers. However, the image taken by conventional cameras contains a large number of redundant background data, resulting in additional computational overhead and longer processing time.

3.2 Event-Based Object Tracking

The event-based object tracking algorithm is still in the research and development stage, which is different from the maturity of the vision algorithm. [2017] introduce a novel soft data association modeled with probabilities. They apply an expectation-maximization (EM) scheme, where given optical flow they compute probabilities (weights) for data association and then they take the expectation over these probabilities in order to compute the optical flow. [2020] represent asynchronous events as Time-Surface with Linear Time Decay. Then feed the sequence of TSLTD frames to a novel Retinal Motion Regression Network (RMR-Net) to perform an end-to-end 5-DoF object motion regression. [2019] realized an attention mechanism by recurrent Spiking Neural Network that implements attractor-dynamics of Dynamic Neural Fields.

4   Method

Figure 2 shows the overall workflow of our UAV detection and tracking method, which is mainly divided into two parts: event data processing and frame sequence processing. The event data is mainly used for the detection and location of moving objects, and the frame sequence is mainly used for the classification of objects.

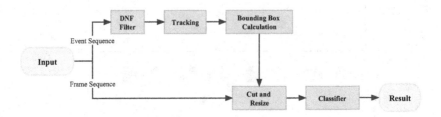

Fig. 2. The overall workflow of UAV detection and tracking methods.

The processing of event data is mainly divided into three stages. The first stage is denoising and moving object detection. The event data collected by DVS will contain a lot of noise. We use the DNF network to filter the noise events contained in it and enhance the event flow generated by moving objects. Then, we use the improved clustering algorithm to cluster the event flow generated by the same moving object and tracking it. Finally, we calculate the position and size of the moving object according to the clustering results and generate the corresponding bounding box. In the video sequence processing part, we cut the image of the moving object region in the corresponding video frame according to the calculated bounding box. Finally, the cuted image is classified and recognized by a classifier to get the category of the moving object.

4.1   SNN-Based Detection and Denoising

We have implemented a DNF structure for UAV detection and background noise filtering based on Spiking Neuron Network. Specific connection structure and synaptic weight enable DNF to enhance the event flow generated by moving objects while filtering noise events.

Figure 3 shows our DNF structure, the network consists of two-dimension layers, the input layer and the DNF layer, with 135 × 240 neurons in each layer. The first input layer can transmit the input spikes to the DNF layer. The DNF layer in the second layer is the core of the whole network. It has excitatory connections (The red arrow) with surrounding neurons and weak global inhibitory connections (The blue arrow).

When an object moves in the field of vision, it will generate spike input on the DNF network at the corresponding location. Because of local excitatory connections, it will generate neuron activation in the corresponding area. The weak global inhibitory can effectively suppress the interference of noise events without affecting the activation of neurons generated by normal motion.

Due to the lack of support for subsequent event input, noise events will be rapidly suppressed by the global inhibition generated by other DNF neurons before reaching the DNF layer neuron activation threshold. For the events generated by moving objects, due to the continuous input of the subsequent event

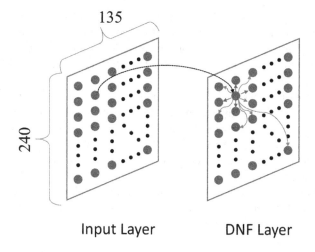

135

240

Input Layer   DNF Layer

Fig. 3. The structure of DNF. (Color figure online)

stream, the weak global inhibition will not be completely suppressed, so multiple active regions can appear at the same time corresponding to multiple moving objects in the scene.

4.2 Event-Based Multi-objects Tracking

We use the clustering algorithm to achieve the merging of event flows and the tracking of objects. The output of DNF is the activation of a series of neurons. The activated neurons in each area correspond to a moving object in the scene. Therefore, we need to combine the activation of neurons generated by the same moving object.

Algorithm 1. Event-based Multi-objective clustering and tracking

---

Input: event stream ϵ
Output: clusters C
 1: **for** e in event stream **do**
 2:     **for** c in clusters **do**
 3:         **if** distance(e,c) $<$ *threshold* **then**
 4:             append e to c
 5:             update c
 6:         **end if**
 7:     **end for**
 8:     **if** No clusters to add e **then**
 9:         create a new cluster add e
10:     **end if**
11: **end for**

Inspired by Density-Based Spatial Clustering of Applications with Noise (DBSCAN) [1996], this paper implements a continuous clustering and cluster tracking algorithm based on AER format data. It does not require a given number of clusters, but only a threshold value. The algorithm can be briefly described as Algorithm 1.

For the set ϵ of all events in a given time window, traverse each event in the order of time stamps. If this is the first event, or the distance from this event to all clusters is greater than the threshold, it will be added to a new cluster. If the distance from this event to some clusters is less than the threshold, it will be added to the nearest cluster. When an event is added to an existing cluster, the data of the cluster is updated. At the same time, with the sliding of the event window, new events are added to the window and the oldest events are removed, so that the real-time update of the event flow is achieved and the continuous tracking of the cluster is also realized.

4.3 Bounding Box Calculation

The bounding box calculation is to calculate the size of UAV in the scene according to the size of the event cluster after clustering. During the flight of UAV, different UAV images size will be generated due to different distances from the camera. If we use a fixed size bounding box, the bounding box will be too large or too small. In order to make the bounding box automatically adapt to the size of moving objects, we propose a object size estimation.

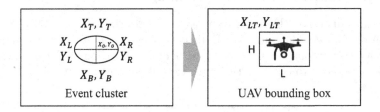

Fig. 4. Bounding Box Estimation.

Figure 4 is the schematic of generating UAV bounding box based on cluster. The event flow output by DNF will be divided into event clusters according to the proposed clustering algorithm. Each event cluster represents a moving object in the scene, And the size of the cluster reflects the size of the moving objects in the scene. We estimate the size of the bounding box by calculating the size of the event cluster. Where $(X_T, Y_T), (X_B, Y_B), (X_L, Y_L), (X_R, Y_R)$ are the coordinates of the top, bottom, left and right endpoints in the same cluster.

4.4 UAV Classification

So far, we have successfully marked all moving objects in the scene. However, these objects may also be flying birds or moving cars (except UAVs). We need a classifier to distinguish UAVs from other objects. Our classification task is just a two-classification task. We only need to distinguish whether moving objects are UAVs. We use SVM as our UAV classifier to distinguish UAVs from all moving objects.

Support Vector Machine (SVM) is a supervised classifier, which can be widely used in statistical classification and regression analysis. In the trained SVM classifier, there is a hyperplane as the decision boundary to divide the object into positive and negative categories. The new sample only needs to be compared with the decision boundary to get the classification results, which is very suitable for the two-classification task and there is almost no computational overhead.

For each object detected in the previous step, we will give a bounding box. This area is slightly larger than the size of the moving objects, ensuring that the entire object is within this area. Then, we cut these regions containing moving objects into new images. We will cut the pictures into two categories, one is UAV, the other is other objects. They are used to train the SVM to realize moving object classification. In this way we can distinguish between UAVs and other objects.

5   Experiment and Result

5.1   Experiment Setup

Dataset. In our method, we need to combine the data of video channel and event channel at the same time. However, the existing multi-mode UAV detection dataset does not contain event data and video data at the same time. We convert video data into DVS event stream through simulation and add event channel for it. Our video data conversion is based on Esim [2018]. Esim is an event camera simulator. It can simulate the working process of the DVS camera, and convert the video pictures taken by the traditional camera into the event stream form taken by the DVS camera.

The data set we use is a 100 s UAV flight video recorded at a fixed-position. The video frame rate is 30 fps, so there are a total of 3000 video frames. In this video the UAV appears in the scene for about 33 s, that is, there are 1000 video frames containing the UAV.

Table 1. Evaluation results of F-E Fusion and other methods.

Method	Parameters	mAP	Inference time	Total FLOPs
faster R-CNN	60 M	**0.72**	1250 ms	156 G
YOLO v3	61.53 M	0.66	520 ms	199 G
YOLO v4	52.5 M	0.68	400 ms	119 G
YOLO-fastest V2	0.25 M	0.23	27 ms	212 M
F-E Fusion	**0.02 M**	0.61	**12 ms**	**8.2 M**

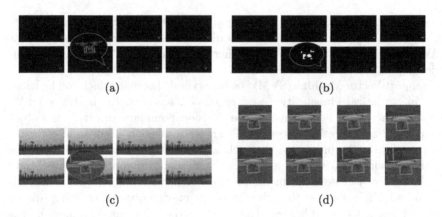

Fig. 5. Result on eight continuous video frames. (a) Shows the convert event flow imaging. (b) Shows the results after DNF filtering. (c) Shows the corresponding rgb image. (d) shows the UAV detected by our method.

5.2   Experiment Result

Performance and Precision. Figure 5 shows the detection and tracking results of our proposed method on eight continuous video frames. Figure 5(a) is the result of the event stream imaging of the original video converted by the Esim simulator, and Fig. 5(b) shows the activation of the DNF layer. It can be seen that there are many noise events in the original event stream, and the noise events are removed after the filtering of the DNF. At the same time, neurons in the corresponding area of DNF are intensively activated by moving objects. Figure 5(c) is the picture taken by the RGB camera corresponding to the event flow imaging. Figure 5(d) is the picture of the moving area containing the UAV obtained by our method.

Our method can effectively detect moving objects in the scene, and recognize the category of the object through the classifier. We compared our method with faster R-CNN [2015], YOLO V3 [2018], YOLO V4 [2020], YOLO-fastest V2 [2021], etc. Compared with the currently widely used YOLO V3 model, our method improves the recognition speed by 40 times and the recognition accuracy remains unchanged. Compared with the current fastest YOLO algorithm YOLO-fastest V2, our method still maintains a high accuracy with a detection speedup by two times. Table 1 shows the evaluation results of our method and other methods.

In our method, we only need to train the final UAV classifier. We use 700 UAV images and 700 random background images to train the SVM classifier. The remaining pictures are used for testing. We use grid search to find the best parameters set for SVM. The final trained UAV classifier has a classification accuracy of 98% between UAV and other backgrounds under the optimal parameter combination ('C': 1000, 'gamma': 0.001, 'kernel': 'rbf').

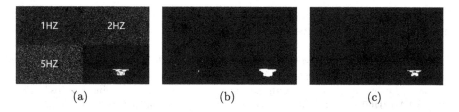

Fig. 6. The filter ability of DNF. (a) Input with different frequency noise, 1 Hz, 2 Hz and 5 Hz respectively. Add in the blank area of input. (b) Filter result without global Inhibitory. (c) Filter result with global Inhibitory.

The Filter Ability of DNF. We evaluated the ability of the DNF model in background activity denoising and detection. We generate Poisson distribution events with different frequencies to simulate DVS background activity noise with different intensities. At the same time, we also compared whether the DNF layer added global suppression to the denoising ability. We simulate and generate noise events at frequencies of 1 Hz, 2 Hz and 5 Hz respectively. As shown in the figure, the filtering results of adding global suppression and not adding global suppression are respectively. We add different noise events in different areas of the picture.

As shown in Fig. 6, the experimental results show that DNF can effectively filter the background noise events. DNF filter without global inhibitory can better fill the outline of moving objects, but it can not completely filter the noise signal with high frequency. DNF filter with global inhibitory has a better noise inhibitory effect, but it will bring high computational overhead. In the actual scene, there are fewer high-frequency noise signals, so we prefer to use DNF filter without global inhibitory.

6 Conclusion

In this paper, we proposed an object detection and tracking method based on the combination of a DVS camera and a conventional camera. We use the feature that the fixed-position DVS only generates event flow for moving objects. On this basis, we can quickly locate the moving objects in the scene. At the same time, we implemented an SNN-based denoising and object extractor. And a clustering algorithm for multi-object tracking. Combining the calculated object position with the high-resolution video frame, we can realize the classification of moving objects. Our proposed method reduces the computational overhead of the traditional detection algorithm in the object location stage. The experimental results show that our method can effectively detect the moving objects in the scene and achieve accurate classification. Compared with YOLO V3, our method improves recognition speed by 40 times. At the same time, our method only needs to train a simple classifier, and the model is greatly simplified. For further work, with the development of DVS, the resolution will be higher and higher. We hope to achieve the classification of moving objects based on event flow completely, without resorting to high-resolution images.

Acknowledgements. Ministry of Science and Technology Innovation 2030- "New Generation Artificial Intelligence" Major Project "Research on Key Technologies for Hardware Security Enhancement of Machine Learning Chips" (No. 2020AAAA0104602). National Natural Science Foundation of China [grant numbers 62032001]. This work was support by Key Laboratory of Advanced Microprocessor Chips and Systems.

References

Abunada, A.H., Osman, A.Y., Khandakar, A., Chowdhury, M.E.H., Khattab, T., Touati, F.: Design and implementation of a RF based anti-drone system. In: 2020 IEEE International Conference on Informatics, IoT, and Enabling Technologies (ICIoT), pp. 35–42. IEEE (2020)

Chang, X., Yang, C., Wu, J., Shi, X., Shi, Z.: A surveillance system for drone localization and tracking using acoustic arrays. In: 2018 IEEE 10th Sensor Array and Multichannel Signal Processing Workshop (SAM), pp. 573–577. IEEE (2018)

Chen, H., Suter, D., Qiangqiang, W., Wang, H.: End-to-end learning of object motion estimation from retinal events for event-based object tracking. Proc. AAAI Conf. Artif. Intell. **34**, 10534–10541 (2020)

dog qiuqiu. dog-qiuqiu/Yolo-fastestv2: V0.2, August (2021). https://doi.org/10.5281/zenodo.5181503

Ester, M., Kriegel, H.-P., Sander, J., Xu, X.: Density-based spatial clustering of applications with noise. Int. Conf. Knowl. Disc. Data Min., 240 (1996)

Evanusa, M., Sandamirskaya, Y., et al.: Event-based attention and tracking on neuromorphic hardware. In: Proceedings of the IEEE/CVF Conference on Computer Vision and Pattern Recognition Workshops (2019)

Girshick, R.: Fast R-CNN. In: Proceedings of the IEEE International Conference on Computer Vision, pp. 1440–1448 (2015)

He, K., Gkioxari, G., Dollár, P., Girshick, R.: Mask R-CNN. In: Proceedings of the IEEE International Conference on Computer Vision, pp. 2961–2969 (2017)

Hu, Y., Wu, X., Zheng, G., Liu, X.. Object detection of UAV for anti-UAV based on improved YOLO v3. In: 2019 Chinese Control Conference (CCC), pp. 8386–8390. IEEE (2019)

Huang, J., Guo, M., Chen, S.: A dynamic vision sensor with direct logarithmic output and full-frame picture-on-demand. In: 2017 IEEE International Symposium on Circuits and Systems (ISCAS), pp. 1–4. IEEE (2017)

Jiang, N., et al.: Anti-UAV: a large multi-modal benchmark for UAV tracking. arXiv preprint arXiv:2101.08466 (2021)

Liu, W., et al.: SSD: single shot multibox detector. In: Leibe, B., Matas, J., Sebe, N., Welling, M. (eds.) ECCV 2016. LNCS, vol. 9905, pp. 21–37. Springer, Cham (2016). https://doi.org/10.1007/978-3-319-46448-0_2

Ma, S., Zhang, Y., Zhu, D., Huang, X.: A method for improving efficiency of anti-UAV radar based on FMCW. In: 2021 IEEE 15th International Conference on Electronic Measurement & Instruments (ICEMI), pp. 109–113. IEEE (2021)

Moeys, D.P., et al.: A sensitive dynamic and active pixel vision sensor for color or neural imaging applications. IEEE Trans. Biomed. Circ. Syst. **12**(1), 123–136 (2017)

Park, S., Choi, Y.: Applications of unmanned aerial vehicles in mining from exploration to reclamation: a review. Minerals **10**(8), 663 (2020)

Pyrgies, J.: The UAVs threat to airport security: risk analysis and mitigation. J. Airline Airport Manage. **9**(2), 63–96 (2019)

Rebecq, H., Gehrig, D., Scaramuzza, D.: ESIM: an open event camera simulator. In: Conference on robot learning, pp. 969–982. PMLR (2018)

Redmon, J., Farhadi, A.: YOLOv3: an incremental improvement. arXiv preprint arXiv:1804.02767 (2018)

Redmon, J., Divvala, S., Girshick, R., Farhadi, A.: You only look once: unified, real-time object detection. In: Proceedings of the IEEE Conference on Computer Vision and Pattern Recognition, pp. 779–788 (2016)

Shi, Q., Li, J.: Objects detection of UAV for anti-UAV based on YOLOv4. In: 2020 IEEE 2nd International Conference on Civil Aviation Safety and Information Technology (ICCASIT, pp. 1048–1052. IEEE (2020)

Suh, Y., et al.: A 1280× 960 dynamic vision sensor with a 4.95-μm pixel pitch and motion artifact minimization. In: 2020 IEEE International Symposium on Circuits and Systems (ISCAS), pp. 1–5. IEEE (2020)

Tsouros, D.C., Bibi, S., Sarigiannidis, P.G.: A review on UAV-based applications for precision agriculture. Information **10**(11), 349 (2019)

Zhao, J., Zhang, J., Li, D., Wang, D.: Vision-based anti-UAV detection and tracking. IEEE Trans. Intell. Transp. Syst. (2022)

Zhi, Y., Zhangjie, F., Sun, X., Jingnan, Y.: Security and privacy issues of UAV: a survey. Mobile Netw. Appl. **25**(1), 95–101 (2020)

Zhu, A.Z., Atanasov, N., Daniilidis, K.: Event-based feature tracking with probabilistic data association. In: 2017 IEEE International Conference on Robotics and Automation (ICRA), pp. 4465–4470. IEEE (2017)

Few-Shot Relational Triple Extraction Based on Evaluation of Token-Level Semantic Similarity

Shuai Jiang, Jiazhe Zhu, and Lianghua He$^{(\boxtimes)}$

College of Electronic and Information Engineering,
Tongji University, Shanghai, China
{2032980,2232934,helianghua}@tongji.edu.cn

Abstract. Relational Triple Extraction refers to extracting entities and classifying relation between different entities from text, which is a nontrivial step in the construction of knowledge graph. However, Traditional relational triple extraction methods require a large amount of labeled data, which is often not available due to the long-tail distribution of entity pairs and relations between entities, thus yielding limited performance of relational triple extraction. In order to address these problems, few-shot relational triple extraction aims at extracting relational triple from text using only few labeled samples. Previous works lack attention on the similarity of token-level information between the query set and support set. Therefore, we propose an evaluation method of Token-Level Similarity of entity tags (TLSM), which exploits the semantic similarity information between tokens in the few annotated samples and unseen samples to improve the accuracy of entity extraction, thereby improving the overall performance of relational triple extraction. In addition, in order to balance the optimization process of two subtasks, entity recognition and relation classification, which have different levels of difficulty, we utilize dynamically weighted balanced loss to enable the model to automatically learn the weight coefficients of the losses of two subtasks. Finally, extensive experiments are conducted on the FewRel dataset to demonstrate the effectiveness of our method.

Keywords: Relational Triple Extraction · Few-shot Learning · Information Extraction

1 Introduction

The construction of knowledge graph is a basic and critical work in the field of knowledge graph. Relational triple extraction is a key technology for building knowledge graphs, which involves relational classification and entity recognition, aiming at classifying the relation described by the sentence and extracting the

---

S. Jiang and J. Zhu—Joint First Authorship.

L. Iliadis et al. (Eds.): ICANN 2023, LNCS 14261, pp. 232–242, 2023.
https://doi.org/10.1007/978-3-031-44198-1_20

entity pair corresponding to the relation. For example, in the sentence "Beijing is the capital of China", we extract the relation "capital", the head entity "Beijing" and the tail entity "China", and finally obtain the relational triple ("Beijing", "capital", "China").

In the previous work, a large number of algorithms based on deep neural network have been applied to relational triple extraction, such as TPLinker [9], CasRel [10], NovelTagging [15], DirectRel [7], etc., and have achieved quite remarkable performance. In particular, the emergence of large-scale pre-trained language models (BERT [3], Roberta [5], etc.) has significantly improved performance. However, most of the models heavily rely on large-scale annotated datasets and struggle to perform well in the few-shot setting. Additionally, these algorithms can only recognize learned entities and relations, resulting in poor performance when facing unseen relations or entities. Therefore, it is non-trivial to study the task of few-shot relational triple extraction.

To address the challenges of few-shot relational triple extraction, MPE [13] has proposed a multi-prototype embedding model based on few-shot learning, and extracts relational triples in an entity-then-relation way. However, it ignores the dependency between relation and entity, thus constraining the performance of relational triple extraction by the prior performance of entity extraction. To solve this problem, the algorithm RelATE [2] has been proposed to extract relational triple in a relation-then-entity way, which means entities corresponding to different relations are extracted independently. In addition, it marks the beginning and the end of entities with the prototypes of "START" and "END" and finally improves the performance of relational triple extraction. However, it does not take into account the token-level semantic similarity between support set and query set, nor does it consider the dependence between the entity sequence labeling, so there still is potential for further improvement in the task of relational triple extraction.

To address the limitations of existing approaches, we propose an evaluation method that assesses the token-level semantic similarity of entity tags. Our method is based on the idea of STRUCTSHOT [11] algorithm and utilizes nearest neighbor classifier, which helps to recognize entities in text. Specifically, we evaluate the semantic similarity between each token in the query sample and each token in the support sample, both of which share the same relation. We then sum the maximum value and the average value of the similarity scores to obtain the prediction score, which improves the accuracy of entity recognition. In addition, as the difficulty levels of two subtasks, relation classification and entity recognition, differ, achieving optimal performance on both tasks simultaneously can be challenging. To address this, we propose a multi-task dynamically weighted balanced loss that enables the model to self-learn the weight coefficients of the losses of two subtasks, so that both subtasks can simultaneously achieve the best performance.

In summary, the main contribution of our work is two-fold as follows:

- An evaluation method of token-level similarity of entity tags is proposed to improve the accuracy of entity recognition;

- A multi-task dynamically weighted balanced loss is proposed to optimize the two subtasks, relation classification and entity recognition, to the optimum at the same time.

2   Related Work

2.1   Traditional Relational Triple Extraction

Traditional relational triple extraction methods can be categorized into two main types: extractive methods and generative methods. The extractive methods can be further classified into two types: the pipeline and the joint extraction methods. The pipeline extraction methods extract entities first and then classify the relation between entities, which suffers from the issue of error propagation. The joint extraction extracts both entities and relation simultaneously, and representative algorithms include TPLinker [9], CasRel [10], etc., which mainly focus on addressing the overlapping problem of relational triples. The generative methods, such as CopyRE [14], and CGT [12], generate all relational triples in the sentence in a sequence-to-sequence (seq2seq) manner. Although these algorithms have achieved acceptable performance, they require large-scale annotated datasets, and cannot handle few-shot scenarios, necessitating re-training the model when encountering unseen relations.

2.2   Few-Shot Relational Triple Extraction

With further research on the task of relational triple extraction, the problem of long-tail distribution of relations and entity pairs is becoming increasingly prominent. More and more researchers have begun to focus on the task of few-shot relational triple extraction. Current research methods can be divided into two types: methods based on transfer learning and methods based on meta-learning. Transfer learning has been a popular approach in addressing the challenges of few-shot relation classification and entity extraction. For example, SDAsh [1] utilizes transfer learning and fine-tuning to achieve few-shot relation classification, TransInit [6] employs transfer learning for few-shot entity recognition, and DAT-Net [16] introduces adversarial training into transfer learning to strengthen the transfer ability of the model.

In recent years, meta-learning has enabled the model to have the ability of "learning to learn", and it has demonstrated effectiveness in solving the few-shot problems in various fields, including images and natural language processing. To tackle the task of joint few-shot relational triple extraction, the MPE [13] algorithm proposes a multi-prototype embedding network based on meta-learning and prototype algorithms. Specifically, the algorithm first extracts entities using a traditional sequence labeling method, and then utilizes multi-prototype embedding to learn the relation prototypes, which improves the accuracy of relation classification. However, the performance of relational triple extraction is constrained due to the prior performance of entity extraction. The RelATE [2]

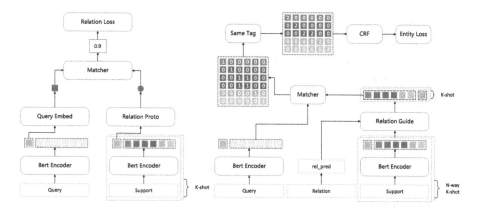

Fig. 1. The overall architecture of our method. Left subfigure is the Relation Classification module. The gray box refers to [CLS] embedding, and the boxes of other colors refer to embeddings of all tokens. In this module, we only use [CLS] embedding to classify the relation of the query sentence. Right Subfigure is the Entity Recognition module. In this module, we only use K support sentences having the same relation as the query sentence to calculate token-level similarity and then identify entities. (Color figure online)

algorithm adopts a relation-then-entity method, which leverages the predicted relation to guide the process of entity recognition, improving the accuracy of entity recognition and then achieving better performance. However, the algorithm does not fully exploit the local contextual information of entities during the instance-level matching and ignores the dependency between entity tags in the entity recognition process.

3 Method

3.1 Problem Definition

Following the classic few-shot task setting, we define the few-shot relational triple extraction problem as an N-way K-shot problem, where N represents the number of different relations in each task, and K represents the number of support samples for each relation (i.e., the number of few annotated samples). Given an unseen sentence belonging to one of the N categories, referred to as the query sample, the objective is to classify the query sentence into the correct relation category according to the meaning it expresses, denoted as r, and simultaneously extract the head entity and tail entity, denoted as h and t, respectively. This results in the formation of a relational triple (h, r, t).

To recognize the entities in text, we use the traditional "BIO" sequence labeling method to label the samples, which means that "BH, IH, BT, IT, O" are used to mark the first token of the head entity, other tokens of the head entity, the first token of the tail entity, other tokens of the tail entity, and non-entity tokens, respectively.

3.2   Instance Encoder

We adopt BERT as the language model to encode contextual information into the embedding vectors. Through BERT, we can obtain the hidden embedding representations $H \in \mathbb{R}^{(n+1) \times d}$ of all tokens and [CLS] token of any sentence $input$ in the support set $\mathbf{S} \in \mathbb{R}^{N \times K \times T_s \times d}$ and query set $\mathbf{Q} \in \mathbb{R}^{T_q \times d}$ as follows:

$$H = \{\boldsymbol{h}_{cls}; \boldsymbol{h}_1, \boldsymbol{h}_2, \ldots, \boldsymbol{h}_n\} = \text{BERT}\,(input) \tag{1}$$

where n denotes the number of the tokens in the sentence, T_s and T_q denote the number of tokens in the query sentence and the support sentence, respectively.

3.3   Relation Classification

Our proposed method first classifies the relation of the query sentence, and then guides the subsequent entity extraction according to the predicted relation. Considering that [CLS] embedding implies rich semantics of sentence instance, we use the mean value of [CLS] embeddings of K support sentences which share the same relation to get the relation prototype $\mathbf{R} = \{\mathbf{R}_i; i = 1, \ldots, N\}$:

$$\boldsymbol{R}_i = \frac{1}{K} \sum_{k}^{K} \boldsymbol{S}_{cls_{i,k}} \tag{2}$$

where $\mathbf{R}_i \in \mathbb{R}^d$ denotes i-th relation prototype, $\mathbf{S}_{cls}$ denotes the [CLS] embeddings of the support sentences.

Afterwards, we feed the [CLS] embedding of the query sentence and each relation prototype into the Matcher network in Sect. 3.5 to calculate the semantic similarity between them, so as to obtain score $m_i^{rel} = \text{Matcher}\,(\mathbf{Q}_{cls}, \mathbf{R}_i)$ of the query sentence belonging to each relation by measuring the similarity, the largest score of which is selected as the predicted category of relation for the query sentence. In this work, cross-entropy loss L_{rel} is adopted to calculate the discrepancy between the relation score and the ground-truth:

$$\mathcal{L}_{rel} = -\sum_{j=1}^{N} y_j \log\,(\hat{y}_j) \tag{3}$$

where $\hat{y}_j = m_i^{rel}$ denotes i-th similarity score, $y_j = 1$ if the relation of the query sentence belongs to class N_j and 0, otherwise.

3.4   Entity Recognition

Since the relation implies semantics of the sentence, we decide to extract entity based on the predicted relation. First, we extract all support sentences $\mathbf{S}_r \in \mathbb{R}^{K \times T_s \times d}$ which share the same relation with the query sentence from the support set $\mathbf{S} \in \mathbb{R}^{N \times K \times T_s \times d}$. Afterwards, we feed the embeddings of the selected support sentences and query sentence into the Matcher Network to obtain the semantic similarity score $m_{i,j}^{token}$ between each token in the query sentence and each token in the selected support sentences:

$$m_{i,j}^{token} = \text{Matcher}\left(\mathbf{Q}_j, \mathbf{S}_{r,k,i}\right) \tag{4}$$

where $\mathbf{Q}_j \in \mathbf{Q}, j = 1, \ldots, T_q, \mathbf{S}_{r,k,i} \in \mathbf{S}_r, k = 1, \ldots, K$ and $i = 1, \ldots, T_s$.

After computing the similarity scores $m^{token} \in \mathbb{R}^{T_q \times K \times T_s}$, along with the corresponding entity tags in the selected support sentences, we group the scores based on the entity tags, and sum the maximum and average values of the similarity scores belonging to the same entity tag. The result is regarded as the probability for each token in the query sentence to tag the entity labels:

$$x_{j,l} = m_j^{token} \cdot \mathbb{1}\{Y_e = l\} \tag{5}$$

$$p_{j,l} = tag\_score = \text{avg}\left(x_{j,l}\right) + \max\left(x_{j,l}\right) \tag{6}$$

where Y_e means the entity tags for each token in the selected support sentence, and $\mathbb{1}$ is an indicator function, $j = 1, \ldots, T_q, l = 1, \ldots, 5$.

Additionally, we adopt Conditional Random Field (CRF), consisting of the emission score and transition score, to constrain the sequence of entities. The emission score captures the compatibility between each token and its assigned entity label, and the transition score captures the likelihood of a particular entity label being followed or preceded by another entity label, enabling the modeling of patterns and constraints in the sequence of labeled entities. By leveraging the CRF, the model can globally optimize the assignment of entity labels, taking into account both local and contextual information. Ultimately, this helps improve the accuracy and coherence of the predicted entity labels.

Therefore, the entity loss can be formulated as:

$$L_{entity} = \frac{e^{(p+f_T(y))}}{\sum_{y'}^{Y'} e^{(p+f_T(y'))}} \tag{7}$$

where the emission score $p \in \mathbb{R}^{T_q \times |E|}, |E| = 5$, and the transition score $f_T(y) = \sum_j^{T_q} p\left(y_j, y_{j+1}\right)$

3.5 Matcher

In order to calculate the semantic similarity between embeddings of the query sentence and the prototype, we employ a Matcher network to achieve it and obtain the probability by measuring the similarity. Given two inputs a and b, we calculate the semantic similarity M as follows:

$$M = [|a - b|; a \otimes b] \tag{8}$$

where $\otimes$ denotes element-wise product, $[.;.]$ denotes concatenation operation.

Afterwards, we feed similarity M into a MLP to get the similarity score m:

$$m = (W_1 M + b_1) W_2 + b_2 \tag{9}$$

where W_1, W_2, b_1, b_2 are all learnable parameters.

3.6 Objective Function

The objective of relation classification is to classify the relation category of the query sentence based on its meaning. If the relation is correctly predicted, the difficulty of the entity recognition task could be largely reduced. To account for the different levels of difficulty in the subtasks of entity recognition and relation classification, we introduce learnable weight coefficients to the losses. By doing so, the model can self-learn to optimize the overall loss. The overall loss can be formulated as:

$$Loss = e^{\lambda_1} L_{rel} + e^{\lambda_2} L_{entity} \tag{10}$$

where λ_1 and λ_2 are all learnable parameters, the initial values of which both are 0.

4 Experiments

4.1 Experimental Setup

Dataset. Same as previous work MPE [13] and RelATE [2], we conduct experiments on the FewRel [4] dataset. The FewRel dataset contains 100 relation types, each relation contains 700 triple instances, and each instance has a pair of entity corresponding to its relation. Since FewRel only discloses the data of 80 categories of relation, we randomly select the instances of 50 relations as the training set, the instances of 15 relations as the validation set, and the rest 15 relations as the test set. The training set, validation set, and test set don't have any overlapping relations.

Evaluation Metrics. Like MPE [13] and RelATE [2], we use Precision, Recall and F1-score to evaluate the performance of the model in the settings of 5-way 5-shot and 10-way 10-shot. During testing, we randomly sample 1000 tasks, with each task containing 5 query samples, and calculate Precision, Recall, and F1-score, which are then averaged to obtain the final result. A relational triple is considered positive if and only if the categories and spans of the head and tail entities are identified correctly and the corresponding relation are predicted correctly.

Hyperparameter. We use Adam optimizer to train our model with the learning rate of 1e-5 for BERT, 1e-3 for other parameters. The maximum sentence length is set as 90. The batch size is set as 1.

4.2 Main Experimental Results

We evaluate the performance of our proposed method against several baselines, including fine-tuning methods and few-shot meta-learning methods: (1) Fine-tune is a method using the BERT language model as the instance encoder, and two MLPs as the entity decoder and the relational decoder respectively. It performs supervised pre-training on the train set, and then fine-tunes the relation

Table 1. Experimental results of relational triple extraction in the setting of 5-way-5-shot and 10-way-10-shot.

Methods	5-way-5-shot			10-way-10-shot		
	Precision	Recall	F1	Precision	Recall	F1
Finetune	15.47	13.00	14.08	12.01	10.40	11.13
Proto	18.29	11.90	14.24	17.08	11.07	13.36
MPE	–	–	23.34	–	–	12.08
RelATE	42.47	**44.23**	43.29	40.47	**42.25**	41.32
TLSM	**54.34**	44.12	**48.23**	**50.07**	41.96	**45.49**

classification module on validation set and test set, which can be regarded as the representative model of the classic "Pretrain + Finetune" architecture; (2) Proto [8] is a method using the BERT language model as the instance encoder, the prototype network as the relation classification module, and "MLP+CRF Decoder" as the entity extraction decoder. The Proto network is typically used as a baseline model for few-shot relation classification and few-shot relational triple extraction. (3) MPE [13] is a representative algorithm for few-shot relational triple extraction that follows an entity-then-relation approach, the entity extraction module of which utilizes traditional supervised sequence labeling method. (Instead of reproducing the algorithm in the original paper, we directly copy the results from the original paper. Some indicators which are not provided in the original paper are represented as "-"); (4) RelATE [2] is a representative algorithm for few-shot relational triple extraction that follows a relation-then-entity approach, using "START" and "END" to mark the start and end of the entity. And TLSM is our proposed method.

The results of the few-shot relational triple extraction are shown in Table 1. It can be seen that:

- Compared with the traditional fine-tuning method, the meta-learning method performs better in few-shot relational triple extraction;
- Compared with MPE using the entity-then-relation method, our proposed method and RelATE adopt the relation-then-entity method, which exploits relation to guide entity extraction and thus obtain better performance;
- Compared with RelATE, our proposed method exploits token-level semantic similarity and captures the dependencies between entity tags by CRF, thereby achieving the state-of-the-art performance and demonstrating the effectiveness of our method.

4.3 Ablation Experiments

In order to evaluate the effectiveness of each module, we conduct the following ablation experiments: (1) -weight: we remove the dynamical weight coefficients of the losses of the two subtasks, resulting in equal weights for the losses of

Table 2. Results of ablation experiment in the setting of 5-way-5-shot and 10-way-10-shot.

Methods	5-way-5-shot			10-way-10-shot		
	Precision	Recall	F1	Precision	Recall	F1
TLSM	54.34	44.12	48.23	50.07	41.96	45.49
-weight	55.83	41.80	47.30	52.07	39.56	44.78
-crf	37.87	40.50	38.83	34.90	38.82	36.63
-relation	53.02	44.50	47.95	48.19	41.34	44.34
-entity	40.31	41.48	40.50	37.86	39.96	38.76
-matcher	38.40	40.74	39.12	34.56	36.39	35.31

the two subtasks; (2) -crf: we replace the CRF loss with a simple cross-entropy loss; (3) -relation: we replace the relation classification matcher metric with the Euclidean distance metric; (4) -entity: we replace the entity recognition matcher metric with the Euclidean distance metric; (5) -matcher: we replace both matcher metrics with the Euclidean distance metric.

The results of the ablation experiment on few-shot relational triple extraction are shown in Table 2. It can be seen that:

- Dynamic weight coefficients effectively balance losses and optimization process of entity recognition and relation classification tasks, thus improving the performance;
- CRF captures the dependencies between entity tags, outperforming the simple cross-entropy loss in the sequence prediction;
- The similarity evaluation module (Matcher) evaluates the similarity between features more effectively than the Euclidean distance metric.

5   Conclusion

In this paper, we propose a token-level similarity evaluation method of entity tags for few-shot relational triple extraction, which enhances the accuracy of entity extraction and thus improves the overall performance of relational triple extraction. In addition, to balance the loss optimization process of two subtasks, relation classification and entity recognition, dynamically weighted balanced loss is proposed to enable the model to dynamically self-learn the weight coefficients of two losses, thus improving overall performance. We also conduct extensive experiments on the FewRel dataset, which demonstrate the effectiveness of our proposed TLSM method for few-shot relational triple extraction.

Acknowledgements. Supported in part by Joint Funds of the National Science Foundation of China under Grant U18092006, in part by the National Natural Science Foundation of China under Grant 62171323, in part by National Key R&D Program of China under Grant 2020YFA0711400, in part by Shanghai Municipal Science and Technology Major Project (2021SHZDZX0100), in part Shanghai Municipal Commission of Science and Technology Project (19511132101), in part by the Changjiang Scholars Program of China, in part by the Fundamental Research Funds for the Central Universities.

References

1. Bengio, Y.: Deep learning of representations for unsupervised and transfer learning. In: Proceedings of ICML Workshop on Unsupervised and Transfer Learning, pp. 17–36. JMLR Workshop and Conference Proceedings (2012)
2. Cong, X., Sheng, J., Cui, S., Yu, B., Liu, T., Wang, B.: Relation-guided few-shot relational triple extraction. In: Proceedings of the 45th International ACM SIGIR Conference on Research and Development in Information Retrieval. ACM (2022). https://doi.org/10.1145/3477495.3531831
3. Devlin, J., Chang, M.W., Lee, K., Toutanova, K.: Bert: pre-training of deep bidirectional transformers for language understanding. In: Proceedings of the 2019 Conference of the North American Chapter of the Association for Computational Linguistics: Human Language Technologies, Volume 1 (Long and Short Papers), pp. 4171–4186 (2019)
4. Han, X., et al.: FewRel: a large-scale supervised few-shot relation classification dataset with state-of-the-art evaluation. In: Proceedings of the 2018 Conference on Empirical Methods in Natural Language Processing. Association for Computational Linguistics (2018). https://doi.org/10.18653/v1/d18-1514
5. Liu, Y., et al.: RoBERTa: a robustly optimized BERT pretraining approach. arXiv preprint arXiv:1907.11692 (2019)
6. Qu, L., Ferraro, G., Zhou, L., Hou, W., Baldwin, T.: Named entity recognition for novel types by transfer learning. In: Proceedings of the 2016 Conference on Empirical Methods in Natural Language Processing. Association for Computational Linguistics (2016). https://doi.org/10.18653/v1/d16-1087
7. Shang, Y.M., Huang, H., Sun, X., Wei, W., Mao, X.L.: Relational triple extraction: one step is enough. In: Proceedings of the Thirty-First International Joint Conference on Artificial Intelligence. International Joint Conferences on Artificial Intelligence Organization (2022). https://doi.org/10.24963/ijcai.2022/605
8. Snell, J., Swersky, K., Zemel, R.: Prototypical networks for few-shot learning. In: Advances in Neural Information Processing Systems 30 (2017)
9. Wang, Y., Yu, B., Zhang, Y., Liu, T., Zhu, H., Sun, L.: TPLinker: single-stage joint extraction of entities and relations through token pair linking. In: Proceedings of the 28th International Conference on Computational Linguistics. International Committee on Computational Linguistics (2020). https://doi.org/10.18653/v1/2020.coling-main.138
10. Wei, Z., Su, J., Wang, Y., Tian, Y., Chang, Y.: A novel cascade binary tagging framework for relational triple extraction. In: Proceedings of the 58th Annual Meeting of the Association for Computational Linguistics. Association for Computational Linguistics (2020). https://doi.org/10.18653/v1/2020.acl-main.136
11. Yang, Y., Katiyar, A.: Simple and effective few-shot named entity recognition with structured nearest neighbor learning. In: Proceedings of the 2020 Conference on Empirical Methods in Natural Language Processing (EMNLP). Association for Computational Linguistics (2020). https://doi.org/10.18653/v1/2020.emnlp-main.516

12. Ye, H., et al.: Contrastive triple extraction with generative transformer. Proc. AAAI Conf. Artif. Intell. **35**(16), 14257–14265 (2021). https://doi.org/10.1609/aaai.v35i16.17677

13. Yu, H., Zhang, N., Deng, S., Ye, H., Zhang, W., Chen, H.: Bridging text and knowledge with multi-prototype embedding for few-shot relational triple extraction. In: Proceedings of the 28th International Conference on Computational Linguistics. International Committee on Computational Linguistics (2020). https://doi.org/10.18653/v1/2020.coling-main.563

14. Zeng, X., Zeng, D., He, S., Liu, K., Zhao, J.: Extracting relational facts by an end-to-end neural model with copy mechanism. In: Proceedings of the 56th Annual Meeting of the Association for Computational Linguistics (Volume 1: Long Papers). Association for Computational Linguistics (2018). https://doi.org/10.18653/v1/p18-1047

15. Zheng, S., Wang, F., Bao, H., Hao, Y., Zhou, P., Xu, B.: Joint extraction of entities and relations based on a novel tagging scheme. In: Proceedings of the 55th Annual Meeting of the Association for Computational Linguistics (Volume 1: Long Papers). Association for Computational Linguistics (2017). https://doi.org/10.18653/v1/p17-1113

16. Zhou, J.T., et al.: Dual adversarial neural transfer for low-resource named entity recognition. In: Proceedings of the 57th Annual Meeting of the Association for Computational Linguistics. Association for Computational Linguistics (2019). https://doi.org/10.18653/v1/p19-1336

GII: A Unified Approach to Representation Learning in Open Set Recognition with Novel Category Discovery

Jingyun Jia[1]([⊠])[iD] and Philip K. Chan[2][iD]

[1] Baidu Research, Sunnyvale, CA 94089, USA
`jingyunjia@baidu.com`
[2] Florida Institute of Technology, Melbourne, FL 32901, USA
`pkc@fit.edu`

Abstract. In this paper, we consider the problem of Novel Class Discovery (NCD) in Open Set Recognition (OSR). Given a labeled and an unlabeled set for training, NCD aims to discover the novel categories in the unlabeled set with prior knowledge learned from the labeled set. Existing approaches tackle the NCD problems under a close-set setting, where only the existing categories from the labeled set and the novel categories from the unlabeled set will occur during the inference. This paper considers a more realistic open-set scenario. In the open-set setting, in addition to the existing and novel categories, some unknown categories absent from the training could be present during inference. To address NCD in the open-set scenario, we propose the General Inter-Intra (GII) loss, a unified approach for learning representations from both labeled and unlabeled samples. The proposed approach discovers novel categories in the training set (NCD) meanwhile recognizes the unknown categories (OSR). We evaluate GII with image and graph datasets, and the results indicate that our proposed approach is more effective than other NCD and OSR approaches.

Keywords: Novel Category Discovery · Open Set Recognition · Representation Learning

1 Introduction

Machine learning models have achieved significant advances in various tasks in recent years. Most of these models are developed under a closed-world assumption and rely on a huge amount of data with human annotations. The real world is an open set, and humans can determine whether images belong to the same category. However, such an open-set setting brings new challenges for machine learning models. First, it is cost-inhibitive to keep manually annotating the emerging new categories. Second, it is unlikely to collect samples exhausting

© The Author(s), under exclusive license to Springer Nature Switzerland AG 2023
L. Iliadis et al. (Eds.): ICANN 2023, LNCS 14261, pp. 243–254, 2023.
https://doi.org/10.1007/978-3-031-44198-1_21

all the classes. In the open-set setting, an ideal machine learning model should automatically discover new categories in the training set without having access to their labels, called novel category discovery (NCD) [Han et al.(2019)]. Meanwhile, the model should recognize the unknown classes absent from the training set, which is referred as Open Set Recognition (OSR) [Bendale and Boult(2016)].

In this paper, we focus on automatically discovering novel categories in a realistic open-set scenario. In the open-set setting, we have labeled and unlabeled samples available for training. Meanwhile, we have unknown samples that are not available in the training process. Our proposed approach has three objectives: classifying the existing categories from the labeled samples, clustering the novel categories from the unlabeled samples, and recognizing the unknown classes absent from the training set. Specifically, we introduce a one-step solution for NCD under the open-set scenario and name this solution general inter-intra (GII) loss. [Hassen and Chan(2020a)] propose inter-intra (ii) loss for OSR with labeled training samples. Ii loss maximizes the inter-class distances and minimizes the intra-class distances in the representation space to achieve inter-class separation and intra-class compactness. We generalize this idea to unlabeled samples in our work. GII consists of three components: intra-class loss for existing categories, intra-cluster loss for novel categories, and inter-category loss for all categories. We calculate their class centroids in representation space for existing categories and minimize the intra-class distance. For novel categories, we first estimate the centroids of the novel categories and cluster assignments via k-means, then we minimize the intra-cluster distance in the representation space. The assumption is that novel categories are disjointed with existing ones, so intra-category loss is designed to maximize the distance between any two categories.

Our contribution includes: first, we propose a unified approach for learning representations from both labeled and unlabeled samples for NCD under an open-set scenario. Second, to the best of our knowledge, we are the first to extend NCD to an open-set setting. Third, we experiment with the proposed approach with image and graph datasets, and the results indicate that our proposed approach is more effective than other approaches for NCD and OSR.

2   Related Work

An **Open Set Recognition (OSR)** task has two objectives: classify the known classes and recognize the unknown class absent from training. We can divide OSR techniques into three categories based on the training set compositions. The first category includes the techniques that borrow additional data in the training set. Dhamija et al. [Dhamija et al.(2018)] utilize the differences in feature magnitudes between known and borrowed unknown samples as part of the objective function. Shu et al. [Shu et al.(2018)] indicate that several manual annotations for unknown classes are required in their workflow. The second category of OSR approaches includes the research works that generate additional data in training data. Most data generation methods are based on GANs. Ge et al. [Ge et al.(2017)] introduce a conditional GAN to generate some unknown samples followed by OpenMax open set classifier. Neal et al. [Neal et al.(2018)] add another encoder network to traditional GANs to map from images to a latent space. The third category of OSR approaches does not require additional data. Instead, it requires outlier detection for the unknown class. Hassen and Chan [Hassen and Chan(2020b)] propose ii loss for open set recognition. It first finds the representations for the known classes during training and then recognizes an instance as unknown if it does not belong to any known classes. Jia and Chan [Jia and Chan(2021)] propose MMF as a loss extension to further separate the known and unknown representations for OSR.

One group of existing approaches solves the **Novel Category Discovery (NCD)** problem by pairing samples and converting the NCD problem to pairwise similarity prediction problem. [Gupta et al.(2020)] utilize the Information Maximization (IM) loss in an ensemble of models to predict the similarity between two data points. [Chang et al.(2017)] propose DAC architecture, which uses the learned label features for clustering tasks. The sample pairs used for training are alternately selected and labeled by the learned features in each iteration. Another group of existing approaches solves the NCD problem using prior knowledge learned from labeled samples. For example, [Han et al.(2019)] use such prior knowledge to reduce the ambiguity of clustering by reducing its KL divergence to a sharper target distribution. [Zhao and Han(2021)] propose to apply dual ranking statistics to transfer the knowledge learned from labeled samples to unlabelled samples for pseudo-labeling. [Liu and Tuytelaars(2022)] propose ResTune to estimate a new residual feature from the pre-trained network and add it with a previous basic feature to compute the clustering objective. [Zhong et al.(2021)] introduce OpenMix to mix the unlabeled examples from an open set and the labeled examples from known classes. They follow a two-stage learning stage for the NCD problem. The model initialization stage is trained on the labeled samples in a supervised way. In the unsupervised clustering stage, they generate mixed training samples by incorporating labeled samples with unlabeled samples. The pseudo-labels of mixed samples will be more reliable than their unlabeled counterparts. In addition to pseudo-pair learning and pseudo-label learning, the loss of OpenMix is applied to the mixed samples.

3   Approach

3.1   Learning Representations of Existing and Novel Categories

Consider we have a labeled collection of instances $D^l = \{(x_i^l, y_i^l)\}_{i=1}^{N^l}$, where $y_i^l \in \{1, \ldots, C^l\}$ is the ground-truth class labels for the labeled samples, and N^l is the number of labeled samples. In addition, we have an unlabelled collection of instances $D^u = \{x_i^u\}_{i=1}^{N^u}$, where N^u is the number of unlabelled samples. Following a common assumption in other works [Han et al.(2019)], we assume that the novel categories are disjoint with the existing ones, i.e., $D^l \cap D^u = \emptyset$, also the number of novel categories C^u is known.

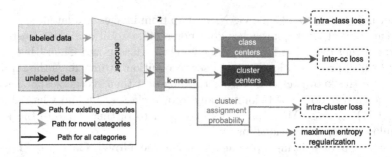

Fig. 1. Illustration of GII architecture for NCD.

Our goal is to model a representation space that separates the existing categories in D^l and the novel categories in D^u. Through such representation space, we can identify if a test instance belongs to one of the existing categories, one of the novel categories, or the unknown class. We propose an end-to-end framework to learn the representations, which provides a one-step solution for NCD under the open-set scenario. The training of the framework consists of three components: intra-class loss for the existing categories, intra-cluster loss for the novel categories, and inter-category loss for all categories. The existing categories are the classes of the labeled samples. The novel categories are the clusters of the unlabeled samples and all categories include these classes and clusters.

Intra-class Loss for Existing Categories. The intra-class component deals with the intra-spread for the labeled samples. One can expect the network to capture some informative knowledge for the existing categories through the training process, which not only helps classify labeled samples but also is beneficial to transfer the basic feature for clustering unlabeled samples. Given a labeled sample x_i^l, we use a network-based trainable encoder $f(\cdot)$ to extract its representation vector z_i^l. Thus, for existing category (or class) j, we find its centroid in the representation space as:

$$\mu_j^l = \frac{1}{N_j^l} \sum_{i=1}^{N_j^l} z_i^l, \tag{1}$$

where N_j^l denotes the number of samples in the existing category j. Then, we measure the intra-class spread as the average distance of labeled instances from their class means:

$$\text{intra-class}_j = \frac{1}{N_j^l} \sum_{i=1}^{N_j^l} \|\mu_j^l - z_i^l\|_2^2. \tag{2}$$

To improve the intra-class compactness, we minimize the largest intra-class spread among the existing categories.

$$\mathcal{L}_{\text{intra-class}} = \max_{1 \leq j \leq C^l} \text{intra-class}_j \tag{3}$$

Intra-cluster Loss for Novel Categories. There are several differences comparing intra-cluster spread with intra-class spread. First, intra-class spread relies on labels to find class centroids. In the intra-cluster spread, we only have unlabeled samples. Thus, we use k-means to estimate the representation of cluster centroids as the centers of novel categories $\tilde{\mu}^u$. Second, we are uncertain which specific centroid is for an unlabeled sample. Thus, we calculate the soft assignment of sample x_i^u based on the distance of its representation z_i^u to the estimated centroids. Since unlabeled samples do not belong to known classes, these samples do not have a soft assignment to known classes. To calculate the soft assignment (probability), we use the softmax of the negative distance of z_i^u from all the estimated centroids. Hence, the probability of sample x_i^u belongs to novel category (or cluster) k is given by:

$$p_{ik} = P(y_i^u = k|x_i^u) = \frac{e^{-\|\tilde{\mu}_k^u - z_i^u\|_2^2}}{\sum_{t=1}^{C^u} e^{-\|\tilde{\mu}_t^u - z_i^u\|_2^2}}, \tag{4}$$

where $\tilde{\mu}_k^u$ is the estimated centroid for novel category k. Similar to the intra-class spread, we measure the intra-cluster spread as the weighted average distance of unlabeled instances from their soft assignments. Suppose we have N_u unlabeled samples, the intra-cluster spread of novel category k is calculated as:

$$\text{intra-cluster}_k = \frac{\sum_{i=1}^{N^u} p_{ik} \|\tilde{\mu}_k^u - z_i^u\|_2^2}{\sum_{i=1}^{N^u} p_{ik}}. \tag{5}$$

Then, we minimize the largest intra-cluster spread among the novel categories to achieve intra-cluster compactness. The differences between the intra-cluster spread in Eq. 5 with the intra-class spread in Eq. 2 are the estimated cluster centroid $\tilde{\mu}_k^u$ and the soft assignment p_{ik}.

$$\mathcal{L}_{\text{intra-cluster}} = \max_{1 \leq k \leq C^u} \text{intra-cluster}_k \tag{6}$$

The cluster centroids are initialized and updated by k-means. To reduce the training time, we use a scheduling function for the k-means. Intuitively, we want to update the centroids more frequently at the beginning of the training. Close to the end of the training, when the network has learned informative knowledge from the labeled samples, and the clusters of the unlabeled samples have been formed for the novel categories, we perform k-means less frequently for the centroids updates.

Finally, to avoid a trivial solution of assigning all unlabeled samples to the same class, we regularize the model with maximum entropy regularization (MER). Specifically, we use the probability p_{ik} calculated from Eq. 4 as the probability of an unlabeled sample x_i^u being assigned to novel category k. MER maximizes the entropy of the output probability distribution:

$$\mathcal{R} = -H(p) = \frac{1}{N^u} \sum_{i=1}^{N^u} \sum_{k=1}^{C^u} p_{ik} \log p_{ik}. \tag{7}$$

Inter-category Loss for All Categories. The above two components shorten the distance between representations of the same categories to ensure intra-class and intra-cluster compactness. To distribute the representations of different categories to different subspaces, we further measure the inter-category separation as the distance between the two closest category centroids. Let μ_c be the centroid of category c, where $c \in \{1, ..., C^l\} \bigcup \{1, ..., C^u\}$. The inter-category separation for category m is defined as:

$$\text{inter-category}_m = \min_{1 \le i \le (C^l + C^u), k \ne i} \|\mu_m - \mu_i\|_2^2. \tag{8}$$

To improve the intra-category separability, we maximize the inter-category separation in the inter-category loss:

$$\mathcal{L}_{\text{inter-category}} = -\min_{1 \le m \le (C^l + C^u)} \text{inter-category}_m. \tag{9}$$

GII Loss Function. The objective function in GII combines three components, and the overall training loss of our unified framework can then be written as:

$$\mathcal{L} = \mathcal{L}_{\text{intra-class}} + \lambda_1 \mathcal{L}_{\text{intra-cluster}} + \lambda_2 \mathcal{L}_{\text{inter-category}} + \lambda_3 \mathcal{R}, \tag{10}$$

where λ_1, λ_2, and λ_3 are regularization parameters set to 1 in all our experiments.

The representation z is learned by three components together. Specifically, $\mathcal{L}_{\text{intra-cluster}}$ is applied to unlabelled data but indirectly uses information from labeled data via z and $\mathcal{L}_{\text{intra-class}}$. The features learned from the labeled data help cluster the unlabeled data. Meanwhile, $\mathcal{L}_{\text{intra-cluster}}$ further reduces intra-cluster spread, which also influences representation z. The influence on representation z from unlabeled samples can benefit not only the representation of unlabeled samples but also the representation of labeled samples. More details are in the analysis in Sect. 4.4. In addition, since $\mathcal{L}_{\text{inter-category}}$ increases separation among classes (existing categories) and clusters (novel categories), it uses information from the labeled data to help separate classes from clusters. GII is a unified approach for learning representations from both labeled and unlabeled samples.

4   Experimental Evaluation

In this section, our proposed GII is evaluated on image and graph datasets. **MNIST** [Ronen et al.(2018)] contains 70,000 handwritten digits from 0 to 9. Each example in the MNIST dataset is a 28×28 grayscale image.

Fashion-MNIST [Ronen et al.(2018)] is associated with 10 classes of clothing images. It contains 60,000 training and 10,000 testing examples. In the Fashion-MNIST dataset, each example is a 28×28 grayscale image.

Microsoft Challenge (MS) [Ronen et al.(2018)] contains disassembled malware samples from 9 families. We use 10260 samples that can be correctly parsed and then extracted their FCGs for the experiment as in [Hassen and Chan(2017)].

Android Genome (AG) consists of 1,113 benign android apps and 1,200 malicious android apps. Our colleague provides the benign samples, and the malicious samples are from [Zhou and Jiang(2015)]. We select nine families with a relatively larger size for the experiment to be fairly split into the training set and the test set. The nine families contain 986 samples in total. We first use [Gascon et al.(2013)] to extract the function instructions and then generate the FCGs as in [Hassen and Chan(2017)].

4.1 Implementation Details

To simulate an open-set scenario, we randomly select six classes from the datasets as existing categories. Moreover, we randomly select another two classes from the datasets as novel categories by removing their labels. These eight classes participate in the training, while the rest are considered unknowns that only exist in the test set.

As shown in Fig. 1, labeled and unlabeled data share the same encoder. For the MNIST and Fashion-MNIST datasets, the padded input layer of the encoder is of size (32, 32), followed by two non-linear convolutional layers with 32 and 64 nodes. We also use the max-polling layers with kernel size (3, 3) and strides (2, 2) after each convolutional layer. We use two fully connected non-linear layers with 256 and 128 hidden units after the convolutional component. Then we have an eight-dimensional representation layer after the encoder. We use the Relu activation function for all the non-linear layers and set the Dropout rate as 0.2 for the fully connected layers. We use Adam optimizer with a learning rate of 0.001. We use a contamination ratio of 0.001 for the unknown class threshold selection. We sort the output probability of training data in ascending order and pick the 0.1 percentile of the probability as the threshold. For the FCG datasets (MS and Android), the padded input layer is in the size of (67, 67). The padded input layer is then flowed by two non-linear convolutional layers with 32 and 64 nodes. We apply the max-polling layers with kernel size (3, 3) and strides (2, 2). We also add batch normalization after each convolutional layer to complete the convolutional block. After the convolutional block, we only use one fully connected non-linear layer with 256 hidden units for the graph dataset. Next, we add an eight-dimensional representation layer after the encoder. We use the Relu activation function and set the Dropout rate as 0.2. We use Adam as the optimizer with a learning rate of 0.001. Finally, we use a contamination ratio of 0.01 for the unknown class threshold selection. Moreover, as mentioned in Sect. 3.1, we use a scheduling function for the k-means updates in the NCD process. In the experiments, we apply k-means every ten iterations in the first

5000 iterations, then reduce the frequency to every 100 iterations in the rest of the training process.

4.2 Comparison Methods

We compare the proposed with ii loss without sharpening on the unlabeled samples (No sharpening), cluster loss, and supervised OSR. For a fair comparison with "No sharpening", we first pre-train the encoder with labeled samples using ii loss [Hassen and Chan(2020b)]. After obtaining the representations of the unlabeled samples, we find the novel cluster centroids and assignments via k-means directly in the representation space without further sharpening. Finally, we apply the same OSR process. Cluster loss is proposed to sharpen the distribution of unlabeled samples through the clustering process [Liu and Tuytelaars(2022)]. We compare our proposed intra-cluster loss with cluster loss by substituting the inter-cluster loss term with cluster loss in our overall loss function in Eq. 10. Moreover, as the cluster loss measures the KL-divergence between two distributions, which is on a different scale with other terms (intra-class and inter-category), we set λ_1 differently for different datasets. That is, all three terms in our GII are based on distances in the same representation space Z. Hence, GII provides a unified approach to representation learning for both labeled and unlabeled samples.

In addition, we experiment on fully supervised OSR and use the results as the upper bounds of NCD and OSR performances. In the supervised OSR experiments, we apply ii loss on eight labeled categories in the training process. The remaining categories are considered as the unknown class.

4.3 Evaluation Criteria

As mentioned above, we simulate an open-set scenario for all the datasets. Moreover, we randomly select two classes in the training set as novel categories and remove their class labels. We simulate three open-set groups for each dataset and then repeat each group 10 runs, so each dataset has results for 30 runs. We calculate the average results of the 30 runs for performance evaluation.

We calculate the accuracy (ACC) scores under different types of categories: existing categories (ACC_E), novel categories (ACC_N) and the unknown category (ACC_U). Specifically, we evaluate the classification accuracy of existing categories and the recognition accuracy of the unknown category. Moreover, we evaluate the model performance on novel categories with clustering accuracy. Clustering accuracy is widely used in NCD problems. To find the optimal match between the class labels and the cluster labels, the ACC of novel categories is defined as $ACC_N = \max_{perm \in P} \frac{1}{N} \sum_{i=1}^{N} \delta(perm(\hat{y}_i) = y_i)$, where N is the total number of unlabeled samples; δ is the Kronecker delta response; $\hat{y}_i$ denotes the predicted cluster label; $perm(\cdot)$ is the permutation operation and P is the set of all permutations of the class assignments in the test set. The score ranges between 0 and 1, and a higher value means better performance. The Hungarian algorithm is used to optimize the permutations for faster computation.

Table 1. The average ACC scores of 30 runs. The upper bounds results are trained with fully supervised learning, and the values in boldface are the highest in each column.

Image Dataset	MNIST					Fashion-MNIST				
	ACC_E	ACC_N	ACC_{E+N}	ACC_U	ACC_{E+N+U}	ACC_E	ACC_N	ACC_{E+N}	ACC_U	ACC_{E+N+U}
No sharpening	$0.733_{\pm0.078}$	$0.800_{\pm0.091}$	$0.697_{\pm0.078}$	$0.767_{\pm0.015}$	$0.615_{\pm0.060}$	$0.598_{\pm0.068}$	$0.668_{\pm0.089}$	$0.539_{\pm0.098}$	$0.786_{\pm0.008}$	$0.468_{\pm0.079}$
Cluster loss	$0.752_{\pm0.161}$	$0.625_{\pm0.125}$	$0.687_{\pm0.166}$	$0.751_{\pm0.031}$	$0.624_{\pm0.127}$	$0.820_{\pm0.062}$	$0.608_{\pm0.104}$	$0.757_{\pm0.052}$	$0.698_{\pm0.049}$	$0.628_{\pm0.042}$
GII (ours)	$\mathbf{0.936}_{\pm0.08}$	$\mathbf{0.854}_{\pm0.088}$	$\mathbf{0.909}_{\pm0.089}$	$\mathbf{0.817}_{\pm0.070}$	$\mathbf{0.810}_{\pm0.069}$	$\mathbf{0.875}_{\pm0.047}$	$\mathbf{0.808}_{\pm0.084}$	$\mathbf{0.847}_{\pm0.051}$	$\mathbf{0.797}_{\pm0.003}$	$\mathbf{0.687}_{\pm0.034}$
Upper bound (supervised)	$0.983_{\pm0.001}$	$0.977_{\pm0.004}$	$0.981_{\pm0.001}$	$0.937_{\pm0.012}$	$0.935_{\pm0.012}$	$0.896_{\pm0.018}$	$0.967_{\pm0.005}$	$0.914_{\pm0.014}$	$0.822_{\pm0.011}$	$0.770_{\pm0.016}$

Malware Dataset	MS					AG				
	ACC_E	ACC_N	ACC_{E+N}	ACC_U	ACC_{E+N+U}	ACC_E	ACC_N	ACC_{E+N}	ACC_U	ACC_{E+N+U}
No sharpening	$0.732_{\pm0.131}$	$0.625_{\pm0.180}$	$0.717_{\pm0.132}$	$0.763_{\pm0.110}$	$0.653_{\pm0.166}$	$0.680_{\pm0.167}$	$0.708_{\pm0.140}$	$0.602_{\pm0.176}$	$0.798_{\pm0.027}$	$0.564_{\pm0.195}$
Cluster loss	$0.880_{\pm0.117}$	$0.602_{\pm0.183}$	$0.818_{\pm0.106}$	$0.758_{\pm0.096}$	$0.742_{\pm0.094}$	$0.779_{\pm0.146}$	$0.601_{\pm0.177}$	$0.734_{\pm0.120}$	$0.773_{\pm0.063}$	$0.684_{\pm0.115}$
GII (ours)	$\mathbf{0.942}_{\pm0.026}$	$\mathbf{0.630}_{\pm0.143}$	$\mathbf{0.895}_{\pm0.054}$	$\mathbf{0.834}_{\pm0.071}$	$\mathbf{0.811}_{\pm0.078}$	$\mathbf{0.944}_{\pm0.013}$	$\mathbf{0.714}_{\pm0.080}$	$\mathbf{0.906}_{\pm0.020}$	$\mathbf{0.831}_{\pm0.048}$	$\mathbf{0.820}_{\pm0.034}$
Upper bound (supervised)	$0.960_{\pm0.016}$	$0.916_{\pm0.035}$	$0.950_{\pm0.020}$	$0.903_{\pm0.035}$	$0.899_{\pm0.035}$	$0.922_{\pm0.012}$	$0.712_{\pm0.080}$	$0.898_{\pm0.021}$	$0.908_{\pm0.013}$	$0.904_{\pm0.012}$

Table 2. The average ROC AUC scores of 30 runs at 100% and 10% FPR. The upper bounds results are trained with fully supervised learning, and the values in boldface are the highest in each column.

	MNIST		Fashion-MNIST		MS		AG	
FPR	100%	10%	100%	10%	100%	10%	100%	10%
No sharpening	$0.439_{\pm0.127}$	$0.004_{\pm0.005}$	$0.418_{\pm0.073}$	$0.003_{\pm0.001}$	$0.528_{\pm0.122}$	$0.007_{\pm0.004}$	$0.293_{\pm0.214}$	$0.000_{\pm0.000}$
Cluster loss	$0.413_{\pm0.231}$	$0.007_{\pm0.009}$	$0.620_{\pm0.084}$	$0.008_{\pm0.003}$	$0.651_{\pm0.271}$	$0.018_{\pm0.015}$	$0.507_{\pm0.283}$	$0.007_{\pm0.015}$
GII (ours)	$\mathbf{0.829}_{\pm0.104}$	$\mathbf{0.047}_{\pm0.016}$	$\mathbf{0.674}_{\pm0.040}$	$\mathbf{0.012}_{\pm0.002}$	$\mathbf{0.858}_{\pm0.086}$	$\mathbf{0.028}_{\pm0.015}$	$\mathbf{0.885}_{\pm0.090}$	$\mathbf{0.016}_{\pm0.020}$
Upper bound (supervised)	$0.966_{\pm0.010}$	$0.078_{\pm0.003}$	$0.676_{\pm0.062}$	$0.015_{\pm0.002}$	$0.945_{\pm0.005}$	$0.062_{\pm0.017}$	$0.963_{\pm0.013}$	$0.052_{\pm0.015}$

To further evaluate our approach on OSR, we measure the AUC scores under 100% and 10% False Positive Rate (FPR). While the AUC score under 100% FPR is commonly used in model performance measurements, the AUC score under 10% FPR is more meaningful for malware detection applications.

4.4 Experimental Results and Analysis

We test our proposed method on image and malware datasets for 30 runs. Table 1 shows the average accuracy scores of different methods. Notably, we measure the average clustering/classification accuracy on the existing/novel set and the combined set (ACC_{E+N}). Moreover, considering an open-set scenario, we measure the average accuracy of the unknown set, and the set contains all the existing, novel, and unknown categories (ACC_{E+N+U}). Comparing the ACC under existing categories (ACC_E) and novel categories (ACC_N), we observe that our proposed GII outperforms both ii loss without sharpening and cluster loss in NCD. Also, comparing the ACC under the unknown category (ACC_U), we observe that GII achieves the best performance in OSR. The upper bound performances are generated from supervised ii loss, where we utilize the labels of novel categories in the training set. We can see that GII has comparable performances with the supervised training in some datasets. In particular, GII obtains higher accuracy than supervised learning in the combined novel and existing categories (ACC_{E+N}) in the AG dataset.

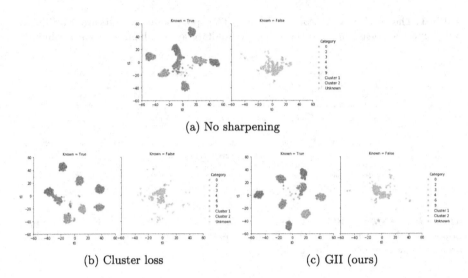

(a) No sharpening

(b) Cluster loss   (c) GII (ours)

Fig. 2. The t-SNE plots of the representations of MNIST test samples.

In addition to the ACC scores, we measure the AUC ROC scores under different FPR values: 100% and 10% in Table 2. The AUC ROC measures OSR at various threshold settings. Similar to the ACC scores, our proposed GII outperforms ii loss without sharpening and cluster loss in the AUC ROC scores. Furthermore, comparing GII with supervised learning, we observe that GII can achieve comparable OSR performance in the Fashion-MNIST dataset.

Our experiment results indicate that GII outperforms ii loss without sharpening and cluster loss in terms of performances in NCD and OSR. Specifically, ii loss without sharpening can be considered as an ablation study to investigate our approach without intra-cluster loss. We plot the t-SNE plots of the representations of samples from different categories in the MNIST test set, as shown in Fig. 2. The left subplots are the representations of the samples from existing categories ("0", "2". "3", "4", "6" and "9") and novel categories ("cluster 1" and "cluster 2"). The right subplots show the representations of samples from unknown categories, which only exist in the test set. Comparing Fig. 2a with Figs. 2b and 2c, we can see that samples from the two clusters result in more compact intra-cluster spread with cluster loss and GII. The reason is that cluster and GII sharpen the distributions of the unlabeled samples while "No sharpening" does not change the distributions of the unlabeled samples. Furthermore, it can be seen that GII forms better clusters compared with cluster loss. GII generates a more discriminative boundary for the samples in cluster 2 (grey) and the samples in class "9" (brown). The reason is that GII forms a tighter cluster for cluster 2. Thus a more accurate cluster centroid is estimated and used in the inter-category loss. Also, comparing the representations in the right subplots, we find that the representations of unknown samples learned by ii loss without sharpening and GII are more concentrated around the origin. In contrast, those learned by GII are more widespread.

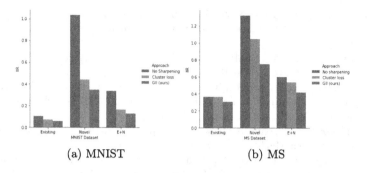

(a) MNIST   (b) MS

Fig. 3. Intra-inter ratio (IIR) of the representations in different categories

Besides visually evaluating representations via t-SNE plots, we also evaluate intra-inter ratio (IIR) [Jia and Chan(2022)] with test samples to measure the representation quality learned by different approaches. IIR measures the representation quality by calculating the ratio between intra-category spread and inter-category separation, and a lower value means better representations. Figure 3 shows the IIR values of different datasets. From Fig. 3, within the novel categories across four datasets, cluster loss or GII has (large) improvements in IIR over no sharpening, which indicates the benefit of representation learning with unlabeled samples via cluster loss or GII. However, GII yields a larger benefit than cluster loss. More interestingly, within the existing categories across datasets, we observe improvements in IIR with GII over no sharpening. That is, the unlabeled samples via GII help improve the representations of samples from labeled classes. Hence, not only the representations of unlabeled samples benefit from representation learning from unlabeled samples via GII, the representations of labeled samples also benefit.

5   Conclusion

We have presented a generic one-step representation learning approach to tackle the challenging problem of novel category discovery under an open-set scenario. Our proposed approach consists of three components. First, we achieve intra-class spread for labeled samples by minimizing the intra-class distance. Second, we estimate the novel category centroids and propose intra-cluster loss for the unlabeled samples to discover novel categories. Third, we separate different categories by maximizing the intra-category distance such that all the categories inhabit the same representation space. Last, we evaluated our approach on image and graph datasets, and the results indicate that the proposed approach obtained superior results in NCD and OSR compared with other approaches.

References

Bendale, A., Boult, T.E.: Towards open set deep networks. In: Proceedings of the IEEE Conference on Computer Vision and Pattern Recognition, pp. 1563–1572 (2016)

Chang, J., Wang, L., Meng, G., Xiang, S., Pan, C.: Deep adaptive image clustering. In: IEEE International Conference on Computer Vision, ICCV Italy. IEEE Computer Society, pp. 5880–5888 (2017)

Dhamija, A.R., Günther, M., Boult, T.E.: Reducing network agnostophobia. Adv. Neural Inf. Process. Syst. **31**, 9175–9186 (2018)

Gascon, H., Yamaguchi, F., Arp, D., Rieck, K.: Structural detection of android malware using embedded call graphs. In Proceedings of the 2013 ACM Workshop on Artificial Intelligence and Security (AISec), pp. 45–54 (2013)

Ge, Z., Demyanov, S., Garnavi, R.: Generative OpenMax for multi-class open set classification. In: British Machine Vision Conference (2017)

Gupta, D., Ramjee, R., Kwatra, N., Sivathanu, M.: Unsupervised clustering using pseudo-semi-supervised learning. In: 8th International Conference on Learning Representations, ICLR, Ethiopia (2020)

Han, K., Vedaldi, A., Zisserman, A.: Learning to discover novel visual categories via deep transfer clustering. In: IEEE/CVF International Conference on Computer Vision, ICCV, Korea (South). IEEE, 8400–8408 (2019)

Hassen, M., Chan, P.K.: Scalable function call graph-based malware classification. In: Proceedings of the Seventh ACM on Conference on Data and Application Security and Privacy, pp. 239–248 (2017)

Hassen, M., Chan, P.K.: Learning a neural-network-based representation for open set recognition. In: Proceedings of the SIAM International Conference on Data Mining, SDM USA. SIAM, pp. 154–162 (2020a)

Hassen, M., Chan, P.K.: Learning a neural-network-based representation for open set recognition. In: Proceedings of the SIAM International Conference Data Mining (2020), pp. 154–162 (2020b). arxiv:1802.04365

Jia, J., Chan, P.K.: MMF: a loss extension for feature learning in open set recognition. In: International Conference on Artificial Neural Networks. Proceedings Part II, pp. 319–331 (2021)

Jia, J., Chan, P.K.: Feature decoupling in self-supervised representation learning for open set recognition. CoRR abs/2209.14385 (2022). arXiv:2209.14385

Liu, Yu., Tuytelaars, T.: Residual tuning: toward novel category discovery without labels. IEEE Trans. Neural Netw. Learn. Syst. **2022**, 1–15 (2022)

Neal, L., Olson, M., Fern, X., Wong, W.-K., Li, F.: Open set learning with counterfactual images. In Proceedings of the European Conference on Computer Vision (ECCV), pp. 613–628 (2018)

Ronen, R., Radu, M., Feuerstein, C., Yom-Tov, E., Ahmadi, M.: . Microsoft malware classification challenge. CoRR abs/1802.10135 (2018). arxiv:1802.10135

Shu, Y., Shi, Y., Wang, Y., Zou, Y., Yuan, Q., Tian, Y.: ODN: opening the deep network for open-set action recognition. In: 2018 International Conference on Multimedia and Expo (ICME), pp. 1–6. . IEEE (2018)

Zhao, B., Han, K.: Novel visual category discovery with dual ranking statistics and mutual knowledge distillation. In: Annual Conference on Neural Information Processing Systems, NeurIPS, virtual, pp. 22982–22994 (2021)

Zhong, Z., Zhu, L., Luo, Z., Li, S., Yang, Y., Sebe, N.: OpenMix: reviving known knowledge for discovering novel visual categories in an open world. In: Conference on Computer Vision and Pattern Recognition, CVPR, virtual. Computer Vision Foundation, pp. 9462–9470. IEEE (2021)

Zhou, Y., Jiang, X.: Android malware genome project (2015). http://www.malgenomeproject.org/

Glancing Text and Vision Regularized Training to Enhance Machine Translation

Pei Cheng[1], Xiayang Shi[1]([✉]), Beibei Liu[2], and Meng Li[2]

[1] Zhengzhou University of Light Industry, Zhengzhou, China
aryang123@163.com
[2] South China University of Technology, Guangzhou, China

Abstract. Bilingual parallel sentences, combined with visual annotations, created an innovative machine translation scenario within the encoder-decoder framework, known as multimodal machine translation. In generally, it was encoded as an additional visual representation to enhance the dependent-time context vector when generating the target translation word by word. However, this approach only simulated the consistency between the visual annotation and the source language and did not sufficiently consider the consistency among the source language, the target language, and the visual context. To address this problem, we proposed a novel method that adds visual features to both the encoder and decoder. In the encoder, we designed a cross-modal correlation mechanism to effectively integrate textual and visual information. In the decoder, we designed a multimodal graph to enhance the related information of vision and text. Experimental results showed that the proposed approach significantly improved translation performance compared to strong baselines for the English-German/French language pairs. The ablation study further confirmed the effectiveness of the proposed approach in improving translation quality.

Keywords: Multimodal · Consistency · Machine Translation

1 Introduction

Multimodal machine translation (MMT) typically involves the integration of information from multiple modalities, such as visual or speech data. The underlying assumption is that the additional modalities (specifically the visual modality in this paper) contain useful alternative information of the textual input. Compared to text-only neural machine translation (NMT), MMT can improve the translation quality by determining the meaning of the text or providing visual contextual information [8]. However, the effectiveness of visual information, and in particular how to incorporate visual information into machine translation, has been seen as a major challenge.

© The Author(s), under exclusive license to Springer Nature Switzerland AG 2023
L. Iliadis et al. (Eds.): ICANN 2023, LNCS 14261, pp. 255–267, 2023.
https://doi.org/10.1007/978-3-031-44198-1_22

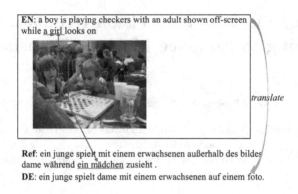

EN: a boy is playing checkers with an adult shown off-screen while a girl looks on

translate

Ref: ein junge spielt mit einem erwachsenen außerhalb des bildes dame während ein mädchen zusieht .
DE: ein junge spielt dame mit einem erwachsenen auf einem foto.

Fig. 1. An example of English (EN)-to-German (DE) MMT, "a girl" in the source sentence should be translated in target sentence.

Previous works [1,18,19] have focused primarily on the source language, largely neglecting the guidance of visual information in the target language. However, it is essential to further strengthen the relation among the source language, target language, and visual information. As shown in Fig. 1, we used parallel sentence pairs from Multi30K[1] to construct a text-only NMT based on the Transformer model [15]. Then, we used the trained NMT to translate a source (English) sentence to a target (German) sentence. It becomes clear that the text-only NMT system cannot translate "a girl," which has strong visual features in the picture. We believe that the visual modality can provide explicit target context that cannot be extracted directly from the text, thereby enhancing the performance of MMT. Therefore, the main motivation of this paper is to exploit the source-visual-target consistency to improve the decoder's text generation.

In this paper, we propose a novel method to improve machine translation generation by exploiting the source-visual-target consistency mechanism. We simultaneously incorporate visual information into the encoder and decoder to maintain consistency among the source, visual information, and target. In the encoder, we introduce a cross-modality relevance framework that considers the relevance of entities between the two modalities and aligns the representation spaces. In the decoder, we compute the semantic similarity between the generated target words and the image label to determine whether relevant target words have been translated or not. To ensure that the most relevant visual objects are used for translation, we introduce a multimodal graph and set a threshold to control the inflow of visual information. We have achieved good results with the Multi30k dataset. The main contributions and novelties of this work are as follows:

– We propose an effective multimodal translation model that exploits source-target-vision consistency to improve translation quality.

---

[1] A widely-used multi-modal dataset [5] to train MMT.

- We provide a cross-modal fusion method that aligns the representation space of visual entities and textual entities.
- We introduce a multimodal graph that uses visual context to guide the generation of target words.

2   Related Work

Multimodal machine translation (MMT) is a cross-modal task within the field of machine translation. Parallel sentences are crucial data for constructing neural machine translation [14], but additional modalities can effectively supplement the context information of pure text machine translation. Early attempts at MMT focused on improving models by incorporating visual features [3]. Current MMT typically uses other modalities (such as visual or voice) to extract useful information to improve text translation. For example, in the case of visual modality, global [19] or local [17] visual information is often added to the model. However, direct encoding of the entire image can introduce additional noise [19]. Huang [7] suggested adding visual features to the encoder in the seq2seq network to enable the decoder to better take into account visual information and the semantic relevance model. Zhou [21] created a visual text attention mechanism to capture words with strong semantic relevance to images. In his work, two multimodal context vectors (global and regional) were computed and then fused to predict the current target word. Previous methods only ensured the combination of visual information and the source language, with no link between the target language and the visual information. While the above methods can implicitly convey information to the decoder, they cannot explicitly establish the semantic relationship between the image and the text. There is a connection in the embedding space between two languages [22], and image information can explicitly strengthen this connection. It is also important to identify the most useful visual information. As shown in [4], irrelevant images have little effect on the translation quality. The experiment in [2] shows that the visual modality is still useful in the absence of linguistic context, but is less sensitive when presented with complete sentences.

Our proposed method not only integrates visual information into the encoder but also uses a graph attention network [16] at the decoder to guide translation with multimodal graphs. The graph attention network can capture node interactions by considering the relationships among each node in the graph. It is widely used in relation extraction and classification tasks. To select the most appropriate text-related information, we use the MBERT model [12]. MBERT is a model that has been pre-trained in language representation. The language representation ability learned through pre-training has achieved excellent performance in various NLP tasks.

3   Proposed Method

As a Seq2Seq model, it contains of an encoder and a decoder. Visual fusion aims to establish a framework of relevance between textual and visual information.

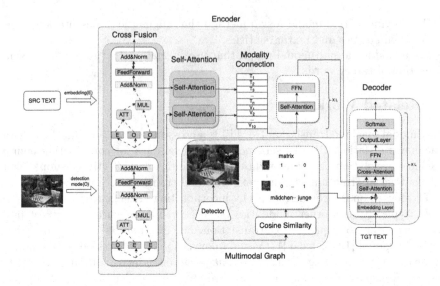

Fig. 2. Diagram of the proposed translation model. **Visual fusion** visual information and text information are aligned by using cross mode. **Multimodal graph**: word vector is generated with the help of MBERT, and the relationship matrix between vision and text is constructed through cosine similarity algorithm

The decoder uses a multimodal graph to strengthen the link with the encoder. Figure 2 shows the architecture we proposed.

3.1 Encoder

The encoder is divided into two parts, feature alignment and fusion. In the feature alignment part, we first obtain data from two modalities. For the visual modality, we use Faster-RCNN to extract visual features from regions of interest. We denote the visual features in an image as $\mathbf{O} = \{o_1 \cdots o_{N^o}\} \in \mathbf{R}^{d \times N^o}$, where N^o is the number of visual objects. We fix N^v by selecting the 10 features with the highest probability in each Faster-RCNN prediction. Each visual feature is a 2048-dimensional vector. To incorporate visual information into contextual representations, we use feedforward layers to project vectors.

For the textual modality, we use positional embeddings. We denote entities in the textual modality with word representation e. To align the visual modality and textual modality in the same vector space, we introduce a visual fusion module. All entities are processed uniformly in this module. We define textual entities as $\mathbf{E} = \{e_1 \cdots e_{N^e}\} \in \mathbf{R}^{d \times N^e}$, where N^e is the number of textual entities.

Cross-modality representation $\mathbf{E}_{\mathrm{cross}}$ and $\mathbf{O}_{\mathrm{cross}}$ are obtained through cross-attention calculation as follows:

$$\mathbf{E}_{\mathrm{cross}} = \mathrm{softmax}(\frac{\mathbf{O}^{\mathrm{T}}\mathbf{E}}{\sqrt{d}}\mathbf{O}) \tag{1}$$

$$\mathbf{O}_{\text{cross}} = \text{softmax}(\frac{\mathbf{E}^{\text{T}}\mathbf{O}}{\sqrt{d}}\mathbf{E}) \tag{2}$$

The cross fusion module consists of a cross-attention representation, followed by a residual connection with normalization from the input representation, a feed-forward layer, and another residual connection normalization. After the cross fusion module, we further apply a self-attention operation to the visual and textual entities, respectively, as follows:

$$\mathbf{S}_e = \text{softmax}(\frac{\mathbf{E}^{\text{T}}_{\text{cross}}\mathbf{E}_{\text{cross}}}{\sqrt{d}}\mathbf{E}_{\text{cross}}) \tag{3}$$

$$\mathbf{S}_o = \text{softmax}(\frac{\mathbf{O}^{\text{T}}_{\text{cross}}\mathbf{O}_{\text{cross}}}{\sqrt{d}}\mathbf{O}_{\text{cross}}) \tag{4}$$

We stack multiple module layers to get a consistent view across all modalities. We call these unified representations entity representations and denote the final expression of all entities as $\mathbf{S} = \text{cat}([\mathbf{S}_e, \mathbf{S}_o])$. Although the representations are separate, they carry information from interactions with the other modality and are aligned in a unified representation space.

In the feature fusion part, we use Transformer encoder modules to fuse the data from different modalities in $\mathbf{S}$. Each layer consists of two sub-layers. The first sub-layer is a multi-headed self-attention:

$$\mathbf{H}^{(l)} = \text{Attention}(\mathbf{S}^{(l-1)}, \mathbf{S}^{(l-1)}, \mathbf{S}^{(l-1)}) \tag{5}$$

where $\mathbf{H}^{(l)}$ is the temporary encoder hidden states, and $\text{Attention}(*)$ is a multi-head self-attention function. $\mathbf{S}^{(l-1)}$ represents the source sentence's representation at the $(l-1) - th$ layer. Particularly, $\mathbf{S}^{(0)}$ is the uniformed representations $\mathbf{S}$ obtained from the visual fusion module.

The second sub-layer is a position-wise fully connected feed-forward network(FFN). The representation of the source sentence at the current layer $\mathbf{S}^{(l)}$ is obtained as:

$$\mathbf{S}^{(l)} = \text{FFN}(\mathbf{H}^{(l)}) \tag{6}$$

where $\text{FFN}(*)$ is a position-wise feed-forward function.

3.2 Multimodal Graph

To establish a relationship between the target language and visual information, we developed a method to fuse the target language and visual information using an undirected graph $G = (Node, Edge)$ which represents connections between multiple modalities. *Node* represents a text node or an image node, and *Edge* represents the edge between nodes. First, we use Faster-RCNN to extract a bag of image objects and their corresponding text labels as candidates for nodes in the graph. We then use MBERT to calculate the similarity between the visual label and the textual representations. If their similarity is greater than the threshold α, the text node and visual node are connected by an *Edge*. Figure 2 shows an example where the phrase *"a girl"* matches an object in the image, resulting in a pair of nodes in the visual-textual graph. The advantage of this multimodal graph is that it can more accurately capture matching information between images and text while reducing noise.

The construction of a multimodal graph is divided into two steps. We use $\mathbf{E}_x = \{e_{x_0} \ldots e_{x_n}\}$ to denote the target language text nodes. The first step uses self-attention to collect messages between nodes within the text modality.

$$\mathbf{C}_x = \text{Attention}(\mathbf{E}_x, \mathbf{E}_x, \mathbf{E}_x) \tag{7}$$

The image nodes are then integrated with the text nodes as follows

$$\mathbf{M}_{x_i} = \sum_{j \in A(\mathbf{U}_{x_i})} \gamma_{i,j} \odot O_j \tag{8}$$

$$\gamma_{i,j} = \text{Sigmoid}(\mathbf{W}_1(\text{cat}[\mathbf{C}_x, O_j])) \tag{9}$$

where $\odot$ is the Hadamard (element-wise) product. $\mathbf{M}$ is a relational matrix. $A(\mathbf{U}_{x_i})$ is the set of visual nodes related to the current text node. $\mathbf{C}_x$ is concatenated with the visual entities O_j. $\mathbf{W}_1$ is a learnable parameter matrix.

3.3   Decoder

The decoder is similar to the encoder. Instead of using text-only information, we incorporate the multimodal graph M into the decoder's input as:

$$\mathbf{E}_{\text{emb}+\text{img}} = \mathbf{E}_{\text{emb}} + \mathbf{M} \tag{10}$$

where $\mathbf{E}_{\text{emb}}$ is the decoder's input. Please note that the complete M only exists during training. The calculation process is shown below:

$$\mathbf{C}_d^{(l-1)} = \text{Attention}(\mathbf{N}^{(l-1)}, \mathbf{N}^{(l-1)}, \mathbf{N}^{(l-1)}) \tag{11}$$

$$\mathbf{D}^{(l-1)} = \text{Attention}(\mathbf{C}_d^{(l-1)}, \mathbf{S}, \mathbf{S}) \tag{12}$$

$$\mathbf{N}^{(l)} = \text{FFN}(\mathbf{D}^{(l-1)}) \tag{13}$$

where $\mathbf{N}^{(0)}$ is $\mathbf{E}_{\text{emb}+\text{img}}$.

Finally, we use the hidden state of the last layer as input and apply softmax to generate the probability distribution of the target sentence and the training goals:

$$P(Y|X, N) = \prod_t \text{softmax}(\mathbf{W}\mathbf{N}^{(\text{last})}) \tag{14}$$

$$\mathcal{L}_f = -\log(P(Y|X, N)) \tag{15}$$

where $\mathbf{W}$ is a learnable parameter.

4 Experimental Results and Analysis

4.1 Datasets

We train our model on Multi30K, which a widely used dataset in multimodal machine translation, which includes image dataset, English text, and their translations(English to French, English to German). We used 29,000 samples for training and 1,014 samples for validation. For testing, we used the WMT2016, WMT2017, and MSCOCO [6] shared tasks. The MSCOCO test set contains 461 more challenging out-of-domain instances with ambiguous verbs. All sentences were preprocessed using BPE (Byte Pair Encoder). We used MOSES scripts to preprocess the dataset and learned a joint BPE code with 10,000 merging operations for both the source and target languages.

Table 1. Experimental results in English-German (En-De) translation tasks.

models	En-De					
	Test2016		Test2017		MSCOCO	
	BLEU	METEOR	BLEU	METEOR	BLEU	METEOR
Text-Only NMT Models						
Transformer	41.02	68.22	33.36	62.05	29.88	56.64
Existing MMT Models						
VAG-NMT	-	-	31.6	52.2	28.3	48
UVR-NMT	40.79	-	32.16	-	29.02	-
Imagination	41.31	68.06	32.89	61.29	29.9	56.57
DCCN	39.7	56.8	31	49.9	26.7	45.7
Ours Proposed Models						
Ours+Faster-RCNN	41.7	**69.5**	34.5	62.1	29.97	56.5
Ours+DETR	41.9	68.7	**34.7**	62.5	**30.01**	56.7
Ours+QueryInst	**42.1**	68.9	34.6	**63.5**	29.4	**56.9**

4.2 Parameter Settings

We followed the configuration described in [10] and experimented with the Transformer Tiny configuration, which is more suitable for small datasets such as Multi30K. We used a 4-layer encoder, 4-layer decoder, and 4 heads. The dimension of the hidden features in the feed-forward layer was 256, and the size of the word embeddings was 128 dimensions. The batch size was set to 64, and the learning rate was set to 0.005. We used Adam as the optimizer, with β_1 set to 0.9, β_2 set to 0.98, and *eps* set to 1e-9. Each batch contains approximately 4,096 source and target tokens. The beam size has been set to 5. Our implementation was based on Fairseq[2] In the training phase, the dropout was set to 0.1. We set

---

[2] https://github.com/facebookresearch/fairseq.

the maximum number of updates to 8000 steps, and training was stopped if the loss did not improve for ten consecutive iterations on the validation set. For evaluation metrics, we perform parameter averaging over the last 10 checkpoints to provide more reliable results. We use BLEU [11] and METEOR [13] to evaluate the quality of our translations.

Table 2. Experimental results in English-French (En-Fr) translation tasks.

models	En-Fr					
	Test2016		Test2017		MSCOCO	
	BLEU	METEOR	BLEU	METEOR	BLEU	METEOR
Text-Only NMT Models						
Transformer	61.8	81.02	53.46	75.62	44.52	69.43
Existing MMT Models						
VAG-NMT	-	-	53.8	70.3	45	31.7
UVR-NMT	61	-	53.2	-	43.71	-
Imagination	61.9	81.2	54.07	76.03	44.81	70.35
DCCN	61.2	76.4	54.3	70.3	45.4	65
Ours Proposed Models						
Ours+Faster-RCNN	62.3	**81.9**	54	76.4	45.2	70.1
Ours+DETR	**62.34**	81.44	54.2	76.3	45.7	**70.5**
Ours+QueryInst	62.33	81.5	**54.4**	**76.9**	**45.9**	69.7

4.3   Main Results

We primarily compare our method with several representative and competitive frameworks, including DCCN [9], VAG [21], UVR-NMT [20], Imagination [6]. The main results of the comparison are shown in Table 1 and Table 2. All models were evaluated on the three test sets for the En-De and En-Fr tasks.

The experimental results showed that, when we used Faster R-CNN to extract visual features, our model achieved an improvement of 0.68 in terms of BLEU score compared to the Transformer model on the WMT2016 En-De task. For the WMT2017 En-De task, this gap was reduced to 1.14. All BLEU scores were higher than in previous work. Compared to our model, the improvements of previous work were very limited in terms of baseline, suggesting that visual features were not fully exploited in their methods. The results are shown in Table 1.

We also investigated the impact of the detection model on translation quality. Here, we report the results of DETR and QueryInst in Table 1. Intuitively, the better performing DETR and QueryInst models provide more complementary knowledge to complete the inadequate text representation. The results show that stronger detection models can capture visual information more accurately, providing richer complementary information to the text. On the WMT2016 En-DE task, DETR improved the BLEU score to 41.9, and QueryInst improved it to 42.1. However, on the MSCOCO dataset, however, performance is comparable to the baseline. This result may be due to the fact that the Multi30K dataset is too small to include enough out-of-domain data. In Table 2, the results for the English to French translation task did not show higher improvements compared to the English to German task. This could be because English and French are more similar in nature, so the role of visual information is limited in this case.

Table 3. Ablation experiments on English-German and English-French translation tasks.

model	En-De WMT2017		En-Fr WMT2017	
	BLEU	METEOR	BLEU	METEOR
Ours	**34.5**	**53.9**	**54.0**	**71.5**
Ours-G_s	34.0	53.29	53.7	71.0
Ours-G_t	33.8	53.6	53.8	70.7
Ours-G_s-G_t	33.9	52.1	53.46	70.5

4.4 Ablation Study

Ablation experiments were carried out to determine the effect of each module on performance. The results are shown in Table 3.

(1)-G_t. In this variant, we removed the multimodal graph between the target and the visual information, while leaving the other parts unchanged. The experimental results show that removing the consistency between the target and visual objects leads to ineffective matching between the image and text objects, resulting in a decrease in translation quality.

Table 4. The impact of incongruent decoding. Here Cong/Icong denotes congruent and incongruent decoding, respectively. The results (BLEU) are measured on En-De Test2017.

System	Mask	
	Cong	Icong
Transformer	33.9	-
Ours_source	34.5	31.3
Ours_target	34.5	30.5
Ours	34.5	30.1

(2)-G_s. In this variant, we removed the information fusion between the source information and the visual information, while leaving the other parts unchanged. This results in the encoder being unable to ensure the consistency between the source language and visual information, leading to a significant decrease in the BLEU and METEOR scores. The experimental results indicate that visual fusion has a greater impact on translation quality.

The results of the ablation experiments suggest that maintaining source-target visual consistency is crucial for improving machine translation performance. However, relying solely on the visual consistency of either the source or the target will only lead to limited improvements in translation results.

4.5   Incongruent Decoding

To understand the sensitivity of the multimodal system to visual patterns, we used inconsistent decoding [2]. Specifically, we reversed the order of visual features, causing misalignment between visual features and text. The integration of visual modalities may worsen the metrics. Table 4 shows that inconsistent decoding leads to significant performance degradation, indicating that our model is highly sensitive to visual features. This is reasonable, as inconsistent visual information is more like noise to the model.

We also investigated the impact of inconsistent decoding on different modules. We found that visual features perform the best when decoding is consistent. When different modules perform inconsistent decoding separately, the performance degrades. Performance is at its lowest when decoding is completely inconsistent. These results suggest that visual information can improve translation performance.

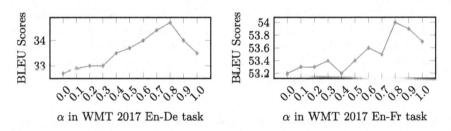

Fig. 3. The effect of the values of threshold α on the test set of WMT 2017 En-De and En-Fr task.

4.6   How the Degree of Visual Introduction Affect the Quality of Translation

We compute the similarity between visual labels and text representations using MBERT. In addition, a threshold is set to control the generation of G. We controlled the flow of visual information by changing the threshold value. As shown in Fig. 3.

We observe that, when the threshold is small, the impact of visual information on translation quality is very limited and may even lead to negative results. In addition, if the threshold is too high, performance also decreases.

This phenomenon indicates that an excessive amount of visual information makes it difficult to correctly select the appropriate information match between the recognition model and MBERT. The presence of inconsistent visual features can introduce noise into the translation process, thereby reducing the quality of the output. It is only by introducing appropriate visual information that translation quality can be improved.

5 Conclusion

In this paper, we propose a novel and effective multimodal translation model that exploits visual consistency between source and target. We used a visual fusion module to better integrate visual information into the encoder, and used noiseless visual object information to better infer context. We introduced a multimodal graph to effectively convey the consistency between visual and textual information to the decoder, thereby utilizing the guidance of visual information to obtain more accurate translation results. Our experiments on the multimodal benchmark dataset show that our model achieved fine results compared to related works. The research results confirm that developing multimodal models for assisting machine translation is a very promising research direction. In future work, we will investigate whether it is possible to effectively use complex background information to further improve the quality of MMT.

References

1. Caglayan, O., et al.: Cross-lingual visual pre-training for multimodal machine translation. In: Merlo, P., Tiedemann, J., Tsarfaty, R. (eds.) Proceedings of the 16th Conference of the European Chapter of the Association for Computational Linguistics: Main Volume, EACL 2021, Online, 19–23 April 2021, pp. 1317–1324. Association for Computational Linguistics (2021). https://aclanthology.org/2021. eacl-main.112/
2. Caglayan, O., Madhyastha, P., Specia, L., Barrault, L.: Probing the need for visual context in multimodal machine translation. CoRR abs/1903.08678 (2019). http:// arxiv.org/abs/1903.08678
3. Calixto, I., Liu, Q., Campbell, N.: Incorporating global visual features into attention-based neural machine translation. CoRR abs/1701.06521 (2017). http:// arxiv.org/abs/1701.06521
4. Elliott, D.: Adversarial evaluation of multimodal machine translation. In: Riloff, E., Chiang, D., Hockenmaier, J., Tsujii, J. (eds.) Proceedings of the 2018 Conference on Empirical Methods in Natural Language Processing, Brussels, Belgium, 31 October–4 November 2018, pp. 2974–2978. Association for Computational Linguistics (2018). https://doi.org/10.18653/v1/d18-1329

5. Elliott, D., Frank, S., Sima'an, K., Specia, L.: Multi30K: multilingual English-German image descriptions. In: Proceedings of the 5th Workshop on Vision and Language, pp. 70–74. Association for Computational Linguistics, Berlin, Germany, August 2016. https://doi.org/10.18653/v1/W16-3210. https://aclanthology.org/W16-3210

6. Elliott, D., Kádár, Á.: Imagination improves multimodal translation. In: Proceedings of the Eighth International Joint Conference on Natural Language Processing (Volume 1: Long Papers), pp. 130–141. Asian Federation of Natural Language Processing, Taipei, Taiwan, November 2017. https://aclanthology.org/I17-1014

7. Huang, P., Liu, F., Shiang, S., Oh, J., Dyer, C.: Attention-based multimodal neural machine translation. In: Proceedings of the First Conference on Machine Translation, WMT 2016, Colocated with ACL 2016, 11–12 August, Berlin, Germany, pp. 639–645. The Association for Computer Linguistics (2016). https://doi.org/10.18653/v1/w16-2360

8. Lee, J., Cho, K., Weston, J., Kiela, D.: Emergent translation in multi-agent communication. CoRR abs/1710.06922 (2017). http://arxiv.org/abs/1710.06922

9. Lin, H., et al.: Dynamic context-guided capsule network for multimodal machine translation. In: Proceedings of the 28th ACM International Conference on Multimedia, MM 2020, pp. 1320–1329. Association for Computing Machinery, New York, NY, USA (2020). https://doi.org/10.1145/3394171.3413715

10. Liu, J.: Multimodal machine translation. IEEE Access, 1 (2021). https://doi.org/10.1109/ACCESS.2021.3115135

11. Post, M.: A call for clarity in reporting BLEU scores. In: Proceedings of the Third Conference on Machine Translation: Research Papers, pp. 186–191. Association for Computational Linguistics, Belgium, Brussels, October 2018. https://www.aclweb.org/anthology/W18-6319

12. Sanh, V., Debut, L., Chaumond, J., Wolf, T.: DistilBERT, a distilled version of BERT: smaller, faster, cheaper and lighter. CoRR abs/1910.01108 (2019). http://arxiv.org/abs/1910.01108

13. Satanjeev, B.: METEOR: an automatic metric for MT evaluation with improved correlation with human judgments. In: ACL-2005, pp. 228–231 (2005)

14. Sun, Y., Zhu, S., Yifan, F., Mi, C.: Parallel sentences mining with transfer learning in an unsupervised setting. In: North American Chapter of the Association for Computational Linguistics (2021)

15. Vaswani, A., et al.: Attention is all you need. arXiv (2017)

16. Veličković, P., Cucurull, G., Casanova, A., Romero, A., Liò, P., Bengio, Y.: Graph attention networks. In: International Conference on Learning Representations (2018). https://openreview.net/forum?id=rJXMpikCZ

17. Wang, D., Xiong, D.: Efficient object-level visual context modeling for multimodal machine translation: masking irrelevant objects helps grounding. CoRR abs/2101.05208 (2021). https://arxiv.org/abs/2101.05208

18. Yang, P., Chen, B., Zhang, P., Sun, X.: Visual agreement regularized training for multi-modal machine translation. In: The Thirty-Fourth AAAI Conference on Artificial Intelligence, AAAI 2020, The Thirty-Second Innovative Applications of Artificial Intelligence Conference, IAAI 2020, The Tenth AAAI Symposium on Educational Advances in Artificial Intelligence, EAAI 2020, New York, NY, USA, 7–12 February 2020, pp. 9418–9425. AAAI Press (2020). https://aaai.org/ojs/index.php/AAAI/article/view/6484

19. Yao, S., Wan, X.: Multimodal transformer for multimodal machine translation. In: Proceedings of the 58th Annual Meeting of the Association for Computational Linguistics (2020)

20. Zhang, Z., et al.: Neural machine translation with universal visual representation. In: 8th International Conference on Learning Representations, ICLR 2020, Addis Ababa, Ethiopia, 26–30 April 2020. OpenReview.net (2020). https://openreview. net/forum?id=Byl8hhNYPS

21. Zhou, M., Cheng, R., Lee, Y.J., Yu, Z.: A visual attention grounding neural model for multimodal machine translation. CoRR abs/1808.08266 (2018). http://arxiv. org/abs/1808.08266

22. Zhu, S., Mi, C., Li, T., Zhang, F., Zhang, Z., Sun, Y.: Improving bilingual word embeddings mapping with monolingual context information. Mach. Transl. **35**, 503–518 (2021)

Global-Temporal Enhancement for Sign Language Recognition

Xiaofei Qin, Hui Wang, Changxiang He, and Xuedian Zhang[✉]

University of Shanghai for Science and Technology, Shanghai, China
xiaofei.qin@usst.edu.cn, obmmd_zxd@163.com

Abstract. The continuous sign language recognition task is challenging which needs to identify unsegmented gloss from long videos in a weakly supervised manner. Some previous methods hope to extract information of different modalities to enhance the representation of features, which often complicates the network and focuses too much on visual features. Sign language data is a long video, as the time span increases, the model may forget the information of early time steps. The long-distance temporal modeling ability directly affects the recognition performance. Therefore, a Global-Temporal Enhancement (GTE) module is proposed to enhance temporal learning ability. Most of the current continuous sign language recognition networks have a three-step architecture, i.e., visual, sequence and alignment module. However, such architecture is difficult to get enough training under current Connectionist Temporal Classification (CTC) losses. So two auxiliary supervision methods are proposed, namely Temporal-Consistency Self-Distillation (TCSD) and GTE loss. TCSD uses two global temporal outputs from different depths to supervise local temporal information. GTE loss can provide a moderate supervision to balance the features extracted by deep and shallow layers. The proposed model achieves state-of-the-art or competitive performance on PHOENIX14, PHOENIX14-T datasets.

Keywords: Sign language recognition · Temporal enhancement · Auxiliary supervision · Self distillation

1 Introduction

Deaf-mute people have serious communication problems in reality. Sign language has become an alternative option for their communication. Sign language is a visual language and users need to transmit information through a series of hand, head and body movements, which makes it difficult for normal people to master. Sign language recognition is beneficial to solve communication problems between two groups.

Sign language recognition can be divided into two categories. Isolated sign language recognition (ISLR) [10] converts a video clip into an independent gloss, and continuous sign language recognition (CSLR) converts a sign language video into a series of glosses, which is more challenging. From the perspective of information distribution, sign language videos are considerably more complex than spoken language. In order to enrich the representation of sign language, some works try to enrich RGB features with different modalities, e.g., C^2SLR [16] uses the pre-extracted keypoint heatmaps to constrain the visual module, forcing visual module to learn the features of the keypoint positions.

Although these methods have some positive contributions, multimodal data increases training complexity and relies on additional function components, such as pose estimation model, depths measurement model, etc. In order to reduce model complexity, some works [8,12] try to extract features from single RGB data. SEN [8] emphasizes some space regions in a self-motivated way, Pseudo-labels [12] uses random fine-grained labels to improve alignment. Remarkably, few of them deal with temporal information from a global perspective. Since the sign language data is a long video, too much attention to local temporal information or spatial information will limit the representation ability of global temporal information. The attention mechanism [1,6,13] has an excellent ability to capture long-distance information. To this end, a Global-Temporal Enhancement (GTE) module is proposed to model global dependency in temporal dimension. Each frame of sign language video contributes differently to the final recognition. GTE can enhance those frames with key information and suppress redundant frames.

Some works [2,7,11] point out that only enhancing the feature extraction module may not be able to fully utilize the capabilities of the three-step architecture. The reason is the current supervision methods are not sufficient to supervise all three steps, therefore, two auxiliary supervision methods are proposed. First, GTE loss is introduced to force the network to learn global temporal information directly. Second, considering that the temporal extraction network consists of multiple modules, different modules output different levels of features, independent calculation of Connectionist Temporal Classification (CTC) [5] loss may cause the network to focus on biased information, so a Temporal-Consistency Self-Distillation (TCSD) method is proposed to make multiple temporal modules more consistent. In summary, the contributions of this paper are as follows:

1. A Global-Temporal Enhancement (GTE) module is proposed, which utilizes attention mechanism to enhance global temporal representation and improve the learning ability of the model.
2. A Temporal-Consistent Self-Distillation (TCSD) method is proposed, which uses two global temporal outputs from different depths to supervise local temporal information. In addition, the GTE loss is also introduced and multiple losses can improve the stability of the network.
3. The GTE module and the auxiliary supervision methods belong to a holistic idea, and depend on each other. The proposed network can achieve high performance on the challenging Phoenix14 and Phoenix14-T datasets.

2   Related Works

The attention mechanism [1] computes an output by learning a set of weights associated with each position of the input sequence. Its excellent sequence modeling ability has inspired many following works. Transformer [13] has shown competitive performance only by attention, which can solve the problem that RNNs cannot be trained in parallel. External attention [6] is a lightweight structure that was originally proposed for image classification, semantic segmentation, etc. It can mine potential relationships across different channels. Attention mechanism has global modeling ability, leading to huge potential in CSLR task where long-distance dependencies are involved.

Auxiliary supervision aims to select an appropriate auxiliary loss to assist the generalization of the main task. Cheng et al. [2] proposed a gloss feature enhancement module and corresponding auxiliary loss provide high quality supervision. Knowledge distillation can also be regarded as a kind of auxiliary supervision method. Zhang et al. [14] proposed the idea of self-distillation, which extracts knowledge from the model itself to realize knowledge transfer between different layers. Hao et al. [7] introduced knowledge distillation method to the CSLR task and achieved good performance. Current main stream three-step architecture of CSLR network has multiple hierarchy parts, making auxiliary supervision a suitable mechanism to improve model performance.

3   Methods

3.1   Network Overview

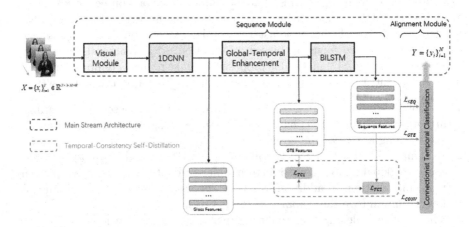

Fig. 1. Overview of our proposed network.

As shown in Fig. 1, the network follows the three-step architecture which consists a visual module, a sequence module and an alignment module. Given an input of T frames RGB sign language video $X = \{x_i\}_{t=1}^{T} \in \mathbb{R}^{T \times 3 \times H \times W}$, the output $Y = \{y_i\}_{i=1}^{N}$ is a sentence composed of glosses, where N represents the length of the sentence. After the sign language video is extracted by the visual module (2DCNN), the feature becomes $F = \{f_t\}_{t=1}^{T} \in \mathbb{R}^{T \times d}$. The sequence module further extracts temporal information, which consists of a local temporal extraction module (1DCNN), a GTE module and a Bi-directional Long Short-Term Memory (BiLSTM). Finally, the alignment module uses CTC to calculate the probability $p = (y \mid x)$ of the predicted gloss sequences.

3.2   Global-Temporal Enhancement

Figure 2 gives the details of GTE module. GTE has a two-branch structure. The first branch is composed of four stacks of Transformer Encoder, which can model global temporal dependencies. The second is an External Attention branch, which can enhance the power of Transformer Encoder by injecting positional information to GTE module.

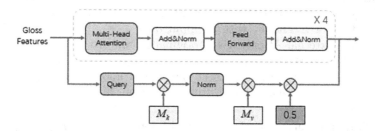

Fig. 2. The structure of Global-Temporal Enhancement.

Transformer Encoder. Compared to original Transformer Encoder, the input embedding and positional encoding are removed in GTE module, reducing the amount of computation and helping the model converge faster. Self-attention plays most of the learning role in GTE. The formula of self-attention is as follows:

$$\text{Attention}(Q, K, V) = \text{softmax}\left(\frac{QK^T}{\sqrt{d_k}}\right) V \tag{1}$$

Q, K, V are linear projections of input with different weights respectively. Q and K perform dot product attention operation, then divided by the square root of their second dimension d_k. After softmax, then multiply V to get the attention matrix.

Multi-head attention projects queries, keys, and values h times with different linear projections, executes the attention functions separately, and finally concatenates them and executes an additional projection:

$$\text{head}_i = \text{Attention}\left(QW_i^Q, KW_i^K, VW_i^V\right) \tag{2}$$

$$\text{MultiHeadAttention}\,(Q, K, V) = \text{Concat}\,(\text{head}_1, \ldots, \text{head}_h)\,W^O \qquad (3)$$

where parameter matrices $W_i^Q \in \mathbb{R}^{d \times d_k}$, $W_i^K \in \mathbb{R}^{d \times d_k}$, $W_i^V \in \mathbb{R}^{d \times d_v}$ and $W^O \in \mathbb{R}^{hd_v \times d}$. Multi-head attention allows the model to focus on different temporal step, which is effective in suppressing redundant and transitional frames. If the input is $F_{1d} = \{f_t\}_{t=1}^{T'} \in \mathbb{R}^{T' \times d}$, after residuals and feedforward, the output of a Transformer Encoder can be calculated as follows:

$$\tilde{F}_{GTE} = \text{LayerNorm}\,(F_{1d} + \text{MutilHeadAttention}\,(F_{1d})) \qquad (4)$$

$$\text{FeedForward}(x) = \max\,(0, xW_1 + b_1)\,W_2 + b_2 \qquad (5)$$

$$F_{ENC} = \text{LayerNorm}\left(\tilde{F}_{ENC} + \text{FeedForward}\left(\tilde{F}_{ENC}\right)\right) \qquad (6)$$

In this paper, the dimension $d = 1024$ to avoid the loss of spatial information, which is consistent with the frame-wise feature dimension of the visual module.

External Attention. To construct the GTE module, the idea of External Attention [6] is borrowed. External Attention uses two linear layers of the same size M instead of K and V, with an input of $F \in \mathbb{R}^{C \times S}$, processing channel dimension C. External Attention was originally proposed to deal with images, not videos. Therefore, this paper processes dimension S instead of C by linear layers M. The idea is to first project the spatial information in each frame, then normalize the temporal and feature dimension, finally project the spatial information again.

In CSLR, the output of 1DCNN can be represented as $F_{1d} = \{f_t\}_{t=1}^{T'} \in \mathbb{R}^{T' \times d}$, while two distinct linear layers can be represented as $M_k, M_v \in \mathbb{R}^{S \times d}$. Unlike the self-attention calculation of the similarity between elements and elements, $(\alpha)_{i,j}$ calculates the similarity between the ith element of the linear layer and the jth line in F_{1d}, M_k and M_v use the same initialization parameters:

$$A = (\alpha)_{i,j} = \text{Norm}\left(F_{1d}M_k^T\right) \qquad (7)$$

$$F_{EA} = AM_v \qquad (8)$$

Since attention is sensitive to data scale, double normalization is used to normalize columns and rows independently. The double normalization formula is as follows:

$$\tilde{\alpha}_{i,j} = F_{1d}M_k^T \qquad (9)$$

$$\hat{\alpha}_{i,j} = \exp\,(\tilde{\alpha}_{i,j}) \,/ \sum_k \exp\,(\tilde{\alpha}_{k,j}) \qquad (10)$$

$$\alpha_{i,j} = \hat{\alpha}_{i,j} \,/ \sum_k \hat{\alpha}_{i,k} \qquad (11)$$

When designing neural network models, many works often add residuals to prevent model learning failures, but GTE module does not follow this case. The input of the GTE module contains local temporal information. Niu et al. [12]

shows that the average length of input video corresponding to one gloss is 12.2 frames. Fixed convolution kernel of 5 in 1DCNN means that the features learned involve frames corresponding to different glosses. Therefore, features may contains some wrong information. Adding residuals at this time will keep error information and interfere with subsequent learning.

After the calculation of the two branches, without using the residual structure, the final output of the GTE is:

$$F_{GTE} = F_{ENC} + 0.5F_{EA} \qquad (12)$$

where coefficient 0.5 is chosen by experiment results.

Since Encoder does not add positional encoding, temporal information may be lost during training. Moreover, due to the inherent requirement of distillation learning, the layer number of GTE cannot be too small. But deepening the number of layers may make the subsequent layers gradually forget the original temporal information. To this end, three measures are adopted. The first and most powerful measure is External Attention. External Attention shares the same input as the Encoder and its outputs are fused at the output stage of GTE. External Attention keeps the most positional information and reduces the influence of fixed convolution kernel size in 1DCNN. Second, due to the existence of TCSD, 1DCNN is taught by GTE and BiLSTM, so that useful temporal information is preserved as much as possible. Third, GTE loss also can be corrected by other CTC losses which might contain more temporal information.

3.3   Temporal-Consistency Self-distillation

Knowledge distillation induces the training of a small model (student) by using a soft target associated with the large model (teacher) as part of the total loss.

For CSLR task, a single loss function often cannot fully capture all aspects of the model that need to be optimized. Each module of feature extraction is responsible for extracting different levels of information, and there are differences between them. At the same time, there is a gradual dependency between them, serving the same purpose of abstracting sign language features. In order to promote the information interaction and consistency between modules, TCSD is proposed.

GTE and BiLSTM with global temporal information are regarded as the teachers, and 1DCNN is regarded as the student. This paper jointly trains the teachers and student networks, and adds auxiliary classifiers after GTE and 1DCNN to obtain auxiliary logits. Generally speaking, shallow features tend to focus on texture details, while deep features pay more attention to abstract semantics. Teachers at different depths can provide their specific knowledge to the student network, thus keeping local and global temporal consistent. The distillation formula is as follows:

$$\mathcal{L}_{TC1} = \text{KL}\left(\text{softmax}\left(\frac{T_1}{\tau}\right), \text{softmax}\left(\frac{S}{\tau}\right)\right) \qquad (13)$$

$$\mathcal{L}_{TC2} = \text{KL}\left(\text{softmax}\left(\frac{T_2}{\tau}\right), \text{softmax}\left(\frac{S}{\tau}\right)\right) \tag{14}$$

Among them, $S = (s_1, \ldots, s_T)$, $T_1 = (t_1, \ldots, t_T)$, and $T_2 = (t'_1, \ldots, t'_T)$ are obtained by 1DCNN, GTE and BiLSTM respectively. Using a higher temperature τ can soften the peak probability and smooth the distribution of labels, and reduce the phenomenon of overfitting.

TCSD utilizes all three temporal modules and regulates the local temporal module through two deep global temporal information, so that the local and global can reach some certain consensus. On the basis of GTE, TCSD is able to further strengthen the global temporal information. Finally, TCSD can also assist CTC losses (see Sect. 3.4 for details) to achieve the desired alignment performance.

3.4   Global-Temporal Enhancement Loss

CTC loss is a loss function for sequence-to-sequence (seq2seq) learning. CTC generates a label for each time step, which can be repeated labels or "blank" labels. "blank" label is a special label for silent time steps and separate continuous repetitions of gloss. "blank" and the gloss vocabulary $\mathbb{G}$ together generate a recognized path $\pi_i \in \mathbb{G} \cup \{blank\}$, π_i denoting the alignment between the input time step t and the corresponding gloss in the target sentence. Under the assumption of conditional independence, given an input sequence X, the conditional probability of path sequence set $\pi = \{\pi_i\}_{i=1}^{T}$ can be formulated as:

$$p(\pi \mid X) = \prod_{i=1}^{T} p(\pi_i \mid X) \tag{15}$$

If the label sequence is y, and the probability of finally predicting the correct sequence is the sum of all possible permutations:

$$p(y \mid X) = \sum_{\phi \in B^{-1}(y)} p(\pi \mid X) \tag{16}$$

Among them, B is a mapping function that removes consecutive repeated words and "blank" symbols in the path. Then the CTC loss can be defined as:

$$\mathcal{L}_{CTC} = -\log p(y \mid X) \tag{17}$$

Min et al. [11] believes that the BiLSTM layer may overfit with partial visual information, for which they introduce 1DCNN loss to enhance visual feature extraction. However, 1DCNN loss alone will limit the attention to the temporal neighborhoods of frame-wise features. Adding supervision to local temporal features will inevitably weaken the model ability to pay adequate attention to the relationship between long-distance frames.

Therefore, a global temporal augmentation loss $\mathcal{L}_{GTE}$ is introduced on top of GTE, forcing the network to make predictions based on GTE feature which has rich global temporal information. The direct supervision of intermediate feature can drive the model to alleviate the information missing due to network deepening. $\mathcal{L}_{GTE}$ belongs to CTC loss, which can be naturally integrated into the final CTC loss during training.

This paper sets a total of three CTC losses in the network, $\mathcal{L}_{SEQ}$ and $\mathcal{L}_{CONV}$ are obtained by BiLSTM and 1DCNN respectively. Combining losses at different levels can force the model to learn more general features, so that temporal information at different depths can be paid enough attention. The final loss function of the overall network is expressed as follows:

$$\mathcal{L} = \mathcal{L}_{SEQ} + \mathcal{L}_{GTE} + \mathcal{L}_{CONV} + \alpha \left(\mathcal{L}_{TC1} + \mathcal{L}_{TC2} \right) \tag{18}$$

4   Experiments

4.1   Experimental Setup

Datasets. RWTH-PHOENIX-Weather-2014 and RWTH-PHOENIX-Weather-2014-T are derived from the German weather forecast sign language records. All videos are recorded in a clean background with a frame number of 25 and a frame size of 210 * 260, including a total of 9 signers. The two datasets each contain 6841/8247 sentences and 1295/1085 sign language vocabulary, divided into 5672/7096 training samples, 540/519 development samples and 629/642 test samples.

Evaluation Metric. Word Error Rate(WER) is used to express the difference between predicted sentences and labels, which is the minimum sum of replacement, insertion and deletion operations required to turn the predicted sentence into a label sentence. The lower WER, the better recognition performance.

$$WER = \frac{\# \text{ sub } + \# \text{ ins } + \# \text{ del}}{\# \text{ reference}} \tag{19}$$

Implementation Details. Resnet18 pre-trained on ImageNet is used as the visual module, and the sequence module consists of three parts: 1DCNN, GTE, and BiLSTM. 1DCNN uses two layers of one-dimensional convolution (kernel size is 5), and each convolution layer is followed by a layer of maximum pooling (pooling size is 2). External Attention linear layer is set to 64. The model loss consists of three CTC losses and two distillation losses. The weight ratios of three CTC losses are the same. The coefficient for both distillation losses is set to 10, and their temperature is set to 8. 40/50 epochs are trained in PHOENIX14 and PHOENIX14-T datasets respectively. The initial learning rate of the Adam optimizer is 0.001, and it decays to one-fifth of the current learning rate at epoch 25 and 35. After the original data is preprocessed, all video frames are adjusted to 256 * 256.

4.2   Ablation Experiment

Ablations on Positional Encoding. The network works better when positional encoding is not used. The reason is that CSLR is a weakly supervised task with only sentence-level annotations. That is, different gloss corresponds to different number of frames, an independent positional encoding for each frame-wise feature will cause disorder. As shown in Table 1, the positional encoding causes ambiguity in model learning.

Table 1. Effects on positional encodering in GTE.

Configurations	Dev(%)	Test(%)
Exist	20.4	21.3
None	**19.8**	**20.9**

Table 2. Ablations of whether GTE and BiLSTM can replace each other(no auxiliary loss).

Methods	Dev(%)	Test(%)
1DCNN + BiLSTM	21.2	22.3
1DCNN + GTE	21.4	22.1
1DCNN + GTE + BiLSTM	**20.2**	**21.3**

Ablations on GTE and BiLSTM. Both GTE and BiLSTM are able to process global temporal information, but they cannot replace each other. As shown in Table 2, when GTE is used to completely replace BiLSTM, the performance of the model decreases slightly. This is because there is no position encoding within GTE, and temporal information may be partially lost. After adding BiLTSM, the temporal information is reorganized and the performance is greatly improved.

Table 3. Ablations on GTE internal structure.

Configurations	Dev(%)	Test(%)
EA	26.9	27.0
ENC	20.3	21.1
EA+ENC	21.9	22.6
Parallelled(res)	20.2	21.1
Parallelled	**19.8**	**20.9**

Table 4. Ablations on ENC layers & heads and distillation coefficient.

layers	heads	$\mathcal{L}_{TC1}$	$\mathcal{L}_{TC2}$	Dev(%)	Test(%)
2	4	10	10	20.2	21.0
2	8	10	10	20.1	20.8
4	8	10	10	**19.8**	**20.9**
4	8	10	20	20.3	21.3
4	8	10	10	20.2	21.1

Ablations on GTE Structure. The parameter amount of External Attention (EA) is very small and inappropriate use may cause model training failure. As shown in Table 3, using EA alone gets much worse results than when only Transformer Encoder (ENC) is used. When the EA and ENC are used in series, the effect is not ideal, and even does not converge in the case of ENC+EA. As the 1st and 2nd of Table 3 shown, inserting EA into the main path of CSLR network will disturb the feature transmission, that is because EA is such a small module that it is not able to handle the abundant information through the main path. But EA has the unique role of preserving local temporal information, and the best results are achieved when connecting them in parallel. The introduction of residuals will disturb the model, as described in Sect. 3.2.

Ablations on ENC Layers & Heads and Distillation Coefficient. As shown in Table 4, the performance will get better when the number of layers and heads increase, however, too much layers and heads will lead to high model complexity, this paper uses 4 layers and 8 heads in ENC. ENC with too few layers and heads will cause insufficient differences between teachers and students in TCSD, which may limit its distillation ability. In addition, when the coefficients of two distillation losses [4] are set the same to 10, model gets the best performance.

Table 5. Ablations on the proposed modules.

Methods	GTE	TCSD	$\mathcal{L}_{GTE}$	Dev(%)	Test(%)
GTE	✓			20.2	21.3
GTE + TCSD	✓	✓		20.1	21.0
GTE + $\mathcal{L}_{GTE}$	✓		✓	20.6	20.8
GTE + TCSD + $\mathcal{L}_{GTE}$	✓	✓	✓	**19.8**	**20.9**

Ablations on the Proposed Modules. As shown in Table 5, when GTE alone is added to the three-step CSLR structure, the model is able to achieve good performance. However, when $\mathcal{L}_{GTE}$ or TCSD alone is further added on the basis of GTE, model performance cannot be further improved obviously. The reason might be $\mathcal{L}_{GTE}$ or TCSD alone cannot achieve good balance between local and

Table 6. Comparison with state-of-the-art methods.

Methods	PHOENIX14				PHOENIX14-T	
	Dev(%)		Test(%)		Dev(%)	Test(%)
	del/ins	WER	del/ins	WER		
SFL [12]	7.9/6.5	26.2	7.5/6.3	26.8	25.1	26.1
FCN [2]	-	23.7	-	23.9	23.3	25.1
STMC [15]	-	25.0	-	-	-	-
VAC [11]	7.9/2.5	21.2	8.4/2.6	22.3	-	-
SMKD [7]	6.8/2.5	20.8	6.3/2.3	21.0	20.8	22.4
SEN [8]	5.8/2.6	**19.5**	7.3/4.0	21.0	19.3	20.7
TLP [9]	6.3/2.8	**19.7**	6.1/2.9	**20.8**	19.4	21.2
DNF* [3]	7.3/3.3	23.1	6.7/3.3	22.9	-	-
STMC* [15]	7.7/3.4	21.1	7.4/2.6	**20.7**	19.6	21.0
C^{2}SLR* [16]	-	20.5	-	**20.4**	20.2	20.4
Ours	5.5/2.9	**19.8**	5.6/3.5	**20.9**	**18.8**	**20.8**

global information. When GTE and two auxiliary supervisions are used together, model achieves the best performance.

4.3   Comparison with State-of-the-Art Results

Table 6 shows the comparison between other state-of-the-art (SOTA) methods and our method, where * indicates using extra clues such as face or hand features. For the PHOENIX14 dataset, our method achieves superior or comparable performance without additional information (pose, hand or face cropping information, etc.). For the PHOENIX14-T dataset, our method achieves the best performance. The method proposed in this paper focus on the processing of temporal information, Fig. 3 gives a visual example of self similarity matrices between baseline [11] and our method, which demonstrates the long-distance modeling ability of the proposed method.

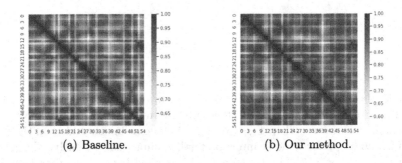

| (a) Baseline. | (b) Our method. |

Fig. 3. Self similarity matrices of output between baseline [11] and our method.

5   Conclusion

This paper first proposes a Global-Temporal Enhancement module, which can enhance model representation ability on global temporal information and alleviate the alignment difficulties caused by weakly supervised characteristic of CSLR task. Secondly, two auxiliary supervision methods are proposed to achieve good balance between local and global temporal information. Extensive ablation experiments verify the effectiveness of the proposed methods. The proposed model can achieve SOTA or competitive performance on the PHOENIX14 and PHOENIX14-T datasets.

Acknowledgements. Funded by National Natural Science Foundation of China (NSFC), Grant Number: 92048205; Also funded by China Scholarship Council (CSC), Grant Number: 202008310014.

References

1. Bahdanau, D., Cho, K., Bengio, Y.: Neural machine translation by jointly learning to align and translate. arXiv preprint arXiv:1409.0473 (2014)
2. Cheng, K.L., Yang, Z., Chen, Q., Tai, Y.-W.: Fully convolutional networks for continuous sign language recognition. In: Vedaldi, A., Bischof, H., Brox, T., Frahm, J.-M. (eds.) ECCV 2020. LNCS, vol. 12369, pp. 697–714. Springer, Cham (2020). https://doi.org/10.1007/978-3-030-58586-0_41
3. Cui, R., Liu, H., Zhang, C.: A deep neural framework for continuous sign language recognition by iterative training. IEEE Trans. Multimedia **21**(7), 1880–1891 (2019)
4. Fukuda, T., Suzuki, M., Kurata, G., Thomas, S., Cui, J., Ramabhadran, B.: Efficient knowledge distillation from an ensemble of teachers. In: Interspeech, pp. 3697–3701 (2017)
5. Graves, A., Fernández, S., Gomez, F., Schmidhuber, J.: Connectionist temporal classification: labelling unsegmented sequence data with recurrent neural networks. In: Proceedings of the 23rd International Conference on Machine Learning, pp. 369–376 (2006)
6. Guo, M.H., Liu, Z.N., Mu, T.J., Hu, S.M.: Beyond self-attention: external attention using two linear layers for visual tasks. IEEE Trans. Pattern Anal. Mach. Intell. (2022)
7. Hao, A., Min, Y., Chen, X.: Self-mutual distillation learning for continuous sign language recognition. In: Proceedings of the IEEE/CVF International Conference on Computer Vision, pp. 11303–11312 (2021)
8. Hu, L., Gao, L., Feng, W., et al.: Self-emphasizing network for continuous sign language recognition. arXiv preprint arXiv:2211.17081 (2022)
9. Hu, L., Gao, L., Liu, Z., Feng, W.: Temporal lift pooling for continuous sign language recognition. In: Avidan, S., Brostow, G., Cissé, M., Farinella, G.M., Hassner, T. (eds.) Computer Vision-ECCV 2022: 17th European Conference, Tel Aviv, Israel, 23–27 October 2022, Proceedings, Part XXXV, pp. 511–527. Springer, Cham (2022)
10. Jiang, S., Sun, B., Wang, L., Bai, Y., Li, K., Fu, Y.: Skeleton aware multi-modal sign language recognition. In: Proceedings of the IEEE/CVF Conference on Computer Vision and Pattern Recognition, pp. 3413–3423 (2021)
11. Min, Y., Hao, A., Chai, X., Chen, X.: Visual alignment constraint for continuous sign language recognition. In: Proceedings of the IEEE/CVF International Conference on Computer Vision, pp. 11542–11551 (2021)
12. Niu, Z., Mak, B.: Stochastic fine-grained labeling of multi-state sign glosses for continuous sign language recognition. In: Vedaldi, A., Bischof, H., Brox, T., Frahm, J.-M. (eds.) ECCV 2020. LNCS, vol. 12361, pp. 172–186. Springer, Cham (2020). https://doi.org/10.1007/978-3-030-58517-4_11

13. Vaswani, A., et al.: Attention is all you need. In: Advances in Neural Information Processing Systems, vol. 30 (2017)
14. Zhang, L., Song, J., Gao, A., Chen, J., Bao, C., Ma, K.: Be your own teacher: improve the performance of convolutional neural networks via self distillation. In: Proceedings of the IEEE/CVF International Conference on Computer Vision, pp. 3713–3722 (2019)
15. Zhou, H., Zhou, W., Zhou, Y., Li, H.: Spatial-temporal multi-cue network for continuous sign language recognition. In: Proceedings of the AAAI Conference on Artificial Intelligence, vol. 34, pp. 13009–13016 (2020)
16. Zuo, R., Mak, B.: C2SLR: consistency-enhanced continuous sign language recognition. In: Proceedings of the IEEE/CVF Conference on Computer Vision and Pattern Recognition, pp. 5131–5140 (2022)

Global-to-Contextual Shared Semantic Learning for Fine-Grained Vision-Language Alignment

Min Zheng[1]([✉]), Chunpeng Wu[1], Jiaqi Qin[1], Weiwei Liu[1], Ming Chen[2], Long Lin[1], and Fei Zhou[1]

[1] State Grid Laboratory of Grid Advanced Computing and Applications, State Grid Smart Grid Research Institute Co., Ltd., Beijing 102209, China
zhengmin@geiri.sgcc.com.cn

[2] Xiamen Power Supply Company, State Grid Fujian Electric Power Company, Xiamen 361004, China

Abstract. The primary requisites of fine-grained vision-language alignment focus on learning effective features to discriminate fine-grained subcategories and aligning heterogeneous data. This paper proposes a global-to-contextual shared semantic learning for fine-grained vision-language alignment method to address the above challenges. Precisely, to enhance the discrimination of features inside intra-modality, this method extracts the global and contextual vision and language features and carries out features joint learning. Further, this method constructs a shared semantic space, which bridges the semantic correlation of heterogeneous data. Extensive experiments demonstrate the effectiveness of our approach.

Keywords: Fine-grained vision-language alignment · Shared semantic learning · Global-to-contextual feature representation

1 Introduction

Vision-language alignment is one of the most fundamental topics with a wide range of multimedia areas, including image-text retrieval, zero-shot learning, and so forth. Various relevant approaches have been proposed over the past several decades [5,7,9–11,15,18]. Most of them focus on extracting the global features of images and texts, and then devise a metric to measure the similarity of image-text pairs. Particularly, some alignment methods [5,7] propose to leverage generative adversarial networks for more robust representations of vision-language alignment. Nevertheless, this issue still faces the challenge of highly similar global geometry and appearance among fine-grained classes. On the other hand, the alignment methods above can not deal with real-world further fine-grained scenarios, e.g., automatic biodiversity monitoring, intelligent retail, intelligent transportation, etc. Therefore, fine-grained vision-language alignment has received attention in recent years. Fine-grained data have the characteristics of slight divergence between different subclasses but large variance within the same subclass. It is essential to learn subtle discriminative detail features that make the subordinate classes different from each other.

L. Iliadis et al. (Eds.): ICANN 2023, LNCS 14261, pp. 281–293, 2023.
https://doi.org/10.1007/978-3-031-44198-1_24

Besides, alignment space construction is still a challenging problem that remains unresolved in fine-grained vision-language alignment. This problem largely depends on capturing and correlating heterogeneous features from different modalities. He *et al.* [17] presented an FGCrossNet, which considers three constraints for representation learning. Zheng *et al.* [19] proposed a discriminative latent space learning that addresses the alignment of heterogeneous data. However, the discriminativeness and relevance of the considered image-text data can be further strengthened by enforcing a shared semantic alignment.

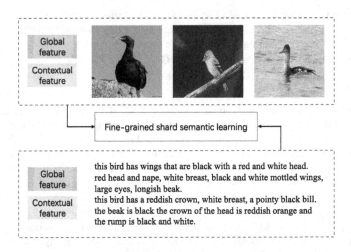

Fig. 1. Overview of the proposed global-to-contextual shared semantic learning for fine-grained vision-language alignment.

This paper proposes global-to-contextual shared semantic learning for fine-grained vision-language alignment, as shown in Fig. 1. Concretely, this method firstly extracts the global and contextual vision features by VggNet deep feature extractor [13] and Transformer model [3], and meanwhile extracts the global and contextual language features by Bag-of-words (BOW) model [4] and Bert model [2]. Then global-to-contextual features joint learning is carried out to enhance the discrimination. Further, to improve the semantic correlation of heterogeneous data and bridge the semantic gap among the modalities, this method presents shared semantic learning, which achieves the relevance of image-text pairs through matrix transformation. Finally, the method returns the candidates by measuring the relevance between image-text pairs. The main contributions of our work can be summarized as follows. (1) We construct the fine-grained contextual vision transformer, which effectively captures the contextual detail dependency of fine-grained image patches. (2) We propose the global-to-contextual shared semantic learning for fine-grained vision-language alignment, which learns discriminative features to distinguish the fine-grained sub-categories and aligns vision-language semantically. (3) Extensive experiments on subcategory-specific and instance-specific tasks demonstrate the effectiveness of our approach. Remarkably, this method achieves a 15% accuracy improvement over the state-of-the-art baselines on the instance-specific task.

2 Related Works

Vision-language alignment establishes relationships between images and texts. Current approaches can be divided into two types: coarse-grained vision-language alignment and fine-grained vision-language alignment. Details are below.

Coarse-Grained Vision-Language Alignment. MHTN [7] proposed to realize knowledge transfer from a single-modal domain to a cross-modal domain and learn cross-modal representation. ACMR [15] aimed to seek an effective common subspace based on adversarial learning. JRL [18] explored the correlation and semantic information in a unified optimization framework jointly. GSPH [10] preserved the semantic distance between the data points, which can be applied to all the scenarios. CMDN [11] exploited the complex cross-modal correlation by hierarchical learning. SCA [9] presented to discover the full latent alignment using image regions and words in sentences as context and infer the image-text similarity. GXN [5] incorporated two generative models into the conventional textual-visual feature embedding, which can learn concrete grounded representations that capture the detailed similarity between the two modalities.

Fine-Grained Vision-Language Alignment. FGCrossNet [17] considered three constraints for better alignment. DLSL [19] proposed a simple yet effective method to directly learn a common latent space by couple dictionary learning to align heterogeneous data. HGR [1] decomposed video-text matching into global-to-local levels and generated hierarchical textual embeddings via attention-based graph reasoning. HANet [16] proposed to make full use of complementary information of different semantic levels of representations for video-text retrieval.

3 Proposed Method

3.1 Problem Formulation

Formally, let $\tilde{V} = \{\tilde{v}_i\}_{i=1}^n$ be a set of global vision features, where $\tilde{v}_i$ denotes the global feature of the i-th image. Let $\hat{V} = \{\hat{v}_i\}_{i=1}^n$ be a set of contextual vision features, where $\hat{v}_i$ denotes the contextual feature of the i-th image. Correspondingly, let $\tilde{T} = \{\tilde{t}_i\}_{i=1}^n$ be a set of global language features, where $\tilde{t}_i$ indicates the global feature of the i-th text. Let $\hat{T} = \{\hat{t}_i\}_{i=1}^n$ be a set of contextual language features, where $\hat{t}_i$ denotes the contextual feature of the i-th text. This method uses pre-trained models to encode images and texts. More precisely, for images, VggNet and Transformer are employed to learn the global and contextual vision features. For texts, BOW (manual feature, not extracted by pre-trained model) and Bert are utilized to learn the global and contextual language features. Details are

shown in Table 1. The goal is to construct a global-to-contextual shared seman-
tic space $Z = \{z_i\}_{i=1}^n$ for $\tilde{V}, \hat{V}, \tilde{T}$ and $\hat{T}$, where z_i represents the semantic feature
of the i-th sample. In this space, we can perform the vision-language alignment
by measuring the similarity among image-text pairs.

Table 1. Key information and notations of initial features.

Type of feature	Notation	Encoder	Dimension
Global vision feature	$\tilde{V}$	VggNet	1024
Contextual vision feature	$\hat{V}$	Transformer	768
Global language feature	$\tilde{T}$	BOW	1000
Contextual language feature	$\hat{T}$	Bert	768

3.2   Fine-Grained Contextual Vision Transformer

The main difficulty of contextual vision feature learning derives from the slight
inter-class distinction and the large intra-class variance of fine-grained subclasses.
This paper remedies the problem by constructing the fine-grained contextual
vision transformer, which can effectively capture the correction of local details
and is conducive to extracting robust fine-grained features. The architecture
is shown in Fig. 2. More specifically, given a fine-grained image, we divide it
into several non-overlapping patches. These patches are then projected to patch
embeddings using a linear layer, and position embeddings are attached ahead
to encode location information. Additionally, a class token is defined to capture
the feature information of patches. Then the class token, patch embeddings,

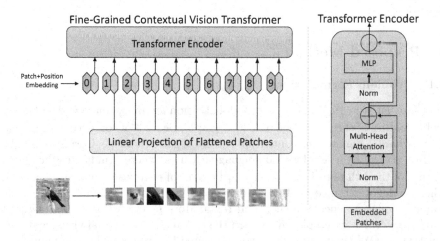

Fig. 2. Architecture of fine-grained contextual vision transformer.

and position embeddings of patches are fed into the transformer encoder. In the transformer encoder, the correlation among patches is established through self-attention, and the feature transformation is realized through the multi-layer full-connected network. Finally, the output representation corresponding to the class token is used as the global feature for the image classification task. In general, the fine-grained contextual vision transformer not only encodes the feature for each patch, but also considers the adjacency among patches.

3.3 Global-to-Contextual Shared Semantic Learning

This method first extracts global and contextual features inside intra-modality samples, and carries out joint learning. Further, this method constructs a shared semantic space, where the relevance among inter-modalities is associated.

Global-to-Contextual Vision Features Learning. The global feature can automatically localize the salient object, learning more refined object-level features, while the contextual feature selects discriminative parts of the object and captures the spatial correlation constraint among parts. The proposed method projects global-contextual features into a shared space to enhance their mutual promotion. Mathematically, the objective function can be formulated as follows:

$$\min_{\tilde{B}^v, \hat{B}^v, Z} \alpha_1 \left\| \tilde{V} - \tilde{B}^v Z \right\|_F^2 + \alpha_2 \left\| \hat{V} - \hat{B}^v Z \right\|_F^2,$$

$$s.t. \quad \|\tilde{b}_i^v\|_2 \leq 1, \quad \|\hat{b}_i^v\|_2 \leq 1, \forall i, \tag{1}$$

where $\tilde{V} \in \mathbb{R}^{j \times n}$ and $\hat{V} \in \mathbb{R}^{p \times n}$ are the sets of global and contextual vision features, j, p are the dimensions of global and contextual vision features and n is the number of samples. $\tilde{B}^v \in \mathbb{R}^{j \times k}$ and $\hat{B}^v \in \mathbb{R}^{p \times k}$ are the bases in global and contextual feature spaces, where k is the dimension of the shared semantic space. $Z \in \mathbb{R}^{k \times n}$ is the common representations of $\tilde{V}$ and $\hat{V}$ in the shared space. $\tilde{b}_i^v$ is the i-th column of $\tilde{B}^v$ and $\hat{b}_i^v$ is the i-th column of $\hat{B}^v$. By forcing the shared semantic features of corresponding $\tilde{V}$ and $\hat{V}$ to be same as Z, the joint learning of global-to-contextual features are achieved. α_1 and α_2 are the parameters controlling the relative importance of the global and contextual features.

Global-to-Contextual Language Features Learning. Similarly, this method projects the global and contextual features into a shared space:

$$\min_{\tilde{B}^t, \hat{B}^t, Z} \beta_1 \left\| \tilde{T} - \tilde{B}^t Z \right\|_F^2 + \beta_2 \left\| \hat{T} - \hat{B}^t Z \right\|_F^2,$$

$$s.t. \quad \|\tilde{b}_i^t\|_2 \leq 1, \quad \|\hat{b}_i^t\|_2 \leq 1, \forall i, \tag{2}$$

where $\tilde{T} \in \mathbb{R}^{j \times n}$ and $\hat{T} \in \mathbb{R}^{p \times n}$ are the sets of global and contextual language features, j, p are the dimensions of global and contextual language features and n is the number of samples. $\tilde{B}^t \in \mathbb{R}^{j \times k}$ and $\hat{B}^t \in \mathbb{R}^{p \times k}$ are the bases in global and contextual feature spaces, where k is the dimension of the shared semantic space. $Z \in \mathbb{R}^{k \times n}$ is the common representations of $\tilde{T}$ and $\hat{T}$ in the shared space.

$\tilde{b}_i^t$ is the i-th column of $\tilde{B}^t$ and $\hat{b}_i^t$ is the i-th column of $\hat{B}^t$. By forcing the shared semantic features of corresponding $\tilde{T}$ and $\hat{T}$ to be same as Z, the joint learning of global and contextual features are achieved. β_1 and β_2 are the parameters controlling the relative importance of the global and contextual features.

Shared Semantic Learning. Due to images and texts being heterogeneous, shared semantic learning is vital to realizing vision-language alignment. This method constructs a common semantic space, where the cross-modal association can be established. In particular, this method introduces the discriminative property to make the semantic space comparable to the fine-grained setting:

$$\min_{\tilde{B}^v,\hat{B}^v,\tilde{B}^t,\hat{B}^t,Z,U} \alpha_1 \left\| \tilde{V} - \tilde{B}^v Z \right\|_F^2 + \alpha_2 \left\| \hat{V} - \hat{B}^v Z \right\|_F^2$$

$$+ \beta_1 \left\| \tilde{T} - \tilde{B}^t Z \right\|_F^2 + \beta_2 \left\| \hat{T} - \hat{B}^t Z \right\|_F^2 + \| H - UZ \|_F^2, \tag{3}$$

$$s.t. \quad \|\tilde{b}_i^v\|_2 \leq 1, \quad \|\hat{b}_i^v\|_2 \leq 1, \quad \|\tilde{b}_i^t\|_2 \leq 1, \quad \|\hat{b}_i^t\|_2 \leq 1,$$
$$\|u_i\|_2 \leq 1, \forall i,$$

where $H = [h_1, h_2, ..., h_{n_s}] \in R^{c_s \times n}$ are the class labels of samples and c_s is the class numbers. $h_i = [0\,0...1...0\,0]$ is a one-hot label vector corresponding to sample x_i, where the non-zero entry indicates the class of x_i. U can be viewed as classifiers in the semantic space. With such formulation, the fifth term in Eq. (3) aims to make the semantic space discriminative enough to classify different classes. It implicitly pulls samples from the same class together and pushes those from different classes away from each other.

Optimization. This method adopts the alternating optimization [6] to solve the closed solution, which initializes all variables to be solved and optimizes them as follows:

(1) Fix $\tilde{B}^v, \hat{B}^v, \tilde{B}^t, \hat{B}^t, U$ and update Z by Eq. (3). Forcing the derivative of Eq. (3) to be 0 and the closed-form solution for Z is

$$Z = (\mathcal{B}^T \mathcal{B})^{-1} \mathcal{B}^T \mathcal{X}, \tag{4}$$

where

$$\mathcal{X} = \begin{bmatrix} \alpha_1 \tilde{V} \\ \alpha_2 \hat{V} \\ \beta_1 \tilde{T} \\ \beta_2 \hat{T} \\ H \end{bmatrix}, \mathcal{B} = \begin{bmatrix} \alpha_1 \tilde{B}^v \\ \alpha_2 \hat{B}^v \\ \beta_1 \tilde{B}^t \\ \beta_2 \hat{B}^t \\ U \end{bmatrix}.$$

(2) Fix Z and update $\tilde{B}^v$. The subproblem is formulated:

$$\min_{\tilde{B}^v} \left\| \tilde{V} - \tilde{B}^v Z \right\|_F^2 \quad s.t. \quad \|\tilde{b}_i^v\|_2 \leq 1, \forall i. \tag{5}$$

This problem can be optimized by the Lagrange dual [8]. Thus the analytical solution for Eq. (5) is

$$\tilde{B}^v = (\tilde{V} Z^T)(Z Z^T + \Lambda)^{-1}, \tag{6}$$

where Λ is a diagonal matrix constructed by all the Lagrange dual variables.
(3) Fix Z and update $\hat{B}^v$. The subproblem is formulated:

$$\min_{\hat{B}^v} \left\| \hat{V} - \hat{B}^v Z \right\|_F^2 \quad s.t. \quad \|\hat{b}_i^v\|_2 \le 1, \forall i. \tag{7}$$

Similarly,

$$\hat{B}^v = (\hat{V} Z^T)(Z Z^T + \Lambda)^{-1}. \tag{8}$$

(4) Fix Z and update $\tilde{B}^t$. The subproblem is formulated:

$$\min_{\tilde{B}^t} \left\| \tilde{T} - \tilde{B}^t Z \right\|_F^2 \quad s.t. \quad \|\tilde{b}_i^t\|_2 \le 1, \forall i. \tag{9}$$

Similarly,

$$\tilde{B}^t = (\tilde{T} Z^T)(Z Z^T + \Lambda)^{-1}. \tag{10}$$

(5) Fix Z and update $\hat{B}^v$. The subproblem is formulated:

$$\min_{\hat{B}^t} \left\| \hat{T} - \hat{B}^t Z \right\|_F^2 \quad s.t. \quad \|\hat{b}_i^t\|_2 \le 1, \forall i. \tag{11}$$

Similarly,

$$\hat{B}^t = (\hat{T} Z^T)(Z Z^T + \Lambda)^{-1}. \tag{12}$$

(6) Fix Z and update U. The subproblem is formulated:

$$\min_U \|H - U Z\|_F^2 \quad s.t. \quad \|u_i\|_2 \le 1, \forall i. \tag{13}$$

Similarly,

$$U = (H Z^T)(Z Z^T + \Lambda)^{-1}. \tag{14}$$

The complete process is summarized in Algorithm 1.

Algorithm 1. Shared semantic learning

Input: Global vision features($\tilde{V}$), Contextual vision features($\hat{V}$), Global language
features($\tilde{T}$), Contextual language features($\hat{T}$), Label matrix(H).

Output: Global vision feature space base($\tilde{B}^v$), Contextual vision feature space
base($\hat{B}^v$), Global language feature space base($\tilde{B}^t$), Contextual language feature
space base($\hat{B}^t$), and Shared semantic space features(Z).

1: Initialize $\tilde{B}^v, \hat{B}^v, \tilde{B}^t, \hat{B}^t, U$ randomly.
2: **while** *not converge* **do**
3:      Update Z by Eq. 4.
4:      Update $\tilde{B}^v$ by Eq. 6.
5:      Update $\hat{B}^v$ by Eq. 8.
6:      Update $\tilde{B}^t$ by Eq. 10.
7:      Update $\hat{B}^t$ by Eq. 12.
8:      Update U by Eq. 14.
9: **end while**

3.4   Cross-Modal Retrieval

In the retrieval phase (images query versus texts gallery), this method uses
VggNet and Transformer to learn global and contextual features, and maps them
into the semantic space:

$$Z_q^* = \arg\min_{Z_q} \alpha_1 \left\| \tilde{V}_q - \tilde{B}^v Z_q \right\|_F^2 + \alpha_2 \left\| \hat{V}_q - \hat{B}^v Z_q \right\|_F^2 + \|Z_q\|_F^2 , \qquad (15)$$

where $\tilde{V}_q$ and $\hat{V}_q$ represent the global and contextual features of query images,
respectively, and Z_q is the corresponding features in the semantic space. Nextly,
we project the gallery texts into the latent feature space by Eq. (16)

$$Z_g^* = \arg\min_{Z_g} \beta_1 \left\| \tilde{T}_g - \tilde{B}^t Z_g \right\|_F^2 + \beta_2 \left\| \hat{T}_g - \hat{B}^t Z_g \right\|_F^2 + \|Z_g\|_F^2 , \qquad (16)$$

where $\tilde{T}_g$ and $\hat{T}_g$ represent the global and contextual features of gallery texts,
and Z_g is the corresponding features in the semantic space. Then this method
employs cosine distance to measure the similarities between Z_q^* and Z_g^*, and
returns the candidates based on the maximum similarity. A similar way can be
conducted for texts query versus images gallery.

4   Experiment

4.1   Experimental Settings

Data Sources. The proposed method is experimented into two tasks:
subcategory-specific and instance-specific. The data sources are summarized as
follows:

- Data source 1: [14] contains 11,788 images of 200 subcategories, 5,994 for
  training and 5,794 for testing.

- Data source 2: [17] contains 8,000 texts of 200 subcategories, 4,000 for training and 4,000 for testing, which describe the subcategory information, such as habitat, eating habit, and background.
- Data source 3: [12] expands the [14] by collecting descriptions. It follows the division settings of [14], containing 11,788 texts of 200 subcategories, 5,994 for training and 5,794 for testing. In each text, 10 single sentence visual descriptions are collected, which depict the appearance information of each instance, such as color and shape.

Task Description. Based on the granularity of descriptions, we divide fine-grained image-text retrieval into two tasks, that is, subcategory-specific and instance-specific. To the best of our knowledge, the instance-specific task is the first proposed in this method. In the former, [14] + [17] are used. In the latter, [14] + [12] are employed. Compared with the subcategory-specific task, the instance-specific task contains more variations and details. Thus the instance-specific task is more suitable for fine-grained cross-domain retrieval.

Evaluation Metrics and Implementation Details. We adopt the mean Average Precision (mAP) as the evaluation metrics. Specifically, we firstly calculate average precision (AP) score for each query, and then calculate their mean value as mAP score. Moreover, all experiments are conducted on a 64-bit Ubuntu 16.04 with 2 Intel 2.40 GHz CPUs, 256 GB memory, and 6 NVIDIA Tesla GPUs.

4.2   Comparisons with State-of-the-Art Methods

In order to better validate and evaluate the proposed method, we conducted comparative experiments on subcategory-specific and instance-specific tasks.

Comparison on the Subcategory-Specific Task. We compare with state-of-the-art methods, including seven coarse-grained methods [5,7,9–11,15, 18] and two fine-grained methods [17,19], as shown in Table 2. The experimental performance of the proposed method exceeds that of all the above methods. This is because the subcategory-specific task focuses on capturing the characteristics of the object itself and the relationship between the object and the environment. While coarse-grained methods are suitable for localizing the saliency object, but ignore the capture of contextual details in fine-grained scenes. In addition, fine-grained methods focus on capturing detailed information and ignore the differences between objects, which draw further apart the inherent characteristic of the slight inter-class distinction and the large intra-class variance of fine-grained subclasses. The proposed global-contextual method can effectively compensate for the shortcomings of both above methods.

Comparison on the Instance-Specific Task. We compare our method with two fine-grained methods [17,19]. Tracing back to the source, FGCrossNet [17] simply and roughly utilizes the full-connected layer to force dimensional alignment of features from different modalities, neglecting to make the alignment space more semantically relevant. In comparison, DLSL [19] proposes an idea of discriminative hidden space alignment, and enhances its discrimination and recognition by adding the discriminative attribute to the hidden space. It

Table 2. The mAP scores comparison on the subcategory-specific task.

Method	Img-to-Txt	Txt-to-Img	Avg
MHTN [7]	0.116	0.124	0.120
ACMR [15]	0.162	0.075	0.119
JRL [18]	0.160	0.190	0.175
GSPH [10]	0.140	0.179	0.160
CMDN [11]	0.099	0.123	0.111
SCA [9]	0.050	0.050	0.050
GXN [5]	0.023	0.035	0.029
FGCrossNet [17]	0.210	0.255	0.233
DLSL [19]	0.318	0.319	0.319
The proposed method	**0.395**	**0.367**	**0.381**

Table 3. The mAP scores comparison on the instance-specific task.

Method	Img-to-Txt	Txt-to-Img	Avg
FGCrossNet [17]	0.328	0.346	0.337
DLSL [19]	0.341	0.349	0.345
The proposed method	**0.412**	**0.376**	**0.394**

Table 4. Ablation studies of features effectiveness on the subcategory-specific task (mAP scores).

Feature	Img-to-Txt	Txt-to-Img	Avg
VggNet+BOW	0.310	0.322	0.316
VggNet+Bert	0.316	0.324	0.320
Transformer+BOW	0.321	0.319	0.320
Transformer+Bert	0.324	0.325	0.325
VggNet+Bert+BOW	0.323	0.324	0.324
Transformer+Bert+BOW	0.382	0.337	0.360
Transformer+VggNet+BOW	0.380	0.336	0.358
Transformer+VggNet+Bert	0.391	0.352	0.372
Ours(Transformer+VggNet+Bert+BOW)	**0.395**	**0.367**	**0.381**

can accurately capture subtle differences between different subclasses. The comparisons of our method against the others are shown in Table 3. On the one hand, our method learns global-contextual features containing multi-view and multi-scale representation. Besides, a shared semantic space is constructed through multiple bases, enhancing the semantic correlation and discriminability between heterogeneous data.

Table 5. Ablation studies of features effectiveness on the instance-specific task (mAP scores).

Feature	Img-to-Txt	Txt-to-Img	Avg
VggNet+BOW	0.329	0.338	0.334
VggNet+Bert	0.332	0.357	0.345
Transformer+BOW	0.345	0.354	0.350
Transformer+Bert	0.352	0.361	0.357
VggNet+Bert+BOW	0.349	0.355	0.352
Transformer+Bert+BOW	0.373	0.368	0.371
Transformer+VggNet+BOW	0.362	0.362	0.362
Transformer+VggNet+Bert	0.407	0.364	0.386
Ours(Transformer+VggNet+Bert+BOW)	**0.412**	**0.376**	**0.394**

Table 6. Ablation studies of the shared semantic learning on the subcategory-specific task (mAP scores).

Alignment	Img-to-Txt	Txt-to-Img	Avg
Features Concentrate	0.310	0.324	0.317
Ours(Shared Semantic Learning)	**0.395**	**0.367**	**0.381**

Table 7. Ablation studies of the shared semantic learning on the instance-specific task (mAP scores).

Alignment	Img-to-Txt	Txt-to-Img	Avg
Features Concentrate	0.346	0.352	0.349
Ours(Shared Semantic Learning)	**0.412**	**0.376**	**0.394**

4.3   Ablation Studies

To comprehensively analyze our method, Table 4, Table 5, Table 6 and Table 7 provide a detailed ablation analysis of the key components of our method. It highlights the importance of global-to-contextual features effectiveness and shared semantic learning block. Experiments demonstrate the proposed method provides progressive improvements over the baseline.

4.4   Hyper-parameter Analysis

Figure 3 shows the hyper-parameter analysis on two tasks. α_1, α_2, β_1 and β_2 are the parameters controlling the relative importance of the global-contextual vision and language features. The best values for α_1, α_2, β_1 and β_2 are chosen by five-fold cross-validation, and the scope of them are set in [0.001, 0.01, 0.1, 1, 10]. In experiments, we set α_1 as 0.1, α_2 as 1, β_1 as 0.1 and β_2 as 1.

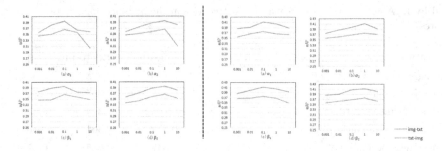

Fig. 3. Hyper-parameters on subcategory-specific and instance-specific tasks.

5   Conclusion

This paper proposes global-to-contextual shared semantic learning for fine-grained vision-language alignment. Specifically, this method extracts global and contextual features of images and texts, respectively, and carries out joint learning to enhance the discrimination of features. Further, this method constructs a shared semantic space to enhance the heterogeneous semantic correlation. Comprehensive experiments demonstrate the effectiveness of this method.

Acknowledgment. This work is supported by the science and technology program of State grid Corporation of China (5108-202218280A-2-234-XG), which is 'Research on Power Hyper-converged Intelligent Computing and Platform Acceleration Technology'.

References

1. Chen, S., Zhao, Y., Jin, Q., Wu, Q.: Fine-grained video-text retrieval with hierarchical graph reasoning. In: CVPR, pp. 10635–10644 (2020)
2. Devlin, J., Chang, M.W., Lee, K., Toutanova, K.: BERT: pre-training of deep bidirectional transformers for language understanding. ArXiv abs/1810.04805 (2019)
3. Dosovitskiy, A., et al.: An image is worth 10x10 words. transformers for image recognition at scale. In: International Conference on Learning Representations abs/2010.11929 (2020)
4. Fei-Fei, L., Fergus, R., Perona, P.: Learning generative visual models from few training examples: an incremental Bayesian approach tested on 101 object categories. In: CVPR Workshop, p. 178 (2004)
5. Gu, J., Cai, J., Joty, S.R., Niu, L., Wang, G.: Look, imagine and match: improving textual-visual cross-modal retrieval with generative models. In: CVPR, pp. 7181–7189 (2018)
6. Hadfield, S., Wang, Z., Bryan O'Gorman, B., Rieffel, E.G., Venturelli, D., Biswas, R.: From the quantum approximate optimization algorithm to a quantum alternating operator ansatz. Algorithms **12**(2) (2019)
7. Huang, X., Peng, Y., Yuan, M.: MHTN: modal-adversarial hybrid transfer network for cross-modal retrieval. IEEE Trans. Cybern. **50**, 1047–1059 (2017)
8. Joo, J.Y., Ilić, M.: Multi-layered optimization of demand resources using Lagrange dual decomposition. IEEE Trans. Smart Grid **4**, 2081–2088 (2013)

9. Lee, K.H., Chen, X.D., Hua, G., Hu, H., He, X.: Stacked cross attention for image-text matching. ArXiv abs/1803.08024 (2018)
10. Mandal, D., Chaudhury, K.N., Biswas, S.: Generalized semantic preserving hashing for N-label cross-modal retrieval. In: CVPR, pp. 2633–2641 (2017)
11. Peng, Y., Huang, X., Qi, J.: Cross-media shared representation by hierarchical learning with multiple deep networks. In: IJCAI, pp. 3846–3853 (2016)
12. Reed, S., Akata, Z., Lee, H., Schiele, B.: Learning deep representations of fine-grained visual descriptions. In: CVPR, pp. 49–58 (2016)
13. Simonyan, K., Zisserman, A.: Very deep convolutional networks for large-scale image recognition. In: ICLR, pp. 1–14 (2015)
14. Wah, C., Branson, S., Welinder, P., Perona, P., Belongie, S.: The caltech-UCSD birds-200-2011 dataset. Technical report (2011)
15. Wang, B., Yang, Y., Xu, X., Hanjalic, A., Shen, H.T.: Adversarial cross-modal retrieval. In: ACM International Conference on Multimedia, pp. 154–162 (2017)
16. Wu, P., He, X., Tang, M., Lv, Y., Liu, J.: HANet: hierarchical alignment networks for video-text retrieval. In: ACM MM (2021)
17. He, X., Peng, Y., Xie, L.: A new benchmark and approach for fine-grained cross-media retrieva. In: ACM International Conference on Multimedia, pp. 1740–1748 (2019)
18. Zhai, X., Peng, Y., Xiao, J.: Learning cross-media joint representation with sparse and semisupervised regularization. IEEE TCSVT **24**, 965–978 (2014)
19. Zheng, M., Wang, W., Li, Q.: Fine-grained image-text retrieval via discriminative latent space learning. IEEE Signal Process. Lett. **28**, 643–647 (2021)

Gradient-Based Learning of Finite Automata

Juan Fdez. del Pozo Romero$^{(\boxtimes)}$ and Luis F. Lago-Fernández

Departamento de Ingeniería Informática,
Universidad Autónoma de Madrid, Madrid, Spain
juan.fernandezdelpozo@estudiante.uam.es, luis.lago@uam.es

Abstract. The inference of regular grammars from recurrent neural networks has usually been a process that is performed after the network has been trained. In this work, we propose two implementations of a recurrent neural network that model the behavior of weighted finite automata. These models are trained through automatic differentiation in order to learn the Tomita grammars, and regularization techniques are explored to ensure determinism. The learned automata are interpretable from the model weights, requiring little to no transformation to be obtained. This brings closer the training and inference phases, thus optimizing the learning process.

Keywords: Weighted Finite Automata · Recurrent Neural Network · Grammatical Inference

1 Introduction

The relationship between recurrent neural networks (RNNs) and finite automata has been a matter of research over quite some time. The oldest reference may be from the original work of McCulloch & Pitts [1], where it was stated that threshold-activated neurons could resemble finite automata. Some years passed before Pollack argued that his *Neuring machine* was Turing universal [2]. The model was a recurrent net, conformed by a finite number of neurons, with threshold and identity activation functions. It was later proved by Kilian & Siegelmann that sigmoidal neurons may also simulate finite automata and Turing machines [3].

But the specific relationship regarding RNNs began after Elman introduced the Simple Recurrent Network (SRN) [4]. Cleeremans et al. studied the relation between this SRN and finite automata [5]. They showed that it could learn to process an infinite number of strings based on a finite set of training examples. It was not long before higher order RNNs were also studied in relation to automata. It was proved that if the neural net was sufficiently trained, the extracted automaton could become a true finite state automaton, by reducing it to the minimal machine of the inferred grammar [6,7]. The approach in [8] suggested that the RNN could be seen as a state machine, its state units and

L. Iliadis et al. (Eds.): ICANN 2023, LNCS 14261, pp. 294–305, 2023.
https://doi.org/10.1007/978-3-031-44198-1_25

weight activations representing the generating automaton. Once the RNN was trained, the automaton could be constructed by determining arcs in its transition diagram, eliminating non-determinism and minimizing states.

Many works have also used external memory modules within a recurrent network, such as stacks, lists or matrices [9]. In the last years, a differentiable Neural Turing Machine was developed by coupling an external memory to a neural network [10].

Another relevant field is Grammatical Inference, a branch of machine learning closely related to Inductive Inference, that aims to represent language, trees, graphs and other structured objects formally. The field was initially dedicated to learning finite state machines, but the interest has extended to context-free grammars and other formalisms over the last decades. Some important algorithms that where originally used to train deterministic finite automata (DFA) were GOLD [11] and RPNI [12]. However, for the sake of this work, we will only review learning techniques related to probabilistic finite automata (PFA), which have a close definition to weighted finite automata (WFA).

In this context, many authors have studied the extraction of a PFA by state merging [13–16] in RNNs. The states may first be obtained by artificially quantizing the RNN activations into a discrete, more interpretable set of states. The first algorithms that did this were ALERGIA [17] and DSAI [18]. Each of them applied different criteria regarding the equivalence of two states in an automaton. Nonetheless, one thing that they had in common was the use of state merging (Stochastic Merge) and folding (Stochastic Fold). Other state merging algorithms considered approaches such as computing distances between two distributions, or applying some sort of heuristic like Minimum Divergence Inference (MDI) [19].

Besides state merging, we can find automata extraction techniques like Angluin's L* algorithm [20] or the KV algorithm by Kearns & Vazirani [21], where the trained RNN is queried to obtain the automaton. A modern variant of the L* algorithm can be found in spectral learning [22,23]. Finally, some more recent approaches have achieved great RNN interpretability, thus simplifying the automaton extraction after the network has been trained. It has been proved that the RNN can directly learn an automaton by applying state regularization [24], or introducing stochastic noise in the activation function [25].

In this work, we propose to involve these previous topics and learn an automaton, more precisely a deterministic WFA, with gradient-based learning. The main and novel idea, is to set the automaton as a RNN, and explore automatic differentiation tools to learn the transition probabilities, which act as network weights. WFA learning through automatic differentiation brings closer the training and inference stages. If we implicitly force the RNN to implement an automaton, the model extraction phase is minimized, if not even omitted. This optimizes the learning process and simplifies the software involved, allowing for easier experimentation. We test our model with the well-known Tomita grammars [26], and show that the inferred WFA are in all cases correct and generalize well to new strings. Moreover, regularizing the transition probabilities leads to determinism and interpretability, with the learned automata being always equivalent to the grammars used for generating the training data.

In the following sections we first review the concept of WFA, and describe our model designs. After that, we explain the methodology and typology of the experiments, followed by the obtained results and a final discussion.

2   Weighted Finite Automata

The notion of a WFA can be explained by first stating what a DFA is. A DFA is a mathematical model that performs a deterministic set of actions as a response to processing some input sequence or string. More formally, a basic DFA can be described by the tuple

$$A = (Q, \Sigma, I, F, E), \tag{1}$$

where Q is a finite set of states, Σ is the input alphabet, $I \in Q$ is the initial state, $F \subseteq Q$ is the set of final states, and $E \subseteq Q \times \Sigma \times Q$ is a finite set of transitions between states. The automaton will perform certain transitions as it goes over a sequence of symbols belonging to the input alphabet, and this process will determine whether or not that sequence belongs to the automaton's language. We will say that a string is accepted if processing it defines an accepting path, which is a sequence of arcs between states that starts at the initial state and ends at any final state. Otherwise we say the string is rejected. The set of all strings accepted by a DFA is called the automaton's language. Thus, these automata are also called acceptors.

WFA are a generalization of DFA that incorporate weights in their transitions [27]. The weights may be probabilities, costs, durations, or any other quantity that may be accumulated when processing an input sequence. This allows the WFA not only to decide whether a string is accepted or not, but also to quantify this decision by means of resources, time, cost, or probability. WFA are closely related to PFA, as mentioned previously, and one can find them in speech processing, natural language processing and optical character recognition [28, 29].

3   Model

We design two equivalent models that implement the WFA as a RNN. The first one considers the weights as probabilities, and the second one as logarithms of probabilities (logprobs).

3.1   Basic Model

Consider the WFA given by

$$A = (Q, \Sigma, I, F, \mathbf{W}), \tag{2}$$

where $\mathbf{W}$ is a $|\Sigma| \times |Q| \times |Q|$ weight tensor that fully determines the automaton's transitions and their associated weights. Let w_{ij}^k represent the components of

$\mathbf{W}$, with $k \in \{1, 2, ..., |\Sigma|\}$ and $i, j \in \{1, 2, ..., |Q|\}$. Then the transition between automaton states q_i and q_j ($q_i, q_j \in Q$) in response to input symbol a_k ($a_k \in \Sigma$) is mediated by the probability p_{ij}^k, which is obtained by applying a *softmax* operation across the third dimension of $\mathbf{W}$:

$$p_{ij}^k = \frac{e^{w_{ij}^k}}{\sum_{j=1}^{|Q|} e^{w_{ij}^k}}. \tag{3}$$

Hence, assuming that at a given time t the automaton lies in the mixture of states $\mathbf{s} = (s_1, s_2, ..., s_{|Q|})$, where $\sum_{i=1}^{|Q|} s_i = 1$, then the next state, after processing the input symbol a_k, will be given by

$$\mathbf{s}' = \mathbf{s}\mathbf{P}^k, \tag{4}$$

where $\mathbf{P}^k$ is a matrix whose elements are the transition probabilities associated to symbol a_k, $(\mathbf{P}^k)_{ij} = p_{ij}^k$. We model this behavior as a RNN module. The input at time t is the one-hot encoded vector $\mathbf{x}^{(t)} = (x_1^{(t)}, x_2^{(t)}, ..., x_{|\Sigma|}^{(t)})$. This vector determines the state transition probabilities by

$$\mathbf{P}^{(t)} = \sum_{k=1}^{|\Sigma|} x_k^{(t)} \sigma(\mathbf{W}^k), \tag{5}$$

where σ is the *softmax* function in Eq. 3 and $\mathbf{W}^k$ is a matrix whose components are $(\mathbf{W}^k)_{ij} = w_{ij}^k$. Given the state probabilities at time t, $\mathbf{s}^{(t)}$, the next state probabilities are then:

$$\mathbf{s}^{(t+1)} = \sum_{k=1}^{|\Sigma|} x_k^{(t)} \mathbf{s}^{(t)} \sigma(\mathbf{W}^k). \tag{6}$$

Finally, the model output for time t is the sum of the state probabilities for all the final states:

$$y^{(t)} = \sum_{i=1}^{|Q|} f_i s_i^{(t)}, \tag{7}$$

where f_i is a binary variable indicating whether or not the state q_i is final. This output represents the acceptance probability that the model assigns to the input string, and can be used to define a cross-entropy loss when taking into account the expected output. Since all the operations in Eqs. 6 and 7 are differentiable, the model weights can be trained using standard gradient descent techniques in order to minimize this cross-entropy loss.

3.2   LSE Model

In a second version of the model we use log-probabilities in order to avoid repeated multiplications by the probability matrices $\mathbf{P}^{(t)}$. Let $\mathbf{L}^{(t)}$ be the logarithm of the transition probability matrix at time t:

$$\mathbf{L}^{(t)} = \log \mathbf{P}^{(t)}. \tag{8}$$

The matrix $\mathbf{L}^{(t)}$ can be directly obtained from the weight matrices as:

$$\mathbf{L}^{(t)} = \sum_{k=1}^{|\Sigma|} x_k^{(t)} \log \sigma(\mathbf{W}^k). \tag{9}$$

Note that the components of $\mathbf{L}^{(t)}$ can also be expressed as:

$$(\mathbf{L}^{(t)})_{ij} = \sum_{k=1}^{|\Sigma|} x_k^{(t)} (w_{ij}^k - \log \sum_{j=1}^{|Q|} e^{w_{ij}^k}), \tag{10}$$

where the last operation is known as *log-sum-exp* (LSE):

$$LSE(\mathbf{W}^k)_i = \log \sum_{j=1}^{|Q|} e^{w_{ij}^k}. \tag{11}$$

We also consider log-probabilities for the vector representing the mixture of states:

$$\mathbf{l} = (l_1, l_2, ..., l_{|Q|}) = (\log s_1, \log s_2, ..., \log s_{|Q|}). \tag{12}$$

Now, the equation that relates the current and the next state vectors, given the transition matrix $\mathbf{L}^{(t)}$, is:

$$l_j^{(t+1)} = \log \sum_{i=1}^{|Q|} e^{\mathbf{L}_{ij}^{(t)} + l_i^{(t)}}. \tag{13}$$

Finally, the model output is computed, as before, as the sum of probabilities over all the final states:

$$y^{(t)} = \sum_{i=1}^{|Q|} f_i e^{l_i^{(t)}}. \tag{14}$$

The two models are equivalent, but the LSE version has the advantage of avoiding repeated multiplications by the probability matrices, which may avoid stability problems when calculating the gradients.

4   Experiments

4.1   Tomita Grammars

Being WFA a generalization of unweighted automata, they have equal or greater representational power. We will develop our experiments with Type 3 grammars, according to Noam Chomsky's Hierarchy. These are known as regular grammars, and one specific set denoted as Tomita grammars [26] has been widely accepted in the grammatical inference field [15].

The set is composed of seven regular languages on a binary alphabet of symbols $\{a, b\}$, whose descriptions can be found in Table 1. The datasets used in the training and test phases have been generated as described in [30], where the symbol $ represents the start of a string. Therefore, the input alphabet is not exactly binary, but rather $\{a, b, \$\}$. The output data is also a sequence of binary labels that indicate, at each time step, whether the string belongs or not to the language.

Table 1. Definition of the seven Tomita grammars

Name	Description
Tomita 1	Strings with only a's
Tomita 2	Strings with only sequences of ab's
Tomita 3	Strings with no odd number of consecutive b's after an odd number of consecutive a's
Tomita 4	Strings with fewer than 3 consecutive b's
Tomita 5	Strings with even length with an even number of a's
Tomita 6	Strings where the difference between the number of a's and b's is a multiple of 3
Tomita 7	Strings generated by the regular expression $b^*a^*b^*a^*$

4.2   Model Training and Evaluation

The training and test phases used these Tomita datasets, splitting them in batches of 32 sequences and length 25. The models were trained with a number of states in the range $[2, 64]$. The final states of each model were generated randomly, with a probability of 0.6, ensuring that at least one final state was defined for each configuration. We consider that both model implementations start with all of the probability on a single initial state q_0. Regarding the model weights initialization, a random uniform distribution was used. Once built, the model was trained by minimizing a *binary cross-entropy* loss using a *Nadam* optimizer, for a maximum of 500 epochs. The model accuracy was binarized with the probability threshold set at 0.5. Finally, the test set was also used during training as a validation set, so that *early stopping* could be applied.

5   Results

In Fig. 1 we show the results of extensive training with the Tomita grammars. It displays barplots of the average model accuracy over 10 executions, for different number of states, obtained with each of the two WFA implementations. The number of states in the automata was increased for each of the implementations, up to a sufficiently large number of 64.

Let us first observe Fig. 1a for the basic WFA model. The results are not consistent on average, even for very simple grammars like Tomita 1. However, for some executions the model is able to achieve perfect accuracy on every grammar but Tomita 5, for which it scores a global maximum of 0.86. We can also observe that the model hardly scores when the number of states grows very big: some of the trained models accuracies stack on a single value.

This does not happen with the LSE implementation, shown in Fig. 1b. At first glance we can notice that simpler grammars like Tomita 1 or Tomita 2, train well with fewer number of states. This is because the minimal automaton needs less states for them (around 2 or 3), and the randomly generated final states are always sufficient, allowing the automata to discriminate those not needed. For higher number of states, we can notice a decrease in the error bar range, meaning that the results are more consistent on average. The model always manages to learn a suitable configuration of states and weights for every grammar, even the hardest ones like Tomita 7. Specifically, with 32 states all grammars are successfully learned.

The LSE implementation is able to achieve better results, and we will execute the remaining experiments with it, leaving the first model behind. Also, a state size of 32 will be used, since it allows for convergence regardless of the grammar.

5.1   Generalizing Over Different Test Sets

The test set used during training in the previous section was the 'big' one, as described in [30]. A trained model was also evaluated on different test sets such as the 'long' (with fewer but longer sequences), or the 'all_a' and 'all_b' sets (with a high density for only one symbol, a or b, respectively).

The results showed that the model was able to generalize over these new datasets, averaging at a perfect accuracy on all of them for every grammar.

5.2   Determinization by Regularization

The trained models already obtain a consistent accuracy of 1, seemingly high, but only because we had set the *binary accuracy* threshold to 0.5 instead of more restrictive levels. This does not imply that the training has reached a point in which the model can be directly interpreted as a deterministic WFA. Even though most of the probability has drifted towards the desired arcs, some of the weights still remain as unwanted small probability transitions (see first row of Fig. 2 as an example for Tomita 3). This uncertainty could be desirable on higher order problems, but regular grammars are well bounded and can be translated as an automaton with deterministic transitions (unique and non-lambda for the Tomita grammars).

We have explored an entropic regularization mechanism on the transition probabilities, that makes the transitions more deterministic by adding the following entropy penalization term to the loss function:

$$R = -\lambda \sum_{k=1}^{|\Sigma|} \sum_{i,j=1}^{|Q|} p_{ij}^k \log p_{ij}^k, \tag{15}$$

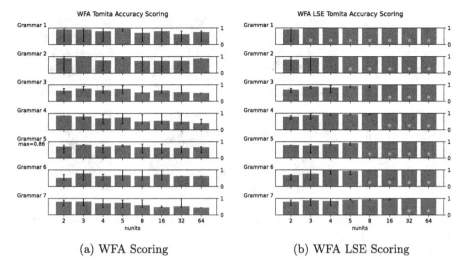

(a) WFA Scoring   (b) WFA LSE Scoring

Fig. 1. Extensive training with the Tomita grammars. Each barplot corresponds to the accuracy on the test set (Y axis), averaged over 10 executions. The error bars indicate the maximum and minimum accuracy obtained for every configuration (X axis). The yellow star indicates that all the executions achieved perfect accuracy. (Color figure online)

where λ is a parameter that controls the regularization strength. If we recall Eq. 3, the transition probabilities are obtained by applying a *softmax* transformation to the weights. This operation is sensitive to addition when the input values are small, and adding a constant to every value will output a smoother probability distribution. These blurred probabilities are not beneficial as they accumulate error in unwanted states of the automaton. Thus, the network is forced to minimize the overall entropy so that the transition probabilities are more skewed.

The results of applying this regularizer on the weights can be seen in the second row of Fig. 2. On *Epoch 1* we can observe the starting probabilities, initialized as mentioned in Sect. 4.2. At *Epoch 80*, both models already score an accuracy of 1, both on the training and test sets. We can see how the weight matrices have structured themselves according to the grammar, but some smaller weights still remain. At *Epoch 200*, the upper matrix has reached a configuration from which it will barely change, whereas the lower matrix keeps on regularizing and lowering the entropy. Finally, if we stretch the training as far as *Epoch 410* (in this case), the desired effect is reached. All the weights have condensed as one per state (row), meaning each input symbol will only be assigned a transition at any state.

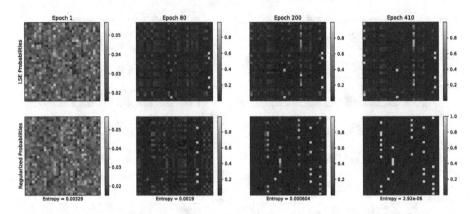

Fig. 2. Entropy Regularization Mechanism. The LSE model was trained with (bottom row) and without (top row) the regularizer. Each panel represents a colorplot of the probability matrix, for input symbol b, at a different training epoch. The model was trained with Tomita 3 and 32 states, for a maximum of 1000 epochs.

5.3 Learned Automata

Once the model had been trained as a deterministic WFA, we extracted the automaton from the model weights. All trained models did not directly correspond to the minimal Tomita automaton, so we performed minimization on each of them. In order to do this, several steps were followed:

- First, we obtained the probabilities by applying a Softmax Transformation to the weight matrices. After that, we rounded the probabilities, which were already quite close to 0 or 1.
- We also discarded $ transitions, since they just indicate the start or end of the string. Therefore, the starting state was no longer q_0 but the one reached after applying the first $ transition from it.
- We obtained the set of unreachable states with a Breadth First Search approach. Those states were later removed from the final automaton.
- Finally, we computed the **equivalent states** by applying Hopcroft's Equivalence Theorem [31]. Those states were then merged together.

The resulting automata were, in all cases, the minimal ones for the Tomita grammars (see Fig. 3).

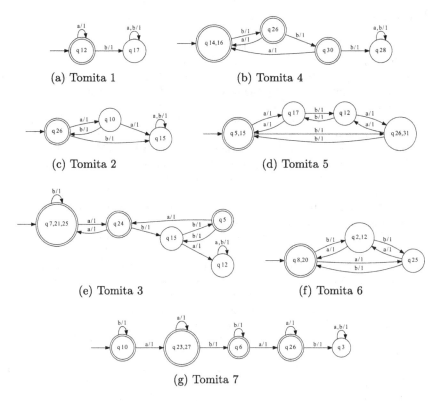

Fig. 3. Learned automata for the Tomita grammars. In each of the plots, a double circle indicates a final state. The transitions are represented as *symbol/probability*, and the lines for the sink states have been merged together (indicated with a comma: $symbol_1, symbol_2$).

6 Discussion

Extracting finite automata from RNNs has customarily been a separate process from the training phase. In this work we have shown that by making the RNN work as an automaton, it is forced to train as one. Moreover, by applying weight regularization techniques the model can learn a deterministic WFA that correctly represents a regular grammar. Determinism allows for a great generalization capability, and the ability to process long input sequences while accumulating little error. The resulting automaton is robust and fully interpretable from the model weights, and can be extracted without turning to complex methods. This effectively brings closer the training and inference phases, and optimizes the learning process.

Acknowledgments. This work has been partially funded by Spanish project PID2020-114867RB-I00, (MCIN/AEI and ERDF - "A way of making Europe"). The authors are grateful to J. Porta-Zamorano for insightful comments and suggestions.

References

1. McCulloch, W.S., Pitts, W.: A logical calculus of the ideas immanent in nervous activity. Bull. Math. Biophys. **5**(4), 115–133 (1943)
2. Pollack J.B.: On connectionist models of natural language processing. Ph.D. Dissertation, Computer Science Dept., University of Illinois, Urbana (1987)
3. Kilian, J., Siegelmann H.T.: On the power of sigmoid neural networks. In: Proceedings of the Sixth Annual Conference on Computational Learning Theory, pp. 137–143 (1993)
4. Elman, J.L.: Finding structure in time. Cogn. Sci. **14**(2), 179–211 (1990)
5. Cleeremans, A., Servan-Schreiber, D., McClelland, J.L.: Finite state automata and simple recurrent networks. Neural Comput. **1**(3), 372–381 (1989)
6. Giles, C.L., Miller, C.B., Chen, D., Chen, H.H., Sun, G.Z., Lee, Y.C.: Learning and extracting finite state automata with second-order recurrent neural networks. Neural Comput. **4**(3), 393–405 (1992)
7. Manolios, P., Fanelli, R.: First-order recurrent neural networks and deterministic finite state automata. Neural Comput. **6**(6), 1155–1173 (1994)
8. Tiño P., Horne, B.G., Giles, C.L., Collingwood, P.C.: Finite state machines and recurrent neural networks-automata and dynamical systems approaches. In: Neural Networks and Pattern Recognition, pp. 171–219. Elsevier (1998)
9. Joulin, A., Mikolov, T.: Inferring algorithmic patterns with stack-augmented recurrent nets. In: Advances in Neural Information Processing Systems, vol. 28 (2015)
10. Graves, A., Wayne, G., Danihelka I.: Neural turing machines. CoRR, abs/1410.5401 (2014)
11. Gold, E.M.: Complexity of automaton identification from given data. Inf. Control **37**(3), 302–320 (1978)
12. Oncina, J., Garcia, P.: Inferring regular languages in polynomial updated time. In: Pattern Recognition and Image Analysis: Selected Papers from the IVth Spanish Symposium, pp. 49–61. World Scientific (1992)
13. Lawrence, S., Giles, C.L., Fong, S.: Natural language grammatical inference with recurrent neural networks. IEEE Trans. Knowl. Data Eng. **12**(1), 126–140 (2000)
14. Jacobsson, H.: Rule extraction from recurrent neural networks: a taxonomy and review. Neural Comput. **17**(6), 1223–1263 (2005)
15. Wang, Q., Zhang, K., Ororbia, II A.G., Xing, X., Liu, X., Giles, C.␣: An empirical evaluation of rule extraction from recurrent neural networks. arXiv preprint: arXiv:1709.10380 (2017)
16. Cohen, M., Caciularu, A., Rejwan, I., Berant, J.: Inducing regular grammars using recurrent neural networks. arXiv preprint: arXiv:1710.10453 (2017)
17. Carrasco, R.C., Oncina, J.: Learning stochastic regular grammars by means of a state merging method. In: Carrasco, R.C., Oncina, J. (eds.) ICGI 1994. LNCS, vol. 862, pp. 139–152. Springer, Heidelberg (1994). https://doi.org/10.1007/3-540-58473-0_144
18. Ron, D., Singer, Y., Tishby N.: Learning probabilistic automata with variable memory length. In: Proceedings of the Seventh Annual Conference on Computational Learning Theory, pp. 35–46 (1994)
19. Thollard, F., Dupont, P., De La Higuera, C.: Probabilistic DFA inference using Kullback-Leibler divergence and minimality (2000)
20. Angluin, D.: Learning regular sets from queries and counterexamples. Inf. Comput. **75**(2), 87–106 (1987)

21. Kearns, M.J., Vazirani, U.: An Introduction to Computational Learning Theory. MIT Press, Cambridge (1994)
22. Ayache, S., Eyraud, R., Goudian, N.: Explaining black boxes on sequential data using weighted automata. In: International Conference on Grammatical Inference, pp. 81–103. PMLR (2019)
23. Okudono, T., Waga, M., Sekiyama, T., Hasuo, I.: Weighted automata extraction from recurrent neural networks via regression on state spaces. In: Proceedings of the AAAI Conference on Artificial Intelligence, vol. 34, pp. 5306–5314 (2020)
24. Wang, C., Niepert, M.: State-regularized recurrent neural networks. In: International Conference on Machine Learning, pp. 6596–6606. PMLR (2019)
25. Oliva, C., Lago-Fernández, L.F.: Stability of internal states in recurrent neural networks trained on regular languages. Neurocomputing **452**, 212–223 (2021)
26. Tomita, M.: Dynamic construction of finite-state automata from examples using hill-climbing. In: Proceedings of the Fourth Annual Conference of the Cognitive Science Society, pp. 105–108 (1982)
27. Mohri, M.: Weighted automata algorithms. In: Droste, M., Kuich, W., Vogler, H. (eds.) Handbook of Weighted Automata. An EATCS Series, pp. 213–254. Springer, Berlin (2009). https://doi.org/10.1007/978-3-642-01492-5_6
28. Mohri, M., Pereira, F., Riley, M.: Speech recognition with weighted finite-state transducers. In: Benesty, J., Sondhi, M.M., Huang, Y.A. (eds.) Springer Handbook of Speech Processing. SH, pp. 559–584. Springer, Heidelberg (2008). https://doi.org/10.1007/978-3-540-49127-9_28
29. Knight, K., May, J.: Applications of weighted automata in natural language processing. In: Droste, M., Kuich, W., Vogler, H. (eds.) Handbook of Weighted Automata. An EATCS Series, pp. 517–596. Springer, Berlin (2009). https://doi.org/10.1007/978-3-642-01492-5_14
30. Oliva, C., Lago-Fernández, L.F.: On the interpretation of recurrent neural networks as finite state machines. In: Tetko, I.V., Kurková, V., Karpov, P., Theis, F. (eds.) ICANN 2019. LNCS, vol. 11727, pp. 312–323. Springer, Cham (2019). https://doi.org/10.1007/978-3-030-30487-4_25
31. Hopcroft, J.E., Motwani, R., Ullman, J.D.: Introduction to automata theory, languages, and computation. ACM SIGACT News **32**(1), 60–65 (2001)

Hierarchical Contrastive Learning
for CSI-Based Fingerprint Localization

Xiangxu Meng[1], Wei Li[1,2](✉) (iD), Zheng Zhao[1], Zhihan Liu[1],
and Huiqiang Wang[1]

[1] College of Computer Science and Technology,
Harbin Engineering University, Harbin 150001, China
{mxx,zhaozheng,lzhlzh,wanghuiqiang,wei.li}@hrbeu.edu.cn
[2] Modeling and Emulation in E-Government National Engineering Laboratory,
Harbin Engineering University, Harbin 150001, China

Abstract. Fingerprint localization based on Channel State Information
(CSI) plays a crucial role in indoor location-based services. Due to the
natural compatibility between offline training and online localization of
CSI-based fingerprint localization and deep learning, recent studies have
shown that introducing the latest deep learning techniques can provide
higher localization accuracy. Most current research efforts in localization have focused on leveraging deep learning advancements to enhance
performance. However, these approaches typically rely on complex techniques and large model sizes, prioritizing model-driven methods over
practicality and real-world deployment capabilities. In this paper, we aim
to improve the localization performance of simple, general-purpose models (*e.g.*, ResNet) through data-driven training paradigms, which align
with the value proposition of real-world applications. Specifically, by constructing positive examples with different signal-to-noise ratios (SNRs)
for contrastive learning, ResNet can learn SNR-robust representations.
Furthermore, we focus on antenna instances (physical components of
CSI) at a smaller granularity to learn scale-invariant representations
through hierarchical loss. In the final location regression fine-tuning process, only a pooling layer and a fully connected layer need to be added to
perform position mapping. Experiments on real-world indoor and urban
canyon datasets demonstrate that our method achieves positioning accuracies of 0.16 m and 0.54 m, respectively, significantly outperforms state-
of-the-art baseline models.

1 Introduction

With the rapid growth of cities, indoor positioning technology is playing an
increasingly important role in real life and has many practical applications,
such as emergency evacuation [9,13] and indoor navigation [7,12]. Due to the
widespread presence of multi-frequency signal sources and reinforced concrete
structures indoors, it is difficult for GPS to provide accurate positioning services
in indoor environments. As a result, mainstream indoor positioning technologies

L. Iliadis et al. (Eds.): ICANN 2023, LNCS 14261, pp. 306–318, 2023.
https://doi.org/10.1007/978-3-031-44198-1_26

currently focus on the use of Bluetooth, WiFi, sound/ultrasonic, pseudolites and geomagnetism to obtain location information. The dominant positioning methods can be divided into geomagnetic positioning and fingerprint positioning.

Geomagnetic positioning is based on the principle of geomagnetism to measure and locate indoor locations. Indoor geomagnetic positioning is more challenging than outdoor geomagnetic positioning (*e.g.*, GPS) because indoor environments often have multiple obstacles and multipath propagation, which can affect the propagation and reception of signals and thus the positioning accuracy. Although researchers have tried various methods to improve accuracy, the results are still unsatisfactory. For example, Chen et al. [1] estimated TOA from the downlink synchronization signal block (SSB) of real 5G NR signals and proposed carrier phase ranging for indoor positioning, but its accuracy was only 0.8 m. In contrast to geomagnetic positioning, the idea behind fingerprint positioning is to use special physical measurements, such as CSI, to construct a location dataset, train it offline and match the location online. Since fingerprint positioning requires fewer base stations, it is relatively easy to deploy. A growing number of scholars have attempted to use fingerprint positioning to achieve high-precision indoor positioning. For example, Gao et al. [4] utilised an modified convolutional neural network that initially focused on extracting features from multiple channels and later interacted between different channel features, which was consistent with the physical characteristics of CSI, achieving a positioning performance with an error of 0.28 m. Ruan et al. [10] improved performance by combining the unique features of LSTM and CNN through a composite approach, achieving the best performance with an error of 0.65 m in indoor environments.

It is clear that current fingerprint positioning technology mainly follows the mainstream thinking of the deep learning community, including improving models and stacking various technologies to improve positioning accuracy. However, this approach is at odds with the practical value-focused nature of fingerprint localisation techniques. The complex techniques and large number of parameters make the technique difficult to apply in practical situations, which is undesirable in a field where practicality is valued.

In this paper, we aim to "arm" mainstream models with advanced training concepts to achieve high-precision indoor positioning. We focus on a "evergreen tree" model, ResNet [5], and propose a training paradigm based on contrastive learning to enhance positioning accuracy. Specifically, we first construct two positive inputs for contrastive learning, which are the same CSI samples at different signal-to-noise ratios. The purpose of this step is to allow the model to learn noise robustness. We then focus the loss function for learning the SNRs invariant representation at a finer granularity (the antenna instance, which is also a physical component of the CSI), and augment the scale-invariant representation by hierarchical loss aggregation. Finally, we use standard regression training to fine-tune the location prediction model (by simply adding a fully connected layer with pooling). Tests on real datasets show that our method can train simple ResNet18 or ResNet34 with high-precision positioning, which significantly outperforms cleverly designed baseline and conventional localization methods. In summary, our contribution is as follows:

1. We propose a training paradigm based on contrastive learning, which enables a simple and generic **ResNet** network to achieve significantly better localization performance than the state-of-the-art baseline.
2. We improve the model's ability to handle CSI at different signal-to-noise ratios by incrementally adding noise to construct positive sample pairs for CSI at different signal-to-noise ratios.
3. We introduce a hierarchical contrastive loss and use antenna-instance loss as a finer-grained loss, enabling the model to learn finer feature representations that are invariant to scale.
4. Experiments on real-world datasets show that our approach achieves significantly better localization performance than all baseline methods.

2   Methodology

The whole architecture of our method is shown in Fig. 1. For each input CSI sample, we encourage a consistent representation at different SNRs. During the contrastive learning phase, the encoder receives the raw input and optimizes it using the hierarchical antenna instance loss. During the fine-tune phase, the encoder receives CSI samples and is fine-tuned using MSE loss.

2.1   Physical Meaning of CSI

The CSI for each antenna and each Orthogonal Frequency Division Multiplexing (OFDM) symbol can be expressed as a column vector in a k-dimensional space:

$$H_{\mathrm{raw}} = (rxGrid)_{k \times 1}/(refGrid)_{k \times 1} \tag{1}$$

where k is the number of subcarriers and $refGrid$ denotes the known pilot. See [4] for more data descriptions.

From the Eq. 1, it can be seen that the columns of the CSI are relatively independent, as they come from different antennas.

2.2   Encoder

Our design philosophy is to create a simple and generalizable model rather than a scenario-specific model. Our encoder is a simple **ResNet** network designed for feature representation extraction. Specifically, in the case of ResNet18, it consists of three main components: a stem layer for input processing, a set of basic blocks for feature extraction and a position regression layer for position estimation. The stem layer includes a convolutional layer with kernel size 7, stride 2, padding 3 and 2D batch normalization, followed by a non-linear activation layer and a pooling layer with size 3, stride 2, padding 1, and dilation 1. We use four basic blocks, each consisting of three 2D convolutions with kernel sizes [3, 3, 1], strides [2, 1, 2] and padding [1, 1, 0]. Each convolution layer has 64 output channels and is followed by 2D batch normalization, with non-linear activation added to the first two convolution layers. The position regression layer includes an

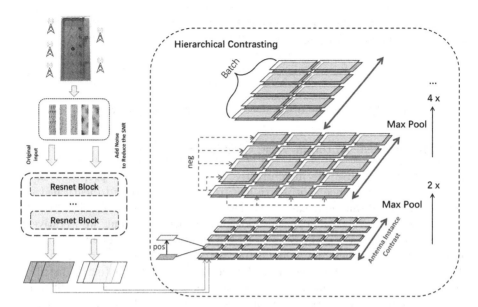

Fig. 1. An overview of the proposed approach, where CSI is extracted from the base station and sent to the Encoder (*e.g.*, a simple ResNet18) along with the noisy input and the original input. Consistency between the two different representations obtained from the encoder is encouraged. The hierarchical comparison on the right is designed to obtain scale-invariant representations by using different levels of instance loss for the antenna instances.

average pooling layer and a fully connected layer for position mapping. The average pooling layer reduces the spatial dimensionality of the feature maps to a fixed size, while the fully connected layer maps the features to position estimates. This description is consistent with the public version of ResNet18 and prioritizes generalizability over model-specific techniques.

2.3   Positive Pairs Construction

Our goal is to construct positive examples by adding noise to the original CSI input, thereby reducing the SNR of CSI and obtaining a consistent representation under different SNR conditions. By enforcing the model to learn a consistent representation between the positive examples and the original CSI samples, the robustness of.the model in different noisy environments is enhanced, allowing it to better adapt to CSI data under various SNR conditions and improving its performance in real-world applications. The probability of x_{pos} being generated from x is defined as $q(\cdot)$, then:

$$q(x_{pos}|x) := \mathcal{N}(x_{pos}; \alpha x, \beta \mathbf{I}) \tag{2}$$

where x_{pos} denotes the positive example, which is compared with x to form a positive pair, and α and β denote the constant scheme, respectively.

Due to the addition of noise, the SNR of the obtained x_{pos} is reduced compared to x. The SNR is calculated as follows:

$$N_{db} = 10 \lg \frac{P_s}{P_n} \tag{3}$$

where P_s and P_n denote the original signal and noise, respectively.

2.4 Hierarchical Antenna-Wise Contrastive Loss

Inspired by recent advances in contrastive learning [14,15]. We propose a hierarchical antenna instance contrastive loss to force the encoder to learn feature representations at different scales. The detailed steps are shown in Algorithm 1. To be precise, for the CSI representation of the encoder output, we iteratively compute the loss shown in the Eq. 4 along the dimension of the antenna instances and sum the output before dividing it by the total number of losses. This allows the encoder to gain a more fine-grained understanding of the potential distribution of CSI from the antenna instances. Hierarchical features can lead to different levels of semantics that have been widely used in various fields of the deep learning community. To our knowledge, we are the first to introduce hierarchical semantics contrastive to CSI deep learning representations.

Algorithm 1: Calculating the hierarchical antenna instance contrastive loss.

1 $HiLoss \leftarrow AiLoss(X, X')$;
2 $d \leftarrow 1$;
3 **while** *antenna_feature_length > 1* **do**
4      $// The maxpool1d operates along the antenna axis$;
5      $X \leftarrow maxpool1d(X, kernelsize = 2)$;
6      $X' \leftarrow maxpool1d(X', kernelsize = 2)$;
7      $HiLoss \leftarrow HiLoss + AiLoss(X, X')$;
8      $d \leftarrow d + 1$;
9 $HiLoss \leftarrow HiLoss/d$;
10 **return** $HiLoss$;

$$AiLoss^{(i,s)} = -\log \frac{\exp\left(r_{i,s}^a \cdot r_{i,s}^b\right)}{\sum_{j=1}^{B} \left(\exp(r_{i,s} \cdot r'_{j,s}) + \mathbb{1}[i \neq j] \exp(r_{i,s} \cdot r_{j,s})\right)} \tag{4}$$

where B represents the batch size, i and j denote the index of the input CSI samples, s represents the index of antenna feature representations, and $\mathbb{1}$ represents the indicator function. As can be seen from the composition of the denominator, we utilize feature representations of other CSI samples with the same antenna index within the same batch as negative samples.

2.5 Fine-Tune in Position Regression

The purpose of contrastive learning is to enable the encoder to learn a CSI feature representation that is invariant to different SNRs, which is "universal" and can be used for other downstream tasks besides location estimation, such as SNR ratio estimation or other practical tasks (requiring only modifications to the fully connected layer). In this paper, we focus on positioning, so in this section, we describe the fine-tuning process of position regression. Defining the model trained by contrastive learning as $model_c$, the loss of position regression is as follows:

$$Loss = \text{MSE}(model_c(X), Y) \tag{5}$$

where Y represents the actual position and MSE represents the mean square error loss function.

3 Experiments

3.1 Datasets and Evaluation Metrics

We validate our approach using datasets that were measured in real-world positioning scenarios. These datasets have been extensively experimented with and validated, and have up-to-date baselines [4]. Additionally, we present the measured scenarios for these datasets, as shown in Fig. 2a depicts a typical indoor scenario. Figure 2b represents an urban canyon scenario where neighboring tall buildings may cause difficulties in utilizing GPS signals due to signal obstruction and interference. The dataset is publicly available and can be found at: https://dx.doi.org/10.21227/jsat-pb50.

The mean error (MeanErr) and root mean square error (RMSE), which are commonly used to assess positioning performance, are defined as follows:

$$\text{MeanErr} = \frac{1}{N_{\text{UE}}} \sum_{i=1}^{N_{\text{UE}}} \left(\left\| S_i - \hat{S}_i \right\|_2 \right)$$

$$\text{RMSE} = \sqrt{\frac{1}{N_{\text{UE}}} \sum_{i=1}^{N_{\text{UE}}} \left(S_i - \hat{S}_i \right)^2} \tag{6}$$

where S_i denotes the actual position of the i-th UE, $\hat{S}_i$ denotes the estimated position of the i-th UE, N_{UE} denotes the number of UEs and $\|\cdot\|_2$ denotes the Euclidean distance.

(a) Indoor scenario   (b) Urban canyon scenario

Fig. 2. Scenario display: The real data collection site is from a building in Beijing, China, affiliated with the Chinese Academy of Sciences.

3.2   Implementation Details

In this study, we use a server equipped with an AMD EPYC 7543 32-Core CPU and an RTX A5000 GPU for simulations. We set the initial learning rate to $1e^{-3}$ and reduce the learning rate by half every 25 epochs when the number of training epochs exceeds 100. We use the Adam optimizer [8] to optimize the model. To ensure a fair comparison, we train our model for 300 epochs, consistent with state-of-the-art work [4]. The default batch size is set to 64. We use datasets consisting of 14,448 and 11,628 CSI matrices for indoor and urban scenarios, respectively. The experimental results of this study show that in both cases, the use of our method significantly improves the positioning performance.

3.3   Quantitative Comparison

We evaluate five different types of positioning methods, including trilateration method (*e.g.*, TDOA), triangulation method (*e.g.*, AOA), hybrid method (*e.g.*, TDoA-AoA), machine learning-based fingerprint method (*e.g.*, KNN), and deep learning-based fingerprint method (*e.g.*, MPRI). In addition, to enrich the baselines, four widely used deep learning models were selected to evaluate their localization accuracy, including ResNet [5], DenseNet [6], EfficientNet [11], MobileFormer [2] and RepLKNet [3]. To thoroughly test the models, we cover all publicly available versions. We test all models in indoor scenarios and select the best-performing models for further testing in the urban canyon scenario.

As shown in Table 1 and 2, our model achieves the best results using the two versions of the encoders (*i.e.*, ResNet18 and ResNet34), which not only outperform their original versions, but significantly exceed all baselines. It's worth noting that the two versions of the encoder chosen also have a low parameter count, with the ResNet18 version having only 5M parameters. This means that our method is highly deployable in practice, as it has a low requirement for computational resources. Furthermore, we visualize the positioning results as shown in Fig. 3, 4 and 5.

Table 1. Mean Error and Root Mean Square Error (m) statistics in indoor scenarios.

Models	MeanErr	RMSE
MPRI	0.28	–
TDoA	0.52	–
AoA	4.43	–
KNN	0.77	–
TDoA-AoA	0.54	–
ResNet18/34/50/101 [5]	0.35/0.27/0.28/0.28	0.62/0.49/0.49/0.50
DenseNet121/161/169/201 [6]	0.47/0.32/0.44/0.41	0.71/0.53/0.65/0.63
EfficientNetb0/1/2/3 [11]	1.13/3.20/6.08/14.23	1.36/3.79/6.95/17.07
EfficientNetb4/5/6/7 [11]	13.92/13.91/13.97/13.94	18.09/18.55/17.25/18.50
RepLKNet31B/L/XL [3]	0.44/0.27/0.31	0.66/0.57/0.55
Mobileformer96/151/214/294 [2]	12.11/11.25/13.24/10.59	14.89/13.11/15.10/13.02
Ours(ResNet18)/(ResNet34)	**0.26/0.16**	**0.48/0.31**

Table 2. Mean Error and Root Mean Square Error (m) statistics in urban canyon scenarios.

Models	Year	MeanErr	RMSE
ResNet18/34/50/101	2016	1.19/0.79/1.02/0.81	1.83/1.04/1.57/1.24
DenseNet121/161/169/201	2017	1.36/1.15/1.40/1.22	2.05/1.51/1.84/1.61
EfficientNetb0/1/2/3	2019	4.81/4.59/5.02/4.99	5.77/5.59/5.97/5.43
EfficientNetb4/5/6/7	2019	6.75/7.58/8.02/8.86	8.16/8.23/9.34/9.57
RepLKNet31B/L/XL	2022	2.97/2.85/3.01	3.97/3.74/4.21
Mobileformer96/151/214/294	2022	13.97/12.58/13.19/10.12	18.30/18.41/17.86/12.09
Ours(ResNet18)/(ResNet34)	–	**0.62/0.54**	**0.81/0.69**

Fig. 3. The visualization of indoor positioning results from left to right are as follows: Ours (with ResNet34 Encoder), ResNet101, DenseNet121, DenseNet161.

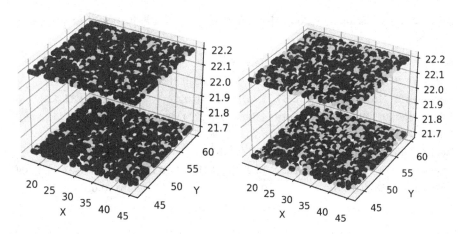

Fig. 4. The visualization of urban canyon positioning results from left to right are as follows: Ours (with ResNet18 Encoder), ResNet18.

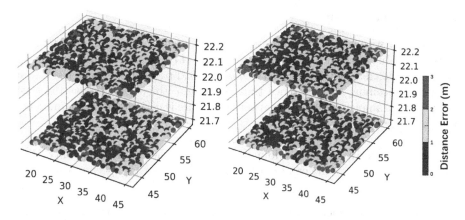

Fig. 5. The visualization of urban canyon positioning results from left to right are as follows: ResNet34, ResNet50.

3.4 Ablation Study

To demonstrate the effectiveness of the whole contrastive learning paradigm, we conduct ablation experiments to explore the specific impact of each design. *Without-progressive* means that noise is not added in a progressive manner, *i.e.*, in Eq. 2, α is set to 1 and β is set to $1e^{-5}$. In the progressive approach, β is progressively increased by $1e^{-5}$ in each training epoch to allow the model to adapt to different levels of noise proportion. As shown in Table 3, in indoor scenes, the positioning accuracy error increases by 0.06 m when using the ResNet18 Encoder and by 0.1 m when using the ResNet34 Encoder as *without-progressive* is used. In urban canyon scenes, when without-progressive is used, the positioning accuracy error increases by 0.30 m using the ResNet18 Encoder and by 0.09 m using the ResNet34 Encoder.

Without-pooling [14] means to using only the contrastive loss without hierarchical pooling to obtain different scales of loss. As shown in Table 3, in the indoor scenarios, the positioning accuracy error increases by 0.11 m when using the ResNet18 Encoder and by 0.16 m when using the ResNet34 Encoder when *without-pooling* is used. In the urban canyon scenario, when *without-pooling* is used, the positioning accuracy error increases by 0.60 m when using the ResNet18 Encoder and by 0.33 m using the ResNet34 Encoder. This implies that learning antenna feature semantics at different scales can provide more knowledge capacity.

Table 3. Ablation study on hierarchical loss and progressively decreasing SNR.

	Indoor	Urban Canyon
without-progressive	0.32(+0.06)/0.26(+0.10)	0.92(+0.30)/0.63(+0.09)
without-pooling	0.37(+0.11)/0.32(+0.16)	1.22(+0.60)/0.87(+0.33)
All	0.26(ResNet18)/0.16(ResNet34)	0.62(ResNet18)/0.54(ResNet34)

3.5   Efficiency Study

In this part, we examine various model-based efficiency metrics in detail. As shown in Table 4, the two Encoders we chose (*i.e.*, ResNet18 and ResNet34) have high efficiency metrics. ResNet18 has only 5 M parameters and is the fastest in terms of training and inference time. Although EfficientNetb0 has the least number of parameters at 4 M, its network structure is designed to make inference and training slower than ResNet18.

By considering both efficiency and accuracy, we can see that some classic models can be active in various domains because of their broad generality. High practical application value can be obtained by designing for specific scenarios.

Table 4. Measures of model efficiency, including the number of parameters (Param), memory usage (Memory (MB)), floating point of operations (FLOPs (M)), training time per one epoch (Training Time (s)) and inference time per one epoch (Inference Time (s)).

Name	Param	Memory	FLOPs	Training Time	Inference Time
ResNet18(**Our encoder**)	5,283,011	1.58	105.48	3.77	0.49
ResNet34(**Our encoder**)	21,292,483	2.52	292.40	6.21	0.68
ResNet50	23,520,451	7.39	326.03	7.79	0.62
ResNet101	42,512,579	10.84	573.15	11.75	0.93
ResNet152	58,156,227	15.05	818.24	17.39	1.31
DenseNet121	6,963,203	34.86	698.66	15.49	1.09
DenseNet161	26,488,035	63.98	1910.00	26.51	2.15
DenseNet169	12,495,747	41.48	829.71	22.20	1.39
DenseNet201	18,104,963	52.61	1060.00	27.06	1.99
EfficientNetb0	4,011,967	5.46	36.72	9.22	0.67
EfficientNetb1	6,517,603	7.70	56.02	12.04	0.96
EfficientNetb2	7,705,797	8.12	65.13	13.18	1.01
EfficientNetb3	10,701,563	10.70	92.67	13.35	0.99
EfficientNetb4	17,554,859	14.26	146.40	14.76	0.99
EfficientNetb5	28,347,795	19.69	232.23	18.83	1.60
EfficientNetb6	40,743,627	25.26	331.04	23.08	1.73
EfficientNetb7	63,795,795	34.03	511.32	28.33	2.12
RepLKNet31B	78,844,547	27.51	1100.00	46.26	2.29
RepLKNet31L	171,142,083	41.26	2340.00	70.90	4.01
RepLKNetXL	333,397,507	56.62	4510.00	122.63	6.61

4   Conclusion

In this paper, we abandon the idea of using special model techniques to obtain sceneario-specific tailored positioning models and instead focus on using simple and general off-the-shelf networks to achieve high-precision fingerprint positioning. To achieve this, we introduce the paradigm of contrastive learning. We construct different signal-to-noise ratio representations of the same CSI sample by manually adding noise and feeding them into the Encoder as a pair of positive samples, thus encouraging consistency in the feature representation between them. This allows the model to adapt to different signal-to-noise ratios. In addition, to obtain scale-invariant standards, we compute losses at different semantic scales and finer granularity of antenna instances. Experiments show that with simple ResNet18 or ResNet34 for hierarchical contrastive learning training can yield excellent performance in terms of efficiency and accuracy.

Acknowledgements. This research was sponsored by National Natural Science Foundation of China, 62272126, and the Fundamental Research Funds for the Central Universities, 3072022TS0605.

References

1. Chen, L., Zhou, X., Chen, F., Yang, L.L., Chen, R.: Carrier phase ranging for indoor positioning with 5G NR signals. IEEE Internet Things J. **9**(13), 10908–10919 (2021)
2. Chen, Y., et al.: Mobile-former: bridging MobileNet and transformer. In: Proceedings of the IEEE/CVF Conference on Computer Vision and Pattern Recognition, pp. 5270–5279 (2022)
3. Ding, X., Zhang, X., Han, J., Ding, G.: Scaling up your kernels to 31x31: revisiting large kernel design in CNNs. In: Proceedings of the IEEE/CVF Conference on Computer Vision and Pattern Recognition, pp. 11963–11975 (2022)
4. Gao, K., Wang, H., Lv, H., Liu, W.: Toward 5G NR high-precision indoor positioning via channel frequency response: a new paradigm and dataset generation method. IEEE J. Sel. Areas Commun. **40**(7), 2233–2247 (2022)
5. He, K., Zhang, X., Ren, S., Sun, J.: Deep residual learning for image recognition. In: Proceedings of the IEEE Conference on Computer Vision and Pattern Recognition, pp. 770–778 (2016)
6. Huang, G., Liu, Z., Van Der Maaten, L., Weinberger, K.Q.: Densely connected convolutional networks. In: Proceedings of the IEEE Conference on Computer Vision and Pattern Recognition, pp. 4700–4708 (2017)
7. Khan, D., Cheng, Z., Uchiyama, H., Ali, S., Asshad, M., Kiyokawa, K.: Recent advances in vision-based indoor navigation: a systematic literature review. Comput. Graph. **104**, 24–45 (2022)
8. Kingma, D.P., Ba, J.: Adam: a method for stochastic optimization. arXiv preprint: arXiv:1412.6980 (2014)
9. Natapov, A., Parush, A., Laufer, L., Fisher-Gewirtzman, D.: Architectural features and indoor evacuation wayfinding: The starting point matters. Saf. Sci. **145**, 105483 (2022)
10. Ruan, Y., Chen, L., Zhou, X., Guo, G., Chen, R.: Hi-Loc: hybrid indoor localization via enhanced 5G NR CSI. IEEE Trans. Instrum. Meas. **71**, 1–15 (2022)
11. Tan, M., Le, Q.: EfficientNet: rethinking model scaling for convolutional neural networks. In: International Conference on Machine Learning, pp. 6105–6114. PMLR (2019)

12. Tavasoli, S., Pan, X., Yang, T.: Real-time autonomous indoor navigation and vision-based damage assessment of reinforced concrete structures using low-cost Nano aerial vehicles. J. Build. Eng. **68**, 106193 (2023)
13. Xie, R., Zlatanova, S., Lee, J.: 3d indoor environments in pedestrian evacuation simulations. Autom. Constr. **144**, 104593 (2022)
14. Yue, Z., et al.: Ts2vec: towards universal representation of time series. In: Proceedings of the AAAI Conference on Artificial Intelligence, vol. 36, pp. 8980–8987 (2022)
15. Zhang, W., Yang, L., Geng, S., Hong, S.: Cross reconstruction transformer for self-supervised time series representation learning. arXiv preprint: arXiv:2205.09928 (2022)

Higher Education Programming Competencies: A Novel Dataset

Natalie Kiesler$^{(\boxtimes)}$ ⓘ and Benedikt Pfülb ⓘ

DIPF Leibniz Institute for Research and Information in Education,
Frankfurt, Germany
kiesler@dipf.de

Abstract. Students' challenges in introductory programming courses have long been subject to research. In fact, learners are faced with cognitively complex tasks, such as modeling and writing programs. At the same time, educators are known to experience challenges with the classification of a competency's cognitive complexity. In this paper, we present a text dataset with competency goals expected in basic programming courses. We then apply a deep learning approach to the dataset to classify the competency-based learning objectives as a use case. A manually annotated dataset of 35 German universities and their learning objectives in 129 introductory programming courses was processed into a machine-readable format to achieve these goals. It contains 1015 competency goals (both in German and English) and their classification into dimensions of complexity. Different state-of-the-art machine learning (ML) models, e.g., BERT, along with Natural Language Processing techniques, i.e., parts-of-speech-tagging, were combined to train a deep learning model in a supervised manner for the classification of competencies. The proof-of-concept shows that knowledge can be derived from the dataset. In the presented use case, the ML classification achieved a maximum accuracy of 81.4%. This work has several implications for educators, as it is the foundation for an application that classifies competency goals according to their cognitive complexity. The dataset can further be used to test language models as a baseline performance task. Moreover, the dataset can be extended, e.g., with data from other countries and languages. The dataset is available online under a Creative Commons license (https://github.com/nkiesler-cs/HEPComp-Dataset).

Keywords: dataset · classification · Learning objectives · Programming education · machine learning · natural language processing

1 Introduction

Developing educational standards and striving for competency has become the focus of many recent curricula recommendations. In the context of computing, the IT2017 [26] and CC2020 report [6] promote that dispositions, together with

© The Author(s), under exclusive license to Springer Nature Switzerland AG 2023
L. Iliadis et al. (Eds.): ICANN 2023, LNCS 14261, pp. 319–330, 2023.
https://doi.org/10.1007/978-3-031-44198-1_27

skills and knowledge, form the three components of competency to accomplish a certain task. Despite its definition and increasing recognition in computing education [24,25], competency has not yet been fully incorporated into study programs, modules or course descriptions. In addition, educators do not necessarily receive the training required for the development of competency-based learning objectives, and how to address them step by step with increasing complexity. Research shows that computing educators experience difficulties when classifying competency-based learning objectives with regard to their cognitive complexity [9,19,33]. This is critical, as educators should be aware of a competency's complexity, and thus what they expect from students. Especially in introductory programming, students do not seem to be able to accomplish certain tasks [3,23], which may be due to unrealistic expectations towards them, i.e., too cognitively complex competency goals.

Therefore, it is the **goal** of the present work to provide a ground-truth dataset as a classification task for the community. The contribution of this work is further due to its potential for educators and secondary researchers, as we:

- provide a manually annotated, mature and provenant empirical dataset with 1015 competency goals from programming education and a methodology for replication studies, e.g., in other countries, languages and other computing areas, and
- propose a use case with a Machine Learning (ML) model to classify programming competencies into categories of cognitive complexity [2] with the help of Natural Language Processing (NLP).

The structure of the paper is as follows: In Sect. 2, competency and learning objectives are briefly defined. The problem is described in Sect. 3, before the data collection and analysis process, and the novel dataset is introduced in Sect. 4 and 5. Then the implementation of ML and NLP approaches and their performance as a first use case is presented in Sect. 6. The paper ends with a discussion of results, conclusions, and perspectives for future work.

2   Competency and Learning Objectives

Weinert [32] defines competency as a set of cognitive abilities and skills that can be learned by individuals to solve problems. In addition, competency comprises the motivational, volitional, and social readiness and capacity to successfully and responsibly perform in various situations. Weinert's definition is reflected well in both the IT2017 [26] and CC2020 [6] definition of competency, which summarize knowledge, skills, and dispositions taken in context of a task. A 2021 ITiCSE working group report adds the integrative nature [24] of competency to this definition, thereby supporting Fink's significant learning model [8] and the human dimension of learning.

Learning outcomes form a common language construct for the representation of competency-based qualifications in formal educational settings. One sentence usually contains exactly one observable learning outcome which is described by an action verb, the learning content object, and, if necessary, the context object [2]. Competency-based learning outcomes can be classified according to the taxonomy developed by Anderson and Krathwohl (AKT) [2]. For example, *CS students are able to decode bit strings as characters or numbers.* The cognitive process dimension "apply" [2] can be derived from the verb "decode". The procedural knowledge dimension [2] how to do something is implied via the "bit strings" and the resulting "characters or numbers". It is thus crucial to transform deviating expressions into the target format, which is especially true for machine readability and further digital processing steps.

3   Problem Description

The data was originally gathered to address a challenge observed in German higher education related to competency-based teaching, learning, and assessing in introductory programming education. Learning to program is still perceived as hard, difficult, and full of unrealistic expectations towards novices. Time and time again, studies have reported that students do not acquire the programming competencies expected from them [3,23]. Thus, there seems to be a gap between what educators expect from novices, and how well students perform in their first programming courses. The dataset was originally collected to (1) model programming competency, (2) analyze the expected competencies with regard to their cognitive complexity, and (3) to reflect on the current state of the art of competency-based learning in German CS higher education programs [11–14].

In the present work, we built upon this primary research, while particularly addressing educators' challenges with the classification of competencies via taxonomies (e.g., AKT). Several studies reveal that cognitive complexity is hard to judge, and that educators tend to downgrade certain tasks and the competencies required to master them [9,19,33]. This underestimation may lead to educators' design of too complex tasks and assessments, students' poor performance, and finally their dropout. Therefore, we start to enable and investigate the classification of competency-based, cognitive learning objectives with the help of ML and NLP approaches. To achieve this, we first have to construct a novel, machine-readable and actionable dataset.

4   Dataset Collection

This section briefly introduces the sampling method of the curricula documents gathered for the primary research [14]. Human subjects were not involved. First of all, a common content area and context were determined. Then types of universities and study programs were selected, before curricula data were collected, and analyzed into categories. For details, we refer to the primary work in which all of the data used herein was gathered and thoroughly described [14].

Determining a Common Content Area: Programming competency is the combination of knowledge, skills, and dispositions related to a programming language, basic algorithms, and data structures, as well as their successful implementation in the context of a specific task. An initial step for the definition of a common content area was the review of the ACM's curricular recommendations including core tiers of CS degree programs [1] to obtain transferable results, independent of specific study profiles or the present case study of Germany. Accordingly, a content area was summarized that resembles the basic components of introductory programming education.

Types of Universities and Study Programs: The search for data was conducted via the "University Compass" [10], which is a database of all German study programs. For the primary research, publicly funded types of universities were considered, meaning full universities and universities of applied sciences. As it was the goal of the primary research to find comparable courses, similar modules across study programs and universities had to be selected that cover the defined content area. Therefore, only full-time Bachelor of Science degree programs in "Computer Science" were considered.

Searching for Modules and Courses: As a next step, introductory programming courses from the first three semesters were selected based on the available study plans and module handbooks of each degree program. Both the study plans and modules were reviewed according to the defined content area. Courses were included in the sample if the mapping had been successful.

Language Transformations: During the data collection process, it became apparent early on that the learning objectives were often not available in the expected format (see Sect. 2). This implied the need to linguistically smooth the data. The goal of the language transformation was to ease the analysis of the data by resulting in a one-to-one correspondence of a learning objective and sentence. In addition, the goal was to obtain syntactically complete sentences without reference elements (so-called "deixis") and thus to ease comprehension prior to the analysis.

Analysis Method and Categories: The 1015 gathered statements on learning objectives were analyzed using the qualitative content analysis method according to P. Mayring [20]. Cognitive objectives were coded by using deductive categories resembling the four knowledge dimensions and six cognitive process dimensions coined within the Anderson Krathwohl Taxonomy (AKT) [2]. Inductive categories representing the competency itself were developed based on the material [22] for cognitive and non-cognitive competency goals, whereas additional subcategories were developed for non-cognitive competencies. Learning objectives lacking the notion of competency were classified as *non operationalized*. The corresponding statements are still part of the dataset. The overall structure of deductive and inductive categories is as follows:

- Cognitive Competencies
    - Knowledge dimensions (deductive [2])
    - Cognitive process dimensions (deductive [2])
    - Inductive categories
- Non-cognitive competencies
    - Inductive categories and inductive subcategories
- Non operationalized

5   Dataset Transformation

The novel dataset of higher education programming competencies is presented next. It is described in terms of the actual data collected from universities and courses, further cleaning and preprocessing steps, as well as the resulting machine-readable structure of the data, and the distribution of categories.

Represented Universities and Courses in the Dataset: The sample comprises a selection of one random full university and one random university of applied sciences per German state. Three additional institutions from the state of Hesse were included due to the primary research's mixed methods approach on the data level [14, 21]. In sum, the CS Bachelor of Science study programs of 35 higher education institutions are part of the sample. 129 courses related to programming are included [14].

Cleaning and Preprocessing: After the primary research had classified competencies into cognitive, non-cognitive, and the non operationalized category, yet another cleaning cycle was conducted to once again verify the classification. The aggregation of data revealed a few examples that required attention and corrections. As part of the data aggregation into a single JSON file, the following additional transformations were applied:

- Replacing German special characters,
- Resolve abbreviations
- Remove hyphenation marks,
- Remove brackets (round and square)

To increase the use cases of the presented dataset, an English translation of each syntactically valid learning objectives was produced with the help of the automated translator DeepL. After a human review cycle and improvements, English translations were added to the dataset. Moreover, we provide Python code for the easy-to-use extraction of competencies and (category) labels, the raw or linguistically transformed text for future research.

Structure of the Data: In sum, 1015 valid statements related to teaching and learning objectives in introductory programming were identified in the sample. The data is available as one JSON file which contains the expected competencies of all 35 institutions, along with their linguistically transformed versions and all of the assigned categories (deductive and inductive). Its structure is illustrated by the following template of a paragraph from a module description containing sentences with multiple learning objectives (see Listing 1.1). By presenting the original text paragraphs and their step-by-step decomposition into full, syntactically valid sentences, every single learning goal can eventually be categorized. Due to the fact that a single sentence of the raw text may contain more than one objective, more than one ID may be contained on the sentence level (line 6, Listing 1.1). The available English translation of each linguistically transformed, valid sentence is added in line 10 (Listing 1.1). In addition to the data, a lookup table is available at the very end of the provided JSON file.

```
1   { "<file id>": {
2       "university": "<university>",
3       "timestamp" : "<timestamp>",
4       "<sentence ids in paragraph>": {
5         "raw_text"        :"<raw paragraph text>",
6         "<sentences' id[s]>": {
7           "text_before"  : "<original sentence>",
8           "<competency id>": { // precisely one
9             "text_transformed": "<transformed text>",
10            "text_en": "<English translation>",
11            "label": [ // one or more labels
12              {<"label type">: {
13                "label_name": "<label name>",
14                "label_id"  : <label identifier>}},
15              ]}}, // more competencies
16        }, // more paragraphs with sentences
17      }, // more files
18    "label_lookup": {
19      "<name>": id,
20      id: "<name>",}}
```

Listing 1.1. Dataset structure (JSON)

Distribution of Categories: The dataset's distribution of competencies within the cognitive domain [2] is illustrated in Fig. 1. 717 of the 1015 syntactically well-formed sentences were classified as cognitive learning objectives and therefore coded along both the knowledge and cognitive process dimensions of the AKT [2]. It is apparent that most of the learning objectives in introductory programming are found within the cognitive process dimension *creating* and the *procedural knowledge* dimension. In 250 cases, the expected competency goal was not operationalized. In addition, 48 sentences were categorized as non-cognitive learning objectives.

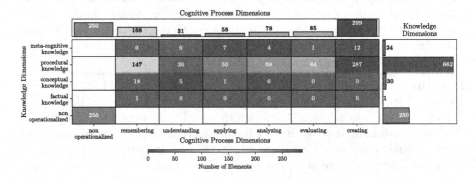

Fig. 1. Distribution of Categories

6   Use Case: Classifying Programming Competencies

To classify programming competencies expressed in natural language we trained and evaluated different machine learning models (i.e., deep learning models) in a supervised manner with the machine-readable dataset described in Sect. 5. As the first and most interesting use case, a classification along the six cognitive process dimensions (*remembering, understanding, applying, analyzing, evaluating, creating*) of the AKT [2] and the *non operationalized* category is performed (see Fig. 1). It is noted that the continuum of cognitive complexity gradually increases, with remembering being the least complex cognitive process dimension. The goal of each tested ML model is to assign the correct label of the corresponding cognitive process dimension for a given competency goal.

6.1 Embedding

Embedding functions constitute a common technique to feed text to deep learning models. Text embedding functions transform words or text into a vector space, whereby similar meanings of samples are closer to each other. We evaluated several pre-trained embedding functions/layers $\mathcal{E}$ with different dimensions (50 and 128), with and without normalization, and trained on different datasets (English Google News 7B corpus, German Google News 30B corpus).

6.2 Models

As a baseline, we trained standard feed-forward Deep Neural Networks (DNNs) to show the superiority of more specialized models. So in addition to standard DNNs, a number of models for special NLP domains were evaluated. The "Bidirectional Encoder Representations from Transformers" (BERT) model [7] is one of the most commonly used models for NLP tasks. The underlying idea of BERT is to mask tokens, and then predict them within the training process. Several different pre-trained and adapted BERT models are available for different application scenarios.

We used the original BERT-Base model, and further evaluated the more simple BERT model versions, e.g., the model defined by Turc et al. [30]. Down-scaled BERT models usually have fewer parameters compared to the standard BERT-Base, saving computational resources. Eleven BERT variants ranging from small (2 transformer layers and a 128 hidden embedding size) to large ones were evaluated (12 transformer layers and a 768 hidden embedding size, see [30]). Similarly, the BERT variant "A Lite BERT" (ALBERT) proposed by Lan et al. [17] aims at the reduction of training parameters. Clark et al. [5] introduced a further BERT variant referred to as "Efficiently Learning an Encoder that Classifies Token Replacements Accurately" (ELECTRA). Another BERT variant is pre-trained on Wikipedia and BooksCorpus. The last variant is also based on BERT and known as "Talking-Heads Attention" [28].

6.3 Part-of-Speech Tagging

To improve the classification accuracy of the German learning objectives, a part-of-speech (PoS) information was added to the learning process [4]. We applied two different PoS tokenizers: The common "Natural Language Toolkit" (NLTK) for English, and the "Hanover Tagger" (HanTa) [31] for the German version of the dataset. Each model was thus trained once with and once without the PoS information to measure the impact of the data enrichment.

6.4   Experiments

Each model was trained for 1000 training iterations with a fixed batch size of 64. This configuration corresponds to approximately 64 training epochs on the entire dataset. To bypass the problem of over-fitting [29], we applied dropout after each layer to all of our models with three different dropout rates $\mathcal{D} = \{0.0, 0.1, 0.2\}$ (0% (off), 10% and 20%). In order to reduce the influence of selecting a suitable learning rate, we vary the learning rate $lr = \{0.001, 0.0001, 0.00001\}$ for AdamW optimizer [18] (an optimization of

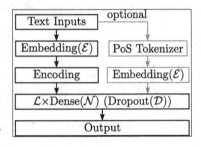

Fig. 2. Model Architecture

Adam [16] with additional weight decay). To assure that random initialization states do not influence the results, we executed each experiment with the same parameters three times with different seeds in each execution. The same procedure was applied to the pre-trained BERT models. To finally achieve the desired classification, standard fully connected feed-forward layers of different quantity $\mathcal{L} = \{1, 3\}$ and different numbers of artificial neurons $\mathcal{N} = \{500, 1000\}$ were evaluated. All evaluated models comply with the architecture illustrated in Fig. 2. We optimized all models with a weighted variant of the sparse categorical cross-entropy loss, which minimized the effects of differently populated classes (see Fig. 1).

To evaluate all deep learning models, we extracted a random subset of 10 samples of each class. Based on these test results, we can draw careful conclusions on the quality of the training process with accuracy as a metric (instead of precision, recall, or F1-scores). More than 4000 experiments were evaluated.

6.5   Experimental Results

As a result of the experiments, we visualize the evaluation of the training process for the best parameter configurations. In the left graph of Fig. 3, the test accuracy of experiments for the German and English version of the dataset is visualized. For each, the German and English data, the test accuracy with PoS tagging (solid lines) and without (dashed lines) is indicated. The maximum accuracy for the English version of the dataset is 81.4% (with PoS), while the German version achieved a slightly lower accuracy of 75.7% (also with PoS). It is clearly visible that the learning process for the English data (red lines) increases faster and earlier. This is likely due to the pre-training of the applied BERT models in English. Another outcome is that the data enrichment via PoS tokenizers seems to support the training process, as the accuracy improved. For the English data, the maximum accuracy without PoS was 78.6%. The German data only achieved an accuracy of 70.0% without the PoS tokenizers.

On the right of Fig. 3, the confusion matrix depicts the classification results for the English data (with PoS) at $i = 250$. It shows that the prediction was flawless for the dimension "evaluating". 9 out of 10 correct predictions were achieved for "non operationalized" learning objectives, and the cognitive process dimension "remembering". Most of the classification errors (4 out of 10) occur in the dimension "applying".

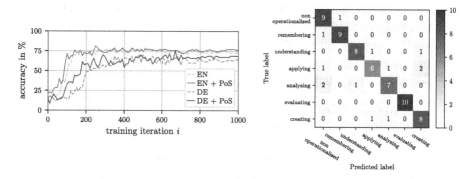

Fig. 3. Prediction trends (left) and confusion matrix (right) (Color figure online)

7   Discussion of Use Cases

In this section, we briefly discuss the dataset's potential, the experiments' results and their implications for various communities. We further outline limitations of this work.

The dataset presented in this work is the first of its kind to represent textual data representing competencies from the context of introductory programming education. It further contains ground-truth categories reflecting programming competencies and their complexity both in German and English language. The proof-of-concept use case of classifying programming competencies via machine learning models revealed that in both the German and the English data, the classification accuracy improved when applying the PoS tokenizers in addition to the pre-trained NLP models. The measured improvements correspond to the number reported by other authors [4]. Predictions for the cognitive process dimension "applying" seem to be most challenging for the ML model with 4 of 10 incorrectly predicted labels. Interestingly, this is also a well-known challenge for human educators who tend to confuse this dimension with "creating" [9, 27].

It should further be noted that the pre-trained models have not been developed for this type of classification task. Therefore, the present classification of competency-based learning objectives via ML approaches constitutes the groundwork for improvements and future applications. By providing the data source of our work, we further aim to engage other (computing education) researchers to adapt the methodology and help us extend the dataset with more valid and classified competency goals from other countries, and languages.

Moreover, the dataset can be utilized by a wider audience, such as the machine learning and artificial intelligence community, as it can serve as a validation dataset for applied text classification or transformation tasks.

Limitations: The dataset was collected from German study programs and modules in 2018, which results in its limitation in terms of the German educational context and time. Moreover, the examples depicted in this dataset reflect only the competencies expected in introductory programming education and not complete CS study programs. This is due to the intense effort that is required for the gathering, transformation, and analysis of such natural language data.

8   Conclusions and Future Work

The presented text dataset reflects on the competency-based learning objectives at German universities, particularly introductory programming education as a common core of CS study programs. It was manually gathered, annotated, and translated with human intelligence. Due to its transformation into a machine readable and actionable format, it can be used by a broad audience, and for various text classification or transformation tasks. The availability of the annotated data along with their classification and an English translation further enables replication studies and other secondary research.

The novel dataset allowed for the analysis of cognitive complexity in the context of introductory programming to make the high level of expectations towards novices explicit. Due to the application of ML and NLP techniques, the automated prediction of a competency goal's cognitive complexity in terms of the AKT dimensions was achieved with an accuracy of up to 81.4%. This benchmark is the first of its kind for this dataset, and thus the starting point for more research and improvements [15]. Generally speaking, the experiments showed that knowledge can be derived from the dataset. To our knowledge, no comparable dataset is currently available.

The text dataset is also considered valuable for future work, such as the transformation of learning objectives into observable, competency-based goals. It can further be utilized by (other) NLP or ML techniques.

References

1. ACM: Computer Science Curricula 2013: Curriculum Guidelines for Undergraduate Degree Programs in Computer Science. Association for Computing Machinery, New York (2013)
2. Anderson, L.W., et al.: A Taxonomy for Learning, Teaching, and Assessing: A Revision of Bloom's Taxonomy of Educational Objectives. Addison Wesley Longman, New York (2001)

3. Bain, G., Barnes, I.: Why is programming so hard to learn? In: Proceedings of the 2014 Conference on Innovation & Technology in Computer Science Education, p. 356 (2014)
4. Cai, X., Dong, S., Hu, J.: A deep learning model incorporating part of speech and self-matching attention for named entity recognition of Chinese electronic medical records. BMC Med. Inform. Decis. Mak. **19**(S2), 101–109 (2019)
5. Clark, K., Luong, M.T., Le, Q.V., Manning, C.D.: ELECTRA: pre-training text encoders as discriminators rather than generators (2020)
6. Clear, A., et al.: Computing Curricula 2020 Paradigms for Global Computing Education. ACM, New York (2020)
7. Devlin, J., Chang, M.W., Lee, K., Toutanova, K.: BERT: pre-training of deep bidirectional transformers for language understanding. arXiv:1810.04805 (2018)
8. Fink, L.D.: Creating Significant Learning Experiences: An Integrated Approach to Designing College Courses. Wiley, San Francisco (2013)
9. Gluga, R., Kay, J., Lister, R., Kleitman, S., Lever, T.: Coming to terms with bloom: an online tutorial for teachers of programming fundamentals. In: Proceedings of the Fourteenth Australasian Computing Education Conference, ACE 2012, vol. 123, pp. 147–156. Australian Computer Society Inc, AUS (2012)
10. HRK, S., Hippler, H.: Hochschulkompass. Online (2018). https://www.hochschulkompass.de/service/impressum.html
11. Kiesler, N.: Kompetenzmodellierung für die grundlegende Programmierausbildung-Eine kritische Diskussion zu Vorzügen und Anwendbarkeit der Anderson Krathwohl Taxonomie im Vergleich zum Kompetenzmodell der GI. In: Zender, R., Ifenthaler, D., an Clara Schumacher, T.L. (eds.) DELFI 2020-Die 18. Fachtagung Bildungstechnologien der Gesellschaft für Informatik e.V., Online, 14–18 September 2020. LNI, vol. P-308, pp. 187–192. Gesellschaft für Informatik e.V. (2020). https://dl.gi.de/20.500.12116/34158
12. Kiesler, N.: Towards a competence model for the novice programmer using bloom's revised taxonomy - an empirical approach. In: Proceedings of the 2020 ACM Conference on Innovation and Technology in Computer Science Education, ITiCSE 2020, pp. 459–465. ACM, New York (2020). https://doi.org/10.1145/3341525.3387419
13. Kiesler, N.: Zur modellierung und klassifizierung von kompetenzen in der grundlegenden programmierausbildung anhand der anderson krathwohl taxonomie. CoRR abs/2006.16922 (2020). arXiv:2006.16922
14. Kiesler, N.: Kompetenzförderung in der Programmierausbildung durch Modellierung von Kompetenzen und informativem Feedback. Dissertation, Johann Wolfgang Goethe-Universität, Frankfurt am Main, January 2022. Fachbereich Informatik und Mathematik
15. Kiesler, N., Schiffner, D.: Why we need open data in computer science education research? In: Proceedings of the 2023 Conference on Innovation and Technology in Computer Science Education, ITiCSE 2023, vol. 1. ACM, New York (2023). https://doi.org/10.1145/3587102.3588860. ISBN: 979-8-4007-0138-2/23/07
16. Kingma, D.P., Ba, J.: Adam: a method for stochastic optimization. arXiv:1412.6980 (2014)
17. Lan, Z., Chen, M., Goodman, S., Gimpel, K., Sharma, P., Soricut, R.: ALBERT: a lite BERT for self-supervised learning of language representations. arXiv:1909.11942 (2019)
18. Loshchilov, I., Hutter, F.: Decoupled weight decay regularization. arXiv:1711.05101 (2017)

19. Masapanta-Carrión, S., Velázquez-Iturbide, J.A.: A systematic review of the use of bloom's taxonomy in computer science education. In: Proceedings of the 49th ACM Technical Symposium on Computer Science Education, SIGCSE 2018, pp. 441–446. Association for Computing Machinery, New York (2018). https://doi.org/10.1145/3159450.3159491

20. Mayring, P.: Qualitative content analysis forum qualitative sozialforschung. In: Forum: Qualitative Social Research, vol. 1 (2000)

21. Mayring, P.: Combination and integration of qualitative and quantitative analysis. In: Forum Qualitative Sozialforschung/Forum: Qualitative Social Research, vol. 2, p. Art. 6 (2001)

22. Mayring, P.: Qualitative Inhaltsanalyse: Grundlagen und Techniken. Beltz, Weinheim, 12. auflage edn. (2015)

23. McCracken, M., et al.: A multi-national, multi-institutional study of assessment of programming skills of first-year CS students. In: Working Group Reports from ITiCSE on Innovation and Technology in Computer Science Education, pp. 125–180. ACM, New York (2001)

24. Raj, R., et al.: Professional competencies in computing education: pedagogies and assessment. In: Proceedings of the 2021 Working Group Reports on Innovation and Technology in Computer Science Education, pp. 133–161. ACM, New York (2021). https://doi.org/10.1145/3502870.3506570

25. Raj, R.K., et al.: Toward practical computing competencies. In: Proceedings of the 26th ACM Conference on Innovation and Technology in Computer Science Education, ITiCSE 2021, vol. 2, pp. 603–604. ACM, New York (2021). https://doi.org/10.1145/3456565.3461442

26. Sabin, M., et al.: Information Technology Curricula 2017: Curriculum Guidelines for Baccalaureate Degree Programs in Information Technology. ACM, New York, December 2017

27. Scott, T.: Bloom's taxonomy applied to testing in computer science classes. J. Comput. Sci. Coll. **19**(1), 267–274 (2003)

28. Shazeer, N., Lan, Z., Cheng, Y., Ding, N., Hou, L.: Talking-heads attention. arXiv preprint arXiv:2003.02436 (2020)

29. Srivastava, N., Hinton, G., Krizhevsky, A., Sutskever, I., Salakhutdinov, R.: Dropout: a simple way to prevent neural networks from overfitting. J. Mach. Learn. Res. **15**(56), 1929–1958 (2014). https://jmlr.org/papers/v15/srivastava14a.html

30. Turc, I., Chang, M.W., Lee, K., Toutanova, K.: Well-read students learn better: on the importance of pre-training compact models. arXiv:1908.08962v2 (2019)

31. Wartena, C.: A probabilistic morphology model for German lemmatization. In: Proceedings of the 15th Conference on Natural Language Processing (KONVENS 2019), pp. 40–49 (2019). https://doi.org/10.25968/opus-1527

32. Weinert, F.E.: Concept of competence: a conceptual clarification. (2001)

33. Whalley, J.L., et al.: An Australasian study of reading and comprehension skills in novice programmers, using the bloom and solo taxonomies. In: Proceedings of the 8th Australasian Conference on Computing Education, ACE 2006, vol. 52, pp. 243–252. Australian Computer Society Inc, AUS (2006)

Higher Target Relevance Parallel Machine Translation with Low-Frequency Word Enhancement

Shuo Sun, Hongxu Hou[(⊠)], and Yisong Wang

College of Computer Science, Inner Mongolia University, National & Local Joint
Engineering Research Center of Intelligent Information Processing Technology for
Mongolian, Inner Mongolia Key Laboratory of Mongolian Information Processing
Technology, Hohhot, China
cshhx@imu.edu.cn

Abstract. Non-autoregressive translation (NAT) has received a surge of
interest due to its success in inference speed by predicting all tokens independently and simultaneously. However, it is difficult for this paradigm
to model the conditional information between words in the target
side, which means its translation accuracy is sacrificed and damaged.
Although many advanced studies are proposed to improve its generation quality, they come at the cost of decoding speed compared to
its counterpart. In this paper, we propose to introduce an evaluation
module to evaluate the NAT generations during training to guide model
parameter update, and as a fine-tuning module during inference to generate plentiful fluency and faithfulness predictions. This recipe can significantly improve the model performance on the basis of ensuring the
decoding efficiency of NAT. Furthermore, to mitigate the large prediction error of low-frequency words caused by knowledge distillation
(KD) in non-autoregressive generation, we supply an enhanced KD to
train NAT students, which exploits the complementarity of bilingual
and monolingual, and transfer both knowledge to the NAT model. We
not only verify our ideas on widely-used WMT14 English-German and
WMT16 Romanian-English tasks, but also make more amelioration on
the low-resource national languages CCMT2019 Mongolian-Chinese and
CWMT2017 Uyghur-Chinese.

Keywords: Non-autoregressive Translation · Evaluation Module ·
Knowledge Distillation · Low-Resource language

1 Introduction

Auto-regressive translation (AT) [1,17] generates target tokens one-by-one with
a sequential manner, which has serious exposure bias and high decoding latency.
To alleviate this problem and accelerate decoding, non-autoregressive translation

L. Iliadis et al. (Eds.): ICANN 2023, LNCS 14261, pp. 331–344, 2023.
https://doi.org/10.1007/978-3-031-44198-1_28

(NAT) [7] is proposed on the premise of the conditional independence assumption, it parallel decodes all target sentence words. However, this paradigm discards the context dependency of the target tokens [9], which reduces the relevance between the generated tokens and resulting translation accuracy hugely decrease.

Stern et al. [16] propose an Insertion Transformer (InsT), which generates target tokens like a balanced binary tree. Besides, Gu et al. [8] further present a deletion operation (Levenshtein Transformer, LevT). It can divide the iterative process into three steps: deletion, placeholder prediction and token prediction, which is more flexible for the adjustment of the translation. Inspired by BERT [2], conditional masked language model (CMLM) is introduced into the NAT model [6], a fraction of target tokens with low prediction probability will be masked and re-predicted in the next iteration and better results are achieved by gradually obtaining more target sentence context dependencies during multiple iterative decoding. However, multiple decoding increases the inference speed and even degrades to the level of auto-regressive Transformer, losing the fast decoding advantage of non-autoregressive models. Therefore, enhancing the context correlation of the single decoding model can improve the translation quality on the premise of maintaining high-speed decoding.

In this paper, we propose to integrate the evaluation module on the basis of the NAT model, which can be evaluated between the relevance of generated words (fluency) and the semantic retention degree of the source language (faithfulness), and adjust the model parameters timely according to the evaluation result. During training, the evaluation module can keep the semantic relations and feature distribution of the target language to continuously enrich the semantic knowledge, which are retained as the model's parameters and used to modify the translation during inference. The quality of the translation generated after one round of decoding can reach a result comparable to that of the multi-round iterative decoding model, and the decoding speed is still more than 6 times higher than that of the auto-regressive model. Furthermore, as the preliminary step for training NAT model, knowledge distillation (KD) [10] has become a necessary paradigm to trade-off between decoding speed and translation quality, which is widely used to construct new training data for model. However, it mainly focuses on the performance of high-frequency words and damages the density estimation of real data, seriously decreasing low-frequency word translation accuracy [3,12]. To this end, this paper makes full use of raw, distill and reverse-distill data according to [4] to rejuvenating low-frequency words. We highlight our contributions as follows:

- We propose integrate the evaluation model to NAT has enable it to improve the context dependency between target tokens while ensuring the decoding speed.
- NAT student uses synthetic distillation data for training to relieve the poor prediction of low-frequency words.
- To firmly reveal our approach, we conduct extensive experiments on two widely used language pairs and two low-resource languages translation tasks.

2   Background

2.1   Non-autoregressive Translation

Given a source sentence $\mathbf{x}$, an AT model predict each target word $\mathbf{y}_t$ conditioned on the prefix words $\mathbf{y}_{<t}$, which suffer from quite time-consuming when generating target sentences, especially for long sentences. In contrast, NAT models use the conditional independent factorization for predicting target words in parallel. Accordingly, the probability of generating $\mathbf{y}_t$ is computed as:

$$P(\mathbf{y}|\mathbf{x}) = P(T_{\mathbf{y}}|\mathbf{x}) \prod_{t=1}^{T_{\mathbf{y}}} P(\mathbf{y}_t|\mathbf{x}, \mathbf{z}) \tag{1}$$

where $T_{\mathbf{y}}$ is the length of the target sentence and each word $\mathbf{y}_t$ are generated independently. Different with AT model, the NAT model has inability to dynamically define the sentence length implicitly through special symbols. Therefore, predicting sentence length is the preliminary step for non-autoregressive translation, and exploiting latent variable $\mathbf{z}$ to model the correlation of the target sequence and predicting the target word without the participation of the prefix words $\mathbf{y}_{<t}$, so as to achieve parallel decoding.

2.2   Knowledge Distillation

Conditional independence assumption prevents the NAT model capturing the target side dependency sufficiently, which leads to serious semantic multimodality. Therefore, sequence-level knowledge distillation [7] is proposed to tackle the above problems. Utilizing bilingual corpus to train a powerful AT teacher model is the initial step and then replace the original target side samples with AT teacher-generated sentences to reduce the modes of training data, which makes NAT easily acquire more realistic probability distribution and achieve significant improvements [15, 18]. Accordingly, the process of knowledge distillation can be defined as follows:

$$Raw = \{(\mathbf{X}_i, \mathbf{Y}_i)\}_{i=1}^{N}, \quad KD = \{(\mathbf{X}_i, AT_{s \to t}(\mathbf{X}_i)) \,|\, \mathbf{X}_i \in Raw\}_{i=1}^{N} \tag{2}$$

where Raw represents the original parallel corpus data and KD represents the sequence-level knowledge distillation data obtained through the AT teacher model. N is the total number of parallel sentence pairs in the training corpus.

3   Methodology

Our work aims to train the NAT student with the authentic and synthetic distillation data to diminish the error prediction of low-frequency words and introduce an evaluation module into the model to further improve the translation quality under the condition of ensuring fast decoding of NAT. The whole architecture is shown in Fig. 1.

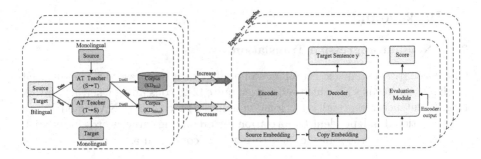

Fig. 1. Illustration of proposed model structure.

3.1 Enhanced Knowledge Distillation

Although standard KD effectively eases the multi-modal of NAT, it may lose important information in the original data during the distillation process, resulting in more errors on predicting low-frequency words. As a data-driven task, the performance of the NAT model heavily relies on the volume and quality of the parallel data. For high-resource translation tasks, external monolingual data as a complement to the original bilingual data have the potential to further improve translation performance. For several low-resource tasks, monolingual data is easier to obtain with several orders of magnitude larger than that of bilingual data, which can effectively alleviate the dependence on bilingual corpus. Therefore, as shown in the left part of Fig. 1, we leverage bidirectional monolingual knowledge distillation to rejuvenate low-frequency words. Specifically, we generate two sets of distillation data based on external monolingual with AT teachers trained on the original bilingual data, and then combined with bilingual KD to obtain the final enhanced KD expressed as (3) and (4):

$$Bili. = \{(\mathbf{X}_i, \mathbf{Y}_i)\}_{i=1}^{N}, \quad Mono. = \left\{(x_q)_{q=1}^{Q} \cup (y_p)_{p=1}^{P}\right\} \tag{3}$$

$$KD_{Enhanced} = (\mathbf{X}_i, AT_{s \to t}(\mathbf{X}_i))_{i=1}^{N} \cup (x_q, AT_{s \to t}(x_q))_{q=1}^{Q} \cup (y_p, AT_{t \to s}(y_p))_{p=1}^{P} \tag{4}$$

where *Bili.* and *Mono.* represent bilingual data and monolingual data (source and target) respectively. N, Q and P indicate the number of bilingual sentence pairs and two monolingual sentences.

3.2 NAT with Evaluation Module

The evaluation module assess the target sentence generated by the NAT from the perspectives of fluency and faithfulness. Both metrics are integrated together to obtain a final score to make a compromise between them. Thus the evaluation module can be logically divided into three layers, which are self-attention layer, cross-attention layer and fusion layer. The definite architecture is shown in Fig. 2.

Different with the self-attention mechanism in the Transformer decoder, the parallel decoding of NAT model non-existent information leakage. Therefore, the self-attention layer in the evaluation module doesn't contain the mask part and thus retains all the information of the entire sentence, which can more comprehensively learn the semantic knowledge and language features of the target language. The self-attention layer calculate the contextual correlation between words to ensure the fluency of the whole translation:

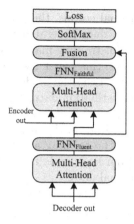

$$C_{fluent} = MultiHead(H_{de}, H_{de}, H_{de}) \quad (5)$$

where H_{de} is the last hidden layer state of the decoder and C_{fluent} is the generated self-attention. Apart from fluency, the generated sentences should also reflect faithfulness so

Fig. 2. Structural view of the evaluation model. Here we omit layer-norm and residual connections for simplicity.

that the entire translation can express the source sentence adequately and accurately in meaning. We regard the evaluation for faithfulness as a translation task, that is to evaluate the probability of converting relevant source information into target words. Specifically, we perform the cross-attention over the source hidden state H_{en} generated by the encoder with the context information of the target sentence in the self-attention layer C_{fluent} to ensure that the generated translation can faithfully express the source sentence:

$$C_{faithful} = MultiHead(C_{fluent}, H_{en}, H_{en}) \quad (6)$$

where $C_{faithful}$ is the generated cross-attention. The two metrics of fluency and faithfulness are traded off against each other to evaluate the generated translation, and the semantic knowledge and other information learned by the two parts are fused by adding a fusion layer. Finally, the evaluation score is obtained through the softmax layer:

$$S = SoftMax(C), \quad C = W_{fluent}C_{fluent} + W_{faithful}C_{faithful} \quad (7)$$

where W_{fluent} and $W_{faithful}$ are linear transformation matrices. $S = [s_1; ...; s_I]^T$ is the last hidden layer state after the softmax layer and s_i is the hidden state for the target word $\mathbf{y}_t$.

3.3   Training and Inference

Training Strategy. The distillation data in this paper can be divided into two parts: KD_{Bili} and KD_{Mono}. The former is generated from original bilingual data and the latter is generated from bidirectional monolingual data with twice the amount of the former. Since the AT teacher model is trained on the original bilingual corpus, the resulting distilled data with higher quality, while the distillation data generated through external monolingual has larger noise, and simply joint training may cause negative effects on the model. Therefore, as shown in Fig. 1, this paper uses the iterative knowledge refinement mechanism to progressively train the model. Specifically, we fist perform BLEU to evaluate monolingual distillation data. The initial epoch utilizes all synthetic distillation corpus KD_{Mono}, and each subsequent epoch **increase** 5% authentic distillation corpus KD_{Bili}, in the meanwhile, **decrease** 10% KD_{Mono} with the lowest BLEU score. The training strategy enables the model to learn more semantic knowledge from large-scale monolingual data while retaining the advantages of original bilingual data.

Loss Function. During training, our method jointly optimizes the translation module and the evaluation module. Specifically, for the translation module, since all tokens in NAT are generated in parallel, it is necessary to predict the length T of the target sentence in advance:

$$\mathcal{L}_{len} = -log P(T|\mathbf{x}; \theta) \qquad (8)$$

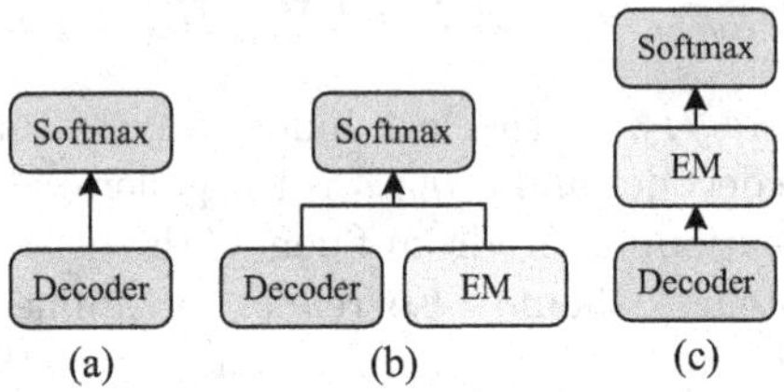

Fig. 3. Different roles of evaluation module during inference.

For generated translation $\mathbf{y}_t$, a cross-entropy loss is employed as

$$\mathcal{L}_t = -\sum_{t=1}^{T} log P(\mathbf{y}_t|\mathbf{x}; \theta) \qquad (9)$$

where $\mathbf{y}$ is the translation obtained by the non-autoregressive translation model. The evaluation module is also optimized via a cross-entropy loss as

$$\mathcal{L}_{em} = -\sum_{t=1}^{T} log P(\mathbf{y}_t^*|\mathbf{x}; \mathbf{y}_t; \theta) \qquad (10)$$

where $\mathbf{y}^*$ denotes the translation generated by the evaluation model. Accordingly, the final loss is

$$\mathcal{L} = \mathcal{L}_{len} + \lambda \mathcal{L}_t + (1 - \lambda)L_{em} \qquad (11)$$

where λ represents the fusion parameter of translation module and evaluation module.

Inference. The evaluation module retains a large amount of semantic knowledge of the target language during training. Therefore, we can regard the evaluation module as a fine-tuning module for test set inference and the process is shown in Fig. 3(c). Namely, the decoder output is input into the evaluation module for fine-tuning and obtaining the final hidden layer state to parallel decoding generates the final translation:

$$C_{em} = SoftMax(EM(C_{en}, C_{de})) \tag{12}$$

where C_{en} and C_{de} represent the state of the last hidden layer of the encoder and decoder respectively and $EM(\cdot)$ denotes the fine-tuning process of the evaluation module.

4 Experimental Setups

4.1 Dataset

We not only conducted experiments on two widely-used NAT benchmarks: WMT14 English-German (En-De) and WMT16 Romanian-English (Ro-En) tasks, but also two low-resource tasks: CCMT19 Mongolian-Chinese (Mo-Zh) and CWMT17 Uyghur-Chinese (Uy-Zh), which consist of 4.5M, 0.6M, 0.25M, and 0.35M sentence pairs, respectively. The validation set contains 3000, 1999, 1001 and 1001 sentence pairs, respectively, with the same number of test sets for each task as its validation set.

The monolingual data is generally the same size as the corresponding bilingual data for fair comparison. We follow [4] to randomly sample English and German monolingual data from News Crawl[1] 2007–2020 and sample Romanian monolingual data from News Crawl 2015. We randomly sample Mongolian and Chinese from CCMT2022 (remove CCMT19) as the monolingual data. As for Uyghur monolingual data, we crawl from publicly available China National Radio (Uyghur)[2]. We preprocess all data via byte pair encoding (BPE) and we use BLEU [13] to measure the translation quality (except for Mo-Zh and Uy-Zh, we use sacre-BLEU [14]).

4.2 Baselines and Implementations

We exploit **Transformer-Base** (Beam Size = 4) as the autoregressive model strong baseline and validate our approach on the initial **NAT** model (Noise Parallel Decoding = 5) and two state-of-the-art NAT models: **MaskPredict** (Iteration Number = 10, Length Beam = 5) and **Levenshtein Transformer**, all baselines (except Transformer) are trained with standard KD. We adopt Adam optimizer [11], $\alpha = 0.9$, $\beta = 0.98$. We set 4000 warm-up steps and the initial learning rate is 0.0004. All the above baselines and our method are based on fairseq[3] implementation.

---

[1] http://data.statmt.org/news-crawl.

[2] http://www.uycnr.com.

[3] https://github.com/pytorch/fairseq.

Table 1. Results on different translation tasks benchmarks. Latency is measured in milliseconds (ms). KD⋆ and IR represent our enhanced knowledge distillation and Iterative Knowledge Refinement respectively. • indicates the same result as the previous row.

ID	Models	WMT14	WMT16	CCMT19		CWMT17	Latency	Speedup
		En-De	Ro-En	Mo-Zh	Zh-Mo	Uy-Zh		
1	Transformer	27.36	35.19	36.91	35.24	38.07	504.7	×1.00
2	NAT	19.74	28.57	29.38	28.63	30.76	64.4	×7.84
3	+EM	21.49	30.15	31.12	29.74	32.73	82.9	×6.08
4	+KD⋆	22.58	31.06	31.59	30.82	33.44	•	•
5	+IR	23.21	31.85	32.05	31.39	34.23	•	•
6	NAT$_{n_{decoder}=7}$	20.08	28.91	29.64	29.01	31.02	72.9	×6.92
7	Mask-Predict	27.19	34.35	31.48	30.72	33.92	307.7	×1.64
8	+EM	29.02	35.79	32.74	31.69	35.27	318.2	×1.58
9	+KD⋆	30.05	36.09	33.59	32.98	/	•	•
10	+IR	31.12	36.62	35.24	34.09	/	•	•
11	Lev-Transformer	27.32	34.31	32.54	30.68	33.75	192.8	×2.59
12	+EM	28.91	35.82	34.31	31.79	34.97	207.4	×2.43
13	+KD⋆	/	36.14	35.06	/	36.22	•	•
14	+IR	/	36.78	35.98	/	37.19	•	•

5   Results and Analyzes

5.1   Main Results

Table 1 lists the results and decoding latency of our method on different baselines and tasks. Encouragingly, we tested the performance of the evaluation module on different baselines and language pairs, our approach improves previous state-of-the-art BLEU on the NAT benchmarks (Line 3, Line 8 and Line 12), reaching a maximum improvement of 1.97 DLEU points (Uy-Zh in Line 3) and fully demonstrating the effectiveness and universality of our approach. It can be seen that the latencies for decoding with Noise Parallel Decoding (NPD) of ordinary NAT is increased since generate multiple sentences, but a speedup of still more than a factor of 7 over autoregressive decoding, sufficiently revealing the advantages of NAT fast decoding (Line 2). By virtue of the evaluation module for fine-tuning during inference, we make a considerable quality improvement with slightly decrease of decoding speed. The improvement on ordinary NAT can reach the same level as that of Lev-Transformer and Mask-Predict, but comparing latencies on the NAT+EM (Line 3) shows a speedup of 3 to 4 times over the above two baselines (Line 7 and Line 11). Since the evaluation module is similar in structure to the Transformer decoder, our model has one more layer of parameters compared with the NAT baseline. To determine whether the performance improvement results from the integration of evaluation module, we add a decoder layer to the NAT baseline and conduct experiments on five tasks. As can be seen from the comparison experiments in Line 2, Line 3 and Line 6, adding one decoder layer also bring improvement but it has extremely weak effects compared to the evaluation module.

Notably, the enhanced knowledge distillation also plays a critical role, which is applicable to different language pairs and models, especially for low-resource translation tasks (Line 4, Line 9 and Line 13). Even though this approach increases the training time, it neither modify model architecture nor add extra training loss, thus doesn't product any external latency, maintaining the intrinsic advantages of NAT models. Furthermore, different training strategies are also shown to be benefit for improving performance. Itera-

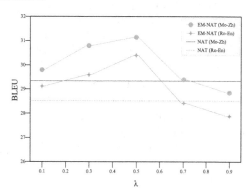

Fig. 4. Performance under different hyperparameters on Ro-En and Mo-Zh.

tive knowledge refinement has better results (Line 5, Line 10 and Line 14) compared with the original joint training because we first uses synthetic distillation data (generated by external monolingual data) for training to learn all semantic knowledge in monolingual data. In each subsequent stage, decrease the synthetic data with lower BLEU scores and increase the authentic distillation data proportionally, which continuously iterated to refine the model's performance. This recipe makes the model has enable to learn more language features and reduce the noise caused by poor quality data.

5.2   Effect of Hyperparameter λ

In this paper, we combine the loss functions of the translation module and the evaluation module as they are trained jointly. We choose linear interpolation for fusion as in (11), to explore the most suitable fusion parameters, we conducted multiple rounds of experiments with different hyperparameters λ (0.1, 0.3, 0.5, 0.7, 0.9) under the same conditions. The experimental results are shown in Fig. 4. It can be seen from the figure that the best effect can be achieved when the value of λ is 0.5. When the weight of the translation module is lower than evaluation module, the model's performance is slightly improved compared with the baseline model. The reason is evaluation module can be regarded as a layer of the translation module, so It have little impact with lower λ. As the weight of the evaluation module gradually decreases, the under-utilization of the it leads to a serious decline in model performance. Therefore, it can be proved that the evaluation module plays a positive and significant role in improving the performance of the model.

5.3   Effect of Evaluation Module During Inference

The evaluation module is reused for fine-tuning translation during inference. Therefore, this paper carries out experiments on the different integration methods of evaluation module and translation module. Figure 3(a) displays that directly use the state of the decoder last hidden layer to generate translation without adding evaluation module. Figure 3(b) integrates decoder hidden layer states and evaluation module states to inference. Figure 3(b) takes the decoder's hidden layer state as input and utilizes the

Table 2. BLEU values of different structures on CCMT19 Mo-Zh and CWMT17 Uy-Zh in the inference phase. (a)(b)(c) corresponds to the three structures in Fig. 3

Models	Mo-Zh	Uy-Zh
NAT	29.38	30.76
NAT+EM(a)	28.92	29.84
NAT+EM(b)	29.75	31.02
NAT+EM(c)	**31.12**	**32.73**

evaluation module to fine-tune and generate translation. The experimental results are shown in Table 2, the performance reaches the best when the evaluation module is used to fine-tune (Fig. 3(c)). Since the model trains the translation module and the evaluation module jointly, there is a certain coupling between them. The translation inference leads to a slight damage of model performance if Fig. 3(a) is used alone and it has improved compared with the NAT baseline when the evaluation model is added for inference. However, compared with the fusion recipe, using evaluation model for fine-tuning translations have the greatest achievements. The reason is that the evaluation model has already learned the linguistic features of the target language and other knowledge during training, so it can fine-tune the translations generated by the translation model according to the reserved knowledge, so as to achieve better results.

5.4   The Fluency and Faithfulness of the Translation

The original intention of introducing the evaluation module in this paper is to expect translations with higher fluency and faithfulness, we assess whether this brings the improvement on the two metrics. According to [5], we test the word repetition rate and n-gram accuracy for fluency. As for faithfulness, the cosine similarity between translation and reference is calculated using the average embeddings of all words. Table 3 reveals the results, the NAT model after fine-tuning the evaluation module can generate translation with higher n-gram accuracy for order 1 to order 4 and the greater accuracy on n-gram indicates higher fluency, especially on 3-gram and 4-gram. Meanwhile, it has the lower word repetition rate implies that the repeated translation issues in NAT parallel decoding is slightly relieved. Besides, our method has a bigger cosine similarity to the reference and this means the generate translation is more faithful in meaning to the source sentence. In conclusion, it proves the effectiveness of our method after fusing the evaluation module, which generate translation with better fluency and faithfulness.

Table 3. N-gram accuracy, repetition rate and cosine similarity on Mo-Zh translation. n-gram accuracy is the ratio of the number of matched n-gram between translation and reference against the total number of n-gram in the translation.

Model	1-gram	2-gram	3-gram	4-gram	Repetition	Cosine similarity
NAT	45.68	37.63	29.32	21.20	10.18	0.749
NAT+EM	46.69	38.31	30.08	22.37	9.71	0.763

5.5 Low-Frequency Word Analysis

To verify the translation effect of low-frequency words during inference, we analyze the lexical accuracy with different frequencies in the test set by taking Mongolian-Chinese translation tasks with low resources as an example. Specifically, we first employ fast-align[4] on the reference translation of the test set to obtain word alignment information, and then perform statistics on the results generated on the test

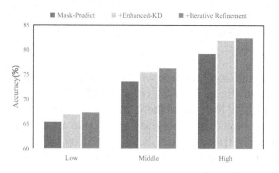

Fig. 5. Accuracy of word translation on Mongolian-Chinese.

set to calculate the accuracy of word translation. The experimental results are shown in Fig. 5. It can be seen that the model trained by standard knowledge distillation has a high translation accuracy in high-frequency words but poor effect on low-frequency words. Adding our enhanced knowledge distillation improve the translation of low-frequency words without reducing the translation effect of high-frequency and medium-frequency words. The reason is that monolingual data and bilingual data complement each other, and low-frequency words in bilingual data may appear more frequently in monolingual data, effectively alleviating the low-frequency word problem. Moreover, monolingual data has better accessibility and scalability, and more monolingual data can be added to improve the model translation quality. Simultaneously, the iterative knowledge refining training strategy alleviates the noise problem of unlabeled data and further improves the translation effect on all word frequencies.

5.6 Case Study

To intuitively reveal the superiority of our method, we list Ro-En and Mo-Zh translation cases generated by different models in Fig. 6. It can be seen that the addition of the evaluation module significantly improves translation fluency and

---

[4] https://github.com/clab/fast_align.

	Ro-En
Source	Anticipăm eradicarea analfabetismului în Timorul de Est în doi sau trei ani de acum înainte.
Reference	We anticipate the eradication of illiteracy in Timor Leste within two or three years from now.
NAT	We anticipate anticipate about East East in two and three years.
NAT+EM	We anticipate eradicate low culture in East in two or three years.
Ours	We anticipate eradicate illiteracy in Timor Leste in two or three years.

	Mo-Zh
Source	ᠬᠢᠩᠭᠠᠨ ᠲᠣᠭᠣᠷᠢᠭ ᠤᠨ ᠳᠠᠷᠤᠭᠠ ᠨᠣᠶᠠᠨ ᠲᠣᠰᠣ ᠵᠢᠩ ᠰᠢᠩᠭᠡᠨ ᠴᠣᠭ ᠲᠠᠢ ᠲᠦ ᠣᠷᠣᠭᠰᠠᠨ ᠢᠶᠠᠷ ᠬᠠᠷᠠ ᠭᠡᠷᠡᠯ ᠳᠦ ᠬᠢᠩᠭᠠᠨ ᠰᠢᠶᠠᠨ ᠳᠤ 《ᠠᠷᠪᠠᠨ ᠪᠦᠬᠦ ᠲᠠᠯᠠ ᠶᠢᠨ ᠪᠦᠷᠬᠦᠭᠦᠯᠲᠡ》 ᠵᠢᠩᠺᠧᠩ ᠪᠠᠷᠢᠯᠭᠠ ᠶᠢᠨ ᠪᠠᠢᠳᠠᠯ ᠢ ᠪᠠᠢᠴᠠᠭᠠᠨ ᠰᠣᠳᠣᠯᠪᠠ ··
Reference	青海省海西州州长诺卫星一行深入和林格尔县调研"十个全覆盖"工程建设情况。
NAT	青海省州长去<unk>检查检查工程建造。
NAT+EM	青海省州长等人去<unk>检查"十个全覆盖"工程建设情况。
Ours	青海省海西州州长等人去和林格尔县检查"十个全覆盖"工程建设情况。

Fig. 6. Translation effects of different models on Ro-En and Mo-Zh.

faithfulness compared with the translation generated by the original NAT model. For Ro-En and Mo-Zh cases, **NAT+EM** has the ability to translate **eradicate** and 建设情况 accurately, meanwhile, reduce the repeated prediction of words, this means that integrate evaluation module mitigates the mistranslation and missing translation of NAT caused by the parallel decoding and discarding the context dependency of the target token, it makes the model pay more attention to semantic coherence in the context generation process and sentence meaning more faithful to the source.

On the basis of adding the evaluation module, further use the synthetic distillation data and the decrease training strategy to make our model have the ability to recognize and translate named entities, such as **Timor Leste** in Ro-En, 海西州 and 和林格尔 in Mo-Zh, which means that more knowledge can be transferred to NAT by employing the distillation data generated by external monolinguals, which lightens the low-frequency word prediction errors, at the same time, our method benefits from the **Decrease** training and reduces the adverse impact of poor quality data on the model, making the translation results more respectful of references.

6   Conclusion

This paper propose to integrate the evaluation module into the NAT model, which can infuse more context dependencies during training and inference, and maintain the advantages of non-autoregressive high-speed decoding while improving the model performance. Experiments have proved that our method can produce translation with better fluency and faithfulness. Furthermore, we also use the distillation data generated by external monolingual to train NAT to soften low-frequency word prediction errors in standard knowledge distillation, which product external latency not at all and maintain the intrinsic advantages of NAT models. We will explore other methods that can further improve the model performance on the basis of one iterative decoding in future work.

References

1. Bahdanau, D., Cho, K., Bengio, Y.: Neural machine translation by jointly learning to align and translate. In: 3rd International Conference on Learning Representations, ICLR 2015 (2015)
2. Devlin, J., Chang, M., Lee, K., Toutanova, K.: BERT: pre-training of deep bidirectional transformers for language understanding. In: Proceedings of the 2019 Conference of the North American Chapter of the Association for Computational Linguistics: Human Language Technologies, NAACL-HLT 2019, pp. 4171–4186 (2019)
3. Ding, L., Wang, L., Liu, X., Wong, D.F., Tao, D., Tu, Z.: Understanding and improving lexical choice in non-autoregressive translation. In: 9th International Conference on Learning Representations, ICLR 2021 (2021)
4. Ding, L., Wang, L., Shi, S., Tao, D., Tu, Z.: Redistributing low-frequency words: Making the most of monolingual data in non-autoregressive translation. In: Proceedings of the 60th Annual Meeting of the Association for Computational Linguistics (Volume 1: Long Papers), ACL 2022, pp. 2417–2426 (2022)
5. Feng, Y., et al.: Modeling fluency and faithfulness for diverse neural machine translation. In: The Thirty-Fourth AAAI Conference on Artificial Intelligence, AAAI 2020, The Thirty-Second Innovative Applications of Artificial Intelligence Conference, IAAI 2020, The Tenth AAAI Symposium on Educational Advances in Artificial Intelligence, EAAI 2020, pp. 59–66 (2020)
6. Ghazvininejad, M., Levy, O., Liu, Y., Zettlemoyer, L.: Mask-predict: parallel decoding of conditional masked language models. In: Proceedings of the 2019 Conference on Empirical Methods in Natural Language Processing and the 9th International Joint Conference on Natural Language Processing, EMNLP-IJCNLP 2019, pp. 6111–6120 (2019)
7. Gu, J., Bradbury, J., Xiong, C., Li, V.O.K., Socher, R.: Non-autoregressive neural machine translation. In: 6th International Conference on Learning Representations, ICLR 2018 (2018)
8. Gu, J., Wang, C., Zhao, J.: Levenshtein transformer. In: Advances in Neural Information Processing Systems 32: Annual Conference on Neural Information Processing Systems 2019, NeurIPS 2019, pp. 11179–11189 (2019)
9. Guo, J., Tan, X., He, D., Qin, T., Xu, L., Liu, T.: Non-autoregressive neural machine translation with enhanced decoder input. In: The Thirty-Third AAAI Conference on Artificial Intelligence, AAAI 2019, The Thirty-First Innovative Applications of Artificial Intelligence Conference, IAAI 2019, The Ninth AAAI Symposium on Educational Advances in Artificial Intelligence, EAAI 2019, pp. 3723–3730 (2019)
10. Kim, Y., Rush, A.M.: Sequence-level knowledge distillation. In: Proceedings of the 2016 Conference on Empirical Methods in Natural Language Processing, EMNLP 2016, pp. 1317–1327 (2016). https://doi.org/10.18653/v1/d16-1139
11. Kingma, D.P., Ba, J.: Adam: a method for stochastic optimization. In: 3rd International Conference on Learning Representations, ICLR 2015 (2015)
12. Lee, J., Tran, D., Firat, O., Cho, K.: On the discrepancy between density estimation and sequence generation. In: Proceedings of the Fourth Workshop on Structured Prediction for NLP@EMNLP 2020, pp. 84–94 (2020). https://doi.org/10.18653/v1/2020.spnlp-1.10
13. Papineni, K., Roukos, S., Ward, T., Zhu, W.: BLEU: a method for automatic evaluation of machine translation. In: Proceedings of the 40th Annual Meeting of the Association for Computational Linguistics, ACL 2002, pp. 311–318 (2002)

14. Post, M.: A call for clarity in reporting BLEU scores. In: Proceedings of the Third Conference on Machine Translation: Research Papers, WMT 2018, pp. 186–191 (2018)

15. Ren, Y., Liu, J., Tan, X., Zhao, Z., Zhao, S., Liu, T.: A study of non-autoregressive model for sequence generation. In: Proceedings of the 58th Annual Meeting of the Association for Computational Linguistics, ACL 2020, pp. 149–159 (2020)

16. Stern, M., Chan, W., Kiros, J., Uszkoreit, J.: Insertion transformer: flexible sequence generation via insertion operations. In: Proceedings of the 36th International Conference on Machine Learning, ICML 2019, Proceedings of Machine Learning Research, vol. 97, pp. 5976–5985 (2019)

17. Vaswani, A., et al.: Attention is all you need. In: Advances in Neural Information Processing Systems 30: Annual Conference on Neural Information Processing Systems, NIPS 2017, pp. 5998–6008 (2017)

18. Xu, W., Ma, S., Zhang, D., Carpuat, M.: How does distilled data complexity impact the quality and confidence of non-autoregressive machine translation? In: Findings of the Association for Computational Linguistics: ACL/IJCNLP 2021. Findings of ACL, vol. ACL/IJCNLP 2021, pp. 4392–4400 (2021)

I²KD-SLU: An Intra-Inter Knowledge Distillation Framework for Zero-Shot Cross-Lingual Spoken Language Understanding

Tianjun Mao and Chenghong Zhang[✉]

School of Management, Fudan University, Shanghai, China
tjmao22@m.fudan.edu.cn, chzhang@fudan.edu.cn

Abstract. Spoken language understanding (SLU) typically includes two subtasks: intent detection and slot filling. Currently, it has achieved great success in high-resource languages, but it still remains challenging in low-resource languages due to the scarcity of labeled training data. Hence, there is a growing interest in zero-shot cross-lingual SLU. Despite of the success of existing zero-shot cross-lingual SLU models, most of them neglect to achieve the mutual guidance between intent and slots. To address this issue, we propose an **I**ntra-**I**nter **K**nowledge **D**istillation framework for zero-shot cross-lingual **S**poken **L**anguage **U**nderstanding (I²KD-SLU) to model the mutual guidance. Specifically, we not only apply intra knowledge distillation between intent predictions or slot predictions of the same utterance in different languages, but also apply inter knowledge distillation between intent predictions and slot predictions of the same utterance. Our experimental results demonstrate that our proposed framework significantly improves the performance compared with the strong baselines and achieves the new state-of-the-art performance on the MultiATIS++ dataset, obtaining a significant improvement over the previous best model in overall accuracy.

Keywords: Spoken language understanding · Knowledge distillation · zero-shot

1 Introduction

Spoken language understanding (SLU) aims to extract the semantic components from user queries [1–7], which is an important component in the task-oriented dialogue systems. SLU typically involves two subtasks: intent detection and slot filling. Intent detection obtains the user's intent from the input utterance and slot filling recognizes entities carrying detailed information of the intent. Deep neural network techniques have achieved remarkable results in SLU, but they require

The original version of the chapter has been revised. A correction to this chapter can be found at
https://doi.org/10.1007/978-3-031-44198-1_43

L. Iliadis et al. (Eds.): ICANN 2023, LNCS 14261, pp. 345–356, 2023.
https://doi.org/10.1007/978-3-031-44198-1_29

extensive labeled training data, which limits their scalability to languages with little or no training data. To address this limitation, zero-shot cross-lingual SLU generalization has received attention, which uses labeled data from high-resource languages to transfer trained models to low-resource target languages.

As deep learning applied to various tasks [8–13], machine translation technique is first introduced in data-based transfer methods to convert source utterances into targets [14–16]. Nevertheless, for some exceptionally low-resource languages, machine translation might be undependable or inaccessible [14]. To tackle this issue, some studies [17] aligned source languages with multiple target languages using bilingual dictionaries to randomly replace some words in the utterance with translation words in other languages, while others [18,19] have applied contrastive learning to achieve explicit alignment and improve performance. However, previous works have neglected the mutual guidance between intent and slots. Normally, intents and slots are related. So it is beneficial to model the mutual guidance between intents and slots in zero-shot cross-lingual spoken language understanding.

In this paper, we propose an intra-inter knowledge distillation framework for zero-shot cross-lingual spoken language understanding termed I^2KD-SLU based on multilingual BERT (mBERT) [20]. mBERT is a pre-trained contextual model trained on a large corpus of multiple languages, and it has shown significant progress in achieving zero-shot cross-lingual SLU. Specifically, for intra knowledge distillation, we apply knowledge distillation between intent predictions or slot predictions of the same utterance in different languages. For inter knowledge distillation, we apply knowledge distillation between intent predictions and slot predictions of the same utterance. Intra knowledge distillation helps to transfer knowledge from different languages and inter knowledge distillation helps to achieve the mutual guidance between intents and slots. Experiment results on the public benchmark dataset MultiATIS++ [16] demonstrate that I^2KD-SLU significantly outperforms the previous best cross-lingual SLU models and analysis further verifies the advantages of our method.

In summary, the contributions of this work can be concluded as follows:

- To the best of our knowledge, we are the first to achieve mutual guidance between intent and slots for zero-shot cross-lingual SLU.
- We propose an intra-inter knowledge distillation framework, where intra knowledge distillation promotes the knowledge transfer and inter knowledge distillation models the mutual guidance.
- Experiments show that our method achieves a new state-of-the-art performance, obtaining an improvement of 3.0% over the previous best model in terms of average overall accuracy of 9 languages.

2 Related Work

2.1 Spoken Language Understanding

Intent detection and slot filling tasks are two typical sub-tasks of SLU [21–23]. While slot filling can be challenging as decisions must be made for each word or token, it is applied in interesting use cases, as noted by [24]. In the past, these two tasks are performed independently, but recent research has shown that jointly optimizing them can improve accuracy [25–29]. Contextual language models have also improved language encoding capabilities for joint NLU models compared to traditional static word embedding approaches. Despite there are lots of remarkable results in SLU, they all require extensive labeled training data, which limits their scalability to languages with little or no training data. As a result, the concept of zero-shot cross-lingual SLU generalization has gained traction, where models are trained using labeled data from high-resource languages and then transferred to low-resource target languages without additional training data. Lately, there have been encouraging results achieved by cross-lingual contextualized embeddings such as mBERT [20]. Several studies have concentrated on enhancing mBERT [16–19,30,31]. However, they both neglect to achieve the mutual guidance between intent and slots. In our work, we tackle this issue by applying intra and inter knowledge distillation.

2.2 Knowledge Distillation

Knowledge Distillation is a technique first proposed by [32]. The goal of knowledge distillation is to transfer the knowledge from a large, complex model which is known as the teacher to a smaller, simpler model which is known as the student. This is achieved by training the student model to mimic the behavior of the teacher model, using either the predicted outputs or intermediate representations of the teacher model. Existing knowledge distillation methods generally fall into two categories. The first category focuses on using dark knowledge [33,34] and the second category focuses on sharing information about the relationships between the layers of the teacher model [35,36]. In our method, we apply knowledge distillation to facilitate knowledge transfer between different languages and achieve the mutual guidance between intent and slots.

3   Method

In this section, we first describe the background (Sect. 3.1) of zero-shot cross-lingual SLU. Then we introduce the main architecture of our framework I²KD-SLU. Finally we introduce the final training objective (Sect. 3.3). The overview of our framework is illustrated in Fig. 1.

3.1 Background

Intent detection and slot filling are two subtasks of SLU. Given an input utterance $\mathbf{x} = (x_1, x_2, \ldots, x_n)$, where n is the length of $\mathbf{x}$. Intent detection is a classification task which predicts the intent o^I. Slot filling is a sequence labeling task which maps each utterance $\mathbf{x}$ into a slot sequence $o^S = \left(o_1^S, o_2^S, \ldots, o_n^S\right)$. Training a single model that can handle both tasks of intent detection and slot

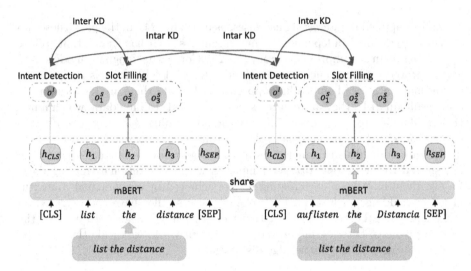

Fig. 1. The overview of our I²KD-SLU. Two models with the same architecture are trained on the original utterance and code-switched utterance, respectively. Intra knowledge distillation helps to transfer knowledge between different languages. Inter knowledge distillation helps to achieve mutual guidance between intent and slots.

filling is a common practice as they are closely interconnected. Following previous work [37], the formalism is formulated as follows:

$$(o^I, o^S) = f(\mathbf{x}) \tag{1}$$

where f is the trained model.

The zero-shot cross-lingual SLU task involves training an SLU model in a source language and then adapting it directly to target languages without additional training. Specifically, given each instance $\mathbf{x}_{tgt}$ in the target language, the predicted intent and slot can be directly obtained by the SLU model f which is trained on the source language:

$$\left(o^I_{tgt}, o^S_{tgt}\right) = f\left(\mathbf{x}_{tgt}\right) \tag{2}$$

where tgt denotes the target language.

3.2 Main Architecture

Inspired by the success of pre-trained models [38–44], we use mBERT [20] obtain the representation $\mathbf{H}$ of the utterance $\mathbf{x}$ by using mBERT [20] model:

$$\mathbf{H} = (h_{\text{CLS}}, h_1, \dots, h_n, h_{\text{SEP}}) \tag{3}$$

where [CLS] denotes the special symbol for representing the whole sequence, and [SEP] can be used for separating non-consecutive token sequences.

For intent detection, we input the utterance representation h_{CLS} to a classification layer to obtain the predicted intent:

$$o^I = \mathrm{softmax}\left(W^I h_{\mathrm{CLS}} + b^I\right) \tag{4}$$

where W^I and b^I denote the trainable matrices.

For slot filling, we follow [45] to utilize the representation of the first sub-token as the whole word representation and utilize the hidden state to predict each slot in the utterance:

$$o_t^S = \mathrm{softmax}\left(W^s h_t + b^s\right) \tag{5}$$

where h_t denotes the representation of the first sub-token of word x_t, W^s and b^s denote the trainable matrices.

We employ the code-switching approach [17] to leverage bilingual dictionaries [46] in generating multi-lingual code-switched utterance $\mathbf{x}'$. We denote the intent prediction and slot prediction of the original utterance $\mathbf{x}$ as o^{Io} and o^{So}, respectively. Similarly, we denote the intent prediction and slot prediction of the code-switched utterance $\mathbf{x}'$ as o^{Ic} and o^{Sc}, respectively. Note that o^{So} and o^{Sc} both consist of all slot predictions in the corresponding utterance.

We apply intra knowledge distillation to promote knowledge transfer between different languages, which includes two components. One is the Jensen-Shannon Divergence (JSD) between the intent prediction of the original utterance and the intent prediction of the code-switched utterance. The other is the JSD between the slot prediction of the original utterance and the slot prediction of the code-switched utterance. The final intra knowledge distillation loss $\mathcal{L}_{intra}$ is computed as follows:

$$\mathcal{L}_{intra} = \mathrm{JSD}(o^{Io}, o^{Ic}) + \mathrm{JSD}(o^{So}, o^{Sc}) \tag{6}$$

We also apply inter knowledge distillation to achieve mutual guidance between intent and slots, which also includes two components. One is the JSD between the intent prediction of the original utterance and the slot prediction of the original utterance. The other is the JSD between the intent prediction of the code-switched utterance and the slot prediction of the code-switched utterance. The final inter knowledge distillation loss $\mathcal{L}_{inter}$ is computed as follows:

$$\mathcal{L}_{inter} = \mathrm{JSD}(o^{Io}, \mathrm{Avg}(o^{So})) + \mathrm{JSD}(o^{Ic}, \mathrm{Avg}(o^{Sc})) \tag{7}$$

where Avg denotes averaging all slots prediction in the utterance.

3.3 Training Objective

Following previous work [37], the intent detection objective $\mathcal{L}_I$ and the slot filling objective $\mathcal{L}_S$ are formulated as follows:

$$\mathcal{L}_I \triangleq -\sum_{i=1}^{n_I} \hat{\mathbf{y}}_i^I \log\left(o_i^I\right) \tag{8}$$

$$\mathcal{L}_S \triangleq -\sum_{j=1}^{n}\sum_{i=1}^{n_S} \hat{\mathbf{y}}_j^{i,S} \log\left(o_j^{i,S}\right) \tag{9}$$

where $\hat{\mathbf{y}}_i^I$ is the gold intent label, $\hat{\mathbf{y}}_j^{i,S}$ is the gold slot label for jth token, n_I is the number of intent labels, and n_S is the number of slot labels.

The final training objective is as follow:

$$\mathcal{L} = \alpha\mathcal{L}_I + \beta\mathcal{L}_S + \lambda\mathcal{L}_{intra} + \gamma\mathcal{L}_{inter} \tag{10}$$

where α, β, λ, γ are the hyper-parameters.

4   Experiments

4.1   Datasets and Metrics

All the experiments are conducted on MultiATIS++[1] [16], which contains 18 intents and 84 slots. Human-translated data for six languages including Spanish (es), German (de), Chinese (zh), Japanese (ja), Portuguese (pt), French (fr) are added to Multilingual ATIS which has Hindi (hi) and Turkish (tr). The statistics of MultiATIS++ dataset are shown in Table 1.

Table 1. Statistics of MultiATIS++

Language	Utterances			Intent types	Slot types
	train	valid	test		
hi	1440	160	893	17	75
tr	578	60	715	17	71
others	4488	490	893	18	84

Following the previous works [18,19,37], we utilize accuracy to evaluate the intent prediction performance, F1 score to evaluate the slot filling performance, and overall accuracy to get evaluation of the overall performance of the model. Overall accuracy represents whether all metrics including intent and slots in the utterance are correctly predicted.

4.2   Implementation Details

In order to help the framework perform well, the model we utilized has $N = 12$ attention heads and $M = 12$ transformer blocks. Following previous work [18], we select the best hyperparameters by searching a combination of batch size, learning rate with the following candidate set: learning rate $\{2 \times 10^{-7}, 5 \times 10^{-7}, 1 \times 10^{-6}, 2 \times 10^{-6}, 5 \times 10^{-6}, 6 \times 10^{-6}, 5 \times 10^{-5}, 5 \times 10^{-4}\}$ and batch size $\{4, 8, 16, 32\}$. α, β, λ, γ are set to 0.9, 0.2, 0.7 and 0.3 in Eq. 10, respectively. We use Adam optimizer [49] with $\beta_1 = 0.9, \beta_2 = 0.98$ to optimize the parameters in our model. The learning rate will decrease according to the

---

[1] https://github.com/amazon-science/multiatis.

Table 2. Experiment results on the MultiATIS++ dataset. The results with "◇" denotes that they are taken from the corresponding published paper, results with [†] are cited from [18], and results with [‡] are cited from [19]. '–' denotes missing results from the published work.

Intent (Acc)	en	de	es	fr	hi	ja	pt	tr	zh	AVG
mBERT[†] [20]	98.54	95.40	96.30	94.31	82.41	76.18	94.95	75.10	82.53	88.42
ZSJoint[‡] [30]	98.54	90.48	93.28	94.51	77.15	76.59	94.62	73.29	84.55	87.00
Ensemble-Net◇ [31]	90.26	92.50	96.64	95.18	77.88	77.04	95.30	75.04	84.99	87.20
CoSDA[†] [17]	95.74	94.06	92.29	77.04	82.75	73.25	93.05	80.42	78.95	87.32
GL-CLeF◇ [18]	98.77	97.53	97.05	97.72	86.00	82.84	96.08	83.92	87.68	91.95
LAJ-MCL◇ [19]	98.77	98.10	98.10	98.77	84.54	81.86	97.09	85.45	89.03	92.41
I²KD-SLU	**98.87**	**98.18**	**98.22**	**98.94**	**86.67**	**82.66**	**97.22**	**85.99**	**89.47**	**92.91**
Slot (F1)	en	de	es	fr	hi	ja	pt	tr	zh	AVG
Ensemble-Net◇ [31]	85.05	82.75	77.56	76.19	14.14	9.44	74.00	45.63	37.29	55.78
mBERT[†] [20]	95.11	80.11	78.22	82.25	26.71	25.40	72.37	41.49	53.22	61.66
ZSJoint[‡] [30]	95.20	74.79	76.52	74.25	52.73	70.10	72.56	29.66	66.91	68.08
CoSDA[†] [17]	92.29	81.37	76.94	79.36	64.06	66.62	75.05	48.77	77.32	73.47
GL-CLeF◇ [18]	95.39	86.30	85.22	84.31	70.34	73.12	81.83	65.85	77.61	80.00
LAJ-MCL◇ [19]	96.02	86.59	83.03	82.11	61.04	68.52	81.49	65.20	82.00	78.23
I²KD-SLU	**96.18**	**86.74**	**85.50**	**84.28**	**73.06**	**74.14**	**82.54**	**68.16**	**83.14**	**81.53**
Overall (Acc)	en	de	es	fr	hi	ja	pt	tr	zh	AVG
AR-S2S-PTR◇ [47]	86.83	34.00	40.72	17.22	7.45	10.04	33.38	–	23.74	–
IT-S2S-PTR◇ [48]	87.23	39.46	50.06	46.78	11.42	12.60	39.30	–	28.72	–
mBERT[†] [20]	87.12	52.69	52.02	37.29	4.92	7.11	43.49	4.33	18.58	36.29
ZSJoint[‡] [30]	87.23	41.43	44.46	43.67	16.01	33.59	43.90	1.12	30.80	38.02
CoSDA[†] [17]	77.04	57.06	46.62	50.06	26.20	28.89	48.77	15.24	46.36	44.03
GL-CLeF◇ [18]	88.02	66.03	59.53	57.02	34.83	41.42	60.43	28.95	50.62	54.09
LAJ-MCL◇ [19]	89.81	67.75	59.13	57.56	23.29	29.34	61.93	28.95	54.76	52.50
I²KD-SLU	**90.04**	**68.01**	**59.76**	**58.03**	**35.08**	**43.02**	**63.02**	**29.31**	**55.06**	**55.70**

step number. For all the experiments, we select the model that performs the best on the dev set in terms of overall accuracy and evaluate it on the test set. All experiments are conducted at an environment older than Nvidia Tesla-A100. The training process lasts several hours.

4.3 Baselines

We compare our model to the following baselines:

- mBERT: mBERT[2] follows the same model architecture and training procedure as BERT [20], but instead of training only on monolingual English data, it is trained on the Wikipedia pages of 104 languages with a shared word piece vocabulary, allowing the model to share embeddings across languages;

---

[2] https://github.com/google-research/bert/blob/master/multilingual.md

- `AR-S2S-PTR`: [47] proposes a unified sequence-to-sequence models with the pointer generator network for cross-lingual SLU;
- `IT-S2S-PTR`: [48] proposes a non-autoregressive parser based on the insertion transformer, which speeds up the decoding progress of cross-lingual SLU;
- `Ensemble-Net`: [31] proposes an effective zero-shot cross-lingual SLU model, whose predictions are the majority voting results of 8 independent models, each separately trained on a single source language, which achieves promising performance on zero-shot cross-lingual SLU;
- `ZSJoint`: [30] proposes a zero-shot SLU model, which is trained on the en training set and directly applied to the test sets of target languages.
- `CoSDA`: [17] proposes a data augmentation framework to generate multi-lingual code-switching data to fine-tune mBERT, which encourages the model to align representations from the source and multiple target languages. For a fair comparison, we use both the en training data and the code-switching data for fine-tuning.
- `GL-CLEF`: [18] introduces a contrastive learning framework to explicitly align representations across languages for zero-shot cross-lingual SLU.
- `LAJ-MCL`: [19] proposes a multi-level contrastive learning framework for zero-shot cross-lingual SLU.

4.4 Main Results

The performance comparison of I^2KD-SLU and baselines are shown in Table 2, from which we have the following observations: (1) The models which applies code-switching method including CoSDA, GL-CLEF, LAJ-MCL and I^2KD-SLU outperform the models which do not use this method. A possible reason is that code-switching produces an implicit alignment, thereby aligning the representations to some degree. (2) Moreover, I^2KD-SLU further improves the performance and obtains a relative improvement of 3.0% over the previous best model in terms of average overall accuracy. The reason is that our method enhance the mutual guidance between intent and slots by intra and inter knowledge distillation, which is helpful to further improve the performance of the model.

4.5 Model Analysis

Effect of Intra Knowledge Distillation Module. To demonstrate the effectiveness of intra knowledge distillation module, we remove it and refer it to *w/o intra KD* in Table 3. We can observe that after we remove the intra knowledge distillation module, the intent accuracy of MixATIS++ dataset drops by 1.45% and the slot F1 of MixATIS++ dataset drops by 3.39%. Moreover, the overall accuracy also drops by 4.68%. These results demonstrate the importance of the intra knowledge distillation in our model, which promotes knowledge transfer between different languages.

Table 3. Ablation results on the MultiATIS++ dataset.

Models	Intent	Slot	Overall
I²KD-SLU	**92.91**	**81.53**	**55.70**
w/o intra KD	91.46(↓1.45)	78.14(↓3.39)	51.02(↓4.68)
w/o inter KD	91.53(↓0.38)	78.26(↓3.27)	51.72(↓3.98)
More Parameters	88.34(↓4.57)	74.84(↓6.69)	46.15(↓9.55)

Effect of Inter Knowledge Distillation Module. To demonstrate the effectiveness of inter knowledge distillation, we remove it and refer it to *w/o inter KD* and the results are shown in Table 3. After we remove the inter knowledge distillation module, the intent accuracy of MixATIS++ dataset drops by 0.38% and the slot F1 of MixATIS++ dataset drops by 3.27%. Moreover, the overall accuracy also drops by 3.98%. We can clearly observe that inter knowledge distillation is beneficial in improving the performance of the model. By applying inter knowledge distillation, the model can predict the intent and slots more accurately, which achieves the mutual guidance between intent and slots.

Effect of More Parameters. Following previous works [27,50], to verify whether the increased parameters of I²KD-SLU lead to the higher performance, we add an additional LSTM layer after the last layer of mBERT and refer it to *More Parameters*. The results in Table 3 show that our method outperforms mBERT with more parameters in intent accuracy, slot F1 and overall accuracy by 4.57%, 6.69%, 9.55%, respectively. These results demonstrate that the improvement of our method comes from the intra and inter knowledge distillation rather than the involved parameters.

5   Case Study

To further demonstrate the superiority of our framework, we present one case in Fig. 2. We can clearly observe that both GL-CLEF and I²KD-SLU predict the

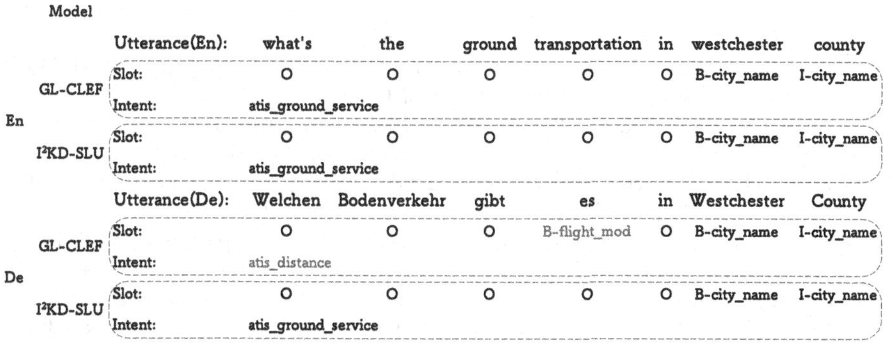

Fig. 2. A case study of our framework and previous best model GL-CLEF. Intents and slots in red are those that are predicted incorrectly. (Color figure online)

slots and intent correctly in English. However, GL-CLeF predicts the slots and intent incorrectly in German, while our model still predicts them correctly. The reason for this is that our model achieve the mutual guidance between intent and slots and promotes knowledge transfer at the same time.

6   Conclusions

In this paper, we propose a novel intra-inter knowledge distillation framework I^2KD-SLU for zero-shot cross-lingual spoken language understanding (SLU), which achieves the mutual guidance between intent and slots and promotes the knowledge transfer between different languages. Experiments on MultiATIS++ dataset show that I^2KD-SLU achieve a new state-of-the-art performance. Model analysis demonstrates the superiority of I^2KD-SLU. In the future, we will explore the effectiveness of our method in other zero-shot cross-lingual tasks to further improve the performance.

References

1. Tur, G., De Mori, R.: Spoken Language Understanding: Systems for Extracting Semantic Information from Speech. Wiley, New York (2011)
2. Young, S., Gašić, M., Thomson, B., Williams, J.D.: POMDP-based statistical spoken dialog systems: a review. Proc. IEEE **101**, 1160–1179 (2013)
3. Cheng, X., et al.: FC-MTLF: a fine- and coarse-grained multi-task learning framework for cross-lingual spoken language understanding. In: Proceedings of Interspeech (2023)
4. Xu, P., Sarikaya, R.: Convolutional neural network based triangular CRF for joint intent detection and slot filling. In: 2013 IEEE Workshop on Automatic Speech Recognition and Understanding (2013)
5. Kim, B., Ryu, S., Lee, G.G.: Two-stage multi-intent detection for spoken language understanding. Multimedia Tools Appl. **76**, 11377–11390 (2017)
6. Gangadharaiah, R., Narayanaswamy, B.: Joint multiple intent detection and slot labeling for goal-oriented dialog. In: Proceedings of NAACL (2019)
7. Cheng, X., Yao, Z., Zhu, Z., Li, Y., Li, H., Zou, Y.: C 2 A-SLU: cross and contrastive attention for improving ASR robustness in spoken language understanding. In: Proceedings of Interspeech (2023)
8. Tian, K., Lin, C., Sun, M., Zhou, L., Yan, J., Ouyang, W.: Improving auto-augment via augmentation-wise weight sharing. In: Proceedings of NeurIPS (2020)
9. Cheng, X., Zhu, Z., Li, H., Li, Y., Zou, Y.: SSVMR: saliency-based self-training for video-music retrieval. In: Proceedings of ICASSP (2023)
10. Tian, K., Lin, C., Lim, S., Ouyang, W., Dokania, P.K., Torr, P.H.S.: A continuous mapping for augmentation design. In: Proceedings of NeurIPS (2021)
11. Guo, R., et al.: Powering one-shot topological NAS with stabilized share-parameter proxy. In: Vedaldi, A., Bischof, H., Brox, T., Frahm, J.-M. (eds.) ECCV 2020. LNCS, vol. 12359, pp. 625–641. Springer, Cham (2020). https://doi.org/10.1007/978-3-030-58568-6_37
12. Tian, K., Jiang, Y., Diao, Q., Lin, C., Wang, L., Yuan, Z.: Designing BERT for convolutional networks: sparse and hierarchical masked modeling. In: Proceedings of ICLR (2023)

13. Yao, Z., Cheng, X., Zou, Y.: PoseRAC: pose saliency transformer for repetitive action counting. ArXiv preprint (2023)
14. Upadhyay, S., Faruqui, M., Tür, G., Hakkani-Tür, D., Heck, L.P.: (almost) zero-shot cross-lingual spoken language understanding. In: Proceedings of ICASSP (2018)
15. Schuster, S., Gupta, S., Shah, R., Lewis, M.: Cross-lingual transfer learning for multilingual task oriented dialog. In: Proceedings of NAACL (2019)
16. Xu, W., Haider, B., Mansour, S.: End-to-end slot alignment and recognition for cross-lingual NLU. In: Proceedings of EMNLP (2020)
17. Qin, L., Ni, M., Zhang, Y., Che, W.: COSDA-ML: multi-lingual code-switching data augmentation for zero-shot cross-lingual NLP. In: Proceedings of IJCAI (2020)
18. Qin, L., et al.: GL-CLeF: a global-local contrastive learning framework for cross-lingual spoken language understanding. In: Proceedings of ACL (2022)
19. Liang, S., et al.: Label-aware multi-level contrastive learning for cross-lingual spoken language understanding. In: Proceedings of EMNLP (2022)
20. Devlin, J., Chang, M.W., Lee, K., Toutanova, K.: BERT: pre-training of deep bidirectional transformers for language understanding. In: Proceedings of NAACL (2019)
21. Cheng, X., Cao, B., Ye, Q., Zhu, Z., Li, H., Zou, Y.: ML-LMCL: mutual learning and large-margin contrastive learning for improving ASR robustness in spoken language understanding. In: Proceedings of ACL Findings (2023)
22. Zhu, Z., Cheng, X., Huang, Z., Chen, D., Zou, Y.: Towards unified spoken language understanding decoding via label-aware compact linguistics representations. In: Proceedings of ACL Findings (2023)
23. Zhu, Z., Xu, W., Cheng, X., Song, T., Zou, Y.: A dynamic graph interactive framework with label-semantic injection for spoken language understanding. In: Proceedings of ICASSP (2023)
24. Gunaratna, K., Srinivasan, V., Nama, S., Jin, H.: Using neighborhood context to improve information extraction from visual documents captured on mobile phones. In: Proceedings of CIKM (2021)
25. Zhang, X., Wang, H.: A joint model of intent determination and slot filling for spoken language understanding. In: Proceedings of IJCAI (2016)
26. Qin, L., Liu, T., Che, W., Kang, B., Zhao, S., Liu, T.: A co-interactive transformer for joint slot filling and intent detection. In: Proceedings of ICASSP (2021)
27. Qin, L., Wei, F., Xie, T., Xu, X., Che, W., Liu, T.: GL-GIN: fast and accurate non-autoregressive model for joint multiple intent detection and slot filling. In: Proceedings of ACL (2021)
28. Xing, B., Tsang, I.: Co-guiding net: achieving mutual guidances between multiple intent detection and slot filling via heterogeneous semantics-label graphs. In: Proceedings of EMNLP (2022)
29. Xing, B., Tsang, I.: Group is better than individual: exploiting label topologies and label relations for joint multiple intent detection and slot filling. In: Proceedings of EMNLP (2022)
30. Chen, Q., Zhuo, Z., Wang, W.: BERT for joint intent classification and slot filling. ArXiv preprint (2019)
31. Razumovskaia, E., Glavas, G., Majewska, O., Ponti, E.M., Korhonen, A., Vulic, I.: Crossing the conversational chasm: a primer on natural language processing for multilingual task-oriented dialogue systems. J. Artif. Intell. Res. **74**, 1351–1402 (2022)
32. Hinton, G., Vinyals, O., Dean, J., et al.: Distilling the knowledge in a neural network. ArXiv preprint (2015)

33. Romero, A., Ballas, N., Kahou, S.E., Chassang, A., Gatta, C., Bengio, Y.: FitNets: hints for thin deep nets. In: Proceedings of ICLR (2015)
34. You, S., Xu, C., Xu, C., Tao, D.: Learning from multiple teacher networks. In: Proceedings of KDD (2017)
35. Yim, J., Joo, D., Bae, J., Kim, J.: A gift from knowledge distillation: fast optimization, network minimization and transfer learning. In: Proceedings of CVPR (2017)
36. Tarvainen, A., Valpola, H.: Mean teachers are better role models: weight-averaged consistency targets improve semi-supervised deep learning results. In: Proceedings of NeurIPS (2017)
37. Goo, C.W., et al.: Slot-gated modeling for joint slot filling and intent prediction. In: Proceedings of NAACL (2018)
38. Dong, Q., et al.: PolyVoice: language models for speech to speech translation. ArXiv preprint (2023)
39. Cheng, X., Zhu, Z., Yao, Z., Li, H., Li, Y., Zou, Y.: GhostT5: generate more features with cheap operations to improve textless spoken question answering. In: Proceedings of Interspeech (2023)
40. Li, H., Cao, M., Cheng, X., Zhu, Z., Li, Y., Zou, Y.: Generating templated caption for video grounding. ArXiv preprint (2023)
41. Li, Y., Yang, B., Cheng, X., Zhu, Z., Li, H., Zou, Y.: Unify, align and refine: Multi-level semantic alignment for radiology report generation. In: Proceedings of ICCV (2023)
42. Zhu, Z., Cheng, X., Chen, D., Huang, Z., Li, H., Zou, Y.: Mix before align: towards zero-shot cross-lingual sentiment analysis via soft-mix and multi-view learning. In: Proceedings of Interspeech (2023)
43. Li, H., Cao, M., Cheng, X., Li, Y., Zhu, Z., Zou, Y.: Semantically aligned and uniform video grounding via geodesic and game theory. In: Proceedings of ICCV (2023)
44. Cheng, X., Dong, Q., Yue, F., Ko, T., Wang, M., Zou, Y.: M 3 ST: mix at three levels for speech translation. In: Proceedings of ICASSP (2023)
45. Wang, Y., Che, W., Guo, J., Liu, Y., Liu, T.: Cross-lingual BERT transformation for zero-shot dependency parsing. In: Proceedings of EMNLP (2019)
46. Lample, G., Conneau, A., Ranzato, M., Denoyer, L., Jégou, H.: Word translation without parallel data. In: Proceedings of ICLR (2018)
47. Rongali, S., Soldaini, L., Montl, E., Hamza, W.: Don't parse, generate! A sequence to sequence architecture for task-oriented semantic parsing. In: Proceedings of WWW (2020)
48. Zhu, Q., Khan, H., Soltan, S., Rawls, S., Hamza, W.: Don't parse, insert: multilingual semantic parsing with insertion based decoding. In: Proceedings of CoNLL (2020)
49. Kingma, D.P., Ba, J.: Adam: a method for stochastic optimization. In: Proceedings of ICLR (2015)
50. Qin, L., Xu, X., Che, W., Liu, T.: AGIF: an adaptive graph-interactive framework for joint multiple intent detection and slot filling. In: Proceedings of EMNLP Findings (2020)

Imbalanced Few-Shot Learning Based on Meta-transfer Learning

Yan Chu[1], Xianghui Sun[1], Jiang Songhao[2,3(✉)], Tianwen Xie[1], Zhengkui Wang[4], and Wen Shan[5]

[1] Harbin Engineering University, Harbin 150001, China
{chuyan,sunxianghui,xietianwen}@hrbeu.edu.cn
[2] CNCERT/CC, Beijing, China
[3] Institute of Information Engineering, Chinese Academy of Sciences, Beijing, China
jiangsonghao@iie.ac.cn
[4] Singapore Institute of Technology, Singapore, Singapore
zhengkui.wang@singaporetech.edu.sg
[5] Singapore University of Social Sciences, Singapore, Singapore
viviensw@suss.edu.sg

Abstract. Few-shot learning is a challenging task that aims to learn to adapt to new tasks with only a few labeled samples. Meta-learning is a promising approach to address this challenge, but the learned meta-knowledge on training sets may not always be useful due to class imbalance, task imbalance, and distribution imbalance. In this paper, we propose a novel few-shot learning method based on meta-transfer learning, which is called Meta-Transfer Task-Adaptive Meta-Learning (MT-TAML). Meta-transfer learning is used to transfer the weight parameters of a pre-trained deep neural network, which makes up for the deficiency of using shallow networks as the feature extractor. To address the imbalance problem in realistic few-shot learning scenarios, we introduce a learnable parameter balance meta-knowledge for each task. Additionally, we propose a novel task training strategy that selects the difficult class in each task and re-samples from it to form the difficult task, thereby improving the model's accuracy. Our experimental results show that MT-TAML outperforms existing few-shot learning methods by 2–4%. Furthermore, our ablation experiments confirm the effectiveness of the combination of meta-transfer learning and learnable equilibrium parameters.

Keywords: meta-learning · few-shot learning · meta-transfer learning

1 Introduction

Few-shot learning has witnessed significant progress in recent years, with existing methods relying on meta-learning techniques [1–4]. During the meta-learning stage, these methods form multiple tasks by sampling from base classes and

---

Supported by the International Exchange Program of Harbin Engineering University for Innovation-oriented Talents Cultivation.

L. Iliadis et al. (Eds.): ICANN 2023, LNCS 14261, pp. 357–369, 2023.
https://doi.org/10.1007/978-3-031-44198-1_30

learn meta-knowledge from source data in the form of good initial conditions, embeddings, and optimization strategies. The resulting model is fine-tuned by learning optimization strategies or feed-forward calculations to solve the target few-shot learning problem without updating the network weights. One representative approach is model-agnostic meta-learning (MAML) [5], which finds the optimal initialization state by learning to make the base learner adapt to new tasks quickly. However, MAML often requires many similar meta-training tasks, making it computationally expensive. Moreover, it models each task using a low-complexity base learner, such as a shallow neural network, thus limiting the ability to train models with more deep and powerful architectures.

Existing few-shot learning methods are based on ideal task settings, such as n-way k-shot learning [6–8]. However, these settings assume consistent categories and instances in each learning task, and the same meta-knowledge can be obtained from each task. In reality, the number of samples and categories in different tasks varies greatly, resulting in task imbalance, unbalanced classification, and distribution imbalance. To address these challenges, we propose a task-adaptive few-shot learning method based on meta-transfer learning, MT-MAML, which combines the strengths of both meta-learning and transfer learning. MT-MAML leverages transfer learning by applying the weights of a pretrained deep neural network to other networks using shift and scaling trainable operations. Meanwhile, meta-learning is employed to learn how to transfer the weight parameters adaptively during few-shot learning, thereby reducing the number of training parameters, mitigating overfitting, and accelerating model convergence.

In summary, our paper presents three contributions:

- We incorporate three balance parameters into MAML to facilitate the proper utilization of meta-knowledge acquired from the training sets.
- We adopt meta-transfer learning to enable the transfer of pre-trained deep neural networks (DNNs). This involves lightweight operations of DNN neurons, reducing the number of parameters and the risk of over-fitting. Furthermore, the weights of the trained DNN remain constant during migration, avoiding the problem of catastrophic forgetting.
- We conduct extensive experiments to validate the effectiveness of combining meta-transfer learning with the newly introduced balance parameters.

2   Related Work

Meta-learning is a task-level learning method that differs from data augmentation [9]. Ma et al. presented a decomposed meta-learning approach that addressed the problem of few-shot NER by sequentially tackling few-shot span detection and few-shot entity typing using meta-learning [10]. Nilesh et al. proposed a method to learn a common set of features from multiple and related tasks and transfer this knowledge to new and unseen tasks [11]. Iwata et al. shared knowledge across supervised learning tasks using feature descriptions written in natural language and improves the predictive performance on unseen tasks with a limited number of labeled data by meta-learning from various tasks [12].

Transfer learning involves the critical tasks of determining what to transfer and how to transfer, as transfer methods vary depending on the source-target domains and the transfer knowledge. In the context of deep models, one effective approach involves the use of a pre-trained model for a new task, commonly known as fine-tuning [13]. It has been demonstrated that models pre-trained on large datasets generally produce superior generalization results compared with models initialized randomly [14]. Another prevalent method is to employ a pre-trained network as the backbone and augment it with advanced functions such as target detection, recognition, and image segmentation.

MAML extracts features and quickly learns new knowledge from tasks while avoiding overfitting enabling direct application to any learning problem and model by training a model with initial parameters to achieve maximum performance on a new task. However, the training of the MAML model does not consider the distribution difference between unseen and training tasks, leading to unbalanced classification, task imbalance, and imbalance of distribution.

3   Methodology

3.1   Model Training Phases

We propose a Meta-Transfer Task-Adaptive Meta-Learning model, which addresses the problem of insufficient feature extraction caused by shallow networks in the MAML model. MT-TAML combines meta-transfer learning with two lightweight parameters to transfer pre-trained deep network weights, while maintaining the network's weight during the transfer process to reduce training parameters. To balance the use of meta-knowledge in tasks, the model adds learnable balance parameters to solve the imbalance problem of few-shot learning. The overall training process is divided into the pre-training, meta-transfer learning, and meta-test phases, as shown in Fig. 1. The pre-training set is Mini-Imagenet, with the low-level network weights fixed as feature extractors. The MT-TAML algorithm then learns Scaling and Shifting (SS) parameters and three balance parameters of feature extractor neurons in the meta-transfer learning phase to adapt quickly to various tasks in unbalanced few-shot environments. The model improves its overall effectiveness by collecting samples with the lowest classification accuracy as the difficult class, creating difficult tasks for training. Finally, the model's classification accuracy is evaluated by meta-testing.

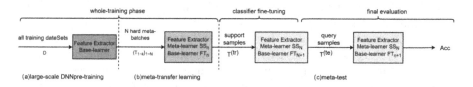

Fig. 1. The whole phases of model training.

DNN Training on Large-Scale Data. In this initial stage, similar to classical pre-training, a meta-training dataset including 64 classes and 600 samples for each class is used. Taking Mini-Imagenet as an example, a 64-class classifier is trained on this dataset. The model training involves randomly initializing a feature extractor Θ and a classifier θ, followed by optimization using gradient descent as shown below.

$$[\Theta; \theta] = [\Theta; \theta] - \alpha_1 \nabla L_D([\Theta; \theta]) \tag{1}$$

where L_D is loss function, D is the dataSet, L_D is as follows:

$$L_D([\Theta; \theta]) = \frac{1}{|D|} \sum (l\left(f_{[\Theta;\theta]}\right)(x), y) \tag{2}$$

At this stage, the feature extractor is learned, which will be frozen for the next meta-training and meta-testing phases. The learned classifier is discarded because the following small sample task contains different classification targets.

Meta-transfer Learning. Following the pre-training phase, the next stage is meta-transfer learning, where a multitude of tasks are employed to learn the optimal scaling and shifting (SS) parameters for the pre-trained DNN parameters. The gradient optimization equation for the basic learner is given as follows.

$$\theta_i = \theta - \alpha_2 \nabla L_{T \text{ (support)}}\left([\Theta; \theta], \Phi_{S\{1,2\}}\right) \quad i = 1, \ldots n \tag{3}$$

where n represents the number of tasks. The test loss is as follows.

$$\Phi_{S_i} = \Phi_{Si} - \mu \nabla_{\phi s i} L_{T \text{ (query)}}\left([\Theta, \theta_i], \Phi_{S_{(1,2)}}\right) \quad i = 1, 2 \tag{4}$$

where S_1 is the scaling parameter and is generally initialized to 1, S_2 is the translation parameter and is generally initialized to 0.

The SS operation can be defined as follows.

$$SS\left(X, W, b; \Phi_{S\{1,2\}}\right) = (W \diamond \Phi_{S_1}) + (b + \Phi_{S_2}) \tag{5}$$

where X is the input, W is weight and b is bias.

3.2   Meta-Transfer Task-Adaptive Meta-Learning

To address class imbalance, we introduce a parameter ω^τ to adjust the learning rate of the base learner based on the size of different classes. Specifically, we utilize a non-negative activation function $g(\cdot) = \text{softplus}(\cdot)$ and a set of scalar $g\left(\omega_1^\tau\right), g\left(\omega_2^\tau\right), \ldots g\left(\omega_N^\tau\right)$ to adjust the gradient descent loss coefficient for each task step, with the goal of improving the training effect of tail classes.

To address task imbalance, we employ a clipping function $f(\cdot)$, which is $\max(0, \min(\cdot, 1))$ and a learning rate coefficient $f\left(\gamma^\tau\right)$ to adjust the learning rate. The idea is to use a higher learning rate when learning a large task and a lower learning rate when learning a small task.

Finally, to address the imbalance of distribution, we introduce a task-dependent variable z^τ and use $g(z^\tau)$ as the coefficient of initialization θ. We aim to use less meta-knowledge when there is a significant difference between the distribution of the training and test set. Conversely, we use more meta-knowledge when the distribution is similar.

Combined with the meta-transfer learning model, the training process can be defined as follows:

$$(\Theta, \theta_0) = g(z^\tau)(\Theta, \theta) \tag{6}$$

$$(\Theta, \theta_i) = (\Theta, \theta_0) - f(\gamma^\tau)\alpha \circ \sum_{n=1}^{N} g(\omega_n^\tau) \nabla_{(\Theta,\theta_0)} L\left([\Theta, \theta_{(\Theta,\theta_0)}; \Phi_{S_{[1,2]}}]\right) \tag{7}$$

$$(\Theta, \theta) = (\Theta, \theta_i) - \mu \sum_{T_i \sim p(T)} L_{T_i}\left(f_{(\Theta,\theta)}\right) \tag{8}$$

3.3 Inference Network

We leverage a framework to model z^τ since it needs to prevent the posterior of z^τ from utilizing the meta-knowledge θ when managing distribution imbalance. Moreover, we allow three balance variables to share the same inference network to minimize the computational cost.

Firstly, we define X^τ is $\{x_n^\tau\}_{n=1}^{N^\tau}$, Y^τ is $\{y_n^\tau\}_{n=1}^{N^\tau}$ for training, $\tilde{X}^\tau$ is $\{\tilde{x}_n^\tau\}_{n=1}^{N^\tau}$, $\tilde{Y}^\tau$ is $\{\tilde{y}_n^\tau\}_{n=1}^{N^\tau}$ for testing. For the sake of convenience, ϕ^τ represent the Integration variables of ω^τ, γ^τ, z^τ.

$$p(Y^\tau, \tilde{Y}^\tau, \phi^\tau \mid X^\tau, \tilde{X}^\tau; \Phi, \theta) = p(\phi^\tau)$$

$$\prod_{n=1}^{N_\tau} p\left(y_n^\tau \mid x_n^\tau, \phi^\tau; \Phi, \theta\right) \prod_{m=1}^{M_\tau} p\left(\tilde{y}_m^\tau \mid \tilde{x}_m^\tau, \phi^\tau; \Phi, \theta\right) \tag{9}$$

However, there is a limitation when using summation pooled DeepSets to describe distributions. If we have a set containing multiple copies of a single instance, its pooled representation will change with the number of copies, even though all sets should be the same from their distribution point of view. Averaging pooling can solve this problem, but does not recognize the quantities in each set. That is important for the imbalance problem. To overcome this, higher-order statistics such as inter-sample variance, bias, and kurtosis are used in addition to the sample mean. Based on the idea that sample variance can capture unbalanced information about tasks and bias can capture unbalanced information about categories, the proposed encoder concatenates these statistics.

$$s_n = \text{StatisticsPooling}\left(\{NN_1(x)\}_{x \in X_n^\tau}\right), \tag{10}$$

$$v^\tau = \text{StatisticsPooling}\left(NN_2(s_n)_{n=1}^{N}\right) \tag{11}$$

Where $n = 1, ...N$ is the number of categories in the task, and NN_1 and NN_2 are parameterized neural networks. Vectors are the final encoded vectors of each task in the data set, and the equilibrium variables are generated through additional affine transformation.

The deep neural network is used to replace the original 4-layer 3×3 convolution layer, and the complex deep neural network is used to make up for the deficiency of feature extraction by the shallow network. In the process of meta-transfer, the parameters of the deep neural network are frozen, and the network parameters that need training are greatly reduced by learning only SS parameters. It effectively prevents over-fitting and speeds up model training.

3.4   Difficult Task-Mining

Online collection and classification of poor samples present challenging tasks that can facilitate faster and more effective learning. Traditional meta-batch processing involves randomly sampled tasks, which results in random difficulty levels. In Algorithm 1, samples with low accuracy in each task are intentionally selected, and their data is recombined to make the task more challenging. The objective is to improve the accuracy of the meta-learner as it learns more challenging tasks.

Each task T consists of two components, namely T(Support) and T(Query), which correspond to support and query sets, respectively. These sets are utilized to update the basic learner's parameters and conduct tests. The basic learner is optimized by using the loss function $L_{T(support)}$, while the SS parameters are optimized by using the last loss function $L_{T(Query)}$. The recognition accuracy of each class can be obtained using $L_{T(Query)}$ of each task, and the class of the sample with the lowest classification accuracy is considered the difficulty class for the current task. After obtaining all the failed classes from the k tasks of the current meta-batch processing, the model training is strengthened by re-sampling from the set of difficult classes to form difficult tasks.

Algorithm 1. MT-TAML

Require: Task distribution $p(\mathcal{T})$ and based on the dataset D, learning rate α_1, α_2, β, μ

Ensure: Feature extractor Θ, classifier θ, SS parameters $\Phi_{S_{(1,2)}}$, balance parameters ω, γ, z

1: Randomly initialize Θ and θ
2: **for** samples in D **do**
3:      Evaluate $L_D([\Theta; \theta])$ by Eq. (2)
4:      Optimize Θ and θ by Eq. (1)
5: **end for**
6: Initialize Φ_{S_1} by ones, Φ_{S_2} by zeros
7: Freeze Θ and reset θ for few-shot tasks
8: Initialize (Θ, θ_0) by Eq. (6)
9: **for** meta datasets **do**
10:     Random sample tasksT from p(T)
11:     **while** not done **do**

12:      Sample task $T_i \in \{T\}$;
13:      Optimize $\Phi_{S_{(1,2)}}$, (Θ, θ_i) and ω, γ, z;
14:      get the return class-hard then add it to {hard}
15: **end while**
16: Sample hard tasks $\{T^{\mathrm{hard}}\}$ from $\subseteq p(T \mid \{hard\})$
17: **while** not done **do**
18:      Sample task $T_j^{\mathrm{hard}} \in \{T^{\mathrm{hard}}\}$
19:      Optimize $\Phi_{S_{(1,2)}}$,(Θ, θ_i) and ω, γ, z;
20: **end while**
21: empty {hard}
22: **end for**

---

4   Experiments

4.1   Dataset and Network Selection

The following datasets are used in the experiments: Omniglot [15], Mnist [16], Mini-Imagenet [17] and Tiered-Imagenet. Meta-DataSet [18] is a collection of datasets, including Omniglot, Describable Textures [19], Quick Draw [20], Fungi [21], and MSCOCO [22], chosen for their accessibility and variety of visual concepts.

RESNET-12 is used as the feature extractor to address the issue of using a shallow network for feature extraction in MAML. This approach enables the pre-training of a parameter on a large dataset. The output feature map is then compressed into feature embedding using an average pooling layer after the four residual blocks.

4.2   Results and Analysis

Two sets of comparative experiments are conducted to verify the different distribution of training and test sets.

Unbalanced Omniglot: We generate unbalanced few-shot tasks based on the Omniglot dataset. Table 1 shows that the prototype network has the best experimental performance under the same distribution of the meta-training set and meta-test set. This is because the Omniglot data set is relatively small, and the performance of advanced algorithms has reached its optimal level. However, MT-TAML has shown improvement compared with the other four baseline algorithms, and its performance difference with the prototype network is negligible. In cases where the meta-training set and the meta-test set do not follow the same distribution, MT-TAML performs the best, which improves the performance by 2% compared with the prototype network of the baseline algorithm.

Tiered-ImageNet: In a similar way, the experiment is conducted using the Tiered-ImageNet dataset. After meta-training, the model's performance is evaluated on Tiered-ImageNet and Mini-ImageNet datasets as test sets. The Mini-ImageNet dataset is also used to simulate an uneven distribution scenario. We

Table 1. Training over Unbalanced Omniglot

Meta Test sets	Omniglot	Mnist
Prototypical-Net(2017)	**98.37 ± 0.05**	82.16 ± 0.19
MAML(2017)	93.38 ± 0.28	79.63 ± 0.33
Meta-SGD(2017)	94.27 ± 0.24	81.00 ± 0.31
MT-Net(2018)	95.41 ± 0.36	81.89 ± 0.54
Meta-baseline(2020)	95.72 ± 0.20	81.90 ± 0.44
Ours(MT-TAML)	97.29 ± 0.31	**84.39 ± 0.48**

conduct experiments on Tiered-ImageNet and Mini-Imagenet, two more complex datasets. As shown in Table 2, due to the larger size of the datasets, the training and testing are divided into more detailed subsets, including both distributed and unbalanced distribution scenarios. The results show that while all algorithms experience a decline in accuracy in these more complex scenarios, MT-TAML outperforms the baseline algorithms, especially in the unbalanced distribution scenario. Compared with the most accurate baseline algorithm, meta-baseline, MT-TAML achieves 3% improvement.

Table 2. Training over Unbalanced Tiered-ImageNet.

Meta Test sets	Tiered-ImageNet	Mini-ImageNet
Prototypical-Net(2017)	65.25 ± 0.74	52.67 ± 0.38
MAML(2017)	66.70 ± 0.40	51.61 ± 0.36
Meta-SGD(2017)	68.16 ± 0.92	56.57 ± 0.37
MT-Net(2018)	69.84 ± 0.79	55.36 ± 0.38
Meta-baseline(2020)	68.32 ± 0.34	57.32 ± 0.46
Ours(MT-TAML)	**71.42 ± 0.78**	**60.67 ± 0.49**

Furthermore, we also test the model on the Meta-DataSet, a new few-shot dataset closer to real-world scenarios and used as a new few-shot learning benchmark dataset. During the testing process, the model is trained on 10-way classification problems with several samples. The first eight datasets of the Meta-DataSet are used in the meta-training stage, and the last two datasets, Traffic Signs and MSCOCO, are used as datasets in the meta-test stage to simulate distribution imbalance.

The experimental results presented in Table 3 demonstrate the effectiveness of MT-TAML in handling imbalance in few-shot learning scenarios. MT-TAML outperforms the baseline algorithms in both the balanced and unbalanced distribution scenarios, with significant improvements observed in the latter. Specifically, in the Unbalanced Omniglot and Tiered-ImageNet datasets, MT-TAML shows superior classification performance. Furthermore, in the Meta-DataSet evaluation, the algorithm's performance is better when the meta-training set and meta-test set are balanced, with an improvement of 1.5% and 4% respectively. This suggests that MT-TAML's consideration of the real situations of task imbalance and its adjustment of balance tasks can effectively improve the performance of few-shot learning.

Table 3. Comparison over Meta-DataSet.

Meta Test sets	Meta-DataSet	Traffic-Signs	MSCOCO
MAML	69.35 ± 0.29	48.69 ± 0.42	41.35 ± 0.56
Prototypical-Net	71.78 ± 0.35	52.35 ± 0.38	48.26 ± 0.60
Meta-SGD	70.26 ± 0.45	53.26 ± 0.55	50.31 ± 0.49
Meta-baseline	71.36 ± 0.65	54.37 ± 0.46	52.26 ± 0.64
Ours	$\mathbf{73.25 \pm 0.58}$	$\mathbf{58.78 \pm 0.52}$	$\mathbf{56.32 \pm 0.68}$

4.3 Ablation Experiments

The effectiveness of integrating meta-transfer learning with the inclusion of learnable equilibrium parameters is confirmed through ablation experiments. In the case of Mini-Imagenet, a 5-way task is employed to carry out the ablation experiment in conjunction with meta-transfer learning. For the Omniglot dataset, a 10-way task is utilized to perform the ablation experiment involving three equilibrium variables.

Effectiveness of Combining Meta-Transfer Learning and Hard-Task Mining. Meta-transfer learning is used to make up for the disadvantage of MAML using 4Conv to extract features and reduce the parameters of a model update to improve the model convergence speed. The results in Table 4 show that learning a pretrained deep network through meta-transfer can effectively improve the experimental accuracy. Hard task mining positively improves experimental accuracy and can be applied to other models as a general strategy.

$g(\omega^\tau)$ **Used to Handle Class Imbalance.** $g(\omega^\tau)$ adjusts the proportion of each kind of gradient descent, as shown in Table 5. The traditional MAML model works well when each class contains only one sample with the equilibrium parameter added. After the sample size of each class increases to 5 and 15, it can be found that the MT-TAML model is superior to the baseline algorithms. Figure 2 further demonstrates the effectiveness of the $g(\omega^\tau)$ equilibrium variable. When there are more samples in a certain class, the value of $g(\omega^\tau)$ is reduced to suppress

Table 4. Meta transfer learning Ablation Experiment (pre refers to pre-training).

Model	Feature abstraction	5-shot
MAML	4Conv	63.12
MAML+hard	4Conv	65.26
MAML	ResNet12(Pre)	68.21
MT-TAML(Ours)	ResNet12(Pre)	71.32
MT-TAML+hard	ResNet12(Pre)	**73.34**

Table 5. Ablation experiment.

Model	Unbalanced classes			task imbalance		
	1-shot	5-shot	15-shot	1-shot	5-shot	15-shot
MAML	**97.87**	95.24	85.21	92.73	96.20	95.62
Meta+SGD	97.35	95.61	89.25	92.52	96.76	98.24
Meta-baseline	97.76	95.88	91.02	93.51	97.35	98.38
Ours	97.56	**96.79**	**91.35**	**94.52**	**97.86**	**98.74**

the empirical loss of that class, in order to balance learning for each category and effectively solve the long-tail problem.

$f(\gamma^\tau)$ **Used to Handle Task Imbalance.** $f(\gamma^\tau)$ is the decay factor of each task's internal gradient descent learning rate. It can be seen from Table 5 that the experimental results after adding parameters are better than the baseline method. In addition, the accuracy of 1-shot is higher than 5-shot and 15-shot, indicating that relying more on meta clearance in small tasks is useful.

Figure 3 shows that it increases with the increase of the task, which ensures that the distance to the initial parameter is as close as possible for small tasks, and more meta-knowledge can be used.

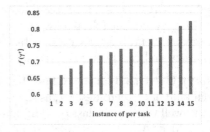

Fig. 2. $g(w^\tau)$ varies with different samples under each class

Fig. 3. $f(\gamma^\tau)$ varies with the size of the task

$g(z^\tau)$ **Used to Handle Distribution Imbalance.** $g(z^\tau)$ balance parameter plays a role in the initialization of model parameters and determines how much meta-knowledge can be used. It can be seen from Table 6 that the problem of imbalance of distribution can be effectively solved by adding the balance parameter.

Table 6. Alation experiment on imbalanced distribution.

Model(k = 5)	Ominglot	Mnist
MAML	98.24	89.05
Meta+SGD	98.29	90.32
Meta-baseline	98.52	90.96
Ours	**98.94**	**92.07**

5   Conclusion

In this paper, we introduced a task-adaptive meta-learning approach, named MT-TAML, which addresses the challenge of using shallow networks for feature extraction in few-shot learning, by combining the strengths of meta-learning and transfer learning. We significantly reduced the training parameters and accelerate network convergence, while also accounting for real-life imbalance scenarios where there may exist tasks with unbalanced class distributions. MT-TAML encodes the data of each task into a vector, which is then used as the initial parameter. We use vector task attenuation and vector base classes generated weighting mask to balance the model's variables and infer the posterior distribution of the variables using the Bayesian framework. In addition, we introduced a training strategy for difficult tasks by identifying the least accurate samples of each class under the query set and using them to strengthen the training of the model. This strategy enables the model to "grow in difficulty" and better handle challenging few-shot learning scenarios. Our experimental results demonstrate that MT-TAML outperforms existing models in unbalanced few-shot learning tasks. We also perform an ablation study to validate the effectiveness.

References

1. Vinyals, O., Lillicrap, T., Blundell, C., Wierstra, D.: Matching networks for one shot learning. In: Advances in Neural Information Processing Systems, pp. 3630–3638 (2016)
2. Santoro, A., Wierstra, D., Botvinick, M., Lillicrap, T.: Meta-learning with memory-augmented neural networks. In: International Conference on Machine Learning, pp. 1842–1850 (2016)
3. Wang, Y.-C.F., Chen, W.-Y., Liu, Y.-C., Huang, J.-B.: A closer look at few-shot classification. In: Proceedings of the International Conference on Learning Representations (2019)
4. Pascanu, R., Andrei, A., Rao, D., Hadsell, R.: Meta-learning with latent embedding optimization. In: Proceedings of the International Conference on Learning Representations (2019)
5. Finn, C., Abbeel, P., Li, H.: Model-agnostic meta-learning for fast adaptation of deep networks. In: International Conference on Machine Learning, vol. abs/1707.09835 (2017)
6. Salimans, T., Kingma, D.P.: Weight normalization: a simple reparameterization to accelerate training of deep neural networks. In: Advances in Neural Information Processing Systems, pp. 901–909 (2016)
7. Satorras, V.G., Estrach, J.B.: Few-shot learning with graph neural networks. In: Proceedings of the International Conference on Learning Representations (2018)
8. Wang, Y.-X., Hebert, M.: Learning to learn: model regression networks for easy small sample learning. In: Leibe, B., Matas, J., Sebe, N., Welling, M. (eds.) ECCV 2016. LNCS, vol. 9910, pp. 616–634. Springer, Cham (2016). https://doi.org/10.1007/978-3-319-46466-4_37
9. Jiang, S., et al.: Explainable text classification via attentive and targeted mixing data augmentation. In: International Joint Conference on Artificial Intelligence (2023)
10. Ma, T., Jiang, H., Wu, Q., Zhao, T., Lin, C.-Y.: Decomposed meta-learning for few-shot named entity recognition, arXiv preprint arXiv:2204.05751 (2022)
11. Tripuraneni, N., Jin, C., Jordan, M.: Provable meta-learning of linear representations. In: International Conference on Machine Learning, pp. 10434–10443. PMLR (2021)
12. Iwata, T., Kumagai, A.: Sharing knowledge for meta-learning with feature descriptions. Adv. Neural. Inf. Process. Syst. **35**, 16637–16649 (2022)
13. Guo, Y., Zhang, L., Hu, Y., He, X., Gao, J.: MS-Celeb-1M: a dataset and benchmark for large-scale face recognition. In: Leibe, B., Matas, J., Sebe, N., Welling, M. (eds.) ECCV 2016. LNCS, vol. 9907, pp. 87–102. Springer, Cham (2016). https://doi.org/10.1007/978-3-319-46487-9_6
14. Huang, J., Wei, Y., Zhang, Y., Yang, Q.: Transfer learning via learning to transfer. In: International Conference on Machine Learning, vol. abs/1707.09835 (2017)
15. Salakhutdinov, R., Lake, B.M., Tenenbaum, J.B.: Human-level concept learning through probabilistic program induction. Science **350**(6266) (2015)
16. Comaniciu, D., Meer, P.: Mean shift: a robust approach toward feature space analysis. IEEE Trans. Pattern Anal. Mach. Intell. **24**(5), 603–619 (2002)
17. Vinyals, O., Blundell, C., Lillicrap, T., Wierstra, D.: Matching networks for one shot learning. Adv. Neural Inf. Process. Syst. **350**(6266) (2016)
18. Triantafillou, E., Dumoulin, V., Xu, K.: Meta-dataset: a dataset of datasets for learning to learn from few examples, arXiv preprint arXiv:1903.03096 (2019)

19. Mohamed, S., Cimpoi, M., Maji, S., Vedaldi, A.: Describing textures in the wild. In: Proceedings of the IEEE Conference on Computer Vision and Pattern Recognition, pp. 3606–3613 (2014)
20. Jonas Jongejan, J.K., Kawashima, T., Fox-Gieg, N.: The quick, draw A.I. experiment, Mount View, CA, vol. 17, no. 2018, p. 4 (2016). Accessed Feb
21. Schroeder, B., Cui, Y.: FGVCX fungi classification challenge 2018 (2018). github.com/visipedia/fgvcx_fungi_comp. Accessed 14 July 2021
22. Lin, T.-Y., et al.: Microsoft COCO: common objects in context. In: Fleet, D., Pajdla, T., Schiele, B., Tuytelaars, T. (eds.) ECCV 2014. LNCS, vol. 8693, pp. 740–755. Springer, Cham (2014). https://doi.org/10.1007/978-3-319-10602-1_48

Impact Analysis of Climate Change on Floods in an Indian Region Using Machine Learning

Sarthak Vage[1], Tanu Gupta[2], and Sudip Roy[1,2]([✉])

[1] Department of Computer Science and Engineering, Indian Institute of Technology Roorkee, Roorkee, India
sudip.roy@cs.iitr.ac.in
[2] Centre of Excellence in Disaster Mitigation and Management, Indian Institute of Technology Roorkee, Roorkee, India

Abstract. Flood is one of the prominent climate-induced disasters (CIDs), which causes enormous damage, financial losses, and casualties every year across the world. The intensities and damages of floods are prone to change due to future climate scenarios. In order to analyze the impact of climate change on flood patterns in the Maharashtra state of India, this research employs machine learning models to analyze historical data and project future floods. In this work, we have defined and used 20 weather parameters based on temperature and precipitation records collected from the India Meteorological Department (IMD) and then to simulate and predict the floods in Maharashtra state. Then we use these parameters to build the machine learning models such as Artificial Neural Network (ANN), Light Gradient-Boosting Machines (LightGBM), and Least Squares Support Vector Machines (LSSVM) for estimating the approximate number of occurrences of floods till 2100 on different shared socioeconomic pathways (SSPs) scenarios. Based on our simulation experiments for data analytics, we found that LightGBM performed the best in the validation phase giving an F1-score of 0.895 and an AUC-ROC score of 0.863. Furthermore, we also used LightGBM for simulations of future scenarios in Maharashtra state. This work introduces a novel approach to predict climate-induced disasters (CIDs), floods in this case, by utilizing data from past disasters, global climate models, and climate change measurements. We believe that the proposed model can be utilized to analyse the impacts of climate change on floods in Maharashtra state and subsequently help the local government bodies and disaster management authorities to plan and prepare accordingly.

Keywords: artificial neural network · climate change · data analytics · disaster risk · flood · machine learning

1 Introduction

Climate change-related disasters including droughts, floods and other extreme events, significantly impact the communities and ecosystems. These impacts can range from property damage and economic losses to adverse effects on natural

L. Iliadis et al. (Eds.): ICANN 2023, LNCS 14261, pp. 370–383, 2023.
https://doi.org/10.1007/978-3-031-44198-1_31

ecosystems and human health, affecting the vulnerable and developed communities. Factors such as rising sea levels, higher temperatures and changing precipitation patterns contribute to the increased frequency and severity of these disasters. According to the Sixth Assessment Report by the Working Group II of the Intergovernmental Panel on Climate Change (IPCC) [10] have been highlighted human-induced impacts of climate change that has led to the emergence of new extreme events in nature. The IPCC's Synthesis Report [11] warns that in the next few years, the Maharashtra state in India, which is our area of study, will likely face severe droughts and massive flooding due to the predicted temperature increase.

The main contributions of this work are as follows:

○ A dataset is proposed that would serve as a repository for all the previous flood locations in Maharashtra with dates from 2001 to 2021.
○ The parameters are defined and used that would work for daily data based on parameters outlined by the Expert Team on Climate Change Detection and Indices (ETCCDI) climate indices [5].
○ Conditional Tabular Generative Adversarial Network (CTGAN) is applied to remove the data imbalance between flooding and non-flooding records.
○ The performances of ANN, LSSVM, and LightGBM classifying models are compared and analyzed to see which models give the best results when trained on the proposed data.
○ The proposed model is simulated on all four SSPs scenarios using the Coupled Model Intercomparison Project Phase 6 (CMIP6) dataset to assess the impact of floods in Maharashtra from 2022 to 2100.

The remainder of the paper is organised as follows. In Sect. 2, a review of recent related work is discussed. Section 3 presents the motivation and problem statement and Sect. 4 provides the details about the datasets used. The architecture of the proposed model is discussed in Sect. 5 and the analysis of the simulation results is presented in Sect. 6. Finally, the paper is concluded in Sect. 7.

2   Literature Survey

Various machine learning models have been applied in recent years to predict and analyze flooding areas and damage. Haggag et al. [9] applied deep neural networks with parameters taken from ETCCDI [5] to create a general model to predict CIDs and then applied for Canada to identify future floods. They got good results with very less miss-classification error value. Islam et al. [12] applied ANN, Random Forests (RF) and Support Vector Machine (SVM) to generate the flood susceptibility maps at the Teesta River basin of Bangladesh. In that case, the Area Under the Curve (AUC) of the Receiver Operating Characteristic (ROC) value was above 0.80 for all the tested models. In their analysis, RF performed the best, closely followed by ANN. Aydin et al. [2] performed a comparative study of gradient boosting techniques like LightGBM and CatBoost along with the other techniques, which includes Gradient Boost (GB), eXtreme Gradient Boosting (XGBoost), RF and Adaptive Boosting (AdaBoost). In their analysis, LightGBM and AdaBoost provides the best results for flood prediction. Anaraki et al. [1] used the Least Squares Support Vector Machine (LSSVM), ANN, k-Nearest Neighbour (kNN) for predicting the rainfall discharge in the future till 2100 using the Coupled Model Intercomparison Project Phase 5 (CMIP5) simulation dataset. They found LSSVM and ANN performing fairly well. Ganguly et al. [8] used Linear Regression (LR), ANN, and RF for the prediction and analysis of flood-affected households. Models which are mostly used are gradient boosting techniques [13,16,17], SVMs [14,24], ANNs [3,7,19,22]. Park et al. [21] used under-sampling to balance out the non-flood and flood datasets as they worked on monthly datasets. However, these are not useful for our work due to extreme imbalance between non-flooding and flooding records.

3   Motivation and Problem Statement

3.1   Motivation

Maharashtra in India is a major agricultural state, and such climate changes could have massive implications for food security and crops. According to the National Disaster Management Authority (NDMA) report, the floods of 2005 in Maharashtra affected more than 3 million people and caused an estimated loss of INR 5000 crore. Moreover, recent floods in July 2021 affected over 200,000 people and caused an estimated loss of Indian Rupees 1000 crore. It can be observed from Fig. 1(a) and Fig. 1(b) that the districts lying in the Konkan region of Maharashtra face many flood events. Although the districts in the rain shadow region of Maharashtra state face droughts regularly, they are also prone to floods in case of untimely rains. Big cities like Pune, Nagpur, Solapur, Mumbai, and other main cities also face flooding due to urbanization. This motivates us to develop a model that can be used to analyse the impacts of climate change on floods in Maharashtra. This will be helpful for disaster managers to make plans for mitigation and prevention measures accordingly.

3.2   Problem Statement

In this paper, we study the impact of climate change on flood frequency in the Maharashtra state of India. Our goal is to determine whether a flood will occur

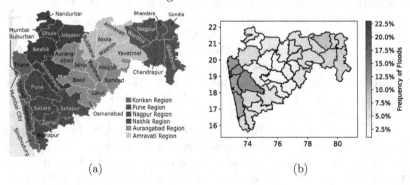

(a)   (b)

Fig. 1. Map of Maharashtra (a) with all districts. (b) flood frequency in last 20 years.

or not under different CMIP6 SSP scenarios from the years 2022 to 2100. We have formulated this as a binary classification problem in which the climate change variables are used as inputs and 0 or 1 as output; where, 0 indicates a non-flood event and 1 indicates a flood event.

4 Description of Datasets

In this section, we discuss the three datasets used for this work.

4.1 Historical Precipitation and Temperature Dataset

A historical dataset of daily precipitation, minimum temperature, and maximum temperature for the years 2001 to 2021 is created for all 35 districts of Maharashtra using the India Meteorological Department (IMD) binary gridded data [20]. The data is collected based on the latitude and longitude of district centers, representing urbanized areas prone to flooding.

4.2 Flood Inventory

As per our knowledge, no previous work has documented floods started exactly on which date and their duration for the district of Maharashtra. A flood repository proposed by Saharia et al. [23] provides the rough estimates of flood events in India from 2001 to 2021 but it lacks proper location details. Therefore, we create a custom flood dataset using the dataset of the work [23] along with various internationally and nationally acknowledged media outlets like FloodList [4]. This dataset comprises of all flood events with their location, date, and duration from 2001 to 2021 for each district of Maharashtra.

4.3 CMIP6 Dataset

The World Climate Research Programme's (WCRP) phase six CMIP6 [6] dataset is used for the analyses of future flood occurrences. CMIP6 has simulations from the latest state-of-the-art climate models. We used bias-corrected climate projections from CMIP6 for South Asia [18], which has better performances. There are 13 models for every country in South Asia, each with five scenarios (SSP126, SSP245, SSP370, SSP585, and historical), having daily precipitation and minimum temperature and maximum temperature from 2015 to 2100. We choose the Beijing Climate Center Climate System Model Version 2 medium resolution (BCC-CSM2-MR) model as it is one of the best-performing models for India, validated by Konda et al. [15] having normalized root mean square error (NRMSE) less than 0.7 and Taylor skill score greater than 0.75.

5 Methodology

This section presents a detailed description of the proposed approach to predict the impact of climate change on floods in Maharashtra. Figure 2 provides the overview of the proposed work.

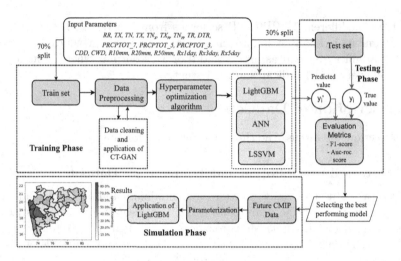

Fig. 2. Overview of the Proposed Methodology.

5.1   Parameter Formulation

ETCCDI [5] has defined 27 core indices developed from temperature and precipitation data. Indices barring RR_i, TN_i, TX_i, CDD and CWD are formulated on aggregation over months and years. As Maharashtra faces heavy rainfall, using monthly values of precipitation and temperature may lead to missing a probable flood event during model training due to their aggregation over a month. Therefore, after trying and testing with them, these indices are converted into a suitable format for our usage keeping their true meaning intact as much as possible. In this work, we have defined and used 20 parameters out of those 27 core indices after finding their correlation with days when flooding occurred. All the parameters with their definitions are shown in Table 1.

5.2   Training Dataset Details

Datasets discussed in Sect. 4 are used to create the final dataset comprising 7670 records for each of the 35 districts in Maharashtra, covering over the years 2001 to 2021. We excluded date column as we are converting the time-series data into stationary form by building these parameters as mentioned in Sect. 5.1. Further, the dataset is split into two subsets with 70% of the data used as the training set and the remaining 30% used as the testing set.

5.3   Data Preprocessing

The main issue with the training dataset is that the output is imbalanced between 0 s and 1 s. For example, in the Mumbai district of Maharashtra, which is prone to severe flooding, out of 7670, there are only 46 records marked as 1s. These imbalances can be observed in Fig. 3(a). To tackle this problem, we use

Table 1. List of parameters used for training of our model.

Parameter	Definition	Formula	Unit
RR_i	Daily precipitation on day i	RR_i	mm
TX_i	Maximum daily temperature on day i	TX_i	°C
TN_i	Minimum daily temperature on day i	TN_i	°C
TX_x	Maximum value of daily maximum temperature in last five days	$max(\{TX_{i-j} \mid \forall j = 1 \text{ to } 5\})$	°C
TN_x	Maximum value of daily minimum temperature in last 5 days	$max(\{TN_{i-j} \mid \forall j = 1 \text{ to } 5\})$	°C
TX_n	Minimum value of daily maximum temperature in last 5 days	$min(\{TN_{i-j} \mid \forall j = 1 \text{ to } 5\})$	°C
TN_n	Minimum value of daily minimum temperature in last 5 days	$min(\{TX_{i-j} \mid \forall j = 1 \text{ to } 5\})$	°C
TR	Number of tropical nights, count of days when $TN > 20°C$ in last 5 days period	$Count(\{TN_{i-j} \mid \forall j = 1 \text{ to } 5 \wedge TN_{i-j} < 20°C\})$	days
DTR	Daily Temperature Range. The mean difference between TX and TN in the last five days, let TX_i and TN_i be the daily maximum and minimum temperature	$DTR = \frac{1}{5}\left(\sum_{i=1}^{5}(TX_i - TN_i)\right)$	°C
$RR7$	Total precipitation in last seven days	$RR7 = \sum_{i=1}^{7} RR_i$	mm
$RR5$	Total precipitation in last five days	$RR5 = \sum_{i=1}^{5} RR_i$	mm
$RR3$	Total precipitation in last three days	$RR3 = \sum_{i=1}^{3} RR_i$	mm
CDD	Maximum length of dry spell, the maximum number of consecutive days with $RR < 1mm$: Let RR_{ij} be the daily precipitation amount on the day i in period j. Count the largest number of consecutive days where:	$RR_{ij} < 1mm$	days
CWD	Maximum length of the wet spell, the maximum number of consecutive days with $RR \geq 1mm$: Let RR_{ij} be the daily precipitation amount on the day i in period j. Count the largest number of consecutive days where:	$RR_{ij} \geq 1mm$	days
$R10mm$	Count of days when $RR \geq 10mm$ within 7 day period: Let RR_i be the daily precipitation amount on day i in 7 day period.	$Count(\{RR_{i-j} \mid \forall j = 1 \text{ to } 7 \wedge RR_{i-j} > 10mm\})$	days
$R20mm$	Count of days when $RR \geq 20mm$ within 7 day period: Let RR_i be the daily precipitation amount on day i in 7 day period.	$Count(\{RR_{i-j} \mid \forall j = 1 \text{ to } 7 \wedge RR_{i-j} > 10mm\})$	days
$Rnnmm$	Count of days when $RR \geq nnmm$ within 7 day period: Let RR_i be the daily precipitation amount on day i in 7 day period.	$Count(\{RR_{i-j} \mid \forall j = 1 \text{ to } 7 \wedge RR_{i-j} > 10mm\})$, $nn = 50$	days
$Rx1day$	Maximum 1-day precipitation in last 5 days	$max(\{RR_{i-j} \mid \forall j = 1 \text{ to } 5\})$	mm
$Rx3day$	Maximum consecutive 3-day precipitation in last 7 days	$max(RR_i), i = 1 \text{ to } 7$	mm
$Rx5day$	Maximum consecutive 5-day precipitation in last 7 days	$max(RR_i), i = 1 \text{ to } 7$	mm

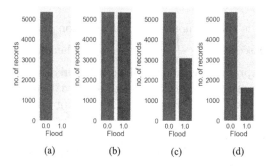

Fig. 3. Training dataset before and after application of CTGAN.

Conditional Tabular Generative Adversarial Networks (CTGAN) proposed by Xu et al. [25]. This algorithm consists of a generator neural network that learns to create synthetic data similar to real data and a discriminator neural network that learns to distinguish between real and synthetic data. We use this synthetic data and fuse it with real data to create a mixed synthetic dataset.

Three types of mixed synthetic datasets are created as follows: with a 50–50 split having 50% of 0 s and 50% of 1 s (Fig. 3(b)), with a 65–35% split which has 65% of 0 s and 35% of 1 (Fig. 3(c)) and with 80–20 split with 80% of 0 s and 20% of 1 s (Fig. 3(d)). ANN, LightGBM, and LSSVM models are trained on these three splits after performing hyper-parameter optimization to check which split works best for all the districts.

5.4 Hyperparameter Optimization

○ **ANN:** After testing several hidden layers, the best-performing neural network for binary classification has five layers: one input, three hidden, and one output layers. The input layer has 512 neurons and the hidden layers has 128, 64 and 8 neurons, respectively. The activation function for the input and hidden layers is "relu", and for the output layer it is "sigmoid."

○ **LightGBM:** In LightGBM, different permutations and combinations are tried for the "learning rate", which affects on normalization weights of dropped trees and the "max_depth" of each trained tree. For all the districts, the best learning parameter lie between 0.01 to 0.3 with "max_depth" of at most 6.

○ **LSSVM:** The LSSVM model has two hyperparameters: C and epsilon. The regularisation parameter C balances training and testing errors, while epsilon determines the generalization capacity of the model for unknown data. The best C value that showed top results for all districts is between1 to 2 and the epsilon value always lie between around 0.2 to 0.4.

5.5 Evaluation Metrics

○ **F1-score:** It is the harmonic mean of precision and recall, and it can be expressed as F1-score $= 2 \cdot \dfrac{\text{precision-recall}}{\text{precision+recall}}$, where precision is the fraction of true positive predictions out of all positive predictions and recall is the fraction of true positive predictions out of all actual positive instances.

○ **Area Under the Curve- Receiver Operating Characteristic (AUC-ROC):** AUC-ROC curve is a plot of the True Positive Rate (TPR) against the False Positive Rate (FPR) at various threshold settings. The AUC-ROC score represents the area under this curve that ranges from 0 to 1, with higher values indicating better classification performance.

6   Results

6.1   Test Results

The testing phase involved reserving 30% of the data and each model is evaluated across all districts in Maharashtra.

Table 2. Performance of the models over Precision and Recall values.

S. No.	District	Precision			Recall		
		ANN	LSSVM	LightGBM	ANN	LSSVM	LightGBM
1	Ahmednagar	1.00	0.90	1.00	0.75	1.00	0.75
2	Akola	1.00	1.00	1.00	0.67	1.00	0.83
3	Amravati	0.64	0.75	1.00	0.75	0.75	0.75
4	Aurangabad	0.67	0.83	1.00	0.99	1.00	1.00
5	Beed	0.62	0.83	0.75	0.75	1.00	0.75
6	Bhandara	1.00	0.75	1.00	0.75	0.75	0.75
7	Buldhana	0.70	1.00	0.98	0.75	0.75	0.77
8	Chandrapur	0.70	0.92	1.00	0.65	0.81	0.88
9	Dhule	0.62	1.00	1.00	0.98	1.00	1.00
10	Gadchiroli	0.69	0.67	0.92	0.75	0.75	0.92
11	Gondia	0.83	0.70	1.00	0.75	0.90	0.70
12	Hingoli	0.69	0.81	1.00	0.80	0.77	0.80
13	Jalgaon	0.83	0.83	0.87	0.75	0.75	0.87
14	Jalna	0.83	1.00	1.00	0.83	0.83	1.00
15	Kolhapur	0.70	0.83	0.87	0.75	0.75	0.88
16	Latur	0.60	1.00	1.00	0.74	0.75	0.75
17	Mumbai	0.66	0.93	0.94	0.74	0.67	0.69
18	Nagpur	0.75	1.00	1.00	1.00	0.75	1.00
19	Nanded	0.98	0.87	0.90	1.00	0.87	0.88
20	Nandurbar	0.75	0.83	1.00	0.67	0.92	0.83
21	Nashik	0.83	0.92	1.00	0.79	0.86	0.86
22	Osmanabad	0.67	0.83	1.00	0.75	1.00	1.00
23	Palghar	0.82	0.82	0.93	0.90	0.72	0.87
24	Parbhani	1.00	0.88	1.00	0.83	0.99	1.00
25	Pune	0.71	0.86	0.81	0.73	0.78	0.85
26	Raigad	0.81	0.87	0.84	0.74	0.64	0.80
27	Ratnagiri	0.71	0.77	0.78	0.71	0.98	0.86
28	Sangli	0.62	0.67	1.00	0.75	0.75	1.00
29	Satara	0.75	0.80	1.00	0.83	0.98	1.00
30	Sindhudurg	0.71	0.87	0.70	0.80	0.83	0.70
31	Solapur	1.00	0.83	1.00	0.99	1.00	1.00
32	Thane	0.82	0.83	0.93	0.90	0.72	0.87
33	Wardha	0.75	1.00	1.00	0.75	1.00	1.00
34	Washim	0.65	0.64	0.99	0.87	0.75	0.76
35	Yavatmal	0.70	0.71	1.00	0.69	0.80	1.00
Mean		**0.766**	**0.850**	**0.949**	**0.796**	**0.845**	**0.868**

Table 3. Performance of models over evaluation metrics F1-score and AUC-ROC score.

S. No.	District	F1-score			AUC-ROC score		
		ANN	LSSVM	LightGBM	ANN	LSSVM	LightGBM
1	Ahmednagar	0.83	0.94	0.833	0.750	0.999	0.750
2	Akola	0.75	1.00	0.9	0.666	1.000	0.833
3	Amravati	0.68	0.75	0.83	0.625	0.795	0.750
4	Aurangabad	0.75	0.95	0.75	0.999	0.999	1.000
5	Beed	0.67	0.90	1.00	0.749	0.999	0.749
6	Bhandara	0.82	0.75	0.83	0.749	0.750	0.750
7	Buldhana	0.68	0.83	0.83	0.749	0.750	0.750
8	Chandrapur	0.72	0.86	0.88	0.625	0.812	0.813
9	Dhule	0.67	1.00	1.00	1.000	1.000	1.000
10	Gadchiroli	0.71	0.70	0.95	0.748	0.749	0.916
11	Gondia	0.75	0.75	0.79	0.699	0.699	0.700
12	Hingoli	0.73	0.77	0.87	0.799	0.899	0.800
13	Jalgaon	0.79	0.79	0.87	0.749	0.749	0.874
14	Jalna	0.83	0.90	1.00	0.666	0.833	1.000
15	Kolhapur	0.72	0.79	0.87	0.747	0.749	0.875
16	Latur	0.67	0.8	0.83	0.499	0.750	0.750
17	Mumbai	0.70	0.74	0.77	0.610	0.666	0.694
18	Nagpur	0.83	0.83	1.00	0.750	0.750	1.000
19	Nanded	0.93	0.87	0.93	0.875	0.874	0.875
20	Nandurbar	0.70	0.88	0.90	0.665	0.853	0.833
21	Nashik	0.81	0.83	0.92	0.714	0.857	0.857
22	Osmanabad	0.83	0.90	1.00	0.749	0.999	1.000
23	Palghar	0.86	0.77	0.90	0.721	0.721	0.888
24	Parbhani	0.90	0.93	1.00	0.833	0.999	1.000
25	Pune	0.72	0.81	0.83	0.721	0.777	0.778
26	Raigad	0.77	0.70	0.82	0.906	0.636	0.772
27	Ratnagiri	0.71	0.85	0.81	0.784	0.998	0.856
28	Sangli	0.67	0.70	1.00	0.749	0.749	1.000
29	Satara	0.79	0.87	1.00	0.833	0.999	1.000
30	Sindhudurg	0.75	0.83	0.70	0.799	0.799	0.699
31	Solapur	1.00	0.90	1.00	0.998	0.997	1.000
32	Thane	0.86	0.77	0.90	0.721	0.721	0.888
33	Wardha	0.75	1.00	1.00	0.750	1.000	1.000
34	Washim	0.71	0.68	0.83	0.624	0.748	0.750
35	Yavatmal	0.70	0.75	1.00	0.699	0.799	1.000
Mean		**0.765**	**0.831**	**0.896**	**0.752**	**0.841**	**0.863**

○ **F1-score:** Across various districts of Maharashtra, we evaluated different models for flood prediction. Among them, LightGBM outperformed achieving the highest F1-score of 1.0 for nine districts and a mean F1-score of 0.895. In comparison, ANN and LSSVM achieved lower mean F1-scores of 0.76 and 0.832, respectively. Table 2 and Table 3 provide a comprehensive overview of precision, recall and F1-scores for each model across all 35 the districts. The results underscore the superiority of the proposed LightGBM method, making it a compelling choice for accurate flood prediction in Maharashtra.

○ **AUC-ROC Score:** Applying LightGBM on all the districts, we recorded AUC-ROC score as 0.863. A total of ten districts recorded AUC-ROC scores greater than 0.9, and the lowest being 0.699. This result is closely followed by LSSVM, in which we obtain a AUC-ROC accuracy of 0.8447. The lowest score is 0.6361 for Raigad district, with nine districts scoring above 0.9, where ANN shows AUC-ROC score of 0.75. Detailed results are given in Table 3.

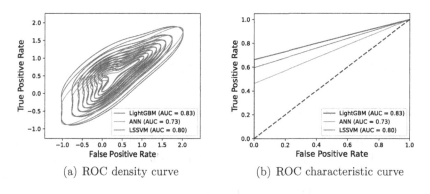

(a) ROC density curve   (b) ROC characteristic curve

Fig. 4. Comparison of the ROC curves for different models.

In Fig. 4(a) and Fig 4(b), LightGBM achieved the highest AUC, indicating its ability to maintain high TPR while keeping FPR low. Considering all means, LightGBM recorded the highest F1-score and AUC-ROC score of 0.895 and 0.8620, respectively. Hence, we use LightGBM to simulate future floods as it performed best in both ROC density and characteristic curves as shown in Fig. 4.

6.2   Simulation Results

For the future simulations we use the bias-corrected BCC-CSM2-MR model of CMIP6 dataset. It has four SSP scenarios and the proposed model is applied to each. The same parameters are then formulated for the future SSP scenarios and LightGBM predicts whether there would be a flood or not on the given date during the years 2022 to 2100.

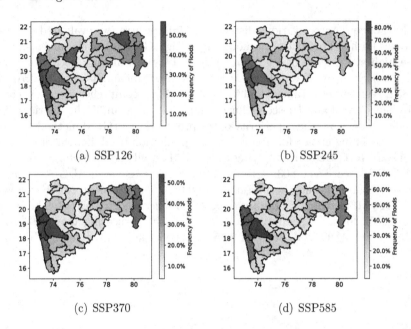

(a) SSP126   (b) SSP245

(c) SSP370   (d) SSP585

Fig. 5. Simulation of the frequency of floods on the CMIP6 dataset.

o **SSP126:** Figure 5(a) shows the SSP126 scenario. In this scenario, the pattern followed in the previous 20 years seems to be repeated, apart from the Aurangabad district, where floods have substantially increased. The Akola district also faces a higher frequency of floods than previously observed. The districts to the west of the Sahyadri range, i.e., Thane, Palghar, Mumbai, Raigad, Ratnagiri, and Sindhudurg, except Sindhudurg, all are bound to face the same frequency of floods over the next 80 years. Ahmednagar, Jalna, Osmanabad, Parbhani, Hingoli, Buldhana, Washim, Nanded, Latur, and Jalgaon districts lying in the rain-shadow areas of Maharashtra will face drought situations and this can be clearly seen in the map, where these districts have very low frequency of floods compared other districts. The far east districts of Maharashtra would face a considerable amount of rains, with Nagpur being one of the biggest cities in India about to face many flooding according to simulations of SSP126 scenario.

o **SSP245:** Figure 5(b) is for the SSP245 scenario, where the flood frequency of all districts of Maharashtra will either remain the same or decreases gradually in the next 80 years. Compared to SSP126, Aurangabad district flood frequency decreased considerably. In this scenario, the district which faced floods in the previous like Mumbai, Palghar, Thane, Raigad, and Pune will face the same flood frequency as in the SSP126 scenario.

o **SSP370:** Figure 5(c) shows the SSP370 scenario. According to this, the rain-shadow districts of Maharashtra would face significantly less amount of floods. However, on the flip side, as these districts usually do not see high precipitation, this situation could also indicate a scarcity of rainfall in the next 80 years, leading to drought-like conditions. Pune district which is considered as one of the important industry hubs of India, is impending a high frequency of floods in the SSP370 scenario. Apart from this, the urbanized Mumbai, Thane, Palghar, and Raigad districts are about to combat the very frequency of flooding scenarios. Moreover, in this scenario, the Gondia and Gadchiroli districts will also face an increase in the frequency of floods.

SSP585: In case of SSP585 scenario shown in Fig. 5(d), the Pune district is about to face a very stark increase in the frequency of floods. Along with all the other districts lying in the west except the Sindhudurg district, we can see a high flood frequency similar to the SSP245 scenario, but comparatively lesser than the SSP370 scenario. All other districts are less prone to floods in this scenario. This could also point to decreasing precipitations in the future.

7   Conclusions

This paper presents a study of the impact analysis of climate change on floods in Maharashtra state of India using a historical dataset of flooding events and daily weather patterns. Three machine learning models namely ANN, LightGBM, and LSSVM are applied using 20 different ETCCDI parameters. The simulation results confirm that LightGBM performs the best with a mean AUC-ROC score of 0.862 and an F1 score of 0.895. Moreover, LightGBM is used to predict future flood events in Maharashtra state under different CMIP6 SSP scenarios. SSP126 and SSP370 scenarios are leading to a much increase in flood events in western and far eastern districts of Maharashtra state, whereas Aurangabad and Pune districts will be having high flood risk in respective scenarios. SSP585 scenario shows a decrease in flood events, but this could also lead to less precipitation, leading to water scarcity in the rain-shadow region of Maharashtra. As a future work, the impact analysis of tidal waves and sea levels can be considered along with climate change data to understand the future flood risks in the districts close to the sea. Moreover, factors like changes in land cover and grasslands in the future will also impact flood events, which may also be considered for further study along with the impacts of climate change in the future.

References

1. Anaraki, M.V., et al.: Uncertainty analysis of climate change impacts on flood frequency by using hybrid machine learning methods. Water Resour. Manage **35**, 199–223 (2021)
2. Aydin, H.E., et al.: Predicting and analyzing flood susceptibility using boosting-based ensemble machine learning algorithms with SHapley additive exPlanations. Nat. Hazards **116**, 1–35 (2022)
3. Bui, Q.T., et al.: Verification of novel integrations of swarm intelligence algorithms into deep learning neural network for flood susceptibility mapping. J. Hydrol. **581**, 124379 (2020)

4. ECMWF: FloodList by European Centre for Medium-Range Weather Forecasts. https://floodlist.com/tag/india. Accessed 30 Mar 2023

5. ETCCDI: Expert Team on Climate Change Detection and Indices (2009). https://etccdi.pacificclimate.org/indices_def.shtml. Accessed 30 Mar 2023

6. Eyring, V., et al.: Overview of the coupled model intercomparison project phase 6 (CMIP6) experimental design and organization. Geosci. Model Dev. **9**(5), 1937–1958 (2016)

7. Falah, F., et al.: Artificial neural networks for flood susceptibility mapping in data-scarce urban areas. In: Proceedings of the SMEES, pp. 323–336 (2019)

8. Ganguly, K.K., et al.: A machine learning-based prediction and analysis of flood affected households: a case study of floods in Bangladesh. Int. J. Disaster Risk Reduct. **34**, 283–294 (2019)

9. Haggag, M., et al.: A deep learning model for predicting climate-induced disasters. Nat. Hazards **107**, 1009–1034 (2021)

10. IPCC: Climate Change 2022: Impacts, Adaptation, and Vulnerability (2022). https://www.ipcc.ch/report/ar6/wg2/

11. IPCC: AR6 Synthesis Report: Climate Change 2023 (2023). https://www.ipcc.ch/report/sixth-assessment-report-cycle/

12. Islam, A.R.M.T., et al.: Flood susceptibility modeling using advanced ensemble machine learning models. Geosci. Front. **12**(3), 101075 (2021)

13. Janizadeh, S., et al.: Mapping the spatial and temporal variability of flood hazard affected by climate and land-use changes in the future. J. Environ. Manage. **298**, 113551 (2021)

14. Khosravi, K., et al.: Flood susceptibility mapping at Ningdu catchment, China using bivariate and data mining techniques. In: Proceedings of the EHCV, pp. 419–434 (2019)

15. Konda, G., et al.: Evaluation of CMIP6 models for simulations of surplus/deficit summer monsoon conditions over India. Clim. Dyn. **60**(3–4), 1023–1042 (2023)

16. Li, X., et al.: Flood risk assessment of global watersheds based on multiple machine learning models. Water **11**(8), 1654 (2019)

17. Mirzaei, S., et al.: Flood susceptibility assessment using extreme gradient boosting (EGB), Iran. Earth Sci. Inf. **14**, 51–67 (2021)

18. Mishra, V., et al.: Bias Corrected Climate Projections from CMIP6 Models for South Asia, June 2020. https://zenodo.org/record/3873998#.ZECpuHZByBI

19. Davoudi Moghaddam, D., Pourghasemi, H.R., Rahmati, O.: Assessment of the contribution of geo-environmental factors to flood inundation in a semi-arid region of SW Iran: comparison of different advanced modeling approaches. In: Pourghasemi, H.R., Rossi, M. (eds.) Natural Hazards GIS-Based Spatial Modeling Using Data Mining Techniques. ANTHR, vol. 48, pp. 59–78. Springer, Cham (2019). https://doi.org/10.1007/978-3-319-73383-8_3

20. Nandi, S., et al.: IMDLIB: A Python Library for IMD Gridded Data, October 2022. https://doi.org/10.5281/zenodo.7205414

21. Park, S.J., et al.: Prediction of coastal flooding risk under climate change impacts in south Korea using machine learning algorithms. Environ. Res. Lett. **15**(9), 094052 (2020)

22. Pham, Q.B., et al.: Flood vulnerability and buildings' flood exposure assessment in a densely urbanised city: comparative analysis of three scenarios using a neural network approach. Nat. Hazards **113**(2), 1043–1081 (2022)

23. Saharia, M., et al.: India flood inventory: creation of a multi-source national geospatial database to facilitate comprehensive flood research. Natural Haz. **108**, 619–633 (2021)

24. Termeh, S.V.R., et al.: Flood susceptibility mapping using novel ensembles of adaptive neuro fuzzy inference system and metaheuristic algorithms. Sci. Total Environ. **615**, 438–451 (2018)
25. Xu, L., et al.: Modeling tabular data using conditional GAN. In: Advances in Neural Information Processing Systems, vol. 32 (2019)

Improving Limited Resource Speech Recognition Performance with Latent Regression Bayesian Network

Liang Xu[1,2], Yue Zhao[1,2(✉)], Xiaona Xu[1,2], Yigang Liu[1,2], and Qiang Ji[3]

[1] School of Information Engineering, Minzu University of China, Beijing, China
zhaoyueso@muc.edu.cn
[2] Key Laboratory of Ethnic Language Intelligent Analysis and Security Governance
of MOE, Minzu University of China, Beijing, China
[3] Department of Electrical, Computer, and Systems Engineering,
Rensselaer Polytechnic Institute, Troy, NY, USA

Abstract. In limited resource speech recognition scenarios, the limited data may result in overfitting and decreased recognition rates when the traditional acoustic features are employed. To enhance speech recognition performance, it is essential to extract representative and robust features from speech signals. This paper explores the latent regression Bayesian network (LRBN) to derive more efficient speech representation from traditional acoustic features to train end-to-end speech recognition models. The LRBN is an effective generative model that captures the inherent dependencies from the original data. To evaluate the effectiveness of LRBN for speech representation, we compare traditional acoustic features and bottleneck features with the hidden features extracted by LRBN. Our experimental results demonstrate that LRBN improves the accuracy of speech recognition on five speech datasets.

Keywords: speech representation · latent regression bayesian network · limited resource speech recognition

1 Introduction

The effectiveness of traditional acoustic features, including Mel-scale Frequency Cepstral Coefficients (MFCCs) and Filter Banks (FBank), in capturing relevant acoustic information has made them widely used for speech recognition tasks. The extraction process of MFCCs features involves the transformation of the speech signal from the time domain into the frequency domain via the fast Fourier transform and mapping to the nonlinear Mel spectrum using auditory Mel filters [14]. After applying logarithmic and discrete cosine transform (DCT), MFCCs are obtained. DCT can eliminate harmonics that are irrelevant

This research was supported by the National Natural Science Foundation of China under Grant No. 61976236.

to phoneme discrimination and preserve envelope information, which is necessary in past probability-based speech recognition. However, it can lead to the loss of some nonlinear information in the speech signal. FBank, on the other hand, differs from MFCCs in that it does not utilize DCT transformation, so it is more correlated and informative. For deep learning models and large-scale datasets, FBank is a more effective acoustic feature [1]. However, traditional acoustic features typically contain only a 20–30 ms speech signal per frame and are susceptible to interference from environmental noise and speaker differences.

Overfitting occurs when a model becomes too specialized in learning noise or randomness present in the training data, instead of learning the underlying patterns that generalize well to new data. In limited resource speech recognition tasks, where the amount of labeled data is limited, models trained on traditional acoustic features may overfit to the training data and perform poorly on new data. These features are highly dependent on the distribution of the training data and may not capture the underlying patterns in speech signals that are useful for generalization to new data. Therefore, it is necessary to extract robust and representative features to improve the recognition accuracy of limited resource speech recognition tasks. To address the issue, researchers have proposed Bottleneck Features (BNF). BNF was originally introduced by Grézl [4] and has been applied to continuous speech recognition. It is an approach that utilizes a pre-trained neural network to extract high-level feature representations of the input data. Existing research [5,11] has established the effectiveness of integrating BNF to enhance the performance of speech recognition systems in limited resource conditions. However, the BNF extracted from pre-trained deep neural networks is typically trained on large annotated speech datasets, which may not capture all the relevant acoustic and linguistic information required for speech recognition tasks with limited resources, particularly when there is a significant difference between the target task and the pre-training dataset. In addition, fine-tuning pre-trained neural networks for BNF extraction is also a challenge, as it requires a large amount of labeled data, which may be scarce.

We propose a method for speech representation using LRBN. Unlike Generative Adversarial Networks (GANs) that employ a simple standardized random vector to model data uncertainty, LRBN is a generative model that effectively captures uncertainty in data. Additionally, classical probabilistic deep generative models, such as Restricted Boltzmann Machines (RBM) and Deep Belief Networks (DBN), ignore the correlation between hidden variables, which weakens their representational power. In contrast, LRBN preserves the dependencies between hidden variables by approximating the true posterior distribution using conditional pseudo-likelihood [9]. Previous studies have demonstrated the superior performance of LRBN in tasks such as image restoration and object recognition, with its strong data representation capabilities [10].

We use LRBN to extract more effective speech representations from traditional acoustic features to improve the performance of speech recognition. By reconstructing speech data and extracting LRBN hidden layer features (LRBN-HF), features dependencies between speech frames can be captured while removing irrelevant information. To evaluate the effectiveness of LRBN for speech representation, two experiments for speech recognition were designed. The first experiment constructed a phoneme recognition model using CNN with MFCCs as the speech feature compared with LRBN-HF, while the second experiment employed the popular Transformer [3] as an end-to-end continuous speech recognition model with FBank and BNF features as speech features compared with LRBN-HF. Two experimental results demonstrate that the proposed LRBN-HF features outperform traditional acoustic features and BNF in speech recognition tasks, thus proving the effectiveness of LRBN in improving speech recognition performance.

The organization of the rest of this paper is as follows: Sect. 2 provides a detailed introduction of the LRBN method and the process of speech feature extraction. Section 3 outlines the experimental setting and discusses the experimental results. Finally, Sect. 4 concludes this paper.

2   Method

We introduce LRBN to extract more effective speech representation from traditional acoustic features. This section begins by presenting the basic principles of LRBN and then applies the LRBN-HF features extracted from LRBN for speech recognition.

2.1   Latent Regression Bayesian Network

LRBN is a generative model composed of visible and hidden layers, where the visible layer X is n_d dimensional and the hidden layer H is n_h dimensional, as illustrated in Fig. 1. The model incorporates directed edges that link each latent variable to visible variables.

LRBN fulfills the chain rule, whereby it represents the visible variables as $x = (x_1, \ldots, x_{n_d})$ and the hidden variables as $h = (h_1, \ldots, h_{n_h})$. The joint probability distribution of all visible and hidden variables can be formulated as the product of the prior probability distribution of any hidden variable and the conditional probability distribution of any visible variable given the values of the hidden variables [16]. The joint probability of x and h is computed in Equation (1),

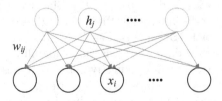

Fig. 1. LRBN structure

$$P(\boldsymbol{x}, \boldsymbol{h}) = \prod_{j=1}^{n_h} P(h_j) \prod_{i=1}^{n_d} P(x_i \mid \boldsymbol{h}) \tag{1}$$

where n_h and n_v refer to the number of hidden and visible nodes, respectively. The joint probability of the visible and hidden variables is represented by $p(\boldsymbol{x}, \boldsymbol{h})$, whereas the prior probability of the hidden variable h_j is denoted as $P(h_j)$. Furthermore, $P(x_i \mid \boldsymbol{h})$ represents the conditional probability of the visible variable x_i given all hidden variables $\boldsymbol{h}$ [17]. Both $P(h_j)$ and $P(x_i \mid \boldsymbol{h})$ follow Bernoulli distribution and can be expressed as Eqs. (2) and (3), respectively,

$$P(h_j) = \sigma(d_j)^{h_j}(1 - \sigma(d_j))^{1-h_j} \tag{2}$$

where $\sigma(z) = 1/(1 + exp(-z))$ and d_j is the deviation of the variable h_j.

$$P(x_i \mid \boldsymbol{h}) = \sigma\left(w_i^T \boldsymbol{h} + b_i\right)^{x_i}\left(1 - \sigma\left(w_i^T \boldsymbol{h} + b_i\right)\right)^{1-x_i} \tag{3}$$

where w_i represents the weight linking the hidden node $\boldsymbol{h}$ with the visible node x_i, while b_i denotes the bias value of the visible node x_i. By integrating Eqs. (2) and (3), Eq. (1) can be derived as Eq. (4).

$$
\begin{aligned}
P_{\Theta_{LRBN}}&(\boldsymbol{x}, \boldsymbol{h}) \\
&= \prod_j \frac{\exp(d_j h_j)}{1 + \exp(d_j)} \prod_i \frac{\exp\left(\left(w_i^T \boldsymbol{h} + b_i\right) x_i\right)}{1 + \exp\left(w_i^T \boldsymbol{h} + b\right)} \\
&= \frac{\exp\left(-\Gamma_{\Theta_{LRBN}}(\boldsymbol{x}, \boldsymbol{h})\right)}{\prod_j (1 + \exp(d_j))}
\end{aligned}
\tag{4}
$$

where $\Theta_{LRBN} = \boldsymbol{W}, \boldsymbol{b}, \boldsymbol{d}$, and

$$
\begin{aligned}
\Gamma_{\Theta_{LRBN}}(\boldsymbol{x}, \boldsymbol{h}) = &-\sum_i \left(w_i^T \boldsymbol{h} + b_i\right) x_i - \sum_j d_j h_j \\
&+ \sum_i \log\left(1 + \exp\left(w_i^T \boldsymbol{h} + b_i\right)\right).
\end{aligned}
\tag{5}
$$

Equation (5) displays a resemblance to RBM's energy function, with an additional term $\sum_i \log\left(1 + \exp\left(w_i^T \boldsymbol{h} + b_i\right)\right)$. This supplementary term offers the capability to capture intricate relationships between hidden variables. In contrast to the RBM, the LRBN model adopts directed connections between hidden and visible nodes, leading to more extensive dependencies between hidden layers [20]. Consequently, the LRBN model can better interpret intrinsic patterns in input data compared to the RBM.

2.2 LRBN for Speech Representation

We applied the speech representation extracted by LRBN for speech recognition. Firstly, we extract the traditional acoustic features and then extract the LRBN-HF feature of each speech with LRBN. The LRBN was trained with unsupervised

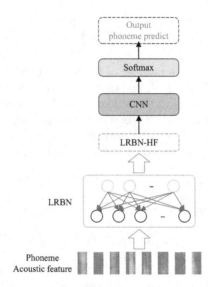

Fig. 2. CNN with LRBN-HF feature for phoneme recognition.

learning, where the mean squared error between the reconstructed and original acoustic features is utilized as the loss function for network training. After the network converged, the values of the hidden nodes are extracted from the hidden layer as the LRBN-HF feature.

Figure 2 shows a CNN that uses the LRBN-HF feature for phoneme recognition. The LRBN-HF feature is inputted into the first layer of the CNN, which generates a set of convolution features using multiple convolutional kernels. The output of the convolution layer is then passed to a pooling layer, which reduces the dimensionality of the feature sequence. The pooling layer's output is utilized as input to a fully connected layer, which maps the input feature sequence to different phoneme labels. Finally, a softmax classifier is applied to the output of the fully connected layer to predict the probability of each phoneme label, and output the most likely phoneme label.

Figure 3 shows a Transformer with LRBN-HF feature for continuous speech recognition. The LRBN-HF feature is subjected to two-dimensional convolution for downsampling before being fed into the encoder section of the model, which consists of multiple layers of blocks. Each block comprises of multi-head self-attention mechanism and a feedforward neural network. The encoder converts the input sequence into a series of high-level abstract feature representations. The output of the encoder is used as the input to the decoder. The decoder also consists of multiple blocks, but each block includes a multi-head encoder-decoder attention mechanism to associate the generated word with the input sequence. The output of the decoder is fed into a fully connected layer for classification, to predict the most likely output label for each time step in the sequence. Finally, the model output is decoded using beam search algorithm to find the most likely output sequence.

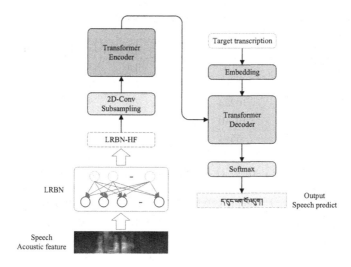

Fig. 3. Transformer with LRBN-HF feature for continuous speech recognition.

3 Experiment

3.1 Datasets

In this work, we evaluated the proposed method using five small-scale speech datasets. The datasets included the TIBMD Tibetan speech dataset [19], the Cantonese dataset [8] from Common Voice, the Zeroth-Korean Korean dataset [18], the Thchs30 Mandarin dataset [15], and the TIMIT English dataset. The TIBMD Tibetan dataset comprises three dialects (Amdo, Kham, and Ü-Tsang) and was recorded by native Tibetan-speaking students. For the experiments, we selected 31.8 h of data from the Ü-Tsang dialect. The Cantonese dataset from Common Voice is a free and open-source speech dataset contributed by volunteers globally, and we used 21.5 h of Cantonese data for experiments. We randomly selected 26.4 h of data from the Zeroth-Korean dataset, an open-source dataset for the Korean language. The TIMIT dataset includes 6300 sentences spoken by 630 individuals from eight major dialect regions in the United States. The Thchs30 dataset, an open-source Mandarin speech dataset comprising approximately 30 h of speech data recorded in a quiet office environment, was used in this work. All speech signals were sampled at 16kHz with 16-bit quantization. Table 1 provides the details of each dataset for the continuous speech recognition experiments.

We randomly selected speech data from TIBMD,Cantonese, Zeroth-Korean, Thchs30, and Librispeech for the phoneme recognition experiment. We used the Montreal Forced Aligner (MFA), which is based on Kaldi, for phoneme segmentation. The speech data for each language were sliced into small phoneme-level segments. Table 2 provides detailed information about the data used for phoneme recognition.

Table 1. Data statistics for the continuous speech recognition experiments

Language	Training data(h)	Training utterances	Testing data(h)	Testing utterances
Tibetan	28.7	25704	3.1	2847
Cantonese	19.4	16884	2.1	1877
Korean	23.8	10224	2.6	1136
Mandarin	27.3	10710	6.8	2678
English	4.7	5544	0.6	756

Table 2. Data statistics for phoneme recognition experiments

Language	Phoneme category	Training data	Testing data
Tibetan	41	457881	40688
Cantonese	71	421865	37461
Korean	46	586958	52166
Mandarin	56	302400	26880
English	69	457257	40630

In addition, we conducted multi-dialect speech recognition experiments on the Ü-Tsang dialect, Amdo dialect, and Kham dialect of the Tibetan language. The data used for these experiments were sourced from the TIBMD dataset. Table 3 provides a detailed overview of the data statistics.

Table 3. Data statistics for multi-dialect speech recognition experiments

Language	Dialect	Train data(h)	Train utterances	Test data(h)	Test utterances
Tibetan	Ü-Tsang	28.7	25704	3.1	2847
	Amdo	11.5	11130	1.3	1237
	Kham	2.5	2302	0.3	256

3.2   Experimental Setup

Experimental Setup of Phoneme Recognition. We used 39-dimensional MFCCs with a window length of 25 ms and a frame shift of 10 ms as input to train the LRBN network. The LRBN comprised a hidden layer with 120 nodes, and unsupervised learning was utilized to train the network. After the network converged, LRBN-HF features were extracted from the hidden layer. A phoneme recognition model based on convolutional neural networks (CNN) was built in this work, with hyperparameters including a learning rate of 0.0008, a batch size of 64, and 100 epochs. The model included 5 convolutional layers, 2 linear layers, and the Rectified Linear Unit (Relu) activation function. A dropout layer was also added between each convolutional layer.

The output layer is a softmax layer, with the number of nodes corresponding to the number of phoneme categories. The Adam [7] algorithm with an initial hyperparameter epsilon of $10e^{-8}$ was used for optimization. To evaluate the phoneme recognition model, recognition accuracy (ACC) was used as the performance metric.

Experimental Setup of Speech Recognition. We conducted an end-to-end speech recognition experiment based on the Transformer model. The speech data were preprocessed by extracting 40-dimensional FBank features with a window length of 25ms and a frame shift of 10ms, and then normalized. We trained the LRBN network using unsupervised learning until convergence and extracted the LRBN-HF features from the hidden layers. We compared the Transformer models using LRBN-HF features, FBank features, and BNF features as inputs. BNF features were extracted using the Shennong library [2], which provides a Python interface for general feature extraction programs. We used the BUT/Phonexia feature extractor [12], which outputs 80 activation values from the bottleneck layer. The hyperparameters of the Transformer model were set as shown in Table 4.

The convolutional layer of the Transformer model consists of two CNN layers with a stride of 2 and a kernel size of 3. The dropout rate is set to 0.1. The channel number is set to 1, with 64 channels in the middle layer and 128 channels in the output layer. The encoder is stacked with 6 layers, each containing 4 attention heads, with each attention head being a 64-dimensional self-attention. These attention heads are concatenated and weighted during the training process, which includes BN (Batch Normalization) [6] to prevent overfitting. We trained the transformer for a certain number of epochs, so no validation set is used in this study. We use words as the basic modeling unit. For testing, we did not use a language model to decode the sentences. The word error rate (WER) is used as the performance evaluation metric for the model, as shown in Eq. (6).

$$WER = \frac{S + D + I}{N} \tag{6}$$

where S represents the number of substituted words, D represents the number of deleted words, I represents the number of inserted words, and N is the total number of words in the reference sequence. The Levenshtein distance algorithm was used to calculate the edit distance.

Table 4. The hyperparameter settings of the Transformer model

hyperparameter	setting
Epoch	100
Learning rate	0.001
Batch size	12
Optimizer	Adam
Dropout	0.1
Warmup steps	12000
Activation	Glu
Label_smoothing [13]	0.1

3.3 Experimental Results and Analysis

We trained a CNN phoneme recognition model with MFCCs and LRBN-HF features and evaluated the accuracy of phoneme recognition, as shown in Table 5. Our experimental results indicate that LRBN-HF features improve the accuracy of phoneme recognition. Specifically, when the model was trained with LRBN-HF features, the accuracy on Tibetan, Cantonese, Korean, Mandarin, and English datasets was 94.66, 64.82, 87.36, 92.04, and 90.53, respectively. Compared to the MFCCs, the accuracy was improved by 37.39, 21.06, 30.93, 18.77, and 27.86, respectively. These results demonstrate that LRBN-HF features, obtained through LRBN, are more robust and better represent speech units, resulting in improved phoneme recognition accuracy.

The end-to-end speech recognition models have been developed using FBank, BNF, and LRBN-HF features, implemented in the Transformer architecture. To evaluate the performance of these models, we conducted speech recognition experiments on five small-scale datasets. The WER was used as the performance metric, and the experimental results are presented in Table 6.

In all five datasets, LRBN-HF features outperformed FBank, with WER reductions of 9.7%, 1.05%, 17.09%, 1.74%, and 7.62%, respectively. This indicates that LRBN is an effective speech representation that can extract representative and stable features. Moreover, compared to FBank features, BNF features achieved better recognition results on the Korean and English datasets, while there was a slight improvement on the Tibetan dataset. However, on the Cantonese and Mandarin datasets, the WER increased. This phenomenon suggests that when the language used for BNF pre-training differs significantly from the target language, it is difficult to effectively capture the target language's feature information, which can deteriorate the model's performance. On the Tibetan, Cantonese, Korean, and Mandarin datasets, the LRBN-HF model outperformed the model using BNF features, indicating that LRBN is superior to the BNF in speech representation. Interestingly, on the English dataset, the WER of the BNF features was 1.74% lower than that of the LRBN-HF features. We analyzed that may be because the BNF pre-training network used a large-scale English corpus, which

Table 5. Comparison of LRBN-HF features and MFCCs features on phoneme recognition accuracy

Feature	ACC(%)				
	Tibetan	Cantonese	Korean	Mandarin	English
MFCCs	57.27	43.76	56.43	73.27	62.67
LRBN-HF	**94.66**	**64.82**	**87.36**	**92.04**	**90.53**

Table 6. Comparison of LRBN-HF features, BNF, and FBank features on WER

Feature	WER(%)				
	Tibetan	Cantonese	Korean	Mandarin	English
FBank	36.86	13.58	41.18	15.43	41.73
BNF	36.77	23.93	29.91	17.44	**32.37**
LRBN-HF	**27.16**	**12.53**	**24.09**	**13.69**	34.11

Table 7. Comparison of LRBN-HF features, BNF, and FBank features on Tibetan multi-dialect

Model	Feature	WER(%)		
		Ü-Tsang dialect	Amdo dialect	Kham dialect
Single-dialect Transformer	FBank	36.86	29.58	86.95
	BNF	36.77	28.92	89.81
	LRBN-HF	27.16	26.33	90.71
Multi-dialect Transformer	FBank	24.06	12.49	39.60
	BNF	22.56	13.45	35.66
	LRBN-HF	19.74	10.57	32.91

kept the source language consistent with the target language, resulting in a significant improvement in recognition performance. However, in practical applications, limited resource languages often lack such large-scale corpus for pre-training networks. Therefore, LRBN has been demonstrated to be an effective speech representation method, providing more useful information for downstream tasks.

In the Tibetan multi-dialect speech recognition experiments, we conducted a comparison of three different features to evaluate their WER in both single-dialect and multi-dialect recognition models. The experimental results are presented in Table 7. From the results of the single-dialect model experiments, it can be observed that LRBN-HF achieved the best performance on the Ü-Tsang and Amdo dialects, reducing the WER by 9.61% and 2.59% respectively compared to BNF. However, the WER on the Kham dialect was higher than the baseline, which we attribute to the relatively smaller size of the Kham dialect data. From the results of the multi-dialect model experiments, the WER for all features were lower than those of the single-dialect model. This is because the multi-dialect model possesses stronger generalization capability, enabling more accurate recognition of differences among different dialects. In the multi-dialect speech recognition model, LRBN-HF exhibited superior performance with the lowest WER. Compared to BNF, LRBN-HF reduced the WER by 2.82%, 2.88%, and 2.75% respectively. This indicates that the LRBN-HF feature can better capture common characteristics among multi-dialect, thereby enhancing the overall performance of multi-dialect speech recognition.

4 Conclusion

This paper investigates the effectiveness of LRBN network for learning more effective speech representation. LRBN-HF is compared with FBank and bottleneck features on limited-resource data for continuous speech recognition. Experimental results show that LRBN-HF features achieve lower word error rates than FBank and BNF features. Additionally, the LRBN-HF features are compared with the MFCCs features for phoneme recognition. The experimental results reveal that LRBN-HF has better phoneme recognition rate, indicating its ability to represent and distinguish speech phonemes. Overall, the experiments on continuous speech recognition and phoneme recognition demonstrate that LRBN networks can effectively capture the dependency relationships between speech frames, making it a more effective method for speech representation.

References

1. Akçay, M.B., Oğuz, K.: Speech emotion recognition: emotional models, databases, features, preprocessing methods, supporting modalities, and classifiers. Speech Commun. **116**, 56–76 (2020)
2. Bernard, M., Poli, M., Karadayi, J., Dupoux, E.: Shennong: a python toolbox for audio speech features extraction. Behav. Res. Methods. 1–13 (2023)
3. Dong, L., Xu, S., Xu, B.: Speech-transformer: a no-recurrence sequence-to-sequence model for speech recognition. In: 2018 IEEE International Conference on Acoustics, Speech and Signal Processing (ICASSP), pp. 5884–5888. IEEE (2018)
4. Grézl, F., Karafiát, M., Kontár, S., Cernocky, J.: Probabilistic and bottle-neck features for LVCSR of meetings. In: 2007 IEEE International Conference on Acoustics, Speech and Signal Processing-ICASSP 2007, vol. 4, pp. IV-757. IEEE (2007)
5. Hermann, E., Kamper, H., Goldwater, S.: Multilingual and unsupervised subword modeling for zero-resource languages. Comput. Speech Lang. **65**, 101098 (2021)
6. Ioffe, S., Szegedy, C.: Batch normalization: accelerating deep network training by reducing internal covariate shift. In: International Conference on Machine Learning, pp. 448–456. PMLR (2015)
7. Kingma, D.P., Ba, J.: Adam: a method for stochastic optimization. arXiv preprint arXiv:1412.6980 (2014)
8. Mozilla: Mozilla common voice. https://commonvoice.mozilla.org. Accessed 21 Feb 2023
9. Nie, S., Zhao, Y., Ji, Q.: Latent regression Bayesian network for data representation. In: 2016 23rd International Conference on Pattern Recognition (ICPR), pp. 3494–3499. IEEE (2016)
10. Nie, S., Zheng, M., Ji, Q.: The deep regression Bayesian network and its applications: probabilistic deep learning for computer vision. IEEE Signal Process. Mag. **35**(1), 101–111 (2018)
11. Padhi, T., Biswas, A., De Wet, F., van der Westhuizen, E., Niesler, T.: Multilingual bottleneck features for improving ASR performance of code-switched speech in under-resourced languages. arXiv preprint arXiv:2011.03118 (2020)
12. Silnova, A., et al.: But/Phonexia bottleneck feature extractor. In: Odyssey, pp. 283–287 (2018)
13. Szegedy, C., Vanhoucke, V., Ioffe, S., Shlens, J., Wojna, Z.: Rethinking the inception architecture for computer vision. In: Proceedings of the IEEE Conference on Computer Vision and Pattern Recognition, pp. 2818–2826 (2016)
14. Tiwari, V.: MFCC and its applications in speaker recognition. Int. J. Emerg. Technol. **1**(1), 19–22 (2010)
15. Wang, D., Zhang, X.: THCHS-30: a free Chinese speech corpus. arXiv preprint arXiv:1512.01882 (2015)
16. Wang, S., Hao, L., Ji, Q.: Facial action unit recognition and intensity estimation enhanced through label dependencies. IEEE Trans. Image Process. **28**(3), 1428–1442 (2018)
17. Wang, S., Hao, L., Ji, Q.: Knowledge-augmented multimodal deep regression Bayesian networks for emotion video tagging. IEEE Trans. Multimed. **22**(4), 1084–1097 (2019)
18. Zeroth Project: Zeroth-Korean: Korean speech recognition corpus for zeroth ASR (2023). https://www.openslr.org/61/. Accessed 21 Feb 2023
19. Zhao, Y., et al.: An open speech resource for Tibetan multi-dialect and multitask recognition. Int. J. Comput. Sci. Eng. **22**(2–3), 297–304 (2020)
20. Zhao, Y., et al.: Tibetan multi-dialect speech recognition using latent regression Bayesian network and end-to-end mode. J. Internet of Things **1**(1), 17 (2019)

Input Layer Binarization with Bit-Plane Encoding

Lorenzo Vorabbi[1,2]([✉]) [iD], Davide Maltoni[2] [iD], and Stefano Santi[1]

[1] Datalogic Labs, 40012 Bologna, Italy
{lorenzo.vorabbi,stefano.santi}@datalogic.com
[2] University of Bologna, DISI, Cesena Campus, 47521 Cesena, Italy
{lorenzo.vorabbi2,davide.maltoni}@unibo.it

Abstract. Binary Neural Networks (BNNs) use 1-bit weights and activations to efficiently execute deep convolutional neural networks on edge devices. Nevertheless, the binarization of the first layer is conventionally excluded, as it leads to a large accuracy loss. The few works addressing the first layer binarization, typically increase the number of input channels to enhance data representation; such data expansion raises the amount of operations needed and it is feasible only on systems with enough computational resources. In this work, we present a new method to binarize the first layer using directly the 8-bit representation of input data; we exploit the standard bit-planes encoding to extract features bit-wise (using depth-wise convolutions); after a re-weighting stage, features are fused again. The resulting model is fully binarized and our first layer binarization approach is model independent. The concept is evaluated on three classification datasets (CIFAR10, SVHN and CIFAR100) for different model architectures (VGG and ResNet) and, the proposed technique outperforms state of the art methods both in accuracy and BMACs reduction.

Keywords: Binary Neural Networks · Input Layer Binarization · Deep Learning

1 Introduction

Deep Neural Networks showed in the last years impressive results, sometimes reaching accuracy better than human level, with applications in a wide variety of domains. These improvements have been achieved by increasing the depth and complexity of the network; such huge models can run smoothly on expensive GPU-based machines but cannot be easily deployed to edge devices (i.e., small mobile or IoT systems), which are typically resource-constrained. Various techniques have been introduced to mitigate this problem, including network quantization [1–5], network pruning [6,7] and efficient architecture design [8–12].

In 2016, Courbariaux and Bengio [13] first showed the potential of the extreme quantization level that uses only 1-bit to represent both weights and

© The Author(s), under exclusive license to Springer Nature Switzerland AG 2023
L. Iliadis et al. (Eds.): ICANN 2023, LNCS 14261, pp. 395–406, 2023.
https://doi.org/10.1007/978-3-031-44198-1_33

activations. By representing +1 with an unset bit and −1 with a set bit, the multiplications of weights and activations can be executed with xnor gates, saving hardware resources and greatly reducing power consumption. Such BNN model was able to achieve comparable accuracy results on small datasets like CIFAR10 [14] and SVHN [15] but on wider dataset like Imagenet [16] a relevant accuracy drop was reported. Recent works [4, 17–25] on BNNs have significantly improved the accuracy on large datasets like Imagenet filling the gap with real-valued networks.

Most of the BNNs do not fully exploit the benefits of 1-bit quantization, since they exclude from binarization the first and last layers that normally work with fixed-point numbers. In general, the number of parameters and the computational effort of the first layer are relatively low compared to intermediate deep convolutional layers employed in VGG [26] or ResNet [27] models, since input data has typically fewer channels (e.g. color images have three channels). This usually leads to deploy the first layer of BNN models using floating-point or quantizing it using 8-bit; the consequence is that two different type of multipliers (8-bit for first layer, binary for the remaining), with different bit widths, are needed to execute the computations leading to a solution which increases the power consumption (8-bit multiplier requires more power than xnor) and consumes more hardware resources (e.g. an FPGA design) than xnor gates. Conversely, the challenge of binarizing both weights and activations in the input layer is due to the small number of input channels [28]. Therefore, almost all the works addressing the binarization of the first layer tried to increase the number of input channels to enrich data representation.

FBNA [28] proposes a two-step optimization scheme that consists of binarization and pruning; during binarization phase the number of input channels is increased by a factor 256× and then, during pruning, lowest bits of input data are dropped away. The constraint of FBNA is that the encoded vector must be a power of two. BIL [29] attempts to directly unpack the 8-bit fixed-point input data, called *DBID*, and adding an additional binary pointwise convolutional layer between the unpacked input data and the first layer to increase the number of channels, dubbed as *BIL*. The authors of FracDNN [30] propose to use thermometer encoding to transform a pixel to a thermometer vector (expanding each input channel to 32 binary channels) that then is transformed to the {−1, +1} bipolar representation.

In contrast with previous works where the number of input channels has been increased, our method directly uses the fixed-point representation of a pixel. The results show that the proposed technique is competitive both in term of efficiency and accuracy. Our contributions can be summarized as follows:

– we propose a general approach to binarize the first layer of a CNN using the native 8-bit fixed-point inputs. We rearrange the 8-bit input data into 8 bit planes, each bit plane is consumed by a binary depth-wise convolutional layer which gives more importance (using a multiplier, actually a shift operation) to the most significant bit planes. Finally, all feature maps are fused together through an addition operator. The entire process, depicted in Fig. 3, does not

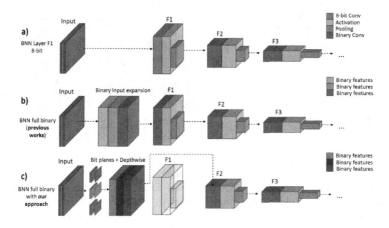

Fig. 1. *(a)* Standard scenario of BNNs where the first convolutional layer is not binarized; weights and inputs are used in 8-bit/floating-point representation. *(b)* Typical approach of the works that binarized the first layer F_1 incrementing the number of input channels; in this case the input expansion is actually an additional layer. *(c)* Our approach, where depth-wise convolutions are applied to input bit-planes and the resulting maps can replace the F_1 layer, producing a more compact model.

rely on floating-point computation, resulting more suitable to be deployed on ASIC or FPGA systems.

– we show that the feature maps resulting from our bit-plane manipulations allow to skip the original[1] F_1 first network layer (see Fig. 1c) with a minimal accuracy loss, leading to a model which uses less BMACs.
– we evaluate our concept on three classification datasets (SVHN, CIFAR10 and CIFAR100 [14]) showing that our solution outperforms all previous methods introduced to binarize the input layer.

2   Method

A common CNN model employed for computer vision problems works with RGB input images; it takes an input volume with three channels ($H \times W \times C$, where C is the number of channels) and extracts the features using convolutional blocks. To increase the receptive field of the network, a sequence of *pooling* operations is used. Each input pixel p is usually a fixed-point integer with 8 bit precision, namely $p = \sum_{m=0}^{7} x_m \cdot 2^m$.

In BNNs, typically the first layer (usually a convolutional one) is not binarized, all the input pixels are processed using 8-bit weights, producing F_1 output 8-bit feature maps (Fig. 1a). The previous works in literature that addressed the problem to generate F_1 binary feature maps, adopted different techniques to increase the number of input channels C (generating a more sparse representation) in order to use binary weights and inputs for layer F_1; usually a good

---

[1] Before the addition of our depth-wise convolutions.

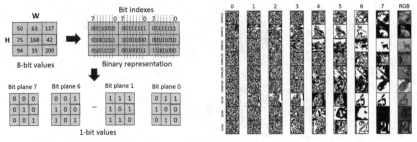

(a) Bit Planes example   (b) Bit Planes on CIFAR10, CIFAR100 and SVHN

Fig. 2. (a) Example of bit plane representation for a 3 × 3 8-bit image. (b) Image representation in bit planes. Each column refers to a bit index extracted from image; for representation purposes, bit 1 is converted to 255 while bit 0 remains 0. In this example all bit planes refer to channel G of RGB images.

tradeoff between accuracy and increment of first layer MACs is to wide the number of channels C by 32× [29,30]. This process is depicted in Fig. 1b, where the increment of input channels leads to a bigger model footprint; in fact, a linear increment of the number of input channels, linearly increases also the kernel parameters of a 2D convolutional layer.

The intuition behind our approach is that, extracting a different bit plane for each bit position, the semantic spatial information is preserved for most of the high index bits (4 to 7), as shown in Fig. 2b. Lower bit indexes (0 − 3) contain less correlated spatial information of image pixels and, depending on the dataset, they can be selectively omitted to further reduce the computational effort. The overall diagram of our method is reported in Fig. 3 and it is composed by the following steps:

1. **Bit Rearrangement:** An input image $\mathcal{I}$ (W, H, C, where C is the number of channels), having M bits for each pixel (usually 8), is rearranged into bit planes (as shown in Fig. 3a); each 8-bit input channel is decomposed into eight 1-bit planes. A bit plane x is a 1-bit map containing only the bit of index x for all pixels (see Fig. 2a). The bit-plane image bp corresponding to channel c can be indicated as $\mathcal{I}(c, bp)$.

2. **Feature Extraction:** Each binary bit-plane is consumed by a binary depth-wise convolution layer that generates **N** feature maps for each bit plane, as reported in Fig. 3b. The output of feature extraction ($\mathcal{FE}$) step can be formulated as:

$$\mathcal{FE}(c, bp) = \gamma(c, bp) \frac{(\mathcal{I}(c, bp) * W(c, bp) + b(c, bp)) - \mu(c, bp)}{\sigma(c, bp)} + \beta(c, bp)$$

(1)

where $*$ is the convolution operator, $W(c, bp)$ and $b(c, bp)$ represent the weights of the depth-wise convolution while γ, μ, σ and β are the Batch

Normalization (BN) [31] parameters; Eq. 1 refers to a single feature map of depth-wise convolution, which is dependent on channel c and bit plane bp. In Eq. 1 the non-linear activation function can be omitted because binarization of activation and weights already introduce non-linearity. The use of Batch Normalization after each binary layer plays a key role in BNNs because it promotes a smoother optimization process allowing a stable behavior of the gradients. BN layer is usually executed in floating-point precision when mixed with binary layers, but the authors of [32] proved that it can be executed with 8-bit fixed point without accuracy loss.

3. **Features Re-Weight:** Following the intuition based on Fig. 2b, where high index bit planes preserve the spatial information of the image, this stage re-weights the feature maps based on the bit plane index. Higher bit planes are multiplied by higher scalar values. In order to simplify this stage, the multiplication can be replaced by a shift operation. The N feature maps of each bit plane are shifted by the same quantity (namely a power of two).

4. **Features Fusion:** The re-weighted feature maps, corresponding to a different 8-bit input channel, are summed to combine the information encoded by different bit indexes and can be expressed as:

$$\mathcal{FWF}(c, bp) = \sum_{i=0}^{M} \mathcal{FE}(c, bp) \cdot 2^i \qquad (2)$$

In Eq. 2 the multiplication by 2^i represents the re-weight of feature maps that can be implemented with a shift operation. The sum instead can be implemented accumulating features over 32-bit register; if the subsequent layer extracts *sign* from inputs, then the 32-bit output maps can be reduced to 1-bit saving memory overhead. The N feature maps corresponding to a different channel are concatenated to create a volume of $N \times 3$ maps that is used to feed the network, Fig. 1c. Such volume of N maps can replace the first layer of the CNN with almost no accuracy loss, as showed in Sec. 4 and, thus reducing the complexity of the overall model. F_1 requires a topology change of the first network layer when its weights and inputs are binarized and the expansion of depth-wise convolutions (Fig. 3b) can be set up in order to keep a number of feature maps equivalent to the layer F_1.

Table 1 reports the MACs of different approaches used to binarize input layer of a CNN, reporting the theoretical speedup of the methods; our solution is clearly competitive, in terms of MACs, with respect to the baseline (input not binarized) and other existing approaches.

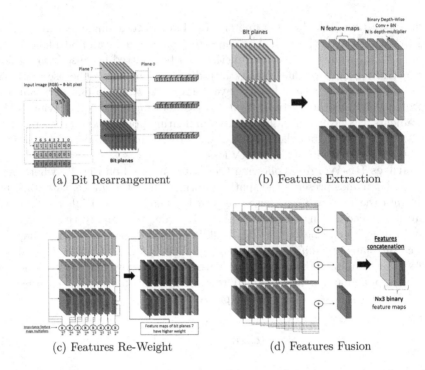

(a) Bit Rearrangement   (b) Features Extraction

(c) Features Re-Weight   (d) Features Fusion

Fig. 3. Binarization process of input layer. (a) shows the rearrangement phase that extracts, for each bit position of the encoded pixel a bit plane. (b) shows the binary depth-convolution block applied to each bit plane; the depth multiplier (N) is an hyper-parameter and it is dataset and model dependent. (c) shows how to weight differently feature maps extracted from different bit planes; maps related to most significant bits receive a higher multiplication factor. In (d), the feature maps related to the same 8-bit input channel are fused together through an addition.

3   Datasets and Implementation Details

We evaluate our method on three classification datasets: CIFAR10, CIFAR100 and SVHN with different BNN architectures. For each model architecture we tested different state-of-the-art binarization techniques of input layer; input binarization does not modify the other layers of the network, which remain unaltered. For each dataset, we conducted our experiments with the same training procedure (same number of epochs, optimizer, learning rate scheduling, loss function) for all topologies without adding distillation losses or special regularization to the overall loss function. The binarization of weights and activations always happens at training time using an approximation of the gradient (STE [34] or derived solution that are model dependent) for *sign* function. The augmentation procedure for all datasets is performed with floating-point arithmetic but, before feeding data to the network, input image is quantized using 8-bit fixed precision. We adopted the following datasets:

Table 1. Comparison of the first layer MACs required by our method with respect to the state of the art solutions. Input data has a shape $H \times W \times C$ $(32 \times 32 \times 3)$ and a precision of M bits; in this example the first convolutional layer has $F_1 = (128)$ filters with size $F \times F$ (3). The expansion channels is $K = 32$ for methods [29,30]. The depthwise multiplier of our method can be chosen as $N_1 = \lfloor \frac{F_1}{C} \rfloor = 42$. We conducted our experiments using also a lower value, $N_2 = 32$ instead of N_1 and only 4 bits of input pixels. P represents the number of bit planes extracted by step 3a.

Method	Type	# MACs	# weights	$\frac{MACs\ method}{MACs\ Baseline}$ [a]	Speedup[b]
Baseline	8-bit	$HWCF^2F_1$	CF^2F_1	$1\times$	$1\times$
DBID [29]	1-bit	$HWCMF^2F_1$	$CMK + F^2F_1K$	$8\times$	$1.12\times$
BIL [29]	1-bit	$HWK\left(CM + F^2F_1\right)$	CKF^2F_1	$10.8\times$	$0.81\times$
Thermometer [30]	1-bit	$HWCKF^2F_1$	CF^2N_1M	$32\times$	$0.27\times$
ours $(P = 8, N_1)$	1-bit	$HWCPF^2N_1$	CPF^2N_1	$2.6\times$	$\mathbf{3.42\times}$
ours $(P = 4, N_1)$	1-bit	$HWCPF^2N_1$	CMF^2N_1	$1.3\times$	$\mathbf{6.84\times}$
ours $(P = 4, N_2)$	1-bit	$HWCPF^2N_2$	CPF^2N_2	$1\times$	$\mathbf{9\times}$

[a] A lower ratio means a higher reduction of MACs.
[b] According to [33] (Fig. 2), the worst case speedup of binary convolution compared to 8-bit is $9\times$.

CIFAR10 and CIFAR100 The RGB images are scaled to the interval $[-1.0 ; +1.0]$ and the following data augmentation was used: zero padding of 4 pixels for each size, a random 32×32 crop and a random horizontal flip. No augmentation is used at test time. The models have been trained for 140 epochs.

SVHN The RGB input images are scaled to the interval $[-1.0 ; +1.0]$ and the following data augmentation procedure is used: random rotation (± 8 degrees), zoom ($[0.95, 1.05]$), random shift ($[0; 10]$) and random shear ($[0; 0.15]$). The models have been trained for 70 epochs.

We evaluated the following networks:

VGG-Small [35] Network structure is the following: $2 \times (128 - C3) + MP2 + 2 \times (256 - C3) + MP2 + 2 \times (512 - C3) + MP2 + FC1024 + FC1024 + Softmax^2$. The VGG-Small model adopted uses the straight-through-estimator (STE) to approximate the gradient on non-differentiable layers [2,34].

VGG-11 [19] Network structure is the following: $64 - C3 + MP2 + 128 - C3 + MP2 + 2 \times (256 - C3) + MP2 + 2 \times (512 - C3) + MP2 + 2 \times (512 - C3) + MP2 + Softmax$ (see footnote 2). Even VGG-11 uses the STE estimator for binarization operation during back-propagation.

BiRealNet [17] It is a modified version of classical ResNet that proposes to preserve the real activations before the sign function to increase the representational capability of the 1-bit CNN, through a simple shortcut. Bi-RealNet

---

[2] $m \times (n - CK)$ stands for m consecutive convolutional layers, each one with n output channels and K kernel size. $MP2$ is the max pooling layer with subsample 2 while FCx is a fully-connected layer having x neurons. $Softmax$ represents the last dense classification layer using softmax as activation.

adopts a tight approximation to the derivative of the non-differentiable sign function with respect to activation and a magnitude-aware gradient to update weight parameters. We used two instances of the network, an *18-layer* and a *34-layer* Bi-Real net[3].

ReactNet [24] To further compress compact networks, this model constructs a baseline based on MobileNetV1 [8] and add shortcut to bypass every 1-bit convolutional layer that has the same number of input and output channels. The 3×3 depth-wise and the 1×1 point-wise convolutional blocks of MobileNet are replaced by the 3×3 and 1×1 vanilla convolutions in parallel with shortcuts in React Net[4]. As for Bi-Real Net, we tested two different versions of React Net: a *18-layer* and a *34-layer*.

4   Results and Conclusions

Table 2. Top1 accuracy (%) results of test set on CIFAR10. In first part we report the result of first test scenario (standard conditions); in second half, the results achieved in the second scenario (reducing the MACs of binarization of input layer).

	VGG-Small	VGG-11	BiReal-18	BiReal-34	React-18	React-34	
DBID [29]$(P = 8)$	84.5	77.6	81.8	85.0	86.0	86.7	
BIL [29]$(P = 8)$	82.0	78.9	81.3	82.2	84.0	83.5	
Therm [30]$(K = 32)$	84.2	80.1	85.2	85.3	86.6	86.6	*1st*
ours $(P = 8, N_1)$	**85.9**	79.1	**87.7**	**88.5**	**89.9**	**90.2**	
baseline	89.2	84.7	89.1	89.3	90.6	90.6	
DBID$(P = 4)$	83.6	76.8	74.9	83.7	83.7	85.3	
BIL$(P = 4)$	80.9	82.4	80.8	82.3	82.7	83.4	
Therm$(K = 16)$	83.8	79.6	84.7	85.9	86.5	86.8	*2nd*
ours$(P = 4, N_2)$	**85.0**	78.3	**86.9**	**87.7**	**88.5**	**89.0**	
baseline	88.3	83.7	87.4	88.3	88.8	89.1	

The validation of our solution has been accomplished through two different test scenarios; in the first one, we compared the accuracy (measured on test set) of our binarization method w.r.t. the state-of-the-arts input layer binarization approaches, keeping unaltered the structure of the network except for the input data binarization layer (first half of Tables 2, 3 and 4). In this first scenario all the 8-bits planes are exploited, layer F1 (Fig. 1) is executed and our proposed solution is able to reach a better accuracy compared to other input binarization methods, closing the accuracy gap with the baseline.

---

[3] Refer to the following https://github.com/liuzechun/Bi-Real-net repository for all the details.

[4] Refer to the following https://github.com/liuzechun/ReActNet repository for all the details.

Table 3. Top1 accuracy (%) results of test set on SVHN.

	VGG-Small	VGG-11	BiReal-18	BiReal-34	React-18	React-34	
DBID [29]$(P = 8)$	94.5	92.2	94.3	95.1	94.9	95.1	⎫
BIL [29]$(P = 8)$	93.5	92.1	94.3	93.4	94.1	94.7	⎬
Therm [30]$(K = 32)$	89.7	88.9	89.2	89.8	89.8	90.2	*1st*
ours$(P = 8, N_1)$	**94.8**	**93.4**	94.3	95.0	**95.1**	**95.7**	⎬
baseline	95.7	95.5	94.3	95.1	95.5	95.9	⎭
DBID$(P = 4)$	94.3	92.1	94.3	94.7	94.8	95.0	⎫
BIL$(P = 4)$	93.4	92.1	94.4	93.5	93.8	94.5	⎬
Therm$(K = 16)$	89.5	88.6	89.8	89.7	89.8	90.1	*2nd*
ours$(P = 4, N_2)$	**94.8**	**93.3**	94.3	**95.0**	**95.1**	**95.7**	⎬
baseline	95.6	95.0	94.4	95.1	95.5	96.0	⎭

Table 4. Top1 accuracy (%) results of test set on CIFAR100.

	VGG-Small	VGG-11	BiReal-18	BiReal-34	React-18	React-34	
DBID [29]$(P = 8)$	53.6	43.1	51.8	58.5	56.3	58.0	⎫
BIL [29]$(P = 8)$	50.0	42.9	52.7	56.0	55.4	55.5	⎬
Therm [30]$(K = 32)$	53.0	43.5	57.2	57.1	57.4	57.9	*1st*
ours$(P = 8, N_1)$	**56.5**	**46.0**	**58.7**	**60.6**	**61.7**	**62.9**	⎬
baseline	60.6	52.3	63.4	65.0	64.9	65.3	⎭
DBID$(P = 4)$	52.3	41.8	50.5	56.5	55.2	56.7	⎫
BIL$(P = 4)$	49.5	42.0	52.1	54.5	52.1	53.6	⎬
Therm$(K = 16)$	52.1	42.6	56.7	54.5	56.8	58.6	*1st*
ours$(P = 4, N_2)$	**54.8**	**44.5**	**57.7**	**59.6**	**60.2**	**62.0**	⎬
baseline	60.3	50.3	60.0	61.7	62.0	63.4	⎭

In the second scenario, to further reduce the MACs of our solution, we propose an optimization of our method that uses only the 4 most significant bits and reduces the depth-wise multiplier from N_1 to N_2 (the reduction to 4 bits is based on Fig. 2b, that shows how the bit planes corresponding to less significant bits convey less information). In the second half of Tables 2, 3 and 4, we report the results of the optimized version compared with other solutions properly modified in order to compute an equivalent number of channels[5]. As reported, our solution is able to preserve the baseline accuracy using less input bits while the other methods get a consistent accuracy drop when reducing input bits and binary channels.

---

[5] For *DBID*, *thermometer* and *baseline* methods, we reduced to 32 the number of output channels of layer $F1$; for *BIL* and *ours*, we skipped the layer $F1$ because the convolution operation is already exploited within the input layer binarization process. For *DBID*, *BIL* and *ours* we used only the 4 most significant bits of input data. For *thermometer* we applied also a reduced expansion factor of $K = 16$.

Differently from other works, our solution re-weights the feature extracted by bit-planes giving more importance to the features corresponding to the most significant bit-planes; this stage contributes to scale down the footprint of our binarization approach simplifying the deployment on resource constrained devices (low-power embedded CPUs). Furthermore, the accuracy of our method is higher than *thermometer encoding* [30], which preserves the feature similarity after binarizing the input layer, as pointed out by Anderson et al. [28].

In conclusion, this paper introduced a novel input layer binarization method that reaches higher accuracy when compared to state-of-the-art solutions reducing the gap to the baseline on average by 2.2% points. Our solution was able to preserve model accuracy when only 4 bits of input pixels are used in the input binarization layer, proving to be more resource-constrained device friendly than existing ones. In the future, we intend to further investigate the latency speedup of our method on real hardware devices like Raspberry Pi Model 3B/4B exploiting the computation capabilities of NEON ARM[6] SIMD engine.

References

1. Choi, J., et al.: PACT: parameterized clipping activation for quantized neural networks. In: arXiv preprint arXiv:1805.06085 (2018)
2. Hubara, I., et al.: Binarized neural networks. In: Advances in Neural Information Processing Systems, vol. 29 (2016)
3. Lin, X., Zhao, C., Pan, W.: Towards accurate binary convolutional neural network. In: Advances in Neural Information Processing Systems, vol. 30 (2017)
4. Rastegari, M., Ordonez, V., Redmon, J., Farhadi, A.: XNOR-Net: ImageNet classification using binary convolutional neural networks. In: Leibe, B., Matas, J., Sebe, N., Welling, M. (eds.) ECCV 2016. LNCS, vol. 9908, pp. 525–542. Springer, Cham (2016). https://doi.org/10.1007/978-3-319-46493-0_32
5. Zhou, S., et al.: DoRefa-Net: training low bitwidth convolutional neural networks with low bitwidth gradients. In: arXiv preprint arXiv:1606.06160 (2016)
6. Han, S., Mao, H., Dally, W.J.: Deep compression: compressing deep neural networks with pruning, trained quantization and Huffman coding. In: arXiv preprint arXiv:1510.00149 (2015)
7. Wen, W., et al.: Learning structured sparsity in deep neural networks. In: Advances in Neural Information Processing Systems, vol. 29 (2016)
8. Howard, A.G., et al.: MobileNets: efficient convolutional neural networks for mobile vision applications. In: arXiv preprint arXiv:1704.04861 (2017)
9. Ma, N., Zhang, X., Zheng, H.-T., Sun, J.: ShuffleNet V2: practical guidelines for efficient CNN architecture design. In: Ferrari, V., Hebert, M., Sminchisescu, C., Weiss, Y. (eds.) Computer Vision – ECCV 2018. LNCS, vol. 11218, pp. 122–138. Springer, Cham (2018). https://doi.org/10.1007/978-3-030-01264-9_8
10. Tan, M., Le, Q.: EfficientNet: rethinking model scaling for convolutional neural networks. In: International Conference on Machine Learning. PMLR, pp. 6105–6114 (2019)
11. Tan, M., Le, Q.: EfficientNetV2: smaller models and faster training. In: International Conference on Machine Learning. PMLR, pp. 10096–10106 (2021)

---

[6] https://www.arm.com/technologies/neon.

12. Hou, Q., Zhou, D., Feng, J.: Coordinate attention for efficient mobile network design. In: Proceedings of the IEEE/CVF Conference on Computer Vision and Pattern Recognition, pp. 13713–13722 (2021)
13. Courbariaux, M., et al.: Binarized neural networks: training deep neural networks with weights and activations constrained to +1 or −1. In: arXiv preprint arXiv:1602.02830 (2016)
14. Krizhevsky, A., Hinton, G., et al.: Learning multiple layers of features from tiny images (2009)
15. Netzer, Y., et al.: Reading digits in natural images with unsupervised feature learning (2011)
16. Russakovsky, O., et al.: ImageNet large scale visual recognition challenge. Int. J. Comput. Vision **115**(3), 211–252 (2015). https://doi.org/10.1007/s11263-015-0816-y
17. Liu, Z., Wu, B., Luo, W., Yang, X., Liu, W., Cheng, K.-T.: Bi-real net: enhancing the performance of 1-bit CNNs with improved representational capability and advanced training algorithm. In: Ferrari, V., Hebert, M., Sminchisescu, C., Weiss, Y. (eds.) ECCV 2018. LNCS, vol. 11219, pp. 747–763. Springer, Cham (2018). https://doi.org/10.1007/978-3-030-01267-0_44
18. Gu, J., et al.: Projection convolutional neural networks for 1-bit CNNs via discrete back propagation. In: Proceedings of the AAAI Conference on Artificial Intelligence, vol. 33, pp. 8344–8351, January 2019
19. Xu, Y., et al.: A main/subsidiary network framework for simplifying binary neural networks. In: Proceedings of the IEEE/CVF Conference on Computer Vision and Pattern Recognition, pp. 7154–7162 (2019)
20. Qin, H., et al.: Forward and backward information retention for accurate binary neural networks. In: Proceedings of the IEEE/CVF Conference on Computer Vision and Pattern Recognition, pp. 2250–2259 (2020)
21. Bethge, J., et al.: MeliusNet: can binary neural networks achieve MobileNet-level accuracy? In: arXiv preprint arXiv:2001.05936 (2020)
22. Bulat, A., Martinez, B., Tzimiropoulos, G.: High-capacity expert binary networks. In: arXiv preprint arXiv:2010.03558 (2020)
23. Martinez, B., et al.: Training binary neural networks with real-to-binary convolutions. In: arXiv preprint arXiv:2003.11535 (2020)
24. Liu, Z., Shen, Z., Savvides, M., Cheng, K.-T.: ReActNet: towards precise binary neural network with generalized activation functions. In: Vedaldi, A., Bischof, H., Brox, T., Frahm, J.-M. (eds.) ECCV 2020. LNCS, vol. 12359, pp. 143–159. Springer, Cham (2020). https://doi.org/10.1007/978-3-030-58568-6_9
25. Shi, X., et al.: RepBNN: towards a precise binary neural network with enhanced feature map via repeating. In: arXiv preprint arXiv:2207.09049 (2022)
26. Simonyan, K., Zisserman, A.: Very deep convolutional networks for large-scale image recognition. In: arXiv preprint arXiv:1409.1556 (2014)
27. He, K., et al.: Deep residual learning for image recognition. In: Proceedings of the IEEE Conference on Computer Vision and Pattern Recognition, pp. 770–778 (2016)
28. Anderson, A.G., Berg, C.P.: The high-dimensional geometry of binary neural networks. In: arXiv preprint arXiv:1705.07199 (2017)
29. Dürichen, R., et al.: Binary Input Layer: training of CNN models with binary input data. In: arXiv preprint arXiv:1812.03410 (2018)
30. Zhang, Y., et al.: FracBNN: accurate and FPGA-efficient binary neural networks with fractional activations. In: The 2021 ACM/SIGDA International Symposium on Field-Programmable Gate Arrays, pp. 171–182 (2021)

31. Ioffe, S., Szegedy, C.: Batch normalization: accelerating deep network training by reducing internal covariate shift. In: International Conference on Machine Learning. PMLR, pp. 448–456 (2015)
32. Vorabbi, L., Maltoni, D., Santi, S.: Optimizing dataflow in Binary Neural Networks. In: arXiv preprint arXiv:2304.00952 (2023)
33. Bannink, T., et al.: Larq compute engine: design, benchmark and deploy state-of-the-art binarized neural networks. Proc. Mach. Learn. Syst. **3**, 680–695 (2021)
34. Bengio, Y., Léonard, N., Courville, A.: Estimating or propagating gradients through stochastic neurons for conditional computation. In: arXiv preprint arXiv:1308.3432 (2013)
35. Zhang, D., Yang, J., Ye, D., Hua, G.: LQ-nets: learned quantization for highly accurate and compact deep neural networks. In: Ferrari, V., Hebert, M., Sminchisescu, C., Weiss, Y. (eds.) ECCV 2018. LNCS, vol. 11212, pp. 373–390. Springer, Cham (2018). https://doi.org/10.1007/978-3-030-01237-3_23

Investigation of Information Processing Mechanisms in the Human Brain During Reading Tanka Poetry

Anna Sato[1]([✉])[iD], Junichi Chikazoe[2][iD], Shotaro Funai[2][iD],
Daichi Mochihashi[3][iD], Yutaka Shikano[4,5][iD], Masayuki Asahara[6][iD],
Satoshi Iso[7][iD], and Ichiro Kobayashi[1][iD]

[1] Ochanomizu University, Tokyo, Japan
{g1920519,koba}@is.ocha.ac.jp
[2] Araya Inc., Tokyo, Japan
{chikazoe_junichi,funai_shotaro}@araya.org
[3] Institute of Statistical Mathematics, Tokyo, Japan
daichi@ism.ac.jp
[4] Gunma University, Maebashi, Gunma, Japan
yshikano@gunma-u.ac.jp
[5] Institute for Quantum Studies, Chapman University, Orange, CA, USA
shikano@chapman.edu
[6] National Institute for Japanese Language and Linguistics, Tokyo, Japan
masayu-a@ninjal.ac.jp
[7] High Energy Accelerator Research Organization, Tsukuba, Ibaraki, Japan
iso@post.kek.jp

Abstract. Recent advances in non-invasive brain function measurement technologies, such as functional magnetic resonance imaging (fMRI) and magnetoencephalography (MEG), and the development of machine learning techniques, including deep learning, have led to increased research on the elucidation and quantitative understanding of information processing processes in the human brain. Since the emergence of word2vec, which represents the meaning of natural language words as vectors, features of language stimuli given to the human brain have been represented using large language models in natural language processing and used to estimate brain states. In this study, we used GPT-2, which is known to perform well as a feature for predicting brain states, and investigated the information processing processes in the human brain when reading Japanese short poems, i.e., tanka poetry. In particular, we investigated the hubness of the regions of interest in the brain by applying the PageRank algorithm. As a result, we have found that the cingulate cortex and the insula, which are said to be related to emotion, have hubness in brain regions, while occipital lobe, which are not said to be related to emotion, have also hubness.

Keywords: Language Processing · Deep learning models · Neuroscience · fMRI · Emotion

© The Author(s), under exclusive license to Springer Nature Switzerland AG 2023
L. Iliadis et al. (Eds.): ICANN 2023, LNCS 14261, pp. 407–418, 2023.
https://doi.org/10.1007/978-3-031-44198-1_34

1   Introduction

In recent years, there has been a growing interest in exploring the relationship between deep learning models (DLMs) and the human brain. DLMs have been developed and inspired by the structure and behavior of the human brain, and have been trained on massive amounts of data, which has allowed them to achieve impressive result in various fields such as computer vision [1–3], natural language processing [4–8], speech recognition [9,10], and many others.

DLMs are also used to facilitate our comprehension of human cognitive processes and cerebral functions. While many studies have been investigated the language processing mechanism using everyday spoken language stimuli, our main objective is to elucidate how humans find the value in verbal arts, which are novels, poems, lyrics and the like. The emotion evoked by varbal arts, unlike that evoked in daily life, cannot be analyzed only through texts. In this study, we employ tanka as our verbal art stimuli, which is a form of Japanese traditional poetry, and will investigate the information processing about "poetic" emotion induced by the stimulus when reading tanka poetry.

2   Related Work

Recent studies suggest that the hidden representations of various DLMs have shown to linearly predict human brain activity [11–13]. Since the introduction of word2vec [7], large language models have been utilized in neuroimaging research to investigate how the human brain processes language [14–20]. By presenting human participants with language stimuli, such as sentences or individual words, and measuring their brain activity, researchers can build models that predict the neural activity patterns in response to these stimuli and decode words and sentences from brain states [20].

Those DLMs have a hierarchical structure, and researchers have been investigating whether the hierarchical structure of DLMs corresponds to the hierarchical organization of the human brain. Convolutional neural networks (CNNs) have been suggested to correspond to the concept of hierarchical processing in human visual processing [21]. Kawasaki et al [22] used a deep learning model to predict brain states under visual and verbal stimuli, and investigated the processing transitions through analysis of these states using representation similarity analysis (RSA) [23]. However, there has been limited research on the relationship between the hierarchy of DLMs and the hierarchy in the human brain under language stimuli.

In this study, we chose GPT-2 as a model for estimating brain activity because it has been shown that the prediction of brain states by using GPT-2 as language features significantly correlates with semantic comprehension [16,18,24]. We will construct an encoding model that predicts brain activity from the feature of each layer of GPT-2 and examine hierarchical processing in the brain when reading a text.

By using a deep learning model that processes natural language as a working model, we investigate emotional activities in the human brain that are similar

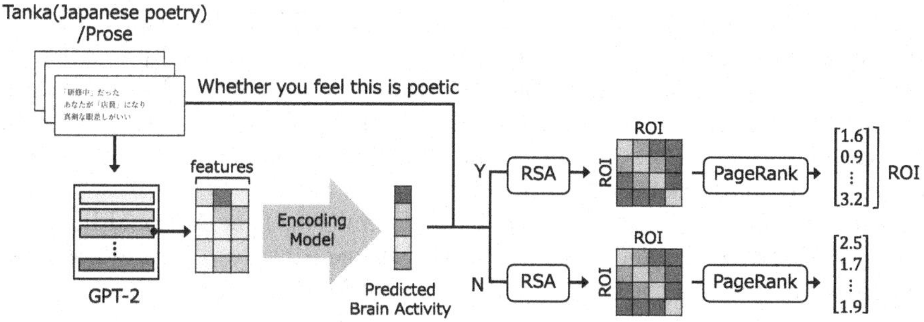

Fig. 1. Overall process: the features of tanka are represented by GPT-2. representation similarity analysis (RSA) is applied to the brain activity data predicted by the encoding model based on the features. The representation dissimilarity matrix (RDM) obtained by RSA is regarded as an adjacency matrix, and the PageRank algorithm is applied to determine the hubness of the regions of interest (ROI) of brain activity stimulated by poetic and unpoetic sentences.

to the sensitivity and sensation induced by tanka, a verbal art form, instead of dealing with emotions expressed as direct responses in the human brain under various stimuli.

3   Analysis of Brain Activity Under Language Stimuli

Figure 1 shows an overview of the method in this study.

To compare brain activities evoked by tanka poetry, and unpoetic sentences, we 1) extract features using tanka poetry that presented in the experiment as input; 2) construct an encoding model to predict brain activity from the features; 3) separate the predicted brain activity under stimuli labeled as poetic or unpoetic; 4) apply RSA to the brain activity and create a RDM that shows the connectivity of ROIs in the brain; and 5) apply PageRank algorithm [25] to the matrix and find the hubness in ROIs.

3.1   Brain Activity Data and Experimental Tasks

Brain activity data were collected from 15 male subjects and 17 female subjects. All subjects are right-handed and native Japanese speakers, aged from 18 to 34 years. Functional scans were collected using a 3.0 T scanner at the National Institute for Physiological Sciences (NIPS) with repetition time (TR) = 750 ms, and voxel size = 2.0 mm × 2.0 mm × 2.0 mm.

As experimental tasks, subjects read and evaluate 300 sentences from the Balanced Corpus of Contemporary Written Japanese (BCCWJ) [26]. The sentence dataset consists of 150 tanka, 31-syllable poems originated in Japan, and 150 prose that have approximately 31 characters. Each tanka/prose was divided into three lines, where only the first line was displayed for the first three seconds, up to the second line for the next three seconds, and all three lines for the following three seconds. In the next three seconds, a slide with the question "Do you feel that this is poetic?" written on it is displayed, and the subjects answers "Yes" or "No" by pressing a button. One trial is conducted in 12 s. These data were collected during six scanning sessions with breaks in between, and each session had 50 trials (25 tanka and 25 prose). The sentences were presented in a different random order for each subject.

The study was approved by the Ethical Committee of the National Institute for Japanese Language and Linguistics, the National Institute for Physiological Sciences of Japan and the Institute of Statistical Mathematics.

3.2　Encoding Model

The method employed in this study to construct an encoding model is the one by Naselaris et al [27].

As a method for constructing the encoding model, linear regression is performed between the features extracted from the data that stimulate the human brain and the brain activity state under stimulation, and weights are learned so that the measured brain activity pattern and the predicted brain activity pattern are close to each other. In general, ridge regression is applied to linear regression, and by observing the regression coefficients, it is possible to observe the behavior of the voxels.

3.3　Representational Similarity Analysis

Representational Similarity Analysis (RSA) uses correlation matrices to measure the degree of similarity or dissimilarity between representational patterns, proposed by Kriegeskorte et al [23,28]. RSA measures the distance between the representational geometries of different brain regions or conditions and calculates the dissimilarity between different neural activation patterns to create Representational Dissimilarity Matrix (RDM) which refers to the matrix of pairwise distance between representational patterns.

In this study, correlation distance (1 − Pearson's correlation coefficient) is used as a measure of similarity. We measure the functional dissimilarity at each time point for each ROI, and then calculate the dissimilarity between the created time × time RDMs to create a ROI × ROI RDM, which represents the connectivity among ROIs (see, Fig. 2). The brain region division atlas used in the experiments was Destrieux Atlas [29] provided by FreeSurfer[1].

3.4　PageRank Algorithm

We used PageRank algorithm to identify regions in the brain that serve as hubs in the linkage among regions of interest (ROIs). The PageRank algorithm [25] is a widely used algorithm for ranking web pages, and outputs a PageRank score which indicates a ranking of importance. The application of the PageRank

---

[1] https://surfer.nmr.mgh.harvard.edu/.

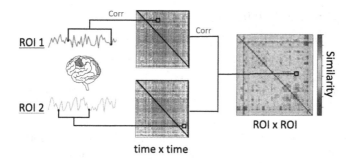

Fig. 2. Creation of a ROI × ROI RDM matrix by RSA

algorithm is not limited to Web networks but can also be extended to social and brain networks [30–32]. The PageRank score of $r_{k+1}(P_i)$ is obtained by a power method as follows.

$$r_{k+1}(P_i) = \sum_{P_j \in B_{P_i}} \frac{r_k(P_j)}{|P_j|}$$

The PageRank score for page P_i is dependent on the PageRank scores for each page P_j contained in B_{P_i}, the set of all pages linking to page P_j, dividing by $|P_i|$, the number of outbound links page P_j.

4   Experiments

4.1   Encoding Models for the Experiments

Encoding models are constructed to estimate the brain state from the features of linguistic stimuli given to the human brain. Specifically, we performed ridge regression from the features extracted from each layer of GPT-2 to brain activity. When a tanka/prose slide was displayed, the language stimulus of t_i is the presented sentence, and when a question slide was shown, the language stimulus is the sentence which is added the question sentence to the preceding tanka/prose.

The features of language stimuli extracted from each layer of GPT-2 are 1024 dimensions, but we reduced them to 300 dimensions using principal component analysis (PCA) to mitigate the risk of overfitting the model. In order to account for the hemodynamic delay when observing blood oxygenation level dependent (BOLD) signal by fMRI, we concatenated seven features from t_{i-9} to t_{i-3} to predict brain activity at time t_i. Of the six sessions, one session was test data and the remaining five sessions were training data for building an encoding model, and then predicted brain activities for all sessions were collected. This regularization coefficient is chosen amongst ten values log-spaced between 10^1 and 10^6 by 5-fold Cross-Validation. For each layer and for each subject, the regularization coefficient is found as the value that led to the best performance with a Pearson correlation between the predicted and measured brain activities.

4.2   Experimental Settings

The features of tanka and prose are represented by GPT-2 in this study. We used a pretrained Japanese GPT-2 model with 24 layers[2], provided by Hugging Face. We fine-tuned GPT-2 on 3571 tanka in BCCWJ that were not used in the experiment. We further fine-tuned GPT-2 for binary text classification for each subject, whether a subject felt it was poetic or not in the experiment. In the second fine-tuning, the training data consisting of 250 sentences, which were displayed during five scanning sessions used for encoding model training. To investigate how information can be changed across each layer of GPT-2, we extracted text features from each layer.

4.3   Results

We analyzed brain activity data from 19 subjects of 32 subjects who participated in the experiment, selected with a statistical threshold of $p < 0.01$. The p-values were calculated as the fraction of 200 random sequences in which the correlation with the measured data was greater than or equal to the correlation between the predicted and measured data. Furthermore, the voxels that were corrected with FDR at $q < 0.05$ and had positive correlation with the measured brain activity were extracted and used for analysis.

In Fig. 3, we show the accuracy predicted by an encoding model. Pearson correlation coefficient was used for evaluating the accuracy. Figure 3a visualizes the prediction accuracy on the cortical surface for one subject. The correlation coefficient between the predicted and mesured brain activity patterns was computed for each voxel and for each scanning session. The average correlation

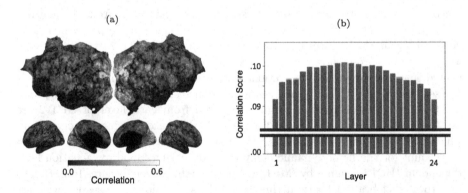

Fig. 3. Performance of the encoding model: (a) Brain map of prediction accuracy for each voxel at the 24th layer. Each correlation coefficient was averaged across the six sessions. (b) Prediction accuracy for each layer. Each correlation coefficient was averaged across the voxels that were FDR-corrected and have positive correlation between the predicted and measured brain activity.

---

[2] https://huggingface.co/rinna/japanese-gpt2-medium.

coefficient across all sessions is then calculated. The map shows only voxels that were multiple-corrected with a false discovery rate (FDR) correction at $q < 0.05$. Fig. 3b shows that the prediction accuracy of each layer of GPT-2. The correlation coefficients for each layer were averaged across subjects, and across those voxels that are FDR-corrected and have positive correlation between the predicted and measured brain activity. The layer with the highest correlation coefficients, which was the 10th layer, is highlighted in red. Prior studies have also reported better prediction accuracy in the middle layer of DLMs [33–35].

We created RDMs for each layer representing the behavior of the ROI in each of the predicted brain activities labeled "poetic" and "unpoetic" based on our experiments. The dissimilarity between 48 RDMs of 2 (poetic/unpopetic) × 24 (the number of hierarchies), each averaged across subjects, was calculated (see, Fig. 4a). Figure 4b shows the results of dimensional compression of the above RDM into three dimensions using UMAP [36].

Next, we applied the PageRank algorithm to a similarity matrix of a ROI × ROI RDM to obtain PageRank scores for each ROI and detect hub regions for each poetic and unpoetic state. PageRank scores were calculated for each state and averaged across subjects. The result of subtracting the PageRank score of the unpoetic state from the PageRank score of the poetic state are visualized in Fig. 5a; the 1st layer as the lowest layer, the 13th layer as middle layer and the 24th layer as the highest layer. The regions colored red have higher PageRank score when the brain feels poetic, indicating that the regions have higher "hubness", while the regions colored blue have higher hubness when the brain did not feel poetic. Figure 5b shows the subtracted PageRank scores after averaged in each regions. We selected four regions where there were significant differences: the cingulate cortex (green), the occipital lobe (orange), the parietal lobe (red) and the frontal lobe (blue). Layers in which significant differences were found were marked with a star ($p < 0.01$, a two-sample t-test).

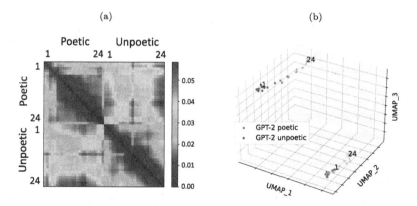

Fig. 4. (a) RDM of hidden layer for each state. (b) The results of dimensional compression of a layer × layer RDM

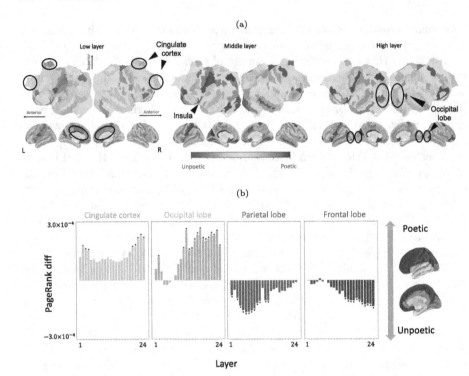

Fig. 5. PageRank scores of poetic state vs. unpoetic state: (a) Brain map of the subtracted PageRank scores at 1st, 13th and 24th layer as low, middle and high layer respectively. (b) The subtracted PageRank scores after averaged in each region(*$p <$ 0.01). (Color figure online)

4.4 Discussion

The information is gradually transitioning in Fig. 4b, indicating that the brain activity that represented by each layer of GPT-2 changes as the hierarchy shifts.

The cingulate cortex that had a high PageRank score in Fig. 5a is involved in a wide range of cognitive and emotional processes. It is said to be the one which plays a key role in attention, decision making, memory, and emotion regulation [37,38]. In a previous study of brain activity during reading of poetry and prose [39], a part of the cingulate gyrus was cited as a brain region that was activated as the emotionality of the text increases. The insula, which also had the same high PageRank score is also said to be an area involved in emotions and experiences [40,41]. In the region around the cingulate cortex and the left insula, the subtracted values were consistently positive through almost all layers.

The occipital lobe's PageRank score was also elevated when participants felt poetic. However, this region is primarily responsible for processing visual information and is typically activated while reading a text, and those well-known functions do not explain why the PageRank score was high when feeling poetic.

In the parietal and frontal lobes, PageRank scores were high in all layers when not feeling poetic (see, Fig. 5b). Further investigation is needed to fully understand these results.

5   Conclusion

In this study, using brain activity data measured by fMRI while reading Japanese tanka poetry and prose, we constructed an encoding model to predict brain state from the features extracted from the hidden layers of a DLM. We especially used GPT-2 to represent the feature of those tanka poetry and prose.

We investigated the ROIs that work as hubs of information connectivity in the brain when feeling poetic by applying the PageRank algorithm to a matrix of connectivity between ROIs. By this, we found a significant importance of the cingulate cortex and the left insula, which has been previously reported to be activated when a person feeling more poetic. On the other hand, we also found results that could not be explained by previous studies, such as the finding of hubness in the occipital lobe at higher layers of GPT-2 and hubness in the parietal and frontal lobes when not feeling poetic. As future work, we will further investigate the results obtained in this study.

Acknowledgement. This study was supported by Inter-University Research Institute Corporation (I-URIC) and the Cooperative Study Program (20-640, 21-543 and 22NIPS630) of National Institute for Physiological Sciences (NIPS). It was also supported by JSPS KAKENHI (21H05060 and 21H05061), JST MOONSHOT (JPMJMS2012) and JST PRESTO (JPMJPR20M4).

References

1. Kolesnikov, A., et al.: Big transfer (bit): general visual representation learning (2020)
2. Dosovitskiy, A., et al.: An image is worth 16×16 words: transformers for image recognition at scale. In: International Conference on Learning Representations (2021). https://openreview.net/forum?id=YicbFdNTTy
3. Goodfellow, I., et al.: Generative adversarial nets. In: Ghahramani, Z., Welling, M., Cortes, C., Lawrence, N., Weinberger, K. (eds.) Advances in Neural Information Processing Systems, vol. 27. Curran Associates, Inc. (2014)
4. Radford, A., Wu, J., Child, R., Luan, D., Amodei, D., Sutskever, I.: Language models are unsupervised multitask learners. OpenAI Blog (2018). https://d4mucfpksywv.cloudfront.net/better-language-models/language-models.pdf
5. Brown, T.B., et al.: Language models are few-shot learners (2020)
6. Pennington, J., Socher, R., Manning, C.D.: Glove: global vectors for word representation. In: Empirical Methods in Natural Language Processing (EMNLP), pp. 1532–1543 (2014). http://www.aclweb.org/anthology/D14-1162

7. Mikolov, T., Sutskever, I., Chen, K., Corrado, G.S., Dean, J.: Distributed representations of words and phrases and their compositionality. Adv. Neural Inf. Process. Syst. **26** (2013). https://proceedings.neurips.cc/paper/2013/file/9aa42b31882ec039965f3c4923ce901b-Paper.pdf

8. Raffel, C., et al.: Exploring the limits of transfer learning with a unified text-to-text transformer (2020)

9. Radford, A., Kim, J.W., Xu, T., Brockman, G., McLeavey, C., Sutskever, I.: Robust speech recognition via large-scale weak supervision (2022)

10. Amodei, D., et al.: Deep speech 2: End-to-end speech recognition in english and mandarin (2015)

11. Holdgraf, C., Rieger, J., Micheli, C., Martin, S., Knight, R., Theunissen, F.: Encoding and decoding models in cognitive electrophysiology. Front. Syst. Neurosci. **11**, 61 (2017). https://doi.org/10.3389/fnsys.2017.00061

12. Caucheteux, C., King, J.R.: Language processing in brains and deep neural networks: computational convergence and its limits. bioRxiv (2021). https://doi.org/10.1101/2020.07.03.186288, https://www.biorxiv.org/content/early/2021/01/14/2020.07.03.186288

13. Yu, T., Shinji, N.: High-resolution image reconstruction with latent diffusion models from human brain activity. bioRxiv (2022)

14. Toneva, M., Stretcu, O., Poczos, B., Wehbe, L., Mitchell, T.M.: Modeling task effects on meaning representation in the brain via zero-shot meg prediction. In: Larochelle, H., Ranzato, M., Hadsell, R., Balcan, M., Lin, H. (eds.) Advances in Neural Information Processing Systems, vol. 33, pp. 5284–5295. Curran Associates, Inc. (2020)

15. Goldstein, A., et al.: Thinking ahead: spontaneous prediction in context as a keystone of language in humans and machines. bioRxiv (2021). https://doi.org/10.1101/2020.12.02.403477. https://www.biorxiv.org/content/early/2021/09/30/2020.12.02.403477

16. Schrimpf, M., et al.: Artificial neural networks accurately predict language processing in the brain. bioRxiv (2020). https://doi.org/10.1101/2020.06.26.174482. https://www.biorxiv.org/content/early/2020/06/27/2020.06.26.174482

17. Schrimpf, M., et al.: The neural architecture of language: integrative modeling converges on predictive processing. Proc. Natl. Acad. Sci. (PNAS) (2021). https://doi.org/10.1073/pnas.2105646118. https://www.pnas.org/content/118/45/e2105646118

18. Caucheteux, C., Gramfort, A., King, J.R.: Gpt-2's activations predict the degree of semantic comprehension in the human brain. bioRxiv (2021). https://doi.org/10.1101/2021.04.20.440622. https://www.biorxiv.org/content/early/2021/04/21/2021.04.20.440622

19. Schwartz, D., Toneva, M., Wehbe, L.: Inducing brain-relevant bias in natural language processing models. Adv. Neural Inf. Process. Syst. **32** (2019)

20. Tang, J., LeBel, A., Jain, S., Huth, A.G.: Semantic reconstruction of continuous language from non-invasive brain recordings. bioRxiv (2022). https://doi.org/10.1101/2022.09.29.509744. https://www.biorxiv.org/content/early/2022/09/29/2022.09.29.509744

21. Eickenberg, M., Gramfort, A., Varoquaux, G., Thirion, B.: Seeing it all: convolutional network layers map the function of the human visual system. Neuroimage **152**, 184–194 (2017). https://doi.org/10.1016/j.neuroimage.2016.10.001

22. Kawasaki, H., Nishida, S., Kobayashi, I.: Hierarchical processing of visual and language information in the brain. In: Findings of the Association for Computational Linguistics: AACL-IJCNLP 2022, pp. 405–410. Association for Computational Linguistics, Online only (2022). https://aclanthology.org/2022.findings-aacl.38

23. Kriegeskorte, N., Mur, M., Bandettini, P.: Representational similarity analysis - connecting the branches of systems neuroscience. Front. Syst. Neurosci. **2**, 4 (2008). https://doi.org/10.3389/neuro.06.004.2008. https://www.frontiersin.org/article/10.3389/neuro.06.004.2008

24. Caucheteux, C., Gramfort, A., King, J.R.: Evidence of a predictive coding hierarchy in the human brain listening to speech. Nat. Human Behav. **7**, 430–441 (2023). https://doi.org/10.1038/s41562-022-01516-2

25. Page, L., Brin, S., Motwani, R., Winograd, T.: The PageRank Citation Ranking: Bringing Order to the Web. Technical report, Stanford Digital Library Technologies Project (1998). http://citeseerx.ist.psu.edu/viewdoc/summary?doi=10.1.1.31.1768

26. The balanced corpus of contemporary written Japanese. https://clrd.ninjal.ac.jp/bccwj/en/

27. Naselaris, T., Kay, K., Nishimoto, S., Gallant, J.: Encoding and decoding in fMRI. NeuroImage **56**(2), 400–410 (2011). https://doi.org/10.1016/j.neuroimage.2010.07.073

28. Kriegeskorte, N., Kievit, R.A.: Representational geometry: integrating cognition, computation, and the brain. Trends Cogn. Sci. **17**(8), 401–412 (2013). https://doi.org/10.1016/j.tics.2013.06.007

29. Destrieux, C., Fischl, B., Dale, A.M., Halgren, E.: Automatic parcellation of human cortical gyri and sulci using standard anatomical nomenclature. NeuroImage **53**(1), 1–15 (2010)

30. Zhu, Q., Yang, J., Xu, B., Hou, Z., Sun, L., Zhang, D.: Multimodal brain network jointly construction and fusion for diagnosis of epilepsy. Front. Neurosci. (2021). https://doi.org/10.3389/fnins.2021.734711

31. Biaobin, J., Kyle, K., David, G., Gribskov, M.: Aptrank: an adaptive pagerank model for protein function prediction on bi-relational graphs. Bioinformatics (2017). https://doi.org/10.1093/bioinformatics/btx029

32. Bin, L., Shuangyan, J., Quan, Z.: Hits-pr-hhblits: protein remote homology detection by combining pagerank and hyperlink-induced topic search. Brief Bioinf. (2020). https://doi.org/10.1093/bib/bby104

33. Caucheteux, C., King, J.R.: Brains and algorithms partially converge in natural language processing. Commun. Biol. **5** (2022). https://doi.org/10.1038/s42003-022-03036-1

34. Caucheteux, C., Gramfort, A., King, J.R.: Deep language algorithms predict semantic comprehension from brain activity. Sci. Rep. **12**(1) (2022). https://doi.org/10.1038/s41598-022-20460-9

35. Huth, A.G., de Heer, W.A., Griffiths, T.L., Theunissen, Frédéric, E., Gallant, J.L.: Natural speech reveals the semantic maps that tile human cerebral cortex. Nature **532**(7600), 453–458 (2016). https://doi.org/10.1038/nature17637

36. McInnes, L., Healy, J., Melville, J.: Umap: uniform manifold approximation and projection for dimension reduction (2018). http://arxiv.org/abs/1802.03426

37. Bush, G., Luu, P., Posner, M.I.: Cognitive and emotional influences in anterior cingulate cortex. Trends Cogn. Sci. **4**, 215–222 (2000)

38. Shackman, A., Salomons, T., Slagter, H., Fox, A., Winter, J., Davidson, R.: The integration of negative affect, pain and cognitive control in the cingulate cortex. Nat. Rev. Neurosci. **12**(3), 154–167 (2011)

39. Zeman, A., Milton, F., Smith, A., Rylance, R.: By heart an fmri study of brain activation by poetry and prose. J. Cons. Stud. **20**(9–10), 9–10 (2013)
40. Kurth, F., Zilles, K., Fox, P., Laird, A., Eickhoff, S.: Kurth f, zilles k, fox pt, laird ar, eickhoff sb. a link between the systems: functional differentiation and integration within the human insula revealed by meta-analysis. Brain Struct. Funct. **214**, 519–534 (2010). https://doi.org/10.1007/s00429-010-0255-z
41. Uddin, L., Nomi, J., Hébert-Seropian, B., Ghaziri, J., Boucher, O.: Structure and function of the human insula. J. Clin. Neurophysiol. **34**, 300–306 (2017). https://doi.org/10.1097/WNP.0000000000000377

Joint Demosaicing and Denoising with Frequency Domain Features

Feiyu Li[1,2] and Jun Yang[2(✉)]

[1] School of Information Science and Engineering,
Zhejiang Sci-Tech University, Hangzhou, China
[2] College of Information Science and Engineering, Jiaxing University, Jiaxing, China
yangj95@mail2.sysu.edu.cn

Abstract. Image demosaicing and denoising play important roles in modern digital camera image processing and have been studied in recent decades. Due to the interference of independent demosaicing and denoising causes color errors and the loss of image details, therefore, the joint demosaicing and denoising problem has been extensively studied. Although the simple combination of existing demosaicing and denoising methods can obtain recovery images, there are still considerable room for improvement. In this paper, we propose an end-to-end frequency domain features network (FFNet) to solve the ill-posed joint problem. Different from previous methods based on spatial domain features, FFNet uses frequency domain information to learn global and local image features, and it is based on the vision Transformer architecture. Our model contains mainly two frequency domain feature blocks: a global Fourier block (GFB) that learns a global frequency domain parameter weight to achieve global attention and a local Fourier block (LFB) based on multi-layer perceptron to enhance local feature learning. These two modules and channel attention are combined into the frequency domain attention block (FAB), which constitutes the core module of FFNet. Extensive experiments demonstrate that FFNet outperforms previous approaches and achieves state-of-the-art performance.

Keywords: Image demosaicing and denoising · joint problem · frequency domain network

1 Introduction

Modern digital cameras are producing increasingly better pictures. To obtain high-quality images from raw sensor data, modern digital cameras need to perform a series of different image reconstruction steps. The sequence of indispensable reconstruction steps is known as the image processing pipelines, where image demosaicing and denoising are very important steps. Therefore, image demosaicing and denoising are classical image restoration problems. Demosaicing aims at reconstructing full-resolution color images from color filter array (CFA) samples such as the Bayer pattern [2]. The Bayer pattern samples the green pixels on a quincunx grid (half of the image resolution) and the red and blue pixels on rectangular grids (a quarter of the image resolution). Meanwhile, in the real world, digital cameras are usually polluted by different kinds of unknown noise that can interfere with the quality of image reconstruction. Most previous demosaicing and denoising methods were usually designed independently and implemented sequentially in image signal processing (ISP). However, the demosaicing color distortion will complicate the denoising process, or the denoising artifacts can be amplified in the demosaicing process. Therefore, joint demosaicing and denoising (JDD) is a very practical problem and has attracted increasing attention in the research community and commercial industry [20, 24, 29, 34].

Recently, JDD based on the deep convolutional neural network (CNN) has exceeded traditional approaches [6, 20, 24, 34]. Considering the difference between different frequencies of images and abundant green channel information, SGNet [24] introduces two self-guidance methods, density-map and green channel guidance to reconstruct image details. Xing and Egiazarian [34] comprehensively studied various solutions for the mixture problem, they used the residual channel connection block (RCAB) [42] as the basic block to extract features and demonstrate the performance improvement between different loss functions. The above methods mainly are based on spatial domain features to restore images.

Attention mechanisms have been widely studied and used, including self-attention and depthwise convolution [3, 5, 25]. In particular, global attention has had significant effects on visual tasks. However, with the expansion of image resolution in the spatial domain, many global attention methods increase the computational complexity of the model and inevitably incur the loss of local information. Inspired by this review paper [22] and GFNet [30], we use the frequency domain features to reconstruct images. Compared with the image spatial domain, frequency domain learning can also achieve the effect of global attention and is more efficient [4, 8, 21, 28, 30, 37]. In this paper, we use the fast Fourier transform (FFT) algorithm to achieve frequency domain feature learning. Our contributions are as follows:

1) We propose a novel frequency domain feature network (FFNet) for joint image demosaicing and denoising, which is based on an end-to-end vision Transformer backbone and does not require extra noise estimation inputs.
2) We design a frequency domain attention block (FAB) that consists of global Fourier and local Fourier blocks, it can enjoy a global receptive field and local feature learning. Meanwhile, we introduce channel attention to FAB to strengthen various feature domain learning.
3) Extensive experiments show that FFNet achieves state-of-the-art (SOTA) results on three JDD datasets and can also process noise-free image demosaicing.

2   Related Work

2.1   Joint Demosaicing and Denoising

Image demosaicing is used to recover full color resolution images from color filter array (CFA) pattern images and is usually performed at the beginning of ISP, where the most popular CFA pattern is Bayer CFA. Therefore, most demosaicing methods have been specifically designed for the Bayer CFA. Existing algorithms can also be classified into two categories: model-based methods and learning-based methods. Model-based methods [11,27,36] focus on the correlations between the spatial and spectral domains to reconstruct images. Early learning-based models are simple and have poor generalization ability lead to cannot effectively restore images [16,32]. Recently, the deep learning methods for image demosaicing have attained SOTA performance [33,35,38,40]. In practical applications, image noise is inevitable during imaging, and this kind of noise seriously disturbs the final visual quality. Gu *et al.* [7] use a denoiser to remove noise. Zhang *et al.* [39] built a residual learning CNN (DnCNN) for Gaussian denoising and attained amazing results.

Some studies have shown that the combined solutions of the mixture problem are better than the traditional sequential solutions [15,29,34]. These end-to-end combined methods can avoid interference between different artifacts in sequence processing. Existing algorithms can also be classified into two categories: model-based methods that use mathematical models and image priors to recover images [9,17,19]. The learning-based methods learned from abundant training data, Gharbi *et al.* [6] trained a deep CNN on millions of datasets and Kokkinos and Lefkimmiatis [20] proposed a majorization-minimization algorithm and a cascade of residual denoising network. Liu *et al.* [24] built a self-guidance network (SGNet) with density-map guidance and green-channel guidance for JDD. Xing and Egiazarian [34] comprehensively studied various solutions. They explored the performance differences between different feature extraction blocks, loss functions and training methods. Janjušević *et al.* [13] proposed CDLNet from convolutional dictionary learning. Although these end-to-end methods can obtain good results, there are still a certain gap for ground truth images.

2.2   Frequency Domain Feature Learning

Discrete Fourier transform (DFT) is widely used in digital image processing. Jiang *et al.* [14] compared the frequency domain difference between real and fake images to recover images through DFT. FNet [21] and GFNet [30] are both efficient FFT models. The former was used for the natural language processing, and the latter was used for image classification. FDA [37] used Fourier domain adaptation for semantic segmentation. Li *et al.* [23] successfully applied the Fourier neural operator (FNO) to zero-shot super-resolution and Guibas *et al.* [8] designed an AFNO for multiple vision tasks by combining GFNet and FNO. Chi *et al.* [4] and Mao *et al.* [28] used a convolutional operator in the FFT to extract features.

3 Methodology

We first introduce our model architecture in Sect. 3.1. Then, we introduce the Fourier filter block (FFB) in Sect. 3.2. Finally, we present our loss functions in Sect. 3.3.

3.1 Model Architecture

Our FFNet uses the vision Transformer architecture as shown in Fig. 1. It consists of three parts: shallow feature extraction, deep feature extraction and color reconstruction. Given a Bayer CFA input image, we first subsample the CFA image into a half-resolution four channels image $I_{CFA} \in \mathbb{R}^{\frac{H}{2} \times \frac{W}{2} \times 4}$, then apply one 3×3 convolutional layer to extract the shallow feature $F_S \in \mathbb{R}^{\frac{H}{2} \times \frac{W}{2} \times C}$, where H and W are the height and width of the full resolution, respectively, and C denotes the channel number of the feature. We then use multiple residual frequency domain attention groups (RFAGs) to further obtain the deep feature F_{DF} from F_S. As shown in Fig. 1, each RFAG contains multiple frequency domain attention blocks (FABs) and one 3×3 convolutional layer. The FAB mainly contains a FFB and a channel attention block (CAB) from RCAN [42], which are shown in Fig. 2a and Fig. 1, respectively. Meanwhile, we use a long skip connection to transfer the shallow feature directly to the color reconstruction module of the model, which can help H_{RFAG} to focus on deep feature learning and stabilize the overall network training. Lastly, we use pixel-shuffle upsampling [31] to reconstruct three-channel full-resolution images I_{HR}.

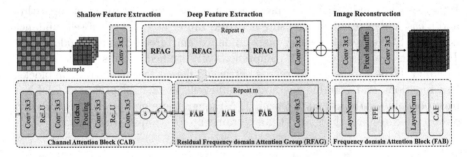

Fig. 1. The top row represents overall architecture of FFNet, and the bottom three modules represent CAB, RFAG and FAB, respectively. In CAB, the ⓢ and ⊗ represent the sigmoid function and element-wise product, respectively.

3.2 Fourier Filter Block (FFB)

The FFB module mainly contains the global Fourier block (GFB) and local Fourier block (LFB), which is shown on the Fig. 2a. The input image features first pass through a 1×1 convolutional layer and a GELU activation function [10] and then enter the GFB and LFB, respectively. Finally, we use a 1×1 convolutional layer to aggregate the features of the GFB and LFB.

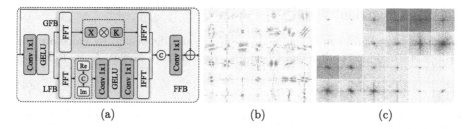

Fig. 2. (a) the structure of FFB, where X represents the frequency domain features, K denotes the learnable filters and ⓒ is the Concatenation. Re and Im represent the real and imaginary parts of FFT, respectively. (b) the frequency domain visualization of GFB stage 5 in FFNet, under 10 noise levels. (c) the frequency domain feature maps of the corresponding stage LFB.

Global Fourier Block (GFB). In DFT, multiplication in the frequency domain is equivalent to circular convolution in the time domain. Therefore, this paper [30] shows that multiplying a frequency domain filter K is equivalent to learning global features. Given the images $x \in \mathbb{R}^{H \times W \times C}$, where $H \times W$ denotes the spatial dimension and C is the number of feature map channels, we first perform a 2D FFT to convert the spatial domain to the frequency domain as follows:

$$X = \mathcal{F}(x), \tag{1}$$

where $\mathcal{F}(\cdot)$ represents the 2D FFT and X is a complex tensor (with the real part and the imaginary part, $X \in \mathbb{R}^{H \times (\lfloor W/2 \rfloor + 1) \times C}$). In the GFB, the computational complexity of FFT and inverse fast Fourier transform (IFFT) are $O(HWlog(HW))$, and the element-wise multiplication is $O(H(\lfloor W/2 \rfloor + 1))$. Therefore, the computational complexity of the GFB is $O(HWlog(HW))$, and the parameters of learnable filter K is $H(\lfloor W/2 \rfloor + 1)C$. Here, it should be noted that since the feature map size of filter K has been fixed during the training stage, interpolation is required so that the feature map size of K corresponds to the resolution of the images in the inference stage.

Local Fourier Block (LFB). In [4,28], they utilize convolutional kernels to learn frequency domain features. Corresponding to the GFB, we characterize LFB as extracting local features in the frequency domain, which is based on the local property of small convolution kernels. Therefore, the LFB consists of two 1×1 convolutional layers as follows:

$$Z_0 = Concat(\mathcal{F}(x)_{real}, \mathcal{F}(x)_{imaginary}), \tag{2}$$

$$Z_1 = Conv_{mlp}(Z_0), \tag{3}$$

where $Conv_{mlp}$ consists of a 1×1 convolutional layer, a GELU activation function and a 1×1 convolutional layer sequentially.

3.3   Loss Function

For the mixture problem of image demosaicing and denoising, we calculate the L_1 loss on the final result images I_{HR} and ground truth images I_{gt} as follows:

$$L_{pixel} = \|I_{HR} - I_{gt}\|_1, \tag{4}$$

We add a frequency reconstruction loss function to strengthen the high-frequency extraction as follows:

$$L_F = \|\mathcal{F}(I_{HR}) - \mathcal{F}(I_{gt})\|_1, \tag{5}$$

where $\mathcal{F}(\cdot)$ represents the 2D FFT. The final loss function in training phase is as follows:

$$L_{total} = L_{pixel} + \lambda L_F, \tag{6}$$

where we set $\lambda = 0.05$ in all experiments.

4   Experiments

In this section, we describe the datasets, evaluation metrics and training details. We then compare the effects of GFB and LFB, as well as the effects of different kernel sizes on LFB. Lastly, we demonstrate the performance of the different approaches for JDD and noise-free demosaicing (DM), respectively.

4.1   Datasets and Implementation Details

Datasets and Evaluation Metrics. We use the DIV2K [1] dataset consisting of 900 2K resolution images (800 for training, 100 for validation). For data preprocessing of denoising, noisy input images are generated by adding Gaussian noise. The noise level is randomly sampled from [0, 20] out of 255. For data preprocessing of demosaicing, we use the Bayer CFA pattern (RGGB) to mosaic the color image. We test the performance of different models on three public datasets: McMaster (McM) [11], Kodak and Urban100 [12]. For the evaluation metrics, the peak signal-to-noise ratio (PSNR) and the structural similarity (SSIM) are used in all experiments. Our code and pretrained models are available at https://github.com/FeiyuLi-cs/FFNet.

Training Details. For data augmentation, the sampled images are randomly cropped to 128×128, and each image patch is horizontally and vertically flipped with a probability of 0.5. The model is trained by the Adam optimizer [18] ($\beta_1 = 0.9, \beta_2 = 0.999$) and runs on one NVIDIA RTX 3090 GPU in all experiments. For JDD problems, we trained the FFNet model for 200 epochs with a batch size of 32. The initial learning rate is set to $5e^{-4}$, which gradually decays to $1e^{-6}$ with cosine annealing [26]. And the DM uses the same training configuration. In all experiments, we set the basic feature dimension to 64.

4.2 Ablation Study

We conducted extensive ablation studies to validate the performance difference between the GFB and LFB and verified the recovery effects between different convolution kernel sizes in the LFB.

Effects of the GFB and LFB. We conducted experiments to demonstrate the effects of the proposed GFB and LFB. The blocks are tested on three datasets at 10 noise levels, which is shown in Table 1. Compared with the LFB, the GFB improves the performance of the model. Although the GFB increases the number of model parameters, the PSNR value on the three datasets increased by 0.03 dB on average, and the training time was shortened by 6 h. Benefiting from the two modules, FFNet obtains a further performance improvement of 0.1 dB on the Urban100 dataset. We show the frequency domain images of the learnable weight from GFB stage 5 in Fig. 2b, and the frequency domain feature maps of the corresponding a McMaster image in Fig. 2c.

Table 1. Ablation study of the GFB and LFB in terms of PSNR.

GFB	LFB	Params (M)	Train Time (H)	McMaster	Kodak	Urban100
✓		13.46	29	33.92	34.13	33.03
	✓	4.92	35	33.88	34.10	33.01
✓	✓	14.65	40.6	**33.95**	**34.16**	**33.13**

Table 2. Ablation study of different kernel sizes of the LFB in terms of PSNR.

Kernel Size	Params (M)	Train Time (H)	McMaster	Kodak	Urban100
3×3 kernel	24.09	45	33.89	34.11	32.99
1×1 kernel	14.65	40.6	**33.95**	**34.16**	**33.13**

Effects of Different Convolutional Kernel Sizes for the LFB. Because the LFB is designed to extract the frequency domain local features of images, we compared the different convolutional kernel sizes using 1×1 and 3×3 kernels. Table 2 shows the performance difference between the 1×1 and 3×3 kernels on three datasets with 10 noise levels. Using the 1×1 kernel is better than the 3×3 kernel, which improves the PSNR by 0.14 dB on the Urban100 dataset. Meanwhile, the training time of the 1×1 kernel is faster than the 3×3 kernel and stores fewer parameters.

4.3   Main Results

In this section, we first compare the results of DM and JDD. Then, we combine image denoising (DN) with our DM model to compare the performance of JDD and independent processing pipelines. To provide a fair comparison, the evaluation results and indicators for all officially publicly provided pretrained models were tested on our computer, and the values of other unavailable models are from the corresponding paper.

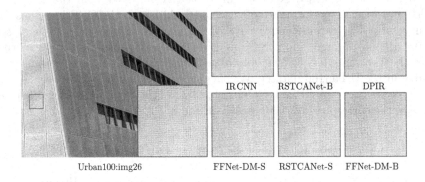

Fig. 3. Comparisons with the other noise-free demosaicing methods.

Table 3. Performance comparison of noise-free demosaicing methods on different datasets. Our FFNet outperforms other models on the Kodak dataset. The top three results are marked in red, blue and green.

Model	McMaster		Kodak		Urban100	
	PSNR	SSIM	PSNR	SSIM	PSNR	SSIM
IRCNN [40]	37.83	0.9643	40.64	0.9819	37.10	0.9760
RSTCANet-B [35]	38.89	0.9689	42.10	0.9892	38.58	0.9821
DPIR [38]	39.39	0.9723	42.30	0.9881	39.31	0.9829
FFNet-DM-S	39.48	0.9718	42.86	0.9900	39.55	0.9839
RSTCANet-S [35]	39.54	0.9711	42.47	0.9897	39.61	0.9846
FFNet-DM-B	39.61	0.9721	42.96	0.9902	39.94	0.9842

Noise-Free Demosaicing. To test the performance of our model for noise-free image demosaicing, we use the same training configuration to retrain the JDD version of FFNet on the noise-free DIV2k dataset, called FFNet-DM-B. Then, we introduce FFNet-DM-S by reducing the number of RFAGs, which only contains three RFAGs and the parameters of the model are halved. In this section, we compare other DM methods, including IRCNN [40], DPIR [38], and RSTCANet

[35], where RSTCANet-B is the basic model of RSTCANet and RSTCANet-S has 3x the model size and computational complexity of RSTCANet-B. The quantitative performance is shown in Table 3. FFNet-DM-B achieves the best results on three datasets, RSTCANet-S achieves the second best results on the McMaster and Urban100 datasets, and the lightweight FFNet-DM-S still attains

Table 4. Performance comparison of JDD methods on different datasets, our FFNet outperforms other models. The top results are marked in **Bold**.

Model	Noise	McMaster		Kodak		Urban100	
		PSNR	SSIM	PSNR	SSIM	PSNR	SSIM
SGNet [24]	5	–	–	–	–	34.54	0.9533
CDLNet [13]		35.27	0.9324	37.03	0.9517	34.59	0.9540
$JD_N D_M$ [34]		36.03	0.9407	36.86	0.9515	35.10	0.9571
FFNet		**36.33**	**0.9438**	**37.20**	**0.9529**	**35.50**	**0.9582**
SGNet [24]	10	–	–	–	–	32.14	0.9229
CDLNet [13]		33.28	0.9048	33.98	0.9136	32.41	0.9294
$JD_N D_M$ [34]		33.72	0.9108	33.88	0.9124	32.84	0.9327
FFNet		**33.95**	**0.9153**	**34.16**	**0.9160**	**33.13**	**0.9352**
SGNet [24]	15	–	–	–	–	30.37	0.8923
CDLNet [13]		31.81	0.8790	32.14	0.8794	30.88	0.9071
$JD_N D_M$ [34]		32.09	0.8837	32.04	0.8766	31.26	0.9103
FFNet		**32.32**	**0.8893**	**32.34**	**0.8829**	**31.55**	**0.9147**

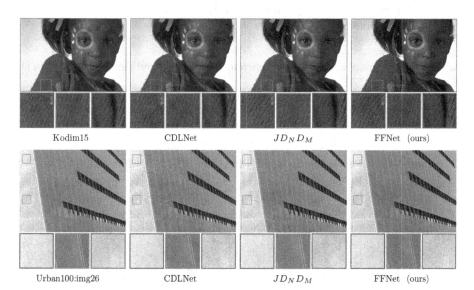

Kodim15   CDLNet $JD_N D_M$ FFNet (ours)

Urban100:img26   CDLNet $JD_N D_M$ FFNet (ours)

Fig. 4. Comparisons with the other JDD methods at 15 noise levels.

significant performance on the Kodak dataset. Compared with DPIR, FFNet-DM-S improves the performance by 0.24 dB on the Urban100 dataset and 0.09 dB on the McMaster dataset. Especially, FFNet-DM-S surpasses RSTCANet-S by 0.39 dB on the Kodak dataset. Figure 3 shows that FFNet-DM-B effectively restore colors and textures in dense grid regions.

Joint Demosaicing and Denoising. For the JDD task, we compare three deep learning models (SGNet [24], CDLNet [13], $JD_N D_M$ [34]) at three noise levels [5, 10, 15], where SGNet does not provide the official model. As shown in Table 4, our model outperforms previous methods on all datasets. It achieves a 0.3 dB gain in PSNR over the previous best model $JD_N D_M$, and SGNet and $JD_N D_M$ require extra noise estimation inputs. Our method effectively removes noise while maintaining fine details, and the visual results under 15 noise levels are shown in Fig. 4. In Row 1, FFNet effectively restores the texture details of the clothing, and the visual effect is more refined and closer to the original image. However, other methods cause a certain degree of mixed distortion. In Row 2, compared to other approaches, FFNet avoids color errors of dense grid regions and restores dense crossbeams in buildings.

In addition, we combine DnCNN [39] (an efficient image denoising model) with our FFNet-DM-B to test the performance of sequential demosaicing and denoising pipelines. The results are compared with our JDD version of FFNet on the McMaster and Kodak datasets, as shown in Table 5. At 10 noise levels, we can observe that the order of DM→DN is better than DN→DM. Although they cannot effectively remove noise, DM→DN avoid color errors. On the contrary, FFNet surpasses two sequential processing modes. We show their visual results in Fig. 5. The reconstruction qualities of the JDD method are significantly better than pipeline modes.

Table 5. Performance comparison of different demosaicing and denoising processes at 10 noise levels.

Pipeline	Method	McMaster		Kodak	
		PSNR	SSIM	PSNR	SSIM
DN→DM	DnCNN→FFNet-DM-B	26.97	0.6608	28.11	0.6732
DM→DN	FFNet-DM-B→DnCNN	28.42	0.6736	28.30	0.6711
JDD	FFNet	**33.95**	**0.9153**	**34.16**	**0.9160**

McM:img1   DnCNN →FFNet-DM-B   FFNet-DM-B →DnCNN   FFNet (ours)

Fig. 5. Comparisons with the different processing pipelines at 10 noise levels.

5   Conclusion

We demonstrated a frequency domain features network (FFNet) that can significantly improve the quality of joint demosaicing and denoising without requiring extra noise estimation inputs. Our model can not only learn global features without losing local information but also be simpler and more effective. Compared with the previous approaches, FFNet uses the vision Transformer architecture and combines frequency domain features and the channel attention mechanism, achieving efficient reconstruction performance. Extensive experiments show that our FFNet outperforms state-of-the-art solutions in terms of both visual qualities and details. In addition, the FFNet-DM-B and lightweight FFNet-DM-S can also restore noise-free mosaiced images. In the future, we will explore more joint problems.

Acknowledgements. This work was supported by the Zhejiang Public Welfare Technology Research Project Fund of China under Grant LGG22F020021 and the City Public Welfare Technology Application Research Project of Jiaxing Science and Technology Bureau of China under Grant 2021AY10071.

References

1. Agustsson, E., Timofte, R.: Ntire 2017 challenge on single image super-resolution: dataset and study. In: Proceedings of the IEEE Conference on Computer Vision and Pattern Recognition Workshops, pp. 126–135 (2017)
2. Bayer, B.: Color imaging array. United States Patent, no. 3971065 (1976)
3. Chen, X., Wang, X., Zhou, J., Dong, C.: Activating more pixels in image super-resolution transformer. arXiv preprint arXiv:2205.04437 (2022)
4. Chi, L., Jiang, B., Mu, Y.: Fast fourier convolution. Adv. Neural Inf. Process. Syst. **33**, 4479–4488 (2020)
5. Dosovitskiy, A., et al.: An image is worth 16×16 words: transformers for image recognition at scale. arXiv preprint arXiv:2010.11929 (2020)
6. Gharbi, M., Chaurasia, G., Paris, S., Durand, F.: Deep joint demosaicking and denoising. ACM Trans. Graph. (ToG) **35**(6), 1–12 (2016)
7. Gu, S., Zhang, L., Zuo, W., Feng, X.: Weighted nuclear norm minimization with application to image denoising. In: Proceedings of the IEEE Conference on Computer Vision and Pattern Recognition, pp. 2862–2869 (2014)
8. Guibas, J., Mardani, M., Li, Z., Tao, A., Anandkumar, A., Catanzaro, B.: Adaptive fourier neural operators: efficient token mixers for transformers. arXiv preprint arXiv:2111.13587 (2021)
9. Heide, F., et al.: Flexisp: a flexible camera image processing framework. ACM Trans. Graph. (ToG) **33**(6), 1–13 (2014)
10. Hendrycks, D., Gimpel, K.: Gaussian error linear units (gelus). arXiv preprint arXiv:1606.08415 (2016)
11. Hirakawa, K., Parks, T.W.: Adaptive homogeneity-directed demosaicing algorithm. IEEE Trans. Image Process. **14**(3), 360–369 (2005)
12. Huang, J.B., Singh, A., Ahuja, N.: Single image super-resolution from transformed self-exemplars. In: Proceedings of the IEEE Conference on Computer Vision and Pattern Recognition, pp. 5197–5206 (2015)

13. Janjušević, N., Khalilian-Gourtani, A., Wang, Y.: Cdlnet: noise-adaptive convolutional dictionary learning network for blind denoising and demosaicing. IEEE Open J. Signal Process. **3**, 196–211 (2022)
14. Jiang, L., Dai, B., Wu, W., Loy, C.C.: Focal frequency loss for image reconstruction and synthesis. In: Proceedings of the IEEE/CVF International Conference on Computer Vision, pp. 13919–13929 (2021)
15. Jin, Q., Facciolo, G., Morel, J.M.: A review of an old dilemma: demosaicking first, or denoising first? In: Proceedings of the IEEE/CVF Conference on Computer Vision and Pattern Recognition Workshops, pp. 514–515 (2020)
16. Kapah, O., Hel-Or, H.Z.: Demosaicking using artificial neural networks. In: Applications of Artificial Neural Networks in Image Processing, vol. 3962, pp. 112–120. SPIE (2000)
17. Khashabi, D., Nowozin, S., Jancsary, J., Fitzgibbon, A.W.: Joint demosaicing and denoising via learned nonparametric random fields. IEEE Trans. Image Process. **23**(12), 4968–4981 (2014)
18. Kingma, D.P., Ba, J.: Adam: a method for stochastic optimization. arXiv preprint arXiv:1412.6980 (2014)
19. Klatzer, T., Hammernik, K., Knobelreiter, P., Pock, T.: Learning joint demosaicing and denoising based on sequential energy minimization. In: 2016 IEEE International Conference on Computational Photography (ICCP), pp. 1–11. IEEE (2016)
20. Kokkinos, F., Lefkimmiatis, S.: Deep image demosaicking using a cascade of convolutional residual denoising networks. In: Proceedings of the European Conference on Computer Vision (ECCV), pp. 303–319 (2018)
21. Lee-Thorp, J., Ainslie, J., Eckstein, I., Ontanon, S.: Fnet: mixing tokens with fourier transforms. arXiv preprint arXiv:2105.03824 (2021)
22. Li, X., Gunturk, B., Zhang, L.: Image demosaicing: a systematic survey. In: Visual Communications and Image Processing 2008, vol. 6822, pp. 489–503. SPIE (2008)
23. Li, Z., et al.: Fourier neural operator for parametric partial differential equations. arXiv preprint arXiv:2010.08895 (2020)
24. Liu, L., Jia, X., Liu, J., Tian, Q.: Joint demosaicing and denoising with self guidance. In: Proceedings of the IEEE/CVF Conference on Computer Vision and Pattern Recognition, pp. 2240–2249 (2020)
25. Liu, Z., Mao, H., Wu, C.Y., Feichtenhofer, C., Darrell, T., Xie, S.: A convnet for the 2020s. In: Proceedings of the IEEE/CVF Conference on Computer Vision and Pattern Recognition, pp. 11970–11980 (2022)
26. Loshchilov, I., Hutter, F.: Sgdr: stochastic gradient descent with warm restarts. arXiv preprint arXiv:1608.03983 (2016)
27. Malvar, H.S., He, L.w., Cutler, R.: High-quality linear interpolation for demosaicing of bayer-patterned color images. In: 2004 IEEE International Conference on Acoustics, Speech, and Signal Processing, vol. 3, pp. iii–485. IEEE (2004)
28. Mao, X., Liu, Y., Shen, W., Li, Q., Wang, Y.: Deep residual fourier transformation for single image deblurring. arXiv preprint arXiv:2111.11745 (2021)
29. Qian, G., Gu, J., Ren, J.S., Dong, C., Zhao, F., Lin, J.: Trinity of pixel enhancement: a joint solution for demosaicking, denoising and super-resolution, vol. 1, no. 3, p. 4. arXiv preprint arXiv:1905.02538 (2019)
30. Rao, Y., Zhao, W., Zhu, Z., Lu, J., Zhou, J.: Global filter networks for image classification. Adv. Neural Inf. Process. Syst. **34**, 980–993 (2021)
31. Shi, W., et al.: Real-time single image and video super-resolution using an efficient sub-pixel convolutional neural network. In: Proceedings of the IEEE Conference on Computer Vision and Pattern Recognition, pp. 1874–1883 (2016)

32. Syu, N.S., Chen, Y.S., Chuang, Y.Y.: Learning deep convolutional networks for demosaicing. arXiv preprint arXiv:1802.03769 (2018)
33. Verma, D., Kumar, M., Eregala, S.: Deep demosaicing using resnet-bottleneck architecture. In: Nain, N., Vipparthi, S.K., Raman, B. (eds.) CVIP 2019. CCIS, vol. 1148, pp. 170–179. Springer, Singapore (2020). https://doi.org/10.1007/978-981-15-4018-9_16
34. Xing, W., Egiazarian, K.: End-to-end learning for joint image demosaicing, denoising and super-resolution. In: Proceedings of the IEEE/CVF Conference on Computer Vision and Pattern Recognition, pp. 3507–3516 (2021)
35. Xing, W., Egiazarian, K.: Residual swin transformer channel attention network for image demosaicing. arXiv preprint arXiv:2204.07098 (2022)
36. Yang, B., Wang, D.: An efficient adaptive interpolation for bayer cfa demosaicking. Sens. Imaging **20**, 1–17 (2019)
37. Yang, Y., Soatto, S.: Fda: fourier domain adaptation for semantic segmentation. In: Proceedings of the IEEE/CVF Conference on Computer Vision and Pattern Recognition, pp. 4085–4095 (2020)
38. Zhang, K., Li, Y., Zuo, W., Zhang, L., Van Gool, L., Timofte, R.: Plug-and-play image restoration with deep denoiser prior. IEEE Trans. Pattern Anal. Mach. Intell. **44**, 6360–6376 (2021)
39. Zhang, K., Zuo, W., Chen, Y., Meng, D., Zhang, L.: Beyond a gaussian denoiser: residual learning of deep cnn for image denoising. IEEE Trans. Image Process. **26**(7), 3142–3155 (2017)
40. Zhang, K., Zuo, W., Gu, S., Zhang, L.: Learning deep cnn denoiser prior for image restoration. In: Proceedings of the IEEE Conference on Computer Vision and Pattern Recognition, pp. 3929–3938 (2017)
41. Zhang, L., Wu, X., Buades, A., Li, X.: Color demosaicking by local directional interpolation and nonlocal adaptive thresholding. J. Electron. Imaging **20**(2), 023016 (2011)
42. Zhang, Y., Li, K., Li, K., Wang, L., Zhong, B., Fu, Y.: Image super-resolution using very deep residual channel attention networks. In: Proceedings of the European Conference on Computer Vision (ECCV), pp. 286–301 (2018)

Knowledge Distillation with Feature Enhancement Mask

Yue Xiao[1]([✉]), Longye Wang[1], Wentao Li[2], and Xiaoli Zeng[3]

[1] School of Electrical Engineering and Information,
Southwest Petroleum University, Chengdu 610500, China
202121000170@stu.swpu.edu.cn, l.y.wang@swpu.edu.cn
[2] Institute of Information Engineering, Chinese Academy of Sciences, Beijing, China
liwentao@iie.ac.an
[3] School of Information Science and Technology,
Tibet University, Lhasa 850000, China

Abstract. Knowledge distillation transfers knowledge from the teacher model to the student model, aiming to improve the student's performance. Previous methods mainly focus on effective feature transformations and alignments to improve distillation efficiency and reduce information loss. However, these approaches ignore the differences between different pixels and layers, which contribute differently during distillation. To this end, we propose the novel knowledge distillation with feature enhancement mask (FEM). The FEM consists of two components: pixel-level feature enhancement mask and layer-level dynamic importance. The pixel-level feature enhancement mask treats target object and non-target object differently during distillation to help the student capture the teacher's crucial features. The layer-level dynamic importance dynamically regulates the effect of each layer in distillation. Extensive experiments on CIFAR-100 indicate that FEM can help the student capture the teacher's crucial features and outperforms previous One-to-One distillation methods even One-to-Many distillation methods.

Keywords: Knowledge distillation · Feature enhancement mask · Crucial feature · Dynamic importance

1 Introduction

Deep learning has gained widespread attention and rapid development in recent years due to its good robustness to the diversity of targets. However, the better performance of deep learning models, the more resources they typically require, which limits their application on resource-constrained equipment such as Internet of Things (IoT) and mobile devices. Therefore, researchers have begun to focus on developing efficient deep learning models that can meet the low power

This work was supported by the National Science Foundation of China (NSFC) under Grant No.62161047.

consumption and real-time requirements of low-resource devices, while minimizing the reduction of model performance. Knowledge distillation [8] was first proposed by Hinton as the mainstream neural network lightweight technique. Its core idea is to use a complex and highly accurate model, known as the teacher model, to guide a simpler and less parameterized student model, allowing the student model to approach the performance of the teacher model.

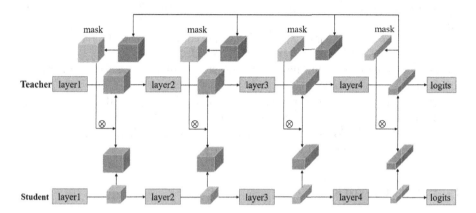

Fig. 1. An overview of the proposed knowledge distillation with feature enhancement mask.

Subsequent research has further developed the concept of knowledge distillation, utilizing intermediate features of the teacher model to guide the student model, rather than just logits. Methods [1,7,13,14,19,22,24] adopt a One-to-One distillation manner, calculating the distance between teacher and student same-level features. Their differences primarily lie in the method of feature transformation and the choice of the distance function. Methods [2,4] indicate that this manual alignment will result in loss of valuable information, hence adopting a One-to-Many distillation manner.

However, these methods focus more on the transformation and alignment between teacher and student features, ignoring differences between different pixels and layers. In computer vision, image content is typically divided into foreground and background, and separating foreground and background is a crucial step in various tasks. A variety of methods have attempted to emphasize the importance of foreground features in object detection distillation field. Chen [3] assigned weights of 1.5 and 1 to the foreground and background respectively during the distillation to increase the importance of the foreground. Li [11] chose to only distill the proposal features generated by the teacher model and the student model. Sun [18] introduced a Gaussian mask to highlight the central region of the labeled object and reduce the background noise around the target region.

Based on these inspirations, we propose a distillation method with feature enhancement mask (FEM). For clarity, it is shown in Fig. 1. FEM employs the last layer of the teacher to generate a feature enhancement mask. Specifically, a positive value will produce a weight of 1.0 while a negative value will produce a weight of 0.5, and all the weights together constitute the mask. For consistency, the masks utilized in previous layers are upsampled and generated from the final layer. In this way, the crucial features will be placed greater emphasis during distillation. Moreover, features from different levels exhibit distinct semantic information and contribute differently to the final prediction. Therefore, dynamic importance is introduced to regulate the effect of different layers during distillation.

Overall, the contributions of this paper are summarized as follows:

1. The feature enhancement mask is proposed to emphasize the teacher's crucial features.
2. Dynamic importance is introduced to regulate the effect of different layers.
3. Extensive experiments are conducted on CIFAR-100 dataset to verify the effectiveness of FEM. They demonstrate that FEM can help the student capture the teacher's crucial features.

2   Related Work

Knowledge distillation (KD) was first proposed by Hinton [8]. It is a technique using both the teacher logits and the ground truth labels to supervise the student's training, which can be formalized as:

$$L_{CE} = -\sum_{i=1}^{N} y_i \log\left(q_i\left(x,1\right)\right),\tag{1}$$

$$L_{KL} = D_{KL}\left(p_i\left(x,t\right)||q_i\left(x,t\right)\right) = \sum_{i=1}^{N} p_i\left(x,t\right)\log\frac{p_i\left(x,t\right)}{q_i\left(x,t\right)},\tag{2}$$

$$L_{KD} = \left(1 - \alpha\right) L_{CE} + \alpha t^2 L_{KL},\tag{3}$$

where t is the distillation temperature to soften predictions. y_i is the one-hot label. $q_i\left(x,t\right)$ is the softened student's prediction while $p_i\left(x,t\right)$ is the softened teacher's prediction.

To further improve KD, recent methods focus on the knowledge contained in intermediate layers. FitNet [14] uses the N-th layer of the teacher to guide the M-th layer of the student. The convolutions are introduced to transform the student's features. AT [24] performs the channel-wise pooling on both student's and teacher's features to produce spacial attention maps. SP [19] calculates the similarity matrices of student and teacher, which models the distribution of the processed data. PKT [13] models the student's and teacher's features as probability distributions and uses KL divergence to measure the similarity between them. VID [1] maximizes the mutual information through variational inference. MGD [22] reduces the channels of the teacher to match the student via the Hungarian algorithm, a parameter-free operation. OFD [7] only distills the helpful information between the teacher and student with proposed Margin-ReLU. The above methods can be formalized as:

$$L_{FD} = \sum_{i=1}^{l} D\left(T_s\left(F_i^s\right), T_t\left(F_i^t\right)\right), \tag{4}$$

where T is the transformation function to transform the features to the target representations. D is the distance function to measure the distance between the teacher and student. FitNet, PKT and SP only select one teacher-student pair, i.e., $l = 1$. While AT, VID, MGD and OFD discard the redundant layers, i.e., $l = min(L_t, L_s)$.

Recent works point out that the above One-to-One distillation methods can not learn the teacher's information adequately. ReviewKD [4] proposes the knowledge review mechanism, utilizing multi-level information of the teacher to guide one-level learning of the student. SemCKD [2] introduces the attention mechanism into knowledge distillation, using all teacher layers to guide a certain student layer. The attention mechanism is used to measure the importance of different teacher layers to the current student layer, which can be formalized as:

$$L_{FD} = \sum_{i=1}^{L_s} \sum_{j=1}^{L_t} \alpha(s_i, t_j) D\left(T\left(F_i^s\right), T\left(F_j^t\right)\right). \tag{5}$$

All previous methods do not discuss the crucial information contained in the teacher, which is found effective to improve the student's performance. This paper focuses on the One-to-One distillation method with crucial feature enhancement mask, which outperforms the above One-to-Many distillation methods.

3 Method

3.1 Feature Enhancement Mask

As demonstrated in Sect. 1, foreground contributes more to object detection than background and is hence treated differently during knowledge distillation. We visualized the intermediate layers of the CNN with channel attention maps [24] (Fig. 2) and found that this conclusion also applies to the image classification. It can be observed that the final layer focuses only on the area near the mouse, while the leaves in the background are abandoned. The student will be unable to capture the teacher's crucial information if all pixels are treated equally during distillation.

However, methods based on anchors and proposals are unavailable in image classification. A different approach needs to be explored to treat target and non-target objects differently. OFD [7] pointed out that the teacher's positive values contain valuable information while the negative values do not. Therefore,

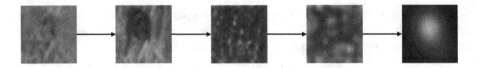

Fig. 2. Visualization of intermediate layers.

it proposed Margin-ReLU (Fig. 3(b)) and partial L_2 to skip the distillation of unnecessary information, similar to the method in [11]. Nevertheless, the research indicates that this distillation manner, *i.e.*, discarding background, is adverse to learning the relation between pixels for the student [20].

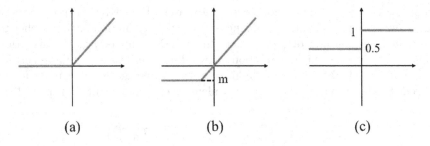

Fig. 3. (a) ReLU. (b) Margin-ReLU. (c) FEM.

The feature enhancement mask (FEM) is proposed to distinguish between foreground and background at the pixel level, with the idea of Gaussian mask [18]. In particular, the teacher's positive feature will produce the weight of 1.0 while the negative feature will produce the weight of 0.5. It is shown in Fig. 3(c) and formalized as:

$$FEM(x) = \begin{cases} 1 & x > 0, \\ 0.5 & x \leq 0. \end{cases} \tag{6}$$

Yosinski [21] found that AlexNet's feature maps from different levels are significantly different. The convolution kernels in shallow layers mainly capture simple features such as edges, textures and colors. The kernels in the middle layers learn deeper semantic information and gradually discard features that are not related to the category. The feature map of the final layer mainly focuses on the target object while discarding the rest information. It is inappropriate to generate masks using shallow layers, since almost all the objects will produce the weight of 1.0.

Therefore, all masks are generated from the final layer, which can be formalized as:

$$M[i] = FEM\left(T_i(F_{L_t}^t)\right) \quad i = 1, 2, \ldots, L_t - 1, \tag{7}$$

where $F_{L_t}^t$ represents the feature of the teacher's L_t-th layer. Assume that $F_{L_t}^t \in R^{b \times c \times h \times w}$ and $F_i^t \in R^{b \times c_i \times h_i \times w_i}$, where b, c, h and w represent the batch size, channels, height and width of the feature. $T_i()$ is the transformation function: $F_{L_t}^t \in R^{b \times c \times h \times w} \rightarrow R^{b \times c_i \times h_i \times w_i}$. Specifically, it consists of a convolution layer to transform c and a linear upsampling to transform h and w. The final layer can directly generate the mask based on FEM without transformation, i.e., $M[L_t] = FEM(F_{L_t}^t)$. Note that the position of feature extraction should be in front of ReLU activation function. Otherwise, the negative features will be filtered out by ReLU, which is similar to OFD.

3.2 Dynamic Importance

CNN typically consists of several convolutional layers, such as Bottlenecks in ResNet [5,6] and Shuffle Units in ShuffleNet [12,25], and the number of pixels contained in features varies significantly with the increasing of the layer. Specifically, features will decrease in width and height to $\frac{1}{2}$ as they flow into the next layer while doubling the number of channels, i.e., shallow layers contain more pixels while deep layers contain less.

As demonstrated in Sect. 3.1, features from different layers exhibit distinct semantic information. Features of the final layer contain category information used for classification and should be emphasized during distillation. However, previous works distilled each layer equally without distinction. The final layer will contribute less during distillation since it has fewer pixels. Therefore, we propose dynamic importance to dynamically regulate the effect of each layer in distillation, which can be formalized as:

$$L_{FD} = \sum_{i=1}^{l} E(i) D \left(T_s \left(F_i^s \right), T_t \left(F_i^t \right) \right) \tag{8}$$

$$= \sum_{i=1}^{l} \frac{D \left(T_s \left(F_i^s \right), T_t \left(F_i^t \right) \right)}{n^{(l-i)}}, \tag{9}$$

where n is the parameter to adjust the importance of each layer. Notably, pixels of each layer have the same importance when $n = 2$ in most cases.

3.3 Loss Function

The loss function of this paper is defined as Eq. (10). For simplicity, the redundant layers are discarded following previous One-to-One distillation methods. The difference is that we discard the shallow layers rather than the deep layers since they contain more valuable information. $M[i]$ is the feature enhancement mask proposed in Sect. 3.1. n is the hyperparameter introduced in Sect. 3.2.

$$L_{FEM} = \sum_{i=1}^{l} \frac{M(i) D \left(T_s \left(F_i^s \right), T_t \left(F_i^t \right) \right)}{n^{(l-i)}}. \tag{10}$$

The total loss function is defined as follows:

$$L_{total} = L_{KD} + \alpha L_{FEM}. \tag{11}$$

L_{KD} refers to the original loss defined as Eq. (3) and α is the hyperparameter to balance the proposed loss.

4   Experiments

In this section, we evaluate the effectiveness of the proposed method through extensive experiments for image classification. We experiment with different network architectures and compare our approach with various distillation methods. Exploratory experiments and visualization experiments are conducted to further analyze the proposed method.

4.1   Experiments on CIFAR-100

Datasets. The CIFAR-100 [10] dataset contains 50,000 images for training and 10,000 images for testing, which are drawn from 100 different classes. Each class has 500 training images and 100 testing images. Each sample is of 32×32 size and RGB color image.

Network Architectures. A variety of representative networks are used for evaluation on CIFAR-100, including VGG [17], ResNet [5,6], WideResNet [23], MobileNet [9,16] and ShuffleNet [12,25]. These networks compose 11 pairs of student-teacher combinations, of which 6 pairs have architectures of the same style, such as: ResNet110/ResNet32, VGG13/VGG8, *etc.*; 5 pairs have completely different architectures, such as: VGG13/MobileNetV2, WRN-40-2/ShuffleNetV1, *etc.*

Compared Approaches

- *Logits distillation* includes KD [8] and DKD [26].
- *One-to-One distillation* includes FitNet [14], AT [24], PKT [13], VID [1] and OFD [7].
- *One-to-Many distillation* includes SemCKD [2] and ReviewKD [4].

Training Details. All models are trained for 240 epochs and the learning rate decayed by 0.1 at the 150-th, 180-th and 210-th epoch. The learning rate is initialized as 0.05, while 0.01 for MobileNet and ShullfeNet. The batch size is set as 64 and the weight decay is set as 0.0005. Stochastic gradient descent (SGD [15]) with momentum is used in all experiments, while the momentum is set as 0.9. α in the loss function Eq. (11) is set as 0.1. For fairness, results of previous methods are all reported in previous papers and combinations that have not been experimented on in papers are denoted by "–".

Experimental Results on CIFAR-100. Extensive experiments are conducted on CIFAR-100 to examine the proposed FEM. The experimental results are reported in Table 1 and Table 2. Table 1 contains the results where teachers and students have the same network architectures. Table 2 contains the results where teachers and students have different network architectures.

According to the distillation manner, previous methods are divided into Logits, One-to-One and One-to-Many. Notably, FEM achieves consistent improvements in all teacher-student pairs, compared with the other One-to-One distillation methods. Our method achieves 1–3% improvements on teacher-student pairs of the same architectures and 1–5% improvements on teacher-student pairs of the different architectures. It strongly supports the effectiveness of FEM. Furthermore, FEM outperforms One-to-Many distillation methods on almost all teacher-student pairs (except for ResNet32×4/ShuffleNetV1), which indicates that emphasizing crucial features in the distillation is more efficient than learning knowledge from other layers.

Table 1. Results on CIFAR-100. Teachers and students have the **same** architectures.

Distillation Manner	Teacher	ResNet56	ResNet110	ResNet32×4	WRN-40-2	WRN-40-2	VGG13
		72.34	74.31	79.42	75.61	75.61	74.64
	Student	ResNet20	ResNet32	ResNet8×4	WRN-16-2	WRN-40-1	VGG8
		69.06	71.14	72.50	73.26	71.98	70.36
Logits	KD	70.66	73.08	73.33	74.92	73.54	72.98
	DKD	71.97	74.11	76.32	76.24	74.81	74.68
One-to-One	FitNet	69.21	71.06	73.50	73.58	72.24	71.02
	PKT	70.34	72.61	73.64	74.54	73.54	72.88
	AT	70.55	72.31	73.44	74.08	72.77	71.43
	VID	70.38	72.61	73.09	74.11	73.30	71.23
	OFD	70.98	73.23	74.95	75.24	74.33	73.95
	FEM	**72.03**	**74.43**	**76.39**	**76.47**	**75.35**	**75.03**
One-to-Many	ReviewKD	71.89	73.89	75.63	76.12	75.09	74.84
	SemCKD	71.29	73.82	76.23	75.86	73.53	74.43

4.2 More Analysis

Distillation Position. As demonstrated in Sect. 3.1, discarding unimportant features is adverse to the student learning the relation between pixels, which will be caused by extracting features after ReLU activation function. In this section, we extract features and generate feature enhancement masks at two positions, before and after the ReLU activation function. The experimental results are shown in Table 3. The results indicate that assigning a lower weight to unimportant features to reduce their impact in distillation is more effective than discarding these features directly.

Hyperparameter Analysis. Dynamic importance is proposed in Sect. 3.2 to regulate the effect of each layer in distillation, where hyperparameter n is introduced. In this section, we set the search space as [1,16] to explore the impact of different values of hyperparameter n on distillation results. The experimental results are shown in Table 4. As demonstrated in Sect. 3.2, each layer has the same effect in distillation when $n = 2$. While the results indicate that students

Table 2. Results on CIFAR-100. Teachers and students have the **different** architectures.

Distillation Manner	Teacher	ResNet32×4 79.42	WRN-40-2 75.61	VGG-13 74.64	ResNet32×4 79.42	ResNet32×4 79.42
	Student	ShuffleNetV1 70.50	ShuffleNetV1 70.50	MobileNetV2 64.60	ShuffleNetV2 71.82	MobileNetV2 64.60
Logits	KD	74.07	74.83	67.37	74.45	68.39
	DKD	76.45	76.70	69.71	77.07	–
One-to-One	FitNet	73.59	73.73	64.14	73.54	68.28
	PKT	74.10	73.89	67.13	74.69	68.88
	AT	71.73	73.32	59.40	72.73	67.15
	VID	73.38	73.61	65.56	73.40	67.94
	OFD	75.98	75.85	69.48	76.82	–
	FEM	77.39	**77.41**	**70.85**	**77.85**	**69.98**
One-to-Many	ReviewKD	**77.45**	77.14	70.37	77.78	–
	SemCKD	76.31	76.83	70.09	77.62	69.00

Table 3. Impact of the distillation positions.

Teacher	ResNet32×4 79.42	VGG-13 74.64	WRN-40-2 75.61	WRN-40-2 75.61	VGG-13 74.64	ResNet32×4 79.42
Student	ResNet8×4 72.50	VGG-8 70.36	WRN-16-2 73.26	ShuffleNetV1 70.50	MobileNetV2 64.60	ShuffleNetV1 70.50
Before	**76.39**	**75.03**	**76.47**	**77.41**	**70.85**	**77.39**
After	76.05	74.36	75.83	76.58	70.56	76.97

Table 4. Impact of the hyperparamter n.

Teacher	ResNet110 74.31	VGG13 74.64	WRN-40-2 75.61	WRN-40-2 75.61	VGG13 74.64	ResNet32×4 79.42
Student	ResNet32 71.14	VGG8 70.36	WRN-16-2 73.26	ShuffleNetV1 70.50	MobileNetV2 64.60	ShuffleNetV1 70.50
$n = 1$	74.10	74.37	76.12	77.23	70.62	76.35
$n = 2$	74.10	74.49	76.05	77.33	70.76	76.87
$n = 4$	**74.43**	**75.03**	**76.47**	77.41	**70.85**	**77.39**
$n = 8$	74.16	74.33	76.24	**77.42**	70.36	77.04
$n = 16$	73.97	75.02	75.89	77.23	70.33	76.28

achieve better performance when $n = 4$ in most cases. It proves that assigning a higher weight to deep layers during distillation will improve the student's performance.

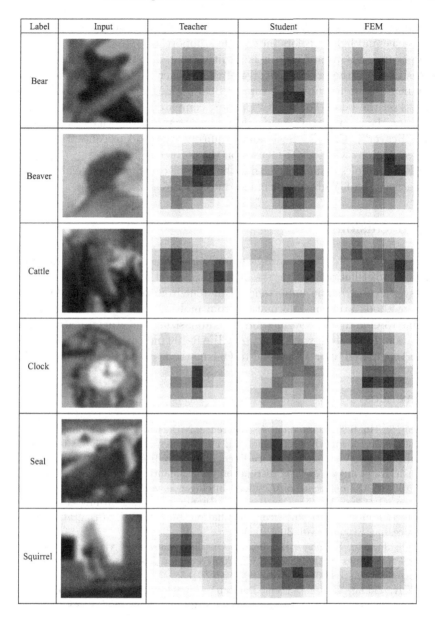

Fig. 4. Channel attention of the last layer(ResNet32 × 4/ResNet8 × 4).

4.3 Visualization

To provide further visual explanation, this section randomly samples several images from the CIFAR-100 dataset and visualizes the final layer using channel attention [24]. The depth of pixel color indicates the importance of that pixel for a model to predict the corresponding label, where darker colors indicate greater importance and lighter colors indicate less importance.

As is apparent from Fig. 4, it is intuitive that the student distilled by FEM focuses more on the crucial features of the teacher while not being affected by other non-crucial features. For input "Bear", FEM focuses more on the head and less on the body. For input "Cattle", compared to the student which only focuses on the right cattle's head, FEM pays attention to both cattle's head. For input "Beaver", "Clock", "Seal" and "Squirrel", the student concentrates on the incorrect regions while FEM focuses on the correct regions.

All the samples demonstrate that the student can capture crucial features of the teacher with feature enhancement mask (FEM).

5   Conclusion

In this paper, we propose a novel Feature Enhancement Mask (FEM) method for knowledge distillation. It consists of the pixel-level feature enhancement mask and layer-level dynamic importance. Different from recent One-to-Many distillation methods utilizing information from multiple teacher layers, we improve the One-to-One distillation method by emphasizing the crucial features during distillation. Extensive experiments on CIFAR-100 indicate the superiority of our method compared to previous One-to-One methods even One-to-Many methods.

References

1. Ahn, S., Hu, S.X., Damianou, A., Lawrence, N.D., Dai, Z.: Variational information distillation for knowledge transfer. In: Proceedings of the IEEE/CVF Conference on Computer Vision and Pattern Recognition, pp. 9163–9171 (2019)
2. Chen, D., et al.: Cross-layer distillation with semantic calibration. In: Proceedings of the AAAI Conference on Artificial Intelligence, vol. 35, pp. 7028–7036 (2021)
3. Chen, G., Choi, W., Yu, X., Han, T., Chandraker, M.: Learning efficient object detection models with knowledge distillation. In: Advances in Neural Information Processing Systems, vol. 30 (2017)
4. Chen, P., Liu, S., Zhao, H., Jia, J.: Distilling knowledge via knowledge review. In: Proceedings of the IEEE/CVF Conference on Computer Vision and Pattern Recognition, pp. 5008–5017 (2021)
5. He, K., Zhang, X., Ren, S., Sun, J.: Deep residual learning for image recognition. In: Proceedings of the IEEE Conference on Computer Vision and Pattern Recognition, pp. 770–778 (2016)
6. He, K., Zhang, X., Ren, S., Sun, J.: Identity mappings in deep residual networks. In: Leibe, B., Matas, J., Sebe, N., Welling, M. (eds.) ECCV 2016. LNCS, vol. 9908, pp. 630–645. Springer, Cham (2016). https://doi.org/10.1007/978-3-319-46493-0_38
7. Heo, B., Kim, J., Yun, S., Park, H., Kwak, N., Choi, J.Y.: A comprehensive overhaul of feature distillation. In: Proceedings of the IEEE/CVF International Conference on Computer Vision, pp. 1921–1930 (2019)
8. Hinton, G., Vinyals, O., Dean, J.: Distilling the knowledge in a neural network. Comput. Sci. 14(7), 38–39 (2015)

9. Howard, A.G., et al.: Mobilenets: efficient convolutional neural networks for mobile vision applications. CoRR abs/1704.04861 (2017)
10. Krizhevsky, A., Hinton, G.: Learning multiple layers of features from tiny images. Handbook Syst. Autoimmune Dis. **1**(4) (2009)
11. Li, Q., Jin, S., Yan, J.: Mimicking very efficient network for object detection. In: Proceedings of the IEEE Conference on Computer Vision and Pattern Recognition, pp. 6356–6364 (2017)
12. Ma, N., Zhang, X., Zheng, H.T., Sun, J.: Shufflenet v2: practical guidelines for efficient cnn architecture design. In: Proceedings of the European Conference on Computer Vision, pp. 116–131 (2018)
13. Passalis, N., Tzelepi, M., Tefas, A.: Probabilistic knowledge transfer for lightweight deep representation learning. IEEE Trans. Neural Netw. Learn. **32**(5), 2030–2039 (2021)
14. Romero, A., Ballas, N., Kahou, S.E., Chassang, A., Gatta, C., Bengio, Y.: Fitnets: hints for thin deep nets. In: International Conference on Learning Representations (2015)
15. Ruder, S.: An overview of gradient descent optimization algorithms. CoRR abs/1609.04747 (2016)
16. Sandler, M., Howard, A., Zhu, M., Zhmoginov, A., Chen, L.C.: Mobilenetv 2: inverted residuals and linear bottlenecks. In: Proceedings of the IEEE Conference on Computer Vision and Pattern Recognition, pp. 4510–4520 (2018)
17. Simonyan, K., Zisserman, A.: Very deep convolutional networks for large-scale image recognition. In: International Conference on Learning Representations (2015)
18. Sun, R., Tang, F., Zhang, X., Xiong, H., Tian, Q.: Distilling object detectors with task adaptive regularization. CoRR abs/2006.13108 (2020)
19. Tung, F., Mori, G.: Similarity-preserving knowledge distillation. In: Proceedings of the IEEE/CVF International Conference on Computer Vision, pp. 1365–1374 (2019)
20. Yang, Z., et al.: Focal and global knowledge distillation for detectors. In: Proceedings of the IEEE/CVF Conference on Computer Vision and Pattern Recognition, pp. 4643–4652 (2022)
21. Yosinski, J., Clune, J., Nguyen, A.M., Fuchs, T.J., Lipson, H.: Understanding neural networks through deep visualization. CoRR abs/1506.06579 (2015)
22. Yue, K., Deng, J., Zhou, F.: Matching guided distillation. In: Proceedings of the European Conference on Computer Vision, pp. 312–328 (2020)
23. Zagoruyko, S., Komodakis, N.: Wide residual networks. In: Proceedings of the British Machine Vision Conference (2016)
24. Zagoruyko, S., Komodakis, N.: Paying more attention to attention: improving the performance of convolutional neural networks via attention transfer. In: International Conference on Learning Representations (2017)
25. Zhang, X., Zhou, X., Lin, M., Sun, J.: Shufflenet: an extremely efficient convolutional neural network for mobile devices. In: Proceedings of the IEEE Conference on Computer Vision and Pattern Recognition, pp. 6848–6856 (2018)
26. Zhao, B., Cui, Q., Song, R., Qiu, Y., Liang, J.: Decoupled knowledge distillation. In: Proceedings of the IEEE/CVF Conference on Computer Vision and Pattern Recognition, pp. 11953–11962 (2022)

Label-Description Enhanced Network for Few-Shot Named Entity Recognition

Xinyue Zhang and Hui Gao[✉]

School of Computer Science and Engineering, University of Electronic Science and
Technology of China, Chengdu, China
kepa0107@std.uestc.edu.cn, huigao@uestc.edu.cn

Abstract. As one of the essential tasks in the context of natural language understanding, Few-shot Named Entity Recognition (NER) aims
to identify and classify entities against limited samples. Recently, many
works have attempted to enhance semantic representations by constructing prompt templates with text and label names. These methods, however, not only distract attention from the text, but also cause unnecessary enumerations. Furthermore, ambiguous label names always fail in
delivering the intended meaning. To address the above issues, we present
a **Label-Description Enhanced Network (LaDEN)** for few-shot named
entity recognition, under which we propose a BERT-based Siamese network to incorporate fine-grained label descriptions as knowledge augmentation. The designed semantic attention mechanism captures label-
specific textual representations, and the distance function matches similar token and label representations based on the nearest-neighbor criterion. Experimental results demonstrate that our model outperforms
previous works in both few-shot and resource-rich settings, achieving
state-of-the-art performance on five benchmarks. Our method is particularly efficient in low-resource scenarios, especially for cross-domain
applications.

Keywords: Named Entity Recognition · Few-shot Setting · Domain
Adaptation

1 Introduction

Typically viewed as a sequence labeling problem [18], Named Entity Recognition
(NER) seeks to tag each label [14] with a specific token. Traditional NER models
suffer from being costly [6,7] and time-consuming with few available annotations,
which yields the concept of few-shot setting.

Metric-based methods have recently shown promising prospects in few-shot
learning. Snell et al. [22] proposed a prototypical network for few-shot NER,
which adopts the nearest-neighbor criterion to match similar features from the
support set. Prior approaches mainly adopted the N-way K-shot method to split
few-shot examples, where N denotes the N classes of the target domain, and K

L. Iliadis et al. (Eds.): ICANN 2023, LNCS 14261, pp. 444–455, 2023.
https://doi.org/10.1007/978-3-031-44198-1_37

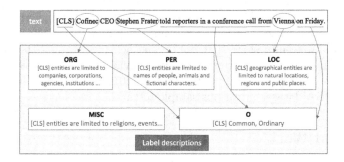

Fig. 1. An example from the CoNLL 2003 dataset. Given a sentence, we use the nearest-neighbor criterion to match similar representations of tokens and label descriptions. (https://www.cnts.ua.ac.be/conll2003/ner/annotation.txt.)

denotes each class has K samples. For the few-shot NER task, it first trains a model with label-set $C^s_{(i)}$ in a source domain, and then tests on a data-scarce target domain with label-set $C^d_{(j)}$. When the domain labels are not necessarily similar, the neural representations can not be improved by updating model parameters and tend to introduce noise. Generalisation of the model remains a challenge in cross-domains with few labeled samples.

Recently, Aly el al. [1] explored the next sentence prediction (NSP) objective of the BERT [5] encoder by incorporating label information to the sentence templates. Nevertheless, every combination inherits unnecessary enumerations. Meanwhile, preparing another encoder is also challenging since the size of label descriptions is considerably smaller than that of the input tokens. Ma et al. [19] introduced label names as prior label knowledge, which contain a wide range of subcategories and fail to convey the intended meaning. For instance, "MISC" in CoNLL 2003 [21] includes religions, events, nationalities and products, etc. As a consequence, they add manual modifications to the definition of label names, leading to a labor-intensive process.

In contrast, using label descriptions is more efficient. First, many data sets post available annotation guidelines with precise label definitions. Second, our experimental results show that the label descriptions hold more semantics than the label names and are more efficient in cross-domain scenarios. As illustrated in Fig. 1, each class is accompanied by a description. The entity "Cofinec" is more approximate to the "Organization" in the common semantic space.[1] Some entities without specific meanings are classified as the negative class "O". In general, the more similar a token is to a label, the more likely it is to be tagged. To conclude, our contributions are as follows:

- We propose a simple but efficient model, LaDEN, which is particularly efficient in low-resource and cross-domain scenarios.

---

[1] We count at the entity level. For instance, both words in "Stephen Frater" are tagged as "I-PERSON". We consider "I-PERSON" to occur once.

- Label description as a knowledge augmentation explicitly enhances the few-shot NER performance without requiring much annotation information.
- Experimental results show that our model achieves state-of-the-art performance on five benchmarks, outperforming previous work by an average of 1.22 to 9.98 F1 points on CoNLL 2003, WNUT 2017, I2B2 2014, NCBI-Disease and JNLPBA dataset in various sample settings.

2   Related Work

2.1   Few-Shot NER

Meta-learning first emerged in computer vision through Matching Networks [25]. Fritzler et al. [9] were the first to apply the prototype-based methods to the task of few-shot NER. Hou et al. [11] delivered label semantics in L-TapNet by a projection function. More recently, prompt-based learning has been successfully adapted to token-level tasks, such as the few-shot NER. By enumerating n-gram spans, Cui et al. [3] employed the prompt-based BART [15] in the NER system. Liu et al. [17] converted the input template into a Question Answering (QA) form and extracted entity spans by fine-tuning the model on SQuAD 2.0. The prompt-based methods, however, are labor-intensive and template-sensitive, and the implicitly injected label knowledge [24] is distracted by the text and cannot be fully exploited.

2.2   Label-Enhanced Knowledge

Some studies have shown that the introduction of explicit label knowledge is crucial for the few-shot performance. Yin et al. [28] and Halder et al. [10] converted label semantics in text classification to a textual entailment problem, predicting the binary probabilities entailed within label descriptions. Ma et al. [19] introduced label names as sentence features and trained two separate BERT [5] to develop knowledge. Li et al. [16] framed the NER task as a Question Answering (QA) problem, utilizing label descriptions as queries to extract entity spans. However, the QA formulation is inefficient since every text has to be encoded with $|C|$ pairs of queries, where $|C|$ denotes the size of the label set.

3   Model

As shown in Fig. 2, It first encodes the input tokens and label descriptions through a shared BERT-based encoder. Next, we devise a semantic attention mechanism and a distance function to capture the semantic associations between similar token and label representations. Finally, we take the maximum value through the linear layer as prediction result.

3.1 Encoding Module

As the size of label descriptions are much smaller than that of the input tokens, training another BERT [5] is inefficient. Inspired by the Siamese network [2], we propose to use the shared BERT encoder to learn text and label representations simultaneously. This structure does not introduce additional parameters and can effectively enhance label semantics.

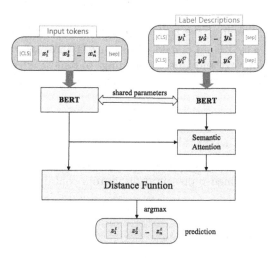

Fig. 2. The architecture of the proposed LaDEN.

Given input tokens X and label descriptions Y, each description is described as a sequence of tokens. For category C, $Y^C = \{y_1^C, y_2^C, ..., y_k^C\}$. The shared BERT-based encoder extracts fine-grained text and label embeddings $f(X) \in R^{b \times n \times d}$ and $f(Y) \in R^{m \times k \times d}$, respectively, where b is the batch size, n is the size of the input tokens, m is the size of the label set, k is the maximum length of the label descriptions, and d is the dimension of the encoder.

3.2 Semantic Attention Module

The semantic attention module aims to enhance semantic relevance of tokens and label representations. To this end, we introduce an attention mechanism to learn label-specific textual features. Firstly, we add a linear transformation to project two representation vectors into a common vector space:

$$g(X) = w_1^T \cdot f(X) \tag{1}$$

$$g(Y) = w_2^T \cdot f(Y) \tag{2}$$

where $w_1, w_2 \in R^{d \times d}$ are trainable weights of the linear classifier. We treat the token embedding $g(X) \in R^{b \times n \times d}$ as query vector Q, and the label embedding

$g(Y) \in R^{m \times k \times d}$ as key vector K as well as value vector V. The attention weight assigned to each value is calculated by the cosine similarity. We also experimented with the dot product operation, but we did not see any performance gain. The reason is that the norm of embeddings dominates the similarity score, while the cosine similarity can be seen as a normalized dot product by L2-normalization:

$$a_{x_i y_j^c} = \frac{g(x_i) \cdot g(y_j^c)}{\|g(x_i)\| \|g(y_j^c)\|} \tag{3}$$

where x_i is the ith token of the text X, y_j^c refers to the jth token of the label description c, and $g(y_j^c)$ is an embedding from $g(Y)$. We perform an attention masking operation on text and label embeddings to remove effects of the padding redundancy. We then incorporate the attention weight into the value vector:

$$g'(Y) = \sum_{c=1}^{m} \sum_{i=1}^{n} \sum_{j=1}^{k} softmax\left(a_{x_i y_j^c}\right) \cdot g(y_j^c) \tag{4}$$

where m is the size of label set, n is the sequence length of input tokens, and $g'(Y)$ refers to fine-grained representation vectors containing label-specific textual semantic features.

3.3 Distance Function

According to the nearest-neighbor criterion, tokens are more likely to be tagged by semantically similar labels. To reduce the dimensionality and promote computational efficiency, the label embeddings is summed over K slots of the attention-based label vectors:

$$h(Y) = \sum_{i=1}^{K} g'(y_i) \tag{5}$$

where K is the maximum length of the label descriptions, y_i is the ith token of each label description, We then define the distance metric to compute the semantic distance between tokens and label vectors:

$$s(X, Y) = w^T (g(X) - h(Y))^2 + b \tag{6}$$

where $s(X, Y)$ is a weighted squared Euclidean distance with trainable weight w and bias b. A higher score of $s(X, Y)$ indicates a higher semantic similarity between the representations of token X and label description Y. If the two embeddings are dissimilar and the original squared distance is large, w would turn negative to make this reasonable. Finally, we apply the softmax function to the prediction matrix $M \in R^{b \times n \times m}$, and take the maximum probability output:

$$z = argmax(softmax(s(X, Y))) \tag{7}$$

3.4 Training

Our experimental setup is in domain adaptation. We first train our model M_s on source domains, and then initiate a new model M_t by the weights of M_s. We further fine-tune M_t on a data-scarce target domain with only a few unseen samples. The token and the label encoder share parameters and update at each iteration, which helps them align the embedding space. Meanwhile, the shared label encoder only requires to generate label representations once and reuses them during inference time, which can significantly reduce memory and improve the inference speed.

Our model is optimized by minimizing the cross-entropy loss. y_i denotes the real probability distribution and z_i denotes the predicted probability distribution. To alleviate the problem of data imbalance caused by excessive negative class ("O"), we set the number of negative class as u, non-negative classes as v and use the weight a_i to adjust the class proportion:

$$\mathcal{L} = -\sum_{i=1}^{m} a_i \cdot p\left(y_i\right) \cdot \log\left(p\left(z_i\right)\right) \tag{8}$$

$$a_u = \frac{v}{u+v} \tag{9}$$

$$a_v = \frac{u}{u+v} \tag{10}$$

4 Experiments

4.1 Datasets

Table 1 summarizes six benchmark datasets for our experiments. (a) OntoNotes [26] contains 18 general domain entities. (b) CoNLL 2003 [21] is gathered from the news domain with 4 classes. (c) WNUT 2017 [4] includes 6 classes from the social media domain. (d) I2B2 [23] is in the medical domain including 23 classes. (e) NCBI-Disease [8] contains a broad disease class for the biology domain. (f) JNLPBA [12] is also in the biology domain with 5 classes.

4.2 Hyperparameters

We use BERT-base-cased[2] as the backbone of all baselines and LaDEN to learn contextual representations. All experiments are implemented with PyTorch and Hugging-Face on a single NVIDIA RTX 3090 GPU. We set the maximum sequence length to 256 and adopt the IO tagging scheme for simplicity. We apply the Adam optimizer [13] with a linear decay schedule and a warm-up at 0.01. We set the batch size to 8 and 4 in low-resource settings. The learning rate of the BERT [5] encoder is 1e−5, and 2e−4 in subsequent layers. We

---

[2] The BERT-base-cased is available in Hugging-Face: https://huggingface.co/bert-base-cased.

first train our model on OntoNotes (the source domain) for 3 epochs, and then fine-tune it on the target domain for 200 epochs. We conduct experiments with $K \in \{1, 5, 10, 20, 50\}$ and use the F1-score as metric. We sample 3 support sets and repeat 5 times with different random seeds.

Table 1. Data summary

Data	Domain	#Classes	#Train	#Test
OntoNotes	General	18	60K	8.3K
CoNLL 2003	News	4	14K	3.5K
WNUT 2017	Social Media	6	3.4K	1.3K
I2B2 2014	Medical	23	56.2K	51.7K
NCBI-Disease	Biology	1	5.4K	0.9K
JNLPBA	Biology	5	18K	4.2K

4.3 Baselines

TransBERT [5] is a BERT model followed by a linear layer. We transfer the bottleneck to fine-tune on the target domain.

NNShot [27] is a metric-learning method based on the nearest-neighbor criterion. It calculates the similarity between the predicted token and all tokens in the support set, and takes the label of the most similar token as prediction.

StructShot [27] is an extension of the NNShot, which captures label dependencies by an abstract transition matrix and a viterbi algorithm during decoding.

TTBERT [19] is a two-tower model, which introduces label names and exploits semantic information via a simple multiply operation. We adopt the IO tagging scheme to keep the consistency of our experimental setting.

4.4 Results

As shown in Table 2, our LaDEN consistently yields the best performance on five benchmarks, i.e., +1.22%, +9.91%, +3.75%, +9.98%, +7.78%, respectively on CoNLL 2003, WNUT 2017, I2B2 2014, NCBI-Disease and JNLPBA.

In low-resource settings, LaDEN performs significantly better than the previous best work, with an average improvement of 9.00 and 6.21 F1 points in 1-shot and 5-shot settings. For the 1-shot setting, similar target labels to OntoNotes such as CoNLL 2003, WNUT 2017 and I2B2 2014 reach the 90.15%, 85.58% and 70.39% performance of the 50-shot setting, respectively. While for datasets without overlaping labels, NCBI-disease and JNLPBA only achieve 50.35% and 66.95% 50-shot performance. This indicates that datasets with similar target labels deliver more knowledge from the source domain, and our label-description based method is particularly efficient by introducing prior label knowledge, even more than half of the resource-rich performance for cross-domains.

In high-resource settings, such as the 50-shot setting, we stay ahead of other models, which validates the effectiveness of our algorithm in both low- and high-resource settings. We also perceive that the growth of our results decreases as more data becomes available, suggesting that LaDEN relies less on prior label knowledge with the amount of data.

TTBERT only performs well on datasets with similar target labels, while the generalization ability becomes poor on the cross-domain datasets NCBI-Disease and JNLPBA, even 1.09 and 4.37 F1 points lower than TransBERT in the 1-shot setting. In contrast, our LaDEN not only performs best in similar datasets, but also proves its superior generalization capability in cross-domain scenarios.

Table 2. Main results of compared models in different settings (k = 1, 5, 10, 20, 50)

Datasets	Methods	1-shot	5-shot	10-shot	20-shot	50-shot
CoNLL 2003	TransBERT	40.92(6.09)	63.38(8.07)	75.68(2.02)	76.95(2.55)	80.24(0.67)
	NNShot	68.22(4.89)	69.15(1.20)	71.55(1.00)	71.68(0.42)	74.47(0.89)
	StructShot	69.54(4.43)	69.94(0.95)	72.34(0.24)	72.62(0.46)	76.08(0.62)
	TTBERT	65.75(2.16)	74.33(4.14)	76.64(1.69)	78.10(1.96)	79.76(1.71)
	LaDEN	**73.10(3.57)**	**75.46(2.15)**	**76.94(1.32)**	**78.34(1.37)**	**81.09(1.03)**
WNUT 2017	TransBERT	19.60(7.88)	21.20(6.72)	25.51(0.97)	33.29(4.58)	36.32(0.24)
	NNShot	22.32(4.62)	24.55(4.28)	27.29(3.34)	25.08(1.47)	25.97(1.32)
	StructShot	24.30(4.49)	26.38(6.04)	30.40(6.41)	28.40(0.48)	29.05(0.83)
	TTBERT	23.09(5.04)	34.61(0.25)	35.01(0.80)	44.19(2.23)	45.86(0.40)
	LaDEN	**42.61(1.94)**	**44.95(2.36)**	**47.24(1.44)**	**48.93(1.39)**	**49.79(2.23)**
I2B2 2014	TransBERT	29.59(2.61)	30.72(1.55)	41.00(5.84)	44.72(4.00)	47.08(3.38)
	NNShot	18.25(0.51)	19.07(1.22)	24.44(0.74)	26.56(4.06)	29.75(2.24)
	StructShot	22.87(1.53)	23.56(1.06)	30.69(1.26)	34.05(4.08)	36.87(3.12)
	TTBERT	37.85(3.40)	42.34(1.62)	49.95(6.28)	53.20(3.31)	55.94(1.81)
	LaDEN	**42.43(0.84)**	**44.46(4.23)**	**53.51(5.12)**	**57.35(4.61)**	**60.28(2.24)**
NCBI-Disease	TransBERT	19.47(1.84)	23.65(5.32)	30.44(9.06)	37.48(5.73)	45.39(0.78)
	NNShot	16.02(2.54)	23.16(7.66)	24.34(4.20)	26.99(3.14)	28.43(4.62)
	StructShot	17.14(3.13)	26.34(6.27)	28.22(2.79)	31.04(3.02)	32.75(2.03)
	TTBERT	18.38(3.41)	16.21(5.15)	28.82(7.44)	39.25(3.96)	49.23(6.28)
	LaDEN	**27.70(4.26)**	**34.42(2.85)**	**47.04(7.30)**	**50.46(2.88)**	**55.01(1.54)**
JNLPBA	TransBERT	27.97(5.36)	29.60(5.10)	37.81(0.72)	41.93(1.55)	48.09(1.49)
	NNShot	12.70(5.43)	14.78(2.95)	16.60(3.60)	17.00(1.92)	18.31(3.20)
	StructShot	14.02(5.78)	17.23(2.22)	19.08(4.30)	19.26(1.85)	22.19(4.48)
	TTBERT	23.60(9.63)	39.06(5.82)	41.06(2.33)	45.49(1.45)	53.71(2.12)
	LaDEN	**38.29(6.35)**	**48.43(1.87)**	**49.10(4.74)**	**53.19(3.96)**	**57.19(1.84)**

5   Analysis

5.1   Variable Analysis in Low-Resource Scenarios

We keep the parameters fixed and set variables to verify the robustness of each module. The results in Table 3 show that these variables lead to a 2.2-5.7 decrease in F1-score:

Sentence-level Features (SLF): It uses sentence-level [CLS] embedding to replace the fine-grained label features. The sentence-level features contain less semantic information than the token-level features, and that fine-grained label knowledge is more essential for subsequent semantic interactions.

Average Pooling (AP): Instead of going through the semantic attention module, it directly averages the fine-grained label features, which performs well in the low-resource setting of NCBI-Disease and inferiorly to LaDEN on the other four datasets. We then conduct supplementary experiment on the 10-shot setting of NCBI-Disease, with performance 5.4 F1 points lower than our LaDEN. One possible reason is that the NCBI-Disease dataset contains only a broad class of diseases, and is thus more sensitive in low-resource settings, making it difficult to distinguish other classes.

Table 3. Model variants in 1-shot and 5-shot settings

	Datasets	SLF	GloVe	AP	MF	LADEN
1-shot	CoNLL 2003	71.38(2.75)	67.87(2.88)	72.11(2.53)	72.46(4.42)	**73.10(3.57)**
	WNUT 2017	40.18(3.39)	33.69(0.95)	38.20(3.81)	41.42(2.88)	**42.61(1.94)**
	I2B2 2014	34.32(2.32)	40.61(4.35)	29.65(1.13)	41.11(1.05)	**42.43(0.84)**
	NCBI-Disease	24.70(3.83)	28.96(3.40)	**29.71(4.62)**	27.09(4.84)	27.70(4.26)
	JNLPBA	33.14(4.24)	24.54(5.01)	27.55(7.19)	30.06(5.52)	**38.29(6.35)**
5-shot	CoNLL 2003	74.26(3.05)	74.40(2.66)	74.47(2.34)	74.56(3.16)	**75.20(1.37)**
	WNUT 2017	44.65(1.35)	40.18(3.52)	41.97(3.94)	44.39(2.74)	**44.95(2.36)**
	I2B2 2014	38.42(5.85)	43.56(6.88)	33.48(3.56)	40.48(5.81)	**44.46(4.23)**
	NCBI-Disease	30.24(2.72)	35.76(2.05)	**37.53(2.81)**	34.98(1.83)	34.42(2.85)
	JNLPBA	42.95(6.00)	41.50(4.13)	39.47(4.64)	43.34(2.90)	**48.43(1.87)**

Multiplicative Fusion (MF): It uses a simple multiplication operation to fuse tokens. From the results, the distance function can effectively align similar representations of tokens and label descriptions.

GloVe Embedding (GloVe): It replaces the shared label encoder with a static GloVe [20] embedding layer.[3] The sharp drop indicates that the contextualized shared BERT encoder can better understand the fine-grained label descriptions.

---

[3] We use the pre-trained 200-dimensional word vectors from Stanford University: https://nlp.stanford.edu/projects/glove/.

All variables are imposed negatively, demonstrating the robustness of our LaDEN. Fine-grained input features allow the shared BERT [5] encoder to better understand the semantics. The subsequent semantic attention module and the distance function capture the semantic associations between similar tokens and label representations. In general, each module complements each other and jointly boost the few-shot NER performance.

5.2 Performance on Label Semantics

To verify the effectiveness of using label descriptions as prior semantics, we set different semantic variables as input to the shared BERT [5] encoder:

Label Names. We replace label descriptions with label names as prior knowledge, and the label name is set to be the same as [19].

Meaningless Labels. We omit specific interpretations of labels and use meaningless labels (e.g., "label descriptions 1", "label descriptions 2") to represent different classes.

TransBERT. We use a single BERT model followed by a linear softmax layer without introducing any label semantics.

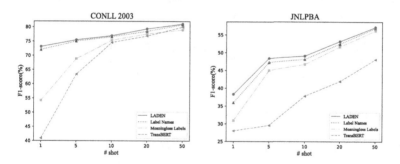

Fig. 3. Label semantics on CoNLL 2003 and JNLPBA in various sample settings

Based on the domain adaptation scenario, we experiment on CoNLL 2003 and JNLPBA, which are similar to and completely different from ontonotes labels, respectively. The experimental results are shown in Fig. 3. In CoNLL 2003, our label-description based method just has a slight advantage over "Label Names" by 0.54%, while for the JNLPBA dataset, our method enables more fine-grained learning, with an average of 1.08% higher than "Label Names". The "Meaningless Labels" without specific semantics are ineffective, making it difficult to interact semantically with the corresponding labels. This illustrates that label descriptions carry more semantics, and the rich semantic knowledge is beneficial for the few-shot setting.

We also observe that similar target domains deliver more knowledge from the source domain, e.g., all labels in CoNLL 2003 are included in OntoNotes except for "MISC". As the amount of data increases, label semantics is no longer decisive and TransBERT exhibits comparable performance to others, even exceeding the performance of "Meaningless Labels" in the 50-shot setting. Furthermore, TransBERT lags far behind other results in JNLPBA, suggesting that prior label knowledge is of vital significance for cross-domains. In contrast, label descriptions deliver the richest semantic information in both few-shot and resource-rich settings, and are particularly efficient in the extreme data-scarce scenarios.

6 Conclusion

In this paper, we propose LaDEN, a label-description enhanced model for few-shot NER. We deliver label descriptions explicitly to fully exploit the label semantics. We propose to use the BERT-based siamese network to encode input tokens and label descriptions individually. The semantic attention mechanism incorporates label-specific textual representations, and the distance function goes further to align similar representations. Label description serves as a knowledge enhancement in the NER system and thus does not require much annotated information, resulting in efficient performance in low-resource scenarios. Our model achieves state-of-the-art performance in various sample settings, and we will continue to explore how to simply and efficiently leverage label descriptions to boost NER tasks in zero-shot scenarios.

Acknowledgements. Our work was supported by Sichuan Science and Technology Program (No.2023YFG0021, No.2022YFG0038 and No.2021YFG0018), and by Xinjiang Science and Technology Program (No. 2022D01B185).

References

1. Aly, R., Vlachos, A., McDonald, R., et al.: Leveraging type descriptions for zero-shot named entity recognition and classification. In: Proceedings of the 59th Annual Meeting of the Association for Computational Linguistics and the 11th International Joint Conference on Natural Language Processing (Volume 1: Long Papers), pp. 1516–1528 (2021)
2. Bromley, J., et al.: Signature verification using a "Siamese" time delay neural network. In: Advances in Neural Information Processing Systems, vol. 6 (1993)
3. Cui, L., et al.: Template-based named entity recognition using BART. arXiv preprint arXiv:2106.01760 (2021)
4. Derczynski, L., et al.: Results of the WNUT2017 shared task on novel and emerging entity recognition. In: Proceedings of the 3rd Workshop on Noisy User-generated Text, pp. 140–147 (2017)
5. Devlin, J., et al.: Bert: Pre-training of deep bidirectional transformers for language understanding. arXiv preprint arXiv:1810.04805 (2018)
6. Ding et al. "Few-nerd: a few-shot named entity recognition dataset. arXiv preprint arXiv:2105.07464 (2021)

7. Ding, N., et al.: Prompt-learning for fine-grained entity typing. arXiv preprint arXiv:2108.10604 (2021)
8. Doğan, R.I., Leaman, R., Lu, Z.: NCBI disease corpus: a resource for disease name recognition and concept normalization. J. Biomed. Inf. **47**, 1–10 (2014)
9. Fritzler, A., Logacheva, V., Kretov, M.: Few-shot classification in named entity recognition task. In: Proceedings of the 34th ACM/SIGAPP Symposium on Applied Computing, pp. 993–1000 (2019)
10. Halder, K., et al.: Task-aware representation of sentences for generic text classification. In: Proceedings of the 28th International Conference on Computational Linguistics, pp. 3202–3213 (2020)
11. Hou, Y., et al.: Few-shot slot tagging with collapsed dependency transfer and label-enhanced task-adaptive projection network. arXiv preprint arXiv:2006.05702 (2020)
12. Kim, J.-D., et al.: Introduction to the bio-entity recognition task at JNLPBA. In: Proceedings of the International Joint Workshop on Natural Language Processing in Biomedicine and its Applications. Citeseer. pp. 70–75 (2004)
13. Kingma, D.P., Ba, J.: Adam: a method for stochastic optimization. arXiv preprint arXiv:1412.6980 (2014)
14. Lafferty, J., McCallum, A., Pereira, F.C.N.: Conditional random fields: probabilistic models for segmenting and labeling sequence data (2001)
15. Lewis, M., et al. Bart: denoising sequence-to-sequence pre-training for natural language generation, translation, and comprehension. arXiv preprint arXiv:1910.13461 (2019)
16. Li, X., et al.: A unified MRC framework for named entity recognition. arXiv preprint arXiv:1910.11476 (2019)
17. Liu, A.T., et al.: QaNER: prompting question answering models for few-shot named entity recognition. arXiv preprint arXiv:2203.01543 (2022)
18. Haitao, L., et al.: TFM: a triple fusion module for integrating lexicon information in Chinese named entity recognition. In: Neural Processing Letters, pp. 1–18 (2022)
19. Ma, J., et al.: Label semantics for few shot named entity recognition. arXiv preprint arXiv:2203.08985 (2022)
20. Pennington, J., Socher, R., Manning, C.D.: Glove: global vectors for word representation. In: Proceedings of the 2014 Conference on Empirical Methods in Natural Language Processing (EMNLP), pp. 1532–1543 (2014)
21. Sang, E.F., De Meulder, F.: Introduction to the CoNLL-2003 shared task: language-independent named entity recognition. arXiv preprint cs/0306050 (2003)
22. Snell, J., Swersky, K., Zemel, R.: Prototypical networks for few-shot learning. In: Advances in Neural Information Processing Systems, vol. 30 (2017)
23. Stubbs, A., Uzuner, Ö.: Annotating longitudinal clinical narratives for de-identification: The 2014 i2b2/UTHealth corpus. J. Biomed. Inf. **58**, S20–S29 (2015)
24. Vaswani, A., et al.: Attention is all you need. In: Advances in Neural Information Processing Systems, vol. 30 (2017)
25. Vinyals, O., et al.: Matching networks for one shot learning. In: Advances in Neural Information Processing Systems, vol. 29 (2016)
26. Weischedel, R., et al.: Ontonotes release 5.0 ldc2013t19. In: Linguistic Data Consortium, Philadelphia, PA, vol. 23 (2013)
27. Yang, Y., Katiyar, A.: Simple and effective few-shot named entity recognition with structured nearest neighbor learning. arXiv preprint arXiv:2010.02405 (2020)
28. Yin, W., et al.: Universal natural language processing with limited annotations: try few-shot textual entailment as a start. arXiv preprint arXiv:2010.02584 (2020)

Landslide Surface Displacement Prediction Based on VSXC-LSTM Algorithm

Menglin Kong[1], Ruichen Li[1], Fan Liu[1], Xingquan Li[2,3], Juan Cheng[1], Muzhou Hou[1], and Cong Cao[1(✉)]

[1] School of Mathematics and Statistics, Central South University, Changsha, China
{212112025,212111114,8201200822,hmzw,congcao}@csu.edu.cn
[2] Peng Cheng Laboratory, Shenzhen, China
[3] School of Mathematics and Statistics, Minnan Normal University, Zhangzhou, China

Abstract. Landslide is a natural disaster that can easily threaten local ecology, people's lives and property. In this paper, we conduct modelling research on real unidirectional surface displacement data of recent landslides in the research area and propose a time series prediction framework named VMD-SegSigmoid-XGBoost-ClusterLSTM (VSXC-LSTM) based on variational mode decomposition, which can predict the landslide surface displacement more accurately. The model performs well on the test set. Except for the random item subsequence that is hard to fit, the root mean square error (RMSE) and the mean absolute percentage error (MAPE) of the trend item subsequence and the periodic item subsequence are both less than 0.1, and the RMSE is as low as 0.006 for the periodic item prediction module based on XGBoost.

Keywords: Landslide warning · Deep learning · Mode decomposition · Time series

1 Introduction

Landslide is a serious natural disasters [1], and large-scale landslides threaten the local ecology and property. An important part of landslide prevention and control is predicting its displacement. Landslide surface displacement data itself is a kind of time series data, which has distinct characteristics, such as being time-sensitive, structural, and almost no update operation [2]. Time series forecasting modelling is mainly aimed at its timeliness and structure, trying to give a reasonable description of its change trend, period and other characteristics, to achieve effective forecasting [3]. Traditional landslide early warning model mostly relies only on the knowledge background of land disasters, due to the scarcity and variability of landslide surface displacement evolution parameters and the

---

M. Kong and R. Li—Contributed equally to this work.

© The Author(s), under exclusive license to Springer Nature Switzerland AG 2023
L. Iliadis et al. (Eds.): ICANN 2023, LNCS 14261, pp. 456–470, 2023.
https://doi.org/10.1007/978-3-031-44198-1_38

complexity of the external environment, the physical model [4] can reveal its evolution mechanism, but it is difficult to obtain accurate prediction effect.

In recent years, variational modal decomposition (VMD) [5] has been widely used in time series data decomposition and prediction because of its ability to divide series data into different sub-series with a clear physical meaning based on frequency. Zhang et al. [6] combined VMD with the optimal combination model for the carbon price prediction tasks and used VMD to complete the decomposition of surface displacement data. Due to its data-driven scalability and powerful ability to fit independent and identically distributed data, the use of machine learning(ML)-based and deep learning(DL)-based methods to predict time series data has become a relatively mature idea, and the methods that have performed better in previous tasks include XGBoost [7], LSTM [8], Prophet [9], support vector regression (SVR) [10], etc. Due to the particularity of geological geomorphology, it is often not feasible to use the same mathematical modelling methods in different regions. In addition, the data used to train the model is likely to not satisfy the hidden assumptions in the model resulting in inconsistency and ultimately unsatisfactory prediction performance.

The key direction of landslide surface displacement prediction is to improve the existing models according to the unique characteristics of each region, and then form a new model that adapts to the characteristics of the data. In this paper, we propose a new prediction framework combining traditional statistical ideas with ML/DL-based time series prediction models, named VMD-SegSigmoid-XGBoost-ClusterLSTM (VSXC-LSTM) for landslide surface displacement time series prediction. The main contributions of this paper are as follows:

- In this paper, we propose a SegSigmoid-XGBoost-ClusterLSTM (VSXC-LSTM) landslide surface displacement time series data prediction framework based on variational modal decomposition(VMD), which is suitable for the characteristics of obvious change trend and abnormal fluctuation of landslide body surface displacement data.
- Different from existing methods, we perform nonparametric tests on each decomposed subsequence during model training to verify its property, which ensures the consistency of the training data and model assumptions.
- We propose a sub-model for modelling irregular subsequences obtained after the modal decomposition of time series data which is named ClusterLSTM.
- Extensive experiments on real-world datasets show our method has good precision and generalization ability. Our VSXC-LSTM framework can provide reliable research materials for experts in the field to study the changes and development of landslides, to achieve effective warning of landslide disasters.

2   Related Work

Due to the variability of landslide surface displacement evolution parameters and the complexity of the external environment, the physical model [4] can reveal its evolution mechanism, but it is difficult to obtain an accurate prediction effect.

Holt [3] applied the double exponential smoothing (DES) method to trend displacement prediction. This method is simple in operation, and has good prediction performance for some specific trend sequences. Cao et al. [11] proposed an extreme learning machine (ELM) method, which takes control factors into account in the landslide surface displacement prediction model. Based on the dynamic characteristics of landslides, Xu et al. [12] used the dynamic model long and short-term memory neural network (LSTM) to predict the cumulative displacement, and the prediction result was more accurate than that of the static model support vector regression (SVR). Huang et al. [13] used a novel recursive neural network to predict the dynamic response of slope, this model is suitable for the case of a large amount of data, and the prediction error is small. In addition, Li et al. [14] proposed a LSTM algorithm based on clustering ideas applied to temporal series anomaly detection, which also has application value in the prediction direction of introducing clustering ideas into LSTM modelling. Krishnan et al. [15] uses deep Kalman filtering for counterfactual reasoning, showing the excellent filtering ability of the Kalman filter algorithm. Cong et al. [16] applies Kalman filtering to monitoring data anomaly detection tasks. Its excellent experimental results prove the feasibility of applying the Kalman filter to anomaly detection in landslide monitoring data. In terms of parameter optimization, Cui et al. [17] proposed that based on spline curve and nested least square support vector regression (LS-SVR) functional parameter optimization, and the stable control of parameter optimization value can be achieved under actual conditions. Traditional ML and DL algorithms need to meet certain conditions to get good prediction results, but in reality, there are often cases where the data do not satisfy the implicit model assumptions, resulting in poor robustness of the model prediction results. However, compared with the existing single-model ML/DL methods, our framework has good robustness while achieving higher precision.

3   Framework

Our goal is to achieve better predictions by integrating models with excellent performance. This paper we propose a SegSigmoid-XGBoost-ClusterLSTM framework, as shown in Fig. 1, which mainly applies modal decomposition and ensemble learning ideas. Firstly, VMD [5] is used to decompose the time series data into three subseries, namely T (trend term), S (period term), R (residual term). Secondly, three subsequence curves are fitted using suitable models (SegSigmoid, XGBoost, ClusterLSTM), respectively. Finally, the three subseries are combined into a prediction sequence and the final prediction result is output.

3.1   VMD Decomposition Based on Genetic Algorithm Parameter

The decomposition of the processed displacement data using the VMD algorithm can obtain more physically meaningful time series components. However, the hyperparameter penalty factor α and ascending step τ in the VMD algorithm will have a greater impact on the decomposition effect, to avoid the modelling bias introduced by artificially determining the hyperparameters, we use

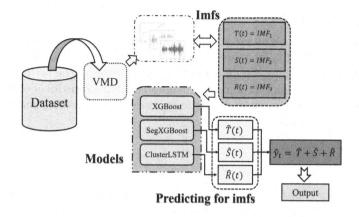

Fig. 1. SegSigmoid-XGBoost-ClusterLSTM model based on VMD

the genetic algorithm (GA) to determine a set of hyperparameter α that make the decomposition effect optimal by iteratively optimizing the fitness function τ. It provides a general framework for solving complex system problems, which does not depend on the specific domain of the problem and has strong robustness.

Completely non-recursive VMD was proposed by Konstantin et al. [5]. In this paper, this method is mainly used to perform modal decomposition of the original surface displacement sequence. Considering interpretability and enforceability, we prescribe the number of decompositions $K = 3$ without losing a large amount of information, which are trend term, period term and residual term, respectively. The detailed steps of VMD are shown in Algorithm 1, where u_k is the centre frequency of the single-component amplitude modulation signal; ω_k is the centre frequency of the single-component FM signal, λ_k is the Lagrangian multiplier, n is the number of iterations, k is the number of subsequences, and ϵ is the tolerance of the convergence criterion.

Algorithm 1. Variational Modal Decomposition

Require: Raw surface displacement data y
Ensure: Trend term subseries T, S, R
1: **Initialize** $\{u_k^1\},\{\omega_k^1\},\lambda_k^1$,n=0,k=1,$\epsilon$=$10^{-7}$
2: **while** $k<3$ **do**
3:     $n = 1$
4: **update** $u_k^{n+1}, \omega_k^{n+1}$
5:     **update** λ_k
6:     **if** $\sum_k \frac{||u_k^{n+1}-u_k^n||^2}{||u_k^n||_2^2} < \epsilon$ **then**
7:         $k = k+1$
8:     **else**
9:         break
10:    **end if**
11: **end while**

3.2 SegSigmoid

The SegSigmoid model is an extension of the traditional logistic regression model, which will be applied to the curve fitting and forecasting tasks of the logistic regression model used for classification tasks, and optimize the prediction effect with appropriate parameters according to different characteristics of time periods of the time series. The essence of logistic regression lies in the Sigmoid function, which is defined as follows:

$$g(z) = \frac{1}{1 + e^{-z}} \tag{1}$$

The characteristic of this function is that the value on the real axis domain is in the interval (0,1] and is not sensitive to maximum and minimum values. The expression of the piecewise logistic regression model is such as the formula (2):

$$g(t) = \frac{C(t)}{1 + exp(-(k + \alpha(t)^t \delta)(t - (m + \alpha(t)^T \gamma))} \tag{2}$$

Inspired by the Prophet algorithm, we propose the SegSigmoid algorithm and introduce anomaly detection ideas of student-based residuals [18] to obtain change point location information.

The student residual can be used to detect outliers, and calculating the residuals such as Equ. (3) and (4), where y_i, $\hat{y}_i$ is the true value of the sequence and the predicted value of the series, respectively. Then, the studentized residual elimination dimensional differences are proposed and the Hat matrix for adjusting the sum of squares of the series residuals in (5) is introduced such as Equ. (6), where n is the sample size, X is the sequence dataset matrix, and h_{ii} is the diagonal element of the Hat matrix. The formula is defined as follows:

$$\hat{y}_i = \sum_{p=0}^{N} a_p x_i^p \tag{3}$$

$$r_i = y_i - \hat{y}_i \tag{4}$$

$$t_i = (n - p - 1)\frac{r_i}{SSE(1 - h_{ii}) - r_i^2} \tag{5}$$

$$H = X(X^T X)^{-1} X^T \tag{6}$$

We define the Bonferroni (BC) critical value to establish a suitable confidence interval in Equ. (7) and (8), where α is the significance level, often set to 0.05, the Bonferroni critical value can be scaled equimetrically using the correction factor β ($\beta = 1/6$). The formula is defined as follows:

$$BC = t(1 - \frac{\alpha}{2n}; n - p - 1) \tag{7}$$

$$- BC(\alpha = 0.05) < x < BC(\alpha = 0.05) \tag{8}$$

3.3   ClusterLSTM

LSTM [8] is a long-short-term memory artificial neural network, which is developed from recurrent neural networks. The proposed ClusterLSTM introduces the idea of clustering on the basis of LSTM, aiming to solve the problem that it is difficult to use a single LSTM fitting with large differences in the scale of different window series. In addition, K-means algorithm is used to realize the clustering of residual term time series data, and shallow LSTMs are established separately for each class to improve the prediction performance.

Specifically, the residual term series obtained from the VMD is first dealt with a white noise test. Then, K-LSTM models with the same structures are initialized, and the residual items of all decomposed training samples within a batch are clustered during the training process, with the number of cluster centers being K, to obtain the partitioned sub-dataset $\{C_1^{res}, \cdots, C_K^{res}\}$. Then the parameters θ_k of the k-th LSTM model are updated as follows:

$$\theta_k^{t+1} \leftarrow \theta_k^t - \alpha \left[\sum_{i=1}^{|C_k^{res}|} \nabla_{\theta_k} Loss \left(R_{i,k}, \hat{R}_{i,k} \right) \right] \tag{9}$$

where θ_k is the parameters of the k-th LSTM model, $|C_k^{res}|$ is the size of the k-th sub-dataset, α is learning rate, $R_{i,k} \in C_k^{res}$ is the groundtruth residual term in the k-th sub-dataset, $\hat{R}_{i,k}$ is the output of the k-th LSTM model. The principle of ClusterLSTM technology is shown in Fig. 2.

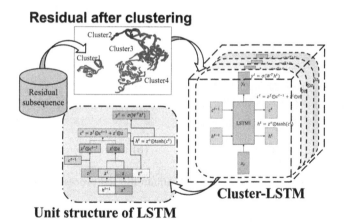

Fig. 2. The framework of our ClusterLSTM

4   Modeling and Results

4.1   Dataset Introduction and Data Preprocessing

The dataset used in this paper is from the relative displacement data recorded by sensors from December 12, 2020, to March 21, 2021, from the N 27°13′57″ and E 109°42′05″ monitoring points in the landslide area of the Niutang Pass Formation in Dashajie Village, Heliao Township, Zhijiang County. Specifically, a total of 2426 pieces of time series data recorded in hours were divided by a threshold of 0.9, the first 2184 pieces of data were used for the training of each machine learning model, and the last 242 pieces of data were used as a test set to verify the accuracy of the model and performed 10-fold cross-validation.

The sensor has measurement errors and process noise when recording landslide motion, so the original displacement data contains many invalid information and interference factors. Before building the model, we first used Kalman-Filter [19] to smooth the noise filtering of the raw data. So we set the variance of the process noise $w \sim N(0, Q)$ to 1, due to the degradation of the measurement accuracy due to sensor ageing, so the variance of the measurement error $v \sim N(0, R)$ is set to 16, and the original data and the filtered data curve are shown in Fig. 3. From Fig. 3-a, we find the Kalman filter retains the characteristics of the original curve to the greatest extent, and does not change the period and trend of the original curve. Observing Fig. 3-b, it can be concluded that the displacement data processed by the Kalman filter has a smoother change trend in the data and shows a more obvious change regularity than the original data.

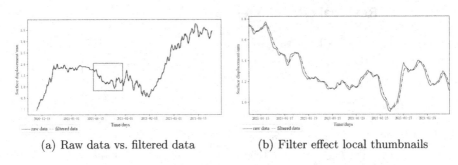

(a) Raw data vs. filtered data   (b) Filter effect local thumbnails

Fig. 3. Sensor raw data and Kalman filtered processed data

4.2   Evaluation Indicators

In order to accurately evaluate the predictive performance of our designed model, the evaluation index is Root Mean Square Error (RMSE) and Mean Absolute Percentage Error (MAPE) as shown in Eq. (10) and (11). Where N is the total sample size of the prediction, and d_i and $\hat{d}_i$ are the true and predicted values of sample$_i$, respectively. The formula is defined as follows:

$$RMSE = \sqrt{\frac{1}{N}\sum_{i=1}^{N}(\hat{d}_i - d_i)^2}; \tag{10}$$

$$MAPE = \frac{1}{N}\sum_{i=1}^{N}\left|\frac{\hat{d}_i - d_i}{d_i}\right|; \tag{11}$$

4.3 VMD Decomposition

Before we use genetic algorithm (GA), we first use VMD to obtain the hyperparameter α. Specifically, we specify the number of components after decomposition $K = 3$, with the reconfiguration mean squared error $(\tilde{y} - y)^2/n$ of the decomposition sequence $\tilde{y} = imf_1 + imf_2 + imf_3$ as the fitness function of the GA: the number of individuals in the population $m = 50$, the number of iterations $niter = 100$, the cross probability is 0.7, and the variation probability is 0.1. Finally, we get the optimal hyperparameter $\alpha = 13.625, \tau = 0.99877$.

The components decomposed by VMD are shown in Fig. 4. The first eigenmode function imf_1 after decomposition is shown in Fig. 4-a, which is smoother than the original sequence y that named trend term T; the second subsequence is shown in Fig. 4-b, exhibits a strong periodicity that named periodic term S; the last subsequence is shown in Fig. 4-c, and it is difficult to observe a more obvious law from the figure, and it is named residual term R.

We use the VMD algorithm to decompose the original sequence into three subsequences, namely: $y_t = T + S + R + e$, where e is the error caused by VMD, this error has been minimized by optimizing the VMD algorithm parameters, and is ignored here. By establishing a time series forecasting model for three subseries, $\hat{T}, \hat{S}, \hat{R}$ are obtained, and then the final predicted value $\hat{y}$ is obtained.

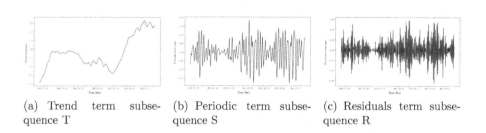

(a) Trend term subsequence T

(b) Periodic term subsequence S

(c) Residuals term subsequence R

Fig. 4. Three subsequences after VMD decomposition

4.4 Trend Term, Periodic Term, Residual Term Test and Model Establishment

(a) Trend Term Testing and Model Building. For the trend term subseries, we first perform the Mann-Kendall test on the sequence. Based on the actual prediction effect, we decided to use SegSigmoid as the trend term prediction model. The trend item modelling process is shown in Fig. 5.

First, the Mann-Kendall tendency test in the nonparametric test is used to determine the trendiness of the target series, and the specific results are shown in Table 1. So we have sufficient evidence to reject the null hypothesis, that the series has a trend, and can be modelled and predicted on this basis. It is observed that the change of the trend term T approximately follows the change law of the cubic polynomial curve $y_t = at^3 + bt^2 + ct + d$, as shown in Fig. 6.

We fit the SegSigmoid function on the training set and calculate the studentized residuals at each moment after cubic polynomial fitting to mark outlier

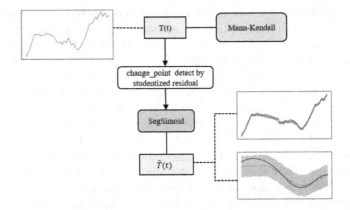

Fig. 5. Trend term testing and predictive modelling process

Table 1. Results of the Mann-Kendall test

Mann-Kendall	original hypothesis	Z statistic	p-value	conclusion
Results	no trend of T	22.059	0.000	Rejection hypothesis

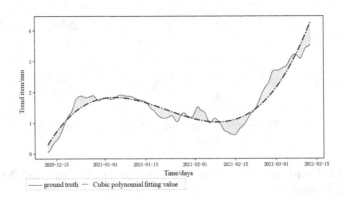

Fig. 6. Cubic polynomial fits the basic shape of a trend term

points and set the set of outliers to the mutation points of the SegSigmoid function. After calculation, the number of mutation points on the training set is 1146, and the growth rate changes δj at the mutation point s_j obeys Laplace $Laplace(0, \tau)$, where τ is 0.5, and the distribution range of mutation points on the training set is 0.95, only change points on the first 95% of the training set.

(b) Periodic Term Inspection and Model Establishment. Periodic term modelling is different from trend term, we first perform an autocorrelation test on periodic term, and then perform the Granger causality test for the proposed hypothesis. Finally, we determine the final prediction model of the periodic term as XGBoost according to the performance of the prediction set. The process of checking and predicting periodic terms is shown in Fig. 7-a. To determine the lagged dependence of terms in the periodic term S, the autocorrelation function (ACF) of the periodic term S is first calculated. From Fig. 7-b, the ACF curve disappears at the lag 48 period, which indicates that the autocorrelation function is truncated at the lag 48 periods, which means that relative displacement at a certain moment is most affected by the displacement data 48 h ago. We assume that the period term S is simultaneously affected by the trend term T, the period term S, the residual term R, and the relative displacement y with lags from periods 1 to 48, so there is a prediction function f that maps the time series component of the lag to the period term S_t of the current period:

$$S_t = f(T_{t-1}, \cdots T_{t-48}, S_{t-1}, \cdots S_{t-48}, R_{t-1}, \cdots R_{t-48}, y_{t-1}, \cdots y_{t-48}) \quad (12)$$

To verify the correctness of this hypothesis, we use the Granger causality test to determine whether the causal relationship between the period term S, T, R; and the results of the Granger causal test with a lag of 48 periods are shown in Table 2. We can see the period term prediction model is statistically significant.

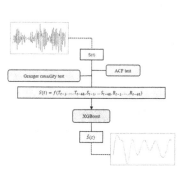

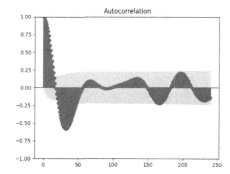

(a) Periodic term testing and prediction process

(b) Periodic term autocorrelation test

Fig. 7. Periodic term

Table 2. Results of Granger causal test under 48-order hysteresis

Test object	Original hypothesis	F statistic	P-value	Conclusion
Relative displacement y	Y is not S's Granger reason	180825.2560	p = 0.0000	Reject
Trend item T	T is not S's Granger reason	26297.4066	p = 0.0000	Reject
Residuals item R	S is not S's Granger reason	548946.1211	p = 0.0000	Reject

After completing the Granger causal test, we use the XGBoost model with excellent performance in a number of similar prediction tasks as the prediction model of the periodic term S and select the same common support vector regression (SVR) model as a comparison.

(c) Residual Term Test and Model Establishment. In view of the problems such as the difficulty of capturing the residual term law, and the suspected white noise, the white noise test is carried out on the residual term subsequence, and the prediction analysis is carried out after confirming that it is a non-white noise sequence. Experiments show that the prediction performance of LSTM directly is poor, so the ClusterLSTM model is introduced and then established separately. The process of testing and predicting residual terms is shown in Fig. 8 and the Ljung-Box test results are shown in Table 3. After testing, it is concluded that there is still a sequence dependence in the residual term R that has not been completely extracted, so the residual term R is a non-white noise sequence.

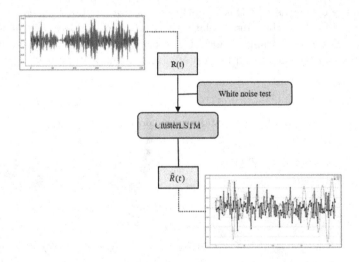

Fig. 8. Residual term inspection and prediction process

Table 3. First-order hysteresis white noise test results

original hypothesis	Ljung-Box statistic	p-value	conclusion
R is the white noise sequence	1817.319	0.00	Rejection hypothesis

Since the data show the characteristics of large-scale differences in different window sequences, we consider ClusterLSTM which first use K-means clustering [20] to aggregate subsequences of similar scales into K different clusters, and then train K-LSTM models with simpler structures on the data in each cluster to enhance the model's perception of data scale changes.

In the experiment, we use 24 as a window length to divide the entire time series into subsequences, and each subsequence as a sample. Then, the t-SNE [21] algorithm is used to convert the 24-dimensional time series samples into the 2-dimensional feature space for visual display, and the visualization effect is shown in Fig. 9. From Fig. 9, time series samples can be roughly divided into four categories, so we set the cluster $K = 4$ in the K-means clustering algorithm. A shallow LSTM with a hidden layer number of 2 and a hidden layer neuron number of 6 is trained for the samples in each cluster.

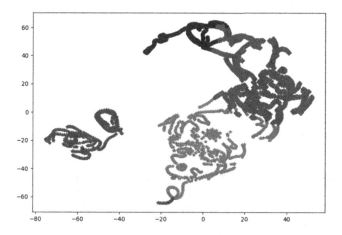

Fig. 9. Distribution of residual term time series samples in two-dimensional feature space

4.5   Series Summary Prediction and Model Validation

According to the principle of time series, the displacements of the trend, period, and residual terms are added together to obtain the displacement prediction value $\hat{y}$, and prediction results are shown in Fig. 10. It can be seen that the predicted values obtained by different forecasting methods have high similarity with the actual values, and the predictions of the overall trend are basically consistent with the actual values, but the predictions of local fluctuations by different methods have great differences, among which the prediction curve obtained by the VSXC-LSTM framework is the closest to the actual value. As shown in Table 4, it show that we propose has achieved the highest prediction accuracy on the two evaluation indicators, which verifies the effectiveness of the method.

In order to further verify the effectiveness and generalization performance of our method, we use the recent relative displacements recorded by sensors from

Table 4. The performance of different total displacement prediction models on the test set

Predictive models	RMSE	MAPE
SegSigmoid-XGBoost-ClusterLSTM	**0.0744**	**0.0177**
SegSigmoid-SVR-ClusterLSTM	0.0924	0.0242
SegSigmoid-XGBoost-LSTM	0.0787	0.0183
SegSigmoid-SVR-LSTM	0.0958	0.0242

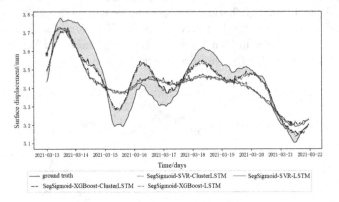

Fig. 10. The performance of different total displacement prediction models on the test set

March 20, 2022, to May 28, 2022, at different monitoring points in the same region as the validation dataset, the results are shown in Fig. 11, similarly, we give a pair of different method combinations on the validation set as shown in Table 5. It can be seen that the prediction framework we proposed still performs well on the new dataset, especially the VSXC-LSTM framework achieves the best on both evaluation indicators. This shows that our method has high prediction accuracy and has robustness for different data sets.

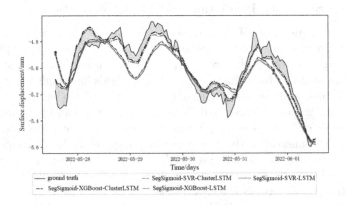

Fig. 11. The performance of different total displacement prediction models on validation sets

Table 5. The performance of different total displacement prediction models on validation sets

Predictive models	RMSE	MAPE
SegSigmoid-XGBoost-ClusterLSTM	**0.0701**	**0.0121**
SegSigmoid-SVR-ClusterLSTM	0.1081	0.0189
SegSigmoid-XGBoost-LSTM	0.0709	0.0122
SegSigmoid-SVR-LSTM	0.1091	0.0189

5   Conclusion and Outlook

We present a framework for predicting the surface displacement of landslides. Our approach uses the Kalman filter to smooth the original sequence, VMD to divide the time series into three subseries, and GA to optimize hyperparameters. We propose the SegSigmoid model for high fitting of the trend term and XGBoost to predict the periodic term. To address the insensitivity of LSTM to the data scale, we introduce ClusterLSTM. Our proposed framework achieves high prediction accuracy and outperforms other models. However, there is still room for improvement, such as reducing the number of independent prediction models and developing an end-to-end training-prediction framework based on neural networks. Additionally, expanding the proposed univariate model to a multivariate prediction model is an essential future task, as soil characteristics, structure, rainfall, and other factors significantly impact landslide displacement.

Acknowledgements. This study was supported by Natural Science Foundation of Hunan Province (grant number 2022JJ30673) and by the Graduate Innovation Project of Central South University (2023XQLH032, 2023ZZTS0304).

References

1. Lu, X., Yuan, Y.: Regional landslide disaster risk analysis based on big data. In: International Conference on Electronic Information Technology (EIT 2022), pp. 717–721. SPIE, Chengdu (2022)
2. Long, J., Li, C., Liu, Y., et al.: A multi-feature fusion transfer learning method for displacement prediction of rainfall reservoir-induced landslide with step-like deformation characteristics. Eng. Geol. **297**, 106494 (2022)
3. Holt, C.C.: Forecasting seasonals and trends by exponentially weighted moving averages. Int. J. Forecast. **201**, 5–10 (2004)
4. Zou, Z., Yan, J., Tang, H., et al.: A shear constitutive model for describing the full process of the deformation and failure of slip zone soil. Eng. Geol. **276**, 105766 (2020)
5. Dragomiretskiy, K., Zosso, D.: Variational mode decomposition. IEEE Trans. Sig. Process. **62**(3), 531–544 (2013)
6. Zhu, J., Wu, P., Chen, H., et al.: Carbon price forecasting with variational mode decomposition and optimal combined model. Phys. a: Stat. Mech. Appl. **519**, 140–158 (2019)

7. Chen, T., Guestrin, C.: XGBoost: a scalable tree boosting system. In: Proceedings of the 22nd ACM SIGKDD International Conference on Knowledge Discovery and Data Mining, pp. 785–794. Association for Computing Machinery, New York (2016)

8. Hochreiter, S., Schmidhuber, J.: Long short-term memory. Neural Comput. **98**, 1735–1780 (1997)

9. Taylor, S.-J., Letham, B.: Forecasting at scale. Am. Stat. **721**, 37–45 (2018)

10. Sanchez, V.-D.: Advanced support vector machines and kernel methods. Neurocomputing **55**, 5–20 (2003)

11. Cao, Y., Yin, K., Alexander, D.E., et al.: Using an extreme learning machine to predict the displacement of step-like landslides in relation to controlling factors. Landslides **134**, 725–736 (2016)

12. Xu, S., Niu, R.: Displacement prediction of Baijiabao landslide based on empirical mode decomposition and long short-term memory neural network in Three Gorges area. China. Comput. Geosci. **111**, 87–96 (2018)

13. Huang, Y., Han, X., Zhao, L.: Recurrent neural networks for complicated seismic dynamic response prediction of a slope system. Eng. Geol. **289**, 106198 (2021)

14. Li, Z., Zhao, Y., Liu, R., et al.: Robust and rapid clustering of KPIs for large-scale anomaly detection. In: Proceedings of the IEEE/ACM 26th International Symposium on Quality of Service (IWQoS), pp. 1–10. IEEE, Banff (2018)

15. Krishnan, R.G., Shalit, U., Sontag, D.: Deep kalman filters. arXiv preprint arXiv:1511.05121 (2015)

16. Cong, T., Tan, R., Ottewill, J.R., et al.: Anomaly detection and mode identification in multimode processes using the field Kalman filter. IEEE Trans. Control Syst. Technol. **295**, 2192–2205 (2020)

17. Cui, Q., Zhang, Y.: Optimization of parameters for FDM process with functional input based on LS-SVR. AIP Adv. **122**, 025108 (2022)

18. Hoaglin, D.C., Welsch, R.E.: The hat matrix in regression and ANOVA. Am. Stat. **321**, 17–22 (1978)

19. Welch, G., Bishop, G.: An introduction to the Kalman filter (1995)

20. Hartigan, J.A., Wong, M.A.: Algorithm AS 136: a k-means clustering algorithm. J. R. Stat. Soc. Ser. C (applied statistics) **281**, 100–108 (1979)

21. Van Der Maaten, L.: Accelerating t-SNE using tree-based algorithms. J. Mach. Learn. Res. **151**, 3221–3245 (2014)

LaneMP: Robust Lane Attention Detection Based on Mutual Perception of Keypoints

Siyuan Peng[1], Wangshu Yao[1,2,3(✉)], and Yifan Xue[1]

[1] School of Computer Science and Technology, Soochow University, Suzhou, China
wshyao@suda.edu.cn
[2] School of Soft, Soochow University, Suzhou, China
[3] Collaborative Innovation Center of Novel Software Technology and Industrialization, Suzhou, China

Abstract. Lane detection is a challenging task that requires predicting complex lane topology shapes in autonomous driving tasks. Some methods use instance segmentation to classify all pixels into lanes and backgrounds; There are also methods that predict each anchor into different lane categories based on the idea of anchor detection. However, these models are less robust and poorly detected. In order to solve these problems, we propose a robust lane attention detection network based on the mutual perception of keypoints (**LaneMP**), which uses the idea of keypoint detection to predict the keypoints on the lane and then clusters these keypoints into lane instances. Since the clustering process depends on the start points, a loss function is designed to guide the network to learn the correct start points. In addition, aiming at some special scenarios, we propose a horizontal stripe attention mechanism, which can adaptively capture the connection among keypoints through local symmetry of lanes, and improve the robustness of the network. Numerous experiments show that the network has an F1 value of 77.11% on CULane and 96.73% on the TuSimple dataset.

Keywords: Autonomous driving · Lane detection · Self-attention

1 Introduction

In the past decade, autonomous driving technology has emerged as significant research in the field of computer vision. In order to ensure the safety of autonomous vehicles, it is crucial for autonomous driving systems(ADS) to accurately understand the spatial information of lanes. Therefore, quickly calculating the shape and position information of lanes from the images acquired by the front camera is a vital step in the ADS, and lane detection requires highly accurate and real-time.

In recent years, most research has approached lane detection as an instance segmentation or object detection problem. SCNN [13] uses multi-class classification to segment pixels into either lanes or background and predicts pixels

© The Author(s), under exclusive license to Springer Nature Switzerland AG 2023
L. Iliadis et al. (Eds.): ICANN 2023, LNCS 14261, pp. 471–483, 2023.
https://doi.org/10.1007/978-3-031-44198-1_39

unrelated to lanes. PointLaneNet [2] predicts lanes based on anchor points, while LaneATT [18] uses anchor lines to expand the feature range of anchors and predict lane instances. However, when facing extreme situations such as road occlusion, these methods tend to perform poorly. In such cases, extracting hidden lane information from images becomes significant.

To address the shortcomings of previous works, we propose a robust lane attention detection network based on mutual perception of keypoints(LaneMP). First, the network employs keypoint detection to predict keypoints on lanes, reducing the computational cost of irrelevant pixels. The keypoints are then clustered into lane instances by their offsets from start points. The start point is defined as the point with the largest y-coordinate among all keypoints on the lane. Additionally, because keypoint clustering depends on start points, we design a loss function to increase the importance of predicting start points. Besides, we propose horizontal stripe attention(HSA) to facilitate local information propagation, so as to handle some special scenarios such as occlusion.

The contributions of this paper are summarized as follows:

1) We propose horizontal stripe attention (HSA) mechanism to enhance the robustness of the model, where the attention range of each keypoint is focused on a rectangular area in the horizontal direction.
2) We design a loss function, named lane focal loss, to increase the importance of predicting start points, and improve the prediction accuracy of the model indirectly, where the range of the start points is assumed in an area within several pixels from the image boundary.
3) The experimental results conducted on TuSimple and CULane datasets demonstrate that our proposed model outperforms most existing models and achieves comparable accuracy and robustness.

2   Related Work

2.1   Lane Detection

Some curve-based methods, such as [4,12,19], regard lane as a continuous curve, using CNN or transformer to encode the image, and then decode out the parameters of the corresponding curve. Additionally, Deeplab-ERFC [3] adopts the multi-class classification to predict the category of each pixel in the feature map. Fast-HBnet [14] combines the input image and the corresponding flipped image to locate the lanes. Due to the small proportion of lane pixels on the feature map, these segmentation-based methods make a lot of invalid calculations. PointLaneNet [2] takes advantage of the anchor concept in [17], and uses each pixel in the feature map as an anchor point to predict the lane. Because the anchor point contains too few lane features due to the linear prior structure of lanes, LaneATT [18] exploits the anchor line instead of the anchor point and extracts the corresponding lane features. However, the long-tail effect of these detection-based methods is obvious, and post-processing methods are required to remove redundant lanes.

Inspired by human pose estimation, some methods regard lane detection as a keypoint detection and clustering problem. PINet [9] utilizes an hourglass network to predict the location information of keypoints on the lane, and predicts an embedding feature for each keypoint by an output branch, then clusters the keypoints with similarity of the embedding features more than the threshold in the same lane instance. Unlike [9] requires additional embedding features, FOLOLane [16] predicts the offset between each keypoint and its neighboring keypoints, and then clusters by gradually extending the adjacent keypoints. However, with the dense dependence between keypoints, FOLOLane [16] may deviate from expectations with some keypoint prediction errors. To avoid this, GANet [20] indirectly clusters keypoints by predicting the offset between keypoints and their corresponding start points.

2.2   Visual Self-attention Mechanisms

The self-attention mechanism focuses limited attention on key information and learns the weight distribution of key information from the input features by weighted summation, and then it applies these weights to the input features to extract more meaningful information from them.

In visual self-attention, spatial feature or channel feature, or a mixture of both, is often used to construct relationships between pixels. SENet [6] uses a scale to control information for all channels. The scale is spread over the spatial extent of the feature map to extract more useful features. Non-local neural network [21] establishes relationships between pixels at different locations by correlations in the spatial distribution of feature maps. But in [21] each pixel focuses on the global scope, resulting in a very intensive computation. To solve this problem, CCNet [7] constructs the contextual information of all pixels in the same horizontal and vertical direction. Each pixel can finally capture the full-image dependencies through its criss-cross path. DANet [5] fuses channel and spatial features to compute the importance of each channel and each spatial location by learning channel weights and spatial weights.

Many lane detection methods, such as ESAnet [10], also use self-attention mechanisms but usually consider local connections within a lane. Inspired by [7,10], we construct associations of keypoints among different lanes in the same horizontal area to better capture useful information among different lanes.

3   Methods

3.1   Overview

The structure of LaneMP is shown in Fig. 1. The point head predicts keypoints in lanes, and in which the keypoints that exceed the threshold are used as candidate keypoints. The offset head regresses the offset between each keypoints and the start points of the lanes. Finally, all the predictions are constructed into lanes by clustering. In addition, we design a loss function to increase the importance of predicting start points. This indirectly improves the performance of the model. We also propose the horizontal stripe attention (HSA) to improve the robustness of the model.

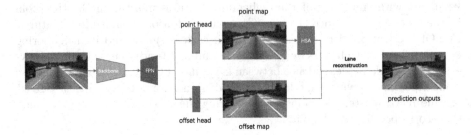

Fig. 1. the structure of LaneMP

3.2   HSA Mechanisms

When driving a car, clear lane markings can be used to assist in identifying partially obscured lanes in extreme situations, such as occlusion. This is because the distribution of keypoints on lanes is sparse, and there is a correlation between keypoints on different lanes in the same horizontal area.

In order to realize the mutual auxiliary detection of lanes in the same horizontal area, the horizontal stripe attention(**HSA**) is designed. In Fig. 2, HSA can construct the relationship of all lanes in the same horizontal area, and collect horizontal context information to enhance the subpixel-level representation ability of the network.

HSA process is following:

1. In order to improve the computational efficiency, the input feature map $f(f \in R^{C \times H' \times W'})$ is downsampled into $f_{ds}(f_{ds} \in R^{C \times P \times W'})$. where H' and W' represent the height and width of the input feature map, respectively; In addition, considering the number of points on the lane, the height of each horizontal strip area is set to 4, so $P = \frac{H'}{4}$. The P indicates the number of horizontal stripes in which the feature map is divided into. Among these stripes, two downsampling operations are used to achieve the preprocessing process of attention. Whereas, the two downsampling operations use two same convolution operations, in which convolution kernel size is $(3, 1)$, the stride is $(2, 1)$, and padding is $(1,0)$.

2. The downsampled feature map f_{ds} first uses two convolutional layers with 1×1 filters to obtain Q,K, where $Q \in R^{P \times W' \times C'}$, $K \in R^{P \times C' \times W'}$, C' is the number of channels. Q,K generate attention map $A(A \in R^{P \times W' \times W'})$ by affine transformation operation, which means the correlation among any point **p** and the total W' points in the same horizontal direction of the point **p**. In addition, the feature map f_{ds} generates $V(V \in R^{P \times C \times W'})$ from a convolutional layer with a 1×1 filter. Finally, the attention-weighted feature

$f_o(f_o \in R^{C \times P \times W'})$ is obtained by matrix multiplication operation between attention map A and V, achieving aggregation in the spatial domain.

3. After constructing attention, the weighted feature f_o upsampled 4x to achieve alignment with the original input feature map f in horizontal direction.

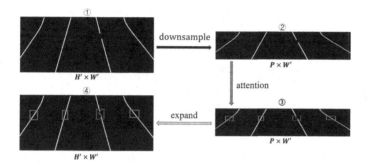

Fig. 2. HSA module. ①-②: $\frac{1}{4}$ downsampling in the horizontal direction; ②-③: the association under the same horizontal area between the unoccluded lanes (blue rectangular area) and the occluded lane (red rectangular area); ③-④: expanding downsampled feature map to input feature map in the horizontal direction.

3.3   Loss Functions

Lane Focal Loss to Predict Keypoints. Due to the design of offset loss, all keypoints are clustered through their corresponding start points to form lanes. This process demands the accuracy of the start points. So, we design a lane focal loss to increase the importance of predicting start points. As shown in Eq. 1, the lane focal loss consists of the weight parameter ζ_{yx} and the general loss function L_f, where H' and W' are the size of the feature map, and (x, y) is the coordinate of the pixels on the feature map. ζ_{yx} is used to increase the start point priority. L_f uses focal loss [11] to solve the imbalance between keypoints and other points.

$$\mathcal{L}_{\text{point}} = \frac{-1}{H' \times W'} \sum_{yx} \zeta_{yx} L_f \tag{1}$$

$$\zeta_{yx} = \begin{cases} a \, , x \in [W'_l, W' - W'_r] \text{ and } y \in [H' - H'_b, H'] \\ b \, , \qquad\qquad \text{otherwise} \end{cases} \tag{2}$$

Based on the distribution of the start points in Fig. 3(a), we assume that the start points in feature maps are concentrated in a small area, which is abbreviated as **start points regions**, as shown in Fig. 3(b). Inspired by [18] setting the image boundary pixels as start points of the anchor line, ζ_{yx} is used to increase the importance of predicting start points.

In Eq. 2, W'_l, W'_r and H'_b represent the left, right and bottom widths of the start points regions respectively; b represents the weight of the start points regions, a represents the weight of other regions. In Fig. 3(b), a corresponds to the white area, while b corresponds to the cyan area. In this article, a and b are set to 1 and 1.5, respectively. Besides, both W_l' and W_r' are set to 5 due to the horizontal symmetry of lanes and H_b' is set to 4, which ensures that more than 99% of the start points is included in start points regions.

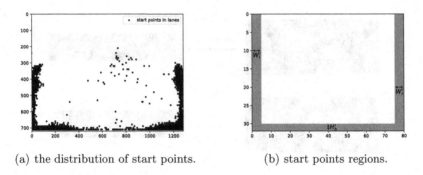

(a) the distribution of start points.   (b) start points regions.

Fig. 3. The real and hypothetical distribution of start points.

$$L_f = \begin{cases} \left(1 - \hat{P}_{yx}\right)^\alpha \log\left(\hat{P}_{yx}\right) & P_{yx} = 1, \\ (1 - P_{yx})^\beta \hat{P}_{yx}^\alpha \log\left(1 - \hat{P}_{yx}\right) & \text{otherwise} \end{cases} \tag{3}$$

In Eq. 3, α and β are both hyperparameters of focal loss, $P_{yx} = 1$ represents (x, y) is the ground truth point, $P_{yx} = 0$ represents (x, y) is the other points, and $\hat{P}_{yx}$ represents the probability that (x, y) is predicted as a keypoint.

Offset Loss to Regress Offsets. The offset loss function takes the start point to represent lane instance and regresses the offset between each keypoint and its start point. The reason why the start point represents the lane instance is that the lane usually extends upwards from the bottom of the image, so the start point tends to be farther apart and less disturbed by other keypoints. In Eq. 4, the meaning of H', W' is the same as in Eq. 1. $\hat{O}_{yx}(\hat{O}_{yx} \in R^{H' \times W' \times 2})$ represents offsets between predicted points and start points in the x-direction and y-direction, and $O_{yx}(O_{yx} \in R^{H' \times W' \times 2})$ represents offsets between ground truth points and start points in the x-direction and y-direction.

$$\mathcal{L}_{\text{offset}} = \frac{1}{H' \times W'} \sum_{yx} \left| \hat{O}_{yx} - O_{yx} \right| \tag{4}$$

The overall loss is shown in Eq. 5, where λ_{point} and λ_{offset} are the weight of the keypoint and offset loss. By adjusting the weights, we achieve comprehensive consideration of keypoints and offset prediction:

$$\mathcal{L}_{\text{total}} = \lambda_{\text{point}} \mathcal{L}_{\text{point}} + \lambda_{\text{offset}} \mathcal{L}_{\text{offset}} \tag{5}$$

3.4   Lane Reconstruction

In the inference stage, the lane construction process needs use the keypoint coordinates and corresponding offset. The entire process is shown in Fig. 4.

First, if the offset between a keypoint and its corresponding start point is less than 1, that point can be preset as a candidate start point P_c. Then, All remaining keypoints are calculated as their theoretical start points P_t based on their offsets. Those points whose distance from the corresponding theoretical start points P_t to the P_c is less than 1 are retained, and the other points are treated as error points. In this way, all preserved start points, including P_c and P_t, are hypothetically concentrated in a area, with the center point of that area considered the actual start points for that lane.

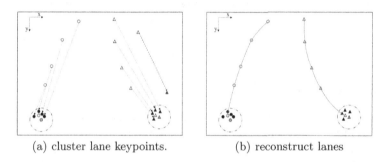

(a) cluster lane keypoints.   (b) reconstruct lanes

Fig. 4. Triangles and circles represent points on different lanes; The hollow point is the predicted keypoint; The solid blue point is the P_c; The solid black point is the P_t; The solid red triangle is the theoretical start point of the discarded, there is no corresponding lane, and the keypoint corresponding to the prediction is discarded; The solid yellow point is the center of all start points. (Color figure online)

4   Experiments Setting

4.1   Datasets

To evaluate the model, we conduct experiments on two benchmarks, including TuSimple [1] and CULane [13]. TuSimple is a real highway dataset comprising 3,626 images for training and 2,782 for testing. CULane contains 88,880 training images and 34,680 testing images, of which test images have 9 different scenarios.

4.2   Evaluation Metrics

CULane. The evaluation involves creating a continuous lane from predicted discrete points and calculating the IoU with ground truth. A predicted lane with an IoU >0.5 is true positive(TP), otherwise, it is false positive(FP) or false negative(FN). We use the F1 score to evaluate model performance in the CULane dataset. As demonstrated in Eq. 6, the F1 score is defined as the harmonic mean of precision and recall.

$$F_1 = 2 \cdot \frac{\text{precision} \cdot \text{recall}}{\text{precision} + \text{recall}} \tag{6}$$

where precision $= \frac{TP}{TP+FP}$, recall $= \frac{TP}{TP+FN}$.

TuSimple. C_{clip} represents the number of correctly predicted points, while S_{clip} is the total number of ground truth points. A predicted point is accurate if it's within 20 pixels to the ground truth point. Besides, in order to be consistent with the CULane standard, we also calculate the F1 score in the TuSimple dataset. So, the predicted lane is classified as a true positive(TP) if the keypoint accuracy rate exceeds 85%. Otherwise, it is false positive(FP) or false negative(FN).

$$accuracy = \frac{\sum_{clip} C_{clip}}{\sum_{clip} S_{clip}} \tag{7}$$

4.3   Implementation Details

ResNet-18 and ResNet-32 serve as the backbone of the LaneMP, with two versions named LaneMP-S and LaneMP-M, respectively.

The input image is cropped to 800 × 320. In Eq. 5, $\lambda_{point} = 1.0$ and $\lambda_{offset} = 0.5$. The hyperparameters a and b in Eq. 2 are set to 1 and 1.5, respectively. The hyperparameters α and β in Eq. 3 are set to 2 and 4. The Adam optimizer [8] and poly learning rate decay are used with an initial learning rate of 0.001. Our method trains for 300 and 80 epochs on the TuSimple and CULane datasets, respectively, with a batch size of 32. In testing, the keypoint threshold is set to 0.4 and T_{dis} is set to 4. Both training and testing are conducted on Tesla-A100 GPUs.

5   Experimental Results

5.1   Results on TuSimple

Table 1 validates the effectiveness of our method on the TuSimple dataset, with an F1 value of 96.73 and FPS(Frames Per Second) of 102, implying the performance of the model as accurate as other methods while also achieving a higher speed. Additionally, the performance of LaneMP-S and LaneMP-M on the TuSimple test set is almost identical, we speculate that this may be due to LaneMP-M being too redundant.

Table 1. The results on TuSimple

Methods	F1	Acc	FP	FN	FPS
SCNN [13]	95.97	96.53	6.17	**1.80**	7.5
UFLDv2 [15]	96.16	95.65	3.06	4.61	312
LaneATT [18]	96.71	95.57	3.56	3.01	250
Fast-HBNet [14]	–	**97.42**	**2.26**	2.61	39
Bézier curve [4]	–	95.65	5.10	3.90	150
PINet [9]	–	96.75	3.10	2.50	25
PointLaneNet [2]	–	95.27	4.94	4.88	111
ESAnet [10]	-	96.12	3.31	4.50	123
LaneMP-S(Ours)	**96.73**	95.77	3.65	2.88	102
LaneMP-M(Ours)	96.71	95.82	3.82	2.75	89

5.2 Results on CULane

Table 2 compares the experimental results of the LaneMP model with others, confirming the superior performance in CULane dataset [13]. Besides, the "Cross" scene lacks lane marks, so the results for this scene only display the FP value.

Some special scenarios in the CULane dataset, especially "Crowded" and "Shadow" scene, the performance of the model is more obvious with other methods, which is mainly attributed to that HSA can assist in predicting some blurred and even invisible lanes in special scenes and lane focal loss can improve the importance of predicting the start points.

Table 2. the results on CULane

Methods	Total	Normal	Crowded	Dazzle	Shadow	No line	Arrow	Curve	Cross*	Night	FPS
SCNN [13]	71.60	90.60	69.70	58.50	66.90	43.40	84.10	64.40	1990	66.10	7.5
UFLDv2 [15]	75.90	**92.50**	74.90	65.70	75.30	49.00	88.50	70.20	1864	70.60	312
LaneATT [18]	75.11	91.17	73.32	65.69	69.58	47.48	86.62	63.07	1059	68.80	250
Fast-HBNet [14]	73.10	91.90	71.60	64.70	66.70	46.80	85.30	65.10	2306	66.70	39
Bézier curve [4]	75.57	91.59	73.20	69.20	76.74	48.05	87.16	62.45	**888**	69.90	150
PINet [9]	74.40	90.30	72.30	66.30	68.40	49.80	83.70	65.60	1427	67.70	25
ESAnet [10]	74.20	92.00	73.10	63.10	75.10	45.80	88.10	68.80	2001	69.50	123
LaneMP-S(Ours)	76.79	91.77	75.74	**69.79**	77.80	50.67	**88.54**	**72.98**	2572	71.20	102
LaneMP-M(Ours)	**77.11**	91.92	**76.40**	68.45	**78.24**	**51.42**	88.10	72.88	2678	**71.53**	89

Nevertheless, the FP value of the model surpasses other methods in the cross scene. This is because both the lane focal loss and HSA module require lanes to function effectively. Thus, the model's detection performance in the "Cross" scene is compromised due to the absence of lane marking.

5.3   Qualitative Results

Fig. 5 reveals the qualitative results of our model and other lane detection models. The first row of pictures in the figure are from the TuSimple dataset, and the others are from the CULane dataset.

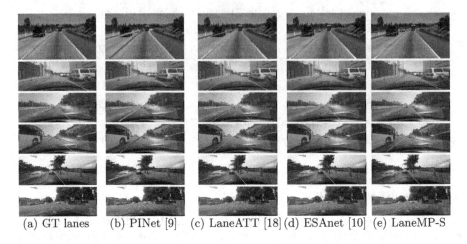

(a) GT lanes   (b) PINet [9]   (c) LaneATT [18] (d) ESAnet [10]   (e) LaneMP-S

Fig. 5. LaneMP and others' qualitative results in TuSimple and CULane

It can be seen that in the face of the shadow and occlusion scenes in the third row and fourth row, the performance of LaneMP is better than other methods. In addition, the model can predict the existing but unmarked lanes in the third row, while there will be misjudgment in the penultimate row. This may be due to some interference with the lane by the rightmost sidewalk. Besides, from the last row of all pictures, the method predicts inexistent lanes in the "Cross" scene. We speculate that it is because the dense white stripes in the zebra crossing interfere with the detection of lanes.

5.4   Ablation Study

We use the CULane dataset for ablation experiments, and all experiments are based on the minimal version of LaneMP-S.

Effectiveness of HSA. Table 3 verifies that HSA improves model performance in three ways: without using attention, using non-local attention, and using HSA.

From the experimental results, it can be seen that when non-local attention is used, the prediction result is better than the method without attention, but because non-local attention is focused on the global scope, it cannot make good use of the characteristics of the lane itself, so compared with HSA, there are still some gaps in the experimental results. Based on the linear shape of lanes, the results in Table 3 show that HSA can effectively utilize the correlation between lanes to adapt to some difficult detection scenarios.

Hyperparameters of Lane Focal Loss. Change the values of a and b in Eq. 2, and verify the different weights of start points in Table 4. In the first row, the values of a and b are the same as 1, which is equivalent to not increasing the importance of predicting start points, and the lane focal loss degenerates into focal loss [11].

Table 3. effectiveness of HSA

Baseline	non-local	HSA	F1
✔			75.50
✔	✔		76.23
✔		✔	**76.79**

Table 4. weights of lane focal loss

a	b	F1
1	1	76.23
1	1.5	**76.79**
1	2	76.63
1	3	76.46

Observing the whole table, lane focal loss can enhance the accuracy of the model. This shows that increasing the importance of predicting start points can enhance the performance of the model to a certain extent. When comparing the results of the last three rows, we can observe that as the importance of predicting start points increases, the experimental results become worse and worse, indicating that increasing the importance of predicting start points does not always improve the performance of the model. This may be because over-enhancing the importance of predicting start points will destroy the balance between keypoints and other points in the lane focal loss.

6   Conclusion

We propose a LaneMP model for lane detection. According to the local symmetry characteristics of lanes, an HSA mechanism is designed to make the model have the ability to deal with extreme scenes such as occlusion. In addition, since the keypoints clustering of lanes is highly dependent on the start points, this paper designs a lane focal loss function, which increases the importance of predicting start points in the loss function, improves the accuracy of predicting start points, and improves the performance of the model indirectly. The experimental results show that the model in this paper can effectively deal with lane detection scenarios that lack sufficient information, such as lane occlusion. The performance is better than many current methods in terms of accuracy and robustness.

Acknowledgements. This work was partially supported by Priority Academic Program Development of Jiangsu Higher Education Institutions (PAPD), Collaborative Innovation Center of Novel Software Technology and Industrialization.

References

1. TuSimple dataset. https://github.com/TuSimple/tusimple-benchmark
2. Chen, Z., Liu, Q., Lian, C.: PointLaneNet: efficient end-to-end CNNs for accurate real-time lane detection. In: 2019 IEEE Intelligent Vehicles Symposium (IV), pp. 2563–2568 (2019). https://doi.org/10.1109/IVS.2019.8813778
3. Fan, Y., Wang, Z., Chen, C., Zhang, X., Lu, Q.: Multi-class lane semantic segmentation of expressway dataset based on aerial view. In: Pimenidis, E., Angelov, P., Jayne, C., Papaleonidas, A., Aydin, M. (eds.) Artificial Neural Networks and Machine Learning - ICANN 2022, LNCS, vol. 13531, pp. 200–211. Springer, Cham (2022). https://doi.org/10.1007/978-3-031-15934-3_17
4. Feng, Z., Guo, S., Tan, X., Xu, K., Wang, M., Ma, L.: Rethinking efficient lane detection via curve modeling. In: 2022 IEEE/CVF Conference on Computer Vision and Pattern Recognition (CVPR), pp. 17041–17049. IEEE (2022)
5. Fu, J., et al.: Dual attention network for scene segmentation. In: 2019 IEEE/CVF Conference on Computer Vision and Pattern Recognition (CVPR), pp. 3141–3149. IEEE (2019)
6. Hu, J., Shen, L., Albanie, S., Sun, G., Wu, E.: Squeeze-and-excitation networks. IEEE Trans. Pattern Anal. Mach. Intell. **42**(8), 2011–2023 (2020)
7. Huang, Z., Wang, X., Huang, L., Huang, C., Wei, Y., Liu, W.: CCNet: Criss-cross attention for semantic segmentation. In: 2019 IEEE/CVF International Conference on Computer Vision (ICCV), pp. 603–612. IEEE (2019)
8. Kingma, D.P., Ba, J.: Adam: a method for stochastic optimization, January 2017. http://arxiv.org/abs/1412.6980
9. Ko, Y., Lee, Y., Azam, S., Munir, F., Jeon, M., Pedrycz, W.: Key points estimation and point instance segmentation approach for lane detection. IEEE Trans. Intell. Transport. Syst. **23**(7), 8949–8958 (2022)
10. Lee, M., Lee, J., Lee, D., Kim, W., Hwang, S., Lee, S.: Robust lane detection via expanded self attention. In: 2022 IEEE/CVF Winter Conference on Applications of Computer Vision (WACV), pp. 1949–1958 (2022)
11. Lin, T.Y., Goyal, P., Girshick, R., He, K., Dollar, P.: Focal loss for dense object detection. IEEE Trans. Pattern Anal. Mach. Intell. **42**(2), 2980–2988 (2020)
12. Liu, R., Yuan, Z., Liu, T., Xiong, Z.: End-to-end lane shape prediction with transformers. In: 2021 IEEE Winter Conference on Applications of Computer Vision (WACV), pp. 3693–3701. IEEE (2021)
13. Pan, X., Shi, J., Luo, P., Wang, X., Tang, X.: Spatial as deep: spatial CNN for traffic scene understanding. In: AAAI, vol. 32, no. 1 (2018)
14. Pang, G., Zhang, B., Teng, Z., Ma, N., Fan, J.: Fast-HBNet: hybrid branch network for fast lane detection. IEEE Trans. Intell. Transp. Syst. **23**(9), 15673–15683 (2022)
15. Qin, Z., Zhang, P., Li, X.: Ultra fast deep lane detection with hybrid anchor driven ordinal classification. IEEE Trans. Pattern Anal. Mach. Intell. 1–14 (2022). https://doi.org/10.1109/TPAMI.2022.3182097
16. Qu, Z., Jin, H., Zhou, Y., Yang, Z., Zhang, W.: Focus on local: detecting lane marker from bottom up via key point. In: 2021 IEEE/CVF Conference on Computer Vision and Pattern Recognition (CVPR), pp. 14117–14125 (2021)
17. Redmon, J., Farhadi, A.: YOLO9000: better, faster, stronger. In: 2017 IEEE Conference on Computer Vision and Pattern Recognition (CVPR), pp. 6517–6525 (2017). https://doi.org/10.1109/CVPR.2017.690

18. Tabelini, L., Berriel, R., Paixao, T.M., Badue, C., De Souza, A.F., Oliveira-Santos, T.: Keep your eyes on the lane: real-time attention-guided lane detection. In: 2021 IEEE/CVF Conference on Computer Vision and Pattern Recognition (CVPR), pp. 294–302. IEEE (2021)
19. Tabelini, L., Berriel, R., Paixão, T.M., Badue, C., De Souza, A.F., Oliveira-Santos, T.: PolyLaneNet: lane estimation via deep polynomial regression. In: 2020 25th International Conference on Pattern Recognition (ICPR), pp. 6150–6156 (2021)
20. Wang, J., et al.: A Keypoint-based global association network for lane detection. In: 2022 IEEE/CVF Conference on Computer Vision and Pattern Recognition (CVPR), pp. 1382–1391 (2022)
21. Wang, X., Girshick, R., Gupta, A., He, K.: Non-local neural networks. In: 2018 IEEE/CVF Conference on Computer Vision and Pattern Recognition, pp. 7794–7803. IEEE (2018). https://doi.org/10.1109/CVPR.2018.00813

LE-MVSNet: Lightweight Efficient Multi-view Stereo Network

Changfei Kong[1], Ziyi Zhang[1], Jiafa Mao[1], Sixian Chan[1(✉)],
and Weigou Sheng[2]

[1] Zhejiang University of Technology, HangZhou 310023, China
sxchan@zjut.edu.cn
[2] The Department of Computer Science, Hangzhou Normal University,
Hangzhou 311121, China

Abstract. Multi-view Stereo(MVS) has been studied for decades as a critical algorithm for 3D reconstruction. Lately, many learning-based methods have improved the reconstruction performance of traditional algorithms, but they pay limited attention to memory consumption and runtime. To address this issue, we propose a novel and effective learning-based MVS framework(LE-MVSNet), based on our exploration of the depth hypothesis and cost volume in this work. Firstly, to decrease the number of depth hypotheses, we establish a more reasonable depth hypothesis space based on its sparse point cloud corresponding to the image set, replacing the previous method of randomly depth hypothesis in evenly divided depth layers within a predefined depth range. Secondly, to reduce memory consumption, we design a lightweight group-wise correlation by compressing the channel of the aggregated cost volumes to one. In addition, for acceleration, we propose SE-UNet, which executes U-Net regularization in the width and height direction, and SE-Net for self-attention in the depth direction. Finally, our method achieves competitive performance on DTU and BlendedMVS dataset with significantly higher efficiency. Compared to MVSNet, our method reduces memory consumption by 52.78% and runtime by 88.57%.

Keywords: 3D Reconstruction · Multi-view Stereo · Depth Map Estimation · Deep Learning

1 Introduction

Multi-view Stereo (MVS) is a procedure of image-based 3D reconstruction: given a series of images and corresponding camera poses, multi-view stereo (MVS) aims to reconstruct a high-precision 3D geometric model by estimating depth maps. Multi-view stereo(MVS) is a critical task in 3D vision, with applications ranging from cultural relics protection [14] to virtual reality. Despite decades of research, MVS remains challenging because of costly runtime and memory consumption. Our paper focuses on the speed improvement and memory reduction of MVS

© The Author(s), under exclusive license to Springer Nature Switzerland AG 2023
L. Iliadis et al. (Eds.): ICANN 2023, LNCS 14261, pp. 484–497, 2023.
https://doi.org/10.1007/978-3-031-44198-1_40

to extend it to edge devices and time-critical tasks such as autonomous driving, robotic navigation and simultaneous localization and mapping (SLAM).

The success of Convolutional Neural Networks(CNN) in almost all areas of computer vision has given MVS problems a whole new way forward. Many learning-based methods [15,26,27] have performed better than some traditional methods [10,20] on MVS benchmarks while paying relatively little attention to memory consumption and runtime. Most current learning-based MVS methods warp source images into the reference camera frustum to form 3D cost volumes, using 3D CNNs to regularize it. 3D CNNs are straightforward for cost volume regularization, but the overhead is significant for devices. Some scholars tried to break through this bottleneck. They propose multi-stage frameworks [12,26] from coarse to fine. While the coarse-to-fine strategy reduces memory consumption, coarse-stage depth prediction may be wrong at large depth intervals, affecting high-resolution depth map prediction after multiple stages.

Our observation is that the unreasonable depth Hypothesis sampling strategy makes the depth plane of the plane sweep algorithm not fit the target object. Most methods uniformly sample depth assumptions within the depth interval given by the dataset, which probably produces many unnecessary depth assumptions. Sparse point clouds can help us determine the approximate location of objects and divide reasonable depth intervals and fewer depth hypotheses. Therefore, some methods [6,11] calculate probability distributions to derive the specific approximate range of depth sampling for each pixel, concentrating as much depth plane as possible on the target object. Camera poses can be gained through cameras, radar, and industrial robotic arms. Due to the cheap cost of cameras, the visual method SFM to calculate the pose of the image set has become the mainstream choice. The traditional MVS algorithm OpenMVS [4] projects sparse points to the reference image to obtain a sparse depth map and then performs triangulation to obtain the initial depth map. In this work, we propose LE-MVSNet, a novel and effective learning-based MVS framework, based on our exploration of more reasonable depth hypothetical sampling strategies to focus on reducing runtime and memory consumption.

The main contributions of this work are listed below:

- To decrease the number of depth hypotheses, we establish a more reasonable depth hypothesis space based on its sparse point cloud corresponding to the image set, replacing the previous method of randomly depth hypothesis in evenly divided depth layers within a predefined depth range.
- To reduce memory consumption, we design a lightweight group-wise correlation by compressing the channel of the aggregated cost volumes to one.
- For acceleration, we propose SE-UNet, which executes U-Net regularization in the width and height direction, and SE-Net for self-attention in the depth direction.
- Our method achieves competitive performance on DTU and BlendedMVS dataset with significantly higher efficiency. Compared to MVSNet, our method reduces memory consumption by 52.78% and runtime by 88.57%.

2   Related Work

2.1   Learning-Based MVS

With the recent rapid development of deep learning, MVS tasks have introduced CNNs and transformers to achieve better reconstruction results. Learning-based MVS approaches warp source images' feature into the camera frustum of the reference image to build 3D cost volumes fused through variance operation [8, 15,27]. This practice transforms MVS into a new task, predicting its depth map for each image.

In this approach, 3D CNNs are a general regularization due to their ability to aggregate features, while the overhead is significant for devices. Some recurrent methods [24,25,28] propose using RNN-CNN hybrid networks to sequentially regularize cost volumes along the depth dimension to mitigate this limitation. R-MVSNet [28] adopts Convolutional GRUs for cost volume regularization. D^2HC-RMVSNet [25] proposes a hybrid module that absorbs the advantages of LSTM and U-Net to regularize cost volumes. AA-RMVSNet [24] proposes an intra-view feature aggregation module and an inter-view cost volume aggregation module, which effectively improves the effect of dense point cloud reconstruction. They can predict depth maps in an extensive depth range with limited memory but sacrifice time.

Multi-stage approaches [5,8,11,12,26] take into account both memory consumption and run time. They foremost estimate low-size depth maps with large depth ranges and then establish a narrow depth range on this depth map to iteratively sample and refine it to generate a high-resolution depth map. CVP-MVSNet [26] form image pyramids and construct cascade cost volume based on the above process. Some methods [8,23,24] introduce attention modules to extract features in the global context and learn the association between 2D features and 3D cost volumes. However, this method may generate mistakes in the coarse stage depth prediction in the large depth range, which affects the high-resolution depth map prediction after multiple stages.

2.2   Depth Hypothetical Sampling Strategy

The plane sweep algorithm [7] divides a continuous depth range into discrete depth planes. CNNs are considered appropriate for classification. For example, softmax predicts the likelihood of each pixel falling on each depth plane to calculate its depth value. Our point is that the essence of the plane sweep algorithm is to test the depth hypothesis. Therefore, establishing a reasonable depth hypothesis is of great significance for the performance improvement of MVS. Some researchers [6,11] have investigated improvements in depth hypothetical sampling for MVS.

Cheng et al. in [6] proposes constructing adaptive volumes using variance-based uncertainty estimates. The adaptive volumes gradually refines the depth interval from a small number of planes in multiple stages, selecting new depth samples based on the confidence of the pixels in the currently estimated depth.

Gao et al. in [11] selects different sampling strategies at different stages: uniform sampling or probability distribution sampling. These methods often take much time to execute the sampling strategy. In contrast, our method can sample fewer and more accurate depth assumptions more efficiently and adaptively select depth division based on image texture information.

3   Method

We intend to design an efficient end-to-end MVS architecture(LE-MVSNet). We chose a flexible and expressive depth map as a scene representation. Given the reference image I_0 and its adjacent graph source image $\{I_i\}_0^{N-1}$, as well as their camera intrinsic and extrinsic parameter matrices, our learning-based MVS framework quickly predicted an accurate I_0's depth map. Fusing all depth maps of the image set can reconstruct a dense point cloud. The architecture of LE-MVSNet is described in Fig. 1. The first step is to extract multi-scale 2D features with CNN and DCN in Sect. 3.1. Then, DSRE adopts sparse point cloud initialization depth hypothetical space in Sect. 3.2. In addition, we adopt group-wise correlation to aggregate cost volumes and SE-UNet to regularize cost volumes in Sect. 3.3. Finally, the winner-take-all strategy regresses to the final pixel-wise depth. Sec3.4 gives our loss function.

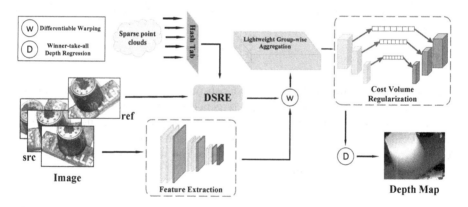

Fig. 1. LE-MVSNet architecture. LE-MVSNet extracts basic features by eight layers CNN and rich features by DCN. The DSRE module establishes depth hypothesis sampling of Gaussian distributions based on sparse point clouds. The lightweight group-wise aggregation module adopts the group-wise correlation to aggregate cost volumes. Finally, SE-UNet regularizes cost volumes.

3.1   Image Features

The essence of MVS is dense matching in multiple perspectives. Therefore, extracting multi-scale features of images is the first step of MVS. We use the

CNN-DCN module to accomplish this task. In detail, we employ the same 8-layer 2D CNN as [27,30] to extract image features.

Untextured and weakly textured areas are well-known challenges in 3D reconstruction. We expect larger receptive fields of convolutions for those regions. In comparison, smaller receptive fields are more needed for regions with rich textures. It is a generic practice [8,22,24] to adjust the receptive field adaptively with DCNv2 [32]. DCN operates deformable convolution to enrich features, which learns extra offsets for sampling position. The deformable convolution is defined as:

$$f'(p) = \sum_k w_k \cdot f(p + p_k + \Delta p_k)\Delta m_k \tag{1}$$

In Eq. 1, f is the feature of pixel p, and w_k and p_k are the convolution kernel parameters and fixed offset, respectively. Δp_k and Δm_k are the offsets and weights resulting from learning deformable convolutions. We only use DCNv2 [32] once after CNN. DCN only once enables adaptive adjustment of accepted domains based on local context at a limited cost.

3.2 Depth Sampling Range Estimation

Most learning-based MVS frameworks [27] typically employ soft-argmax operations to regress probability bodies to obtain depth maps based on plane sweep stereo [7]. In other words, the soft-argmax operation calculates expectations in the direction of depth:

$$D = \sum_{d=d_{min}}^{d_{max}} d \cdot P(d) \tag{2}$$

where, d_{max}, d_{min}, and the division of depth planes are what we focus on optimizing. A sparse point cloud $\{p_{w,i}\}_0^n$ is generated while the SFM algorithm calculates the camera pose in the visual method. Depth sampling range estimation(DSRE) module guides establishing these three elements by sparse point clouds. Firstly, we convert the sparse points of the world coordinate system to the camera coordinate system:

$$P = \begin{bmatrix} x \\ y \\ z \\ 1 \end{bmatrix}^T = [R\, t]\, P_w \tag{3}$$

In Eq. 3, P and P_w are homogeneous coordinates in the camera frame and world coordinates, respectively. R and t are rotation and translation matrices in the exterior parameter matrix, respectively. We only record the depth of the sparse point$\{P_{d,i}|P_{d,i} = z, z > 0\}_{i=0}^n$ in the reference image viewing angle. Although the points are sparse, this step can be run in parallel. Because in Colmap [20], SFM algorithms usually store sparse point clouds in Sqlist. In addition, we modified

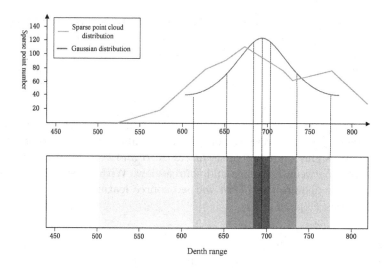

Fig. 2. Distribution of scan1's sparse point cloud over the depth range in DTU dataset [1]. The DSER module uses the Gaussian distribution to fit this probability distribution. Finally, sampling on the Gaussian distribution obtains the depth hypothesis.

the SFM algorithm to use hash tables to record sparse point clouds for parallel computation. Consequently, the depth hypothesis range$[d_{min}, d_{max}]$ is inferred:

$$\begin{cases} d_{min} = \alpha \cdot min\{P_{d,i}\} \\ d_{max} = \beta \cdot max\{P_{d,i}\} \end{cases} \tag{4}$$

In Eq. 4, α and β are relaxation coefficients used to expand the depth range acceptance domain to a limited extent. For the division of the depth hypothesis, we assume that it follows the Gaussian distribution $G \sim N(\mu = \frac{d_{max}+d_{min}}{2}, \sigma^2)$ according to its uncertainty [16]. It is very appropriate to use the Bayesian neural network BNN to predict the depth interval distribution from $\{p_{d,i}\}_{i=0}^{n}$. In Fig. 2, we designed BNN with only one hidden layer: the input size is the number of depth points in the reference image, and the output size is the number of depth intervals $D = 96$. The probability distribution of the output also follows the Gaussian distribution. DSRE module is self-contained. In Fig. 1, it can compute in parallel with feature extraction and warp operations. Therefore, DSRE modules only introduce limited memory consumption without affecting runtime time. This module establishes fewer and more accurate assumptions, which can reduce the runtime and memory consumption of later cost establishment and regularization.

3.3   Cost Volume

Most current learning-based MVS methods [24,26,27,30] construct front-to-parallel planes (3D cost volumes) for sampled depth hypotheses and feature maps based on plane sweep stereo [7]. MVSNet [27] is the first to introduce 3D cost volumes from the field of binocular stereo matching to MVS. It is a prerequisite for accelerating one-to-many feature matching tasks with GPUs. Similarly, we apply differentiable warping to convert source images to the reference perspective.

$$p_{i,j} = K(RK_0^{-1} \cdot p_{src} \cdot d + t) \tag{5}$$

Equation 5 describes the pixel p_{src} of source images converted to the corresponding pixel $p_{i,j}$ in the reference perspective via differentiable warping. K_0 and K_i are references and source intrinsic matrices. R and t are rotation and translation matrices between reference and source view. With differentiable bilinear interpolation, we acquire the $i-th$ warped source feature maps and the $j-$th depth hypothesis $F_i(p_{i,j})$.

Cost Aggregation. This step aggregates multiple source images to form a single cost per pixel p and depth hypothesis D_j. Previous practices [26,27,30] used variance to calculate feature volumes based on the assumption that all views should be equally important. Taking into account factors such as occlusion, literature [31] points out that the higher similarity between views should have more weight in the aggregation. We use group-wise correlation [22,23,31] to measure visual similarity between reference features and source volumes in an efficient way:

$$S_i(p,j)^g = \frac{G}{C}\langle F_0(p)^g, F_i(p_{i,j})^g \rangle \tag{6}$$

where $g = 0, 1, 2, ..., G-1$. $S_i(p,j)^g \in \mathbb{R}^G$ represents the inner product of F_0 and F_i in the depth direction in the i-th group. This is a straightforward approach because the local maximum similarity can represent the relationship between the views. $\sum S_i(p,j)^g$ is the sum of the similarities of the i-th group. Then, the weighted average of all the F_i yields the corresponding 3D cost volume **C**:

$$\mathbf{C} = \frac{1}{N-1} \sum_{k=1}^{N-1} max\left[\sum S_i(p,j)^q\right]\Gamma_k \tag{7}$$

In this way, those critical views receive more significant weight. Compared with the original group-wise correlation method, we reduce the channel of the aggregated cost volumes to 1. Compared to calculating variance, lightwight group-wise correlation does not incur much memory consumption.

Cost Volume Regularization. Our observation is that there is less noise in the height and width directions and more noise in the depth direction. Therefore, depth D and height H ,width W should not be regularized simultaneously. 3D CNNs [3,8,27] are usually adopted to cost volume $C \in \mathbb{R}^{B \times C \times D \times H \times W}$ regularization to smooth out the final depth map. We propose SE-UNet, which executes U-Net regularization in the width and height direction, and SE-Net [13] for self-attention in the depth direction. SENet was the winner of the last ImageNet competition. It is ideal for focusing on correlations between depth planes in a cost volume. The importance of each depth is automatically obtained by learning to increase the valuable depth and suppress the less helpful depth. In Fig. 1, we bridge SENet three times on 3D U-Net. Our introduction of SENet only brings a limited amount of parameter improvement, which significantly affects the performance improvement of the model.

3.4 Loss

Like most existing learning-based MVS [22,26,27], we use the L1 norm to calculate ground truth and estimated depth. We also introduced focal loss [17] to strengthen oversight of unconfident areas. [8,11]demonstrated the effectiveness of focal loss [17] in MVS. Our loss is defined below:

$$Loss = \lambda \cdot L_{fl} + \sum_{p \in \Omega} \|D_{GT}(p) - D(p)\|_1 \tag{8}$$

In Eq. 8, L_{fl} is focal loss, and λ balances L_{fl} and L1 norm. GT is ground truth measurements. Ω is the valid set of pixels with GT. The loss L_{fl} is defined as:

$$L_{fl} = -(1 - P(p))^2 log(P(p)) \tag{9}$$

In Eq. 9, $P(p)$ stands for confidence in predicting pix p's depth and is the probability sum of the four depth hypotheses closest to $D(p)$.

4   Experiments

4.1   Datasets

The DTU dataset [1] is a large indoor dataset for MVS. Hence, it is possible to obtain the internal and external parameters of the camera at different viewing angles of each object. The dataset consists of 124 scenes, each shot from 49 or 64 locations, including a wide variety of objects, corresponding to the number of RGB images in the scene or scan, to solve MVS problems, each with an image resolution of 1600 × 1200 pixels. We use official evaluation metrics to evaluate our proposed method in the DTU dataset [1] with other learning-based methods. **Acc.** and **Comp.** are the accuracy and completeness scores of the model reconstruction, respectively. **Overall** is the average of the two indicators.

BlendedMVS [29] is a new large-scale dataset for MVS. The dataset contains 113 different scenes with a variety of different camera tracks, each consisting of 20 to 1000 input images. The BlendedMVS dataset does not give ground truth point clouds for quantitative evaluation. To prove the scalability of the network, we test the model on the BlendedMVS dataset, which train on the DTU dataset.

4.2   Implementation Details

We implement LE-MVSNet with Pytorch [18] and train it on the DTU dataset [1]. We apply COLMAP-SFM [19] to acquire sparse point clouds We set the number of input images $N = 5$, and the image resolution is 640×512. We choose $\alpha = 0.98$ and $\beta = 1.02$ in DSER and $\lambda = 0.5$ in Loss. The model is trained with Adam for 40 epochs with an initial learning rate of 0.001, which decays by a factor of 0.5, respectively, after 10, 16, 22, and 28 epochs. The batch size is 4 on 1 NVIDIA RTX 3090Ti GPU.

4.3   3D Reconstruction Performance

Table 1. Quantitative results of different methods on the DTU evaluation set [1]. The runtime is measured by the input image resolution of 1600×1200.

	Methods	Acc. (mm)	Comp. (mm)	Overall (mm)	Runtime
Traditional	Camp [2]	0.835	0.554	0.695	–
	Furu [9]	0.613	0.941	0.777	–
	Tola [21]	0.342	1.190	0.766	-
	Gipuma [10]	**0.283**	0.873	0.578	–
	Colmap [20]	0.400	0.664	0.532	–
Learning-based	MVSNet [27]	0.396	0.527	0.462	1.93 s
	R-MVSNet [28]	0.383	0.452	0.417	3.65 s
	Point-MVSNet [5]	0.342	0.411	0.376	3.35 s
	Fast-MVSNet [30]	0.336	0.403	0.370	0.6 s
	CVP-MVSNet [26]	0.296	0.406	**0.351**	1.29 s
	Vis-MVSnet [31]	0.369	0.361	0.365	5.23 s
	D^2HC-RMVSNet [25]	0.395	0.378	0.357	8.0 s
	AA-RMVSNet [24]	0.376	**0.339**	0.357	26.3 s
	Ours	0.438	0.394	0.416	**0.24 s**

We compare LE-MVSNet with traditional methods [2,9,10,20,21] and recent learning-based methods [5,24–28,30,31]. The results of the quantification are shown in Table 1. Our approach achieves a competitive effect in completeness. On the DTU dataset [1], we visualize 3D dense point clouds by Fast-MVSNet and LE-MVSNet. In addition, we qualitatively compared CVP-MVSNet on the Blendmvs dataset [29]. Our solution results in more prosperous and complete point clouds. In Fig. 3 and Fig. 4, our method retains more detail at the boundary with other efficient MVS method [26,30]. As an efficient MVS framework, the 3D reconstruction performance of LE-MVSNet is acceptable.

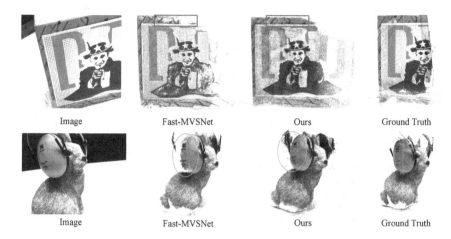

Fig. 3. Qualitative comparisons with Fast-MVSNet of Scan13 and Scan 33 in the DTU dataset [1].

Fig. 4. Qualitative comparisons with CVP-MVSNet in the BlendedMVS dataset [29].

4.4 GPU Memory and Runtime

The input image resolution in Table 1 is 1600×1200. Notably, the inference time of our method is 0.24 s, which is faster than previous methods. We compare memory consumption and runtime with several learning-based MVS methods: MVSNet [27], Fast-MVSNet [30]and CVP-MVSNet [26]. As shown in Fig. 5, memory consumption and runtime increase linearly with image resolution. At a resolution size of 1152×864 (51.8%), memory consumption and runtime are

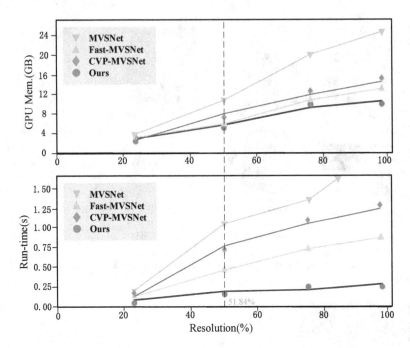

Fig. 5. Relates GPU memory and runtime to input resolution. The maximum image resolution is $1600 \times 1200(100\%)$.

reduced by 52.78% and 88.57% compared to MVSNet, by 5.26% and 53.85% compared to Fast-MVSNet, by 68.80% and 63.08% compared to CVP-MVSNet. In summary, our method is more efficient regarding memory consumption and runtime than the previous method.

4.5   Ablation Study

We perform ablation experiments to verify the effectiveness of each component in LE-MVSNet. The implemented baseline is basically based on MVSNet [27], measured by our experimental environment. The input image resolution is 1152×864. As shown in Table 2, DCN enriches features, resulting in a 15.2% improvement in completeness with a small amount of time and memory consumption. Memory consumption and runtime are significantly reduced after applying DSRE. It is mainly due to the simplification of the depth assumption. Lightweight group-wise correlation(LG) considers the inconsistency of view weights, which effectively improves the completeness and accuracy of the model. In addition, LG replaces variance aggregation cost volume, which can effectively reduce memory consumption. SE-UNet dramatically reduces the runtime of 3D CNNs at the cost of adding only a few parameters.

Table 2. Ablation study on DTU dataset. The input image resolution is 1152×864.

Model Settings				DTU Benchmark				
DCN	DSRE	LG	SE-UNet	Acc. (mm)	Comp. (mm)	Overall (mm)	Mem. (Mb)	Time(s)
				0.467	0.497	0.482	10847	1.05
✓				0.452	0.422	0.437	10924	1.08
✓	✓			0.446	0.418	0.432	6768	0.71
✓	✓	✓		0.441	0.405	0.423	5047	0.33
✓	✓	✓	✓	0.438	0.394	0.416	5121	0.12

5   Conclusions

In this paper, we have proposed LE-MVSNet, a novel and efficient learning-based MVS architecture. Inherited from the traditional 3D reconstruction pipeline, LE-MVSNet applies sparse point clouds to accelerate MVS for the first time. The DSRE module uses BNN to learn the probability distribution of sparse point clouds to optimize deep hypothesis sampling. Besides, We apply SE-UNet to regularize 3D cost volumes aggregated by lightweight group-wise correlation. Extensive experiments have been conducted on DTU and BlendedMVS datasets and demonstrate that our model dramatically improves the reconstruction speed of MVS and is more suitable for memory-limited devices. Our attempt will provide some insights and inspire researchers to reconsider the role of sparse point clouds in MVS frameworks. Our results in a resolution of 1600×1200 reach 0.24 s, but real-time high-resolution reconstruction still requires effort.

Acknowledgements. This work is partially supported by the National Natural Science Foundation of China (Grant Nos. 62176237 and 61906168), Zhejiang Provincial Natural Science Foundation of China (Grant No. LY23F020023), the Hangzhou AI major scientific and technological innovation project (2022AIZD0061) and the "Pioneer" and "Leading Goose" R&D Program of Zhejiang Province (Grant No. 2023C01022).

References

1. Aanæs, H., Jensen, R.R., Vogiatzis, G., Tola, E., Dahl, A.B.: Large-scale data for multiple-view stereopsis. Int. J. Comput. Vision **120**, 153–168 (2016)
2. Campbell, N.D.F., Vogiatzis, G., Hernández, C., Cipolla, R.: Using multiple hypotheses to improve depth-maps for multi-view stereo. In: Forsyth, D., Torr, P., Zisserman, A. (eds.) ECCV 2008. LNCS, vol. 5302, pp. 766–779. Springer, Heidelberg (2008). https://doi.org/10.1007/978-3-540-88682-2_58
3. Cao, C., Ren, X., Fu, Y.: Mvsformer: multi-view stereo by learning robust image features and temperature-based depth. Trans. Mach. Learn. Res
4. Cernea, D.: OpenMVS: multi-view stereo reconstruction library (2020). https://cdcseacave.github.io/openMVS

5. Chen, R., Han, S., Xu, J., Su, H.: Point-based multi-view stereo network. In: Proceedings of the IEEE/CVF International Conference on Computer Vision, pp. 1538–1547 (2019)

6. Cheng, S., Xu, Z., Zhu, S., Li, Z., Li, L.E., Ramamoorthi, R., Su, H.: Deep stereo using adaptive thin volume representation with uncertainty awareness. In: Proceedings of the IEEE/CVF Conference on Computer Vision and Pattern Recognition, pp. 2524–2534 (2020)

7. Collins, R.T.: A space-sweep approach to true multi-image matching. In: Proceedings CVPR IEEE Computer Society Conference on Computer Vision and Pattern Recognition, pp. 358–363. IEEE (1996)

8. Ding, Y., et al.: Transmvsnet: global context-aware multi-view stereo network with transformers. In: Proceedings of the IEEE/CVF Conference on Computer Vision and Pattern Recognition, pp. 8585–8594 (2022)

9. Furukawa, Y., Ponce, J.: Accurate, dense, and robust multiview stereopsis. IEEE Trans. Pattern Anal. Mach. Intell. **32**(8), 1362–1376 (2009)

10. Galliani, S., Lasinger, K., Schindler, K.: Massively parallel multiview stereopsis by surface normal diffusion. In: Proceedings of the IEEE International Conference on Computer Vision, pp. 873–881 (2015)

11. Gao, S., Li, Z., Wang, Z.: Cost volume pyramid network with multi-strategies range searching for multi-view stereo. In: Advances in Computer Graphics: 39th Computer Graphics International Conference, CGI 2022, Virtual Event, September 12–16, 2022, Proceedings, pp. 157–169. Springer (2023). https://doi.org/10.1007/978-3-031-23473-6_13

12. Gu, X., Fan, Z., Zhu, S., Dai, Z., Tan, F., Tan, P.: Cascade cost volume for high-resolution multi-view stereo and stereo matching. In: Proceedings of the IEEE/CVF Conference on Computer Vision and Pattern Recognition, pp. 2495–2504 (2020)

13. Hu, J., Shen, L., Sun, G.: Squeeze-and-excitation networks. In: Proceedings of the IEEE Conference on Computer Vision and Pattern Recognition, pp. 7132–7141 (2018)

14. Jianguo, L., Dexin, C.: Multi-view 3d reconstruction for the research of buddhist archaeology. Universum Humanitarium (En) **1**, 84–96 (2017)

15. Jie, L., Zhang, H.: Psp-mvsnet: deep patch-based similarity perceptual for multi-view stereo depth inference. In: Artificial Neural Networks and Machine Learning-ICANN 2022: 31st International Conference on Artificial Neural Networks, Bristol, UK, 6–9 September 2022, Proceedings, Part I, pp. 316–328. Springer (2022). https://doi.org/10.1007/978-3-031-15919-0_27

16. Kendall, A., Gal, Y.: What uncertainties do we need in bayesian deep learning for computer vision?. In: Advances in Neural Information Processing Systems 30 (2017)

17. Lin, T.Y., Goyal, P., Girshick, R., He, K., Dollár, P.: Focal loss for dense object detection. In: Proceedings of the IEEE International Conference on Computer Vision, pp. 2980–2988 (2017)

18. Paszke, A., Gross, S., Massa, F., Lerer, A., Bradbury, J.P.: An imperative style, high-performance deep learning library. In: Advances in Neural Information Processing Systems 32

19. Schonberger, J.L., Frahm, J.M.: Structure-from-motion revisited. In: Proceedings of the IEEE Conference on Computer Vision and Pattern Recognition, pp. 4104–4113 (2016)

20. Schönberger, J.L., Zheng, E., Frahm, J.-M., Pollefeys, M.: Pixelwise view selection for unstructured multi-view stereo. In: Leibe, B., Matas, J., Sebe, N., Welling, M. (eds.) ECCV 2016. LNCS, vol. 9907, pp. 501–518. Springer, Cham (2016). https://doi.org/10.1007/978-3-319-46487-9_31

21. Tola, E., Strecha, C., Fua, P.: Efficient large-scale multi-view stereo for ultra high-resolution image sets. Mach. Vis. Appl. **23**, 903–920 (2012)

22. Wang, F., Galliani, S., Vogel, C., Speciale, P., Pollefeys, M.: Patchmatchnet: learned multi-view patchmatch stereo. In: Proceedings of the IEEE/CVF Conference on Computer Vision and Pattern Recognition, pp. 14194–14203 (2021)

23. Wang, X., et al.: Mvster: epipolar transformer for efficient multi-view stereo. In: Computer Vision-ECCV 2022: 17th European Conference, Tel Aviv, Israel, 23–27 October 2022, Proceedings, Part XXXI, pp. 573–591. Springer (2022). https://doi.org/10.1007/978-3-031-19821-2_33

24. Wei, Z., Zhu, Q., Min, C., Chen, Y., Wang, G.: Aa-rmvsnet: adaptive aggregation recurrent multi-view stereo network. In: Proceedings of the IEEE/CVF International Conference on Computer Vision, pp. 6187–6196 (2021)

25. Yan, J., et al.: Dense hybrid recurrent multi-view stereo net with dynamic consistency checking. In: Vedaldi, A., Bischof, H., Brox, T., Frahm, J.-M. (eds.) ECCV 2020. LNCS, vol. 12349, pp. 674–689. Springer, Cham (2020). https://doi.org/10.1007/978-3-030-58548-8_39

26. Yang, J., Mao, W., Alvarez, J.M., Liu, M.: Cost volume pyramid based depth inference for multi-view stereo. In: Proceedings of the IEEE/CVF Conference on Computer Vision and Pattern Recognition, pp. 4877–4886 (2020)

27. Yao, Y., Luo, Z., Li, S., Fang, T., Quan, L.: MVSNet: depth inference for unstructured multi-view stereo. In: Ferrari, V., Hebert, M., Sminchisescu, C., Weiss, Y. (eds.) ECCV 2018. LNCS, vol. 11212, pp. 785–801. Springer, Cham (2018). https://doi.org/10.1007/978-3-030-01237-3_47

28. Yao, Y., Luo, Z., Li, S., Shen, T., Fang, T., Quan, L.: Recurrent mvsnet for high-resolution multi-view stereo depth inference. In: Proceedings of the IEEE/CVF Conference on Computer Vision and Pattern Recognition, pp. 5525–5534 (2019)

29. Yao, Y., et al.: Blendedmvs: a large-scale dataset for generalized multi-view stereo networks. In: Proceedings of the IEEE/CVF Conference on Computer Vision and Pattern Recognition, pp. 1790–1799 (2020)

30. Yu, Z., Gao, S.: Fast-mvsnet: sparse-to-dense multi-view stereo with learned propagation and gauss-newton refinement. In: Proceedings of the IEEE/CVF Conference on Computer Vision and Pattern Recognition, pp. 1949–1958 (2020)

31. Zhang, J., Yao, Y., Li, S., Luo, Z., Fang, T.: Visibility-aware multi-view stereo network. arXiv preprint arXiv:2008.07928 (2020)

32. Zhu, X., Hu, H., Lin, S., Dai, J.: Deformable convnets v2: more deformable, better results. In: Proceedings of the IEEE/CVF Conference on Computer Vision and Pattern Recognition, pp. 9308–9316 (2019)

Lightweight Reference-Less Summary Quality Evaluation via Key Feature Extraction

Shunan Zang[1,2], Chuang Zhang[1(✉)], Jingwen Lin[1,2], Xiaojun Chen[1],
and Shuai Zhang[1]

[1] Institute of Information Engineering, Chinese Academy of Sciences, Beijing, China
{zangshunan,zhangchuang,linjingwen,chenxiaojun,zhangshuai}@iie.ac.cn
[2] School of Cyber Security, University of Chinese Academy of Sciences,
Beijing, China

Abstract. One of the main problems with automatic text summarization is the lack of a "gold standard" for summary quality evaluation. ROUGE [9] is the most widely used evaluation metric for summary quality. However, its evaluation merely concentrates on reference summary and overlap features of sentences rather than focusing on more critical semantic features. Some other exiting methods have issues with improper noise handling and high cost. To solve these problems, we propose a lightweight reference-less summary quality evaluation method (**SE-tiny**), which evaluates the summary from two aspects: the summary's self-quality and the degree of matching the features of the summary with the key features of the source text. Then, we optimize computational efficiency and space cost. Compared with existing methods, **SE-tiny** improves the quality of evaluation and reduces the cost. Besides, our method does not rely on reference summaries and can be generalized to evaluation on summarization datasets. For the goal of reproducibility, we make the **SE-tiny** project's code and models available.

Keywords: Automatic Text Summarization · Reference Less Summarization Quality Evaluation · Summarization Datasets

1 Introduction

In text summarization tasks, evaluating summary quality is a challenging challenge that severely limits model performance development. Three questions need to be clarified before we can evaluate summary quality. (1) What is a summary? The summary is not the same length as the source text and contains a limited amount of information. The summary is a collection of key information in the source text, rather than an abstraction of all the information. (2) How do humans evaluate a summary quality? Humans evaluate the quality of a summary in two steps, first evaluating the summary's self-quality, and then judging how well the summary matches the key information in the source text. (3) What kind of summary evaluation method is good? A good summary evaluation method should

L. Iliadis et al. (Eds.): ICANN 2023, LNCS 14261, pp. 498–510, 2023.
https://doi.org/10.1007/978-3-031-44198-1_41

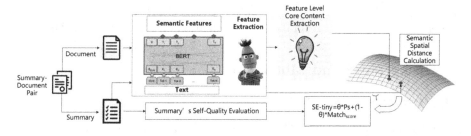

Fig. 1. *SE-tiny* architecture

minimize the cost while evaluating the summary quality comprehensively and accurately.

The two primary types of summary evaluation methods are reference-based and reference-less. The former completely depends on the quality of the reference summary, which is costly and labor-intensive. The latter uses the source text information to match the summary, saving the cost of the reference summary. However, current reference-less methods share common drawbacks. Firstly, the noise information in the source text is not handled well, which affects the evaluation results. Second, the amount of information in the summary differs from that in the source text. Using all the semantic information of the source text to match the summary not only violates human logic but also fails to generate correct matching results. Furthermore, most of the well-performing reference-less methods are based on complex models, which incurs a large cost.

In response to the above problems, we propose *SE-tiny*. Taking inspiration from human evaluation, the method is divided into three steps. (1) Evaluate the summary's self-quality in terms of compression ratio, fluency, and readability. (2) To acquire the representations of the summaries and source texts, we first map them to the feature space. Then, we extract key features from the features of the source text (simulate the extraction of key information from the source text during the human evaluation) and use these key features to perform similarity calculations with the features of the summary. This not only increases evaluation accuracy, but also aligns with the logic when humans evaluate summaries. Moreover, compared to existing methods that directly match summary and entire source text information, this method greatly simplifies computation. (3) We adopt a linear method to fuse the results of step1 and step2. Besides, we use two lightweight language models, n-gram and BERT-base [3] to reduce the cost of model loading. Experimental results show that *SE-tiny* not only guarantees the quality of the evaluation but also reduces the cost.

Contributions. (1) We propose a lightweight reference-less summary quality evaluation method (*SE-tiny*), which fully utilizes the source text information, removes noise, and conforms to the logic of human evaluation. (2) We optimize *SE-tiny* from two aspects: the computational complexity and the cost of the model. (3) We construct a high-quality dataset (*SE-tiny-db*) for evaluation of reference-less summarization and a reference-less summary evaluation system

(**SE-tiny-S**) that can be easily invoked. (4) Since **SE-tiny** does not rely on reference summaries, we generalize it to evaluation on summarization datasets.

2   Background and Motivation

2.1   Reference-Based Evaluation Metric

Model-Free Metrics: ROUGE [9] is a widely used metric, which evaluates summary using the co-occurrence of n-grams between machine summary and reference summary.

Model-Based Metrics: ROUGE-WE [13] uses the Word2Vec, and cosine distance to calculate the similarity of the two words, and then obtains the similarity between the machine summary and the reference summary. ROUGE-G [17] is a summary evaluation metric based on graph semantic matching. BERTScore [22] uses the contextual embeddings in the BERT [3] to represent the words and then calculates the similarity between the machine summary and the reference summary by the cosine similarity. MoverScore [23] calculates the similarity between the machine summary and the reference summary by the Word Mover distance. Based on MoverScore [23], Clark et al [2] use SMS and S+WMS to divide the text into multiple sentence vectors or a mixture of sentence vectors and word vectors to perform similarity detection on longer continuous text content. Clark et al [21] have proposed a content-based weighted generative summary evaluation metric.

These metrics can partly solve the quality evaluation problem of summary, but they have the following drawbacks. (1) These methods rely on reference summaries which are costly and labor-intensive, and the evaluation results completely depend on the quality of the reference summary. (2) The information in the source text is greatly wasted. (3) Model-based evaluation methods have a large cost, which is not conducive to practical use. Therefore, the researchers proposed the reference-less evaluation metrics.

2.2   Reference-Less Evaluation Metrics

Model-Free Metrics: Louis et al. [12] first introduce a reference-less summary evaluation method that uses JS divergence to determine whether the word distribution in the machine summary is similar to the word distribution in the source text.

Model-Based Metrics: Chen et al. [1] have proposed a summary evaluation method based on a question answering system. SummaQA [16] uses generated summaries to answer cloze-style questions, and evaluates summary quality by reporting F_1 overlap scores and QA model confidence. SUM-QE [20] uses the BERT [3] to evaluate the quality of summary in five dimensions: grammar, redundancy, clarity of reference, content relevance, and article organization. Kryscinski et al. [7] present a method based on the factual content of the source text, using machine summary to match multiple text fragments extracted from the source text. SUPERT [4] is an evaluation method for reference-less multi-document summaries. LS_Score [19] is an unsupervised evaluation method based on contrastive learning, which combines semantic and linguistic dimensions to evaluate the summary, and uses contrastive learning to optimize the model. QuestEval [15] uses a question answering(QA) system to assess the semantic match between the source text and the summary. Finally, the F1-score between the predicted answer and the real answer is used as the semantic matching degree between the summary and the source text.

Motivation: Although these metrics no longer rely on reference summaries and utilize source text information, they also suffer from the following drawbacks. (1) The noise information in the source text is not well handled, which affects the evaluation results. (2) Using all the semantic information of the source text to match the summary is not only inaccurate but also fails to generate correct matching results. (3) Model-based evaluation methods have a large cost, which is not conducive to practical use. In order to overcome the above problems, we propose a lightweight reference-less method *SE-tiny* for summarization quality evaluation.

3   Method

In order to overcome the shortcomings in the above analysis, we propose *SE-tiny*. We divide the summary evaluation into the following two dimensions: (1) Summary's self-quality dimension. (2) The matching dimension of the summary and the source text. Based on the evaluation dimensions proposed above, *SE-tiny* is divided into the following three steps: (1) Summary's self-quality evaluation. (2) Calculate the similarity between the summary features and the key features extracted from the source text. (3) Integrate the scores of step1 and step2. The details are as follows.

3.1   Summary Self-quality

The summary's self-quality is mainly divided into compression ratio, readability, and fluency. The compression ratio is a static metric and can be directly calculated. In order to reduce the model cost while maintaining the evaluation quality, we use the summary sequence S as input, and obtain the probability value of the sequence S through a trained n-gram language model (CNN/DM) to represent the readability and fluency scores. Furthermore, considering that the n-gram model is unfriendly to long summaries, we add a penalty factor.

   step1: For summary sequence S, the compression ratio is denoted as "Compress(S)". If "Compress(S)" within [0.75-0.98], continue to the next step, otherwise the quality score of the summary is 0.

   step2: We fuse the probability values of the unigram (S_{g1}) and bigram (S_{g2}) outputs of the sequence S as readability and fluency scores (P_s). Adding a penalty factor for text length reduces the unfriendly of n-grams for long summaries.

$$P_s = Min\_max(\alpha \lg S_{g1} + \beta \lg S_{g2} + \eta |S|) \tag{1}$$

Where $|S|$ is the text length, α, η is tuning parameters, $\alpha + \beta = 1$ here. $Min\_max(*)$ is a normalization function.

In the current summarization evaluation, only human scoring can be regarded as the "gold standard". We use the Spearman correlation between our method and human scoring (**SE-tiny-DB**) to analyze the value of α, η. The specific analysis results are shown in Fig. 2. We can find that the Spearman correlation is the highest when $\alpha = 0.401, \eta = 0.429$ here.

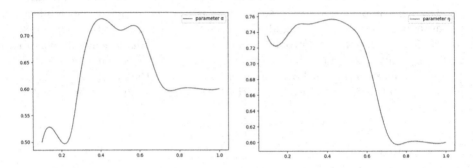

Fig. 2. The effect of parameter α and η on **SE-tiny**. The abscissa is the α and η value, the ordinate is the Spearman correlation between our method scores and human scores (**SE-tiny-DB**).

3.2   Matching Degree

We use the BERT [3] contextual embedding to represent the summaries and the source texts. In order to conform to the logic when humans evaluate summary, we extract key features from the features of the source text to perform similarity calculations with the features of the summary. This eliminates noise, improves evaluation quality, and reduces computational cost. The specific method is as follows:

Text Preprocessing: The preprocessing part removes stop words, prepositions, and some content-independent words.

Feature Extraction: For the bridge between text and features, we choose a lightweight language model BERT-base [3]. S and D represent summary and source text, respectively. $BERT(S)$ and $BERT(D)$ represent the feature representations of S and D. $BERT(*)$ is obtained through the token-level feature representation by using the BERT-base [3].

Extraction of Key Features: The feature vectors of the source text are $T = [t_1, ..., t_n]$, and the key feature vectors of the source text are $K_i = (k_1, ..., k_w)$.

Stack the m key features as a key content matrix $K = [K_1, ..., K_m]$. We define the approximative token vector $\tilde{t}_i$ for the token t_i as the optimal linear approximation given by key feature matrix: $\tilde{t}_i = \tilde{\alpha}_i K$, where $\tilde{\alpha}_i = argmin\|t_i - \tilde{\alpha}_i K\|_2^2$, $\| * \|$ is the Frobenius norm of a matrix. We use the key feature matrix to approximate the features of the source text and minimize the approximate representation error (E).

$$E = \sum_{i=1}^{n} \|t_i - \tilde{t}_i\|_2^2 \tag{2}$$

$$K = argminE(K) \tag{3}$$

Without loss of generality, we make the key feature vectors $[K_i]_{i=1}^{m}$ to be orthonormal. Then this optimization problem can be solved by Singular Value Decomposition (SVD). $T = UWV^T$, WV^T is an approximate representation of T. We denote key feature vectors ($[K_i]_{i=1}^{m}$) of the source text by the first m vectors of V^T. The W as the weight matrix of V^T. This ensures approximate representation error is minimized.

Calculate Spatial Distance: We calculate the cosine distance between the key feature vectors of the source text and the feature vectors of the summary to indicate the matching degree. Map the distance into [0, 1] to get the $Match_{score}$.

We use the Spearman correlation between our method and human scoring (**SE-tiny-DB**) to analyze the value of m, and the specific analysis results are shown in Fig. 3. We can find that the spearman correlation is the highest when $m = 4$.

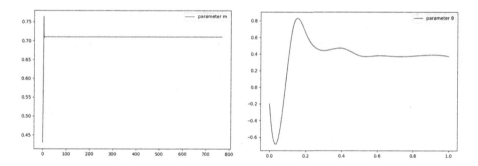

Fig. 3. The effect of parameter m and θ on **SE-tiny**. The abscissa is the m and θ value, the ordinate is the Spearman correlation between our method scores and human scores (**SE-tiny-DB**).

3.3   SE-Tiny Score

We adopt a linear approach to fuse the scores obtained from the above two dimensions.

$$SE_{tiny} = \theta P_s + (1 - \theta)Match_{score} \tag{4}$$

Where θ is a tuning parameter. We use the Spearman correlation between our method and human scoring (**SE-tiny-DB**) to analyze the value of θ, and the specific analysis results are shown in Fig. 3. We can find that the spearman correlation is the highest when $\theta = 0.13$.

4   Experiment

We verified **SE-tiny** from four aspects: correlation, actual effect, cost and cross-datasets transferability. Select the commonly used evaluation metrics ROUGE [9], MoverScore [23], BERTScore [22], LS_Score [19] and the current best performing metric QuestEval [14] as the baselines for evaluating metrics. Select Transformer [18], Presumm [10], Bart [8] and SimCLS [11] as baselines for generating machine summaries. For specific model parameters, please refer to Appendix A.

4.1   Evaluation Dataset

Since there is currently no high-quality dataset for reference-less summary evaluation methods, we constructed a dataset (**SE-tiny-DB**) dedicated to evaluating reference-less summary and invited 6 linguists to score the <summary-document> pairs. The specific scoring standard are as follows.

(1) Summary Self-quality Evaluation:

step1: If the compression ratio of the summary is in the range of [0.75-0.98], the next scoring is performed, otherwise it is directly scored as 0.

step2: We count the frequency of occurrence of disfluency in the summary as f. $f \geq 5$: 0 points; $f = 4$: 1 points; $f = 3$: 2 points; $f = 2$: 3 points; $f = 1$: 4 points; $f = 0$: 5 points. We got the fluency score ($Score_{fluency}$) based on the above standard.

step3: We count the frequency of incomprehensible occurrences in the summary as r. $r = 5$: 0 points; $r = 4$: 1 points; $r = 3$: 2 points; $r = 2$: 3 points; $r = 1$: 4 points; $r = 0.5$ points. We got the readability score ($Score_{readability}$) based on the above standard.

(2) Evaluation of Matching Degree: The percentage of the summary covering the key content of the source text is denoted as k. $k < 1/5$: 0 points; $1/5 \leq k < 2/5$: 1 point; $2/5 \leq k < 3/5$: 2 points; $3/5 \leq k < 4/5$: 3 points; $4/5 \leq k < 1$: 4 points; $k = 1$: 5 points. We got the matching degree score ($Score_{match}$) based on the above standard.

(3) Dataset Construction Process: Our data source comes from the existing datasets CNN/DM [6] and Newsroom [5]. Specific steps are as follows:

step1: We divided linguistic experts into two groups. The first group of experts scored the data in **SE-tiny-DB** according to the scoring standard. The second group of experts checked the scoring results of the first group.

step2: The two groups of experts exchanged and repeated **step1**.

According to the established scoring standard, the summary data scores in CNN/DM [6] and Newsroom [5] are concentrated in the range of [2, 5] points, which is not conducive to our use. In response to this situation, we have processed the summarization data in *SE-tiny-DB*. The processing methods include: deleting some key points in the summary, rewriting the summary to make it difficult to understand, rewriting the summary to make it less fluent, etc. After these processes and repeating the scoring steps, we get the final dataset, and the statistical results of the dataset are shown in Table 1.

Table 1. Statistics of the distribution of data in *SE-tiny-DB* on each score.

	0 points	1 point	2 points	3 points	4 points	5 points
Fluency	178	417	472	500	408	43
Readability	127	305	582	532	402	70
Matching degree	122	308	526	476	486	100

4.2 Correlation

Correlation with Human Metrics. Human metrics are the current "gold standard" for summary quality evaluation. We selected fluency, readability, matching degree and composite score for correlation calculation (Spearman) on *SE-tiny-DB*. The specific results are shown in Table 2. Compared with other methods, *SE-tiny* has the highest correlation with human metrics, which fully reflects the superiority of our method.

Table 2. Correlation (Spearman) evaluation of *SE-tiny* and some baseline methods with human scoring. Total represents the composite score of human metrics

	Fluency	Readability	Match	Total
ROUGE-L(F)	0.37	0.34	-0.10	0.28
MoverScore	0.35	0.31	0.28	0.27
BERTScore(F)	0.18	0.23	0.31	0.25
LS_Score	0.42	0.46	0.64	0.53
QuestEval	0.49	0.51	0.70	0.68
SE-tiny	**0.66**	**0.55**	**0.78**	**0.71**

4.3 Scoring Effect

In order to verify the actual scoring effect of *SE-tiny*, we use our method and some baseline methods to score the machine summaries generated by the text summarization models. The specific scoring results are shown in Table 3. We can find that the evaluation results of *SE-tiny* are consistent with the quality of the models.

Table 3. The actual scoring effect of ROUGE, BERTScore (F), and *SE-tiny* on the machine summaries generated by the text summarization models.

	ROUGE-1	ROUGE-2	ROUGE-L	BERT(F)	*SE-tiny*
Lead3	40.42	17.62	36.67	75.16	61.42
TextRank	35.23	13.90	31.48	65.71	56.89
Pointer	39.34	17.21	35.23	76.54	63.76
Transformer	39.66	17.19	36.66	87.68	68.47
BertSumAbs	41.72	19.39	38.76	88.26	69.18
BertSumExtAbs	43.23	20.24	39.63	88.22	70.91
Bart	44.39	21.21	41.28	88.33	69.16
SimCLS	46.67	22.15	43.54	89.24	71.85

4.4   Model Cost

A good evaluation model needs to have less cost, we calculate the cost of various methods to complete the evaluation of 10K <summary-document> pairs. The specific results are shown in Table 4. Compared with model-based evaluation methods, *SE-tiny* saves time and has less space cost.

Table 4. Model cost comparison

	ROUGE	BERTScore	LS_Score	*SE-tiny*
Time (s)	<300	8,418	9,761	**4,181**
Space (MB)	<10	4,280	3,525	**716**

4.5   Cross-Datasets Transferability

A good evaluation method should also have good transferability. In order to verify this feature, we train SE-tinyon two datasets CNN/DM [6] and NEWS-ROOM [5], and then evaluate the data quality of SE-tiny-DB and calculate the correlation (Spearman) with human scoring. SE-tiny-DB in 4.1 above contains part of the data in CNN/DM [6] and NEWSROOM [5] after scoring. The specific experimental results are shown in Table 4. Both SE-tiny-CNN/DM and SE-tiny-CNN/DM* are the correlation score between CNN/DM [6] scoring results and human scoring, SE-tiny-CNN/DM is trained using CNN/DM [6] data, and SE-tiny-CNN/DM* is trained using NEWSROOM [5]. Both SE-tiny-NEWSROOM and SE-tiny-NEWSROOM* are the correlation score between NEWSROOM [5] scoring results and human scoring, SE-tiny-NEWSROOM is trained using NEWSROOM [5] data, and SE-tiny-NEWSROOM* is trained using CNN/DM

[6]. We can find that the scoring results in other datasets are similar to the scoring results trained in this dataset. This fully demonstrates the transferability of our method.

Table 5. Cross-datasets transferability

	Fluency	Readability	Match	Total
SE-tiny-CNN/DM*	0.63	0.64	0.75	0.74
SE-tiny-CNN/DM	0.67	0.58	0.78	0.76
SE-tiny-NEWSROOM*	0.53	0.54	0.61	0.56
SE-tiny-NEWSROOM	0.57	0.60	0.68	0.62

5   Conclusion

SE-tiny is a lightweight reference-less summary quality evaluation method based on key feature extraction. By matching the summary features with the key features of the source text, this evaluation method conforms to human evaluation logic, eliminates noise, improves evaluation quality, and reduces the cost. Experimental results show that our method outperforms existing model-based summarization evaluation methods in both performance and cost. At the same time, our method does not rely on reference summaries and can be generalized to evaluation on summary datasets.

6   Limitation and Future Work

Our method is a general approach, effective for commonly used summarization data, but lacks specificity for domain-specific summarization data evaluation. In order to overcome this shortcoming, more algorithms for specific domains need to be proposed in the future.

With the improvement of computing power, more and more large models have been proposed (Chat-gpt, GPT-3 etc.), but when the model develops to a certain scale, how to reduce the cost of the model while ensuring the quality of summarization evaluation is also an area for future development. In addition to the pruning algorithm, reducing overhead directly from the model architecture is also a future trend. In the future, we hope to propose more lightweight and efficient summarization evaluation algorithms.

References

1. Chen, P., Wu, F., Wang, T., Ding, W.: A semantic qa-based approach for text summarization evaluation. In: McIlraith, S.A., Weinberger, K.Q. (eds.) Proceedings of the Thirty-Second AAAI Conference on Artificial Intelligence, (AAAI 2018), the 30th innovative Applications of Artificial Intelligence (IAAI 2018), and the 8thAAAI Symposium on Educational Advances in Artificial Intelligence (EAAI 2018), New Orleans, Louisiana, USA, 2–7 February 2018, pp. 4800–4807. AAAI Press (2018). https://www.aaai.org/ocs/index.php/AAAI/AAAI18/paper/view/16115

2. Clark, E., Celikyilmaz, A., Smith, N.A.: Sentence mover's similarity: automatic evaluation for multi-sentence texts. In: Korhonen, A., Traum, D.R., Màrquez, L. (eds.) Proceedings of the 57th Conference of the Association for Computational Linguistics, ACL 2019, Florence, Italy, 2–7 July - 2 August 2019, Volume 1: Long Papers, pp. 2748–2760. Association for Computational Linguistics (2019). https://doi.org/10.18653/v1/p19-1264

3. Devlin, J., Chang, M., Lee, K., Toutanova, K.: BERT: pre-training of deep bidirectional transformers for language understanding. In: Burstein, J., Doran, C., Solorio, T. (eds.) Proceedings of the 2019 Conference of the North American Chapter of the Association for Computational Linguistics: Human Language Technologies, NAACL-HLT 2019, Minneapolis, MN, USA, 2–7 June 2019, Volume 1 (Long and Short Papers), pp. 4171–4186. Association for Computational Linguistics (2019). https://doi.org/10.18653/v1/n19-1423

4. Gao, Y., Zhao, W., Eger, S.: SUPERT: towards new frontiers in unsupervised evaluation metrics for multi-document summarization. In: Jurafsky, D., Chai, J., Schluter, N., Tetreault, J.R. (eds.) Proceedings of the 58th Annual Meeting of the Association for Computational Linguistics, ACL 2020, Online, 5–10 July 2020, pp. 1347–1354. Association for Computational Linguistics (2020). https://doi.org/10.18653/v1/2020.acl-main.124

5. Grusky, M., Naaman, M., Artzi, Y.: Newsroom: a dataset of 1.3 million summaries with diverse extractive strategies. In: Walker, M.A., Ji, H., Stent, A. (eds.) Proceedings of the 2018 Conference of the North American Chapter of the Association for Computational Linguistics: Human Language Technologies, NAACL-HLT 2018, New Orleans, Louisiana, USA, 1–6 June 2018, Volume 1 (Long Papers), pp. 708–719. Association for Computational Linguistics (2018). https://doi.org/10.18653/v1/n18-1065

6. Hermann, K.M., et al.: Teaching machines to read and comprehend. In: Cortes, C., Lawrence, N.D., Lee, D.D., Sugiyama, M., Garnett, R. (eds.) Advances in Neural Information Processing Systems 28: Annual Conference on Neural Information Processing Systems 2015, pp. 7–12, 2015. Montreal, Quebec, Canada, pp. 1693–1701 (Dec 2015), https://proceedings.neurips.cc/paper/2015/hash/afdec7005cc9f14302cd0474fd0f3c96-Abstract.html

7. Kryscinski, W., McCann, B., Xiong, C., Socher, R.: Evaluating the factual consistency of abstractive text summarization. In: Webber, B., Cohn, T., He, Y., Liu, Y. (eds.) Proceedings of the 2020 Conference on Empirical Methods in Natural Language Processing, EMNLP 2020, Online, 16–20 November 2020, pp. 9332–9346. Association for Computational Linguistics (2020). https://doi.org/10.18653/v1/2020.emnlp-main.750

8. Lewis, M., et al.: BART: denoising sequence-to-sequence pre-training for natural language generation, translation, and comprehension. In: Jurafsky, D., Chai, J., Schluter, N., Tetreault, J.R. (eds.) Proceedings of the 58th Annual Meeting of the Association for Computational Linguistics, ACL 2020, Online, 5–10 July 2020, pp. 7871–7880. Association for Computational Linguistics (2020). https://doi.org/10.18653/v1/2020.acl-main.703, https://doi.org/10.18653/v1/2020.acl-main.703

9. Lin, C., Hovy, E.H.: Automatic evaluation of summaries using n-gram co-occurrence statistics. In: Hearst, M.A., Ostendorf, M. (eds.) Human Language Technology Conference of the North American Chapter of the Association for Computational Linguistics, HLT-NAACL 2003, Edmonton, Canada, 27 May - 1 June 2003. The Association for Computational Linguistics (2003). https://aclanthology.org/N03-1020/

10. Liu, Y., Lapata, M.: Text summarization with pretrained encoders. In: Inui, K., Jiang, J., Ng, V., Wan, X. (eds.) Proceedings of the 2019 Conference on Empirical Methods in Natural Language Processing and the 9th International Joint Conference on Natural Language Processing, EMNLP-IJCNLP 2019, Hong Kong, China, 3–7 November 2019, pp. 3728–3738. Association for Computational Linguistics (2019). https://doi.org/10.18653/v1/D19-1387

11. Liu, Y., Liu, P.: Simcls: A simple framework for contrastive learning of abstractive summarization. In: Zong, C., Xia, F., Li, W., Navigli, R. (eds.) Proceedings of the 59th Annual Meeting of the Association for Computational Linguistics and the 11th International Joint Conference on Natural Language Processing, ACL/IJCNLP 2021, (Volume 2: Short Papers), Virtual Event, 1–6 August 2021, pp. 1065–1072. Association for Computational Linguistics (2021). https://doi.org/10.18653/v1/2021.acl-short.135

12. Louis, A., Nenkova, A.: Automatically evaluating content selection in summarization without human models. In: Proceedings of the 2009 Conference on Empirical Methods in Natural Language Processing, EMNLP 2009, 6–7 August 2009, Singapore, A meeting of SIGDAT, a Special Interest Group of the ACL, pp. 306–314. ACL (2009), https://aclanthology.org/D09-1032/

13. Ng, J., Abrecht, V.: Better summarization evaluation with word embeddings for ROUGE. In: Màrquez, L., Callison-Burch, C., Su, J., Pighin, D., Marton, Y. (eds.) Proceedings of the 2015 Conference on Empirical Methods in Natural Language Processing, EMNLP 2015, Lisbon, Portugal, 17–21 September 2015, pp. 1925–1930. The Association for Computational Linguistics (2015). https://doi.org/10.18653/v1/d15-1222

14. Rebuffel, C., et al.: Data-questeval: A referenceless metric for data-to-text semantic evaluation. In: Moens, M., Huang, X., Specia, L., Yih, S.W. (eds.) Proceedings of the 2021 Conference on Empirical Methods in Natural Language Processing, EMNLP 2021, Virtual Event / Punta Cana, Dominican Republic, 7–11 November 2021, pp. 8029–8036. Association for Computational Linguistics (2021). https://doi.org/10.18653/v1/2021.emnlp-main.633

15. Scialom, T., et al.: Questeval: summarization asks for fact-based evaluation. In: Moens, M., Huang, X., Specia, L., Yih, S.W. (eds.) Proceedings of the 2021 Conference on Empirical Methods in Natural Language Processing, EMNLP 2021, Virtual Event / Punta Cana, Dominican Republic, 7–11 November 2021, pp. 6594–6604. Association for Computational Linguistics (2021). https://doi.org/10.18653/v1/2021.emnlp-main.529

16. Scialom, T., Lamprier, S., Piwowarski, B., Staiano, J.: Answers unite! unsupervised metrics for reinforced summarization models. In: Inui, K., Jiang, J., Ng, V., Wan, X. (eds.) Proceedings of the 2019 Conference on Empirical Methods in Natural Language Processing and the 9th International Joint Conference on Natural Language Processing, EMNLP-IJCNLP 2019, Hong Kong, China, 3–7 November 2019, pp. 3244–3254. Association for Computational Linguistics (2019). https://doi.org/10.18653/v1/D19-1320

17. ShafieiBavani, E., Ebrahimi, M., Wong, R.K., Chen, F.: A graph-theoretic summary evaluation for rouge. In: Riloff, E., Chiang, D., Hockenmaier, J., Tsujii, J. (eds.) Proceedings of the 2018 Conference on Empirical Methods in Natural Language Processing, Brussels, Belgium, 31 October - 4 November 2018, pp. 762–767. Association for Computational Linguistics (2018). https://doi.org/10.18653/v1/d18-1085

18. Vaswani, A., et al.: Attention is all you need. In: Guyon, I., et al. (eds.) Advances in Neural Information Processing Systems 30: Annual Conference on Neural Information Processing Systems 2017 (December), pp. 4–9, 2017, Long Beach, CA, USA, pp. 5998–6008 (2017). https://proceedings.neurips.cc/paper/2017/hash/3f5ee243547dee91fbd053c1c4a845aa-Abstract.html

19. Wu, H., Ma, T., Wu, L., Manyumwa, T., Ji, S.: Unsupervised reference-free summary quality evaluation via contrastive learning. In: Webber, B., Cohn, T., He, Y., Liu, Y. (eds.) Proceedings of the 2020 Conference on Empirical Methods in Natural Language Processing, EMNLP 2020, Online, 16–20 November 2020, pp. 3612–3621. Association for Computational Linguistics (2020). https://doi.org/10.18653/v1/2020.emnlp-main.294

20. Xenouleas, S., Malakasiotis, P., Apidianaki, M., Androutsopoulos, I.: Sumqe: a bert-based summary quality estimation model. CoRR abs/ arXiv: 1909.00578 (2019)

21. Xu, X., Dusek, O., Li, J., Rieser, V., Konstas, I.: Fact-based content weighting for evaluating abstractive summarisation. In: Jurafsky, D., Chai, J., Schluter, N., Tetreault, J.R. (eds.) Proceedings of the 58th Annual Meeting of the Association for Computational Linguistics, ACL 2020, Online, 5–10 July 2020, pp. 5071–5081. Association for Computational Linguistics (2020). https://doi.org/10.18653/v1/2020.acl-main.455

22. Zhang*, T., Kishore*, V., Wu*, F., Weinberger, K.Q., Artzi, Y · Bertscore: evaluating text generation with bert. In: International Conference on Learning Representations (2020). https://openreview.net/forum?id=SkeHuCVFDr

23. Zhao, W., Peyrard, M., Liu, F., Gao, Y., Meyer, C.M., Eger, S.: Moverscore: Text generation evaluating with contextualized embeddings and earth mover distance. In: Inui, K., Jiang, J., Ng, V., Wan, X. (eds.) Proceedings of the 2019 Conference on Empirical Methods in Natural Language Processing and the 9th International Joint Conference on Natural Language Processing, EMNLP-IJCNLP 2019, Hong Kong, China, 3–7 November 2019, pp. 563–578. Association for Computational Linguistics (2019). https://doi.org/10.18653/v1/D19-1053

Limited Information Opponent Modeling

Yongliang Lv[1], Yuanqiang Yu[1], Yan Zheng[1], Jianye Hao[1(✉)], Yongming Wen[2], and Yue Yu[2]

[1] Deep Reinforcement Learning Lab, Tianjin University, Tianjin, China
{lvyongliang,yuyuanqiang,yanzheng,jianye.hao}@tju.edu.cn
[2] Science and Technology on Information Systems Engineering Laboratory, Beijing Institute of Control and Electronics Technology, Beijing, China

Abstract. The goal of opponent modeling is to model the opponent policy to maximize the reward of the main agent. Most prior works fail to effectively handle scenarios where opponent information is limited. To this end, we propose a Limited Information Opponent Modeling (LIOM) approach that extracts opponent policy representations across episodes using only self-observations. LIOM introduces a novel policy-based data augmentation method that extracts opponent policy representations offline via contrastive learning and incorporates them as additional inputs for training a general response policy. During online testing, LIOM dynamically responds to opponent policies by extracting opponent policy representations from recent historical trajectory data and combining them with the general policy. Moreover, LIOM ensures a lower bound on expected rewards through a balance between conservative and exploitation. Experimental results demonstrate that LIOM is able to accurately extract opponent policy representations even when the opponent's information is limited, and has a certain degree of generalization ability for unknown policies, outperforming existing opponent modeling algorithms.

Keywords: opponent modeling · contrastive learning · general policy

1 Introduction

Opponent Modeling [2,4,7,12] is an important branch of Multi-Agent Reinforcement Learning aimed at utilizing opponent information to model the opponent in order to maximize self (i.e., the main agent's) reward, particularly when the opponent policy is non-stationary. However, existing opponent modeling approaches heavily rely on the completeness of opponent information, rendering them limited in accuracy and effectiveness when opponent observations and actions are unknown. To address this issue, we propose the Limited Information Opponent Modeling (LIOM) algorithm, which models the opponent policy solely based on the main agent's historical observations. We divide the problem into two stages: offline training and online testing.

© The Author(s), under exclusive license to Springer Nature Switzerland AG 2023
L. Iliadis et al. (Eds.): ICANN 2023, LNCS 14261, pp. 511–522, 2023.
https://doi.org/10.1007/978-3-031-44198-1_42

During the offline training stage, we aim to learn a powerful general policy on a given set of opponent policies, which can approximate the optimal response policy of any known or unknown opponent as closely as possible. This requires an accurate and generalizable representation of opponent policies as support. To this end, we propose a novel policy-based data augmentation approach that interacts with opponent policies with various augmentation policies to generate trajectories for constructing positive and negative samples. We then extract cross-episode trajectory representations self-supervisedly via contrastive learning as opponent policy representations. Then, the opponent policy representations are further inputted into the reinforcement learning algorithm for learning the general policy. The advantage of the general policy lies in its ability to generalize to an infinite number of opponent policies, implying no need for relearning against new individual opponent policies during online testing.

During the online testing stage, we encode the recent historical trajectories into opponent policy representations and use them as additional inputs to the general policy. This dynamic response allows us to handle non-stationary opponent policies. Furthermore, to deal with difficult-to-generalize opponent policies, we dynamically update a weight based on the reward, which selects between a conservative Nash equilibrium policy and an exploitative general policy. This ensures the lower bound of expected returns.

This paper presents two innovative contributions: (1) opponent modeling is performed only based on self-observation, which renders our approach adaptable to almost any environment. (2) a novel policy-based data augmentation technique is proposed, which allows for independent extraction of policy representations without being influenced by policies it interacts with. Moreover, we introduce a classic algorithm EXP3 to address the trade-off between conservative and exploitation during online testing.

We compared the performance of LIOM with multiple algorithms in two classic reinforcement learning benchmarks, Kuhn Poker and Soccer. Our results demonstrate that LIOM outperforms existing opponent modeling algorithms in terms of performance against both "seen" and "unseen" opponents.

2   Related Work

2.1   Opponent Modeling

Early opponent modeling research primarily focused on simple environments with fixed opponent policies. With the introduction of non-stationary environments, existing opponent modeling can be categorized into two approaches: implicit modeling and explicit modeling.

Implicit opponent modeling refers to extracting opponent information for representation learning during training. He et al. [4] proposed an end-to-end training approach by merging the opponent's observation with the agent's observation using a deep neural network. Hong et al. [7] further incorporated opponent action information and fitted the opponent policy through a neural network. Considering that the opponent may also have learning behaviors, Foerster et al. [2]

leveraged recurrent reasoning to estimate the parameters of the opponent policy network and maximize the agent's reward. Raileanu et al. [9] took a different perspective, considering the opponent policy network parameters of the agent's own policy and using opponent observations to make decisions.

Explicit opponent modeling refers to the explicit modeling of opponent policies, dividing opponent types, and online detection and response during the interaction process. Rosman et al. [10] first proposed bayesian policy reuse for multi-task learning, while Hernandez-Leal et al. [6] extended this to multi-agent systems by using MDPs to model opponents and adding a detection mechanism for unknown opponent policies. In more complex environments, Zheng et al. [12] used neural networks to model opponents and introduced a rectified belief model to improve opponent detection accuracy and speed. Building on this work, Yang et al. [11] introduced the Theory of Mind approach to defeat opponents using higher-level decision-making methods in cases where the opponent is also using an opponent modeling method.

2.2 Contrastive Learning

As the most prevalent self-supervised learning algorithm in recent years, contrastive learning aims to learn common features among similar instances while distinguishing dissimilar instances. Oord et al. [8] initially proposed InfoNCE loss, which encodes time-series data. By segregating positive and negative samples, it can extract data-specific representations. Following this approach, He et al. [5] achieved high performance in image classification by enhancing the similarity between the query vector and its corresponding key vector, while reducing similarity with the key vectors of other images. From the perspective of data augmentation, Chen et al. [1] applied various transformations such as random cropping, inversion, grayscale, etc., on images, and extracted invariant representations through contrastive learning. Subsequent works have made further improvements, achieving performance levels comparable to supervised learning algorithms on certain tasks.

3   Methodology

We introduce our main algorithm LIOM, the offline training in Sect. 3.1 and the online testing in Sect. 3.2.

3.1   Offline Training

This section first introduces a novel policy data augmentation method. Then, we introduce the encoder training based on contrastive learning, where the opponent policy representation can be obtained from historical trajectory data. The policy representation will assist in training the general response policy and solving online execution policies.

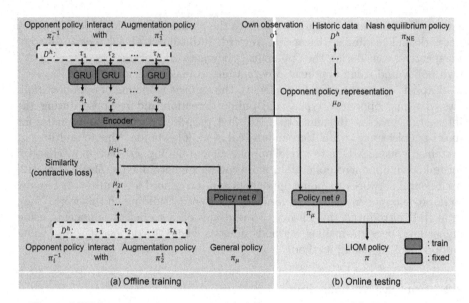

Fig. 1. LIOM consists of two stages: (a) Offline training and (b) Online testing.

Data augmentation is widely used for representation extraction, where it can extract important features while disregarding irrelevant information. In contrastive learning, data augmentation is mainly used to create positive and negative samples. However, the opponent's policy representation cannot be learned independently, it can only be extracted from interaction trajectories. We thus define a policy that interacts with an opponent's policy as an *augmentation policy*. We use some pure policies as augmentation policies since they take deterministic actions and have a minor effect on the trajectory representations' distribution.

By treating the interaction with an augmentation policy as a form of data augmentation, we can define a policy-based contrastive loss. For a given N opponent policy set, we randomly choose two augmentation policies to interact with the opponent policies. Then, the obtained trajectories are encoded to form the set of trajectory representations $\{\mu_1, \mu_2, ..., \mu_{2N}\}$, where μ_{2k-1} and μ_{2k} are generated by the same opponent policy. The loss function can be defined as:

$$L = \frac{1}{2N} \sum_{k=1}^{N} [l(2k-1, 2k) + l(2k, 2k-1)], \tag{1}$$

where:

$$l(i, j) = -\log \frac{\exp(s_{i,j}/\tau)}{\sum_{k=1}^{2N} \mathbf{1}_{[k \neq i]} \exp(s_{i,k}/\tau)}. \tag{2}$$

Here $s_{i,j}$ represents the cosine similarity between trajectory representation μ_i and μ_j, and τ is the temperature coefficient.

Due to the unknown observation information of the opponent, inferring the current opponent policy from a single-episode trajectory is challenging. Therefore, it is necessary to extract cross-episode opponent policy representations. The specific procedure is illustrated in Fig. 1(a). Let h denote the number of game episodes required to learn the policy representations. For a N opponent policy set $\{\pi_1^{-1}, \pi_2^{-1}, ..., \pi_N^{-1}\}$, we randomly select two augmented policies π_1^1 and π_1^2. Let opponent policy π_i^{-1} interact with augmented policy π_1^1, and randomly sample a trajectory set $D^h = \{\tau_1, ..., \tau_h\}$. For each trajectory, we use GRU to extract the features:

$$z_t = f_{\text{GRU}}(\tau_t). \tag{3}$$

It is necessary to further encode and aggregate the representations z_t obtained from trajectories. In this paper, we employ the mean operation for aggregation due to simplify the expression:

$$\mu_{2i-1} = \frac{1}{h} \sum_{t=1}^{h} f_{\text{MLP}}(z_t). \tag{4}$$

Similarly, opponent policies interact with the augmented policy π_1^2 to construct a set of trajectory representations $\{\mu_1, ..., \mu_{2N}\}$, based on extracted features. By minimizing contrast loss (Eq. 1), we can obtain the opponent policy encoder $f_\phi(\cdot)$ in offline stage:

$$\mu_D = f_\phi(D). \tag{5}$$

After that, the opponent policy representation μ is regarded as labeled information, which assists the agent to make optimal responsive decisions against different opponent policies. This is particularly important in scenarios where the opponent's observations are unknown.

The core idea is to select an opponent policy π_k^{-1} and interact with it, storing the trajectory information τ in the historical trajectory set D_k. Before each episode of the game starts, the historical trajectory D_i^h for the current episode is selected from D_k. The opponent policy representation μ is generated based on D_i^h and a pre-trained opponent policy encoder $f_\phi(\cdot)$, and then it is combined with the observation o_t^1 of the main agent as a new observation to the critic and policy networks for training, and the network parameters are updated using the SAC algorithm. The main advantage of training a general policy lies in enabling the opponent policy encoder to obtain relatively accurate representations of unknown opponent policies, improving generalization.

3.2 Online Testing

This section first introduces the representation extraction method for online opponent policies. Then, we discuss the choice between conservative and exploitative policies and present a dynamic response policy that maximizes expected rewards.

Using the opponent policy encoder f_ϕ obtained in the offline training phase and the general policy π_μ, LIOM can respond to the opponent policy in online

---

Algorithm 1: LIOM(testing)

Require: Nash equilibrium policy π_{NE}, general policy π_μ, opponent policy encoder $f_\phi(\cdot)$, opponent policy set Π^{test}, number of testing episodes T, trajectory length H, number of steps behind h, EXP3 parameters $p = [0.5, 0.5]$, $s = [0, 0]$, $\rho = 1$, $\eta = 0.1$.

1: **for** testing episode $i = 0 \cdots T - 1$ **do**
2:      Initialize history trajectory set $D = \emptyset$
3:      **if** $i < h$ **then**
4:          Choose to interact with opponent using π_{NE}, generating trajectory τ_i.
5:          $D \leftarrow D \cup \tau_i$.
6:      **else**
7:          Cut out historical trajectory D_i^h for current episode from D.
8:          Generate opponent policy representation $\mu = f_\phi(D_i^h)$.
9:          Update probability distribution p according to Eq. (6).
10:          Choose policy π_i for this episode based on probability distribution p, generating trajectory τ_i.
11:          Update score s based on chosen policy and Eq. (7).
12:          **if** $\pi_i = \pi_\mu$ **then**
13:             $D \leftarrow D \cup \tau_i$.
14:          **end if**
15:      **end if**
16: **end for**

---

testing. For opponents with continuously changing policies, the agent fits the opponent policy representation μ using the recent h episodes of historical trajectory D^h. The real-time calculated μ is then used as the input of the general policy π_μ to continuously adjust the currently used policy, achieving the optimal response to the current opponent. However, for unknown opponent policies, although the general policy and policy representation theoretically have certain generalization capabilities, the agent still cannot guarantee to respond to any unknown opponent policy. A conservative and stable policy is, therefore, necessary to handle this situation.

To maximize expected return during online testing, the algorithm needs to balance between the conservative policy π_{NE} and the exploitative policy π_μ. This scenario can be modeled as a classic Multi Armed Bandit (MAB) problem, that is, how to quickly converge to the higher expected return policy when the return distribution for choosing policies π_{NE} and π_μ is uncertain. We choose to use the EXP3 algorithm to solve the problem. The EXP3 algorithm dynamically maintains an action probability distribution p, and the probability of choosing action a in the ith selection is given by:

$$p_i(a) = (1 - \eta)\frac{(1 + \rho)^{s_i(a)}}{\sum_{j=1}^K (1 + \rho)^{s_j(a)}} + \frac{\eta}{K}, \tag{6}$$

where K is the number of actions, and ρ and η are hyperparameters, s represents the score of each action, which is also dynamically maintained:

$$s_{i+1}(a) = s_i(a) + \frac{\eta r}{K p_i(a)}. \tag{7}$$

Here, a is selected based on the distribution p, and r is the reward obtained in this selection. In theory, the EXP3 algorithm's regret R_n^* has a lower bound:

$$R_n^* \geq c\sqrt{nK}, \tag{8}$$

where n is the total number of selections, and c is a constant.

Combined with the policy representation estimation and policy selection algorithm EXP3, we can obtain the online part of the LIOM algorithm. As shown in Algorithm 1, at the beginning of testing, LIOM uses the Nash equilibrium policy for a period of interaction. On the one hand, the algorithm needs enough data to construct the historical trajectory set D. On the other hand, using the Nash equilibrium policy for exploration is a more stable approach when there is less information about the opponent. When there is enough data, only the trajectory data of interactions between π_μ and the opponent will be kept in D to avoid the influence of trajectory data with different distributions on the performance of π_μ. It is worth noting that the exploration factor η should not be set too large or too small. Due to the possible changes in the opponent's policy, the exploration of policy selection should be ensured as much as possible.

4 Experiments

The purpose of our experimental research is to compare the performance of various methods when facing online adversarial scenarios with known, unknown, and non-stationary opponent policies. Additionally, we analyze the effectiveness of policy representation and the balance between conservative and exploitation.

4.1 Experimental Setup

Environments. We employed two classic multi-agent adversarial environments, Kuhn Poker [3] and Soccer [12]. Kuhn Poker is a simplified version of Texas Hold'em environment where each player chooses one card from J, Q, and K, and subsequently selects pass or bet in a turn-based manner. The rules is presented in Table 1, where ± 1 represents $+1$ for the player with a higher card value, and -1 otherwise. Soccer is a partially observable environment, as illustrated in Fig. 2, where the attacker (red) moves towards the goal along any path while the defender (blue) tries to stop them, and can only observe the position of the opponent when they are nearby. The winner receives a reward of 1, while the loser receives -1. We selected player 1 in Kuhn Poker and the defender in Soccer as our main agents to control. Due to the unknown hand cards or positions of the opponent, this presents a multi-agent competition problem with limited opponent information.

Table 1. Kuhn Poker rules

Player 1	Player 2	Player1	Reward
pass	pass		±1
pass	bet	pass	$(-1, 1)$
pass	bet	bet	±2
bet	bet		±2
bet	pass		$(1, -1)$

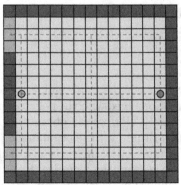

Fig. 2. Soccer configuration

Opponent Policies. For each environment, we have designed six opponent policies with distinct styles denoted by $\{\pi_0, \pi_1, \cdots, \pi_5\}$. Among them, policies $\{\pi_0, \pi_1, \pi_2\}$ constitute the visible policies and are used to form the training set Π^{train}, while policies $\{\pi_3, \pi_4, \pi_5\}$ serve as invisible policies. During online testing, we evaluate the effectiveness of various algorithms on three categories of opponent policy sets: "seen", "unseen", and "mix".

Comparing Methods. The following policies will be compared in LIOM:

- NE: Nash equilibrium policy, a conservative policy that can be solved through self-play and other methods.
- ORACLE: Oracle policy refers to a policy that is aware of the opponent policy type and trains separate policy networks for each type of opponent policy. It can be considered as the best response policy.
- DRON: An implicit opponent modeling algorithm that uses opponent information as an additional input to the network during offline training.
- Deep BPR+: An explicit opponent modeling algorithm that selects the best response from the offline-trained policy library using a Bayesian belief model. It can learn new response policies and update the policy library by detecting unknown opponents online.
- LIOM w/o EXP3: Only use the general policy π_μ to combat the opponent, where μ is jointly calculated based on historical trajectories within several episodes.

4.2 Online Testing with Fixed Opponents

In this experiment, we demonstrate the average rewards of different methods in online testing against three categories of opponent policy sets ("seen", "unseen" and "mix").

Based on the average rewards on Kuhn Poker presented in Fig. 3, LIOM exhibits performance inferior only to the best response policy across all types of

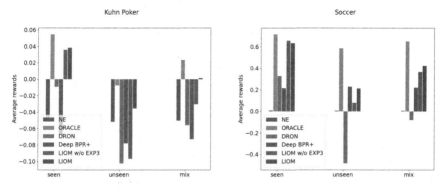

Fig. 3. The average rewards of different methods when facing three categories of opponent policy sets in online testing.

opponent policy sets. In the "seen" setting, LIOM performs similarly to LIOM w/o EXP3, indicating that when facing known opponent policies, LIOM tends to select strategies with stronger exploitation to achieve best responses. Moreover, LIOM outperforms DRON significantly, demonstrating the effectiveness of offline opponent policy representation extraction across episodes. In the "unseen" setting, LIOM w/o EXP3 outperforms DRON, suggesting that the general policy π_μ possesses better generalization capability, while LIOM surpasses LIOM w/o EXP3, owing to the lower bound on LIOM's performance guaranteed by EXP3, which can handle difficult-to-generalize opponent policies. In the "mix" setting, LIOM approaches the ORACLE policy for the known opponent type, indicating that the opponent policy representation μ inferred from limited opponent information by contrastive learning can effectively describe both known and unknown opponents, thereby assisting the general policy π_μ in making decisions.

Based on the average rewards on Soccer shown in Fig. 3, we arrive at conclusions similar to those on Kuhn Poker. The only difference is that in the "unseen" setting, Deep BPR+ performs slightly better than LIOM due to its capability of online learning against unknown opponent policies. However, the existing opponent modeling methods heavily rely on the completeness of opponent information, leading to a significant degradation in modeling accuracy when the opponent information is limited. Therefore, considering all settings, LIOM demonstrates superior performance.

4.3   Analysis of Opponent Policy Representations

In this experiment, we further analyse the effectiveness and generalization of offline-extracted opponent policy representations on Kuhn Poker, as it offers a straightforward parameterized approach to define opponent policies. Figure 4 shows the true distribution of six opponent policies, as well as their representation distribution in the representation space extracted by offline contrastive learning. Note that, the training of the opponent policy encoder only use $\Pi^{train} = \{\pi_0, \pi_1, \pi_2\}$.

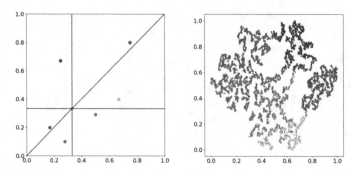

Fig. 4. The true coordinates (left) and representation distributions (right) of different opponent policies in Kuhn Poker.

Figure 4 shows that the distribution of opponent policy representations, as depicted, closely aligns with the true distribution. This indicates the accuracy and generalization of opponent policy representations extracted through contrastive learning. As policies cannot be directly represented, Fig. 4 displays the distribution of trajectory representations obtained from interacting with a randomly augmentation policy. In fact, opponent policy representations computed by different augmentation policies exhibit similar distributions, and the distribution of opponent policy representations is almost independent of the choice of augmentation policies. This is because, through contrastive learning, we only extract the portions of the trajectory representation that are relevant to opponent policies.

Table 2. Average rewards in the interaction with independent opponent policies.

	π_0	π_1	π_2
NE	-0.046 ± 1.308	$-0.042 + 1.274$	0.058 ± 1.143
ORACLE	0.068 ± 1.498	0.065 ± 1.673	0.031 ± 1.295
DRON	0.069 ± 1.509	0.025 ± 1.466	-0.122 ± 1.301
Deep BPR+	-0.106 ± 1.507	-0.063 ± 1.43	-0.035 ± 1.307
LIOM w/o EXP3	0.057 ± 1.505	0.031 ± 1.49	0.02 ± 1.297
LIOM	0.055 ± 1.457	0.04 ± 1.456	0.018 ± 1.282
	π_3	π_4	π_5
NE	-0.061 ± 1.11	-0.051 ± 1.175	-0.043 ± 1.206
ORACLE	0.026 ± 1.335	-0.039 ± 1.113	-0.01 ± 1.42
DRON	-0.156 ± 1.258	-0.093 ± 1.337	-0.058 ± 1.377
Deep BPR+	-0.039 ± 1.31	-0.098 ± 1.427	-0.097 ± 1.379
LIOM w/o EXP3	0.0 ± 1.326	-0.137 ± 1.349	-0.153 ± 1.364
LIOM	0.008 ± 1.291	-0.065 ± 1.163	-0.049 ± 1.197

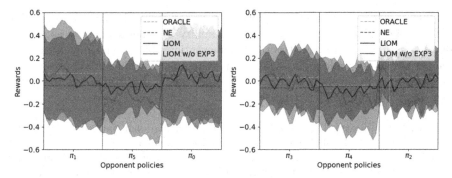

Fig. 5. The reward curve of online testing with non-stationary opponent policies in Kuhn Poker.

To further illustrate, we show in Table 2 the average returns of various algorithms interacting with specific opponent policies. Compared to DRON, LIOM w/o EXP3 performs better when facing unknown opponent policy π_3, indicating that the learned opponent policy representation has certain generalization ability. However, LIOM w/o EXP3 performs worse on opponent policies π_4 and π_5 than LIOM, which is consistent with the proximity relationships between different opponent policies as depicted in Fig. 4. This also indicates the necessity of introducing the EXP3 to balance conservative and exploitative policies.

4.4 Online Testing with Non-stationary Opponents

In this experiment, we present the reward curve against non-stationary opponents. As shown in Fig. 5, LIOM is capable of inferring the current opponent's policy representation μ based on the recent historical trajectory data D, which serves as an additional input to the general policy π_μ. Thus, it can dynamically respond to non-stationary opponent policies, and its average performance is comparable to the best response policy ORACLE. Additionally, LIOM selects between conservative Nash equilibrium policies and exploitative general policies using EXP3, so that the expected reward falls between the two, but guaranteeing a lower bound on the reward when facing unknown opponents.

5 Conclusion and Future Work

In this paper, we propose a policy-based data augmentation method that achieves offline cross-episode opponent policy representation extraction through contrastive learning. Our approach does not rely on the completeness of opponent information and can infer the current opponent's policy representation through limited information. By introducing additional policy representations, a general exploitative policy is trained offline. We also use EXP3 to balance between conservative and exploitation. Results from online testing demonstrate that LIOM exhibits high expected returns and strong generalization ability.

Future work may involve exploring the relationship between constructing offline policy sets and the generalization ability of general policies, as well as developing methods for constructing augmentation policies in complex environments. We aim to build a diverse and complete policy set for both opponent and augmentation policies. As problem scales increase, it may require us to further decomposition of complex policies.

Acknowledgements. This work is supported by the National Natural Science Foundation of China (Grant No.62106172), the "New Generation of Artificial Intelligence" Major Project of Science & Technology 2030 (Grant No.2022ZD0116402), and the Science and Technology on Information Systems Engineering Laboratory (Grant No.WDZC20235250409, No.WDZC20205250407).

References

1. Chen, T., Kornblith, S., Norouzi, M., Hinton, G.: A simple framework for contrastive learning of visual representations. In: International Conference on Machine Learning, pp. 1597–1607. PMLR (2020)
2. Foerster, J.N., Chen, R.Y., Al-Shedivat, M., Whiteson, S., Abbeel, P., Mordatch, I.: Learning with opponent-learning awareness. arXiv preprint: arXiv:1709.04326 (2017)
3. Fu, H., et al.: Greedy when sure and conservative when uncertain about the opponents. In: International Conference on Machine Learning, pp. 6829–6848. PMLR (2022)
4. He, H., Boyd-Graber, J., Kwok, K., Daumé III, H.: Opponent modeling in deep reinforcement learning. In: International Conference on Machine Learning, pp. 1804–1813. PMLR (2016)
5. He, K., Fan, H., Wu, Y., Xie, S., Girshick, R.: Momentum contrast for unsupervised visual representation learning. In: Proceedings of the IEEE/CVF Conference on Computer Vision and Pattern Recognition, pp. 9729–9738 (2020)
6. Hernandez-Leal, P., Taylor, M.E., Rosman, B.S., Sucar, L.E., Munoz de Cote, E.: Identifying and tracking switching, non-stationary opponents: a Bayesian approach (2016)
7. Hong, Z.W., Su, S.Y., Shann, T.Y., Chang, Y.H., Lee, C.Y.: A deep policy inference q-network for multi-agent systems. arXiv preprint: arXiv:1712.07893 (2017)
8. Oord, A.V.D., Li, Y., Vinyals, O.: Representation learning with contrastive predictive coding. arXiv preprint: arXiv:1807.03748 (2018)
9. Raileanu, R., Denton, E., Szlam, A., Fergus, R.: Modeling others using oneself in multi-agent reinforcement learning. In: International Conference on Machine Learning, pp. 4257–4266. PMLR (2018)
10. Rosman, B., Hawasly, M., Ramamoorthy, S.: Bayesian policy reuse. Mach. Learn. **104**, 99–127 (2016)
11. Yang, T., Meng, Z., Hao, J., Zhang, C., Zheng, Y., Zheng, Z.: Towards efficient detection and optimal response against sophisticated opponents. arXiv preprint: arXiv:1809.04240 (2018)
12. Zheng, Y., Meng, Z., Hao, J., Zhang, Z., Yang, T., Fan, C.: A deep Bayesian policy reuse approach against non-stationary agents. In: Advances in Neural Information Processing Systems, vol. 31 (2018)

Correction to: I²KD-SLU: An Intra-Inter Knowledge Distillation Framework for Zero-Shot Cross-Lingual Spoken Language Understanding

Tianjun Mao and Chenghong Zhang

Correction to:
Chapter 29 in: L. Iliadis et al. (Eds.): *Artificial Neural Networks and Machine Learning – ICANN 2023*, LNCS 14261, https://doi.org/10.1007/978-3-031-44198-1_29

The original version of chapter 29 was inadvertently published with some wrong information in Section 4.1 and 4.2. This has been corrected.

The updated version of this chapter can be found at
https://doi.org/10.1007/978-3-031-44198-1_29

Author Index

© The Editor(s) (if applicable) and The Author(s), under exclusive license
to Springer Nature Switzerland AG 2023
L. Iliadis et al. (Eds.): ICANN 2023, LNCS 14261, pp. 523–525, 2023.
https://doi.org/10.1007/978-3-031-44198-1

Printed in the United States
by Baker & Taylor Publisher Services